MASON

Mason's bookplate by A.R.D. Fairburn

MASON

The Life of R.A.K. Mason

Rachel Barrowman

VICTORIA UNIVERSITY PRESS

VICTORIA UNIVERSITY PRESS
Victoria University of Wellington
PO Box 600 Wellington

National Library of New Zealand Cataloguing-in-Publication Data
Barrowman, Rachel, 1963–
Mason : the life of R.A.K. Mason / Rachel Barrowman.
Includes bibliographical references and index.
ISBN 0-86473-463-8
1. Mason, R. A. K. (Ronald Allison Kells), 1905-1971.
2. Poets, New Zealand—20th century—Biography. I. Title.
NZ821.2 B—dc 21

'Ron Mason' by Hone Tuwhare is reprinted on pp.399–400
by kind permission of the author and Random House NZ Ltd.
(Original version from *Something Nothing*, Caveman Press, Dunedin, 1974;
reprinted in *Hone Tuwhare: A Biography* by Janet Hunt,
Godwit Press, Auckland, 1998.)

Published with the assistance of a grant from

ARTS COUNCIL OF NEW ZEALAND *TOI AOTEAROA*

Printed by Astra Print, Wellington

Though my soul is not to save
    boldly march I to my grave
    through this hostile country here
    prey of doubt and pain and fear

—R.A.K. Mason, 'Stoic Marching Song'

Contents

List of Illustrations

Mason and Dorothea, 1941

Portrait of Mason by Bert Tornquist, 1942

Jean Alison, Blackwood Paul and Mason at the Centennial Exhibition, Wellington, 1940

Mason's house at Crown Hill

Mason and Dorothea at the Bay of Islands, May 1949

Mason and Dorothea at Redvale, 1950

China Society delegation outside Peking, 1957

Still from *Inside Red China*, Hayward Film Productions, 1957

Portrait by Clifton Firth for the *Collected Poems* (1962)

Launch of the *Collected Poems*, Dunedin, July 1962

Mason at Charles Brasch's Broad Bay crib, 1964

Mason in Auckland, 1971

Mason in Dunedin, 1963

Acknowledgements

THIS BOOK began as a collaboration with John Caselberg, who had been working for some twenty years on a biography of R.A.K. Mason. It soon became apparent, however, that our views of Mason and of the nature of the biographer's task were too different for this arrangement to be satisfactory for either of us, and we agreed that I would continue to work on my biography independently. This text, and its version of Mason, are my own, but I am indebted to John for agreeing to my involvement in the first place, and for allowing me to continue to have access to his research material. This material, deposited in the Hocken Library, includes, most valuably, correspondence and notes from interviews with a great number of people: Mason's family, friends, colleagues and contemporaries. John began his research in the 1970s, not many years after Mason died, and many of these people are no longer alive.

My second debt is to my brother Fergus Barrowman at Victoria University Press for suggesting the project, and for his ongoing encouragement. Thirdly, I want to thank Stuart Strachan, Hocken librarian and trustee (with John Caselberg) of the Mason papers, for his support of the project; and his staff for making the Hocken such a pleasant place to work. Special thanks to Louise Sinclair for following up last-minute queries, and to Linda Tyler, curator of pictorial collections. Thanks too to the staff of the Alexander Turnbull Library, especially the manuscripts department.

For sharing their memories of and thoughts about Mason I am grateful to Jean Bartlett, the late Bill Pearson, Keith Maslen, Jocelyn Harris, John Griffin, Jennifer Barrer and Kay Flavell. I wish to thank especially A.R.D. Fairburn's daughters and executors of the Fairburn Literary Estate, Dinah Holman and Janis Fairburn, for the exciting discovery of Mason's letters to Fairburn, and for their hospitality; also for permission to reproduce Mason's gothic bookplate and for searching out the photograph of Teddy Roussel. Others who have assisted my research include Hugh Price, Peter Simpson, Michael King, Stephen Hamilton, Simon Sigley, Jane McCartney, David Colquhoun, Doug

Munro and David Grant. Thanks to the staff of the Putaruru Timber Museum and staff of Lichfield School for helping me to find the photograph of Mason and Aunt Foster at Whakarewarewa.

I began this project with the support of a grant from Creative New Zealand, and the J.D. Stout Research Fellowship at Victoria University of Wellington for 2000. I am grateful to Creative New Zealand and the Stout Trust for these awards, and to Vincent O'Sullivan and Lydia Wevers, successive directors of the Stout Research Centre, for generously providing me with a room to work in for the duration of the project. For their hospitality, many thanks to Rosalie Somerville in Dunedin and Tom Dignan in Auckland; for his impeccable editing and the index, Andrew Mason; for reading and commenting on the draft, Bill Manhire. Thank you to everyone who has listened to me talking about Mason for the last three and a half years, above all Ross Somerville, without whose support this book would not have been written.

Rachel Barrowman
August 2003

I

The Beggar

ONE DAY, or perhaps it was one evening, during the second half of the 1920s, a young man stood at the end of Queen's Wharf on Auckland's Waitemata harbour. He was slightly built, with short, coarse black hair and far-seeing green eyes. He wore a black raincoat and carried a walking stick in one hand. At his feet lay a bulky rucksack. He was perhaps twenty years old, or twenty-two. He stood quite still for a while, looking out at the uncannily symmetrical volcanic profile of Rangitoto Island while he finished a cigarette, drawing the smoke through nicotine-stained teeth. Then he bent down and took from his rucksack a bundle of paper: copies of a booklet of poems he had published, at his own expense, two or three years earlier and couldn't sell. Perhaps he paused and opened one, and read a few lines, before he threw them, handful by handful, into the sea.

The story of how R.A.K. Mason dumped 200 copies of his first book, *The Beggar*, into Auckland harbour, out of disappointment, disgust or despair because no one would buy it, is a legend in New Zealand literary history. It is a symbol of a time — the 1920s and 1930s — when a true, vital, native literature struggled to be written or heard in a provincial and puritanical country. Mason on Queen's Wharf is the archetype of the poet ignored by a society which he in turn despised. It was first told by his friend Rex Fairburn in an article he wrote about Mason for the *New Zealand Artists' Annual* in 1929. Their mutual friend and fellow poet Geoffrey de Montalk, when he read this in London the following year, responded with a 114-line satirical poem lambasting, in his own inimitable style, a crass, materialistic, repressed and repressive society's neglect of its creative sons (himself included).[1]

The story may be apocryphal. Another, less romantic version has Mason at home in Ellerslie bundling the *Beggars* into a fire in the washhouse copper and a family member fortuitously calling by in time to rescue a dozen. In another story he threw copies of the *Penny Broadsheet*, published later the same year, at the pigeons from a first-floor window of the Ferry Buildings on the Auckland waterfront, where he was working as a Latin tutor at a cramming school.[2] Was he speaking of *The Beggar* or some other failed publishing venture when he remarked to Denis Glover in 1937, 'Actually I have dozens of copies somewhere, but I do not like to spoil their innocent beliefs'?[3] Whether or not the story is literally true, it contains a poetic truth: it is more meaningful as myth than it may be as history.

The poet Allen Curnow, whose critical writings in the 1940s largely defined the theme and parameters of New Zealand literary historiography for the next three or four decades, counted *The Beggar* as the founding document of New Zealand literature, and Mason as the country's first 'real' poet. The nationalist critical orthodoxy of which Curnow has been seen as the author has since been vigorously challenged, but his assessment still essentially stands: Mason as a poet remains a seminal and central figure in New Zealand literature. But he is at the same time curiously peripheral. His tough, knotty, powerful and elusive poems do not lend themselves to simple or literal readings, about place and time any more than about the poet. They are at once intensely personal and universal. Mason himself disavowed any consciously nationalist intentions, and rejected any such interpretations of his work. He published quite a small number of poems, all when he was young: almost all of those on which his reputation is based were written between the ages of eighteen and thirty. *No New Thing* (1934), which contains most of them, is almost as rare and legendary as *The Beggar*. In the second half of his life he published virtually no poetry, and wrote little. In the histories his name routinely appears alongside those of the others who made up the literary fraternity of mid-twentieth-century New Zealand, but in reality he was somewhere else: outside, or at the edge of the circle. The 'mysteriously remote' Mason, Glover wrote of him.[4] In 1951, when nearly everyone who was anyone in New Zealand letters gathered in Christchurch for the second New Zealand writers' conference, Mason was not there.

Mason was not only a poet, and his is not only a literary story. Politics prompted him to turn the focus of his creative energies away from poetry in the second half of the 1930s, when he became involved in left-wing theatre. His socialist beliefs were formed by his early twenties, and he retained them all his life. In the early 1930s he briefly joined the Communist Party, and he remained closely associated with it for many years. During the Second World War he edited the weekly which replaced the banned Party newspaper the *People's Voice*. For ten years after the war he worked for the Auckland General Labourers' Union, on the militant left wing of the New Zealand labour movement. In the 1950s he became involved in the fledgling New Zealand

China Society, and visited China in 1957. He wrote during these years, but not poetry. Mason's story is also a story of the left and the labour movements, through the fervent, hard, treacherous and disillusioned years of the Popular Front, the Second World War, the beginning of the Cold War and the 1951 waterfront lockout.

Still, the core of Mason's life and his interest remains his poetry: his finely formed sonnets, tough, sardonic love poems, grim meditations on death and betrayal that startle by their maturity and power. They are remarkable poems, immediately striking yet complex in meaning, technically assured, infused with a deep knowledge of English and classical literature, brilliant and disturbing. And they appeared seemingly out of nowhere in the 1920s – as, in Curnow's often-quoted but indispensable words, 'something different, something/ Nobody counted on'.[5]

Where that poetry came from is part of the puzzle of Mason. Why he stopped writing it is another – or perhaps the same one. Was it because of 'the failure of a gift', to quote C.K. Stead?[6] Did Mason simply and deliberately abandon poetry for politics; or did his poetic gift fall victim to his increasing involvement in politics from the 1930s, when, in his own words, he sought 'to bring my artistic feelings into line with my intellectual knowledge', to reconcile his literary self and his socialism?[7] Did the poet fail because of politics; or did politics fill the space when the poetry failed? Twenty years later, Mason himself hinted at more prosaic reasons to explain his lapse into poetic silence when he blamed it on 'the tecoma hedges' (he also worked for some years as a landscape gardener) – his lack of time, energy and money.[8]

The answer is in all of these. It is in the nexus of the disparate spheres of his life. And somewhere deeper and darker altogether.

In the last decade of his life Mason was treated for manic depressive illness. The diagnosis came late, but the signs were always there: in the puzzling patterns of behaviour, the missed opportunities, failures of confidence. In the seeming contradictions: between the gentleness of his character, the fierceness of his politics and the control of his poems; between his sardonic toughness and his nervousness; his quick, biting humour and his sombre intensity; his openness and air of distraction. And in the poems themselves: the combination of compulsiveness and control, their structural ambiguity, in the way their literariness feels 'so strangely at odds with what is being said', as Charles Brasch once observed.[9]

Family pressures were also part of Mason's burden. There was his father's death (some have conjectured suicide) when Mason was eight years old, his very close – too close – relationship with his mother, and his equally complicated relationship with his older brother, Dan, a disgraced lawyer, a charmer and a rogue, in whose shady business dealings Mason became involved in the 1930s. Here is a retelling of another legend of New Zealand literary history, the brief, bright life of the Auckland university literary magazine *Phoenix*: some of the meetings of the *Phoenix* committee when Mason was the editor in 1933 were held in Dan Mason's dingy sharebrokers' office downtown. The deep sense of personal betrayal that Mason felt at his brother's dishonesty was to be repeated twenty years later in his experience in the Auckland General Labourers' Union.

The tension between politics and poetry is only one clue to the meaning of Mason's life, and source of his struggle. That 'far-pitched perilous hostile place' that became a leitmotif of New Zealand literary nationalism was also 'the dark cave at the corner' of a troubled mind.[10]

2

Penrose and Lichfield

1905–16

MASON'S FOUR grandparents travelled to New Zealand in the nineteenth century from England, Scotland and Ireland. Their stories, and those of their families, are the stories of many: of innkeepers, soldiers and farmers, mothers and wives; of struggle, achievement and sadness; of lives changed and families disrupted by distance and death – stories at once ordinary and extraordinary. Mason would find in them some meanings for his own.

His maternal grandmother, Eliza Forbes, made the journey from Scotland as a nine-year-old with her parents and five sisters and brothers.[1] Born in 1831, she was the first child of Margaret Ross Cooper, a farmer's daughter, and Robert Forbes, who had been married the year before in the coastal parish of Pitsligo in the eastern Highland county of Aberdeenshire, and ten years later joined the Scottish diaspora, the exodus of tens of thousands of Highland Scots south or abroad in the eighteenth and nineteenth centuries in response to the Highland clearances and periods of economic distress. Many, at first, went to America. In the mid-nineteenth century, the countrywide famine of 1836–37, triggered by two successive crop failures – the worst subsistence crisis in thirty years – created a receptive audience for the promoters of free and subsidised emigration to the new, distant colonies of Canada, Australia and New Zealand.

Robert Forbes's occupation was recorded as agricultural labourer when he embarked with his family in the autumn of 1840 on the New Zealand Company ship the *Slains Castle*. They were bound for Wellington, but on arriving there late in January 1841 the passengers were encouraged by government representatives to go north to Auckland, which had recently been declared capital of the newly annexed colony (to the chagrin of the New Zealand Company directors) and where wages were higher and land cheaper. All of Mason's immigrant forebears were to settle in Auckland. He was to live there almost all his life.

Robert Forbes took up a 'suburban farm' at Epsom, and in late 1842 became innkeeper of the One Tree Hill Inn. Although officially the capital, Auckland in 1842 was just a town, with a population of 1500. Epsom, four miles south, represented its frontier fringe. Two years later Robert and his family moved further out to Onehunga, on the shore of the Manukau harbour. He acquired a bush inn licence, which allowed him to sell spirituous liquor to travellers, and opened the New Leith Inn in a raupo whare near the beach. In 1845 he purchased eight acres of surrounding land from Ngati Whatua, paid for, according to family lore, by selling Margaret's jewellery.

When he died of apoplexy in 1849 Robert Forbes left his widow with seven children and a battle to retain the land, which she fought with spirit, though not success. The Crown's pre-emptive right to purchase Maori land, which had been waived by proclamation in 1844, was reinstated in 1846. The land claims commissioners who investigated settler purchases decided in favour of Robert Forbes but he died before the title deed could be issued, and the governor, George Grey, decreed that Margaret could keep only an acre and a half. When surveyors arrived to mark out the land she ordered them off, pulled up the survey pegs and tore up the flags, dressed her children in their Sunday best and drove to town to see the governor in person to ask permission to address the Legislative Council to plead her cause. 'I gied him a bit o' ma Scotch tongue,' the family version of the story goes, 'and it did me gude.' The plight of the poor but feisty widow battling against the 'arbitrary, unprincipled and despotic' behaviour of Governor Grey attracted much sympathy in the community and in the Legislative Council, where a petition was presented on her behalf, but was declined. Later she was able to buy back some of the land when it was put up for auction. She sold the liquor licence in 1857 and supported her family by farming, running a herd of fifty cattle. She died in 1877, and Forbes Street in Onehunga commemorates her name.[2]

In 1849, the year of her father's death, the Forbeses's first-born, Eliza, had married William George Vernon, a young Scotsman who worked as a sawyer at Te Huia, near the Manukau harbour entrance. They had a son, born in January 1850. In June William was killed felling timber. Eliza rowed his body back to Onehunga.

Five years later she married George Kells, himself a widower with two children. He was an Irishman, born in Collon, County Louth, in 1821, the second of the five sons of Jane Rogers and George Kells, a farmer originally from County Fermagh. Jane was from a Dublin family of money and education, who were not pleased by her marriage to a farmer's son: her brothers studied at Trinity College, two becoming ordained ministers. The five Kells brothers all joined the British army and sailed to New Zealand with the 65th Regiment of Foot on the troop-ship *Java* in 1846. Two companies disembarked at Kororareka in the north, where the government and Hone Heke maintained an uneasy peace following the war of 1845–46, and the remainder at Auckland. In March 1847 a detachment was sent to Wanganui, where they engaged in a desultory battle with a Maori party blockading the town in which Thomas, the oldest of the Kells, was wounded. His uniform, preserved in the Wanganui Museum, attests that the brothers were big men: Thomas was six foot four. Three of them settled in Wanganui. George was invalided and discharged in 1849 and took up land in the military pensioner settlement of Howick, southeast of Auckland, where he married the daughter of the local innkeeper, Amelia Lewis. Three children were born, one dying in infancy, before Amelia herself died from consumption in 1853.[3]

Eliza Vernon and George Kells, Mason's maternal grandparents, were married at St Peter's Anglican Church, Onehunga, on 2 June 1855. They developed a farm at Pakuranga, and had six children, a son and five daughters, of their own. Mason was to admire his Kells grandfather, whom he never knew, as embodying the best Celtic and colonial qualities of fairness and tolerance: 'a leader of soldiers yet one who had striven to avert the hated looming of war and had from it only hardships, save that the other side gave him life for the friendship he had had with them'.[4] George was quick to enlist when fighting broke out in Taranaki in 1860, joining the Otahuhu Royal Cavalry Volunteers, and was commissioned a lieutenant in the Auckland militia in April 1860. During the war in Waikato in 1863–64 he was at Drury as captain in charge of the No.6 Company of the Transport Corps. 'I never recovered from the effects of the Waikato War', he later wrote to one of his sons. Nevertheless, he became an established figure in the institutions of civilian life. By 1882 he owned just over a thousand acres. He was elected a highway trustee and chairman of the local Highway Board and became a Justice of the Peace, defending the colony against frontier lawlessness – in particular the problem of roaming horses. In 1884 he wrote indignantly and at length to the *Auckland Weekly News* about his struggle to keep them off the roads and his land:

> I have had a stick shaken over my head on the public road, my life threatened, my gates removed and broken, my fences wilfully set on fire, my wife and children grossly insulted by a parcel of ignorant boors, and a few nights ago I was brought up in state to the top of Pigeon Mountain, and there shot and then burned, with lots of beer to cool me as I was being consumed. . . . I

spent a good part of my young days in the wilds of the County Clare, among
the 'Terryalts,' and I declare their conduct was mild compared with the ruffians
growing up in some parts of New Zealand.[5]

In March 1890 he applied for and was denied compensation for military
services, under an act passed in 1888. Soon afterwards he suffered a stroke,
and remained partially paralysed until his death in January 1891. Eliza applied
three more times for compensation, unsuccessfully. The Pakuranga farm passed
to the son of her husband's first marriage.

When a new school opened in 1873 at Panmure, three miles from
Pakuranga towards Auckland, the first name written in the register was that
of George and Eliza's third daughter, the six-year-old Jessie Forbes Kells.[6]
She grew to be a young woman of striking looks and character: handsome,
clever and vivacious. She had dark olive skin 'like a gypsy' and extraordinary
flashing eyes, 'big violet blue eyes' that looked right through you. 'I'm sure
she had second sight', one of her nieces would remember. 'Aunt Jessie was a
real hoot . . . she had these dramatic flairs' and tumultuous emotions, but 'a
kind of mystery attached to all this . . . she was quite odd'. She became
engaged to a young man, but he went off to America to make his fortune,
and returned too late.[7] From 1892 until August 1898 Jessie worked as a librarian
at the Auckland Public Library, in the imposing French Renaissance-style
building in Wellesley Street, opened in 1887, which also housed the municipal
offices. The building of a new library had been prompted by George Grey's
decision to leave to the city his valuable collection of books, incunabula and
manuscripts: by the time of his death in 1898 he had gifted 14,000 volumes.
In December 1892 the ageing politician had presented Jessie with a copy of
his biography, *The Life and Times of Sir George Grey*, inscribed 'To Miss Jessie
Forbes Kells, in recognition of the assistance she has offered the Librarian –
Sir George Grey, December 25th, 1892.'

It was at the library that Jessie met Frank Mason, a young man who was
studying to enter his father's chemical manufacturing and hairdressing business.
They were married in 1898.

Frank Mason's mother, Annie, had been born on board the ship on which
her parents, Walter and Ellen McCaul, left Scotland in 1849. Ellen was the
eldest of four children of Annie McDonnell and Duff Laing, an Edinburgh
type-founder. After the death of her husband in 1828, Annie Laing settled in
the textile town of Paisley, near Glasgow. She married again and had three
more children. She appears to have been working as a cook in a public house

before she and her second husband, James Cox, sailed from Greenock in June 1842 on the *Argyll*, the second of the first four ships to bring immigrants directly to Auckland. Her daughter Ellen, however, stayed in Paisley, where she had married Walter Allison McCaul. In 1849 they sailed on the *Victory* for Melbourne, and in May 1850 arrived at Auckland with their infant daughter Annie on the *Moa*. Walter started a tailoring business in High Street. A son was born before Ellen died in childbirth. Walter later remarried. An entrepreneurial type, he went into the auctioneering and land agency business and coastal trading, worked a claim with his son during the Thames goldrush in the late 1860s and later 'tried some experimental boring for coal in New Lynn'. 'Wattie' McCaul died at New Lynn in 1904, and was remembered by the *New Zealand Herald* as a well-known early identity – his name 'identical with the city's foundation' – though having been for the last twenty years 'practically a recluse, on account of a growing infirmity which affected his lower limbs so gradually that at first he was unable to walk without a stick, then a stick and a crutch, and latterly two crutches; but . . . he maintained until the last a sunny and contented mind'.[8]

His eldest daughter, Annie, was married at the Auckland Registry Office on 24 October 1871 to Thomas Mason, a chemist who had emigrated to the colony with his father in 1863 from Nottingham. The pride that his grandson, as a poet and socialist, would take in his Scottish and Irish ancestry was matched by his disdain for the English. He preferred the idea that he was in fact descended from Huguenots, and insisted that his grandfather looked like a Frenchman: short with a small dark beard. Thomas's father, William, had been born in Woolwich, London – once a centre of displaced Huguenots – in 1803, and some time later moved to Nottingham. Although too young to be press-ganged into service in the Napoleonic wars, he was old enough to witness the widespread unemployment and poverty they caused, and to know of the Luddite movement which began in the Nottinghamshire textile factories in 1811. In 1828 he married Elizabeth Turner in the nearby town of Duffield in Derbyshire, and they had two sons: Thomas (born 1833) and John (born 1841). William Mason, his obituary in the *Auckland Evening Star* would record, 'was for many years engaged as city missionary in Nottingham, where his name was familiar to thousands of the humbler classes of the large manufacturing town. He took a very active part in establishing ragged schools and night classes for the education of working men.'[9]

The Masons came to New Zealand with the Albertland special settlement scheme: an idealistic and ill-fated plan to establish a non-conformist co-operative settlement at Kaipara, north of Auckland. It was the brainchild of a Baptist minister's son and newspaperman from Birmingham, William Brame, and was launched in 1861 to mark the forthcoming bicentenary of the expulsion of non-conforming ministers from the Church of England. The name Albertland, honouring the recently deceased prince consort, was chosen by a close vote over Cromwell and Milton by the members of the settlement association. John Mason, the younger of the two sons and a hairdresser by trade, sailed with the first party of Albertlanders on the *Mathilda Wattenbach* in May 1862. Thomas, with his father, William's second wife and their young son, followed on the fifth Albertland ship, the *Tyburnia*, which docked at Auckland on 5 October 1863 after spending a month quarantined off Rangitoto Island because of an outbreak of smallpox on board.

Albertland was a manifest failure. The land that the association's agents had chosen was remote and of poor quality: 70,000 acres of scrubland stretching 30 miles along the swampy shores of the Kaipara harbour, as inappropriate for a co-operative community as it was inhospitable to agriculture. Half of the 3000 intended settlers never went to Kaipara; of those who did, only half persevered. The later arrivals, such as those on the *Tyburnia*, were met at Auckland by the disillusioned who had already abandoned the promised land. William Mason and his family stayed in Auckland, while Thomas disappeared up north for a while to avoid being conscripted for the Waikato war. William acted as a city missionary in Auckland for several years and later in Thames, where he died in 1879. 'As a colporteur he has trudged many a weary mile to take the "glad tidings" to isolated homesteads', his obituary recorded. 'He was known by all acquainted with him as a kind-hearted man, strong in faith, of earnest address, and full of sympathy for the most humble of the industrial classes, among whom the best years of his life have been spent.'[10]

John and Thomas went into partnership in a hairdressing business in Auckland's Queen Street, later adding a 'perfume manufactury' which fronted onto Lorne Street behind the salon. The firm intended, the *Auckland Weekly News* reported in 1882, to 'manufacture all kinds of distilled perfumes, washes, pomades, and cosmetics' and 'to foster local industry by utilising all the local products which can be used in the manufacture of perfumery, as well as those from the islands and Australian colonies'.[11] J. & T. Mason won medals for their products at the Auckland Agricultural and Pastoral Show in 1883, the New Zealand Industries Fair in 1885 and the 1886 Colonial and Indian Exhibition in London.

After their marriage in 1871, Thomas and Annie Mason had bought a property at 4 Smith Street, Ponsonby. Their first child, Frank (Francis William), was born on 17 January 1872, and followed by three more sons and three daughters, one of whom died in the diphtheria epidemic that swept Auckland in 1885. Frank attended Beresford Street Primary School, and Auckland Grammar School in 1887 and 1888. He was then sent to work at Mitchelson's General Store in Dargaville, north of the Kaipara, as the 'Long Depression' (fifteen years of economic stagnation starting about 1879) continued. His sister Winifred later commented: 'What a wicked thing it was to send a boy of 16 alone to such a place, where almost the whole population were hard bushmen and gumdiggers: they taught Frank to *drink*.'[12] When he returned to Auckland he trained to enter the family business. His occupation was recorded as 'perfumer' when he married Jessie Kells at the Auckland Registry Office on 2 September 1898. He was twenty-six; Jessie was thirty-two.

JESSIE AND Frank Mason lived at first in Mt Roskill Road, where Jessie's mother, Eliza Kells, was also living. In 1899 Frank bought the Trocadero Dining Rooms at 126 Queen Street, not far from the perfume manufactory, and the couple ran this for two or three years, with Jessie cooking and serving the meals. Their first child was born on 21 March 1900. He was named Walter Thomas Foster Kells Mason, but would always be called Dan. In 1902–03 they lived in Avondale, before moving to Penrose to a property that belonged to Jessie's Aunt Bella and her husband. It was there that their second son, Ronald Allison Kells Mason, was born on Tuesday, 10 January 1905. Ronald was the name of Frank's youngest brother (who was known, however, as Roy); Allison came from his great-grandfather McCaul. The family knew him as John.

Penrose in 1905 was a rural district: a basin of 'grass-land, scrub and stony outcrops'[13] surrounded by the volcanic cones of Mt Smart (Rarotonga), the fine profile of One Tree Hill (Maungakiekie) to the north-west, and the bulkier, quarry-scarred Mt Wellington (Maungarei, or 'watchful mountain') to the north-east. Southwards the land slopes gently down to Onehunga wharf and the Manukau inlet. East, beyond Maungarei, lie Pakuranga, Pigeon Mountain and Howick. To the south-west stand the cones of Mangere and Puketutu Island. The summit of Mt Wellington gave, the missionary Samuel Marsden had remarked, a 'grand and nobly pleasing' view.[14]

The house at Penrose, which Jessie purchased in 1906, stood well back from the road 'among lava country', surrounded by trees and garden, with a pony, fowls and house-cows. The 14-acre property included a scoria quarry, a valuable asset. The household was cheerful and disorderly. At night by kerosene lamplight Frank would joke good-humouredly while Jessie played the piano and crooned in her deep, beautiful voice, 'like Dame Edith Evans'. At gatherings of relatives and friends, folk and popular songs were sung and poetry recited. Dan was the confident, talkative one. His brother would be remembered from this time for his gentle, generous nature: 'the dearest and loveliest natured child that I have ever had anything to do with', one cousin would recall. When Jessie served up strawberries he would count how many on his plate and how many on Dan's, then take a spoon and put an extra one onto Dan's. 'He always seemed to me to be smiling.' He was also a precocious reader, remembered (by another cousin) 'reading to my father when he was four years old' and reciting poetry to his brother while Dan milked the cows. He was always reading, and 'seemed to learn without being taught'.[15] Mason himself would later state:

> I was always encouraged, from an early age, to take an interest in books. I learnt to read before I went to school. And my people threw their library open to my brother and me. The works of Shakespeare, Dickens, Sir Walter Scott, Robert Burns and others, were always available to us. I don't remember when I didn't take an interest in them.[16]

From Penrose the family would make visits by horse and gig or on foot to Great-aunt Bella's in Onehunga; by train and tram into the city and then by ferry across the Waitemata harbour to see Aunt Alice, Jessie's youngest sister, in Northcote; and most frequently to Annie and Thomas Mason's in Ponsonby. Grandfather Mason, who had grown 'sick of religion', spent the last three years before his death in 1909 bedridden with rheumatoid arthritis, administering 'modest amounts' of Hennessey's Three-Star Brandy as a sedative. Annie was a member of the Church of Christ and a staunch temperance supporter. It was perhaps to Thomas Mason's death that his grandson referred thirty years later when he wrote of his clear and possibly earliest memory of when he was 'four or five years old, when I was ruefully learning that there were in this world grim-becoming horrors that no mother could rescue me from'.[17]

In 1912 Mason was sent to live with his aunt, Isabella Foster Kells, and attend school at Lichfield in southern Waikato. Dan had gone there before him, in 1907, but returned to Auckland after a term and was enrolled at Panmure school. (Whether his aunt sent him back, or Jessie called him back, or whether he simply insisted on leaving is not known.) Ron stayed with Aunt Foster for four years, going home to Penrose for some of the holidays. Later, as a young man, he would return there regularly to work during the summer. Lichfield was a tiny, remote rural settlement, on the edge of a 'bleak treeless . . . landslip-scarred' plateau which stretched east to the Mamaku ranges and the Rotorua lakes; to the south and west lay 'a vast expanse of tussock, fern and scrub'.[18] It was reached from Auckland by train to Putaruru, then by horse-drawn vehicle four and a half miles south towards Tokoroa and Taupo, in winter an all-day journey. 'None of the kids I went to school with there had ever seen the sea.' 'When the sun shines it is absolute Paradise', Mason would later describe Lichfield to a friend.

> Just at the moment – 6.45 p.m – the sun is declining: the east is all a tranquil brown rolling away to vague purple mountains, the west is a bright glitter of green and gold. The only sound is that of a lark's song and the confused roaring of wind in the trees. Trees everywhere – tall pines and cascading silver poplars overshadow the house and in front of me as I write on the verandah are great, warm-looking dark soft plantations of pines.[19]

Lichfield, another ill-starred colonial dream, had been founded in the 1880s as in effect a company town by the Thames Valley Land Company, which had purchased 300,000 acres to develop into a cattle and sheep station. It was planned on the model of an English country estate. The original survey described a large township centred on a cathedral square, with a handsome homestead for the manager, a clubhouse for the expected English farm cadets, a hotel, hall, and cottages for the workers. It was named after the cathedral town in England. 'Possibly it may have attained that distinction too', its historian would drolly remark, 'if the railway for Rotorua had not made a detour over the Mamaku range from Putaruru.'[20] More serious, in addition to the deepening depression of the late 1880s, was the 'bush sickness' that afflicted much of the volcanic land of the central plateau and Bay of Plenty. Not until the mid-1930s would it be discovered that the sickness which wasted cattle and ruined livelihoods and speculative schemes was caused by a cobalt deficiency in the soil. The Thames Valley Land Company went bust in 1891, and the land was re-surveyed by the government in 1905–06.

Foster Kells, Jessie's eldest sister, had gone to Lichfield in 1889 at the invitation of their uncle, the then manager of the estate, to take sole charge of the school. At that time the settlement was still thriving on the promise of prosperity: there was a two-storey hotel, stores, a butcher's shop, railway houses (for the railway had once gone as far as Lichfield) and a bank; there were tennis and pheasant-shooting parties and all-night dances and 'it was nothing to see 40 or 50 settlers with their buggies at the station'.[21] Foster Kells remained Lichfield's teacher until her retirement at the end of 1913, but continued as the town's postmistress until 1926. The post and telegraph agency was housed in a lean-to at the back of the school, which had originally been the community hall; a short distance away stood the cottage in which Miss Kells, and for four years her nephew, lived.

Lichfield in 1912 consisted of a stone store, the school and house, and a handful of farm houses or cottages. It was a frontier life. Wood was gathered and chopped daily, water was heated and food cooked on a wood-fired iron stove, clothes were washed in a wood-fired copper. Aunt Foster was upright, Anglican and devout. Each Sunday she set out the lectern and candles in the schoolhouse for the church service and provided meals for the visiting clergymen. '[M]y rigid mid-Victorian aunt', Mason would later refer to her.[22] Without doubt it was a lonely life for a seven-year-old boy. The school had between ten and twenty pupils. It also housed an 850-volume library that had been donated in the 1880s, and included 'books of reference and many classics among those of a lighter nature'.[23]

For a school composition early in 1913, at the age of eight, Mason composed an obituary:

> in memory of my dear cat Gutsy Porter, known as Fluffy to most others, aged about nine months. He was only about nine months old, and an ordinary grey-and-white cat, yet during his short life, so playful his nature and so pretty his looks, he was feared and liked by all who knew him. On account of his good qualities I had taken him, in preference to nine others, for he was a cat in a hundred, but as the poet [Burns] says 'The well laid plans of men and mice, gang aft agley'. Born in the year 1912, of a family of 4, 'Guts,' early showed a roving and adventurous spirit. Hardly were his eyes open, when he showed his abundance of mischief, love and kindness. There are many famous cats in history, good and bad – Dick Whittington's, the Cheshire cat, Puss-in-Boots and many others – but I am sure none were better or more dearly loved than my ain, plain, 'Guts.' There are many unknown heroes, whose graves are marked by a wooden cross or other simple thing – perhaps nothing. There are others, less good and brave who are decorated with medals.[24]

In the autumn of that year news came to Lichfield of Frank Mason's death. In the late morning of Friday, 25 April the doctor was called to Penrose and found Frank semi-conscious, exhibiting symptoms of severe opium poisoning: 'His pupils were contracted to a pinpoint, his breathing was very strenuous, his face purple.' Jessie had first called the family. Frank's uncle James McCaul arrived at the house around 9.30. Frank told him that he had taken opium and whisky because 'I could not sleep. I took some through the night and still could not sleep so I took some more this morning', McCaul later reported at the inquest. 'I said "Frank you have taken too much." He said "You needn't be frightened about me Jim". "I have often taken it before and I know how much is safe as well as a doctor."' In the form of laudanum, a tincture of opium diluted in wine or spirit, the drug was in common use as a sedative. There was an empty four-ounce bottle beside Frank's bed. Jessie and his uncle gave him a mixture of salt and water and mustard to induce vomiting before calling the doctor, who administered coffee and permanganate of potash and left about 1.30 with 'reasonable hopes of his recovery'. At 5 o'clock he was called back when Frank collapsed and stopped breathing. He could not be resuscitated. At the inquest the local constable stated: 'I have known the deceased for a number of years and I am of the opinion that he took this drug as a medicine. He was always of a cheerful disposition but weak sighted and always trembling.' His son too suffered from this, especially in times of illness or stress: his hands always shook, Mason's friends would repeatedly observe. The mention of trembling invites speculation about alcoholism, but it is possible that both Mason and his father had some form of benign essential tremor.

The coroner found that Frank Mason's death was 'accidental and was caused by his taking an overdose of Opium for Sleeplessness'.[25] He was buried at Purewa cemetery on the Sunday.

Dan was in his third year at Auckland Grammar School in 1913. It is not known whether he stayed home that Friday, how much he learned of the inquest, or what he may have told his younger brother. The family never spoke of the circumstances of Frank's death. Jessie never remarried. She 'thought the sun rose and set on Frank',[26] and after his death she focused her love on her sons – perhaps excessively so. Many years later, when writing of his time in Lichfield as a boy, Mason simply recorded: 'I should mention that my mother was widowed during my time at Lichfield.'[27] But as a young man he wrote this fragment of verse in his notebook:

> Now fatherless & fruitless
>   the old despair again
>   greys all my life: and bootless
>   the torment sweeps my brain:
>   who can uproot the rootless
>   tree of pain?
>
> Who can track down the fiddle
>   whose tune shatters my days:
>   who drive into the middle
>   of the tormented maze:[28]

He stayed with his aunt for another two and a half years. War broke out in Europe, and news came to Lichfield of other deaths. Auntie Fos 'sat in the little telegraph office knitting soldiers' socks as she waited for telegrams from the War Office', which she then delivered in person, often walking miles in the dark and mud and wet.[29] By day the locals gathered at the school waiting while she sorted the mail. Uncle Roy Mason, after whom Ron was named, was among those wounded at Gallipoli on 25 April 1915.

Shortly before he left Lichfield, in October 1915, Mason was treated to a Labour weekend excursion to Rotorua. 'Dear Mother and Dan,' he wrote home. 'Where do you think we have been? We have been tourists for a while'. They travelled by train to Rotorua, stopping overnight at the Grand Vue boarding house before going on to Ohinemutu and visiting Whakarewarewa. He described with excitement and in careful detail his first visit to the thermal wonderland that lay two and a half days' journey from Lichfield: 'hot pools, naked Maoris, the old and new churches, carved Maori houses and a statue of Queen Victoria. . . . coloured sands . . . sulphur and boiling pools'. It rained steadily. On the morning they left, he 'went and stood in the warm steam' of the tiny geyser opposite the hotel.[30]

In December he returned to Penrose, and in 1916 was enrolled for his final year at Panmure District School, where his mother and Dan had gone and Aunt Foster had started her teaching career. The school lay a few miles over rough road east of the Penrose farmlet, close to the base of Mt Wellington, whose volcanic slopes the boys spent much time exploring. A popular place was a fumarole on the western flank of the mountain known as the 'fairy hole', a domed fissure four to five feet in diameter with sides that sloped inwards then went straight down some forty feet, widening at the bottom: 'a fatal step for the unwary sheep on the mountain'.[31] Thereabouts and over the pitted scoria slopes skulls were commonly found. Maungarei had been the site of one of the last inter-tribal Maori battles on the Tamaki isthmus in the 1820s. 'Path grey & fibrous like an old cave-found skull', Mason would later write in his notebook.[32]

3

The boy with manly hair

1917–22

IN 1917 Mason wore the uniform of a Grammar boy – blue flannel shirt and navy serge shorts, plain black stockings and serviceable boots – and went to school by train with Dan from Penrose station. Dan was a prefect in his upper-sixth year. Another new boy, Robert Burton, with whom he would travel to school on and off for the next five years, first knew Ron as 'merely the younger brother of Walter Thomas Foster Kells Mason, an exalted personage in a straw boater'. Tall and broad-shouldered, Dan was an excellent tennis player and a member of the senior shooting team; handsome and well-mannered, with his mother's beautiful speaking voice, he was 'a man of the world among a class of boys' in the eyes of his younger form-mates. At the end of the year, 'the final apotheosis', he gained a university scholarship, albeit with the lowest marks of the thirteen successful scholars.[1]

From Newmarket station the boys walked across Broadway and along Teed Street, 'past tiny cottages with perhaps an old man sitting in the sun, or a slattern on an old verandah', up past Secombe's brewery and the tall yellow house of the French consul, to Mountain Road. Along the way 'the fennel grew wild and rank by the metal road . . . we sometimes crushed it in Maths for impure diversion'.[2] When Frank Mason had attended Auckland Grammar the school was in Symonds Street, on the eastern ridge overlooking the central city, the harbour and the Domain, but it had been usurped from this prime site by Auckland University College. The year 1917 was Grammar's second in Mountain Road, Mt Eden. The new school – a grandiose building in Spanish-mission style, with pillared and colonnaded arches, Marseilles tile roof and Moorish domed towers – was completed during the year with the installation of gas lamps in the assembly hall, but it was several more years before the broken volcanic ground was finally levelled to make rugby fields. It was a school which placed equal emphasis on scholarship and sport, and on inculcating the values of moral integrity and responsibility, manliness and patriotism. Mason's years there were the last years of J.W. Tibbs, headmaster since 1893: a 'muscular Christian', Beatrice Webb had described him then.[3]

He was a tall, powerfully built man, a little stooped by this time, with piercing, deep-set eyes and a clipped, silver-white moustache. Dignified, genial and charismatic, he governed the country's largest school with a paternal hand.

Next to the school was the Auckland prison, a grim stone edifice. Prisoners worked in the school grounds, constructing the stone wall between school and prison: on the western side of the building lessons were conducted over the din of the stone-crushers. Executions created a palpable atmosphere of mingled fascination and fear. Three were carried out during Mason's school years. But war cast a larger and darker shadow. Robert Burton's brother Ormond (later a prominent Christian pacifist) was already fighting in France. At morning assembly, after the Bible lesson and school prayer, Tibbs read out the names of old boys and staff killed, wounded or missing in action; one morning he announced the death of his own son. By the end, 278 old boys had been killed or were missing, and five of the seventeen masters who had enlisted were dead.

Mason was in the top third form in 1917. He came in the bottom third of the class in English, French, maths and science, higher in Latin, and in 1918 was placed in 4B. 'I was a . . . skinny, lonely, ill-fitting little wretch', he later described himself then.[4] Robert Burton would remember him, at first, as 'pleasant and cheerful and ready of speech, though not unduly', modest, sensitive and retiring. Norman Leonard, a fellow traveller on the train and Mason's 3A classmate, an older, 'level-headed' boy, found him (although perhaps this was a later year) 'a bit odd – a loner', 'a most unusual type' who 'had little time for organised games'.[5] But in 3A there was at least one other of his kind: Ted Blaiklock, another boy with a nascent love of literature and Latin. They met on the first day, in Blaiklock's recollection, suffering their initiation under the same tap at the hands of fourth-formers. They discovered a mutual disdain for muscular sports and scorn for trigonometry, and produced a handwritten broadsheet which the form master swiftly suppressed. The next year Mason wrote the 4B form notes for the official school magazine, the *Chronicle*, and won the form prize for English, Latin and French.

School closed early that year, a few days short of the armistice on 11 November, not in celebration but as a precaution against the influenza epidemic that swept through New Zealand in 1918 and was at its virulent peak that summer. Several thousand died. A cousin of Mason's would remember 'Smith St. [Ponsonby] with somebody in bed in every room . . . My father, Walter, May & Roy Mason all got it. Dan too, I *think*.'[6] Nor was the war quite over.

Soon the family received news that Uncle Tom, whom Dan and Ron had farewelled from the wharf in the winter of 1918, had been killed in action at Le Quesnoy, in his first action, seven days before peace was declared.

Prize-giving was postponed until Easter 1919. Mason, who as an adult was to be an extremely nervous public speaker, relived the experience five years later in a classic dream of anxiety and inadequacy:

> I was going up to get my prize at school. . . . I had to climb up on to a platform and shake hands with the Chairman of the Board of Governors and go down the other side. Well, that was all right, but half-way up I realised that I only had on a little grey rib-knitted under-flannel and to make things worse Robinson Crusoe who was sitting in the front row, though I hadn't noticed him, had got hold of one end of a bit of wool and the jersey was unraveling with every step I took. Fortunately the Chairman yelled out 'Daniel de foe,' and I saw he was man Friday. He pointed to the eagle on a crest on the honours board at the back of the stage and it suddenly jumped out and turned into a parrot which crowed three times and denied Christ. Then I grabbed an M.A. gown from a master to cover my nakedness, fell down the steps – and woke up just before I hit the bottom.[7]

He was back in the top form in 1919, together with Blaiklock. Their form master was H.J.D. ('Porky') Mahon, who took English: a liberal, tolerant and urbane teacher who enjoyed reading to the boys aloud, giving virtuoso performances of plays (taking all the parts himself), and had a special love of poetry – the boys memorised hundreds of lines. Out of class Mason and Blaiklock 'talked much of poetry and . . . ate lunch together on an outcrop of stone in that rugged playground'.[8] A preference for literature over sport was enough to set one apart in such a school; Mason was also one of the few boys who swapped chemistry for history in his senior years.

Dan, meanwhile, was cutting a dash at university, taking law and developing a reputation as wild and irresponsible. Five years older, he was as different from his brother in personality as they were apart in years: clever and dilatory while Ron was polite and studious. In the opinion of many in the family, Jessie favoured Dan. He rode to his early morning and evening lectures on a motorbike; later she bought him a Ford Beauty. One winter night, probably in 1919, he rode drunkenly up Anzac Avenue, with a friend (who was already on crutches from a football injury) riding pillion, into the tailboard of a fish wagon. Bloodied and bruised, the pair climbed back on and continued up

Symonds Street and down Queen Street, cheered on by passing picture-goers who took them for students staging a varsity stunt, before they were stopped and taken to hospital. Jessie and Ron collected Dan the next day, his head swathed in bandages. According to one family account, it was the head injury he suffered that night that disrupted Dan's university studies for the next few years. Perhaps Mason had this incident in mind when he later wrote: 'The future historian will take as the token of our downfall a crouching goggled common fool sprawled between the handles of a motor-bike.'[9] In subsequent years Dan's irresponsible behaviour was to cause the family considerable distress.

Ron was absent from school for the third term of 1919, from 14 August. Perhaps he had some mysterious illness; his classmates never knew. Ted Blaiklock would later speculate on what personal crisis had occurred that turned Mason from the 'quaint and sunny boy of 3A' whom he had first known – 'gay and carefree . . . sharp-tongued and satirical' – into the troubled, gloomy young man he would later recognise in his poetry.[10] There may have been a crisis of a more prosaic kind: the family's economic troubles. Jessie was by then working in a dining and tea rooms at the Otahuhu saleyards, serving meals during the weekly stock sales at Westfield. The house at Penrose, as Ron's friend Norman Leonard remembered it, was always 'in the most extraordinary muddle', and Jessie he recalled as a large, formidable and courageous woman, 'battling to run a restaurant to pay for the schooling of her two sons'.[11] A handyman-gardener, an Englishman named Nicholas Williams but known as Dick, also lived on the Penrose property, and early in 1919 Jessie took in a student boarder. Since Frank's death Annie Mason had given Jessie £5 a week – 'an average working man's wage' – and purchased surplus eggs and butter from the farmlet. When she died in September 1918, her will left Frank's share of her estate to Jessie, but her daughters, as trustees, ceased the regular financial support, perhaps because Dan was by then at university supported by his scholarship and could soon be expected to be earning himself.[12]

Or was it, as some have speculated, in this year that Mason first learned of the circumstances of his father's death? Did he wonder if it had been, in fact, suicide? Was there a sudden change in disposition, as Blaiklock believed (although he himself did not return to school in 1920, and was not to know Mason personally again for another several years)? Robert Burton would also wonder about 'that hidden part of his life' and his nervous tension and insecurity, and remembered 'a bad cry for help' one day, in 1918 or 1919, when Jessie arrived at his house to ask him to stay the weekend with Ron and he refused, 'scared of what I was going to find'.[13] Jessie later told a friend of Mason's how as a boy he would sometimes shut himself in his room for days at a time.[14]

MASON RETURNED to school in 1920 to repeat his fifth-form year, and made the most important friend of his youth, perhaps of his life. 'I had previously been aware of this tall good-looking lad with the curly hair and the prominent nose', he later wrote of the beginning of his friendship with Rex Fairburn. 'I well remember my pride and joy when this friendly giant took me under his wing.'[15] This was a little too self-effacing. Their appreciation of the relationship was mutual. To each the other became a mentor and best friend.

Fairburn was a year older than Mason. He had grown up in Parnell, in Lichfield Street, in a household at least outwardly more conventional than Mason's; his father was a sugar company clerk. Both temperamentally and physically they were opposites. Fairburn was large and lanky, physically strong, rumbustiously energetic, and good at sport. Mason was small and slight and disinclined to games or physical activity of any kind, except walking. At the beginning of 1920 the Fairburn family had moved from Parnell to Green Bay on the northern shore of the Manukau harbour. It was reached by train from the city, but the two boys habitually walked the ten miles between their homes. Epic walks were to become a lifelong habit of both. Fairburn was gregarious while Mason was reserved. But they shared a feeling of apartness. As fifteen-year-olds, their bond was at once vague and close: a common outlook on the world, instinctively sensed. 'For all our differences, we were heretics & rebels.'[16]

They had a distant family connection, too, as they were to discover some years later – or so the story has been told. Resting in St Thomas's churchyard one day while out walking, they pulled away the grass overgrowing the tombstone by which they sat and read the name Mathilda Jane Fairburn, who had died aged 17 in 1851. 'She's my relative', said Fairburn, 'and Mason surprised him even more by saying, "Yes and she's mine also".' Mathilda Lewis, who had married John Fairburn, Rex's great-uncle, in 1851 (she died the same year), was the sister of Amelia Lewis, the first wife of Mason's grandfather George Kells.[17]

There was literature, too. Mason, more widely read, introduced Fairburn to his already impressive knowledge of the classics. Fairburn wrote the 5A form notes for the final term on a Greek mythological theme. Mason appeared as Salmoneus, 'a lad of small stature, distinguished by his manly hair. He was attentive and eager to learn, and his work, when it could be read, vied with that of the best. But one fateful day, when told to "go hard," he went so far as to imitate lightning, and was struck down for his daring.'[18] He had by now adopted the distinctive hairstyle that he would keep for the rest of his life: brushed straight back from his forehead, 'tar-brush fashion'. It was 'a device to make him seem taller', one friend suspected.[19] Fairburn featured as a crack swimmer in the class notes Mason wrote for the second term, which took the form of a short play, prefaced by an epigraph from Homer and concluding with a stanza from Horace, in which an old boy, in the character of the cheerful idiot, visits the class and is hounded from the room at the mention of maths and science.

They were both abysmal at maths. Fairburn finished the year in last-equal place in the class, and Mason shared the second-lowest mark. By failing maths they failed the Matriculation exam. Fairburn decided to leave school, and took a job his mother had found him as a clerk in the New Zealand Insurance Company office in Queen Street.

Mason returned to school in 1921, to the upper sixth form, taking the train each day from the slightly closer station of Ellerslie. For in October 1920 Jessie had bought a five-acre property at 451 Great South Road, several miles nearer the city than the Penrose farmlet.[20] The property included a small house which could be let to tenants, along with a large, rambling, kauri-built homestead named 'Kohatu', meaning stone or rock ('on the rocks', Mason would refer to it in the 1930s, because they always were). The house stood at the end of a curving drive lined with pohutukawa and other native trees. 'Kohatu' remained Jessie's home for the next twenty-seven years, Mason's for nearly twenty.

While he continued to disdain sport, he took part in extra-curricular competition as a proficient debater, and began contributing regularly to the school *Chronicle*. In 1920 he had led the successful affirmative team in 5A's first debate, on the proposition 'That the supremacy of the sea must yield to the supremacy of the air', and written a humorous sketch for the *Chronicle* about 'The Boy with the Bad Memory' who writes away for Professor X—'s Marvellous Memory Course. In 1921, when he spoke for the negative in a debate on whether the British Empire was justified in building a fleet of super-Dreadnoughts, his friend Norman Leonard judged his speech 'the best of the day'.[21] But he did poorly in his exams that year, coming at or near the

bottom of the class in all his subjects. In the second term he had composed
the form notes in the style of *Pilgrim's Progress*:

> Now at last was the goal in sight and the prize in view, far in the distance, so
> that each man laboured to perfect himself to pass through the last and narrowest
> gate of all. For this gate was marked 'Exit,' and gave on to the shadowy plains
> of 'Work' and 'Varsity.' But the prizes were marked 'Varsity Schol.,' and
> seemed to me but poor rewards for so much labour, so that I contrived to
> loosen the burdens with which I was laden, and I walked on with the band,
> but not of them.[22]

He went back, though, in 1922 with the aim of matriculating and gaining
a university scholarship, like Dan. In the upper sixth's first-term debate that
year, on the proposition 'That the pen is mightier than the sword', he led the
negative team. The *Chronicle* reporter appreciated his 'conversational and easy'
style: 'his speech showed thought and humour. In summarising for his side he
maintained that the man with the sword speaks in a language that appeals to
all men for all time. The average man cannot appreciate Aeschylus and
Sophocles, but he can appreciate Leonidas and his 300. Their heroism will be
remembered longer than the "monumentum" of Horace.'[23] Appropriately,
Mason's team lost. To the *Chronicle* he contributed a humorous piece about
the agonies of mid-winter mornings (of 'frost and ice and frozen water-taps,
and fog and a sun that looks like an aluminium frying-pan'),[24] and a poem on
the school's motto, 'Per Angusta Ad Augusta'. But the clue to his vocation
was the translation of Horace's ode 'O Fons Bandusiae' which he produced
for his Latin master, Ken Dellow, during an exam in the second term that
year. This was the earliest poem that he would include in his first published
collection two years later. Mason's version of Horace's hymn to the fountain
of Bandusia was elegant, jaunty and precocious, with the mixture of strength
and lightness, formal mastery and colloquial feel that was to distinguish his
maturer work:

> O, fair Bandusian fountain,
>   Which clearer art than glass,
> To thee I shall account on
>   The next day that may pass;
> To thee I shall devote, then,
> As sacrifice, a goat, then,

Which dreams in vain love-battles; whose forehead is just curving
With young rough horns: such I shall give to thee who art deserving
Of unmixed wine with flowers for decoration serving.
O, fount Bandusian, that's what I shall do!
. . .

The technical accomplishment of the poem lies in the handling of rhythm: in the balance of short and long lines, and the use of the feminine rhymed couplets of each stanza to effect the transition from the short lines of the quatrain to the long six-beat measure. In Allen Curnow's appreciation, it was 'warm, brilliant and lively'.[25] Mason would later describe it when he first published it as '*Spiritually Rendered Into English Verse*. Fairly closely after: "Heigh-ho, My Fancy."'[26]

In the form notes he wrote for the final term he cast himself as a butler, forty years in the future, who works for a former 6A classmate – unbeknown to the latter. Nor does anyone else recognise him when his employer holds a class reunion. The butler wryly observes his old schoolmates – the staid judge, the portly doctor, the retired missionary, the faded film star – while they wonder what became of 'xy': 'last seen selling peanuts in a Sydney street'. Finally, 'I turned and went my weary way, wondering why I had paid so little attention to the solid things in life and so much to the gathering of rosebuds'. He signed this piece 'Herrick, I think'.[27]

The year ended with the unveiling of a memorial to the fallen of the First World War, and the final prize-giving presided over by Tibbs, who was retiring after thirty years. In the scholarship examinations Mason gained the second-highest mark in the country in English, and his combined results in English, Latin and French gave him over 300 marks more than the lowest-ranking of the successful scholars to qualify for university entrance. But he had failed maths again. In his testimonial Tibbs wrote: 'He is a lad of more than average ability in literary accomplishments; and he seems to me to have special gifts for journalism, which he hopes to take up as a profession.'[28]

4

In the Manner of Men

1923–25

WHEN SCHOOL closed at the end of 1922 Mason went down to Lichfield to stay with Aunt Foster and work on the nearby farms haymaking, as he would for most of the next seven summers. It was hot, hard work, alongside 'wise weather-beaten shrewd, sometimes sombre men', itinerant farm labourers mostly[1] – except when it rained and there was little to do except read, and write. When he could borrow a horse he would go riding, which he loved. In the evenings he went for solitary walks around 'The Square', a ten-acre block of rough paddocks surrounded by exotic trees (part of the original Thames Valley estate). He sent off a contribution to the *New Zealand Herald*, and received a rejection letter a few days before he returned to Auckland at the beginning of February 1923.

It was a tough time to be looking for his first job. A brief period of post-war prosperity had been brought abruptly to an end by the slump of 1921–22. Rehabilitation schemes were interrupted and new farmers – returned soldiers already struggling on poor, isolated, uneconomic blocks – were forced off the land. In the towns, wages fell, unemployment rose and bankruptcies spread. Conditions eased in a few years, but the 1920s remained a decade of economic insecurity, political instability, and widespread disillusionment that peace had not brought what it had promised.

From February until May Mason was employed as a relieving teacher at Mt Albert Grammar School. In the winter he worked in a surveyors' office (Harrison & Grierson in the Victoria Arcade in Queen Street). He had asked Tibbs to intercede with the University of New Zealand on his behalf, hoping to be granted provisional matriculation, but was disappointed. 'I am sorry nothing can be done in favour of R.A.K. Mason', the registrar replied, 'as he failed altogether in Mathematics in the Scholarship examination': he had scored 7 per cent.[2] Tibbs encouraged him to try again, but Mason did not study maths this year. In September he applied for a temporary teaching position at Seddon Memorial Technical College (near the university college on Symonds Street). On the back of his rejection letter he wrote these lines:

> So they took him & him they rewarded
> In the manner of all men at last:
> They took him & cruelly corded
> To the five & faggot right fast
> And his torture their pleasure afforded
> Till the even skies were o'ercast
> Who had dared to leave the old sordid
> And evil ways of the past.
> The Virgils [. . .] starve in our English streets,
> But oh, Maecenas, hard you are to find![3]

Maecenas was the patron of Horace and Virgil.

In the spring of 1923 Mason had several books of good quality blank paper prepared at a commercial bindery. Into two of them he copied a collection of poems, entitled 'In the Manner of Men', which he described as 'a small part of the unaided literary labour of almost exactly a year on the part of a youth of 18'.[4] Using for some reason the pseudonym 'V.R.N. Bird', he sent one copy to R.A. (Dickie) Singer, a prominent criminal lawyer of progressive views, an amateur actor and a published poet himself. The other he sent to Henry Hemus, a retired civil servant and member of the Grafton Shakespeare and Dramatic Society (which Fairburn and probably Mason joined around this time). Both books were subsequently lost, and only five of the poems would he later republish. But his surviving notes to the collection suggest its range and intention, and the character of the apprentice poet, at once sure of his purpose and striking a pose.

The notes begin (in mid-sentence) with some general remarks about style. Mason aimed to avoid

> flamboyant descriptive words & therefrom decoct poetry in the style of the early Swinburne or Kipling – earth's most dangerous models. For my part, I have usually employed only the simplest metres in original work (Namby–Pamby metre especially), so as to ensure the impossibility of writing twaddle or bombast. As to the vocabulary, I have endeavoured to keep it as free as possible from fine-sounding, meaningless phrases.

He opened the book with a group of translations from Horace: 'These I hope to extend & have indeed increased by two: Eheu fugaces & Carminum ii vii O Saepe mecum.'[5] The translations have been lost, but there is a clue here to

Mason's appreciation of the great Latin lyricist. It was not so much the light, celebratory tone of 'O Fons Bandusiae', which he had so brilliantly captured in his schoolboy translation, that attracted him. 'Eheu Fugaces' is an ode on the inevitability of death, a subject that Mason would make particularly his own. 'Deeper side of Horace – man haunted by fear of Death', he wrote in his notebook. 'I must kill for you Horace and cause Virgil to cease to be.'[6]

Horace, and Latin generally, would remain a deep influence on Mason's poetry, but one felt more in his style than in his subjects: his denseness of language and elusiveness of meaning, his swift ambiguities. The closer one reads Mason, C.K. Stead has observed, the harder he becomes to understand.[7] This is also true of Horace, a poet notoriously difficult to translate well with his allusiveness and delicacy, as Mason went on to observe here: 'Suffice it to say that it is pretty well agreed that there exists no readable translation of Horace: I therefore thought it no presumption to attempt translations which will at least make readable English, though not absolutely strictly literal renderings, and even containing additions which I have thought fit to make.' The Loeb Classical Library, which was then the standard edition of Latin literature, scarcely made the attempt, but interpreted the odes, in parallel text editions, in serviceable but clumsy English prose.

Mason followed the translations with two sonnets, entitled 'The Four Limbs of the Heretic' and 'I Send My Mind Aquest'. The first, of which he gave a detailed exegesis, was written, he explained, for the reader 'of imagination', who 'might take pleasure in seeing the swords suddenly leap out of the fog at the dimly-seen heretic: he leaps back & upward while the swords strike fire from the rock. Then, with neither the heretic nor pursuer in sight, the voice of the vengeful pursuer comes rolling up through the fog . . .'. Notice, he remarked, 'how the whole action is confined to a short incident' and 'how shadowy it all is'. The second, he apologised,

is difficult, apparently a grave fault. But there is a great difference in being obscure over a simple statement, and over a difficult & intricate thought worked out in so involved a form as the Sonnet. I meant to express a mood to which I am often subject: I often feel great natural indignation at the vice & folly of others, and seek to relieve my feelings by anger against them. But my mind refuses to condemn them, saying your attack is unmerited: for after all, we are servants of Fate, and each of these but a blind helpless instrument of environment & circumstance. Then my mind says to me: These men are helpless, but what of you? Are you not wrong & foolish in thinking that you should attack & judge your fellow-creatures: they know no better, but you who are wiser, you alone are foul.

A draft of the poem has survived among Mason's unpublished manuscripts, with the title 'Dejected in Defeat from having Nothing to Assault':

> I send my mind aquest early & late,
>> Urged by man's folly, greed, & seething reek,
>> That in his vice & bestialness it may seek
> That I may hate as oft as I wish to hate.
>
> But it returning, me doth contemplate
>> Reproachfully, and bitterly doth speak:
>> 'Wouldst deem hate-worthy men who are but weak,
> Frail victims of a common crushing fate?
>
> Fool! I have found those men you would despise –
>> The lecherous, the murderer, they who howl
> Incessant everything beneath the skies –
>> all pure & but seem dark from Destiny's scowl,
> But thou, who dost them meet for scorn surmise,
>> Thou – thou alone – of earthly things art foul.'[8]

The poem he would reject, but the anxiety remained.

He would republish the next three, 'Sonnets of the Ocean's Base', which treat a traditional metaphor of classical and Romantic literature – the ship as a being on the voyage of life or society under threat, the sea as signifying chaos or death – and show specific textual influences from Shakespeare, Shelley, Keats and again Horace. The metaphor recurs in Mason's notebooks: 'The ship of my soul, trapped far from land, is sinking beneath the battering of their huge waves . . .', 'We are submarines sunk at the bottom of this sea of air, and cruising blindly round knowing that the sea must some day crush us.'[9] The three sonnets, however, he presented as exercises, explicitly abjuring interpretation. 'In these 3 poems alone', he wrote, 'I have abandoned myself to pure creative imagination, untramelled by thought. It seems to me as though there are a few organ-notes there, notably in the octave of the second':

I strayed where sunk fleets slept, all filled with jars
    Of jacinth, silver, sunset-gleaming gold,
    Half-hidden in leather slowly growing mould,
Or royally lying in great, beaten bars.

And there were swords, and shields, and scimitars
    That in the grey sea-twilight glimmered cold,
    As adoration paid by Eremite old,
Bending his body down to distant stars.

The other two poems from 'In the Manner of Men' which were to remain in Mason's published oeuvre, 'Lullaby' and 'The Beggar', were of a different order. These are cursing poems, whose effect is achieved by the counterpoint of violent sentiment and the lyric form, and by their taut, sure rhythm. 'Lullaby' employs a classical theme and archaic language, but its meaning is direct and earnest. The speaker, an outcast or rebel, heaps vengeance on his oppressor:

Didst not o mine enemy
    think in pleasant death to lie
    shrined in pomp-girt cemetery?

I have taken pick and spade
    digged you out whence you were laid
    midst the moan your money made

Digged you out whence you were shrined
    I whom thing with scarce a mind
    all long lifetime you did grind

Down to filthed machine-like toil
    black with muck and reek of oil
    digged your proud corpse from proud soil
. . .

'The Beggar', while similarly bitter in tone, is a more sophisticated poem in its ironic reversal of the situation, for here it is the victor who curses the outcast, blind and crippled beggar:

Curse the beggar in the street
  That he has less joy than I,
As, at these fine old trees' feet,
  Body-satisfied, I lie.

He it is whose threne sobs thin
  All adown this lovely dale;
Till slight pleasure grows rank sin
  'Gainst Pan's pipes his pipes prevail.

He it is, with loathsome mien,
  Gibbers by the sweeping car,
As, for joy, we steal between
  Fields where frail pools sleeping are.

He hath damned my fine-bound book
  And my pleasantness of meat –
Blasted, by his withering look,
  All that once I glad could greet.

Curse the beggar in the street:
  Curse the beggar that he die:
Curse him for his shrivelled feet
  And his cruel, sight-striving eye.

Mason was right to be most pleased with this one. It 'may be compared with "There Is An Old Etruscan". I like it very well. Is not "frail" the mot juste for quiet, unruffled shimmering pools lying in hot sunshine like great teacups? Sight-striving also, is that not expressive of the agony as if the eye were rebelling always against its fate, not merely passive as blind would suggest. Enough', he continued, in a tone of feigned modesty. 'I do not like puffing myself. I could not do it all except under the decent guise of a double barrelled nom-de-plume. But there are many unpalatable tasks for him who would serve Literature.'

Dickie Singer responded warmly, but his encouragement was not the kind the young poet was hoping for. He would not be Mason's Maecenas. 'I am always prepared to help anybody in your position and with your aspirations', he wrote to him in December, saying that the volume showed 'excellent promise', but 'I am bound to tell you that I am not quite rich enough to justify me in giving you five pounds as the price of the book. It may quite possibly happen that in years to come there will be considerable accretion to your estimated value, but after all, the gamble would be upon me'. He advised Mason to get a job. 'I see no reason why, in a country like this, notwithstanding your poetic vein, your muscles should be neglected, nor why a reasonable occupation which will return you a living should prevent you from continuing your literary efforts.'[10]

BY THIS TIME Mason had begun keeping a writer's notebook. He wrote down fragments of verse, short sketches, epigrams and aphorisms, 'Fag-ends of conversations, extracts from books . . . word-sketches of faces, characters, landscapes', observations about politics and poetry, the nature of humanity, the meaning – or absurdity – of life as it appeared to a well-read, introspective, troubled young man. He also wrote on the backs of envelopes and letters, on stationery left over from his father's business or from Dan's various enterprises, on tram tickets or whatever else came to hand: 'old ragged edges of newspapers – bits torn out of books'.[11] Throughout his life he would write using pencil in preference to pen, his gaunt, upright script fading and shrinking to illegibility on scraps of brown newsprint or card. About 1930 he collected and neatly copied his jottings into five loose-leaved 'books', using the backs of letterhead paper for Leighton Laboratories, Manufacturing Chemists of Hamilton.

The earliest of these notebook entries that can be precisely dated were made in February 1923, just after Mason had returned to Auckland from Lichfield. Then, according to his later annotation, 'I was making the book an interchange of letters between [a] N.Z. man and [a] German doctor, but I gave this up because of ignorance of Germany.' He cast himself as a young poet who discussed his work with his correspondent and sent him poems; the doctor, whose side of the correspondence is only implied, sent him advice and books. 'Many thanks for your kind letter', the poet wrote, ' – also for books. I have shown the latter to a friend of mine who is rather an expert in that line, and he is wildly enthusiastic about them, especially the one containing translations from Heine, which he has borrowed'. ('Isn't it funny', he digressed on the subject of lending books, 'people are so lax about books and umbrellas and defrauding the Government? And have you noticed how hard it is to post a letter that anyone gives you to drop in the box?') He continued:

And you know I find it very hard in writing to know just how to punctuate properly, especially just where I ought to put the commas. Also paragraphing puzzled me for a long time. I read the grammar-books, but they didn't help much, so I just gave it up and sort of trusted to luck. With poetry I was worried to get the lines the right length so that the rhymes would come just in the proper place. However, that tumbled out all right. I found there was no use worrying, for at times I couldn't possibly manage to get a line right for all the struggling in the world; and at others I just couldn't go wrong and all went well without any worry – though for the life of me I can't reason how it is done at such times as it *is* done. All these rules and things for writing seem to be either no trouble or of no account when you are full of yourself and going full speed ahead, so I don't think I shall worry myself so much about them in future. . . . henceforth let my motto be 'Rules to Hell'.[12]

But Mason himself was anything but careless about the art of poetry. He was working at it, and took his vocation with all the seriousness of his years. Writing to Henry Hemus, he discussed the efficacy and validity of rhyme, about which 'I myself have had some doubts', he confessed before elaborating five points in its defence. 'It may be said that rhyme ruins many verses. For my own part, I am content to let it. One aims at the small amount of perfection, not at the large amount of mediocrity': 'I intend to make myself master of the most difficult forms of art, before I try the easier, so that it shall not be said that "I write 'vers libre' because I have not the brains enough to write rhyme."' Hemus found the young man 'idealistic to a degree that is remarkable at your years'.[13]

The imaginary German was not his only confidant. Rex Fairburn, still working as a reluctant insurance clerk, remained his closest friend. About this time the two of them – Fairburn more enthusiastically – became involved in amateur theatre. This was one of the few interests that Fairburn shared with his accountant-father, who had designed the family home around a two-storey auditorium. Fairburn became juvenile lead for the Grafton society, appearing in plays by Shakespeare, Barrie and Milne in the St Andrews Hall in lower Symonds Street. Mason's interest in the theatre was to find its more natural outlet in writing. He already had 'a few tales & plays to my credit', he had stated in his note to 'In the Manner of Men'.

At Lichfield again over the summer of 1923–24 Mason experienced what was probably his first romantic attachment, falling briefly in love with a cousin who was visiting Aunt Foster. Fairburn, who was embarked on his own, more enduring first romance, which would inspire his first, tentative efforts at poetry, wrote to him in teasing sympathy from the insurance office. 'I Received your lewd epistle today and was subject to considerable questionnings as to who the mutt was who wrote it. I told them all, sparing no details and their mirth turned to pity instantly. . . . As you say, it's a hell of a life. Why can't a man be decently & comfortably dead & done? Your lysol suggestion is excellent, but suicide is so *vulgar*!' He then discoursed for several more paragraphs on death and the soul, before signing himself 'F. Achates' – the faithful friend of Aeneas in Virgil's *Aeneid*.[14] This is the earliest surviving piece of a voluminous correspondence in which, over the next several years, Fairburn indulged his philosophising bent and ribald wit in long, rambling letters to his friend. Mason's letters to Fairburn were shorter and fewer. 'Here I go & open my Geom. book to-day in Pork's room & discover this letter', he began one of the first he sent him (in 1921). 'I can see I'll really have to be a poet so as to have something to blame my memory on to.'[15] The letter containing his Lysol suggestion has not survived.

Back in Auckland after the harvest season Mason found a job teaching Latin at the University Coaching College. It was unrewarding work, intellectually and financially, and he was to do it for more than six years. It was part-time and irregular and paid poorly; the students were cramming for school or university exams. But he was good at it. He loved Latin, and was a patient, generous teacher. The college was run by Horace Holl, a Cambridge graduate and mathematician, and a passionate alpinist who had climbed extensively in the Swiss Alps, and in New Zealand claimed some kind of record by reaching the summit of Mt Cook twice in a fortnight. Each year he held a summer school for his pupils at Tongariro National Park. The rest of the time the college was conducted in offices on the first floor of the Ferry Building, the large brick transport terminus on the waterfront at the bottom of Queen Street. There was time between classes to visit the public library. Among other things Mason was reading at this time, he kept up with the Sydney *Bulletin*, whose 'Red Page' had for many years been a valuable outlet for the publication and discussion of New Zealand as well as Australian literature, and with the monthly *London Mercury*, which published and reviewed new English and American writing, albeit from a quite conservative editorial position (its founder and editor, the Georgian poet J.C. Squire, had no time for modernism).

Meanwhile, he and Fairburn planned newspapers of their own. A monthly or three-weekly arts review had been Mason's last idea (in the winter of

1923): 'a sort of cross between the aforementioned "London Mercury", the "Smart Set Magazine" (H.L. Mencken of U.S.A.) & "The Triad"', written entirely by themselves. 'We could adopt a high-tone, anti-democratic tone – "to uphold fearlessly & without regard to class or creed etc etc etc."' Fairburn had had in mind a sports weekly.[16]

At lunchtime and after work the two regularly met at the corner of Exchange Lane and Queen Street. In the weekends they walked, 'partly for the pleasure of it and partly because we usually didn't have the fares to do anything else'. They walked between the city and Ellerslie and Green Bay, to Mt Albert, where Rex's girlfriend, Irene Jenkin, lived, and further afield, back and forth across the undulating volcanic landscape of the Auckland isthmus. They walked and 'talked of everything under the sun . . . questioned all assumptions and . . . questioned all authority', two earnest young men with Housman in their pockets and a deepening awareness and indignation that the world was not as they thought it should be.[17] They talked about poetry and philosophy, and railed against the smugness, hypocrisy, narrow-mindedness, conservatism and shallow materialism of post-war New Zealand, a society ruled by '[m]en who consider the world was made and the stars ranged in order to facilitate the transport of pigs between Taupiri and Wairoa.' 'N.Z. has three idols', Mason observed, '– dairy-farming, footballers, and profit – the cow, the bullock, the gilded calf.' He wrote withering comments in his notebook on the middle class, the capitalist, the conventionally minded – the kind of people with whom Fairburn worked in the insurance office, and Mason had briefly at Harrison & Grierson: 'Standardised and carefully synchronised souls'; 'Kiplingesque beef-and-beer Briton'; 'He was straight – and oh, so narrow'; 'Mr. Harren, though a Mayor, yet was almost certain that a man who deals with sonnets is a writer of some sort.' They had grown up during the grim, jingoistic, messy years of the First World War and its aftermath, and took a cynical view of imperialism and patriotism, subjects which featured frequently in Mason's notebook conversations. 'The blind nations of Europe have blundered into war: we New Zealanders feel called on to justify our taste in ancestors by aiding England. The bloody investment of the Maori Wars is now paying its dividend in blood. Oh luckless sons of Atreus!'[18] In time their instinctive sense of revolt would follow different paths, but for the moment they were heretics together.

'SPEAKING of umbrellas,' Mason wrote to the German doctor, 'I am working out a little epigram – haven't got it properly fixed yet – about the rain falling

on the just and unjust man alike, but it will usually be found that the unjust
man has the umbrella of the just man. Sounds clumsy put that way, but I
think I can work it up until it is quite neat. Well, I shall close this dreary
account of dreary weather with a piece of poetry. It was most effortless in the
writing. I call it In Perpetuum Vale, after the last line of a magnificent poem
by Catullus (No. CI).'[19] 'In Perpetuum Vale' was one of the poems Mason
collected together to make his first publication proper, *The Beggar*, which he
had printed in the winter of 1924 by local booksellers and publisher–printers
Whitcombe & Tombs. It was 'a small waistcoat-pocket volume', measuring
four inches by five, bound in brown paper covers and containing eighteen
poems 'pleasingly printed' in tiny, 9-point type.[20] It cost him, according to
one account, £20 – at least two months' salary from Holl's. He sold it for a
shilling a copy.

   Along with the title poem he included his favourite (the second) of the
three ocean sonnets from 'In the Manner of Men', the inspired rendering of
Horace's 'O Fons Bandusiae' and a translation from the French, François
Coppée's 'J'ai crié dans le solitude' (I cried out in the wilderness), and fourteen
new poems which dealt with death and fate, the loneliness of the outcast and
the failure of belief. These were not unusual preoccupations for an eighteen-
or nineteen-year-old. There was, though, something more than unusual in
the intensity, the harshness of imagery, the bitterness of taste – the cumulative
impact of what his closest friend would later describe as Mason's 'smouldering
pessimism' – and in the technical sureness of the writing. It was a remarkable
literary début. In the restrained but admiring assessment of the *Auckland Star*,
there was 'a touch of distinction in his verse which lifts it above the ruck'.[21]

   At the front of the book Mason placed the 'sight-striving' outcast, the poet–
beggar. Next, a sonnet about the failure of belief, the first three stanzas of
which declared with increasing stridency a position of agnostic humanism –

> I am not stone, not adamant, not steel,
>   Am no undutiful clod, but all a man . . .
>
> And I would break a valiant lance for truth,
>   And against wrong wield an unflagging sword . . .
>
> And ever would be strong as granite crag
>   Assailed by weak, pale, wan, dead-grass fire . . .

– only to undercut this conviction in the final couplet, a puzzled expression of doubt. 'The Agnostic', as one of his earliest critics fairly observed, 'as you probably know, is an exercise';[22] but in its rhetorical structure it suggests where, in part, the source of Mason's 'touch of distinction' lay. As here, Mason's poems are characteristically dramatic, a quality they share with Latin verse. At their best they succeed, and disconcert (whether by instinct or design has been a matter of critical debate), by swift, subtle underminings of the rhetorical gesture – in C.K. Stead's words, by their 'meaningful ambiguity': 'Mason's instinct is to embody dramatically what he sets out to deny.'[23] 'Old Memories of Earth' does so with a seeming casualness which makes it arguably the best poem in *The Beggar*:

> I think I have no other home than this.
>> I have forgotten much, remember much,
>> But never have I any memories such
> As others feign they have of lands of bliss.
>
> Perhaps they have done, again will do what
>> They say they have – mayhap quaffed godly drink;
>> But I have not communed with gods, I think,
> And, even though I live past death, will not.
>
> I rather am for ever bondaged fast
>> To earth, and have been. So much untaught I know.
>> Slow, like great ships, I have often seen go
> Ten priests – ten each time – round a grave long past.
>
> And I recall – I think I can recall –
>> Back even past the time I started school,
>> Or went a-Crusoëing in the corner pool
> That I was present at a city's fall.
>
> And I am positive that, yesterday,
>> Walking past One Tree Hill and quite alone,
>> To me there came a fellow I have known
> In some old times, but when I cannot say.

We must have been great friends, though, I and he,
　　Otherwise I should not remember him,
　　For everything of the old life seems dim
As last year's deeds recalled by friends to me.

The narrator appears to set out to assert that there are no gods and no after-
life, but his narrative contradicts him. The poem's peculiar force lies in his
hesitancy and humbleness, in its rhythm of thinking aloud, in its shifting
between certainty and doubt, and its casual intermingling of past and present,
classical and colloquial – of the concrete present (One Tree Hill and the
corner pool) and a vast, mythic past (in some old days, at a city's fall, round a
grave long past).

　'Wayfarers' with similar deftness conflates biblical, classical and contemporary time into the poet's imaginative world:

That I go out alone to them it seems,
　　Because they see none with me in the way:
Not know men that the fabrics of my dreams
　　Are less intangible to me than they.

Not know that I have heard and seen Christ break
　　The bondage of His tongue-tied sightlessness;
Have walked with firm-faithed Mary to the stake
　　And kissed the hem of martyred Flora's dress,

And I in Lichfield often-times have been
　　With Thomas Chatterton at suicide;
Have Gaius Marius in Minturnae seen
　　For many hours by Waitemata's tide.

Burnt Dian's temple down at Otahu,
　　And slain Herostratus at Papatoi;
Have here, in Penrose, brought Æneas through
　　To calm Ausonian lands from boisterous Troy.

Here the poet claims companionship with a cast of the defeated and outcast:
with the saint Mary and the martyred goddess of spring;[24] with Chatterton,
poet and suicide at seventeen; with the proletarian Gaius Marius, Roman

consul and emperor, in the days of his downfall, a fugitive in the coastal marshes of Minturnae; with the slave Herostratus; and with Virgil's homeless wanderer, Aeneas. Mason's schoolfriend and fellow Latinist, Ted Blaiklock, would later read in this poem a clue to the emotional crisis that he believed Mason had suffered in his teenage years, during his mysterious absence from school. It lay not only in his identifying with the young, dead Chatterton: 'What curious strife of soul', Blaiklock wondered, lay behind his identifying with Herostratus, then 'striking the villain down' at Papatoetoe?[25] The same, perhaps, that concluded 'Sonnet of Brotherhood', a poem about the bonds of common humanity, with a powerful image of alienation that would become Mason's most frequently quoted lines:

> Here, in this far-pitched, perilous, hostile place,
> This solitary, hard-assaulted spot,
> Fixed at the friendless, utter verge of space.

Mason's classical learning was everywhere in these poems: in their rhythm, vocabulary and word order, their temper, their characters, and sometimes in more direct literary associations. Three sonnets collectively entitled 'Miracle of Life', a meditation on chance and mortality, may have had their genesis in the great philosophical poem of Lucretius, *De Rerum Natura*, a work which Mason studied. 'I am prepared to go to a great deal of trouble to win even such a poor & limited appreciation of Lucretius as is possible for me to-day living in a mechanical age among an isolated & only half civilised people', he wrote in his notebook.[26] 'The Lesser Stars' took its cue from the last ode of Horace, 'Exegi monumentum': 'I have raised myself a monument more lasting than bronze and higher than the royal site of the pyramids', it begins (in Mason's own translation). His own poem was an elegy for the ordinary: 'We are they who are doomed to raise up no monuments/ to outlast brass'. In the poem later titled 'Herostratus at Ephesus' he treated the same theme but took the part of Herostratus, who razed the temple of Diana solely to preserve his own name, and exulted in his arrogance:

> Spit at me – scorn me – spurn me – strike me down,
> Heirs to Oblivion, mine is still the crown –
> Ephemeral ones, still deathless fame my lot.
> . . .

> This outcast, reviled, mocked, and despised fool,
> Alone inherits immortality.

Catullus, original master of the epigram, love poet and satirist *extraordinaire*, provided the title of 'In Perpetuum Vale', from the line 'atque in perpetuum, frater, ave atque vale' (now and for ever, my brother, hail and farewell), but the stronger literary reference here is to Tennyson's 'The Lotos Eaters'. The sound of the poem, however, is Mason's own. It states its theme, man's mortality, with the muscular rhythm and economy of the earlier 'Lullaby' and 'The Beggar', and through a characteristic dramatic irony in that it is spoken from beyond the grave:

> Bruised – bruised – bruised – bruised.
> Wrathfully the sods have used
> This poor, mouldering self of mine,
> That I, fool, once thought divine.
> Bitterly the bleak sods fell.

> I no hint of asphodel,
> Amaranth, ambrosia, moly,
> Paradise, nor heaven holy,
> After those long pangs have found,
> But the cold clutch of cold ground.

In 'After Death' Mason treated his favourite subject in a different tone:

> And there will be just as rich fruits to cull,
> And jewels to see;
> Nor shall the moon nor the sun be any more dull;
> And there will be flowers as fine to pull,
> And the rain will be as beautiful –
> But not for me.

The feel of this poem lies in the lyrical evocation of sensual pleasures denied, rather than in the abrupt denial of the refrain (from Thomas Beddoes, another poet who had a preoccupation with graves and death). Still, the point is no less plain: 'The ghastly realisation that Death is not just a subject for disinterested speculation but a machine made to kill all men, to murder me. Not an easy piece of material to cut precious sonnets out of, but an entangling choking shroud.'[27]

'You see, I am afraid it is a bit too pessimistic', Mason's imagined poet observed to the Geman doctor,

> but somehow or other when I start to write poetry it always does seem to turn out that way. However, I feel vaguely that this will strengthen me up and take the flabby thoughts out of me; besides, it will be all the better when I do come round to the proper way of writing, because then I will sort of have tokens of my former sins to be able to hang up in the church as a visible sign of repentance. I do try and I sometimes do write poems about pleasant things, but somehow they don't seem very good. The optimistic things that I see and read and think and do all seem to slide away from me when I sit down to write poetry – it's not the same way with prose. I am very worried about it because I do want to brighten life and make this world a better place for my being in it.

He also wrote: 'You are a misanthropist, a pessimist. No, I damn well wish I could be – it would be easier for myself and I should be less of a man of melancholy.'[28]

THE BEGGAR was the book that Mason reputedly threw into Auckland harbour, in a gesture of disgust or despair. 'He had foolish dreams – wildly, madly, bitterly impossible dreams – dreams of an age where the highest learning and art and literature were on at least an equal footing with the lowest ranks of trade and commerce and politics.'[29] It was a bravura performance: both the poetry and his melodramatically tossing it into the sea. Critic and poet Allen Curnow, in an often-quoted phrase, was subsequently to find in *The Beggar* the emergence of New Zealand's 'first wholly original, unmistakably gifted poet'.[30] Leaving aside, for the moment, the critical debate over the way in which this statement fixed Mason in the construct of literary nationalism, it contains some literal truth. He was unmistakably gifted. And, although no more 'wholly original' than any poet, he was something different on the local literary scene. In 1924 the most important recent publications of New Zealand poetry were B.E. (Blanche) Baughan's fourth volume, *Poems from the Port Hills* (1923), and Eileen Duggan's first (*Poems*, 1922). Baughan wrote rhapsodic, at times transcendent, poetry informed by a Whitmanesque belief in the need for a new poetic in a new land; Curnow thought her much-anthologised 'A

Bush Section' from the 1908 volume *Shingle-short and Other Verses* 'the best
New Zealand poem before Mason'.[31] Duggan was a deeply religious,
whimsical, often sentimental poet in the Georgian style, who would later
write patriotically about New Zealand but who in her earliest poems looked
to her family's Irish heritage. Mason may have read these and other volumes
of contemporary local verse – journalist O.N. Gillespie's *The Road to Muriwai*
(1922), perhaps, and probably S.C. August's *Stewart Island Verses* (1923), whose
author sent him a copy (and asked for an autographed copy of *The Beggar* in
return) – but it left no traces in his own.

Mason does appear to have known and been impressed by the earlier
work of A.H. Adams, whose *Collected Poems* had been published in Australia
in 1913. Their work has at least a 'temperamental affinity' in their fascination
with death, their empathy with outcasts and their atheistic humanism, and
perhaps in some more direct associations: Mason's 'After Death', critics have
observed, may owe something to Adams's 'After'. Adams, who had lived
mainly in Sydney after 1898 and was for a time editor of the *Bulletin*, was
influenced by the Australian bush-ballad tradition and he described a harsher,
more melancholy New Zealand than the vast bulk of colonial verse, which
was sentimental, derivative and decorative. But Mason took little from the
shallow pool of New Zealand poetry; there was little in it for him to take. His
sources lay in the deeper traditions of classical and English literature.

The question of influence, of where poetry came from, troubled him. He
wrote in his notebook: 'Certain passages in authors are neither plagiarized
nor even imitated, yet they are vaguely reminiscent. Thus one feels that when
Milton wrote "Lawrence, of virtuous father virtuous son", he was dimly
aware of Horace's "O filia pulchrior" and that Rossetti's "Blessed Damozel"
might never have been written, certainly not in its present form, but for the
old ballad, "Good King Wenceslas looked out."' And: 'Stevenson's method
of learning to write by "playing the sedulous ape" was never mine. I was
protected against it in youth by my laziness, in maturer years by my knowledge.
This laziness, I may say, is the essence of art – just waiting placidly till the
ideas float along.' But this, Mason knew, was disingenuous. Elsewhere he
came closer to describing the nature of literary creation: 'Momentary inspiration
regulated by previously assimilated art.' Writing to his friend and fellow poet
Geoffrey de Montalk some years later, he advised him: 'why be diffident
about one bloody echo, when anybody worth a damn is rotten with
them?'[32]

How many copies of *The Beggar* he had printed, and how many were sold, is not known. But the book was not totally ignored as the legend implies. An anonymous benefactor sent him £3. It received an appreciative, if slightly patronising, notice in the *Auckland Star*, where it was reviewed in the same column as *Random Rhymes* by James H. Elliot of Hamilton – 'a fluent sentimentalist and a facile philosopher, but hardly a poet', whose poems had titles such as 'Lament and petition of a thirsty cow'. The reviewer then turned to *The Beggar*, the work of 'a young writer with a different outlook and method. His work has the crudity of youth, but also its intensity and its promise.' However, 'Mr. Mason is inclined to brood too much on "graves and epitaphs." He will find out that life holds more than gloom, and will realise that when a poet writes about the processes of mortality he should select carefully. There is unusual promise in his verses, and work and experience should take him up the hill.'[33]

Other readers were similarly both impressed by his achievement and worried by his turn of mind. A teacher at Auckland Grammar wrote to him: 'I have just read with delight, half-a-dozen times over, your very remarkable poems. I took them to school to-day and read several of them to my colleagues round the luncheon table. . . . Remarks are made about the morbidity of much of the sentiment', although he himself was not concerned by this:

> a work of art should be judged on its craftsmanship and not on its morals. And you quite surprise one with the apt word the telling phrase the bold metaphor. I can only say 'maete virtute'. Indulge your fine fancies and express them in untrammelled verse. Never mind if you shock respectability and convention. Do not however let your musings on the gruesome and grotesque spoil your own enjoyment of the delights which life offers. You are entitled to happiness & you should look upon it as your birthright.

He enclosed a shilling for an extra copy to give to Mr Browne, one of the maths masters, 'who has a good taste in literature with all his sines & cosines'.[34]

Mason had also taken the enterprising initiative of sending fifty copies of *The Beggar* to London: to Harold Monro, publisher, poet and proprietor of the famous Poetry Bookshop in Bloomsbury. The Poetry Bookshop was a mecca for young and aspiring writers, students and visiting literati from abroad. Monro hosted weekly poetry readings, opening each session with a recital of Shelley's 'Hymn to Intellectual Beauty'. He was an important figure on the Georgian literary scene, and his patronage was not exclusive. T.S. Eliot and

Ezra Pound were among those who read their work at the Poetry Bookshop, Robert Frost and D.H. Lawrence among the writers to whom he let the two attic rooms above it for a nominal rent. As an editor, 'his gloomy pessimism was persuasive'.[35]

He wrote back to Mason on 27 December 1924, apologising for his seeming neglect in not having done so before. It was not through 'lack of appreciation or carelessness. By no means. I admit that when I first opened your parcel of 50 copies I felt bored and indifferent, because so much that is worthless is fired in here in such a manner. But when I had read your letter and your printed matter (I can't call it even a book-let) I felt grateful and contented.' His letter was intended to be encouraging and helpfully critical. He recognised, he told Mason, 'a strong affinity between us', although hastening to add that it was the skill as much as the sentiment of the poetry that had impressed him, its 'inventiveness of rhythm & stanza-form'. He liked best ('in their order in the book'): 'After Death' (for its 'restraint'), 'Old Memories of Earth', 'The Lesser Stars', 'In Perpetuum Vale', the first sonnet under the title 'The Miracle of Life', 'The Spark's Farewell to its Clay' and 'Latter-day Geography Lesson'. 'The Beggar' was 'good enough to annoy most people, but not quite good enough to please those whom it would not annoy'. 'In Perpetuum Vale' 'begins splendidly', but he criticised the last twelve lines (which Mason subsequently removed from the poem) 'where you begin philosophising'.

'I am sorry for you, very', he remarked, 'though (is it a platitude?) loneliness is always good discipline.' Monro himself had begun writing poetry as a lonely teenager. He spent some time living in Italy, indulging a romantic and vaguely socialist idealism – imbued with 'the mind-climate of the new century with its expectation of joy and freedom, expressed through Fabianism and Utopianism, through Tolstoyan settlements, garden cities and vegetarianism tea-rooms, through Shelley's Spirit of Delight and the Spirit of Ecstasy on the new Rolls Royce' – before returning to England in 1911 to do something practical for the cause of popularising poetry, founding the *Poetry Review* and *Poetry and Drama* and the Poetry Bookshop.[36] His own writing was darker and more bitter than most of the 'Georgian' verse of his contemporaries. Monro had felt profoundly his loss of religious faith when in his twenties, and he recognised in himself the tendency to gloom and introspection which, in his later life, contributed to his alcoholism. '[O]n the basis of kindred mentality alone, I could not fail to be sympathetic toward your verse', he told Mason, wondering if he had ever visited the Poetry Bookshop.[37]

Having had no time to secure Mason's permission, Monro had taken his own initiative and placed two poems in the November 1924 issue of the *Chapbook*, originally a monthly and by then an occasional anthology of new verse published under the Poetry Bookshop imprint to 'encourage new talent and to introduce to the public writers and artists of genuine originality, whether unacknowledged or acknowledged'.[38] He chose 'Latter-day Geography Lesson', which, in Mason's own description, '[d]eals with a schoolteacher taking his little ch[ar]ges round the ruins of London: he is chafing to soar into pedantic pseudo-poetry but is always brought back by their playing the bloody fool' – a lighter take on the themes of mortality and mutability that dominate *The Beggar*.[39] The poem brings to mind Macaulay's New Zealander standing in some future time on London Bridge sketching the ruins of St Paul's Cathedral (Mason's latter-day visitors are Eskimos) and, when the Eskimo master instructs one boy to 'stop poking/ your thumb through the eyes of that skull', perhaps his own childhood clambering over the pitted scoria slopes of Mt Wellington. Mason would later describe it as his own favourite (or at least, 'I used to like it').[40] The other poem Monro selected was a short untitled poem which followed 'In Perpetuum Vale' in *The Beggar*, and which he read as an epilogue to that poem and printed under that title.[41] Mason would later call it 'Body of John':

> Oh! I have grown so shrivelled and sere,
> > *But the body of John enlarges,*
> And I can scarcely summon a tear,
> > *But the body of John discharges.*
>
> It's true my old roof is near ready to drop,
> > *But John's boards have burst asunder,*
> And I am perishing cold here a-top,
> > *But his bones lie stark hereunder.*

It is a simple, powerful, disturbing and elusive poem, all the more so when read in the light of its personal resonances: that John was the name by which Mason was known in his family, and also the name of a cousin (the first son of Frank Mason's Uncle John) who had drowned in 1884 at the age of eleven. (An unpublished poem, similarly structured and entitled 'Progress', has for John the name Ben – a Benjamin is the youngest or favourite son.) Mason appears to have expressed some reservations about the poem, for Monro advised him not to revise it: 'I think these two stanzas about the best thing in the book – mysterious sombre realism in a strangely successful rhythm.' 'Don't be angry with me', Monro entreated him, and enclosed 'a miserable little cheque of a guinea'. He hoped to see more of Mason's work, but counselled him: 'please, in your loneliness, don't run too fast, or you may lose your breath'.[42]

Mason cannot have been unhappy with Monro's letter, nor with his poems being published, with or without his permission, in the *Chapbook* alongside such names as T.S. Eliot, Richard Aldington, Anna Wickham and the Sitwells. Nor with the guinea. But he did not reply to Monro. Perhaps it was simply that he never got around to it – he was, throughout his life, a terrible correspondent and a procrastinator. His friends perpetually complained about what one called his 'constitutional incapacity to write letters'.[43] 'Write, you bugger', Fairburn would conclude his own. Even the letters Mason did write he did not always post. An entry in his notebook reads: 'Census before last – earnest intellectual – put myself down as poet. Next time I looked on this as affectation and wrote wharf-lumper. But this time I feel that this was even greater pride O Diogenes and out of respect to my damnable habit of dilatoriness I write myself as Procrastinator. Must be a bit of a puzzle to classifying officials.'[44] Or perhaps there was more to his behaviour than carelessness or procrastination. 'My life has been full of such missed opportunities', Mason once commented (although in jest).[45] This might have been one.

'WE DANCE across the tight-rope to our death.' 'And when they buried him the grave was so deep that no man could see the bottom of it.'[46] The notebook writings that Mason kept and carefully transcribed in his early twenties are as witty as they are dark and cynical. They show his humour – albeit often of a bitter, sardonic kind – and taste for satire, his enjoyment of language, punning and word-play. But he wrote often about death: throwaway bits of verse, and images of disturbing starkness.

Tick-tock old clock –
  What's that square hole yonder?
Tick-tock tick-tock
  What's it for I wonder.

One second nearer
It is growing clearer
Look how its sides crumble
Save me for I stumble.

All my strength is leaking away through a great hole in my back. My life is oozing out of a ragged tear at the base of my back-bone. The tail of my shirt is soaking up my life-blood.

Broken nerveless shivering friendless
   he went into the endless
   nothing of the grave.[47]

'What a death-obsessed young man he was', a close friend would later remark.[48] He made a number of entries in the character of an old man and poet who is lying on his deathbed musing on, among other things, reputation and posterity, which both trouble and amuse him.

Sadist and sentimentalist, joker and tragedian, cynic and idealist, glutton and ascetic – I am dying.
   I must die before the week is out, the doctors say, but there is no need for them. I know even better. I know death will come before the day leaves me.

How ghastly to think that a ray from the early-risen sun may yet poke the snotty eyes of an old Professor till he wakes to unglue his dirty nose and ungum his bleary eyes, belch, trouser goosey legs, coat scrawny arms and dodder down to bleat about me to a flock of University students – morons, half-wits, cretins, bone-heads, unreported idiots and border-line cases.

It is some consolation to know that in some thousands of years from now a piece of dust that is stung by old memories and yearns for its kindred may find a congenial resting-place in an old neglected Masonic book in some quiet slumbering library.[49]

In the spring of 1924 Mason had five new poems commercially printed on a single folded sheet of card: a *Penny Broadsheet*. Robert Burton, his friend from Grammar School days, and by then at Teachers' Training College 'full of purpose and scorning drifters', met him one day selling them on Queen Street and bought one, more out of sympathy than admiration ('Did I pay a penny or threepence?'). Then, he 'rather looked down on the shiftless Ron'; later, he would wonder 'what integrity of purpose made him do that?'[50] The *Penny Broadsheet* was dedicated 'To (?) the unknown Hero who sent me £3 in appreciation of "THE BEGGAR," . . . as a Token of Gratitude to himself (and

a Hortatory Example to Other People!)' On the back was an advertisement:
'If you are anxious to help the cause of young New Zealand Literature, buy
"The Beggar". A rather remarkable LITTLE BOOK. Price One Shilling. POST
FREE – from the Author'. On the front Mason placed 'A Song of Allegiance',
a strident declaration of his vocation and homage to his literary mentors. The
boldness of the statement, however, is confused by the poem's shifts in tone:
the young poet toils on stoutly with bloodied knees, sings boldly in a voice
cracked and harsh.

> Shakespear, Milton, Keats, are dead:
> Donne lies in a lowly bed.
>
> Shelley, at last, calm doth lie,
> Knowing 'whence we are, and why!'
>
> Byron, Wordsworth, both are gone:
> Coleridge, Beddoes, Tennyson.
>
> Housman neither knows nor cares
> How this 'heavy world' now fares.
>
> Little clinging grains enfold
> All the mighty minds of old
>
> . . . They are gone; but I am here,
> Stoutly bringing up the rear.
>
> Where they went at limber ease
> Toil I on with bloody knees.
>
> Though my voice is cracked and harsh,
> Stoutly in the rear I march.
>
> Though my song have none to hear,
> Boldly bring I up the rear.

Within the literary fraternity to which Mason here claims allegiance, it was Shelley, the Romantic revolutionary, and Housman, the 'modern stoic',[51] with whom he most closely identified. Of Shelley he wrote in an early entry in his notebook:

> It is no shame for a man to say that he finds Byron too mundane, Milton too tedious, Tennyson too proper, Browning too hard, Swinburne wishy-washy, to say that he cannot read Wordsworth – strange man if he could! – or that Keats's lips are too wet for his liking. All these things you may do with impunity, but he would be indeed a bold man who declared he did not like Shelley. With his fierce passionate virile love of beauty and liberty he is the symbol of Poetry for ever. I cannot imagine myself worshipping any other writer – even Shakespear is too shadowy – but I can quite easily see myself in a slightly different state of life erecting altars at which to worship Marlowe and Shelley. 'His meanest lyric has an epic sweep about it.'[52]

With Housman, the Latin scholar and writer of spare, nostalgic lyrics, Mason found a closer affinity of outlook and tone. Housman's simple, melancholic poems, written largely in ballad form, expressed both a delight in the sensual world and a pervading sense of death, and a classical, especially Latin, influence in their mode of expression and Horatian taste for irony. *A Shropshire Lad*, first published in 1896, was a book that earnest and literary-minded young men like Mason and Fairburn carried in their coat pockets. Fairburn was later to say that Mason wrote the whole of *The Beggar* before he had read *A Shropshire Lad*; yet one of Housman's verses (the final stanza of xxv) could well have provided the cue for 'Body of John'. Housman, Mason told a friend in 1930, would be his desert island poet, 'perhaps rather than all the rest of English poetry put together. . . . Housman is the real man – unmoved, strong and stoical'.[53] In an article published in the *Auckland Star* in 1929, he wrote of Housman's 'splendid fiery lyrics and the gloriously-disciplined audacities', and of Housman's pessimism:

> wistful, now ironic, now brutal, now tender, but always it is tinged with gloom. . . . It is no mere coincidence that he so often hints at Ecclesiastes. He sees all things 'in the light of eternity' as Spinoza said. All the trouble and sorrow were here yesterday and will be here tomorrow. There is no remedy. . . . All that he knows and loves is but a small bright patch on a great landscape around which stretches the vast desert of annihilation. His towns are always

falling, his soldiers gird on useless swords, his lovers waste their sighs, good causes go down, and all things are in vain. He is haunted by the thought of fine lads who are hanged or crucified, and die cursing their luck.

'For a man in whose soul the dark angel has taken up his abode there is surely nothing more depressing than easy recommendations to be optimistic', the article began. 'In hours of gloom we turn to those who sing of the times when they too walked in the dark lands and drank the bitter waters – to the great pessimists like Lucretius, Shakespeare, de Vigny and Hardy.' Mason wrote of Housman's 'sombre power, and strange wayward beauty and the exquisite, relentless rise and fall of his language'.[54] A comment on Housman he made many years later also identifies an essential quality of his own poetry: 'You can see a happy blending of popular and classical attitudes in that great thing of Housman's, "Epitaph on an Army of Mercenaries." It can be read, in my way of thinking, in two separate, indeed contradictory, ways, resulting in a third, ironical, philosophical overtone. That, in turn, has a sort of stabilising – not soothing – effect.'[55]

Thematically, the poems in the *Penny Broadsheet* were of a piece with *The Beggar*. 'A Fragment' treated the subject of physical love for the first time, although it was not a love poem, but paired love with death and dramatically mingled past worlds with the present in its poetic moment in a similar way to 'Wayfarers'. There was a richly imagined and (unusually) unironic poem on a religious theme, Mary soothing the feet of Christ; a sonnet, 'of my Everlasting Hand', on fate and mutability, the vastness of time and the smallness of man (with evident echoes of Lucretius and Shelley); and lastly, Housmanlike, 'A Doubt':

> I do not know
>   When I was told
> That men must go
>   To glut the mould.
>
> Oh! was I told,
>   Or did I know
> I must grow old,
>   And earthward go?

I cannot say
> If youth knows or learns
That man the clay
> To clay returns.

'I have long ago given up the worship of a god', one of the characters in his notebook declared, probably a year or two before this poem was written. 'I searched and could find no perfection in any deity and so I have abandoned them all. I am alone – a solitary pariah. I have grown so oblivious of right and wrong, so cynical that I could commit murder and not be troubled in my soul. Poor clay toy creature of Eternity.' He also wrote: 'Belief is being ignorant and denying it: agnosticism is being ignorant and respectfully admitting it: atheism is being ignorant and glorying in it. Religion is man's supreme impertinence: belief is a gesture of insult to God. One only thing justifies it – the pleasure it gives men.'[56] Did Mason's deep scepticism about the Christian religion derive from some early, traumatic crisis of faith? According to one story, told by an aunt (his father's sister Winifred), he had been 'terribly' disillusioned when, as a young boy, 'he got friendly with an Anglican vicar' but when he 'told the vicar what an inspiration his sermons were the vicar had laughed at him and said "I don't believe a word of it" . . . What a terrible thing [that] a vicar should talk to a young boy like that. It was a wicked thing.'[57] In his notebooks Mason twice described an incident in which a young boy is disabused of his belief by a perfidious parson, and he jotted down passing cynical remarks on the institution of religion: 'Clergymen and other licensed buffoons', 'this nincompoop-turned-pontiff', 'Company-commander Christ, D.S.O., O.B.E.'.[58] Interviewed late in his life, he would deny having had a strong religious upbringing, while acknowledging the literary influence of the Bible on his writing: 'The classics of literature with which I was acquainted, from an early age, would include the Bible and, more particularly in my case, the New Testament. I didn't have religion rammed down my throat, but I was familiar with the New Testament, and naturally used its imagery; perhaps, to some extent, its words.'[59] In fact he understates the presence of religion in his poetry: in its imagery, in poems which directly treated biblical themes (if rarely in so straight a manner as 'Oils and Ointments' in *Penny Broadsheet*), in the recurring presence of the figure of Christ – not a divine Christ, but the beggar–poet–outcast Christ: 'Christ the man persecuted by men and betrayed by God'.[60] He was fascinated by the intermingled horror and humour of the crucifixion, several versions of which appear in his notebooks. The following unpublished poem, 'Gaudeo Quod Nescio', was probably written about 1923:

> They urge on me for worship & for praise
>   A gross, material, unmystical & sly,
>   Shrewd, bargainer with a usurous, reckoning eye
> Demanding all in adulation raise
> Their hands: a cruel snarer-God who lays
>   His gins and pitfalls and doth ambushed lie
>   For captures: who doth amass upon high
> The record of each tripping in life's maze
> To damn men for them after run their days.
> This is the narrow god they give, but I,
>   Content not, still ideal-questing cry:
>   'Let me conclusions lack: for there be ways
>   And ways: and I should rather worship a blind haze
> Than your clay gods of creed & certainty.'[61]

Also written in the 1920s was the blunt, bleak and bitter 'Lullaby and Neck-verse', with the same structure as 'Body of John', which he would publish only much later:

> Oh snuggle down, my baby, your cheek is soft and warm
>   *A stubble beard unkempt*
> And sleep you now soundly safe on your mother's arm
>   *Wild oats have threshed out hemp*
>
> Ah nestle down safe on your loving mother's knee
>   *There is not any hope*
> While Jesus watches over you, who died on Calvary
>   *A lank snake of a rope.*

In his notebooks he usually treated the subject in a more jocular tone: 'For some reason or other Deities are becoming scarce. In the last month not one has been reported either in Rotokawa or Mangonui or indeed in the whole province of Ingoa.'[62]

The *Penny Broadsheet* attracted another brief but kind notice in the *Auckland Star.*

The poet, especially the young poet, has a particularly hard job to get a hearing, and he cannot be blamed if he occasionally adopts unconventional methods. We know one New Zealand poet who takes his wares round from door to door, and why not? Food is sold that way, so why not food for the mind? Mr. R.K. [*sic*] Mason, the Auckland poet whose little volume, 'The Beggar,' we noticed recently, has issued a penny broadsheet containing five short poems. This is not the first venture of the kind in Auckland, but we doubt whether any previous ones have been so good in quality. Mr. Mason's faults of youth still hang about him, but his work is improving.[63]

Eventually, it seems, Mason also sent copies to Harold Monro, but not for a year or more. In October 1925 Monro wrote to him once more, puzzled and disappointed by Mason's silence: 'I simply cannot understand at all why I have not had any letter or manuscripts from you in response to the letter I wrote you last January [*sic*] and of your receipt of which I seem to have sufficient evidence in the fact that the cheque I enclosed has passed through the Bank.' He would have liked to include some more of Mason's work in the *Chapbook* which had just gone to press. 'Perhaps the fact is that you were offended or annoyed at my treatment of your poems in the last CHAPBOOK. I admit I took a good deal of risk in dealing with them as I did, but I relied I suppose on your trusting sufficiently in my judgment.' (There is no evidence, however, that Mason had been offended.) 'Meanwhile I have recommended your book to several people and have sold I think about twenty copies. I shall fully expect to hear from you.'[64]

5

Poets and princes

1926–27

MASON HAD spent some of his time during 1925 studying maths, probably with the help of Horace Holl's Matriculation primer. In December he sat the university entrance examination for the third time, and passed. Fairburn made a desultory effort, at his friend's urging, and failed. In the new year Mason enrolled at Auckland University College in Latin, French and history. He had just turned twenty-one. ('Shall I ever forget your 21st birthday?' Fairburn wrote, homesick in England, six years later, but how they had marked the occasion he did not record.)[1]

It was a significant moment for the university too. In March 1926 the new arts building on Princes and Symonds streets was at last completed and opened, provoking controversy for its flamboyant 'wedding cake' tower and native embellishments which earned it the architectural tag 'Maori Gothic'. It was the college's first purpose-designed permanent building, and it gave a noticeable stimulus to student activity and morale. Still, there could never be more than a semblance of 'student life' when fewer than a fifth of the college's thousand-odd students were at university full-time. Most worked by day as teachers, or law clerks like Dan, and attended lectures by night.

The 1920s in the history of Auckland University College were unexciting years. One of the few centres of intellectual vitality was the Classics Department. The recently appointed professor, A.C. Paterson, came from the University College of Transvaal, which he had left after twelve years in alarm at the rise of Afrikaner nationalism. A short and paunchy Scotsman, he was a gifted linguist (an 'acknowledged authority' on Arabic and African as well as classical languages, the London *Times* would write in his obituary in 1932), a rigorous scholar and an exacting teacher who believed that a thorough grounding in syntax was the basis of good classical scholarship. 'He did not bring authors to life and relevance . . . He analysed, ruthlessly, their language.'[2] In 1926 the first-year class analysed Cicero and Virgil.

The professor of French, Maxwell Walker, by contrast, was notoriously lazy, a large, hearty man with a drinker's complexion who was known to read

Kipling at Rotary Club dinners. His one published work was *The Art of Delivery*, a treatise on the technique not of lecturing but of bowls; he was rumoured to mark exam scripts at the Bowling Club bar. History was in the hands of the handsome, eloquent and charismatic J.P. Grossmann, estranged husband of the New Zealand novelist Edith Searle Grossmann, a man of progressive views – he was 'especially eloquent over liberators like Garibaldi'[3] – and something of a rogue. Unbeknown to the college governors when they appointed him, he had left his first academic job at Canterbury College when he was sentenced to two years in gaol for fraud; he was soon to embroil Auckland University College in the biggest scandal in its history.

At the end of this year Mason passed his exams in Latin and French, but did not sit history, in which he had failed terms – the beginning of an erratic academic career of his own.

While Mason was teaching at Holl's and studying, Fairburn languished in the uncongenial employ of the insurance office. He had been granted a 'partial pass' in the Matriculation examination and enrolled in economics, but this was as far as he would go in pursuit of a degree – he dismissed university education as 'bourgeois'.[4] In the winter of 1926 Mason persuaded his friend to join him in a market-gardening venture. They purchased a few hundred onion seedlings and planted them out at Ellerslie, but when it came to weeding Fairburn refused. Mason would later recall his mother 'reduced to tears of helpless laughter as she stood on the verandah and Rex stood in the garden demonstrating with gestures and actions that onion weeding could best be conducted by short, stumpy men. As for men of over six feet to bend way down to the earth and separate the weeds from the poor little plants was just a plain, blunt, practical impossibility.'[5] Mason, as well as Fairburn's father, despaired of his impractical attitude to the question of making a living. Literary schemes were more to his liking.

In July Fairburn had introduced himself by letter to another young poet, Geoffrey de Montalk. They had been in the same class one year at Remuera Primary School, he reminded de Montalk, and although they had not met since he had heard of him from time to time, 'mostly from R.A.K. Mason whom I have known in a fidus Achates sort of way for six or seven years'.[6] De Montalk's father was an architect and sometime farmer, neither with conspicuous success. His grandfather, a Polish aristocrat-in-exile, had taught languages at Auckland University College in the 1890s; his mother's family had money. Since leaving school he had been variously engaged as a teacher, a milkman and a clerk, studied languages at university in Wellington and

Christchurch and theology at Auckland. By then living in Christchurch, he
was handsome, eccentric, married and unemployed. By the end of 1926 he
had taken a job in a lawyer's office, which he confessed that he enjoyed, but
his serious mission was poetry. 'So R.A.K.M. is your Aeneas', he replied to
Fairburn. He had yet to find either an Achates or an Aeneas of his own, but
he was supremely confident that he – and Mason and Fairburn – had been
'anointed to the ways of poetry' by the gods.[7]

In their ensuing correspondence, Fairburn and de Montalk compared notes
on politics, poetry and philosophy, women and sex. They exchanged poems
and frankly criticised each other's efforts; de Montalk found Fairburn too
'Brookey'. Fairburn professed communism, while de Montalk declared himself
a monarchist and discoursed at length on religion. 'So you're a socialist, you
silly ass', he wrote. 'If your motto is "épatez les bourgeois" why exactly are
you writing to me?'[8] Their political views were completely at odds, and over
time de Montalk was to grow increasingly strange in his aristocratic pretensions
– eventually, once he had abandoned the dull, philistine colony for Europe,
donning crimson robes and growing waist-length hair and declaring himself
heir to the Polish throne. But for the moment the two had something in
common, Fairburn recognised, in their commitment to 'the emancipation of
the artist & the spread of Beauty', and their 'personal rebellion against the
ugliness and hypocrisy of it all', the miserable, conforming culture of the
New Zealand middle classes: 'the brutal doltish lumpishness of the wowseristic
bourgeoisie', in Mason's typically savage expression.[9]

It is not clear whether de Montalk had yet met Mason. He did know Dan,
however, and he knew Mason's poetry. 'I used to tell his brother that he
wasn't a poet,' he remarked to Fairburn in August, 'and even though he may
not be of Tennysonian stature, I now realise that I was talking through my
hat. He is far better than, say, Walter de la Mare.' Mason would be flattered,
Fairburn replied: de la Mare was a poet he 'rather admires'.[10] De Montalk
wrote to Mason, apparently for the first time, in October to tell him so himself,
with uncharacteristic modesty. Much later in his life de Montalk would recall
that he met Mason some years earlier, in 1923 or 1924, but his letter suggests
otherwise, or that, if he did know him, it was not well: 'As I have learnt a
great admiration for your poetry, I suppose I need no excuse for writing to
you', he began. 'I believe nearly every other line of your Beggar and Broadsheet
are monumental and wish I could say as much for my own lines.'[11] A few
months later he would offer Mason some criticism and advice that made
plain the temperamental and artistic distance between them, although his

admiration was not diminished. He had been 'reading and re-reading your classic "The Beggar"' and had to tell him that he did not like 'those two bloody awful verses at the end of "In Perpetuum Vale"' – the short poem which Mason later called 'Body of John' and which Harold Monro had thought the best thing in the book. De Montalk went on:

> To be realistic it is not sufficient merely to be disgusting. I can see the point – that there is nothing evil under the sun; true enough. But are there not enough and to spare of people who are ready to dwell on that side of life? The mere plebs are willing enough to see the beauty of decay, smuttiness, lust; *our* job is to make their decay a new birth, their smuttiness a delicacy of expression, their lust a love of Love. It is for us to show the man with the muck-rake that there is by his side an angel with a shining crown. . . . If you chaps are not absolutely in Love with a philosophy of Despair, I can honestly recommend you to read up the old systems of the East . . . You will find there the explanation of the seeming inconsistencies of Life.[12]

Mason was as usual a more reticent correspondent, but the three – de Montalk, Fairburn and Mason – maintained a somewhat curious friendship, largely by mail, for the next half-dozen years. De Montalk could hardly have been more different from Mason in his character: his confidence contrasted with Mason's doubt, his flamboyance with Mason's reticence, although they shared the seriousness with which they regarded poetry. With the flagrant self-regard and lack of judgment that were part of de Montalk's charm and eccentricity, and which Mason regarded with amusement, he was convinced of their collective brilliance. 'I have a reprehensible ambition to father the New Zealand school of poets,' he declared to Fairburn, 'in my opinion a very great school. W.B. Yeats is our only rival.'[13] He addressed his letters to Mason, 'R.A.K. Mason, Poet, Ellerslie', and those to Fairburn likewise until Fairburn asked him not to because of the effect it had on his father, to whom a letter lying around addressed to his son as a poet was worse than 'the red rag to Bonzo'; 'Also he can't stand a bar of R.A.K.'.[14]

Fairburn had written a review of *The Beggar* which he submitted to the *Times Literary Supplement*, adopting a 'faintly patronising' tone ('"we expect great things from Mr. – I almost said Master – Mason"') which he thought the paper would recognise as its own, but it was not printed. By September 1926 there was talk of a book. 'I had an idea the other day', he wrote to de Montalk. 'Why not publish (in England, & in tip top style) a volume of

poems comprised of selected items from yourself, Mason, Rudd, myself, &
possibly one or two others, say five in all. Call it "Five New Zealanders" or
some such title, and make a point of our youth'. Mason was already in contact
with Harold Monro, who seemed 'very very enthusiastic about him, & seems
very keen on booming young poets. We might get a preface by such a man as
Bernard Shaw or Squire or Mencken (all very helpful to struggling amateurs,
I understand)'. 'By splitting the expense, & making the volume fairly thin,
we might be able to afford a really decent binding.'[15] Maxwell Rudd was a
former schoolmate of Mason's and a friend of de Montalk's. He had been in
Mason's fourth form at Auckland Grammar before his family moved to
Dunedin, and was by then back in Auckland living unhappily with his strictly
Methodist father (a shipping company manager) and stepmother, and working
for the Public Trust. It had been while searching titles in the Land Registry
Office that de Montalk, when working as a law clerk in Auckland, met him
two or three years earlier. Rudd was quiet and intense, with 'strange, large,
blue eyes' and a fascination with the lost city of Atlantis. He had written
about a dozen poems that reminded de Montalk of the Belgian symbolist
Maeterlinck and Yeats. De Montalk thought him 'the world's greatest
poet'.[16]

On 23 September 1926 Rudd died of pneumonia in Avondale Mental
Hospital. His death both grieved and angered Mason. He blamed it, as did de
Montalk, on the damage inflicted on a sensitive, creative personality by an
unsympathetic family, society and church. Fairburn, although he had not
known Rudd, was moved to remark on the lonely and embattled life of the
New Zealand poet: 'We are a small band and can help each other so much
that we must keep as many links intact as possible.' Melodramatically, he
found something significant in the date of Rudd's death, which was also the
date of birth of de Montalk's baby daughter: 'The 23rd Sept. has always had
a peculiar ring to me' – 'Before I left, I said to R.A.K. . . . that if anything did
happen – boat blown off her course & delayed by bad weather, and we were
at sea on the 23rd, he would understand if anything should happen in the
high tragedy line.'[17]

FAIRBURN WAS by this time on Norfolk Island, 'beachcombing'.[18] He
had left Auckland in mid-September, having been thinking of 'clearing out',
at least temporarily, since July – perhaps to Tahiti, like his literary hero Rupert
Brooke, but he didn't speak French. Norfolk Island was not exactly a palm-
fringed tropical paradise, but it had a reputation for abundant cheap alcohol

and carefree ways. He was taking 'a hell of a lot of books', he had told de Montalk, and was planning three months of solid reading, a little painting and writing.[19] In fact, his Norfolk vacation was motivated primarily by the need to resolve his unsatisfactory relationship with his girlfriend, Irene Jenkin, his frustration at their three-year platonic attachment having been inflamed by his correspondence with the more worldly de Montalk, who was by then separated from his wife and daughter and an enthusiastic advocate of free love.

Meanwhile, Mason was unhappily in love himself. The object of his affection was a young woman named Lola Mousseler, beautiful and half-French, whom he had met earlier that year. He sent her an aggrieved and passionate letter in October, 'Seeing that you never give me a chance to talk to you. . . . This is not one of my usual – You know: when you have let me grow half-crazy with pain, I weigh in with some erotic, idiotic, erratic, and ecstatic effusion', but he was suffering in loneliness and longing.

> . . . have you ever had an irresistible desire to talk earnestly with someone who doesn't want to speak to you? If you ever really want to hurt yourself, try taking a good walk, eagerly thinking all the time 'To-night, the priest will hear confession, and cleanse me' – but put a locked door (or a priest who is bored or busy) at the journey's end. . . . I want spiritual consolation – I want sometimes to talk with all the honesty and depth that I can. You have taught me to need you in this, and you have denied me the opportunity. . . . Either comfort my soul – or you are no friend of mine. I'm not trying this torture any more . . . Don't treat me as you are: I don't deserve it.[20]

Lola replied with light-hearted sympathy: 'Bonjour cher monsieur le Poète. . . . Poor tormented Soul! be of good courage! and believe me I love no man and have no intention, for the present, of thinking of that passion which is burning you up to a flaming spark of unreasonableness!' She returned his letter. On the back of hers Mason pencilled: 'an over-supply of the milk of human kindness on the mind as to cause milk-fever' and 'The cold sap of Death is creeping up my trunk.'[21] Elsewhere in his notebook he once wrote: 'She was running a great risk of waking up to find a poisoned poet dangling from her doorknob', and 'she' may have been Lola.[22]

He gave another account of the affair to Fairburn. 'Strange girl. It comes as a nasty blow to my perfectly beautiful childish cynicism to find that a woman does not necessarily chase the male.' But '[t]his woman business is beginning to worry me', he admitted, referring not only to Lola, for it appears that he was being courted himself: 'At present I am busily occupied in dreading lest I be dragged into some permanent attachment (c.f. Dan), or even into an entanglement. Can you, as man to man, tell me of anything on God's earth so bloody unromantic as love. It's all right when you're no good for anything else, but in youth, my oath! Deadening, soul-destroying, fettering.'[23] An encounter with Lola and another of her admirers in town one day prompted an angry tirade about social convention, and everything about New Zealand that he and Fairburn both so despised:

> Want to get right away from this bloody burg – into the wilds or go to London or Paris. Bloody stinking little brainless narrow-minded suspicious unintellectual priggish snobbish half-pie undistinguished boastful unamusing unmusical low-spirited sporting racing dancing sottish parson-ridden bigoted Puritanical Reason-hating true-blue-British, Fought-for-my-flag-on flood-and-field, class-ridden avaricious, greedy, money-grubbing, newspaper-believing persecuting reactionary Tory Votes-for-Coates orthodox Prussian mob-minded conservative, prunes-and-prisms, conventionality-ridden – bloody bastard of a town.[24]

But the hurt was deeper and more personal than his indignation lets on. In despair one night and unable to sleep, he had gone out and caught a horse he had seen wandering on the road in the afternoon and ridden bareback seven miles to Green Bay and back. He confided this to Fairburn, swearing him to secrecy.

Fairburn wrote a few days after he reached Norfolk, describing the pine-clad island with all the lyrical enthusiasm of the first-time traveller. It was, he imagined, 'something like Sicily or some other beautiful corner of the Mediterranean', but 'Don't imagine I have been Don Juanning all over the place'.[25] He formally renounced his interest in the onion crop, but several weeks later asked to borrow a pound. Mason obliged, even though he can hardly have had any money to spare. A few months later he wrote to Horace Holl asking for a rise: 'I have been advised on good authority that I have an almost certain chance for a secondary school position', which would pay £200 a year, while 'my present salary, which works out at under £2"5"0 per week, does not so much as cover ordinary living expenses. Even for purely business purposes and in justice to you, I should dress well, read widely, and fulfil certain social and academic duties, but at present I have not the money to do so.'[26] Whether he got the rise is not known. Fairburn spent the last of Mason's pound playing poker on the boat back home.

'When I get back,' he had written to de Montalk before Christmas, 'R.A.K. and I are probably going off on a walk around the back country of the North Island for six weeks or two months. I will have no money left . . . and R.A.K. will probably be stoney also. We will be out and out tramps, stealing, begging, sleeping under haystacks, and having a free time all round. I shall drop occasional notes to you on the backs of bits of brown paper and wrappers off cigarette packets, writing with a burnt match or a pin dipped in blood.'[27] But when he got back, towards the end of January, Mason was in Lichfield. 'You bugger', Fairburn berated him. 'I fully expected your delicately chiselled features to be glowering at me over the edge of the wharf. When are you coming back?' A few days later he wrote from Mason's house, where he had spent the night and had a heart-to-heart talk with Mason's mother: 'Everybody seems to be messed up in a love affair at present.'[28] Fairburn had had a passionate romance with a 'Sydney society girl' just before he got the boat home from Norfolk, but they were destined never to meet again. He did not, meanwhile, appreciate Mason chiding him over his treatment of Irene. This was not the only time that Fairburn's love affairs and Mason's disapproval of them would cause tension between them. '[W]ho the hell are you to be delivering moral uplift lecturettes on Primal Passions?' demanded Fairburn. 'Aren't you just about as bloody-well fixed as anyone ever could be? . . . you know bloody well that the only grounds you have for considering yourself a suitable counsellor are those of personal (and disastrous) experience.'[29]

Lola replied in February to another impassioned letter, which Mason would refer to casually a few years later as having been written 'under the influence of two months solitude' in Lichfield and 'damn near proposing matrimony'.[30] She rejected him again, with kindly intentioned words that are unlikely to have consoled: 'I admire your cleverness and see a great future for you in the world of letters', and for 'all the compliments which you so lavishly confer upon me I humbly thank you. For the hours of lost sleep, the heart aches, the moments of despair that I have unknowingly caused you I offer you a heart full of sympathy.' But they could only be friends. 'So Ronald shake your self together . . . Show us [Lola and her mother] your inner self, your *real* self – the man of poise. Don't let Rex influence you to throw unbalanced opinions right and left and swear at things you really love and admire.'[31] Fairburn correctly discerned that Lola thought him a 'conceited fool'.[32]

Fairburn continued to be as close a friend as Mason would ever have. As for who was the stronger influence on whom, for good or bad, Arthur Fairburn, like Lola, was in no doubt. '[T]he old man always looked to make of me a fine little golf-playing Conservative, and he regards you as the Serpent', Fairburn later remarked to his friend.[33] Eventually his father banned 'that scrubby Mason'[34] from the Fairburn home. Rex, however, remained a welcome and regular visitor at Mason's. 'Thank God', he wrote to de Montalk, 'there are a few of us in N.Z. together. Imagine life for either R.A.K., you, or me without the spiritual consolation & moral support of the other two.'[35] He meant poets, but his father was also suspicious of Mason's unconventional home and increasingly left-wing political views.

IN 1927 Mason enrolled in English I, history again, Latin II and French II. In Latin he met an old friend. Ted Blaiklock, his 3A classmate, was a new lecturer at the college, and on his way to a chair. He would later remember Mason from this time as 'my perverse and irregular student in the Classics Department. He did well, became quite an authority on Suetonius (who was not on the syllabus), and needed all the protection that I could give him, for old acquaintance's sake, from the wrath' of Professor Paterson.[36] They did not become close again; their interests, aside from Latin, had diverged too far – Blaiklock had become a Baptist. But he thought highly of the quality of Mason's classical scholarship, and would try hard to help him into what might have been an academic career. They were reading Cicero ('that windbag', in Mason's view[37]) and Juvenal (that most savage of satirists) that year. In English, in a syllabus otherwise heavily philological, the literary period of study was the seventeenth century: Milton, Dryden and Herrick.

Fairburn was unemployed and bored: gardening, cultivating his loneliness, still acting and producing for the Grafton Shakespeare and Dramatic Society, although even this was beginning to pall. He told de Montalk in May that 'R.A.K. and I are going to try to write the next Varsity play. . . . a satire on human foibles . . . [i]n the Voltaire manner', but there is no evidence that they did.[38] As always, they walked. One June weekend, in 'abominable weather', they left some friends in Mt Albert at eleven o'clock on Saturday night, Fairburn reported to de Montalk,

> & set off for [Mason's] dump in Ellerslie. When we got to the Royal Oak, he
> suggested a walk, so we set off. We went through Onehunga & across the
> bridge & up Mangere Mountain. It was delightful up there, with romantic
> groves of macrocarpas and the dim moon shining over the Manukau. We

descended the far side of it and went away out the Ihumata [sic] Peninsula, which looked at that hour exactly what I should imagine the bog country of Ireland to be like, the sort Synge talks about. On the way home we were drenched by a terrific rainstorm. We hit the hay at half past five & slept till 1 o'clock. Then, since the afternoon was apallingly [sic] filthy, we read & smoked till 10 last night & tumbled in again.[39]

De Montalk was unimpressed. Walking was one of the many things on which he and Mason and Fairburn disagreed. De Montalk was a motor car man ('for the car brings new poetry to the earth'), while they despised cars and their owners as symbols of bourgeois smugness and Babbitry: 'He is true lord of creation who owns a good motor-car', Mason wrote in his notebook (he was never to own a car himself, nor obtain a driver's licence).[40] '[D]amn you Wordsworthian poets!' de Montalk snorted. 'Driving itself is one of the most beautiful pleasures yet known to man!' He greatly admired

Mason's motor-car lines, –
    'And still shall the car sweep along as lovely a line
      But not for me' –
    and 'Gibbers by the sweeping car'
that is the sort of thing we want, not the moon and nightingale touch.'[41]

On this they were agreed.

In town, when not lunching with their women friends at Milne and Choyce, Mason and Fairburn went slumming, mixing with the poor and down-and-out, 'yarning' with prostitutes and the unemployed. They made a particular friend of Charlie, a well-known local 'character', a homeless returned soldier who slept during the summer in the Grafton cemetery and in winter under the grandstand at the Ellerslie racecourse. They had met Charlie one night the previous September, not long before Fairburn left for Norfolk, when they were thrown out of a meeting in the Town Hall held by the travelling evangelist Gipsy Smith. Mason, Fairburn and his younger brother Geoff had gone along with the intention of exposing the man as a charlatan and his mission as a racket. At the back of the packed hall, Mason had barely risen to his feet to ask a question when the evangelist started up the orchestra to lead the singing. When Mason tried to speak again he was set upon by half-a-dozen 'muscular Christians'. 'There was a struggle and, amid the uproar which ensued, could be heard a voice calling out something to the effect that

"These Christians are strangling me.'" A policeman was called, and the three found themselves on the pavement outside with Charlie, who had risen to support them and been thrown out too. Mason and Fairburn defended themselves in letters to the *New Zealand Herald* signed 'Veritas Prevalebit' and 'Civis Romanus Sum'. 'Allow me to make a confession of my ghastly guilt, as far as my trembling hands will allow me to push my sinful pen', wrote Mason. 'Let me admit that I am the black-hearted scoundrel whose blackguardly ruffianism so disrupted Mr. Smith's meeting' – and the words 'anent strangulation', he noted, had been correctly reported.[42]

Baiting Christians was evidently a favourite diversion. One July day in 1927 he and Fairburn attended 'the daily prayer meeting in the Baptist bagnio' (the Baptist tabernacle on Queen Street), where among those present was 'the leader of the gang of brothel-skunks that fired us out of Gipsy Smith's meeting'. They 'completed the afternoon by a visit to the Auckland City Mission and then to the Lunatic Asylum, where we yarned for an hour to an old chap' who had once been a gardener for the Fairburns.[43]

THEY MADE another real friend around this time, Clifton Firth. He was their contemporary in age and comrade in spirit, the odd son out in an established wealthy family, whose money came from trade and manufacturing: his father and two younger brothers established the Firth Concrete Company. He was working as a freelance graphic designer and photographer from a studio in Swanson Street, just off Queen Street, reading and writing poetry (none of which was ever published) and looking for friends to share his interests in politics and art. He noticed Mason one day when he was walking along Queen Street with Merton Hodge, a fellow art student (and future playwright). Who, Firth asked his companion, was that chap with the black hair sticking up and the rustic walking-stick? He's a poet, Hodge told him, he's published a book. When he encountered Mason face to face outside the Bank of New Zealand a few days later, Firth introduced himself and asked where he could buy the book, and Mason duly brought a copy of *The Beggar* around to his studio, inscribed 'To one saved soul in this city of sodomites'.[44]

Mason introduced Firth to Fairburn, and the pair became a threesome. They made a striking trio: Firth slim, bespectacled, always elegantly dressed, alongside the tall (over six foot three), affectedly outlandish Fairburn in his flapping blue greatcoat and baggy suit, and the shorter, stockier Mason, 'shabbily homespun' with a black raincoat over one shoulder and a walking-stick. 'He never dressed properly, poor lad, never had decent clothes', Irene later remembered of Mason.[45] Yet it was not only that he could not afford, or that he disdained, flash clothes. He would always be careless of his appearance – he had a habit of leaving his shoelaces undone. Firth's first name was Reginald and they called themselves the Three Rs or the Three Kings: Ronald, Reginald and Rex. Much time was spent in the Swanson Street studio over the next few years, talking and drinking. Firth and Fairburn 'started an argument regarding Classicism and Romanticism' (Clifton was the Classicist and Rex the Romantic), which continued for years until it became 'something like the old dynastic wars of the Middle Ages', Mason later recalled.[46] Firth would remember Mason during these years as witty and fun: 'He never stopped laughing. He was inordinately funny', as well as being 'the gentlest person I've ever met'.[47]

'During this period', Mason later recorded, 'I became acquainted with prevalent radical and socialist doctrines, first through books and discussions with Clifton Firth . . . and Rex Fairburn; then through contact with radical groups, particularly the then-new N.Z. Communist Party. I "contacted" this through the Rev. William Monckton, who was tutoring me in Greek: he sent me, at a peak point in the Sacco-Vanzetti agitation, to see the then National Secretary of the Party'.[48] Mason did not in fact enrol in Greek at university until 1929. But the sentencing and execution of the two Italian-American anarchists Nicola Sacco and Bartolomeo Vanzetti, whose case had become a *cause célèbre* for the left worldwide, took place in 1927. The 'then-new' Communist Party of New Zealand was in fact newly re-established (in December 1926), having disbanded to become a branch of the Communist Party of Australia two years earlier. It had been founded in April 1921, at a meeting in the Socialist Hall in Wellington. It was not only a far-flung outcome of the 1917 Russian revolution, but also the latest in a succession of tiny radical and Marxist groups that had been formed in New Zealand since the 1890s. It contained, uncomfortably and at times acrimoniously, a range of ideological positions and political programmes – Bolshevist, socialist and syndicalist – and in 1927 had some 100 members, most of whom were probably quite young.[49] The 'national secretary' whom Mason was sent to see was the secretary of the Auckland branch, Dove Myer Robinson, who was in his late twenties and managed his father's pawnbroking shop in Queen Street (later he was Auckland's mayor).

At university in 1927 Mason also met Sid Scott, who was studying for a Diploma in Social Science while working in his father's grocery store in Onehunga, and who became the Auckland branch secretary of the Party in

1928. He would become one of the Party's most prominent, and controversial, national figures. Mason gave a pen portrait of Scott in the novel he started writing a few years later, as a soap-box orator on Quay Street: 'a slick-haired, rather over-dressed young man of about 25 who was obviously a bit depressed because his carefully-prepared squibs were, for some reason, failing to do more than fizzle. He wore a gallant but slightly uneasy look, as of an arrested innocent whose arguments fall on ears inexplicably deaf.' The crowd's attention was drawn instead to another speaker: 'One of the most ardent Communists. . . . A little old blue-eyed man with sparse white hairs sticking straight up on a pink scalp – the strongest of American accents & a wealth of dry homely illustrations – "I.W.W." stamped all over him.'[50] This was Dick (Daddy) Scholefield, a former 'Wobbly' agitator (that is, a member of the American syndicalists the Industrial Workers of the World, or IWW), who lived in the communal house in Newton Road that was, in 1930, the Party's *de facto* Auckland headquarters (home to four bachelor comrades, 'a large black cat and a coffee-coloured Pekingese').[51]

Quay Street West, 'opposite the wharf sheds & outside the shipping-offices',[52] was the city's open forum, venue for impromptu orations and political demonstrations. During 1927 the Auckland Communist Party held a series of open-air meetings in support of the 'Hands off China' campaign (against Britain's suppression of China's rising nationalist movement) and the Sacco-Vanzetti defence, for which 1500 people attended one rally. It was the first year that the tiny New Zealand Communist Party made any public impression beyond the periodic arrest of its members for selling 'seditious' literature. Mason did not join the Party at this time, but he was to be closely associated with it for many years. Reading, contact with radical groups and arguments with like-minded friends, slumming among the poor in the city streets and working alongside rural labourers in Waikato – all contributed to the formation of his political views, to the belief in socialism that he would retain all his life. So, in a more fundamental way, did his nature: an instinctive sensitivity to injustice and empathy with others; the generosity, simplicity and honesty of his manner; and his fierce anger. His socialism came as well, in part, from his home. In later years he was to emphasise his Irish and Scottish heritage as the basis of his political radicalism.

Dan, too, was developing an interest in politics, though of a different colour. In November 1928 he was to stand for election in Manukau for the United Party, newly formed around the remnant of the old Liberals. He campaigned for better transport, a post office in Panmure and the installation of slot telephones throughout the district, and recklessly accused the government of illegally spending £25,000 of petrol-tax revenue on electioneering. The absence during the election of the sitting member, Labour's W.J. Jordan, at the Empire Parliamentary Conference in Ottawa led some observers to suggest that Dan's candidacy was opportunistic. Reports of his meetings alluded to 'numerous rumours' circulating about him in the electorate, to which he replied that 'if he were to give credence to half the statements he had heard he would drive himself mad within a short time. The electorate were quite at liberty to know all about his past life' – of which nothing more was revealed.[53] United were the unlikely winners in the election, in what was largely a protest vote against the Reform government (Labour came in third). Mason was present at the meeting when the ageing United leader, Sir Joseph Ward, inadvertently promised to borrow £70 million immediately instead of over ten years, misreading his speech notes and clinching the election. Dan gained 2908 votes, more than 3500 behind Jordan, who increased his majority by three and a half times.

JESSIE MASON wrote to friends overseas in May 1927: 'The unemployment is great. It is many, many years since N.Z. has gone through such trying times. . . . People are rallying round . . . but there are many, I fear, who quite forget the hungry & homeless. . . . What a terrible lot there is to do for others in this world'. As for herself, she had had 'a very bad run of health – my heart is very bad'. She had collapsed in town and her doctor had advised her to 'go right away from it all; but my purse will certainly not allow even a very small trip', as 'We have had a lot of unfortunate happenings in the financial line.' The sprawling house and large section at Great South Road had become a burden. But of her sons she reported proudly: 'Ronald is still at Holl's, he is hoping to see England when he gets through his B.A. if all goes well. Foster [Dan] is Managing Clerk for J.J. Sullivan, the big Criminal Lawyer here, & is kept most awfully busy.'[54]

Two days later, on 27 May, Horace Holl was drowned on Mt Ruapehu. He had been making for Holl's Camp on the southern slopes of the mountain, his regular base for assaults on the summit, of which he was said to have made more than fifty. But it had been a month of unusually heavy rain, and he was swept away while attempting to cross the Mangaturuturu Stream. His first assistant, David Faigan, a young graduate of the University of Otago, took over running the college. Mason was 'second in command (now)', Fairburn reported to de Montalk, and 'busy as hell'.[55]

In Christchurch, de Montalk was making up his mind to go to London, to introduce 'the young group of New Zealand poets', led by himself, to England and the world. He had had second thoughts about the plan to publish a book together in London. They would be better to follow Mason's example, he told Fairburn, and publish their work in New Zealand first, to test the waters of public taste and loyalty 'in the land where it is made' (besides, it would be cheaper and easier). 'We . . . should call ourselves the Something Brotherhood . . . or band or Sons of Something or other' – 'Please trot along some suggestions for a name'.[56] He was already planning a volume of his own, undeterred by sympathetic warnings from Mason about how much trouble it would cause him. His was to be 'a huge tome compared to Mason's, though I would not care to assert that the poetry is as good'.[57]

Meanwhile de Montalk was assiduously promoting *The Beggar*, which he had decided 'ranks with Flecker and Rupert Brooke'. At a literary evening in March he read 'The Beggar' and 'After Death', which 'were subjects of wild enthusiasm'. He had bought two copies of the book himself and energetically recommended it to others: 'My plan is to get people to go into W.&T.s and buy it, or else to collect the bob from them and buy it for them.' Did Mason know that Whitcombe & Tombs were selling the book for 1s 6d, while he had priced it at a shilling: 'who is getting the extra sixpence, he or they?' When the shop sold out, he asked Fairburn to tell Mason to send down some more.[58]

'How do you mean 50% of New Zealanders have not read "The Beggar"?' Fairburn responded, misunderstanding de Montalk's remark that 50 per cent of New Zealanders should have read it but hadn't. 'At the very outside, .08% have read it, which means that 99.92% have not. That is allowing 50,000 people who are capable of reading it in N.Z.. Great isn't it?' By this calculation Mason had sold, or circulated, forty copies of the book, besides the ones he sent to London, in three years. In de Montalk's view the problem lay with the poet as well as the philistines. Mason had been too modest, his book was too small: 'the dash thing isn't conspicuous enough, and therefore these fools think it can't be any good'. 'There are few people who have enough common sense that they cackle such a deal about, to realise the greatness of such a wee book at one shilling.'[59]

Early in May 1927 de Montalk sent Fairburn and Mason a copy of his own book, hot off the press. Entitled *Wild Oats: a sheaf of poems*, 'by Geoffrey Wladislas Vaile Potocki de Montalk, Prince Potocki', it was elegantly printed, in a 'Limited and First Edition' of 200 copies, on thick, unnumbered, quarto-sized pages, covered in aristocratic purple suede and bound with a purple tassel – completely the opposite of Mason's small, plain, error-ridden *Beggar* and *Broadsheet* – and priced at 10 shillings. In his introduction ('Envoy') de Montalk set out his aristocratic credo ('I am here as the poet and protagonist of the abused upper castes') and his nationalist literary mission:

> I am convinced that there is in New Zealand a cultured class large enough and discriminating enough not only to pay the cost of publishing, as it gradually appears, our national literature, but also handsomely to reward the creators of that art. This volume is evidence of my faith in my countrymen, and is their chance to prove whether or not they really want us, their young poets, to stay here and to work here, building up a national literature, or to take our magic lyres to older and lovelier lands.

Of the poems themselves, he noted that they were the product of his youth and should be 'compared with the work of, say, Coleridge, at such an age'. There was nothing modest about de Montalk – except in his acknowledgement that Mason's poems were possibly better than his own.[60]

Fairburn too regarded *Wild Oats* as 'the test. If they [the New Zealand public] accept that and support it, I will consider that they deserve to have other stuff printed here. If, however, they don't take much notice, I will *vow* never to publish anything in N.Z. myself, never to lose any opportunity of dissuading others from doing it, and in general take no notice whatever of my native country.'[61] De Montalk had sold eighteen copies by the end of May. But, for all the bravado and the challenge of his introduction, he was not the kind really to care how many people bought his books. As he reminded Mason, they were poets by divine right and privilege: 'we shall from the mere public get nothing but blows – but from the earnest lovers of beauty we shall get an unsought renown, and a very sweet mead of thanks before the high Gods'.[62]

Reciprocating de Montalk's efforts on his own behalf, Mason undertook to review *Wild Oats*. He gave it 'some classy write-up', Fairburn told de Montalk, but the press would not print it.[63] Mason remonstrated with Alan Mulgan, the literary editor of the *Auckland Star*, that if the paper was happy to 'lavish any amount of space on your [de Montalk's] private affairs' it could give some to his poetry. By 'private affairs' he was referring to de Montalk's marriage, which was in the newspapers in September 1927: he had left his wife, Lilian Hemus, and their two-year-old daughter Wanda, and had spent a night in gaol on a charge of assault, which was subsequently withdrawn. Lilian was by that time petitioning in the Supreme Court for the restitution of conjugal rights. The press made much of de Montalk's styling himself a Polish count, his devotion to poetry and his vaunted intention to follow the 'road to Samarkand' – London and literary fame. Mulgan replied to Mason that in his belief it was more important to be a good citizen than a poet, and clearly his friend had married for money only to abandon his family once he had spent it. This in a way was true. De Montalk had lost some thousands of pounds belonging to Lilian in his failed milk-delivery business. After that, she complained, he had done nothing but sit around the house writing poetry.[64]

NEWSPAPERS were up there with evangelists as the objects of Mason's and Fairburn's contempt. They were the organs of the blustering, smug, conservative ruling classes, pedlars of gossip and reaction. Lying awake one night when Fairburn was staying at Mason's, they graded the local specimens: 'the "Sun" is dirty: the "Star" grubby: and the "Herald" filthy'.[65] In fact they had some respect for Mulgan's literary page, and they were too hasty and too harsh in condemning the *Sun*. Sister paper of the *Sun* in Christchurch, the Auckland *Sun* was launched in March 1927 with an avowedly 'independent' editorial policy and a Friday literary page that pledged to support new New Zealand writing, poetry especially. The literary editor, Ian Donnelly, who had been a schoolfriend of de Montalk's in Christchurch, wrote some himself, of which Mason was dismissive. He described Donnelly to de Montalk as 'the Lost-Atlantis and Bacon-Shakespeare boy. Ian is a damn fine chap, and no fool and I like him immensely, but really a casual stroll in the Celtic twilight has not made him a poet'.[66] True to its intention, the *Sun* in the 1920s played an important role in supporting a nascent New Zealand literary movement, as 'the one and only daily to pay serious attention to literary work – poems, short stories, articles – garnered in from the stores of New Zealand writers', in the words of the poet and journalist Iris Wilkinson (Robin Hyde).[67] It paid five shillings for a poem and around thirty shillings for an article. Fairburn's poems began appearing regularly, and reviews and articles occasionally, from July 1927, as he contemplated a career as a freelance journalist. The *Sun* offices on Wyndham Street became another downtown haunt, and Fairburn also played for the *Sun* rugby team.

Mason's contributions were less frequent. Two of his poems were printed in October 1927. 'Stoic Marching Song', two short, hard stanzas, expressed one of his most characteristic poetic moods, gritted teeth in the face of death, a hostile world and uncaring gods:

> Though I have no soul to save
> Boldly march I to my grave
> Through this hostile country here,
> Prey of doubt and pain and fear.
>
> Son of sorrow, sire of sods,
> Still I gird back at the gods,
> Boldly bear five foot eleven
> Despite Hell and Earth and Heaven.

It shared the 'Poet's Corner' on 7 October with Fairburn's 'After Death', a romantic and clichéd treatment of this theme, and 'Chrysanthemums' by A. Gladys Kernot, which was as much a contrast to Mason's grim verses as could be imagined and, most likely, more to the taste of the *Sun*'s readers:

> The prima donna, Summer, all her bouquets threw away;
> Upon the garden beds they lie, dishevelled, in the rain.
> She said that she was coming back – her promises were gay –
> I wonder shall I see her bright chrysanthemums again? . . .

The next week Donnelly printed Mason's 'Man and Beast', another meditation on the common fate of us all, in the 'inevitable, ultimate,/ Dark realms lying underground'. He treated the subject in a lighter mood in a few lines in his notebook:

> We all must pass the terminus
> We all must get the worm in us
> To riot round and squirm in us.[68]

The pair were not too disdainful to continue to submit their poems to the *Star* as well. Mulgan printed four poems by Mason between September 1927 and February 1928, three of which Mason would later republish, including 'The Leave-taking', on burying a dead friend. The fourth, which he would not, was a sonnet which ends with a favourite metaphor:

The seas whereon my poor spirit is tossed
By huge storms in whose idiotic force
That plunges in mad and overwhelming riot
My being's scattered, and my soul is lost.[69]

In September 1927 he sent two contributions to the Labour Party newspaper the *New Zealand Worker*, under the pseudonym 'Porta Ipse'. One was a review of a book about the recent British coalminers' strike, and the other a satirical piece collating 'impressions as to the present state of Russia' gleaned from 'the immortal pages of that noble, cultural, honest, true-minded, fascinating – shall we say omniscient – organ of enlightenment, "The New Zealand Herald"'. This was his first piece of political journalism.[70]

THERE WERE still plans for the book that had been talked about a year earlier – '"Four New Zealanders" or something', by this time, with poems by Mason, Fairburn, de Montalk and Rudd – although Mason was less enthusiastic about the project than his friends. Fairburn wrote encouragingly to de Montalk in July: 'Do it in an original form, & make it plain that we are young & struggling (one, alas, no longer.). When you go to England what about taking a selection & trying to get some publisher to do it at his own expense? They do, you know, sometimes. We might manage to create a stir.'[71] In October de Montalk arrived in Auckland on his way to the world. The country had failed the test: 'In spite of the fact that a few Wild Oats have sold, I fail to see that New Zealand wants us'.[72] He spent a few weeks in Auckland, staying some of the time with Mason, the rest with Fairburn. 'He fought with me, he fought with Rex, he fought with the porters down at the railway station, he fought with the tramwaymen, he fought with everybody under the sun, everybody liked him very much, detested his opinions, [and] waved him goodbye to England.'[73] He paused briefly in Sydney, where he took a job selling Eureka vacuum cleaners and contemplated staying for a year or so and starting a literary journal. 'Dear old Lenin', he addressed his first postcard to Mason, from on board the *Oronsay* off Colombo in late December. 'I don't think you'd remain a Communist long on this ship – unless, of course, you travelled First Class.'[74]

He had failed to persuade anyone to go with him, although Fairburn had been talking about leaving 'this intellectual rathole', this 'spiritual cesspool', for some months. He would follow de Montalk, but not for another three years. For now he had no money, among other obstacles. And '[i]f you think

R.A.K. has stayed in Auckland for the sheer joy of it, you are mistook. As a matter of fact he is at present slaving like a navvy to get his degree, so he will have a chance of being independent of this bordello.'[75] For some reason, Mason did not sit any of his exams that year, despite having gained terms in three subjects. Dan passed five of his six papers. He would not complete his degree, but was soon embarked on what was to be a short and ignominious career in the law.

6

Why we can't write for nuts

1928–29

DOWN TO Lichfield Mason went for the harvesting season at the end of
1927. This time he invited Fairburn down too. He would try to find him
some work, he wrote to him from Aunt Foster's, but there was not much
available, and 'it's bloody hard labour and liable to start hay-fever', he warned.
But they could walk a bit, and go riding. They should walk back to Auckland
'by some roundabout route', via Raglan or Whakatane, say, and 'you could
write it up for the "Sun" and so make yourself financial'.[1]

He installed Rex in an abandoned and semi-derelict stone store, popularly
known as the Bank, a remnant of Lichfield's prosperous days which now
provided shelter for passing swaggers. There was no question of Fairburn
staying with Aunt Foster, as 'for once he had met a woman whom even his
ease could not melt' (although 'you might . . . win your way to her heart
with an axe – I mean, chop wood for her until she loves you', Mason
suggested).[2] The Bank was currently occupied by a sometime 'rabbiter,
"hobo," railway porter, bushman, hawker, harvester, road-mender, carter,
[and] slaughterman' named George Parkes, a 'lean aquiline nosed, sunbaked
man' who fancied that he bore a striking resemblance to Julius Caesar, drove
'the most decrepit of old, old Model T Fords', and delighted his new friends
with his store of anecdotes, bushman's philosophy, 'strange expressions' and
literary gleanings from the pages of the *Bulletin*.[3] He was, Mason would later
remark, 'my first close acquaintance with a casual rural worker', a type that
would later recur in his writing.[4]

George and Ron and Rex 'got on marvellously', smoking and drinking
tea and yarning into the evenings. Fairburn's harvesting season, however, was
short. Incapacitated by hayfever, within a week he had retreated to Auckland,
where he stayed briefly at Great South Road. 'Poor Rex', Jessie reported to
Lichfield, 'has awful hay fever still & seems to want to sleep all the time.'[5]
Fairburn did turn the experience into an article for the *Sun*, writing only
semi-facetiously of the arcadian scene, quoting Housman and making light of
his affliction, although it was a subject on which he was sorely sensitive (Mason's

account of it to Irene was emphatically '*not* appreciated').[6] It was, in fact, not only hayfever that had defeated him, but, as Mason had predicted, the work. 'I don't know how the hell . . . you can do 9 1/2 & 10 hours forking,' Fairburn confessed. 'Probably *you* don't know'. But Mason enjoyed it: 'it's great fun to do some hard work after so much bloody reading, writing, talking, thinking, teaching', he would write to de Montalk a few years later. 'I love it' – except when digging out ragwort, 'a cursed weed . . . which infests these parts'.[7]

De Montalk, having arrived in England, continued his efforts to promote Mason's poetry, and Fairburn's and his own, in his self-appointed role as 'your London ambassador'. If necessary he would take the castle by force, he wrote to Fairburn in April – if talent and charm and bombast didn't do it. 'And as soon as I am inside I create you and Ronald assistant Kings – unless you get there first, in which case you are expected to do the same – and then we issue jointly several death warrants against some "giants" of English literature, and after that we reign merrily. . . . Which ever of us arrives first will help the other, won't we, and Ronald?'[8] He had met Harold Monro and been unimpressed: Monro was nice but 'very ordinary', with a 'small, unintellectual, Scottish mind', and he was no poet. Instead it was Humbert Wolfe, another minor poet of the Georgian/Poetry Bookshop circle whom he had met early in February, on whom de Montalk now placed his hopes for the future of New Zealand literature. He had dashed off a postcard to Mason immediately: 'he knew all about you, and told me all about your poems before I even mentioned your name. The "Body of John" upset him, but he got over it as I did, and I believe he thinks you are not too worse.'[9] Three weeks and another meeting with Wolfe later, he reported still more excitedly: 'I used the phrase "New Zealand poet" and before I knew where I was he had taken it for granted I meant you, and he knew all about you, and held forth about your highness for some length of time.' He had also remarked on 'the fact that you neglected to correspond properly with H.M. and seemed amazingly indifferent to notice in high quarters. . . . He spoke of your laxity in pursuing the Monro lead as "mysterious", in fact you were an intriguing mystery all round.'[10]

Mason was to receive two more letters from Monro, to which he did not reply, while Monro's estimation of his 'young friend' remained undiminished. When asked by the *Spectator* in March 1928 to write an article on a contemporary poet, Monro offered to do a more general one instead, 'in which I would include Roy Campbell, Quennell, a young New Zealander named Mason and perhaps one or two other people who might be termed followers of Rupert Brooke, either on account of their similarity or their divergence' (the paper, however, asked for something on Flecker).[11] 'I have been pretty bloody in not writing to him even when he does things for me', Mason would later admit to de Montalk, ' – and what he has done has helped me more than I can show – given me confidence and courage in the dark days.'[12] In 1928, de Montalk saw the poet he admired most in New Zealand inexplicably squandering his god-given talent, not to mention his obligation to the rest of the group. 'Now look here old boy', he remonstrated. 'I submit it is about time you started to take yourself seriously as a poet. At least you might have a complete folio of your own works instead of all that morass of scrap paper you use for scenery at Ellerslie. Why not have enough conceit to make a copy of a projected book?'[13] Conceit was something de Montalk had more than enough of; Mason little.

Mason was not writing much at that time, in fact – not poetry, at any rate. He was sick of, but persevered with, tutoring at Holl's: teaching conjugations and declensions to the sons and daughters of Auckland's middle and upper classes, whom he so despised, in 'the bare ink-stained desert of a cramming school'.[14] He was also tutoring some economics and civics by then. And he was busy at university, having enrolled in seven papers that year: English I, History I, Latin II and French II, all repeated from the previous year, plus Economics I for his BA and Political Science I and Economics II for a Diploma in Social Science. He would pass his exams in all of them except English, which he appears not to have sat. Perhaps this time it was simply that the subject did not interest him. The literary period of study in English I in 1928, and the special field of interest of the professor – the gentlemanly, doddery C.W. Egerton, one of the college's founding staff – was the first half of the eighteenth century, the 'Age of Pope' and the Augustans, which Mason despised: 'the awful era of standardised poetry . . . when most poets did as they were told (and consequently ceased to be poets)'. This Mason wrote in an article he contributed to the *Sun* literary page in June 1928, in response to one from S. Anderson of Horahora entitled 'Freak English', a tirade against the 'asinine', 'queer cult' of free verse complete with a couple of stanzas of spoof Ezra Pound.

Mason's reply was a measured essay in literary history. It concerned him not that the writer 'really prefers strict formalism (and there I am with him)', but that he was ignorant. Explaining that free verse was not a modern or pernicious invention of the French, he traced its development from Greek literature and in French from the seventeenth century and La Fontaine. In English literature 'the use of lines of irregular length with the rhymes occurring in any order (or even without rhyme at all) is so ordinary' – from Milton, then Blake, the Romantics, Shelley and Southey, to contemporary writers, including Lawrence, Giovanetti and Maurice Baring – 'that it seems strange to find men regarding it as a spasmodic outbreak peculiar to modern times'. Nor should free verse be feared as a threat to the healthy development of New Zealand literature, for 'the curse of our native writers lies in the want of proper originality, not in the presence of too much. We are in no danger of imitating the follies of the wilder Americans'. Who, the reader is left to wonder, or expected to know, was the New Zealand writer he considered its 'one outstanding example of daring originality (as apart from mere eccentricity)' and 'our one great writer'?[15] Mason did not respond in his turn to S. Anderson's reply, which declared that the function of poetry was to soothe and distract, as 'an anodyne and an opiate': 'In the main, thought in poetry is merely an accidental by-product'. Clearly he, or she, would not have abided Mason's poetry.[16]

IN DECEMBER 1928 the *Sun* published the first proper review of Mason's poems. It was the third article in a series of ten by Ian Donnelly under the title 'Of N.Z. Poets', which aimed to showcase the 'younger' writers, beginning with Jessie Mackay (described as New Zealand's most popular poet) and Eileen Duggan (its 'finest'). Mason was introduced as a contributor to the *Chapbook* – only later, Donnelly claimed, perhaps disingenuously, had he learned that Mason was not a young Englishman but an Auckland student – and 'one of the most original minds in the young New Zealand literary movement'. Donnelly admired his '[g]ood, angry cynicism', 'hard thinking' and 'brooding mind'. 'He is not influenced in any marked way by English contemporary poetry, having struck out for himself with a melancholy philosophy that makes a direct appeal. There is nothing pretty-pretty in his work, and many readers will not find his philosophy particularly attractive. He is blind to the comforts of life, and prefers to engage himself with pessimistic speculations.'[17] Donnelly, in fact, had consulted Mason about the article and Mason had suggested – 'Pardon my presumption' – that he take as his theme

> pessimism objectified always in various moods: – nihilistic ('In Perpetuum Vale' – if properly punctuated it shows the boy quite at his best), agnostic ('A Doubt' – simple thing in broadsheet): gently pessimistic, brooding 'white',

'Virgilian' melancholy (After Death – p.5 and The Lesser Stars – p8.): spirit-
destroying humour (The Latter-day Geography Lesson is first class stuff – just
about as good as I could wish for). Pessimism that of classical scholar . . . If
you want a relief from this 'Anatomy of Melancholy' try 'Tribute'.[18]

Donnelly got the message.

For all his welcoming Mason's 'original turn of mind', however, Donnelly
found it necessary to defend him on the grounds of respectable precedent
('there is not much honey-dew about Hardy, A.E. Housman, and some other
established men'), and noted that he was a traditionalist in his use of classical
forms ('He feels himself that he owes a great deal to the Romans, Catullus in
particular'). The article quoted extracts from Monro's letters to Mason and
from four poems in The Beggar, and two short stanzas which Mason would
place (slightly revised) at the beginning of his next collection, and which here
were entitled 'Preface to the Book of Pessimism':[19]

> If the drink that satisfied
> The son of Joseph when he died
> Has not the right smack for you,
> Leave it for a kindlier brew.
>
> For my bitter verses are
> Sponges steeped in vinegar.
> Useless to the happy-eyed
> But handy to the crucified.

'[W]ith the peculiar strength of his mind, and his aptness for originating forms,'
Donnelly concluded, 'there seems to be every hope that he will accomplish
some really memorable verse. Philosophic poets are rare in these days, but he
is certainly one.'

Among the other poets featured in the series were Fairburn, whom
Donnelly appraised, less enthusiastically, as strongly influenced by the Georgians
(having 'the same happy gift of selecting slender yet beautiful themes. . . . Mr.
Fairburn, as a poet, has no grave concern with the major tragedies of life', but
rather excels 'in the little, unambitious lyrics'), and de Montalk (a 'provocative
and original thinker', his poems were 'carefully wrought' and 'strongly
flavoured with philosophical mysticism'), Robin Hyde, and a handful of other,
since-forgotten names. Donnelly would not claim that here was yet a 'definite

school of writing', but considered them a group of young poets who had in different ways 'broken away from the first tradition' represented by Alexander and Currie's recent *Treasury of New Zealand Verse* (1926), the second edition of their 1906 collection, and who deserved an anthology of their own. 'Perhaps some literary philanthropist will aid this last assault against those who say that the young New Zealanders have accomplished nothing of worth in poetry.'[20]

But literary philanthropists were thin on the ground, as Mason and his friends well knew, and their own small anthology was still just an idea. Fairburn had also been talking about starting a literary journal, mention of which prompted de Montalk into extravagant schemes of coming back and founding one himself: 'It'd be something quite original. . . . Include everything from my Royalism and theosophy, to your aristocracy and Ronald's Communism and atheism . . . Spice with advanced tendencies in music (C. Scott – Scriabin – Stravinski) and a sound all-round contempt for dullness in every branch of Art. Think of it! Our own theatre, later on – plays by you and Ron; poetry evenings by all of us. New Zealand, a modern Athens.'[21] Five days later he told them he was not coming back to New Zealand – and he did not, for another fifty-five years. He began learning Polish, and spent the second half of 1929 in Lithuania in search of his royal inheritance. But he remained, for the moment, as committed as ever to his personal crusade on behalf of New Zealand literary nationalism. 'We, I think, between us, form a grand and unique group – I mean the New Zealand poets. All so young, so fair to look at, and gifted with so great a strain of song – so well-witted, so full of hope.'[22] He caused a stir early the following year when he was reported in the New Zealand press to have remarked during a lecture at Foyle's bookshop that New Zealand had poets greater than Shakespeare. What he had really said, he wrote in his defence, was that New Zealand boasted the greatest living group of poets in the world today. 'In my own heart', he could not refrain from adding, 'I believe myself greater than any European poet, except "Shakespear".'[23] He sent back poems and articles describing his meetings with famous writers for Fairburn to submit to the *Sun*. He also sent his friends advice on what they should be reading, and two copies of Joyce's *Ulysses*, which was banned in New Zealand. A university friend of Mason's would later remember borrowing his copy, 'a bulky quarto paperback with a pale blue cover, looking rather like a telephone directory'.[24] Irene recalled that he and Rex would not let her read it.

For his part, Fairburn had sent off an article on Mason and the Wellington poet Eileen Duggan to the newly established London weekly *Everyman*, but

without result. He had more success with a piece on Mason which he submitted
to Pat Lawlor's *New Zealand Artists' Annual* for 1929. Lawlor was an unlikely
ally. A journalist of twenty years, a bibliophile and a Catholic, he represented
in many respects the literary and social values that Mason and Fairburn despised.
But he was an energetic and dedicated, and often controversial, figure in the
small circle of New Zealand letters for many years. The *Annual*, which he
had founded in 1926, succeeded and was modelled on the New Zealand
edition of the Australian humorous magazine *Aussie*, which he had also edited.
It contained mainly cartoons and comic and middle-brow journalism, with
just a smattering of more serious literary contributions. In the absence of a
proper literary journal, however, it was the next best thing to the weekly
literary columns or half-pages of the *Star* or the *Sun*.

In his article Fairburn cast Mason as an antipodean Housman, 'one of the
"lean and swarthy poets of despair"', who 'is in revolt against life, and resorts
to a smouldering pessimism, ranging from wistful melancholy to out-and-out
rancour, using it homeopathically as a drug in order to escape from reality.
This *weltschmerz* becomes in Mason, as it does in Byron, Heine, Housman,
and all pessimists, thoroughly romantic in its expression'. He quoted 'After
Death' and the 'Sonnet of Brotherhood' in full. It was here that the story of
The Beggar's watery end originated: 'I remember meeting him one day, and
his telling me, half in sorrow and half in relief, that he had just been down to
the end of Queen's Wharf and had disposed of a bundle of two hundred.
"Thank God I've got a few of them off my mind, anyway!".' It was 'a tragic
thing', Fairburn lamented, 'that a book of this sort should find its way into
the hands of only a scattering of people in all Australasia.' To this neglect he
attributed the poet's 'almost unbroken silence during the intervening five
years'.[25]

The article sparked a flutter of interest in the book, which Mason may not
have appreciated. Lawlor asked for an autographed copy. He had requested
something for the *Annual* but Mason told him that he was 'writing little at
present. I still have a few copies of the "Beggar" left, but am not anxious to
get rid of them, as they are so full of mistakes and of stuff that would have
been better left unprinted.'[26] The young editor of an Australian literary
magazine sent three shillings for two copies, and the Georgian Bookshop in
Invercargill ordered three. The story of Mason tossing the book into the
harbour also inspired de Montalk to write, in the small hours of a London
morning, a long, lewd, satiric poem about the fate of the young poet in
'God's Own Country', 'that snobbish little nation' of philistines and wowsers.[27]

WHY WE CAN'T WRITE FOR NUTS *1928–29*

DOUGLAS GLASS, another young New Zealander abroad and a friend of de Montalk, wrote to Mason in April 1929: 'I never see anything of yours in the Sun. How is this? Rex and Geoffrey often get in.'[28] It was not only that Mason was not writing much. The *Star* printed his article on Housman, 'An English Pessimist: Great verse in little space', and a lighter contribution on harvesting in January 1929, and later that year a bleak sonnet on the insignificance of human life:

> Of all our toil and skill and pride and hope
> And hate and plots and love and piety,
>
> . . .
>
> A little while with godly foes to cope,
> Then pass like cloud-shadows on a blind sea.[29]

In June he sent two poems to the *Sun*. 'Flattering Unction', published on 28 June, was a Shakespearean sonnet (the title is from *Hamlet*) on a Catullan theme, juxtaposing the desire for immortality and sexual gratification.[30] The second, 'The Young Man Thinks of Sons', was rejected. It was a more frankly worded poem about sex and mortality, a bitter denial of propagation:

> Did my father curse his father for his lust I wonder
>   as I do mine
> and my grand-dad curse his sire for his wickedness his weakness his blunder
>   and so on down the whole line.
>
> Well I'll stop the game break the thread end my race: I will not continue
>   in the old bad trade:
> I'll take care that for my nerveless mind weakened brain neglected sinew
>   I alone shall have paid.

Horace gave the Latin cue here. In Mason's 1818 school edition of Horace he marked the last line of Ode 6, Book 3, 'Delicta maiorum': 'Our parents' age, worse than our grandsires', has brought forth us less worthy and destined soon to yield an offspring still more wicked' (as translated in the Loeb edition). 'I like "The Young Man Thinks of Sons" tremendously', Percy Crisp, the editor of the *Sun*, wrote back to Mason, 'but won't be able to use it. As you know, the N.Z. general reader bucks like a broncho [*sic*] at the mention of lust'.[31]

Lawlor felt no need to apologise when he returned two contributions
from Mason in June the following year: a poem 'on reading which few New
Zealanders would remain unshocked' and a 'brilliantly written article the
sentiments of which however I largely disagree with'.[32] What poem this was
is not clear. The article, entitled 'Why We Can't Write for Nuts', was a
savage attack on the local literary culture: on the conservatism of editors and
the insipidity of the writing they encouraged by publishing it, 'that almost
unmitigated mass of sickliness which we so loftily dub "New Zealand
Literature"'. 'The gentlemen whose sacred mission it is to direct literary
standards in N.Z.', Mason wrote, '(I shall name none – for reasons connected
with the law of libel) are for the most part old men (or youths prematurely
old) who have never even studied literature deeply. It goes without saying
that scarcely one of them could write a decent line himself'. They liked
anything that was old and regarded most modern writers as 'nasty-minded
neurotics, dabblers in sex and free-verse, railers at our established institutions,
sceptics, scoffers, iconoclasts, perverse, destructive, and generally unclean. . . .
No wonder the young writer of promise so rarely fulfils that promise. . . . It
is only out of questioning and free room for the honest expression of doubt
that any great art can arise. But we are so conventional and timid'. He referred
to Crisp having demurred at printing 'The Young Man Thinks of Sons': 'I
answered "Hang it, what could be more orthodox? Can't you see it's a strong
plea for chastity" (Quaintly enough I happen to support that old-fashioned
doctrine even in this age of moving pictures and garbled Freud). He smiled
wearily and said: "Yes, but what New Zealander will remain unshocked if
you talk of 'the lust of my loins'"?' There had been a time when New Zealand
writing showed some 'independent spirit' – 'uncouth, maybe, but a potential
basis for glorious originality when enlightened' – but

The wild colonial boy is no more born – Babbitt inherits his land. The fat,
stodgy, pudgy little thoughts of Suburbia prevail and swamp out both the
native wit of the pioneer and the scholarly courage of the study. . . . If we are
to get anywhere we must develop freedom, and boldness, and vigour in our
thinking. Of course fools will interpret this according to their folly. Inevitably
such an upsurge would involve an accompaniment of crudeness and clumsiness
with outbursts of brutality masquerading as strength – it might possibly mean
no more than that. But certainly our present stagnation is spiritual death.
Certainly nothing could be worse than the present position and the existing
spirit – this mealy-mouthed, conscience-canting, sickly, goody-goody, namby-

pamby, weak and watery, sheltered school-girl, bourgeois drawing room, Sunday-school picnic, mothers' meeting spirit that is all powerful among the generation of to-day.[33]

Mason can hardly have been surprised that the article was rejected. He wrote back to Lawlor with some cheek:

Really your strictures on my moral obliquity make me feel quite sinister. . . . Sorry I can't try again: I did not understand yours was the type of magazine where contributors have to gauge the editor's tastes. . . . The article is infinitely better than some of my trashier stuff which you persist in admiring. I could do you others, but I fear they would not fit – I am amusing myself at the moment with a thesis on the personal religion of Cicero – or I could do a little thing on the sexual psychology of Catullus, or I should just love to see in print my learned analysis of the position of patriotism in the light of modern international developments. . . . but if that article would shock what would these do? Should be delighted to foregather with you if in Auckland at any time. Only I warn you – do not expect to find any Fancy's child warbling his native wood-notes wild about me. I am just reading Havelock Ellis – The Dance of Life – which I can thoroughly recommend if you haven't read it.'[34]

Despite this exchange the two remained on cordial terms.

Mason had also offered the article to Percy Crisp, who wrote to him a few months later to apologise: he had intended to print it but had 'lost sight of it for a while .... and now it is too late!'[35] It was too late because the *Sun* had just closed down, in September 1930, a casualty of the worsening economic crisis. It had been unable to find sufficient advertising to sustain itself as Auckland's third daily newspaper as the Great Depression deepened.

HAROLD MONRO had written his third letter to Mason in April 1929, sending 'a recent list which may interest you'. He was evidently almost as neglectful a correspondent as Mason himself: 'I believe it is my turn to write to you as a year or two ago I had a letter from you [which he had since lost] with some printed poems [presumably the *Penny Broadsheet*].' The same month Douglas Glass wrote to Mason from London. He had met Monro, who told him that he had now sold about ninety copies of *The Beggar*. 'If you do not care to keep it up with Monro,' Glass urged Mason, 'why not drop me a line and send me some of your recent MSS. I may be able to do something for

you over here for I know a great number of people in the swim.' He had
been trying to do the same for de Montalk, 'but most of the people that I
have shown his work were not impressed.'[36]

Mason received one more letter from Monro, his would-be London patron,
in the New Year of 1930: 'It is ages since we have corresponded. I have heard
of you however through two people who know you, at any rate one named
A.G.D. Glass who is a journalist and I think the other must have been a
strange individual called Geoffrey de Montalk.' He was writing, again
somewhat apologetically, to tell Mason that he had included two of his poems
in an anthology that was coming out that month (November 1929). 'There
was no time to communicate with you and I wanted very much to represent
you by one page at any rate so I chose two poems that went well on one page
together, namely THE SPARK'S FAREWELL TO ITS CLAY and THE MIRACLE OF
LIFE' (the first part only of both). The book was entitled *Twentieth Century
Poetry*, and was being published by Chatto and Windus in its 3s 6d Phoenix
Library. 'Please, whatever happens, don't be angry about this. I assure you
they are very worthy, though you yourself may now think them juvenile.'[37]

The anthology, which was to be reprinted four times in the next two
years, represented seventy-seven poets, all except for Mason British or Irish
(though four were of American origin, including Eliot and Pound), and a
'portentously prolific' period, the defining event of which Monro identified
as the First World War: 'for the young authors who suddenly (as it were)
burst out in flame through a fierce indignation against the war are like a
central pivot to the period, and were more than partly instrumental in the
fresh impulse given, thus, indirectly, to our English poetry'. Among the poetic
trends of the period he noted the 'habit of sharp contrast and of anticlimax'
(also, he regretted, a continuing prominence of nature poems – there were
still far too many starlings in English verse). He refrained from discussing the
'controversial' subject of free verse. But he was prepared to pick that T.S.
Eliot would prove to be as influential in the following ten years as Housman
and Brooke had been up to 1920. 'To-day we have each our *Waste Land*, and
the strong influence of Mr. T.S. Eliot, and a few other poets, chiefly
unacknowledged in Georgian circles, is more indicative of future tendencies
than any other recognizable Signpost.'[38]

Mason was in Lichfield, and half-way through a letter to de Montalk,
when his copy arrived early in January. 'Anthologies are usually unspeakable,
but I must admit I like this one – perhaps I am blinded by my own vanity. Of
course, some things are too well-known' (he noted poems by Ralph Hodgson,

Chesterton and Housman's 'Epitaph on an Army of Mercenaries', 'though that is perfect'). 'Also some is not good enough to be there in my opinion', including pieces by Masefield, John Freeman and Roy Campbell. 'Still, on the whole it's the best collection I know. Introduced me to some damn fine new men – Gerard Manley Hopkins gets a queer grip on me'.[39] He copied these comments into a letter to Fairburn, with suggestions for a review Fairburn might write. 'I must admit that The Hollow Men has me beat in places', he added, '– though I like it queerly – but that is the only thing at all hard to make out.'[40] The book appeared in the Auckland shops in the first week of February, and was noticed in a short article in the *Sun* ('New Zealand Poet Honoured. Represented in anthology') and by one sentence in the *Star*.[41] Fairburn too was struck, though puzzled, by Hopkins, included by Monro as belonging temperamentally to the twentieth century and not the nineteenth; and, although he evidently did not write the review, he was unrestrained in his congratulations to his friend. 'Now looky here, I'm not given to passing (or pissing) idle compliments and vague sentimentalities, but those two things of yours are about as good as anything in the book. . . . They hit me where I live. I've always liked them (among others), but when I see them alongside the rest I get a new light on them. Theyre [*sic*] sure good, bo, and then some.' 'For God's sake', he urged Mason, 'collect all your scraps of poems together and let me type them out.'[42]

MONRO'S LETTER to Mason had continued: 'I have constantly meant to correspond with you again and particularly to enquire if you had written any further poems. I hope you have not been overwhelmed by an uncongenial life. You seemed to me so full of promise and I have sold most of the 100 copies of your little book and will send you a cheque as soon as I hear that we have your correct address.' Mason did write in reply to Monro this time, so he told de Montalk; but as he never posted his letter to de Montalk it is likely that he never sent Monro's either.

His university year ended in disappointment. He had sat and passed his finals in Latin III, French III and Political Science (he did not sit Greek, although he had gained terms). In Latin he gained the top marks in New Zealand, 'his margin . . . over the second candidate being the unprecedented one of seven per cent', Professor Paterson recorded. 'Only a technicality deprived him of the Senior Scholarship so well and decisively won.' He had qualified for a scholarship by 'over 20 marks – by far the largest margin I have ever known in this examination'.[43] The technicality was that he had not completed his degree. Having failed terms in History I in 1928, although he had passed the final exam, he was not credited with the nine subjects required for a BA.

At the end of the year he resigned from Holl's – a reckless move, perhaps, at that time. Perhaps he had simply had enough of it. From Lichfield, in the midst of the harvest, he wrote to de Montalk early in January 1930: 'Other years I have done it for love, very largely, but this year it is a case of bitter constraint and dire occasion drear [he is quoting Milton]. For I have thrown up teaching.'[44]

7

The Book of Pessimism

1930

MASON STAYED in Lichfield for four months this time, to his mother's distress. 'I am already missing you', she wrote to him a few days after he had gone. 'My dear good son you have been *so* good to me – & some day I hope to repay you. Don't stay too long away . . . I think I shall not need to be such a strain & drain on you this year.'[1] But she did need the money he sent – and he needed to be away. This long Lichfield summer was one of his happiest there. 'I am in clover', he wrote to Fairburn, 'never so happy, fit and prosperous.'[2]

He had approached the Workers' Educational Association (WEA) offering to give a course of lectures on Latin literature, but was turned down: 'lack of funds would prevent any experiment in this direction just now', he was advised.[3] The ambition he had had when he left school for a career in journalism had been dispelled by his deepening cynicism about newspapers. 'Utterly abandoned rags like the Herald are all right', he remarked to de Montalk.

> But things with a glimpse of the light like the Sun – they are the snares about the feet of the young men. Have just enough of pseudo-taste to encourage decent people to pander to them. I hope I never have to write another line for a newspaper all my life long: they inevitably debase your vigour: the mere thought of them serves to turn your pen insensibly towards journalism – and journalism is the utter antithesis of what writing ought to be.[4]

'The Greeks had temple-prostitution, the Romans crucifixion, but neither of them had newspapers', he wrote in his notebook.[5] He planned to get a labouring job when the harvest was over, then go back to university to finish his degree 'and get a post-graduate scholarship the next'. A scholarship would pay his passage and £200 a year for two years' study in England or Europe. But he was ambivalent about this prospect – remote though he believed it to be, for only three travelling scholarships were awarded nationally each year.

Of course he should like to see London, he told de Montalk, but 'the prospect of England appals me'. His political antipathy towards the place many New Zealanders still referred to wistfully as 'Home' — he saw it as a capitalist, colonising, class-ridden country — had been only reinforced by the disillusioned reports he and Fairburn had received from their friend, who had found London at first to be squalid, ugly and expensive, no place for aristocrats or poets at all. And Lichfield exerted a special hold: 'After all, this is my own native land and all that; and I rather fancy that a man can never *feel*, never be moved or gripped by any land unless he has been brought up in it.' He told de Montalk: 'I often think of you as I roam by some secluded and delightful solitude; with affection not unmixed with a sense of arrogance that after all perhaps I have made the better choice.'[6] But he was not sure, and he would continue to be alternately drawn to and repelled by the idea of London: the centre of things, the literary metropolis.

Nor was it only a matter of choice. January was unusually wet — the second-wettest January on record, in fact, after 1923 — which meant that there was little work and a lot of time for reading, walking and writing, including letters: 'some of them in belated answer to those sent me a couple of years back', and the 26-page letter he composed to de Montalk over the course of two weeks, but neglected to send — while de Montalk was inquiring of Fairburn, 'What . . . of Ronald? Is he dead? Or slumbereth he only?'[7] 'Read a lot of Milton, Plato and Virgil at first,' he reported, 'but found my mind was turning a pure snow-white: a little Horace to bring me back to normal, and then some of that black-hearted, calumniating (but gloriously powerful) bastard Tacitus to put a bit of malignity in me.' He was reading Suetonius's Caesars ('it's huge; they talk about Lytton Strachey as though his biographies had audacities!'), Petronius, Catullus ('in prose, mind'), Tibullus ('not so good'), the *Pervigilium Veneris* and *The Golden Asse*; Housman and Stendhal.[8] He had his mother collect his Latin dictionary from the binders ('It's pretty heavy, I warn you'[9]) and send it down along with the five volumes in the 'damned fine' Loeb library that he had received as a university prize given by Professor Paterson. He asked de Montalk to send him books from the Poetry Bookshop. He had sold the five copies of *Wild Oats* that de Montalk had left with him and, to save the expense of transferring the money he owed him (£2 3s 6d, he calculated), told de Montalk to take it from what he himself was owed by Harold Monro from sales of *The Beggar* — and if there was any credit left asked him to get him some, or any, of 'Joyce, Pomes Penyeach, Rosenberg, Hardy's Collected Poems, Wilfred Owen, T.S. Eliot, Aldington, Flint, Charlotte Mew,

Sitwells' – all poets represented in *Twentieth Century Poetry*. 'Collected Poems if you can – at all costs none of those bloody selections. If you can't manage on the above, use your discretion; something "advanced" and out-of-the-way for preference.'

The long-planned New Zealand anthology, meanwhile, was 'in a state of chaotic half-completion' but 'no one seems to want to touch it', he reported to de Montalk, although de Montalk was no longer part of this scheme. It was now to include Mason, Fairburn, Rudd and Firth, and another mutual friend, Carl Straubel. Straubel was teaching in Palmerston North but soon disappointed Mason and Fairburn by taking a job with the Christchurch *Press*: 'was showing distinct signs of better things a year ago. Now he will just turn into a glib slick man about town with the proper witticism about the latest scandal and the correct thing to say about the newest book'. In this letter Mason also gave de Montalk, for the first time, his candid opinion of *Wild Oats*. The introduction was 'bloody', and much of the poetry was 'immature', but he singled out one poem as 'splendid', one fine, one magnificent and several good. Several others, however, were spoiled by 'an abominable pettiness – obtrusion of your own pet fads and fancies – Hierarchika, for example: it just exactly reminds me of one of those Socialist poems – too long have the People suffered, ground down by the Lords of the Land sort of stuff, only written, of course, from another point of view'. Whereas, for his own part, 'I may have radical sympathies, and write articles for the N.Z. Worker, but I don't write "rhymes of the under-dog" (dedicated to all who toil, 3rd edition, price 3/6 post free). Get me.'

He was writing, though. When he resumed the letter six days later he copied into it the poem he had written the night before, on his birthday. 'How soon hath Time the suttle theef of youth Stoln on his wing my five and twentieth year!' he remarked, misquoting Milton. The poem was called 'Christ on the Swag':

> His body doubled
> under the pack
> that sprawls untidily
> on his old back
> the cold wet dead-beat
> plods up the track.

The cook peers out:
    oh, curse that old lag –
    here again
    with his clumsy swag
    made of a dirty old
    turnip-bag.

Bring him in, cook,
    from the cold level sleet:
    put silk on his body,
    slippers on his feet;
    give him fire
    and bread and meat

Let the fruit be plucked,
    and the cake be iced,
    the bed be snug,
    and the wine be spiced
    for the old cove's night-cap –
    for this is Christ.

– 'not good', he demurred, 'don't be surprised that it's somewhat in the slangy style beloved by Australian bush-bards. I'm doing a lot in that line. The fact that somewhat similar-looking stuff has been done to death by Colonials does not worry me a damn.'[10] This was to become one of his best-known poems. He was to point out, when discussing it many years later, that the scene related more particularly to the depression of the 1890s than 1930, and elaborated on the context in more abstract political terms as being 'a patriarchal economy in the fullest form that we have had it, where a high degree of social equality may exist even alongside economic inequality, a characteristic that tends to persist in peculiar forms in many ways in New Zealand'. The cook, 'somewhat like a court jester or fool in Elizabethan drama', has the right to abuse everyone and everything, including the principle of hospitality; he transgresses, however, by dismissing the stranger as an 'old lag'. Mason noted too the mingling of local symbols (the fruit being picked, the cake iced) with the general (fire and bread and meat) and exotic (silk and spiced wine), which serve to prepare the reader for the revelation in the final line.[11] Fairburn, when he was trying to place the poem in English journals a

THE BOOK OF PESSIMISM 1930

few years later, took the liberty of retitling it 'The Man on the Swag', for 'I refuse to allow others to be robbed of the kick in that last line by anticipation.'[12] Mason was eventually to publish it as 'On the Swag'.

It may also have been the first poem in which he adopted certain stylistic features – the hanging indent, 'copied from certain reprints of Horace', and minimal punctuation 'largely moulded on that of the Authorised Version and the Anglican Prayer Book' – which would characterise all of his printed poetry from about this time on, recognising how the clear typographical style strengthened the impact of his precise handling of rhythm, vocabulary and line length.[13]

He was sending poems to Fairburn as well, along with 'little scrapbook gems', and manuscripts home for Dan to have typed. 'Christ on the Swag' was very likely one of the two poems Fairburn responded to in a letter he sent to Lichfield in March: 'The two poems you send are great, lad. They really are. No sentimental gush about it. Particularly the one about Xt. That last line has a bigger kick to it than any I've ever read. And the thing has such a tide of symbolism running through it too, that it hits me right where I live.'[14] Possibly Mason had also sent 'Nails and a Cross', another poem about Christ which he wrote at Lichfield on 1 March 1930 (although it was not to be published until many years later). The voice of the poem is the crucified son, the tone sardonic:

> . . .
> And I see, if I squint, my blood of death
> drip on the little harsh grass beneath:
> and friend and foe and men long dead
> faint and reel in my whirling head:
> and while the troops divide up my cloak
> the mob fling dung and see the joke.

But the second poem Fairburn referred to was more likely to have been 'Ecce Homunculus', a better poem on the same theme, which Mason was to include in his next published collection:

> Betrayed by friend dragged from the garden hailed
>   as prophet and as lord in mockery
>   hauled down where Roman Pilate sat on high
>   perplexed and querulous, lustily assailed
>   by every righteous Hebrew cried down railed

against by all true zealots – still no sigh
escaped him but he boldly went to die
made scarcely a moan when his soft flesh was nailed.

And so he brazened it out right to the last
still wore the gallant mask still cried 'Divine
am I, lo for me is heaven overcast'
though that inscrutable darkness gave no sign
indifferent or malignant: while he was passed
by even the worst of men at least sour wine.

'The other poem hurts me', Fairburn wrote. 'The last three lines have a terrible bloody power. Perhaps it's the mood I'm in. They have an echo of the awful strife of Free Will and Destiny, mirrored in such a way that, as I say, it hurts me to read them. . . . there is a strain of *pessimism*, *real* pessimism, in them. Not the dust and ashes sort. The other, deeper sort. "We are to the gods as flies to etc" . . . Only subtler.'[15]

Mason was worried about Fairburn, who '[s]eems to be worrying,' he observed to de Montalk, 'just sort of slops along from week to week without any ambition', failing to appreciate, as Mason did, the importance of 'little simple things to do – things whose completion gives you a sort of minor triumph . . . something solid to hang on to, and keep you from drifting. . . . So even such a petty thing as getting a degree I do not despise – once I did in my wisdom, but now I do not in my greater wisdom.'[16] In February, Fairburn announced that he was going to Hollywood to seek his fortune, divulging this plan to Mason and Clifton Firth in strictest confidence – and defensively, correctly anticipating their cynical response, for to go to Hollywood would be for them to step into the very jaws of capitalism and cultural philistinism, as Fairburn knew, insisting that his intention was purely mercenary. His Hollywood plan may well have been influenced by Firth, in fact. While Mason was in Lichfield and Fairburn languishing in New Lynn, Firth was spending the summer of 1929–30 at Tokaanu, on the southern shore of Lake Taupo – from where he visited Mason in February – working for the American film director Alexander Markey on *Hei Tiki*, a romantic Maori drama (also known, for its British release, as *Primitive Passions*). It was the suave, swashbuckling and controversial Markey's second New Zealand film. He had been fired from the first (in 1928) by Universal Studios after filming became mired in delays, cost overruns and cultural misunderstanding. This time Markey had local finance, but *Hei Tiki* was no happier an experience for his Maori hosts and cast than his previous venture, which had eventually been completed without him and released as *Under the Southern Cross*. Nor was it a happy experience for Firth, who described the company to his friends as 'fools and cranks . . . Table rappers, Theosophists, devotees of New Thought, wets and leeches of the lowest order'. He advised Fairburn to 'go up and crawl out of Lake Taupo pretending he is John the Baptist or a Dawn-Spirit and they will worship him and give him all they've got'. Yet it did not entirely dampen his enthusiasm for film-making, nor Fairburn's Hollywood dream.[17]

Mason, meanwhile, was nurturing an equally romantic dream of himself and Fairburn going to live in the south of France – 'influence of Monty', Fairburn surmised, for de Montalk had soon abandoned London for Paris, which he found cheaper and more congenial for the pursuit of a life of 'aristocratic paganism'.[18] There were other possible reasons for the allure of France for Mason, however, and not only the French novels he was reading at that time.

IN THE letter he never sent to de Montalk, Mason also wrote briefly about his love life: 'funny thing, but I have only been intimate with three girls, and all half French'. Lola had married about two years before – 'knocked me up absolutely' – but was separated by then, with a child, and unhappy. Jessie worried that he was still in love with her, but she need not have. His current interest was Marie Gaudin: 'Fine girl – intelligent and honest . . . Have known her some 2 1/2 years now, and like her more as time goes on.'[19] She was a few years older than Mason and a journalist (assistant 'lady-editor') on the *Auckland Star*. He had met her through the Grafton Shakespeare and Dramatic Society, where she had once played juvenile lead opposite Fairburn in Clemence Dane's *A Bill of Divorcement*. The eldest of four 'beautiful and talented' sisters, she lived with her family on the North Shore, where Mason became a frequent visitor to their convivial, intelligent and always open home. 'He loved our family', she would later recall. 'My father was a bit of a socialist, my mother a John Bull.' Marie in turn became friends with Jessie.[20] 'As intellectual and platonic as these things can be', Mason described their relationship to de Montalk, ' – which is probably much more than you think possible and much less than I do.'[21] They remained less than lovers and more than friends for ten years. Marie, a mutual friend later commented, was the love of his life.[22] When he met her in town he would bring armfuls of pale pink Dorothy Perkins roses from the Ellerslie garden. On Saturdays he and

Fairburn would meet her at the *Star* office in Shortland Street and they would set off walking. 'Ronald and Rex and I were a sort of trio', she said, except when they stopped at a pub for a drink and she would wait outside. She wrote poetry too, which she would dedicate, when it was published years later, to her two young poet-friends.

The poems Mason sent with his letters to Marie this summer – and asked her to type out for him in triplicate – were not poems about the suffering Christ, but love poems, of a sort. One was 'Thigh to thigh', one of several on the theme of frustrated passion that would be included in his next collection:

> Thigh to thigh and lip to lip
> > in the long grass we lie:
> > the cup brims high but we dare not sip.
>
> Girl, don't you think that we were meant
> > to take it and drink,
> > to blend and sink back in drowsed content.
>
> But the seconds pass, the moment's gone
> > and the rustling grass
> > breathes a dead mass and an orison
>
> And two night-owls toll from a star-lit bough,
> > dirge-voiced the waves roll
> > as though a soul were passing now.

'Incidentally the incident is *quite* imaginary', Mason remarked, 'I'd never have done a thing like that – I'd have sipped.'[23] 'Lugete o Veneres', a surviving draft of which is dated 20 March 1930, was another narrative of unrequited love, in which a boy pines for the girl on the next-door farm whose family is moving away. 'The title from Catullus', he explained to Fairburn, ' – great psychologist and poet, no philosopher. Cat. Housman and Baudelaire three poets I like best.'[24] The poem characteristically mixes literary diction and rough colloquialism:

> . . .
> mark how dejected tormented he lies poor lad while his shivers
> > run and shake his fat arse:

a space let us mourn this tortured boy here who slobbers and quivers
while we laugh at the farce.

It is a harsh poem, an ironic parody of Catullus's: the lament for Lesbia's loss
of her virtue. There is a much softer feeling in 'Nox Perpetua Dormienda',
which could have been the poem Mason was referring to in a letter to Marie
earlier in March. It is another Catullan poem about longing which plays, like
'Thigh to thigh', on the juxtaposition of sensuality and death. It has the added
title in an early typescript 'Erotica Episode No. 1':

Your eyeballs dark like a deep black pool in the night
that is lit by the steadfast fire of a handful of stars,
flecks of gold upon ovals of ebony, trees half alight
vaguely touched by the wandering beams from distant cars:

Those eyes that now shine like some enduring god's earnest
of rest beyond this world's storms and a tranquil haven
shall fall from their impotent sockets: and, only, their burnished
splendour shall make a feast for the worm and the raven.

Some eager-eyed traveller then or peasant in ploughing
will find that which once wore those exquisite eyes and dear
hands and sweet hair – gutted shrine to whose goddess once vowing
great oaths I came: then that man will flee you in fear.

We shall be no good then save to cower and crouch
naked bone turning green like verdigrised silver or polished
by the rain blind dumb bone lying cold on its earthy couch
when all this goodly garment of flesh is demolished.

What will it help us then girl not to have loved,
chill and exposed to the rain or cramped and deep-sodded
wet to the bone of a truth and mute and unmoved
then whom will it help that we loved not when we were bodied?

'Got quite away from me', he wrote to Marie. 'I wanted it to be more
economical in words and more ascetic in metre, but I could feel it foaming
up into a windy froth of verbiage.'[25]

But there was, he assured her, little to tempt him in Lichfield, where the girls '[m]ostly run to fat stolidity and either piety or wild promiscuity – or sometimes both. The drink is dear and rot-gut, so my only weakness is my daily ounce of tobacco and a growing disposition to stop in the middle of the road to lay down and argue the point with myself.' He had left her his university library card while he was away, recommending the Loeb Latin volumes ('do be sure to read the "Satyricon" of Petronius, the first book of Suetonius "Lives of the Caesars", the book with Catullus, Tibullus, and the "Pervigilium Veneris" in it, and Plato "the Apology" & "Crito"') and Tawney's *Acquisitive Society*. She shared his political sympathies, up to a point, and in his letters from Lichfield he unburdened to her some of his anger and indignation at the world:

> My God, my dear, how I should love to have a gang of about 40 of the foulest of the insipid, mealy-mouthed, platitudinous mealy-mouthed (that's twice) windy-brained newspaper-minded offspring of unmarried parents that infest Auckland (I can think of some particularly choice specimens among my old pupils) and make 'em toil for ten hours a day with the realisation that they were damned lucky to get work at all. There wouldn't be quite so much smug, self-satisfied braggadocio and canting humbug about them at the end of a month. . . . I have a brainless, sookey-sookey slab of a cousin, tasteless as lukewarm water or an unsalted egg and that nonentity draws 295 per annum for being listless in the Lands and Deeds (you see, if you understand the proper use of terms, that I am no Socialist).[26]

He wrote about his gardening (his peas, he told his mother, were thriving in spite of Aunt Foster having 'prophesied woe, destruction, blight, pestilences and desolation over them') and his reading ('Why is it that all the great writers have been rank rebels'), and about the social and political conservatism and insularity of small-town New Zealand.

> My aunt, poor simple soul, slaved all her life for a pittance: she sops up the Herald (reads nought else, save a few pious tracts exhorting her to save her soul, not to commit adultery, and contribute literally to funds for such objects as converting the Chinese from Confucianism to that wierd [sic] farrago of superstition and rationalism which constitutes Anglicanism). And she reads with glee and exaltation [sic] the little paragraphs describing how a man was offered work and would not take it: cackles with respectable venom (I know

it is not her genuine self, but big-advertisers'-propaganda influence) when she reads of how some labourer attempted to live without work and failed.[27]

Marie kept an eye on Jessie while Mason was away. He sent her money from his harvest earnings and asked her to take his mother shopping, because 'If I send her the money she will squander it on some such senseless extravagance as paying the mortgage-interest.' 'Your rustic adorer, Ronald', he signed his letters ('I nearly signed myself "John": have just written to Mum and find it hard to remember just who I am to whom').[28] He would not publish until many years later the poem he addressed to her, 'Ad Mariam':

> You are Jezebel, Thais, and an iniquitous thing:
> > all chaos flows from your dark unwounded side:
> > you are that wanton who will bear dire ruin to the king,
> > then vouchsafe to a called-in sot what the king was denied.
>
> You came and the sweet is sour, the light is murk:
> > you are that defiled Tullia who drove unheeding
> > through her father's skull: long years in the dark you work
> > to exult at last where Agamemnon lies bleeding.
>
> You are all evil desires, the fount of all sin,
> > and – rot! you're a friend whom I found tapping austerely
> > at a laggard morning typewriter when I called in
> > for a cup of tea, and now you sit a trifle severely
>
> And chat about this and that . . . oh thou Messalina
> > clad in purple of annihilation, abominable silk,
> > vile adulterous beacon to evil, death-goddess, Faustina,
> > take me rack me madden Hell-doom me and pass the milk.[29]

MASON'S relationship with Edwynna Roussel – Teddy – was more complicated. He had known Teddy for six years, since she was thirteen and he had first started teaching her at Holl's. She was nineteen now, young, pretty and vivacious, with a willowy figure and large, languid eyes – 'the sweetest of young things', he described her to de Montalk, as sweet as the letters she wrote him, full of adolescent effusion and real affection.[30] Mason was to Teddy a teacher and mentor, 'best friend' and confessor, and something more. '[Y]ou have made me what I am', she told him, more than once, ' – all and every decent instinct I ever had was but the flower of some carefully planted remark of yours', 'you Viper – you Latin-master'.³¹

What Teddy was, or had been, to Mason is more difficult to discern. 'You pair of fauns', Fairburn wrote to him after a friend had reported seeing Mason and Teddy together in the back seat of Dan's car. 'Why didn't you do the thing properly and bind leaves in your hair and place a large representation of Bacchus on top of the hood.'³² But it was Fairburn who spent two weeks over the New Year, while Mason was in Lichfield, holidaying with Teddy and her mother at the beach settlement of Maraetai. It rained there too, but not enough to prevent Teddy from getting so badly sunburnt that she had to be taken back to Auckland by ambulance, while Fairburn took the family car, the first time he had driven in his life. And it was Fairburn who fell most heavily for Teddy's charms. Before they left for Maraetai, Fairburn and Teddy, along with Jessie and Irene, had seen Mason off on the train to Lichfield, then the four had gone to have morning tea, during which Jessie – mischievously, Fairburn believed – pressed him about his holiday plans, of which he had told Irene nothing ('Atmosphere electrical. Nearly drank the Worcester sauce in mistake for coffee'³³). Teddy, also relating this incident to Mason, indignantly denied that she and Irene were rivals for Fairburn. But Fairburn thought he knew better. 'Don't talk about it in your cups, my boy,' he wrote a few weeks later, 'but the fact is that you and I have got the old lady so she doesn't know if she's going or coming. We (you, more particularly, of course) have made the child such an exotic product of our own microcosmic world that it is now almost impossible for her to associate successfully with any other brand of homo sap.'³⁴

Her 'remarkably worthless parents' (in Mason's words) wanted her married, but not to any penniless, poetry-writing, bohemian types like Mason or Fairburn. There was a suitor on the scene, named Stanley: 'He has money & mother is out for blood', Teddy told Mason. But she was adamant that she would not marry for money. 'That is why *I* sometimes think *I* am a fool not to marry you – or Rex, and save you & myself from that particular kind of hell. When I think of the beasts of girls lying in wait for you two kids, I sweat – they would fleece you of all you had, and then torture you – they have about as much sympathy and understanding of artistic temperament as an ordinary clothes peg'. And not for the first time she told him to 'mind *your* eye'.³⁵

Along with Marie, Teddy kept a solicitous eye on Jessie while Mason was in Lichfield, and she was indignant about the family burden he carried. It was she who wrote to tell him, in February, that his mother was seriously ill. She was suffering from inflammation of the liver but refused to see a doctor, and she was worried about the family's financial situation. The large house was empty and tenants were difficult to find: 'if we can let the big place again, & then this one, it would be wiser for us to make a move into town or somewhere – but I want to know what *you* say. . . . you, being the business man of the Family', she wrote to him.[36] Mason felt that he should go back (and that they should sell the house) but was reluctant to leave before the harvest was over. Teddy was infuriated: 'Can you tell me why Dan can't look after and generally tend your mother – why must you always throw yourself into whatever trouble comes along – Really, Dan makes me ache from my head down, or my toes up – Why can't he be unselfish for a change . . . You are the main-spring of the whole darn family – why can [*sic*] he big-brother you – instead of you being a sort of wet-nurse to him – she wrote, mixing a metaphor and slanging the poor man's family.'[37] But it was a fair question.

In late February, to escape the intentions of her parents and the attentions of Stanley, Teddy took a job as a governess to three 'terribly English' children in the Bay of Plenty, 150 miles away. ('In a way I am rather glad', Fairburn professed.[38]) It was not work to which she was particularly well suited, as the children's mother, Pia Richards, also realised, but she found the girl charming and Teddy remained with them for the rest of the year, returning to Auckland for a few days' holiday each month. The Richards family had recently moved to New Zealand from England and were living on a citrus orchard at Welcome Bay, just outside Tauranga. They were well travelled, sophisticated and literary. Robin Richards had been business manager of the *London Mercury* in partnership with J.C. Squire. Pia was the daughter of the poet, novelist and essayist (and old friend of Harold Monro) Maurice Hewlett. She was in her mid-thirties, '*well* educated, jolly clever, speaks French and German as she does English – lived in both countries for ages', Teddy reported, rather dazzled. They had 2000 books, 'most of them given by the authors'. Teddy arranged for Mason to visit on his way back to Auckland in April, and the Richards family became long-standing friends. 'Be natural & your self', she counselled him. 'Remember you *must* listen to Robin & *that you want to go to England to do literary work* – he knows the ropes & loves talking of it.'[39]

Like Teddy, Mason found Robin Richards 'a stunning chap', while he, she reported, admired Mason's poems in *Twentieth Century Poetry*, although he thought Monro 'rather an old ass'. That he had been 'messed up in the war' – shell-shocked – also engaged Mason's sympathy. When Robin lost his licence for a year for drunken driving, Mason responded to Teddy with a bitter tirade against war and ignorance, 'brutality and cant' and 'malignant respectable righteous tongues':

> Yesterday was Anzac Day and I've just had a good sickener of what can be done in the way of rant and slobbering sentimentality – and all the time you know that they are full of the narrowmindedness which condemns the scape-goats when they go a bit wrong (I never knew a man who genuinely fought and didn't lose his grip a fair bit) and of the bigoted stick-in-the-mud ignorance which made the last mess so successful an abomination and will probably do the same again soon. Pardon me if I preach a bit.[40]

In March, while Mason was still in Lichfield and a few days after Teddy had been back for her first holiday in Auckland, Fairburn wrote to him: 'I have fallen in love with Ed. Now, I know that you will not get up and cheer about that, because you will probably be jealous. But dont be, just yet.' Being in love with Teddy, he explained, 'has no parallel in my experience, either first- or second-hand'. 'It isnt the same as your being, or anybody else.' He wanted to marry her but knew his situation was hopeless; her parents hated him. He was in such despair that even Housman was no help: 'I suppose you, in your moments of deepest depression, can read Housman, and get homeopathic relief from the man. I always have. But when I turned to that this time . . . I found myself taking him literally, and going further under. Dont think I am piling it on to impress you, or enjoying myself in an inverted and dramatic fashion, Byron-like, when I tell you that for four days I was in the most desperate fear of going mad'. He also feared Mason's reaction. 'If you are in love with her yourself by any chance, do whatever you like, of course. But dont chuck any spanners merely because you think we're on the wrong track. . . . When are you coming home? God, boy, I'm in a mess.'[41]

Until their eventual, lasting estrangement a few years later it was the Teddy affair that most tested Mason's and Fairburn's friendship. Mason was jealous, as his response to Fairburn's impassioned confession and plea only just reveals, and he disapproved: 'I don't know what I am going to do (that is at once a confession of ignorance and a squeal of pain – must be read both ways). I hope to hop down and see Teddy for a few days. Fear not, I chuck no spanners, but, as I have told you before and repeat, I am going to warn her against your good faith unless backed by works.'[42] Fairburn replied to him angrily and resentfully: 'You really *mustnt* . . . set up as a sort of policeman to watch over Teddy and see that I Do The Right Thing. Its not done. . . . I *cant* stand the idea of your acting as her unofficial guardian. I am not a child, and I am not a blackguard'. Not for the first time Mason had chastised his friend for his indolence and suggested he look for a job (indeed, he was trying to find one for him). 'But take our respective records', Fairburn shot back. 'I have worked for five and a half years in a town job which I didnt like. I have spent the three since then in educating myself – also in doing a bit of loafing; but not altogether without profit. You reversed things. You went to school for the first three, and worked in a bloody awful job for the five and a half (isnt it?). You have now chucked it. So, in a sense, we are level. So dont call me a waster and a wont-work yet awhile.'[43]

Over the next few months Mason was to receive both Fairburn's and Teddy's accounts of their brief (and platonic) but tempestuous and painful affair – tempestuous and painful on Fairburn's part at least. 'Rex never took the faintest interest in my mind', Teddy wrote, three days after Fairburn. 'In my look – *Oh! Yes* – but I might have been bird-brained. *You* are my downfall'. A month later she confessed: 'I'm falling in love with him – thanks to the prize asses – ma & pa'. In May she recounted a dream: 'I married to Rex – happy & unhappy – you unhappy and showing it – Rex unhappy & taking it out of [*sic*] me, you silent and *very* darling to me – *Me* wishing God had made me two – or rolled you & Rex [into] one – or best of all that I could be for both – *My God* – what a dream.' 'Ronald', she wrote on another occasion, 'you don't mind my using you as a sort of cross between a mental wastepaper basket and a priest, do you? – I mean, it does not offend you acutely if I pour my worries over you – complain if it does – but I have dark suspicions that you like it.'[44] By May Fairburn was consulting a lawyer to see how he could get around Teddy's father, whom both he and Mason despised: 'a nasty unwholesome sort of person' with 'a slightly criminal cast of mind', Fairburn described him; 'Bon bourgeois papa the centre of the universe', Mason wrote in his notebook.[45] The situation was to resolve itself only when Fairburn finally made good, in August, his long-standing and frequently declared intention to leave 'this disgusting treacly mess called Auckland'. 'I *must* leave New Zealand', he had announced in his love-stricken letter to Mason in March, still with Hollywood in mind.[46] Three months later – egged on by de Montalk – he was on his way to London.

MASON ARRIVED home from Lichfield, via Welcome Bay, towards the
end of April. He had missed the train, 'but, between you and me,' he told
Teddy, 'I pretty well meant to. Walked and trained and cadged lifts to Waihi',
where he put up at a hotel. There he

> had a big bottle of beer, didn't go to bed, but went down to the lounge like
> a damn fool. A new publican had just come in, the old one had not gone
> away, there was a commercial [traveller] there . . . and like an ass I went in to
> the Bar to have a couple before I went to bed. And I found I had known the
> new publican in Auckland, and that I almost knew the commercial: the old
> publican shouted and the new one shouted and finally the police came in and
> put his helmet on the counter and he helped to make things go with a great
> swing. . . . I grew more and more exquisitely gentle and learned: I delivered
> profound economic discourses, cunningly gagging when I got into a corner
> in a way that I'd never dare to if sober. About 11 I found myself wanting to
> recite Horace, so decided to pull out, as I know that's the sign that I'm
> getting paralytic.

The next morning he woke 'quite O.K. except for a corrugated palate and
granulated throat. It was a case of walk now, want to or not, so the most
distinguished sociological expert that had ever visited Waihi started off for
home on foot.' He got a lift almost to Paeroa, but ended up walking the
breadth of the Hauraki Plain – 'Long straight dusty stretches, you know, with
cars rolling past' – pausing at Kerepehi, where a friend of his and Fairburn's,
art student Guy Mountain, was working as a surveyor's assistant for the summer.
By nightfall '[t]he road was just stunning, after being dreary all day – cool and
winding and dark and hilly and solitary'. When a car finally did pull up – 'me
in the lime-light looking picturesque with staff, haversack and uplifted hand'
– the driver turned out to be an old school friend: 'Jolly trip in car.'[47]

Disaster awaited him. 'Lord what a mess to land into at home. People had
pulled out from big house [which they were now trying to sell], leaving it in
an indescribable state: Mum frightfully ill.' Dan's mess was bigger. He had
'staked all on a big company, neglecting his other work: they had just crashed'.[48]
Mason made his own inquiries and he believed that Dan was not to blame.
But worse was to come. The full extent of Dan's disaster was to unfold over
the following months, and would burden the family for years.

Dan had advanced from law clerk to being a practising lawyer. Although
not completing his degree (which was not a professional requirement), he

had enrolled as a solicitor of the Supreme Court in April 1928, and set up in practice on his own account – as W.T.F. Kells Mason – with his offices in His Majesty's Arcade on Queen Street. If Dan was not a crooked lawyer, he was at least a negligent or perhaps just a stupid one. The Auckland District Law Society first received a complaint about him in August 1929, from a funeral director after he had neglected to pay out a deceased estate to the beneficiaries. The auditor sent in by the society to investigate his accounts in the early months of 1930 found difficulty in locating Dan, let alone getting assistance from or information out of him, and discovered serious irregularities in his accounts. He had not been keeping a personal bank account separate from his trust account, and regularly received and paid out money without entering it in his books. He had been practising without a practitioner's certificate, and ignored three demands for payment of his fee before the Law Society filed a charge of contempt against him in the Supreme Court in May 1930, for which he paid a fine and costs of £8 16s as well as the outstanding fee. On 19 August the court found Dan guilty of 'gross professional misconduct' and recommended that he be suspended or struck off.

The case went before the Court of Appeal, which considered evidence from four clients who were pursuing claims against Dan; one had been receiving part payments of the money owed him from Jessie. The money Dan lost at this time also included the sum Aunt Foster had lent him to set himself up in practice. In his defence, Dan insisted that he had been unaware of the deficiencies in his paperwork, having left it in the hands of an employee while he had been tied up with the affairs of Associated Investment Underwriters (N.Z.) Ltd of Hamilton, by which he was engaged in December 1929, and which went into liquidation in April the following year. This was the company he had 'staked all on'. The affidavit of the company's accountant was the only one made in support of Dan: he had been busy 'night and day', including weekends, straightening out its affairs, 'and by his unrelaxing energy and tact did much to avert a collapse involving thirteen companies which would have caused a parallel to the Hatry collapse in Great Britain, his efforts subsequently causing him to have a breakdown'. This was perhaps an unfortunate comparison: the sensational collapse of the fraudster Clarence Hatry had wiped 12 per cent off the value of the British stockmarket in September 1929, destroying livelihoods and bringing widespread personal distress to Hatry's many small investors (this was just a teaser, though, for the New York stockmarket crash in October which set in train the slump that became the Great Depression). In March 1931 the Court of Appeal upheld the findings of the Supreme Court, suspended Dan from practice until 31 December 1931, and ordered him to pay £61 to the Auckland District Law Society. He never practised as a lawyer again.[49]

Mason had quickly lost any illusions about what had been going on. The report he gave to Fairburn, after the preliminary hearing in the Court of Appeal, expressed how hurt he was by Dan's deception:

> During his brief but gay experience with the Law he has (1) embezzled £300 – and £50 – and probably another £300 (2) spent £400 and £50 (3) contracted a nice little pile of debts to be paid by Nell [Dan's girlfriend] and us and (4) left a splendid shining trail of documents unstamped, cases not seen to &c &c &c.
>
> All told this has (1) literally sent the mater nearly crazy besides impoverishing her utterly hopelessly (2) forced us to crawl on our bellies to half N.Z. (3) impoverished Auntie Fos and, I should say, killed her (4) wasted the best of Nell's life (5) made me old, sour & hopeless. . . .
>
> It is painful to realise you have been the goat – I now see that, put coolly, I have been a very convenient gull for Brother Dan for more years than I care to count. But no more! The opportunities are mostly gone, of course, but any luck which does chance my way stays mine. And if any bugger comes along & claims kinship with me on the Mason side I'll blow his apologies for brains out first of all before we start talking business, just to save trouble.
>
> Some people have had the brilliant idea of putting Dan in clink, but unfortunately it hasn't yet come about – which just shows you that justice is really never done. . . .
>
> Don't be surprised if you see me blow in some day: shall get out of this if I possibly can and everybody can go to Hell. . . .
>
> Now *mark this*. In my old days I may have canted about one's duty to others, the need of work & self-sacrifice and all that common cant. Forgive me: I didn't know, but now I have learnt. Don't ever trouble to pay for the knowledge with your own experience, but take my humble life.
>
> Enjoy yourself & express yourself – but don't let the second interfere with the first. I've learnt my bitter lesson a bit too late to be any good to me – for God's sake don't you fall into my error. Yes I know you warned me all right, but I was a blind fool.

He signed this letter 'Yours in venom'.[50]

But Dan's debacle and Jessie's health were perhaps not the only things

causing him distress when he arrived home from Lichfield, or so a letter
Teddy wrote him in early May suggests. 'Ronald, dear, you do worry me
when you talk of hells on earth, and common-place squabbles and things like
that – why shouldn't two people live happily? – why should being together
push them apart? – why should being everything to each other, make them
nothing? . . . I can't think you believe that really – do you? Oh! Ronald I do
love you so, and when you think like that, it shows how unhappy you must
be inside. Be like Rex – when you are unhappy, spread it, and then everyone
around you will *make* you happy in self-defence.'[51]

MASON CLEANED up the house, managed to pick up some private and
casual tutoring through Dave Faigan at Holl's, and went back to university as
he had planned. He enrolled in four papers for the Diploma in Social Science,
and repeated Greek History, Art and Literature, which would have completed
his degree had he sat the exam. At the invitation of a fellow student, Alun
Richards, a Christian pacifist, he helped to establish and became secretary of
a free discussions group called the Open Forum.

He continued working on the novel he had begun in Lichfield in January,
and would work on intermittently through the following year. Like many
first novels, it was semi-autobiographical, as the notes he appended to it many
years later elaborated. Also like many first novels, it was never finished. Its
working title, 'Dreams Come True', was taken from a poem by Fairburn
which had won the *Sun*'s Christmas poetry competition in 1929. It is set in
Auckland and concerns four main characters, two boys and two girls: John,
from the country; the Communist Reporter; Viola Gould, a pretty but shallow
working-class girl; and Nell, who resembles Marie Gaudin.

It opens in a place very like Lichfield. John, who is in his early twenties
(and closely based on a Lichfield acquaintance), lives with his 'cold and
evangelical' mother and 'subdued and rather ineffectual father' on a poor,
remote, southern Waikato farm. His parents pine for their previous life of
English gentility and have sheltered John from the coarseness of rural New
Zealand society, while he longs for a more fulfilling life. He is a weak, naïve,
earnest character – sympathetically but not kindly drawn – but has initiative
enough to make up his mind to leave the backblocks and go to Auckland,
where he takes a room in a boarding house in Grafton and tries to break into
journalism. He manages to sell only an occasional ill-paid article, while '[m]uch
of his rather ample spare time is spent rather aimlessly in wandering round,
seeking some sort of "literary" job, reading at the Public Library. . . . attending

odd lectures provided by rather "dim" characters in uncomfortable, out-of-the-way halls. . . . He also catches glimpses of University life, which he feels is really daring.'[52]

John makes two woman friends: Nell, a 'lady-journalist' who lives across the harbour in Takapuna; and Viola, who lives in the poorer but closer suburb of Grey Lynn, and with whom, for little reason other than that it is more convenient, he falls rather pathetically in love. Viola is a cruel portrait of a clever, flirtatious but shallow-minded young woman whose only interest is in getting a husband: an 'insipid little blond . . . you know, the girl with the wind-blown bob', Mason described her to Marie.[53] She was based ('quite unfairly', he later admitted) on a cousin of his 'with tinges of a couple of others, girls with whom I had in fact unhappy, though brief love affairs' – evidently Lola and Teddy.[54] Her family is a caricature of jolly working-class domesticity. To John their 'shabbily ugly but comfortable and cheerful' household is a haven from the 'pinched aridity', 'solitariness and skimpy meals, decorum and stiffness, stinginess, antagonism, and depression' of the boarding house. Mrs Gould, with her 'fat common face', enormous chest, 'bad leg' and proletarian patois, turns out huge batches of scones, 'great puddings thick with fat', dumplings and 'sponge cakes made with butter', while John pays court to Viola. When, after some weeks of inept love-making ('an occasional long silence, which he filled up with a stare intended to be soulful and eked out with noisy sighs'), he finally lands his first kiss, he believes that he is in love and that they will, therefore, get married.

He also believes that he is educating Viola, while she humours his intellectual pretensions as 'at least once a fortnight they would trudge off to some dingy and draughty Church-hall or poverty-stricken class-room and there on hard bentwood chairs or benches hear the illustrious interpreted by the timid local illuminati, those who will never die murdered by those who have never lived'. The lecturers Mason describes, with his cynical eye and withering invective, were caricatures of men like J.W. Shaw and A.B. Chappell, both ministers and newspaper columnists (writing under Maori pseudonyms, an affectation of late-colonial, 'Maoriland' literary culture) whom Mason and Fairburn disdained, and 'poor, well-intentioned, devils with a badly-nourished, well-drubbed look – cowed-looking but overbearing professors, old newspaper men in badly-paid but responsible jobs, "stickit ministers" . . . nerve-starved teachers from school or college watering down their already watery textbooks'. John listens to it all dutifully, only once becoming excited, 'when a foreign professor lectured on Shelley. For a while John sat with eager eyes

and sounding heart; then without warning his mind surged up and swayed
and fainted in realms so strange they filled him with fear. But the professor
went back to the South, and Death came down once again upon the city, and
John was no more troubled by the breath of life.' Viola, meanwhile, is ever
moved to such feeling only by the 'pictures': 'the cheap melodrama, the
florid music, and the garish tawdriness' of 'third-rate Hollywood or Elstree'.
When John admits to her that he is not earning enough money from his
writing for them to get married just yet, she swiftly and brutally drops him
and becomes engaged to a motor-salesman.[55]

Mason tired of the rather pallid John in the course of working on the
novel, and its focus shifted to the other pair. The more sophisticated, but also
unsatisfied Nell, to whom John turns (after several pages of love-sickness),
likes him and is 'sympathetic with, although slightly contemptuous of, his
rather weakly aspirations' and his innocent earnestness.[56] When John describes
to her the depths of his despair she can only laugh at his self-pity and assure
him that everyone feels that way sometimes: 'When men are up some quiet
gully shooting, they often think how easy it would be to end it all now in
such a way that it would seem like an accident. And women often feel how
withered and futile life is, and look at the deep and think "I might as well fix
it now." . . . do you think we couldn't all just drop the oars & bed and drift
on to the rocks? Don't you know how much we'd all just like to lie down on
it – just let ourselves go & not care?'[57] 'Am putting you in almost holus-
bolus', Mason told Marie.[58] Nell is smart, articulate, forthright and opinionated.
Although she is attracted to John, she has more in common, as Mason himself
did, with the character of the Communist Reporter (once named as Dick
Grafton), whom he later glossed as 'a conscious type of the intellectual radical
of the time, moving from intellectual and individualistic cynicism to throw in
his lot with the working class movement, yet never becoming quite of it'.[59]

Much of the remainder of the novel, as far as it went, consists of Nell and
the Reporter's witty, sparring dialogue (based, Mason tells us, on his and
Marie's own). She questions his commitment to the revolution, he teases her
for her ardent feminism, and they both confront their similar dilemmas:
whether to stay and fight, or leave like so many others. 'Leaven all goes to
England', Nell remarks. 'That is if it can rake up the dough.'

> You know, New Zealand reminds me sometimes of Russia before the
> Revolution, as the writers describe it. Not so bad, of course, but the same
> hopelessness, the same apathy & despair. . . . Same pallid ineffectual intellectuals

with too much goodness ever to [do] any real good. Same rigid dragooning of heresy. Same incompetence & corruption in high places with no one daring to speak out. Same ignorant pigs of business-men scrambling for swill: and same mob of poor wailing because they are shut out from a place at the trough. Ugh! Same gang of yokels plodding in the fields till they are too tired to think anything save envy & hatred – and then only under newspaper direction.

'And dark over it all is the same vast spirit of untamed Nature, hovering like a malignant spirit', the Communist Reporter interposes. 'No wonder Katherine Mansfield found her spiritual relations among the Russians'. 'I'm going to get out before I go soft', the Reporter declares – to England, or France, or perhaps Russia, or '[f]ind some show down in the Islands, if they're not all thoroughly mucked up by missionaries & traders'. But Nell is not so sure that she could leave her family and friends, and 'the country you have learned to love – the land itself, I mean'.[60] She is also torn between the fulfilment of a career and family – the woman's dilemma – and, while she shares the Reporter's political analysis, cannot follow him to the extreme of communism. (Perhaps, Mason wrote later about himself and Marie, 'she subconsciously resented too the fact that I was making too much sacrifice' to radical politics.)[61] In the Quay Street scene, Nell is out walking with her older, sophisticated and acerbic friend Elaine and is shocked and angered to see the Communist Reporter up on the soapbox delivering a speech denouncing capitalist wars – adopting, she notices, a 'plebeian pronunciation' and simpler manner of speaking than his normal speech. She finds herself equally appalled by his revolutionary talk and her friend's well-bred unconcern. The Communist Reporter, meanwhile, struggles to reconcile his career, communism, and his love for Nell . . . 'So they brewed coffee & made toast & sat around the fire, fighting back misery.'[62]

'Dreams Come True' was far from finished when Mason abandoned it, consisting of a dozen 'episodes' in various stages of completion, some little more than notes. In the conclusion, John went back to the farm to help his parents, at Nell's urging, while her relationship with the Reporter continued, until 'After one talk, they go for a moonlight stroll and their underlying passion breaks through in an interlude which both know to be final'.[63]

IN AUGUST Fairburn left for London, assisted by money from an aunt and de Montalk's flat to stay in when he got there. He farewelled his friends on a 'wet miserable August evening' of drink and talk in Clifton Firth's Swanson Street studio. At about eleven Mason and Fairburn left to walk back to Ellerslie.

> When we got there it would be about 1 o'clock in the morning, we decided it was a lovely night and we hadn't finished talking and we probably wouldn't see each other again ever, perhaps for years so we'd go home and have a yarn for a little while further and so we walked up to the top of Mt Smart . . . and we sat there and we went on talking and we talked till the moon went down over the Manukau and the sun started to come up over the Waitemata and we went home still talking and we had breakfast . . . I think we both had a sort of feeling 'well, that's the end of a sort of an epoch for us'.[64]

Fairburn was homesick by the time he got to Melbourne. But London dazzled him. His first letters back to Mason were full of the wonder and urgency of it: 'God, this London is a staggering place! . . . my breath is taken away a hundred times a day by its sheer beauty. You are out of place in N.Z.. You *must* come here, and taste it. You'll love it. I think I told you I saw all those M/S copies of poems at the Br/Museum. Milton, Donne, Byron, Shelley, Keats, Brooke ("The Soldier") Flecker ("Oak & Olive") and a dozen or two others. *Thrrrilling*!!' Later: 'For God's sake try to get a travelling scholarship or something & come and join me.'[65]

'Buck up about Dan', Fairburn added in his first letter from London. 'I don't know what's happened by the time you get this, but *don't* worry too much about it.' 'Your letter arrived yesterday', he wrote to Mason in December. 'It was right welcome. I was beginning to fear for you. You seem to be in a fairly cheerful mood. For God's sake stay in it, and don't let things get you under. There's no call for it.'[66] But Dan's catastrophe had taken Mason far enough under to cause him to throw away his university year. 'Missed badly', he wrote: 'worked, but felt too utterly hopeless to sit when the time came. Bang goes a chance of that scholarship I had done so much for – also of ever getting a decent teaching job.' There had been another blow as well. Professor Paterson had let Mason know that he was taking sabbatical leave the following year, and Mason 'had half counted on getting the job of assistant-lecturer: one is always appointed'. But this time, for reasons of economy, none was.[67]

The promise and then loss of a university position was a disappointment that Mason was to feel acutely in years to come. Paterson thought him well suited to an academic career. In the testimonial he gave him he stated:

Amongst the many brilliant students I have had during 25 years of teaching work I should assign a very high place to Mr. R.A.K. Mason. . . . [He] is a young man of exceptional powers and attainments. Although his scholarship is fine & extremely accurate, he is no pedant; he is a man of independent judgment who thinks for himself and examines a problem from every side, while his gift of literary appreciation and his faculty of expression should combine to make him a quite unusually stimulating and inspiring teacher. He is among the very best of our younger graduates and I venture to think that the institution which secures him will deserve congratulation.[68]

But it was not be. Instead he was applying for a position with the WEA, Mason told Fairburn, but was not hopeful. 'I have a superstitious feeling that nothing I do will succeed.'[69]

In November Teddy told Mason she was leaving too, for France first and then London. She was to miss him more than he would her. 'Ronald you've brought me up – who else *ever* did anything for me?' she wrote from Tauranga, in a letter in which she reproached herself for not listening enough to his troubles when he always had listened to hers. 'I didn't know exactly what Stoic meant so I looked it up in the Concise Oxford I found it between stodgy and stoke but it didn't tell me much – . . . Ronald you are so calm about not seeing me any more that I know that either you don't care a hang about me *or* that you care lots and lots.'[70]

8

The islands

1931

'POOR, ILL, and lonely', Mason went in the New Year of 1931 not to Lichfield but to Samoa, for 'the first holiday of my life'.[1] Teddy lent him the money for his boat fare, but it was through another of Mason's pupils that his ten-week sojourn in Samoa came about. During 1930 he had been teaching Olive Nelson, one of the daughters of Olaf Nelson, exiled leader of the Samoan nationalist movement. It was Nelson who suggested that Mason visit the Islands, perhaps simply because he needed a holiday, although Mason also went with a purpose. In the job application he wrote shortly before he left he stated that he was 'at present working on . . . an investigation of a Polynesian racial problem' and 'just starting for Tonga and Samoa'. 'This Polynesian business is rather fascinating', he remarked to Fairburn. 'Had I a year, some cash for books, Nelson & his organisation openly helping me, and no great worries, I could really make rather a marvellous thing of it.'[2]

Even before he became acquainted with the Nelson family, Mason would have known something of the unhappy history of New Zealand's adminis-tration of Western Samoa, a small cluster of rugged volcanic islands 1800 miles and several days by steamer north-west of Auckland. It was 'a sorry tale of imprisonments, fines, banishments, deportations, raids, special ordinances, dog-shootings, and Samoan-shootings', in Mason's own words,[3] culminating in Black Saturday, December 1929, when a peaceful procession in the capital Apia was fired on by military police. Among his papers Mason kept a flyer for a meeting held by the New Zealand Samoa Defence League in the Auckland Town Hall in March 1929. While he did plenty of basking in the balmy tropical sun while he was in Samoa, he also spent a good part of his time learning more about its political affairs.

New Zealand had accepted only reluctantly, in 1920, its League of Nations mandate over the islands which it had taken from Germany during the First World War. Samoans already resented their new colonial ruler for its clumsy wartime administration, and more deeply for the devastating impact of the influenza pandemic of 1919, in which almost a quarter of the islands' population died – the highest fatality rate suffered by any nation in the world – as a direct result of New Zealand's failure to quarantine the ship *Tahune* (while neighbouring American Samoa, where the *Tahune* was not allowed to berth, escaped the epidemic virtually unscathed). Then Major-General G.S. Richardson arrived, a former British Army officer who was appointed New Zealand's third resident administrator for Samoa in 1923: a charming but vain, ambitious and arrogant man with no previous experience of colonial administration, who set about 'modernising' the islands' political and social structure as efficiently as he could. Richardson, and thus the New Zealand government, dismissed the nationalist Mau movement, formed in 1926, as a pawn of the Samoan 'half-caste' community in their own pursuit of political power, and particularly as a pawn of Olaf Nelson. They were wrong: the Mau was a genuine nationalist movement which commanded wide popular support for its campaign of cheeky defiance and passive resistance to colonial rule. But Nelson, although not actually a member of the Mau, as he was only half-Samoan, was its undisputed leader. He was the richest and most powerful man in Samoa, having profited during the war from the copra trading business he inherited from his Swedish-born father. His house Tuaefu rivalled Robert Louis Stevenson's Vailima, by this time Government House, as Apia's social centre. He was as large physically as he was powerful politically, and estimated to weigh over twenty stone. 'Henry VIII was nothing to Mr Nelson', one English observer wrote.[4] He was also well travelled and articulate, egotistical and bombastic, like his nemesis, Richardson. It was in his offices on the Apia waterfront that the Mau movement was founded, and his company made the Mau police uniforms – resplendent violet-blue lava-lava with white piping and white shirts. He had pleaded the Mau cause, unsuccessfully, before the League of Nations in Geneva and the Privy Council in London. Mason found him 'very clever, entertaining & likeable'.[5]

Samoan affairs had been given scant attention in New Zealand, except by the Labour and Communist Party papers, before Nelson set himself up in exile in Auckland in 1928, after he was deported from Samoa, and established the New Zealand Samoa Defence League and *New Zealand Samoa Guardian*. However, the findings of the Royal Commission of 1927, which vindicated the New Zealand administration and sent Nelson and other Mau leaders into exile, had been reported in the daily press. The nadir of New Zealand's well-meaning, but misguided and inept, administration of the islands came on 28 December 1929, when an unarmed Mau procession was fired on by panicked New Zealand military police and at least eight Samoans, including the high chief and Mau leader Tupua Tamasese, were killed. Mason was later to write a short play based on this event. He commented caustically on Samoa in his long, unposted letter to de Montalk, which was written a week after Black Saturday:

> Do you hear anything about N.Z.'s Empire all-of-its-own. – you know, part of the 1/4 million square miles (is my figure right?) that we boys of the bull-dog breed got as our reward for fighting in the cause of Democracy, Honour, Justice – oh, you know the rigmarole. . . . I wouldn't give N.Z. (Britain either, for that matter) charge of a shit-house. The Government consists solely of a dying dodderer – social conditions are getting bloodier – politics slimier than ever – why the Hell we can't try to get some elements of decency into our own affairs without this self-conceited white-man's-burden stuff! . . . I reckon we ought to give Samoa back to the people who could at least run it reasonably decently.[6]

Mason left Auckland on Saturday, 27 December 1930 on the Pacific Islands trading steamer the *Tofua*, in the company of '3 boys, two Chinese, a girl & Mr. Sutherland', who shared his cabin, 'an old Scot from the lonely end of Viti Levu'. He was enchanted by the sea, the islands, and the adventure – his first trip abroad. 'You could have done almost the whole voyage in a dinghy', he wrote to Jessie.

> After we left Auckland we steamed through island after island: most beautiful. We all stood & watched the Poor Knights – the last of New Zealand – disappearing in the South about 8.30 just as night was falling. There was not a ripple on the water and the ocean was covered with long sea-lanes of absolute glass. . . . We lost New Zealand at night-fall on Saturday & saw no land again till day-break on Wednesday. . . . We seemed to be for ever climbing up a long low slope to a misty green sky which never got any closer. Sometimes a breeze sprang up and the sea got choppy but usually there was just a lazy swell.[7]

He found a favourite spot on the foredeck, perched on a coil of rope in the bows, where he spent hours watching the sea or yarning to the sailors on look-out during the night.

They made first for Fiji, where Kandavu, off the southern coast of Viti Levu, appeared as 'a grey-blue cone smudged on the horizon at dawn: gradually

it grew plainer & you could see the valleys and the low land running East.
These islands look blue-grey in the distance and golden-green near at hand.
New Zealand hills look purple in the distance & hard brown close up'. He
spent New Year's Eve and the next two days looking around Suva (it was 'full
of slums and low quarters'), before the *Tofua* steamed on to Levuka on the
nearby island of Ovalau, having taken on board a party of Fijian labourers and
a crowd of Tongan and Samoan deck passengers, 'a Tongan high chief, three
Samoan medical students, two lousy Hindus returning to Bombay with their
pile, a white engineer with his Tahitian wife & five small brats, & a big dark
mill-hand who says sometimes he comes from the Channel Islands, sometimes
from Hawke's Bay'. While they paused at Levuka he had time to climb a
'rocky hill' to gain a view: 'a most glorious sea-scape. The open sea was the
gentle rolling tropical blue: then the white & silver of breakers on the reef:
inside the reef the water is (as always) perfectly calm and most marvellously
coloured – all the purple and scarlet and green and azure in creation,
undisturbed save by a few canoes with triangular sails beating up from the
West.' Their next stop was Tonga, where the steamer navigated the beautiful
archipelago of Vava'u, fifteen miles through 'a narrow winding lane of rocky
islands' whose sides fell straight down to the sea, and that night he was treated
to a Tongan feast: 'chicken, pork, cooked cocoa-nut, bananas, taros & yams',
laid out on the floor on banana leaves. 'I began with half a cooked chicken
and yams'. Tonga, he decided, 'must be about the happiest lands in the world'.
They reached Apia, Samoa's sole town, by night beneath a 'few soft heavy
clouds & the rest of the sky one powder of soft stars', and waited until daylight
to land. By morning the town appeared 'glorious . . . low tropical buildings
under the palms on the sea-front. Then low hills covered with palms & sloping
up to cloud-capped mountains' – '"soft" is the only word for everything
here: people & earth & sea & sky'.[8] He took his first-ever photographs in
Samoa, but none has survived.

MASON STAYED for the length of his time in Samoa with George
Westbrook, an old trader whom he later described (in the preface he would
write to Westbrook's memoirs) as 'the most perfect figure of a John Bull in
the world. A face like weathered stone set on a solid neck: close-cropped,
grey bullet head: bright eyes looking out honestly from under thick grey
brows. Short, sturdy, bluff, genial, hospitable – the typical Englishman of the
adventurous school'. The 'poor old cuss is really almost mad, as he knows',
he wrote to his mother.[9] Westbrook could have been a character out of a

South Seas novel. He had left England as a sea cadet at the age of sixteen, deserted his ship in Auckland and spent the rest of his life knocking about the South Pacific, living in the Marshall, Caroline and Ellice islands, Rotuma and Wallis Island, before settling in Samoa in 1891. He had worked as a trader and planter, clerk and customs officer, beekeeper, hotelier, Church Missionary Society agent and insurance broker; he had met Robert Louis Stevenson and Jack London. In 1923 he had been one of three Europeans elected to the Samoan Legislative Council, from which time he became passionately committed to the nationalist cause; this led him to neglect his business, and he was declared bankrupt. He became a compulsive writer of letters to newspaper editors, officials and politicians, and Samoa's self-appointed local historian. Now in his seventies, in failing health but with a fighting spirit, he tapped away at his rusted second-hand typewriter recording his life story, which Mason had offered to help him with. Mason tried to make order of the reams of badly typed letters, articles and reminiscences, and slept 'on the broad green upper verandah almost overhanging the tide. Behind us palms and broad-leaved trees rolling up to the mist-wreathed mountains of Upolu's interior: before us the many-coloured harbour crawling over reef and shoal and the ribs of shattered warships'.[10]

When not working with Westbrook, Mason spent his time 'consorting with the heads of the "rebel" natives, going to half-caste parties, yarning for long with old traders and whites who had gone half-native'.[11] He walked 'for miles through coconut & cocoa' and met German and Australian planters; across the island to Siumu, where he found the Mormon mission; to the eastern end of Upolu, from where he could just see American Samoa. He visited Nelson's abandoned house, a 'huge turreted place between a wooded hill and a swiftly-running stream and looking out over trees to the sea' – it had 'a small but first-rate library, mainly South-seas & Maori stuff. Shame to see two pianos, billiard-table & all those books & furniture going to waste.' He made the pilgrimage to Stevenson's grave, 'just a slab of concrete roughly coffin-shaped', up a rough dirt track behind Vailima.[12] '[M]y closest personal contact with classical Scottish tradition', he was to write many years later, came when he asked the eighty-six-year-old chief Tuimaleai'ifano, 'a mutual friend of Stevenson's and my own, what Stevenson looked like, and he nodded with a smile, replying "Just like you".'[13]

He discussed political affairs with high chiefs and Mau leaders (Faumuina, Mata'afa and Malietoa), met the New Zealand-educated anthropologist Felix Keesing and was invited to a house-warming hosted by a German-Samoan:

'Quite a jolly crowd, but very bitter against New Zealand (But then, for one reason or other, most people here are – white, castes, and Samoan)'.[14] But it was not all politics. His strongest impressions would remain the 'miraculous' beauty of Samoa and the Samoans, 'such tall, graceful, proud-looking people as they wander along in their spotless shirts and lava-lavas' (but 'screamingly funny when they get themselves up for Church'), and their 'exquisite artistry' – 'that so few people should create so much beauty. As a community we New Zealanders ought to sit at their feet and humbly learn just what can be done by sheer simplicity without sacrificing one jot of utility.'[15]

And he really was having a holiday, he assured his mother: 'Nothing at all ever happens here. I am too utterly fat & lazy to walk more than a 100 yards. I mostly sit in the shade & smoke & sweat & watch the sea. It is about 100 feet from our front-verandah and I couldn't sleep now if I didn't hear the swishing of the sea near at hand and the distant thunder on the reef.' For a while at least he relished the tropical climate, even though it had rained steadily for the first five days he was there: 'The sweat is running down on to the paper & I did not know I could feel so well.' 'Everything would be perfect if I were only sure you were not worrying.'[16]

Jessie's letters to Mason were full of her missing him. 'My own dearly loved Son', she wrote at the beginning of January. 'By the *Calendar* it is *seven days* since you left; but by my *heart* it is *seven years*.' 'This is your tenth week away,' she wrote at the beginning of March. 'I could count the minutes on one hand that I have not thought of you.' Later: 'I am a *dead* woman without you – night after night, not to hear that little whistle & footstep'.[17] She sent him a poem:

> There is a lad called R.A.K.
> Who off in Lichfield did make hay –
> And now in Samoa he does stay
>   But 'Jess' wants him, 'Samoa' –

Now how is that dearest? *There's* where your poetry comes from.

There was an emotion in her letters that expressed more than just her missing his company, and his care:

Yes dear I *know* you are tired of my 'eating dirt' – but you see it never choked me – it would have done so years ago only for my loving & wonderful son, who always cleared it away & made my path easy; & *nothing* I have done or suffered has seemed *anything* at all, because of your great unselfishness & love & devotion, & whatever happens, you will always *know* that not *once* have you failed me in *any* way; tho' I *know* & *appreciate* how much sacrifice you have had to make to do all these things for me; the grief of the past years has only been that I have had to call on you to bear *so much*, & that I could do so little in return. Jack you have been wonderful, & I feel sure that in the years to come, you will feel glad that you have been such a comfort to me; each day I think more & more of your Goodness. . . . God bless & keep you – Join in the services & ask God to look after Mother, & He will.[18]

Mason knew that she was being looked after in more immediate ways: both Teddy and Marie rang Jessie regularly and took her out. 'Marie seems so anxious to befriend me – sort of *Mother* to me'. And: 'Every one is kind to me & all keep saying "Cannot even *imagine* you without Ronald".'[19]

They both worried about Dan. 'Whose mug is he at the moment? And the mythical millions ..... ?' Mason asked, while Jessie wrote, 'Dan requests that you get all information you can re banana growing'.[20] Mason was also anxious to hear news about the application for the position of tutor-organiser for the WEA in Hamilton, which he had sent off before he left. In his application he stated both his literary and political qualifications: 'an excellent firsthand knowledge of Latin and French literatures: of English from origins, but particularly of Elizabethan and modern writers. I also have a good general knowledge of other literatures in translation, particularly German and classical Greek', and 'a good non-partisan knowedge of politics'.[21] 'I am still hoping against hope', he wrote to his mother towards the end of January, but Jessie's next letter told him that he had been unsuccessful: 'a Dr. Beaglehole got it – there were 27 in for it'. Norman Richmond, director of the WEA for the Auckland district, assured her that Mason 'came well up, but Beaglehole had great scholarship & experience & older; said no one should be ashamed of being beaten by him' – 'I do not know who this Beaglehole (lovely name) is at all, but supposed to have great attainments.'[22] He was a young New Zealand history graduate (only a few years older than Mason, in fact) not long returned from post-graduate study at the London School of Economics, who would later be recognised as the country's pre-eminent historical scholar.

BY THE END of February Mason was '[s]ick & tired of the tropics', and as keen to get home to New Zealand as he was also sorry, nevertheless, to be leaving Samoa. 'If you haven't let the place when I get back, I might have a shot at growing vegetables', he told Jessie. 'I do feel so much happier & more satisfied at getting this trip.'[23] But the romance of the Islands, the pleasure of the tropical climate, and the novelty of his first-ever holiday had worn off. Writing a few months later to a friend who was considering taking a teaching job in Apia, he warned him about the heat ('I thought I liked heat, but it was terrible, and I was glad with a vengeance to get back to New Zealand'), the politics, the bigoted and boring white population ('as far as company goes, you would do just as well if you confined yourself to a set of small-town snobs in N.Z.') and Apia itself: 'a town with no clubs, no pubs, scarcely any library, no decent restaurant overpowered with hills almost on top of it, where you are confined to a dozen whites mostly minor officials and clerks, and there is a nasty note of hatred under the whole box of tricks'.[24] Still, he thought he might go back and live in the Islands for a year or two one day, and indeed had made inquiries about a teaching job in Tonga. He had told Jessie that he was writing to the Bishop of the Western Pacific, whom he had met on his way over, offering to set up a European school in Nuku'alofa, 'but want a guarantee of £350 & free house' and a contract for two years. He clearly envisaged that Jessie would go too: 'If by any remote chance it did happen to come off we could go to N.Z. once a year. Wouldn't be ideal, but needs must . . . .'[25] It didn't come off, and Mason was never to return to the Pacific.

He sailed for Auckland early in March (nearly missing the boat), taking with him Westbrook's memoirs and half a dozen paintings that Westbrook had brought back from his sister's house in London in 1924, when he made his first trip home, and thought might be by William Hogarth. Mason took the paintings, badly affected by their exposure to tropical conditions, to A.J.C. Fisher, director of the Elam School of Art, who, after 'much rubbing them with spit', decided that three of them were 'probably genuine Hogarths' and recommended that they be sent to England for restoration and sale.[26] The president of the Auckland Society of Arts, E.B. Gunson, agreed to put up the finance in return for a third of the profit from the sale, while Mason politely suggested to Westbrook that it would be fair if he and Fisher shared five per cent: 'We are both poor men', he explained, and any money he received he would be sending to 'a girl in France who lent me £25 to pay my fare to Samoa' – Teddy.[27] However, the scheme was abandoned when Gunson learned that Westbrook was a declared bankrupt – he would have risked being sued for knowingly selling a bankrupt's property. (The paintings, which were evidently not by Hogarth, ended up back in Apia in the possession of Westbrook's son.)

The book proved to be a more protracted but equally disappointing affair. It was 'practically finished', Mason advised Westbrook a few weeks after he got home, despite having lost his reading glasses in Samoa and being unable to do any work on the boat and for several days after.[28] A month later he wrote apologising for taking so long: initially he had thought that the old man's tales as he had written them 'were only worth revising and correcting, but now I have seen that we can make a proper classic out of them. I am leaving your own stuff as untouched as I can, but adding from your clippings, my own impressions, and old books.' He did background research, and organised, edited and completely retyped Westbrook's material, having bought himself a typewriter when he got home (a new Imperial Portable for £9 wholesale, on credit). To finish it off he needed only a biographical outline from him and some dates to get the stories in proper order, he told Westbrook, a request repeated in July and again in August. 'I am a bit of a pessimist, but I feel reasonably sure that by the time I've given it a final polish the English critics will look on it as a minor classic.'[29]

A year later Mason sent Westbrook the completed typescript, which he had entitled 'An Old Trader in the South Seas. Being The Record of my Adventures while Trading in the Pacific Islands from the 'Seventies', by G.E.L. Westbrook, edited with a preface by R.A.K. Mason. 'It has been a Hell of a job – thanks largely to my procrastinating and unmethodical habits', he admitted to Fairburn.[30] His preface minced no words about New Zealand's shameful conduct over Samoa, even though the narrative did not extend that far. Mason had decided to take the story only up to Westbrook's arrival in Samoa, after which it became, as he frankly told him, 'less interesting', largely because of Westbrook's obsessive interest in Samoan politics and in vindicating his own role therein: 'try to get rid of that oppressed feeling and don't take your politics too seriously', Mason told him – ironic advice, perhaps, coming from him.[31] He was modest about his role as editor:

> I have left it the plain tale he wrote – the simple and straightforward narrative, the Homeric not unspiced with the Rabelaisian. You need not fear to find those romantic embellishments of the stock traveller in the South Seas, who goes home and empties his whole pepper-pot of adjectives over the scrag of lean meat he has got on a through trip. All my work has been to arrange and, here and there, condense.

This was the last mail Westbrook received from Mason, although he saw him when he visited Auckland at the end of 1932 (bringing with him armloads more research material, with books full of newspaper clippings). Eventually his reminiscences were published, but not the book Mason had prepared.[32] In February 1933 Westbrook was approached by an American journalist and writer of 'romantic fiction', Julian Dana. Dana had been put onto Westbrook by the American consul in Suva, whom he had asked for help after his publisher commissioned him to write 'a tale of the South seas', where he had never been. Through flattery, the offer of a new typewriter, a camera and a trip to San Francisco, the promise of sales in the several thousands and the prospect of film rights worth up to £100,000, Dana persuaded Westbrook to sign a contract giving him rights to 'all auto-biography, biography, or any other manuscript or idea suggested or written by' Westbrook, and to hand over the typescript Mason had prepared. Dana was not content to promise Westbrook that his book would be a 'minor classic': 'the record of your more than half century of adventure where the seas swirl under a burnished sun and hurricanes storm up to the Feet of God will be one of the greatest epics of the South Seas.'[33]

Westbrook made no mention of Mason when he replied to Dana, eagerly accepting his proposal, although he subsequently acknowledged that it was Mason who had suggested that he write up his reminiscences for publication in the first place, and he was anxious that his young friend receive due credit for his 'valuable' and 'friendly' assistance.[34] In June 1933 he wrote to Mason to tell him that he had agreed to Dana's offer, 'mentioning you as a man of literary ability', and asked him to send Dana everything he had: he suggested that Mason ask Dana for a payment of £50 for his labours. When he had not heard from Mason by December, Westbrook interpreted his silence – which may have been only characteristic negligence – as pique. 'If you had responded with a good grace to my letter in place of taking the huff as you evidently have done I would have forwarded you copies of the whole of my correspondence with Dana, which I feel sure would have appealed to you as genuine . . . By your not replying to either myself or Mr Dana I could only come to the conclusion that you had washed your hands of me, and did not any longer study my interest.'[35]

While Westbrook set to work on volume two, Dana rewrote 'An Old Trader', which he found charming but lacking in 'glamour and color',[36] and retitled it 'Vanished Years in the South Seas – an autobiography of George Westbrook as told to Julian Dana'. When it failed to find a publisher he rewrote it again (adding a 'psychological angle', as advised), renegotiated his agreement with Westbrook increasing his share of the royalty from 10 to 30 per cent, and signed a contract with Macmillan assigning the copyright to himself. Westbrook never saw this contract, nor the completed manuscript, which was published with the title *Gods Who Die: the story of Samoa's greatest adventurer* in 1935. It was clearly based on Mason's version, although the nature of Dana's input is immediately apparent from his chapter titles: 'The devil's grave', 'The isle of serpents', 'Duel at dawn', for example, in place of Mason's more prosaic 'Incidents and adventures', 'More about the Marshalls' and 'Some "old-timers"'. Westbrook's name appeared on neither the jacket nor the title page. Westbrook died in 1939, embittered by many things but not least by the lost promise of literary fame and fortune. The book had not sold well – nowhere near the 20,000 or more copies he had been told it would – and fewer than 3000 were printed. He had received £75 in royalties, but had gone into debt on the promise of much more. Dana's fictional preface, describing his meeting Westbrook in the lobby of an Auckland hotel on his way home from Samoa to San Francisco, was only salt in the wound. Dana had never met Westbrook, nor had he ever been to Samoa or Auckland. Nor did he ever send Westbrook a new typewriter. Mason's view of this episode of literary skulduggery and breached trust, and the cavalier appropriation of his own hard work, is not known.

9

On the swag

1931

IN MARCH 1931 Mason was pleased to be back from Samoa, and rejuvenated by the experience: 'I had lost all heart in everything until the Samoan trip bucked me up.'[1] He was working on 'a book of short stories which will make the cows sit up if I ever get them finished', he told Westbrook. He was 'Also thinking of publishing another book of poetry', at Fairburn's urging from London. 'You will be delighted to learn I am utterly reforming in the matter of tidiness and even making a cheap filing-cabinet for myself. Am tidying up the deposit of years'.[2] In his notebook he recorded this account of the writer's spring-clean:

I have been clearing up the five years accumulation of papers in my desk. Letters left unanswered – portraits of the love of the year before last . . . – pipes, candlesticks – a watch I searched the house for – tobacco, loose and in tins – innumerable boxes of matches & cigarettes – prophylactics, contraceptives, cork-screws, empty flasks – half-full flask (loud Hallelujahs!) – tickets for theatre, tram, bus, boat, train. Books – many of them lent to me and should have been returned long ago: too late now – already sworn that I must have returned them long ago – not going to lose both book and last shreds of reputation for veracity. Any rate – who has conscience in books? Or deals with Government – or women (for last Ovid –).

The matrix of it all – papers, papers, papers. Dusty in top strata, crawling with filth on bottom – jump up and bark at you: Notes on old tickets – on old ragged edges of newspapers – bits torn out of books – scrawled on labels. Notes. Fragments of epics in three books. Notes scribbled and now undecipherable. Twist him and turn him and hold him up to the light in hopes he may turn out valuable. Just manage to make him out: Meet V.R. 12.40 outside G.P.O. Curse: half-an-hour lost. Who the Hell was V.R. anyway? Or is it really U.R. which would mean Ursula Richmond?

Number codes to which I have forgotten the key.

Things readable but deplorable. Looked marvellous at the time. Treatises on political and religious and philosophical subjects elucidating at great length points I could now sum up in a sentence – or which are no longer comprehensible at all.

The good things abandoned as being worth more favourable moments (which never came) the bad things worked out fully and neatly copied – quite legible but not worth reading.

Oh Christ, how depressing. Was I more of a bloody fool then than I am now? And what of next year. Filthy. Got sick of it – started to burn indiscriminately. Left higgledy-piggledy muck half-sorted all over the room. Went & had drink at pub. Back at night. Same again.

All jumbled with pure ephemeridae – notes for trip, record of poker-scores, golf-scores, walks, notes from friends. My soul is like a dark unfathomed pool three pairs of pyjamas grey socks get pants cleaned sausages Jim Corner at ten Or the unbridled license of a fool Ring 126 Wed re interest.

Ciphers – key long forgotten. Fag-ends of conversations, extracts from books, meanings of words, drawings, word-sketches of faces, characters, landscapes – filth, balls.

How bad – much jotted down for passing amusement, admittedly – now valued at any account. But oh how tarnished the treasures of ten years ago. Will that which I cherish so warmly to-day be valued at nothing to-morrow (Te-tum-te-te-tum-te-te-tum-te-te-tum and the something or other my sorrow – Byron at his bloodiest. Or Tom Moore). Why worry? We'll be damnably mouldy a hundred years hence.

And I'm damnably grubby and grimy to-night. Need a bath but haven't the spirit. Dirty to bed and bad dreams of sinking in a papery morass.[3]

As for work, he wrote to Westbrook: 'My own prospects are looking brighter than they have for many a long day. Actual cash is still scarce, but at any rate I am on scratch, instead of being far behind it, as I have been for so long.'[4] He had been struck on his return by the visible evidence of the worsening economic depression, at how much more desperate – 'bloody', as he and Fairburn would have put it – things had become in even the few months he had been away. 'It seems strange to see in our native Auckland boys and women playing the fiddle for money in the streets, men selling fruit on the pavements, old crones diving into rubbish-baskets for a few rejected newspapers, men sneaking scraps of food out of "Keep our city clean"s.' Two months later: 'Doss-houses and soup-kitchens multiply.'[5] He was fortunate, however, to get some tutoring work from Dave Faigan at Holl's and with the

Nelsons. It was 'One of the few things that wax fat and flourish under present conditions' – presumably, he supposed, because people felt more urgently the importance of giving their children a good education when jobs were so scarce. 'I do a fair bit of reading, writing, gardening, and walking. Get a fair bit of work and would be in a reasonably decent way if I had not borrowed money to keep a friend out of gaol . . . now of course the poor devil cannot pay me and it has been keeping me poor for all my work.'[6] It is easy to speculate that this 'friend' was Dan, whose case in the Court of Appeal was heard at the end of March. Mason's relatively sanguine outlook on things was not to last, however, as the Depression bit deeper.

He enrolled at university again but not for post-graduate studies, to the disappointment of his old friend and teacher Ted Blaiklock, who, like Paterson, held high hopes of his wayward pupil's academic career. 'Mr. Blaiklock is *most* anxious for you to go in for this Post Graduate Scholarship – thinks you have a great chance', Jessie had written to him in Samoa. 'Says Prof. Paterson [who was by that time in England] is so keenly interested in you; & he wishes you would write him a line'.[7] Blaiklock sent Mason an exasperated note:

Will you ever have to be driven & kicked & goaded on to seek your own good fortune? Are you taking Honours this year? If so why not present for the first week? Silly ass, doesn't the sure prospect of a post-grad. schol. attract you? 'Not got Greek, couldn't take Humanities at Oxford.' Well get the Schol & study Political Economy or any other fool thing you like. For goodness' sake try to break through this apathy to all the higher aspirations of the soul. There are things in life worth the dust. Throw your pipe away, buy a hat, cut out the Bolshies, get up early, have a cold bath & pull yourself together & turn up at the Honours class for a golden future.

It was signed 'Your sincere but disgusted well-wisher E.M. Blaiklock'.[8]

Mason did not take honours; he enrolled in ethics and economic history for the Diploma in Social Science instead. He wrote to Fairburn casually, a few weeks after the term began: 'I have given up any save the very remotest ideas of going Home. Look a bloody fool I have chucked away my divine opportunities at Varsity and now must spend the rest of my days as an underling and consider myself bloody lucky when I can get somebody to be under.'[9] To Teddy he remarked, enviously, wistfully, a few weeks later: 'Gad, how I envy you your trip. Have always longed to see France'.[10]

He would never go to either England or France. Blaiklock was not the only one of his friends who would see here not just one more instance in a pattern of missed opportunities, but something more troubling, perverse: opportunities that were perhaps wilfully missed. Then, too, the economic depression, compounded by the financial morass that Dan had got the family into, would have made going to Europe at that time a remote if not impossible dream, even if Mason remained ambivalent about it. He never paid Teddy back the money he had borrowed to go to Samoa, although she asked: he would have if he had ever had the money to send, he apologised in the last letter he wrote to her, in April 1933. He had just opened his first savings account: it contained £3.[11] Moreover, the economic burden of financially supporting the household was perhaps not the only family tie that held him: according to some who knew the family well, Jessie would never have let him go.[12]

HE REPORTED to Fairburn in April 1931 on extracurricular goings-on at the university college: 'there has been a horrid outburst of something beastly at the dump – I mean our Alma Mater. It has been variously defined, but for my own part I have dark suspicions that it is something perilously like intelligence.'[13] A poem of Fairburn's published in the annual student literary review, *Kiwi*, in 1930 had offended some of the professors by referring, poetically but unequivocally, to sex, and the editor had been reprimanded. In March the Professorial Board banned the first issue of the Student Christian Movement magazine, *Open Windows*, because it contained two articles on D.H. Lawrence. Then Mason 'strolled all unconscious into the storms and tumult' when he agreed to give a talk to the Literary Society on James Joyce, which was '[p]romptly banned' after the professor of English borrowed and read a copy of *Ulysses*.[14] These were early skirmishes in the battle of minds and morals that enlivened the college and scandalised the tabloid press in the first half of the 1930s, in which Mason was to play a larger part.

Later that year *Kiwi* published a poem of Mason's, 'Wise at Last', and a short story, 'Springtime and the Sick-bed', which had won the annual fiction prize. 'Wise at Last' iterated his now-familiar stoicism, but the feeling here was new: the poem's tone is light, its diction simple (almost child-like), its attitude off-hand. The narrator considers the wrongs of the world, which once would have moved him to anger, but now he can adopt an attitude only of weary and almost casual resignation. There is no sense here of struggle, or ambiguity, or despair:

. . .

Still the wise and stout
 of heart and good
 and strong are cast out
 to want for food.

Of all this wrong
 I have no least doubt:
 but I have long
 been wearied out

. . .

I sit in the sun
 and take my rest:
 when all's said and all's done
 negation is best.

'Springtime and the Sick-bed' was a darker affair. A man decides to abandon his invalid wife, bedridden and pain-racked by chronic asthma, after years of giving up his life (as he now realises) to her care. In the cold clear air of an early spring morning, as he splits kindling in the backyard, he comes to the sudden realisation 'that all his life of self-sacrifice was only a sham and hypocrisy. . . . He had often wrung his hands for death to give her rest: now he saw that it was his own rest that he wished for.'[15] The story is a Joycean moment of epiphany, its form an interior monologue. Marie Gaudin would later recall that when Mason showed it to her she commented, 'I didn't know you felt that way about your mother', to which he replied, 'I didn't know you were so clever.'[16]

 Marie had been down to stay with the Richardses at Welcome Bay while he was away, and met with Pia's approval. 'I love your Miss Gaudin – she is a darling', Pia wrote to him. 'Why don't you try & make her marry you?' To which Mason only jested in reply.[17] Pia would continue to take a friendly interest in his romantic affairs. She invited him down to stay too, although 'Of course I am quite aware that the attraction of Tauranga' – 'your young protégé', as she called Teddy – 'has now transferred itself to the high seas'.[18] Teddy had left soon after Mason got back from Samoa. They were never to see each other again. He wrote to her in May, when she had not long arrived in London, a typical letter to the traveller from one left behind with nothing to report: 'Nothing worthy of record ever happens. I just work eat sleep, drink, play, and fool round as usual: do a thousand ridiculous things such as refraining from falling in love . . . my infernal arrogance won't allow me to let anyone see that I feel so much the loss of one small young piece of femininity.'[19]

If her parents' intention in sending Teddy to London had been to get her married, they were soon satisfied. Within a week she had had a proposal. She saw Fairburn in June, and found that he was 'in love with somebody else . . . He is now on his way to some cottage to write a novel'.[20] By the end of that month she was engaged to 'a *very* nice young man' she had met at an East Africa dinner at the Savoy, 'just a sweet kid – only twenty-six', who was going out to Kenya. She left London, newly married, in September. 'Oh! how I wish you were here', she wrote to Mason from on board their ship off Port Said. 'It's priceless being married – simply priceless.' She had already asked if he could come out and join them: 'if you sent money etc to your mother could you come? There is a very good job vacant Geoffrey tells me.'[21]

She sent him half a dozen letters from Africa – excited, loving and increasingly lonely letters, each time asking him to come and see her. The last was in September 1932:

I miss you *terribly* . . . I miss our walks and I miss you showing me things and telling me things. . . .

Don't you *ever* want to curl up and smoke your filthy pipe and 'talk about yourself' – (which was really talking about me) – don't you? Don't you ever want me, just a weeny bit?

Just run away – and come here and you shall stay with us and see our little house – its so sweet – all cosy and small – and you shall talk for hours to me & we shall go for walks on the plains – and see zebra and buck and sometimes we shall see a giraffe perhaps – and I'll show you wild flowers and pretty little coloured birds, and wild cats and you shall hear hyena's howling in the night and you shall shiver and pull the bed-clothes up – Don't you want to come? . . . Oh! *misery* I'm making myself homesick for you . . .

Oh! Ronald, I love you!! Is it wrong to say that when I'm a respectable married woman? If it isn't, forgive me – I want to see your ugly mug again too!!!

Your hair & your green eyes and your tobacco stained tooth – and your silly narrow womans hands and your short trousers and turned up toes and the whole of you – and your old rain-coat for fine days and your stick for wet

– and your little book of Latin tags and your Housman – and your green
fountain-pen and your loads of blue pencils that stain everything, and your
tram-ticket-appointment-books, and the funny little cage you keep your watch
in (as if you think it will beat itself out) – and your swinging walk.[22]

He replied to her only once. But he wrote a poem for Teddy: a beautiful,
puzzling, elusive poem of absence and regret. He titled it 'Amores VI' when
it was first published in 1933:

> Be swift, O sun
> > lest she fall on some evil chance:
> > make haste and run
> > to light up the dark fields of France.
>
> See already the moon
> > lies sea-green on our globe's eastern rim:
> > speed to be with her soon:
> > even now her stars grow dim.
>
> Here your labour is null
> > and water poured upon sand
> > to light up the hull
> > which at dawn glimmers on to the land:
>
> And here you in vain
> > clothe many coming sails with gold,
> > if you bring not again
> > those breasts where I found death of old.
>
> Why bring you ships
> > from that evil Dis of a shore
> > if you bring not the lips
> > I kissed once and shall kiss no more:
>
> O sun, make speed
> > and delay not to send her your rays
> > lest she be in need
> > of light in those far alien ways.

That you may single
    my love from the rest, her eyes
    her wide eyes commingle
    all innocence with all things wise:

Rain drops at eve fall
    in your last rays no lovelier:
    her voice is the madrigal
    at your dawn when the first birds stir.

Be swift, O sun,
    lest she fall on some evil chance:
    make haste and run
    to light up the dark fields of France.

HE WAS more assiduous in writing to Fairburn – relatively speaking, at least, and Fairburn too would in time come to reproach Mason repeatedly for his silence, as he too grew increasingly homesick. 'At present you are a ghost, flitting moth-like across my vision with a tuppenny stamp attached, about once in six months', he wrote in August.[23] He found that Firth was an even worse correspondent. The 'Chosen Ones' were being scattered, as he had remarked to Firth in the summer of 1930, but by more than distance by this time. Within six weeks of arriving in London, Fairburn had fallen out with de Montalk after an argument about a girl, and they saw little of each other thereafter. Nor did de Montalk continue to correspond with Mason.

Fairburn's expatriate experience was the opposite of de Montalk's. De Montalk had loathed London at first, but he was sure of his repudiation of New Zealand and he was eventually to find his particular, peculiar place in England (and later France). Fairburn at first loved London, although always with an underlying feeling of insecurity and loneliness. On Armistice Day he visited Kew Gardens and nearly wept, he told Mason, in the New Zealand corner of the Temperate House – he stole a sprig of tea-tree – and pronounced that he had now experienced what it felt to be an exile: it brought, instead of unhealthy melancholy, 'a feeling of romantic dignity'.[24] He was soon disillusioned by the literary world. Harold Monro was 'definitely homosexual' and an alcoholic, while '[h]alf the intelligentsia are nancy-boys' (a deepening and vitriolic homophobia revealed itself in his letters from London). Economic conditions were 'absolutely bloody': 'Theres not one artist who isn't living on cheese-parings.'[25] But there was none of the tawdriness and fustiness and uptight puritanism of New Zealand: London was fun, much like he imagined the Restoration period must have been. He accidentally sent Teddy the first page of a letter addressed to Firth which described a carnivalesque atmosphere of sexual and social freedom; what does 'fucking' mean? Teddy asked Mason.[26] But Fairburn never saw himself as a permanent exile, and the longer he stayed away the surer he was that he would go back to New Zealand.

Fairburn, like de Montalk, had gone to London with the dream of launching himself and his friends to acclaim in the literary metropolis. Shortly after he arrived, six of his poems and two of Mason's, 'After Death' and 'The Beggar', were included (without permission) in a new anthology of New Zealand verse published by Dent in London, edited by Wellington journalist Quentin Pope.[27] It represented the work of fifty-six contemporary New Zealand poets. But this was not the company in which they wished to be seen. 'The bloody thing is called "Kowhai Gold" (which speaks for itself)', Fairburn complained. And so it would, as a critical shorthand for all that literary historians in later years would disdain in New Zealand poetry of the 1920s: its insipidity and preciousness, its pale Georgianism. And it was full of mistakes – 'fourteen mistakes in punctuation in my own section', Fairburn expostulated to Mason – and 'chock full of all the women poetasters' (misogyny was another of Fairburn's less attractive, maturing traits).[28] Nevertheless, he felt compelled to respond to a 'vile sneering' review in *New Zealand News* by the expatriate poet D'Arcy Cresswell, whose own work had been omitted after a public disagreement with the editor, and gave Mason 'a good boost'.[29]

In December 1930 Fairburn had his first book published, at his own expense and through de Montalk's agency, by the Columbia Press, who had already printed a volume of de Montalk's. His would be 'better than Monty's as regards binding, printing etc.', he told Mason, echoing de Montalk's competitive remarks about *Wild Oats* and *The Beggar*. It was a guinea edition of 25 copies. He was eager to do the same for Mason and urged him to send him his poems, along with some autographed copies of *The Beggar* 'if you can rake them up'. By late January Fairburn had secured £5 in subscriptions, 'repayable to whatever extent may be possible out of sales returns – and no harm done if not a copy is sold'. '*Please* send them along', he begged. 'I'm *dying* to do it.'[30] He had a while to wait. In April Mason wrote: 'I may be sending you some Mss. as soon as I have learnt how to operate this machine' – his new typewriter – 'without letting it lead me astray. At present I am always being forced to alter my sentences in order to cover up the mistake I have just made.' 'Am quite sure that I should never get into the way of actually composing on the typewriter', he added. 'I am so busy writing that the sense just wanders at its own sweet will' – like Wordsworth's Thames.

A month later Mason sent off a 'big batch' of stories – 'fables & tales', he described them – not for Fairburn to see through the vanity press but to try to place in the literary journals, suggesting the *Adelphi*, the *London Mercury* and 'the Americans'. 'Sell the bloody things for me, sen[d] me a copy of the thing they appear in and keep a third of the net rake-off for yourself' – 'At fair prices this lot ought to bring £50!' Clearly, he regarded this writing differently from his poetry: 'I can simply do these things to order: demand for poems does not affect supply.' And circumstances by then demanded that writing was work. There was a note of desperation, although it was casually put: 'I'm afraid some of it is rather impossible stuff to get rid of, but, if you feel like it, try hard. . . . Keep them moving briskly, use every base wheedle that you can think up, influence . . . anything you like. If they object to a thing in its present form, let them have at it, hack, hew, lop, prune, and generally bebang the thing to their heart's desire. But they must pay, pay, pay . . . '. If Fairburn had reasonable luck with these, 'I can soon find time to send you enough to put a few books out. Short stories, poems, essays, and I'd get a novel finished if I found I were getting anything out of the business. As it is, I'm so damnably near the bread-line that I'm scrounging for sixpences all the time.'[31] To George Westbrook he wrote a few weeks later: 'I have never before had to worry so much whether I got anything out of writing or not, just pottered along for my own amusement. But things are so deplorable now that I really hardly know how to get money to take me in to work.'[32] It was, however, not only money that he needed, he confessed to Fairburn, but 'also a bit of encouragement and some sort of feeling that I do count for at least two bits in the scheme of things . . . Also a chance to sneer (even if it were only privately) at a pack of bastards.'[33]

Fairburn did what he could, refusing to take more than 10 per cent for his efforts, but warned Mason not to be too hopeful: 'everybody here is scrounging hard, and it's very difficult to get stuff accepted'.[34] In the end he was able to place one poem from the collection which Mason would send him the next year, just before he left to come home. 'The Man on the Swag' was accepted by A.R. Orage's new *New English Weekly* in 1932, but 'they are not paying for stuff at present, unfortunately', Fairburn apologised, ' – but neither is anybody else, virtually'.[35] He had also sent a selection of his own and Mason's poems to Oxford University Press, for an anthology they were publishing for the English Association. Ian Donnelly had been commissioned to provide New Zealand material for this anthology back in 1929, and had sent some of Mason's work then. But it did not come out until 1934, as *The Modern Muse: poems of today British and American*, with one short poem by Mason, 'On a Dead Cripple' (which he did not include in his own new collection).

Among the writing he was doing around this time were some prose dialogues, aphoristic in style and in subject similar to his notebook jottings: perhaps it was these he had described to Fairburn as 'rather impossible stuff to get rid of'. His short stories evidently were as well. Of the ten stories written in 1931–32 which he collected under the title 'Men and Things', three he would publish at home in the student literary press, but the rest have not survived. 'His End was Peace', which appeared in the Literary Club magazine in July 1932, was, like 'Springtime and the Sick-bed', a dream of escape or release. An elderly farmer – tall and strong still, but weathered by years of hard outdoor work (possibly based on Mason's maternal grandfather, George Kells) – meets a swagger crossing his land. He is tantalised by the idea of the swagger's life of simplicity and self-reliance, and drawn to thinking about his own: 'fifty years of battle against Nature and his fellow-men . . . He had land and wealth, office and position, family and dependants, yet they were all but goads and rods to him. The more he won, the more he had to fret him'. Abandoning the presidential report for the Farmers' Union he had been on his way home to prepare, he sets out across 'the back' – rugged land with '[b]arren knife-edges scored with ravines', precipitous sheep tracks, fallen trees and charred stumps, the still-visible scars of forest clearance – into a fierce gale. Resting finally in a sheltered grassy hollow beneath a majestic burnt tree-trunk, lying back and gazing skywards, he experiences a moment of epiphany:

> let insanity flow in to calm him. He was floating face-downward on a slowly-moving, grey waste: he looked on every side to espy some island or shore, some source or terminus, but there was nothing save the flat, toneless vast. As far as he could see, it drove on, without colour, without form, without horizon, without intermission, beginning, or end . . . and he knew that his self had dissolved and been absorbed into the nothingness and uncoloured void . . . Long he lay thus, pouring with the stream.

He walks home, speechless, eyes smiling. His wife thinks he has gone mad, the doctor tells her that he has suffered a stroke, but he knows that he has

found his peace.[36] '[A]bout 15 pages and smelling strongly of the devil', Mason
described this story to Fairburn.[37]

AT THE END of April Fairburn had moved from London to a cottage on
the outskirts of the village of Wootton Rivers in Wiltshire. He went with
Jocelyn Mays, a New Zealander who had been studying in London at the
Slade School of Art – the 'somebody else' Teddy had referred to. The rent
was cheap and they managed a subsistence existence while Fairburn dabbled
in painting, wrote poetry and started a novel. They were deep in literary
country and he made pilgrimages to Stonehenge (where he spent an
uncomfortable night on the same stone altar as Tess), to Hardy's birthplace,
and on Keats's trail to Lulworth Cove, which he found at low tide was 'to
Piha what a daisy is to a sunflower'.[38] In August they discovered that Jocelyn
was pregnant, and in November they married. Fairburn divulged this news
to his friend with some embarrassment, for Mason regarded marriage (as
Fairburn had too) with Shelleyan and socialist scorn. 'A close corporation of
two legally empowered to add', he once wrote in his notebook. 'A knot
which makes the Gordian knot look like a granny-knot'. And: 'After a long
discussion on matrimony the other night an old chap had the last word. In
half-sentimental fashion he sighed and remarked: Well, perhaps after all the
best way is the good old-fashioned idea of getting a virgin and breeding from
her.'[39] He was ambivalent about Fairburn's situation, however, as Fairburn
was himself. 'Feel uneasily that you are quite right,' Mason responded, 'but
I'd never make up my mind for matrimony. All the same I'd probably be
secretly glad if that which I call my mind were forced into it – provided, of
course, it were really a love-affair. You can keep this confession (which I shall
sign) and use it against me at any time', he added flippantly.[40] In January
Jocelyn replied to a letter from Mason about her pregnancy: 'I would rather
you had congratulated me than sympathised though.'[41] Fairburn had at first
told Mason that they did not want to keep the baby. 'Suave, mori magno
turbantibus . . . ', Mason had greeted this news, quoting Lucretius (A joy it is,
when the strong winds of storm/ Stir up the waters of a mighty sea/ To
watch from shore the troubles of another), but 'There is not a little of nasty
envy in it'.[42] Jocelyn also told Mason, 'in confidence', that when Edwynna
had come to see Rex and 'he found that things had altered, he thought of you
& told her the best thing for her to do was to return'.

As the Depression deepened, Fairburn's initial exhortations to Mason to
come to Europe 'as soon as you bloody-well can' turned to warnings to stay

away, while Mason was writing to Fairburn warning him not to come home.[43] 'For God's sake contrive to keep away from this unhappy little land for another year at all costs', Mason wrote in May. 'Do anything, but don't come here. You'll be sorry if you do, my son', suggesting 'Why don't you try to see Russia properly?' There were now 38,000 officially registered unemployed in New Zealand, but in reality probably twice that number out of work, he reckoned. 'Believe me this is no place for a gintleman at the moment.'[44] O.N. Gillespie, an older journalist they both knew, had 'not had a day's work since the "Sun" shut up shop' the previous September and was on relief. Mason viewed with cynicism the desultory efforts of the government to deal with the crisis: a 'pitiful' relief works scheme, 'no good either to the men on it or to the country as a whole', and the risible attempts of civic authorities to raise public morale: 'This week is Auckland['s] 90th birthday and they have organised a "Cheer-up Week" to keep the urban rabble in psychological order.' A neighbour who had worked for years for one of the big department stores was now selling Art Union tickets; another after fourteen years with the Railways was peddling bootlaces.[45]

His own situation was scarcely better. 'Instead of getting 6 or 7 quid a week as I should have done with luck, I have been scraping along on a couple', he told a friend in Samoa. They had let half their house, to a 'poor devil of a Scottish engineer' who had also had no work for months. 'The people whom we owe money are at us all the time, while we get nothing from those who [owe] us. My brother can scarcely buy a meal', yet he was owed, Mason said, well over a thousand pounds.[46] Jessie continued to be sick, the property was 'a curse', and Dan continued to cast around for fast and foolproof schemes to repair his fortunes, 'though I am thankful to say he is not actually producing any bills at the moment', Mason reported to Fairburn. 'Personally, I go out a fair bit – it's the only way to stand up against things when they become so thick.'[47]

> Stiffened so rigidly,
> Poor and unwell,
> Shivering frigidly,
> Sadder than Hell

he signed off one letter (after Thomas Hood).[48]

He still had some tutoring work, but not enough; and he wrote occasionally for the Labour Party paper the *New Zealand Worker*, but they could not afford to pay. In August, for example, he contributed a review of a recent article in the *London Mercury* by the Russian literary historian and critic Prince Mirsky on 'The present state of Russian letters'. Mason wrote of the influence of pre-revolutionary Russian writers – the 'dark, brooding, grotesque loveliness and a strange, compelling power' of Tolstoy, Gogol and Dostoevsky which was so marked an influence in the work of '[m]ost English novelists or short-story writers of any worth', although 'we must admit that they suffered from an excessive pessimism, and at times morbidity' as a result of the tyranny of bureaucracy and the indifference of the masses – before quoting at length from Mirsky on the cultural changes brought by the revolution.[49] The same month he spoke to the university college Literary Society on 'Laws for N.Z. Literature' and 'made things hum: it divided em into warring factions, it seemed', he reported to Fairburn. He told the students: 'If you desire to write, go out among men; spend your time talking to bargees.'[50] He was reading Sinclair Lewis (*Babbitt*) and James Cabell's *Jurgen* at this time. '[T]he more I see of the present-day yanks the more I like 'em', he commented to Fairburn, who had just sent him Hemingway's *Farewell to Arms*.[51] Meanwhile, his poem 'Christ on the Swag', along with one by Fairburn, was read during a public lecture on New Zealand literature by Alan Mulgan, which Mason thought was 'amazingly good'.[52]

He was still working on the Westbrook memoir too, and meanwhile had an article on the unveiling of a missionary memorial in Samoa accepted by the *Auckland Star*, while 'a ripping article' about the Samoan political situation was turned down by the *New Zealand Observer* but published in Nelson's *New Zealand Samoa Guardian* and in *Farming First*.[53] Donnelly at the *Sun* rejected a Westbrook piece, feeling it lacked 'vitality . . . the chronicle is just a bit pedestrian'.[54] On the larger study of Pacific problems he had been planning, however, Mason had made no progress. '"The realisation of ignorance is the beginning of knowledge"; so I have at least learnt something from my trip', he commented wryly to Felix Keesing.[55] Writing, he was finding, was a hard way to make a living, even had it paid. 'I have been at this infernal machine for five hours to-day, and am absolutely losing my grip of it in weariness,' he concluded a letter to Westbrook.[56]

As ever, he went walking, 'into the country a lot mainly with old John'. This was probably Jack Stewart, an 'advertising man' with whom, Mason would later recall, he formed an unlikely and lasting friendship.[57] But it was not the same as when Fairburn had been there. One December day he walked over to Green Bay to visit Irene Jenkin, and afterwards wrote nostalgically:

'Think of pushing y/self on your belly to the very edge of the browned, crackling grass on some great cliff: then look down through the scarlet pohutukawa (they are all out in full blaze) at a blue sea creaming on a white curve of beach. . . . Walked home along the coast at night with a great guinea of a moon burning behind the dark pines by Avondale. Thought much of old times in a mood of gentle Virgilian melancholy.'[58]

He was gardening, too, not only because he enjoyed it. 'How amusing to use your garden for commerce', Pia Richards observed. 'Asparagus is the stuff.'[59] As well as vegetables, he told Fairburn in December, he had planted 'enough tobacco to last me (in theory) for a twelve-month'. Not being able to afford to buy tobacco was one of the hardest deprivations, he found. Dan, as well as desperation, may have inspired Mason's tobacco-growing experiment. 'Brother Daniel', he reported, 'is climbing steadily de profundis financialibus: Christ knows how he has done it, but from the midst of his absolute and universal smash he has organised an absolutely first-rate tobacco company.' He had 210 acres planted at Brigham's Creek (Whenuapai), and the 'moderation & shrewdness he is showing are rather remarkable. Of course, if he prospers he will no doubt degenerate: but I shall try to establish myself before he does that. I feel a little prosperity would not ruin my character.'

There was a '[s]ort of domestic and peasant economy returning', Mason observed, more seriously. Home-brewing was all the rage, while shares in investment schemes were selling well: 'Capitalism does seem to be generating its own toxins: the trouble is it's such a damn long time dying.' Clifton Firth, he had informed Fairburn the previous November, the ardent socialist, 'floats companies consisting of himself at a rate of one (approximately) every 2.784 days and spends on advertising prodigious sums which are better put out on good liquor.'[60]

ONE OF THE entrepreneurial Firth's latest ventures in the winter of 1931, in which Mason had had a part, was an 'experimental' film that Firth was making in partnership with a flamboyant young Australian, Robert Steele (later to make a career in Auckland as a photographer, documentary-film director and bon vivant). Entitled Shattered, the film (which has since been lost) was claimed to be 'the first photo-play to be made here with synchronised sound'.[61] Co-written by Firth, possibly with help from Mason, it dealt with the aftermath of the First World War, which was a subject on which Mason felt deeply (he had been strongly recommending to his friends Richard Aldington's novel Death of a Hero). Shattered followed three New Zealanders who enlist and fight in the trenches in France. One in particular, a young captain, is so traumatised by the experience, his morale 'shattered', that he 'returns a changed man, with no desire to resume his former occupation. His gratuity is soon spent on riotous living and he is reduced to poverty', and becomes involved in a murder. Mason played the part of a communist agitator, although his name did not appear among the cast members listed in the reviews, most of them well-known actors on the Auckland amateur stage.[62] It was filmed mostly in a disused warehouse in Sandringham, in 'the Continental style – quick, flashing shots, requiring little in the way of background' (such as trenches), although the passenger liner *Rangitane* served as the troop-ship and a full stand of punters at the Ellerslie racecourse as unwitting extras, while Queen Street businesses 'lent their most up-to-date window backgrounds for interior sets, when an atmosphere of something approaching Hollywood was required'.[63] The film had a five-night season at the Town Hall Concert Chamber in October, but was not a great success. The acting was commended but, as the *New Zealand Observer* remarked, '16 millimetre-film is quite useless when it comes to a matter of exhibition in a large hall. . . . it was sometimes inaudible, sometimes practically invisible, and when to these drawbacks were added very frequent breaks in the film, one could not wonder that the audience sometimes laughed in the wrong places'.[64] The fledgling company had announced plans to make two feature films a year on 'subjects of Imperial interest',[65] but there were no more, and *Shattered* was the beginning and the end of Mason's movie career.

He briefly contemplated a political career. Mason was one of 'two or three' people approached by the Farmers' Union to stand as independent candidates for Parliament in the general election in December 1931, 'expenses paid so long as we emphasised the importance of putting our primary industries on a sound footing', he told Fairburn. 'Rather appeals to me, so you may yet see fulfilled my old intention of standing as Country Party candidate for City Central.' He did think about it, he told Westbrook (in confidence), but declined.[66] Dan too had evidently abandoned his fleeting political aspirations. At the poll Labour increased its representation by four seats to twenty-four, and 34 per cent of the vote, the largest gained by any single party. But the conservatives, United and Reform – 'that mob of vulgar cows', Mason called them – held comfortably onto power in a newly forged Coalition Party.[67] The Coalition government continued to respond to the economic crisis with timid, orthodox and ultimately inflammatory methods: devaluation, cutting salaries and wages, and drafting the jobless into demoralising make-work relief schemes ('Sort of combination of Samuel Smiles and Peter Kropotkin'[68]). 'It is a wonder that there has not been more trouble here', Mason remarked to Westbrook. 'The Communists are very active with processions, agitation and demonstrations.'[69]

The Communist Party profited from the Depression, in a manner of speaking. Its membership increased from some 100 (or fewer) at the beginning of the 1930s to 350 in 1935; 60 per cent of its members in this period were unemployed.[70] It was instrumental in the formation of the Unemployed Workers' Movement in 1931, and prominent in the Labour Defence League and the anti-eviction campaigns, supporting workers and unemployed who were being evicted weekly from substandard housing in working-class suburbs like Freemans Bay because they could no longer pay their rent. Party members were regularly arrested at demonstrations or on street corners selling the *Red Worker*. 'You could rot in Freeman's Bay & they'd never smell you in Remuera', Mason wrote in his notebook –

> Dear land, to which of old my fathers came
> to-day enslaved to cant & sold to shame
> where smug snug ranters soft-wrapped in fat ease
> recommend the starving to Diogenes.[71]

The Depression had a lasting and embittering impact on Mason. It deepened his awareness of the injustice and inhumanity of capitalism, intensified his hatred of those who profited from it, and hardened his anger. It turned his politics further to the left and impelled him further into political activity. He suffered himself, and he empathised with the suffering of others. '[A]ny sensitive person', he would later observe, 'had to react to the strange horrors of that time.'[72] Fairburn reacted differently. He became more conservative while he was in England, repudiating his youthful profession of communism. By the end of 1931 he was writing long letters to Mason and Firth explaining his new world-view, earnestly arguing his case against theirs. Being in England, he told them, and feeling a part of history (in a way, presumably, that one did not out in the colonies) forced one to 'take a rule in life'. He declared his faith to be in the supremacy of the spirit and the imagination rather than in the masses, and told them they should be reading Lawrence, Blake and Nietzsche, not Lenin: 'Forget your false Tartar gods', 'forget Russia & the economic interpretation on history & etc'.[73] He had made some investigations, he said, and concluded that Russia promised not deliverance from all social evil but the tyranny of scientific materialism over the individual and the artist. He was also reading Oswald Spengler and Nikolai Berdyaev. His letters to Firth had an angry and reproachful tone that was missing from those he wrote to Mason, possibly because Firth had not written to him for two years, and when he did he compared Fairburn's poetry unfavourably with de Montalk's. It was possibly also because he found Firth's more dogmatic expositions of Marxism more goading, and because his bond with Mason went deeper. 'I am really an anarchist, I fear', he told Mason: he looked forward to 'the complete breakdown of human society, so that the individual would (perhaps) be freed from all social restraint'.[74] In fact, he would soon become a convert to Social Credit. Politics, not women, was to cause an irreparable breach between Mason and his closest friend, but not yet.

AT THE END of the year Mason attended the WEA's annual, week-long summer school at Paerata, where he had been invited (at short notice) to give a lecture. The school was held at a private Methodist boarding college, amid undulating farming country 30 miles south of Auckland. His Samoan holiday appears to have broken a pattern, for he seems never to have gone back to Lichfield to work over the summer again.

At the summer school he spoke on 'The theatre of the future', to which he was to become deeply committed in the coming years. Already he had begun writing plays. One that he had written during the previous year, but was never performed, was 'This Bird May Swing': a one-act play with a message, despite his protestations to the contrary. 'The play may be regarded as a piece of "propaganda", but that is not the intention, which is purely aesthetic', his 'producer's note' stated. 'The conversation is not necessarily intended to be naturalistic.' The action takes place outside a courthouse during the trial of a young man for the murder, by poisoning, of his jilted lover: the case was based on an incident that had occurred in Samoa while Mason was there. The central character, a court reporter, is awaiting the verdict and discusses the case and its implications, the wrongs and stupidities of the legal system and the social order, with his friend, the Surveyor, and other passing observers who are foils for his progressive views. He believes that it was not murder but a suicide–revenge, and that an innocent man will hang. The Reporter, who is in his early thirties, bitter, cynical and a socialist, resembles the Communist Reporter in 'Dreams Come True'. 'Reporting a case?' the Surveyor asks him. 'Aye,' he replies, 'aiding a fearless, altruistic, and broad-minded Press in its pure, noble, and selfless task of edifying and enlightening a cultured, wise, and virtuous democracy. In other words, sedulously copying down the dirty details of a degraded murder-trial to serve up in undigested gobbets for greasy suburbans to gloat over at to-morrow's breakfast-table.' He has learnt not to have opinions in his job, not to think about the relation between crime and society. 'But just now this case has stirred me up. I can't help somehow wanting to do something active about it all – kick down all the social rottenness somehow, all the ignorance and cant and bigotry and hypocrisy and greasy, lying, unctuous, smeary, Rotarian humbug.' The Surveyor is quietly amused by his young friend's bitter idealism.

> Rep: There must be some outburst of fiery wisdom . . .
> Sur: (Interrupting). Yes, yes. But who's it to come from? Press? Church? Parliament? Or perhaps the Universities – but I descend to the farcical.
> Rep: (Laughing). Universities, that's a good one. No, there are only two forces bringing life to-day – women and workers.

Their conversation turns to the ethics of capital punishment. '[W]e don't cancel evil just by doing evil to the evil-doer', the Reporter declares. 'Socrates knew that . . . No, we must check crime at its source':

> it nearly all comes from sexual and economic troubles that we are all to blame for, all of us. If we cared to think it all out – or even just apply the knowledge we have, we could fix it. But we prefer to keep our knowledge in cold storage for students, and punish a few poor devils for the communal crimes. Men don't think, can't think, won't think, daren't think – no brain, no spine, no spunk, no guts.
> Sur: Your argument boils down to this – we take one man and make him suffer as a scape-goat for the crime and criminal folly of the lot of us.
> Rep: (eagerly). Now you're getting it. Every gaol-bird is Christ

and he takes from his pocket a copy of the *Hammer* and reads out a poem, 'Our Sacrifice'. The last stanza reads:

> The hangman fumbles,
>   the hangman lingers
>   and knots his fingers,
>   while the priest mumbles
>   of what god hallows

> the fruit the gallows
> gives for offering.

The play ends with the pronouncement of the verdict of guilty and the anguished cry of the accused's mother: 'Oh Christ, oh Christ.'[75]

After the New Year he went on to stay with the Richardses in Tauranga, where Jessie wrote to him:

> Well my Dear son, I can only wish you may have something better in this coming year than in the last one, & to thank you for your great kindness to me – Do not imagine for one moment that I am not aware of all you have given up & had to fight against – but I am sure *your* life will be a great one; & that a reward will come to you. I realize how far short I have come in being able to do all for you that I wished, but my darling son, I did *my best*, poor as it may seem to you. I feel confident things are coming better.[76]

He had taken down with him the Christmas shopping Pia had asked him to do for her. Until the Richardses moved to Auckland a few years later, he regularly sent books that she wanted, advised her on the children's education, and set Latin exercises for her by mail. 'To the Same-Day Latin Service', she addressed one letter. He invited her in return to stay at Ellerslie whenever she was in Auckland: 'things are never within of [sic] miles of being straight,' he warned, 'but if you do not mind that overmuch you will find this fairly handy to town'.[77] She enjoyed discussing literary matters with him. Her letters suggest that she found in Mason a confidant of a kind, although in a different way from Teddy. She could not take seriously his politics, however, about which she would tease him – not unkindly, and not unperceptively either: 'You are so strangely romantic in politics & so unromantic in art & literature; it seems odd to me that you should fondly think that feeding the hungry & starving the overfed will immediately create contented people. . . . You are a pure Tolstoyan. My father used to say that Tolstoy & St. Francis were the only two real Christians since Christ. You must be the third.'[78]

10

A crack-brained socialist

1932

'I HAVE been putting my ounce of enthusiasm for the last 3 or 4 months into putting my chaos in order', Mason wrote to Fairburn in May 1932. 'Out of it all I have carved a book of poems I sent you, a book of stories and one of plays which I am keeping to work over.'[1] By March 1932 he had got together the new collection of poems that Fairburn had been waiting for a year earlier. He titled it *No New Thing*,[2] and drafted a letter to send to the poet Robert Graves, care of Graves's literary agents, J.B. Pinker and Sons in London, asking him, if he was interested, to communicate with his friend Rex Fairburn in Clench Common. (Fairburn had by this time moved to a larger run-down farm cottage near Marlborough, where he and Jocelyn were anxiously awaiting their baby.) 'I think you could get rid of five hundred copies at six shillings', Mason wrote. '[Y]ou can rely on a fair number of extraordinary sales owing to the fact that I am a New Zealander. For one thing, it is so remarkable that anyone here should do anything decent. Again, there [are] a certain number of collectors here who will buy it just to add to their collection of New Zealand books, even if they do not appreciate it.' (He was thinking, perhaps, of Pat Lawlor among others.) He introduced himself as a teacher of Latin, 'just twenty-seven', and the author of *The Beggar*, which had given him much trouble to get published but had been 'praised in England'.[3]

Mason had heard about, though he was not likely to have seen, the publications of the Seizin Press which Robert Graves and Laura Riding had established in 1927: small, hand-printed fine editions, thus far mostly of their own poetry. They had been living in Majorca for two and a half years by 1932, and one of the four books they published there was a collection of letters by their New Zealand friend, film-maker Len Lye. It appears, however, that Graves never saw *No New Thing*.

Fairburn had another plan. While in London he had become friends with Charles Lahr, a socialist, owner of the Progressive Bookshop in Holborn and occasional publisher under the imprint Blue Moon Press. He conducted much of his literary business and held court to young writers and politicos in the public bar of the Red Lion across the road from his shop, which was where Fairburn met him. He was planning to publish a booklet of Fairburn's satirical poems: 'squibs (as vicious as possible)' aimed at members of the literary establishment,[4] a genre to which Fairburn found his verbal wit and rude humour well suited, and which was much in vogue in the 1930s (but not one in which Mason would write, except in his notebooks). 'Looky here, do you want a book of poems published?' Fairburn asked him in March, just as Mason was preparing to dispatch his package to Graves. 'Because I think I might be able to do it, through Lahr. What about sending me a complete set of them typed'.[5] Mason sent them (along with the letter he had written to Graves) by return mail, instructing Fairburn to 'Beg, beseech, plead with, go on your knees to Lahr. I don't give a damn what sort of get-up the thing has. Yes I do. I want it cheap if possible. Brown-paper cover, for all I care, and printed on sanitary paper.'[6]

Fairburn was as enthusiastic as ever when the poems arrived: 'I shall not rest content until I see them in print, recorded once for all. . . . Whether the poems are widely noticed, here or in NZ, they put you in a position to defy the ephemeral foes of the world you inhabit. You can gibe at them and cast eternity in their teeth.' He was less sure about Mason's prose preface, however, which he suggested be either headed 'Mainly for New Zealanders' or omitted altogether. Mason's sarcastic dig at local critics and sensibilities, while reminding him painfully of home ('Chappell, Mulgan, et hoc genus omni'), would be largely superfluous over there, he told him, where minds were not so narrow. 'The poems', Mason wrote,

> are too deeply soaked in an ancient tradition to hope to escape the charge of modernism: they are too strongly imbued with religious sense to hope to escape the stigma of impiety. Still I fear that, for once, wallowers in self-righteousness must forgo their other customary pleasure – that of screaming against sexuality. My apologies: there was no definite intention of depriving worthy people of so dear a pleasure – it is entirely the fault of my artistic canons.[7]

He would later remove this paragraph when the collection was eventually published, although not for the reasons that Fairburn objected to it: for the moment he demurred, while Fairburn hoped that he would not mind if he at least edited it a little.

Lahr, however, was by this time 'up to his ears in debt' and in no position to do the book. Nor was Humbert Wolfe, who had been such a fan of *The Beggar*, although he 'seemed impressed' with the clutch of poems Fairburn had sent him and '[s]poke of trying to place them separately';[8] he didn't, however. Nor did Lahr publish Fairburn's lampoons. Next Fairburn tried Chatto and Windus, where he had met one of the editors, Harold Raymond, who also turned the book down. 'They are pungent and vigorous, but the publication of poems by unknown writers is in these days the grimmest of prospects', he apologised. He would, on the other hand, be interested in any of the prose works Fairburn had mentioned – 'some memoirs of a Stevensonian Samoan, some short stories, and a novel'. Especially the novel, 'for it is obvious that there is stuff in your friend's mind' and it was easier to sell poetry if the writer had an established reputation as a prose writer first: 'A sad reflection, that; but alas! true.'[9] Mason understood this, but it was not advice he found helpful. 'I know that from a sales point of view the prose should precede this book,' he acknowledged when he approached another publisher in November, 'but from a psychological point of view, foolishly enough, I find it impossible. Life is too stagnant.' The publisher was Terry Bond, a New Zealander who had established a small publishing house, Boriswood, in London in the 1920s, and whom Mason had met recently in Auckland, when Bond had agreed to consider his book or else pass it on to an agent for him. Mason was explicit about the kind of volume he had in mind: 'something cheap and simple, as it seems only a fair thing to the poorer readers. I myself, as a reader, resent the guinea vellum bound limited edition touch. Paper covers seem quite good enough' (he cited 'Faber & Faber's pamphlets' as an example).[10] But again he was disappointed, and *No New Thing* went back into the bottom drawer. Whether or not he had had the means, he was in no mind to do it himself as he had eight years earlier, when he was young and foolish (as he might have said), with *The Beggar*. That, he had written to Robert Graves, had been published 'in half-pie fashion . . . hopelessly mismanaged, and gave me a lot of trouble with a loss of money'.[11]

Fairburn's letters also informed Mason of the death from tuberculosis of his old benefactor Harold Monro in March 1932, at the age of just 53, and of the relative indifference to his passing of the literary community. 'He had been regarded for long enough as an object of pity', consumed by alcoholism, his business still failing, no longer at the centre of things.[12] 'Needless to say, I wish I had written to H.M. now', Mason responded to this news. 'I don't know what he was, except that he was damn decent to me, and I should have liked to show him a bit of gratitude somehow.'[13]

MEANWHILE de Montalk, their once poet-in-arms and fellow crusader against the puritans and philistines, blazed briefly but spectacularly, for the last time, into Mason's and Fairburn's orbit in the early months of 1932, in a scandal of his own making that was effectively to end his own brilliant (as he believed it to be) literary career. In January he was arrested and charged with uttering and publishing an obscene libel. He had gone with Douglas Glass to a linotype-setter with a group of poems entitled 'Here Lies John Penis', which he planned to have printed as a broadsheet and distribute privately among his friends; the linotype-setter, however, took them to the police. The poems included a translation of Rimbaud's ode to a codpiece, a parody of Verlaine, and three short verses which alluded to unsuccessful amorous adventures of Fairburn's (playing on the title of Fairburn's book, *He Shall Not Rise*) – 'all poor' except the Verlaine, remarked Fairburn, who was amused rather than offended when he received a copy from Charles Lahr, who had later had them published in Paris.[14] But in another way this was de Montalk's greatest moment. His case was heard in the Old Bailey magistrates' court in February, observed with amusement by the press and alarm by the literati. 'The Count' appeared in his by then customary royal attire: wine-red cloak, silk scarf and sandals; Glass accompanied him in a matching cape and scarf in white and black. The judge was notoriously conservative. Still, de Montalk might not have been treated so harshly if he had not facetiously asked for six years in Buckingham Palace; he was sentenced to six months in Wormwood Scrubs.

Despite the comedy, the case became a *cause célèbre* for a literary community growing increasingly worried about the threat to freedom of expression in a time of political extremism and social unrest. At Glass's instigation, a meeting was held at the home of Leonard and Virginia Woolf, an appeal was launched and subscribed to by writers of the likes and reputation of J.B. Priestley, W.B. Yeats, H.G. Wells, T.S. Eliot, E.M. Forster, Housman and Walter de la Mare, and a celebrated lawyer engaged. Meanwhile de Montalk, in characteristic fashion, sat in prison feeling disgruntled that his defenders appeared to be more interested in the principle than in himself as a poet and prince – which they were: 'It is a pity it wasn't a real poet who came up against the authorities,' Lahr commented to Fairburn.[15]

Fairburn kept Mason informed of events as they played out, or at least the slightly confused version that reached Clench Common, and asked him to spread the word to those who should know ('Mulgan, Marie Gaudin &c &c &c.').[16] De Montalk's appeal was heard in March, and failed. Mason duly sent a 'strong letter' to the *Star*, focusing on the issue of freedom of expression and quoting from the clippings Fairburn had sent him: de Montalk, he wrote, 'was working on certain well-established psychological and artistic theories, which, however we may personally consider them wrong, are undeniably his sincere opinion'.[17] For himself, he worried about the trouble *No New Thing*, which he had just posted off, might land him in. But Fairburn assured him that Monty's was a special case and that there was nothing in his own poems that could cause offence in a country where one could see 'contraceptive literature and apparatus simply *piled* up in the windows' of the bookshops and chemist shops on Charing Cross Road, and where 'it is unnecessary to begin a discussion on James Joyce by determining whether or no he is pornographic. Intelligent people raise their eyebrows & gape blankly if you come out with irrelevancies of that sort.'[18]

For de Montalk the experience was embittering and traumatic. It strengthened his contempt for and self-conscious alienation from middle-class (especially English) society, and made him even more of an eccentric than he already was. After his release from prison (at the end of June), he spent two years in Poland, where he worked as a journalist and was fêted by the literary community. When he returned to England in 1935 he bought a printing press and founded the *Right Review*, an intermittent political and literary journal in which he espoused monarchist, anti-Semitic and pro-fascist views, and surrounded himself with a retinue of acolytes and fellow aristocrats *manqués*. In 1939 he crowned himself Wladislaw V, King of Poland, Hungary and Bohemia. He became more extremely, or at least more overtly, right-wing in a decade in which, against the background of economic crisis, rising fascism and impending war, most Western intellectuals, writers and artists – such as Mason – moved to the left.

Fairburn, on the other hand, was meandering off down the side road of Social Credit. He was reading *Das Kapital* in the early months of 1932, while sending his friends literature about Major Douglas's theories of monetary reform – anticipating the revolution, but only as an expedient. He had met Douglas in London (probably early that year), and was looking forward, he told Mason in June, to coming home to New Zealand to build a nationalist, Social Credit, anti-communist movement there. 'The fight, you say, is Communism v. Capitalism. No, not quite', he wrote, the real fight when it came would be between 'Communism and Fascism + Social Credit + Hitlerism'.[19] Fairburn's letters home during 1932 had an increasingly apocalyptic tone. 'Don't you fret your little heart about capitalism being a long time dying', he wrote to Mason. 'Its not decaying. It's collapsing. . . .

For the immediate future, look to a complete smash of Western Civilisation – inside five years – maybe in two or three years. Mark my words.' There was 'an End-of-the-world psychology among all the intelligentsia'. 'Perhaps you dont see, out there in NZ, away from Europe as you are, just what is happening. What is indisputably, unmistakably, inevitably happening. We are ending': 'It won't be a question of a World Revolution, and a Communist State. Its a question of another Dark Age.'[20] For all Fairburn's propensity to tendentiousness and over-statement (and his confusion), he had caught the *Zeitgeist*.

Mason's letters to Fairburn assured him that New Zealand was as boring and bloody as ever ('Your letter the other day indicated very well the desert nature of the Waste Land', Fairburn replied[21]). But even there, at the far periphery of the world, it sometimes seemed – to those who were looking for it – that the revolution was at hand. In April Mason sent Fairburn news of rioting in Auckland. He was not there, but Clifton Firth was, when a demonstration of the unemployed turned ugly: windows were smashed the length of Queen Street and shops looted. On the evening of 14 April some 15,000 unemployed had marched from the bottom of Queen Street to the Town Hall, where police prevented them from joining a meeting of Post and Telegraph workers protesting against wage cuts. Nearly 80,000 were officially out of work by then, and tension was rising: there had already been skirmishes on the streets. The trouble started on 14 April when police batoned to the ground Jim Edwards, a communist and Unemployed Workers' Movement activist, as he addressed the crowd, and batoned him again when he stood, bloodied, and exhorted them to restrain their anger – in vain. The crowd stripped the picket fence of the City Mission of its palings and broke 250 windows, leaving 'trails of loot hanging out like ends of sausages'.[22]

The next night Mason and Firth went into town and were in Karangahape Road, the working-class shopping area at the top of Queen Street, when trouble flared again, although it was less violent this time. The normal throng of Friday night shoppers had been swelled in expectation of another stoush; it was rumoured that the Huntly miners were coming to town. Mounted Waikato farmers rode up Queen Street in a dramatic but unnecessary show of strength. The crowd jostled with police, marines with fixed bayonets, and special constables – civilians armed with batons whom the government had been recruiting since March. A large number of students from the university and grammar schools were among those who enrolled: 'University riff-raff & such-like scum of the earth', Mason described them to Fairburn.[23] One was

Dan. Mason and Firth watched from the pavement as the girls from the factories of Newton hurled rocks and insults at the Grammar and King's boys. 'What an opportunity you missed of becoming a clean, decent citizen, and restoring yourself to respectability and public favour, when you omitted to join the specials!' Fairburn jested. 'What a Godsend for Dan!'[24] But even he felt he had missed something.

For Mason, the riots crystallised his political views. 'I have had it delicately hinted from high places that I am under special surveillance', he confided to Fairburn. 'Not that I have any real connection with the donnybrook – I only wish I had.' He wrote a few weeks later:

> You called yourself an anarchist in a recent letter. I have often thought of myself as one – in fact, I read all the Kropotkin I could lay my hands on & had a huge admiration for Bakunin six years ago almost. But it has no more to do with practical politics than the White Rose Leaguers or Monty's monarchism. When it comes to the business, the fight is Communism v Capitalism – it is that, we cannot help it – and my sympathies are with the Bolshies. If I had ever slit the navel-string binding me to the family, I should be a practical revolutionary. As it is, I can do nothing much, but try to help where I can.[25]

Not even Mason's discouraged and discouraging reports from the outpost, however, deflected Fairburn from his decision to come home, which he had reached by the end of July. He felt the need to justify this decision to his friends, listing six reasons including family, the political and economic situation, the English weather (1932 had seen the wettest summer there for forty years) and, not least, his loneliness and 'the promised joy of smelling your filthy tobacco smoke and hearing Clifton speak on grave matters'.[26] It was Mason he missed above all. 'My God, I wish I were nearer to you, mein friend!' he wrote in January that year.

> But you are 14000 miles away. Or 8000. . . . You know, I was just thinking of it today as I was digging in the garden. (This is March – the month of planting – and I am digging over the whole of our new garden.) I thought, here am I, at ten o'clock in the morning, in the middle of England, digging in my garden with a spade. Just twelve hours later there will be another fellow, standing feet to feet with me, 8000 miles away, digging in a garden in Ellerslie. Like two sentries, two sages, posted at opposite ends of the earth, watching

the decay of an era. . . . Curse it, but I do miss you dreadfully. I feel it – just as strongly as ever – as a bereavement, in the real sense of the word, to be away from you.

'Why have you written so seldom during the last year?' he demanded in June. 'It was four months since I heard from you last, until I got a letter last mail. I know you dislike writing . . . But I needed your letters – some sort of contact with you – very badly at times'. In July: 'No letter from you, so I suppose you are embroiled in a bloody revolution, or have taken that job.'[27]

MASON HAD, reluctantly, taken a job. In addition to some casual tutoring, for the next three or four years he was employed as company secretary for several business ventures in which Dan was also involved, working from a small and shabby office in the Premier Building on the corner of Queen Street and Durham Street East (opposite Whitcombe & Tombs), from which Dan was working as a sharebroker and a manufacturers' agent, with a company named Mason Sterling & Co. The building housed several lawyers, accountants and insurance offices and the Auckland Private Detective Agency. Mason's correspondence in these years – between 1932 and 1935 – was written on a variety of letterheads, including Kay Robot Air-Pilots Ltd, the New Zealand Underwriting and Development Corporation, Premier Bonds, Provident Bonds, Market Research Ltd and International Concessions, as well as Mason Sterling & Co, all with the same address. His friends were never quite sure just what the brothers' business was: something shady, many thought.

Official records for only two of these enterprises can be traced. Kay Robot Air-Pilots Ltd was a company floated in March 1934 to manufacture an automatic compressed-air stabiliser for aircraft, developed by the famous aviator Cyril Kay. It lasted in business for eighteen months, during which Kay's invention was overtaken by the development overseas of a gyroscopic stabiliser, the basis of the modern autopilot.[28] International Concessions Ltd, a more successful enterprise for a time, was possibly an initiative of Mason and Firth's. The company was registered in September 1932 and may have been some kind of sports-gambling venture. Mason was the secretary and Firth was employed as the promoter, receiving payment in shares; by the end of 1933 they had covered the country and sold nearly 40,000 shares. Dan was broker for both these companies. Another is believed to have been an illegal lottery franchise.[29]

Mason cannot have felt comfortable with participating in some possibly dodgy capitalist enterprise. He did not, in fact, really want a job at all, as he confessed to Fairburn, but had been under 'some slight social pressure' to take one. He was happy enough living at home on £1 a week, spending his mornings helping his mother around the house, his afternoons in the garden, his evenings reading and writing, going into town once or twice a week to see Firth and Marie and to visit the library, and waiting to hear news of *No New Thing*. 'If I had a book or so to my name (and maybe 20 quid odd) I could face the world, the flesh, and the family with a bolder front.'[30] But there was Jessie to support, and Dan's creditors to keep at bay.

Mason had also just been appointed the new editor of the university Literary Club magazine, which had been launched at the beginning of the year – and was to cease abruptly at the end of the next. This was not a paying job, but he was to invest much energy and expectation in it over the next eighteen months, and it brought him into contact with a group of younger writers who collectively were to form the core (or a good part of it) of the New Zealand literary establishment a decade on. He made friends here, and found literary supporters. It was his only formal connection with the university by then, for he had not enrolled that year – having given up for good, it would seem, the dream of a scholarship and perhaps an academic career.

The magazine was called the *Phoenix* – a 'bloody awful title', Pia Richards remarked to him in her characteristically frank way[31] – but it was at least an improvement on the editor's first suggestion, *Farrago*, in the aggrieved opinion of the magazine's founder, designer and printer, Bob Lowry. He had planned to be the editor as well but the secretary of the Literary Club, James Bertram, had 'snatched' it from him, for the time being: when Bertram left for Oxford in the middle of the year to take up a Rhodes scholarship, Lowry intended to snatch it back.[32]

Lowry was a second-year arts student, and aspiring printer, publisher and typographer, who had ambition and self-confidence to spare. He had bought himself a printing press while he was still a schoolboy at Auckland Grammar (a Golding hand platen and a single font), displaying a precociousness in his chosen field to match Mason's, and was well up with the modern revolution in typographical design and technology, with the work of Stanley Morison and the new Monotype fonts. It was Lowry who had approached the Literary Club committee in his first term in 1931 and offered to put his press and expertise at their disposal. A number of plans and ambitions were invested in the *Phoenix* – as would be much myth-making, subsequently, in the narrative of New Zealand literary history – to which Mason would add his own. Lowry's ambitions, covering all bases, were to start a revolution in the local printing and publishing industry (such as there was), to establish a New Zealand university press, and to encourage New Zealand literature. He also wanted to start a social and political revolution, and was to join the Communist Party in due course, although for the moment he was as interested in the ideas of the French philosopher Henri Bergson as he was in those of Lenin and Marx. 'This reconciliation of the intellectual and the emotional is to be the Big Mission of my Junior Adelphi next year (with a circulation of about 50). Ah, impetuous Youth!' he wrote to his schoolfriend and fellow printing enthusiast Denis Glover (who was at Canterbury College in Christchurch), modestly identifying his planned magazine as a successor to the monthly which John Middleton Murry and D.H. Lawrence had founded in 1923.[33] Although he didn't like the editor – 'Mr. Blooming Bertram', an 'affected coxcomb' with 'anaemic literary taste': 'He's going to spoil the whole business by making the rag the most hopelessly highbrow thing you ever saw in your life', he complained to Glover – they were at one on the philosophical affiliations of the magazine.[34] Its title, cover device and motto, the lofty statements and even the title of the introduction to the first number, which came out in March 1932, explicitly declared its allegiance to the spirit of the *New Adelphi*, 'the most distinguished literary periodical of the last decade'. The *Phoenix* would aim to sweep away the grey cloud and dusty air of Victorianism and Georgianism from New Zealand letters, as the English modernists had done in that country twenty years before. This was to be no ordinary undergraduate magazine: its purpose 'may be variously described – in descending order of grandiloquence – as the integration of national consciousness, the focussing of contemporary opinion upon local needs, the creation of cultural antennae, the communication of definite standards of taste, the "redeeming of the times"'.[35]

In keeping with these bold ambitions, the first number was heavy on comment and comparatively light on literature. Jack Bennett, another Rhodes scholar, wrote on the need for 'sincere and intelligent' criticism in New Zealand letters. Lowry, quoting Bergson, called for the integration of human consciousness through a synthesis of philosophy and literature. Bertram summarised Berdyaev's analysis, in *The Challenge of Russia*, of the fundamental opposition between communism and the individual. There was also a congratulatory foreword from D'Arcy Cresswell, who had just returned to New Zealand in the role of 'successful poet' and as such, for all his eccentricities (and the doubtful quality of his verse), became something of a role model for this younger generation. (Cresswell had been hawking his poems door to door and lane to lane around England several years before de Montalk and Fairburn, had earned considerable acclaim in London for his autobiography *A Poet's Progress* (1930) and was now busy shocking the locals with satirical essays in the Christchurch *Press*.)

It was all a little too serious and modish, the *New Zealand Herald* remarked, but then 'Most young people who are worth their salt are in revolt against something or other'. The *Phoenix* was a promising start, 'gaily-clad' and 'printed with industry and enthusiasm'.[36] Student reviews were less indulgent, complaining that the literary content did not match the editors' high-minded intentions. Mason described it to Fairburn as 'rankly smelling of the "Adelphi"', but for all its faults 'quite the best thing to date in N.Z.', and suggested that Fairburn contribute something on English literary life.[37]

Bertram had written to Mason in January asking for something for the first issue: 'anything – verse or prose, original work or criticism, even a piece of anything you've been saying (Laws for N.Z. Literature?) . . . you've *carte blanche* to write on James Joyce or Professor Anderson' (of philosophy, the most conservative of the college professors). 'I really shouldn't ask you to let your stuff appear in a rag', Bertram added shyly, addressing Mason as an elder poet: 'I honestly believe this will be quite good.'[38] He was still hoping for a short story in the second week of March, when the issue was already overdue. Instead Mason sent him a poem from *No New Thing*: 'Stoic Overthrow', a sombre, bleak poem which evokes a familiar spirit of pessimism in a mythical setting – the aftermath of a battle as a defeated army stoically waits for its people and land to be overrun. For the rest, though, the literary content of the first *Phoenix* was notable only for some of the earliest published poems of Allen Curnow, who had come up from Christchurch the year before (leaving a job on the *Star*) to enrol at St John's Theological College: 'he's quite a cut above ours', Lowry remarked to Glover.[39] Bertram was not yet so sure, finding Curnow's poems a little too Eliot-ish.

Mason did speak about Joyce, however, when he went down to Hamilton in May to give a lecture to a WEA class, at J.C. Beaglehole's invitation. His subject was 'Modernism in literature'. 'Bring in Aristophanes if you like, and be as rude as you like', Beaglehole had told him: 'a charge of dynamite on literature wd. do Hamilton good. I have no doubt that you can fire it.'[40] But it is hard to imagine that Mason would have scandalised even provincial Hamilton – although he may have challenged them – with his lecture, which was a sociological reading of the defining features of the literature of the past

forty years. It was a well-known paradox, he observed, that art from one age
to the next was both universal and particular: that 'A.E. Housman is the same
as Catullus, only different', and that 'qualities arousing wrath of old women
in petticoats against James Joyce are the same qualities of greatness as brought
querulous protests from moralists against Shakespeare'. 'Manners, morals,
clothes, institutions, twirl round like weathercocks or whirligigs in history,
but art remains – littera scripta manet', because it dealt with 'the strongest,
deepest, most abiding instincts of humanity'. This alone was the test of art,
while 'artificiality and shallowness, such as distinguish ages like the Augustan
or Victorian mean speedy death'. The great characteristic of the modern age
was the realisation of change, and the greatest poet of change, he argued – the
greatest of those who 'turn all their power to finding out more and more
about the stream', among them Lawrence, Yeats and Housman – was Joyce.
And of the social forces that had influenced the literature of the modern age
– including the decline of liberal-conservatism and the rise of socialism, the
emergence of women, and the declining power of the church – the most
important was the development of the science of psychology. The insights of
psychologists into the subconscious had produced 'a wise, deep, fine
interpretation of the human mind such as only the great Greeks ever dreamt
of in the past', which in turn had deepened and introduced an 'almost mythical'
dimension to literature, in the work, for example, of Joyce, Virginia Woolf
and Dorothy Richardson.[41]

   It was in his short stories, which he himself described (to one publisher) as
'fairly "advanced" psychological studies',[42] rather than in his poetry, that
Mason's interest in Joycean modernism at that time – in 'that fantastic twilit
jungle where amid the mops and mows of nightmare apes and owls Mr.
Joyce and the Lancashire lout prance hand-in-hand to the sweet pipings of
Professor Freud', as he jotted in his notebook – was most evident.[43] Not,
however, in the form of experimenting with stream-of-consciousness narrative
(apart from one piece of notebook parody). The second issue of the *Phoenix*
opened with the story Bertram had been hoping to get out of him for the
first, 'His End was Peace', and included a review by Bertram of prose writing
in the four university college literary reviews of 1931 which singled out Mason's
'Springtime and the Sick-bed' as the brilliant exception among the usual
mediocre and unmemorable lot. 'This seems to me a small masterpiece', he
wrote, 'perhaps a little Joycian [sic] (the early Joyce of *Dubliners*)', but Mason
was 'a strong enough individualist to absorb any such influence. This short
study of a man deserting an invalid wife is superbly nimble in conception,

and as inevitable in its movement as the death that is never far from its pages.'[44]
He looked forward – vainly, it was to prove – to a rumoured collected volume
of Mason's short stories.

By the time the second *Phoenix* appeared, dated July but in August, Bertram
had left for Oxford and Mason had been chosen as editor in his place. There
is no evidence that Lowry resented this, despite having coveted the position
for himself – indeed, he would later say that it was he who proposed Mason
for it, although others recalled that Bertram did. 'He's a crack-brained socialist,
with some literary ability', he reported enthusiastically to Glover, 'and he's
certain sure to land Phoenix into a rough-house with the College authorities',
something Lowry was looking forward to.[45] There were to have been three
*Phoenix*es a year (one each term), but Mason was formally appointed editor
only in October, and began planning for the next issue to come out in the
first term of 1933.

In the meantime, the 1932 *Kiwi* was out in the third term, with Mason's
'Christ on the Swag', 'Their Sacrifice' (a revised version of the poem from
'This Bird May Swing') and 'Youth at the Dance', a more recent poem in
which the bleak pessimism of 'Stoic Overthrow' has been replaced, it seems,
by a mood of revolutionary optimism – of redemption rather than defeat.
'Youth at the Dance' has been described as Mason's most explicitly 'political'
poem, the one which most directly expressed his 1930s left-wing convictions
– too simplistically so for most critics, who would prefer his spiritual uncertainty
to his political faith, although Curnow would appreciate its 'universal quality,
the echo of a pulse-beat of history in the poet's mind'.[46]

> Get your machine-guns manned
>   for a new way of war:
>   can you not understand
>   that here a foe is at hand
>   you have not fought before.
>
> Young blood, in the dance
>   you are graceful and well-groomed
>   and move with an elegance –
>   ah! is it not evil chance
>   that your blood and grace are doomed?

Come, young blood, leave your prattle
> for the machine-gun's chatter:
> now your tamed and trusted cattle
> turn like an old bull to battle
> and rip their lords to tatters.

The lone hand digging gum
> and the starving bushie out-back
> girls from the stews and the slum
> and the factory-hell . . . up they come
> to the tune of the devil's attack.

Their faces are more scarred
> than a miner's boot and rough
> as a quarry-face and as hard
> as a hammer-head, and good tarred
> canvas is not more tough.

Jean Alison, the secretary of the *Phoenix* committee – who was to become a close friend of Mason – would later speculate that the immediate inspiration for this poem was a chance meeting with her and some friends one evening when they were on their way to a dance. Mason declined to join them (he was a hopeless dancer, she recalled). Another friend remembered him being persuaded to go along and sitting in the gallery all evening watching the dancers with disapproval.[47]

IN OCTOBER Fairburn arrived home, with Jocelyn and their baby daughter, a pile of Social Credit pamphlets, and cartons of cigarettes which he smuggled past the customs officers in the baby's pram, whereas books by Tolstoy and H.G. Wells were confiscated. Mason was on the wharf to meet him, along with Firth. They resumed their old habits of walking and talking, of earnest, night-long disputations about poetry and politics, especially by this time the latter, about the wrongs of the world and what to do about them. But it was not the same, and it was not to last. Fairburn found relief work chipping weeds by the side of the road, and devoted his evenings to campaigning for the Social Credit movement. In 1934 he got another relief job as secretary of the Farmers' Union, which had become a leading proponent of Douglas Social Credit in New Zealand. Mason had no time for this. Monetary reform, he later wrote, 'was no great message to bring from abroad. The country was deluged with Douglasite outpourings. Infested with its devotees. You couldn't get down the street for them. . . . At every lamp-post someone would pin you down while he popped imaginary cheques into mythical banks and then ducked round the back to espy the banker creating credit.'[48] In retrospect he was to look back on Fairburn's espousal of Social Credit as 'damn nonsense'; at the time he regarded it as 'a form of betrayal'.[49] There was no sudden excommunication, however, rather a widening and lengthening distance: they simply saw each other less and less. 'While he was away, our opinions just sort of drifted apart', Mason reported to Teddy in April 1933, 'and now we disagree too much altogether.'[50]

Fairburn wrote a poem for Mason in England, which he had sent to him earlier that year, entitled 'Lines for a Revolutionary'. Mason would later read this as a tacit recognition that his path had been the right one and Fairburn's wrong, and as representing for Fairburn 'the parting of the ways'.[51] Or perhaps, rather, it was Fairburn's tribute to his friend's strength and clarity of conviction at a time when he was still struggling to find his own. The poem Mason had written for Fairburn, 'Ad Regem. To R.F.', belonged to an earlier time, to their younger selves, when poetry and youth bound them together more strongly than the politics that pushed them apart:

> They set up monuments on some public site
>   in crumbling stone, or perdurable bronze,
> to rescue one hour longer from the night
>   the memory of our local paragons.
>
> but what need we such paltry honour attain
>   to save us from that sea Oblivion,
> which, with its swirling waves and midnight mane,
>   across the poor, wrecked, past comes plunging on
>
> For I somehow think that we two silly devils
>   will be remembered when their metal's rotten,
> that men will read about our brainless revels,
>   our follies, when their wisdom is forgotten.[52]

11

Romantics and revolutionaries

1933

MASON WAS several years older than the students who worked on and gathered around the *Phoenix*: in his late twenties, and not a student any more himself. They knew him – some of them, at least – as a published poet; they had read his poems and stories in *Phoenix* and *Kiwi*, had possibly heard of *The Beggar* and *Penny Broadsheet*, and of his inclusion in Monro's *Chapbook* and anthology. For aspiring poets like themselves, he was an example to be admired or held in awe. But when they would later remember Mason from these *Phoenix* years it was first for the aggression and anger of his politics. 'He was so fierce', Jean Alison wrote in *Landfall* after his death:

> a crusading rebel filled with the controlled intensity of feeling which gave his poems their power. His long dark face expressed his nervous intense nature. His eyes could be compassionate or suffering but his full strongly-marked lips curled often in contempt. A home-made fag hung on his lower lip, accentuating with its smoke the frown between his tormented eyes. His coarse dark hair was cut short and stood upright like an iron crown. His manner of speaking and his words were often harsh and biting, his humour had a savage quality. I once commented to him that New Zealanders smiled too easily. Ron bared his strong carnivorous teeth and replied that the human smile was really a snarl, primitive man in us showing his fangs to frighten a possible enemy.

Yet his anger, she learned, was 'the rage of outraged tenderness'.[1]

She had first met Mason at her friend Elsie Farrelly's basement flat in Wynyard Street, just across the road from the *Phoenix* printery. Mason and Fairburn were there, and sat on the bed and argued about Social Credit and Marxism all night while the others sat on the floor and listened. (They never talked about their poetry, Elsie recalled.) She would remember being taken to Clifton Firth's 'modern flat' by Mason and Lowry and the young men explaining Marx to her, and sitting with Mason in the shadow of the Queen

Victoria statue in Albert Park while he read aloud from the *Communist Manifesto*, 'full of missionary zeal'. There was 'a certain grim aspect to him'.[2] Ian Milner, a fellow poet and radical, and editor of the Canterbury student newspaper and *Review*, met Mason briefly in Auckland in the summer of 1932, and would later describe him thus: 'Long, lean face, gashed lines below the cheeks, pugnacious nose, firm jaw, full sensual lips, but clenched in a hard line that could twist suddenly into a snarl of indignation, upstanding crop of jet-black hair . . . and the eyes, dark intense luminous, that looked straight at and into you' (like Jessie's). Like Jean Alison, he was struck by Mason's peculiar mixture of hardness and tenderness, posturing and nervousness: 'his sardonic toughness' was the other side of 'a reserve of compassion for human suffering, about which he knew a lot in his own life'.[3] 'I did not "swallow Marx whole" and from that build up my ideas of the world', Mason himself later said. 'I did learn the nature of society from observation and bitter experience. Later I discovered that the only philosophy which corresponded to practical reality was the Marxian.'[4]

While his new young friends may have been impressed, Pia Richards found his deepening political conviction tiresome. It was the fault of an over-developed ego, she thought: 'Your ideas (whatever they are – a mixture of crude nihilism with a truly touching & naïf idealism) have always been too young for your age. That is because you do not allow yourself to take advantage of other men's work & thought but insist on laboriously finding out things for yourself – (I wonder you don't dig with a stick or sleep on the floor until at the age of 70 a spade or a bed dawns in your inner consciousness).' He ought to stop thinking and read for a year – Aldous Huxley, and J.B.S. Haldane, Ford Madox Ford and Joseph Conrad – 'to make you feel smaller than even a New Zealander. And if you have to change some ideas – change them. Don't be afraid. I suppose you feel that it is a pity to waste them – but try & get over your Scotch ancestry.' She was missing his intellectual company. 'I should simply adore to have a conversation with you – it would be very stimulating', Pia wrote to him in October 1932. 'I think that since I have known you your interests have considerably narrowed – when you first came here in Miss Roussel's day you did not care so passionately about the lower classes or want so ardently to raise them to the bourgeois level as you do now.'[5]

PHOENIX WAS due out at the beginning of the first term, and Lowry wanted everything in by the end of January. At the New Year Mason was 'tearing his hair' with nothing in front of him except 'wads of second-rate verse'; Lowry printed 'some highly aesthetic rejection slips'.[6] The printery was in a small room in the basement of the university science building on Symonds Street, cramped and chaotic, 'its walls covered with triolets, lino-cuts, lampoons and Lowry jokes', prone to flooding when the chemists upstairs let their sinks overflow ('much paper was spoilt').[7] The first issue had been produced in even more exiguous circumstances – half on Lowry's own hand-press, the rest at a commercial printery in Paeroa when he was home for the summer holidays, using a motley collection of type, and he had been embarrassed enough by the result to print a disclaimer. For the second he had persuaded the Students' Association to buy a new press: not the new £285 Dawson, Payne & Elliot cylinder press he really wanted (the 'very latest' model), but a second-hand treadle-platen for a sixth of the price. But with this and a good supply of new type, along with experience, *Phoenix* improved typographically issue by issue. He changed its look too, while Mason changed the content. Lowry had set out to revolutionise local printing and book design, and it is fair to say that, in terms of *Phoenix*'s influence, he did.

Mason had accepted the editorship on the condition that he would have complete editorial control subject only to supervision by the *Phoenix* committee, which was a sub-committee of the literary committee of the Literary and Dramatic Club. Its members included Hector Monro, a future professor of philosophy whom Mason had known for four or five years, and Monro's best friend, future publisher Blackwood Paul – 'those strangely matched Dioscuri', Bertram would later describe them: Monro 'shaggy, solid', sharp and satirical, Paul 'light, tripping, with his pixie's face under dark hair and his gleaming spectacles'.[8] Other members were Allen Curnow, serious and self-assured and wont to 'declaim his latest poem at the drop of a hat'[9] – who knew of Mason only as the author of two sonnets in *Twentieth Century Poetry*, the anthology that had introduced him to Eliot and the Imagist poets; Jack Bennett, a brilliant classics scholar who was to become an Oxford don; Rona Munro, with whom Mason was for a while enamoured ('How lovely – I think your Miss Munro sounds delightful and just right for you', Pia Richards wrote approvingly[10]); and Jean Alison, the secretary, who worked in the university library and with whom most of the young men were in love (Mason too, in due course). He had made clear his objection to editing-by-committee and they met only rarely, in the printery or in one of the Students' Association rooms – once in the Haeremai Club room, where there were no chairs and they perched self-consciously on beer barrels while Mason led a discussion on how to encourage serious writers. They met at least once in the office of Mason Sterling downtown. It was here that Curnow first met him, 'sitting behind a little grille making out receipts on yellow paper'. When he introduced himself Mason pushed under the grille to him a poem, badly typed on the same yellow paper: 'Be swift o sun'.[11]

Lowry had been spoiling for a fight, and was not disappointed. Already the previous year the college had been embroiled in a series of controversies over academic freedom, precipitated not by the students but by members of the staff. A left-thinking lecturer in philosophy, R.P. Anschutz, had written a foreword to a pamphlet by Communist Party member Nellie Scott (wife of Sid Scott) recounting her recent trip to Russia. This provoked the ire of the Minister of Education: what, he asked the college authorities, was a person who had something good to say about the Soviet Union doing teaching in a New Zealand university college? 'The ten years that the Russians have spent getting out of their mess, we have spent in getting into ours', Anschutz had written, and he was hardly the only one thinking so at a time when Western countries were still in the grip of the Depression, the Soviet Union appeared to have solved unemployment, and many people with open minds – not only card-carrying communists – wondered why. Then, in May 1932, J.C. Beaglehole, by this time a lecturer in the History Department, and WEA director Norman Richmond sent a letter to the press entitled 'Communism and hysterics', prompted by the statement made by a judge when sentencing two men to six months' gaol for importing seditious literature, that it was the communists and their pamphlets who were responsible for the disorder that had just been witnessed on Queen Street. The *Herald* and the *Auckland Star* turned the letter down but it was published by the *New Zealand Worker*. Beaglehole and Richmond had also asked the college's ageing president, George Fowlds, to sign it. Instead he issued the famous Fowlds Memorandum, reminding his staff of their responsibilities in the exercise of academic freedom, which were, in his view, 'intimately related to the question of fitness for tenure'.[12] Beaglehole and Richmond formally protested and a few months later Beaglehole lost his job – which is to say, his temporary lectureship was 'retrenched' on the grounds of economy, prompting much suspicion and agitation. (Lowry was one of the history students who petitioned the college council on his behalf.) Many were outraged but few surprised when Beaglehole was not shortlisted for the vacant history chair at the end of the year.

Mason had been promised 'something rubicund' by Beaglehole and Richmond for his first *Phoenix*, but they were too tired, they said.[13]

Nevertheless there was still plenty to offend those who were easily offended. He prefaced it, mischievously, with a comment made by George Fowlds, at an earlier time in a long career of working for progressive causes, that unrest among the masses in the civilised world was justified by social conditions. Mason's editorial notes stated that this was 'our first regular issue', and in what he apologised was '[s]o long a statement of policy' made it clear that this *Phoenix* was different from the first. 'This is a forum, a battle-ground, an arena', open to any argument that was 'sufficiently active, vigorous, and stimulating' and well-written: 'Only please remember that this is 1933, the Five-Year Plan is a matter of history, not of argument, and Nudism has now been a matter of calm discussion with sensible people these many years. There is no room here for the spinsterish monasticism of the newspapers.' He intended *Phoenix* to be 'an organ of creative thought', as of course had the editors of the first *Phoenix*, but Mason's tone was more strident, his interests more political, his intentions more engaged.[14]

His editorial notes continued with a warning 'on the present trend of the Dominion. That trend is bad. Such social organisation as we had is breaking down. Slowly but steadily comes the advance of bankruptcy, poverty, misery, crime, insanity. An ever-increasing number of New Zealanders are being reduced to levels which would have turned the stomach of an Athenian slave.' With economic hardship, discontent 'grows apace'; with 'the intensification of depression comes an ever-deepening sense of crisis ahead'. The world was dividing into two hostile camps: those who feared the coming crash and were turning to fascism, and those who hoped for it and were turning to communism. 'This is no time to be studying the tonal value of the minor works of T.E. Brown. It is the greatest hour in history. . . . the hour for realism is at hand.'[15]

The new editorial style was matched by Lowry's typography. The type was larger and heavier (12 point Gill sans-serif); the page bigger, margins wider and paper thicker; the title page had a striking asymmetrical design, reminiscent of contemporary German typography; the phoenix was a more aggressive and stylised bird. (Lowry's friend Glover helped with the printing, having come up from Christchurch to compete in the boxing at the university Easter tournament.)

That most of the contributors to the issue were not students was, Mason explained, because the 'university men' had had, apparently, neither the time, energy nor inclination to write, rather than because of any policy of positive discrimination. But equally he had a broader, populist conception of the magazine in mind than merely an undergraduate literary review: 'We shall confine ourselves neither to the academic nor even to the business man. They may have the monopoly of privilege, they have no monopoly of wisdom. Rather it is true that there are as good brains to be found on the wharf, down the stokehold, in the slave-camp, in the mines'.[16] He included an article on 'Art in the world of crisis' by an unemployed friend, Jack Prince, who quoted Lunacharsky on Marxism and art, welcomed the revitalisation of art in the Soviet Union which was 'arising from the soil of the masses' (while bourgeois artists, the capitalist world crumbling around them, retreated into vagueness and inanity), and declared that, especially at this time while the new world was still to be won, art was propaganda. Clifton Firth contributed an aphoristic essay (the first part of two) on Russian cinema, which began as a primer on Marxism before analysing Western cinema as an instrument of exploitation, arguing that 'the cinema as an art-form is possible only in Russia' because there films were the voice of the people: whereas the Hollywood cinema was all 'Punch kick thrills heart-tugs sins and sadism', Russian films showed 'the actualities of workaday life'.[17] (Part two, in the following issue, would be a more challenging analysis of the theory and technique of avant-garde film-making.) An article entitled 'Free Men', 'an equally dogmatic dissertation on the Com-munist mechanist philosophy', in the opinion of the *Auckland Star*, was written by Firth and Mason (on Firth's initiative) under the pseudonym 'Group A'.[18]

Mason, as 'J.P.', contributed a scathing review of *New Zealand Plain Talk*, a new fortnightly paper promoting Social Credit, a movement he described as anti-Semitic and proto-fascist, a revolutionary-reactionary doctrine calculated to appeal to the desperation of the petty-bourgeoisie, whose misguided dreams of social advancement (on which the social stability of capitalism depended) had been dashed by the Depression; thus had the National Socialists risen to power in Germany. *Plain Talk*, not an official organ of the Social Credit movement, was an easy target for Mason's sharply sardonic pen – even its typography, which was 'as weakly sensational as the contents. Matter is thrown in higgledy-piggledy. . . . Types are jumbled in meaningless fashion. Paragraphs in italics are as common as swastikas or cartoons with hook-noses. Some pages are veritable hedgehogs of exclamation-marks.' He ridiculed the local 'Hitler-Douglasites' and their recent, inaugural national summer camp at Okoroire.[19] (Fairburn, who was to respond to Mason's review in the next issue, had been there.) Books briefly reviewed included *Soviet Russia and the World* by Cambridge economist Maurice Dobb, and *Experimental Cinema* No.4;

James Joyce and the Plain Reader, and *Introduction to Psycho-analysis for Teachers*; *Hunger and Love* by Lionel Britton, 'the first truly proletarian novel in England', and *New Zealand Best Poems* 1932, edited by Charles Marris, the first number of an annual anthology and showcase of new verse, in which the reviewer, James Bertram, found too much of the same old weakly derivative Georgian fare.

In its literary content *Phoenix* mark two was not so radically different from *Phoenix* one. There were no socialist poems or rhymes for the under-dog or proletarian novels in progress, or at least Mason had found none that he considered worth publishing. Insofar as the literary spirit of *Phoenix* was revolutionary, it was the same revolution, against the insipid kind of colonial versifying represented by Marris's *Best Poems* and Pope's *Kowhai Gold*, as Mason and Fairburn had been engaged on for several years already. Mason solicited two poems from Fairburn, one of which ('Deserted Farmyard') embarrassed the Professorial Board, which passed a motion expressing its strong disapproval of 'those portions of "Phoenix" which offend against the canons of decency and good taste'.[20] Both poems had been written in Clench Common and responded to an atmosphere of rural and social decay and psychological stress, a kind of desperate eccentricity, which had brought to Fairburn's mind – helped him to understand, he thought – the melancholy despair of Housman. There was a short story and a poem by Ian Milner, the one a gently sardonic tale of youthful idealism in conflict with social reality, the other an elegy for the dead of the last war.

Mason's contribution was 'In Manus Tuas, Domine', from his still-languishing collection *No New Thing*. This poem was thematically similar to 'Stoic Overthrow', evoking an impending catastrophe, but with a stronger register of foreboding and fear; it had a mythical feeling lent by its classical allusions but a very immediate sense of urgency and panic. Here was none of the upbeat socialist optimism of 'Youth at the Dance', but it expressed no less the spirit of the time.

> O Christ our Lord, where art thou tarrying?
>> our enemies have girdled us about
>> enclosed us in a little narrowing ring
>> put all our faint-heart allies to the rout:
>> nightly and day obscenities they sing
>> our piety towards thee to mock and flout:
>> now now if ever is it time, o King,

to put thy hand forth to save thy few devout.
Lord, Lord, not the wickedest child our dames have borne
the most ungrateful in our whole wide land
would see us perish in this hope forlorn
and not so much as raise a little hand,
if doing that would rescue us from the scorn
of conquerors death or the captive brand:
save thou then, Lord, or our nation's waning horn
shall perish utterly with this our band.

Nine hundred years, Lord, faithfully we have served
we and our fathers full nine hundred years,
in direst tribulation we have not swerved
in trial in pagan war in blood in tears:
thinkest thou we at our death-gasp have deserved
to call on him who sways the world, yet not hears
but leaves his flock to the kind mercy of the curved
scimitars and sharp hissing swords and straight spears?

Thou wilt not let these foul swine in to swill
in our old cities, spoiling the whole sum
of forty generations' toil . . . the shrill
locust-like trumpets why have they ceased their hum,
as ere a storm the singing winds grow still
and all the woods unnaturally are dumb . . .
o Lord our Christ, they are storming up the hill:
curse you, o Christ, a continent they come.

THE ISSUE came out late, with two pages missing, replaced by an inserted slip informing readers 'that the article which formerly occupied pages 35 and 36 has been removed by order of the Students' Association Executive of the Auckland University College'.[21] Here was the stoush that Lowry had been hoping for, but it was not after all with the university authorities. The magazine had been printed and a few copies already bound when the president of the Students' Association, Martin Sullivan – an arts and theology graduate who had just been appointed to his first ministry – visited the printery, read the proofs, and demanded that the article be removed. (It was an action he would look back on years later, when he was Dean of St Paul's in London and writing his memoirs, with astonishment.) Lowry stole the pages back from the locked room where Sullivan had hidden them, but the forces of squeamishness and suppression prevailed, much to Mason's delight. Two hastily convened meetings of the executive endorsed the president's stand, while Mason and Lowry secured the right to draw attention to this flagrant display of 'moral indignation and virtuous obscurantism'[22] and violation of freedom of expression with their explanatory insert, which left everyone wondering what the offending article had been about.

That was a good question. Entitled 'Groundswell', it was a short, densely written, confusing mixture of sexual-psychological, economic and political analysis, which seemed to be arguing that New Zealand could only free itself from its colonial condition (of 'physical and mental masturbation') and inherently reactionary culture ('we are breeding little Fascists furiously out of our decay') by releasing 'the pent splendid force of sex'.[23] Whatever the point, it was two words in particular that Sullivan took offence at, as Mason later recounted: one 'a grim pun on the fact that syphilis has been forced by European imperialism on the weaker peoples of the world', the second 'the scientific term for the trick practised by Onan as explained in Genesis xxxviii.9' – namely, syphilisation and masturbation.[24] The author was Eric Cook, a former student, unemployed teacher and member of the Communist Party ('a quiet, swarthy young man living in Christchurch, reputedly under the grandstand at the Riccarton Racecourse', Mason later described him); he intended to continue with 'a more detailed strategic survey' in forthcoming issues.[25] Mason didn't particularly like the article (nor did Lowry), but thought it was well written and provocative, and Cook was a stalwart of the left-wing movement – 'self-sacrificing, tireless and utterly devoted to any such radical cause'.[26] They printed the article separately as a broadsheet, while *Phoenix* itself sold out.

The weekly tabloid *New Zealand Truth* helped things along with its front-page banner headline of 31 May: 'N.Z. Universities Hotbeds of Revolution. Red hot gospels of highbrows', adorned with a cartoon depicting flames leaping from the top of a red-brick building, over an article deploring the 'sneers, jeers, bellicose blasphemies, red rantings and sex-saturated sophistries of young men and women who are graduating to become the leaders of the community tomorrow' – a piece of invective and paranoia that was impressive even by *Truth*'s standards.[27] It was not only, although primarily, *Phoenix* which had provoked this outburst. In April Canterbury's version of the *Phoenix*, *Oriflamme*, had been banned after its first issue because of an article entitled

'Sex and the undergraduate', and in May the militantly left-wing paper of the Free Discussions Club at Victoria University College, *Student*, was suppressed by the Students' Association. Sex and sedition, it seemed, were breaking out everywhere. Mason was only partly amused. 'Yes, Truth is a scream', he remarked to Jack Stewart. 'But, to my mind, no funnier than the Herald or Star under similar circumstances – and a bloody side more frank.'[28]

Other commentators were less choleric: disapproving, perhaps, but not shocked by *Phoenix*'s polemical turn. The *Star* thought its determination to be a battleground of ideas admirable, but it was a shame that 'They have allowed their "arena" to be narrowed to a Communist's soap box': praising the Soviet Union was quite all right, so long as there was some balance (the paper speculated that the suppressed article may have contained 'a too-violent attack on Stalin').[29] Similarly, Charles Marris in *Art in New Zealand* commended 'the iconoclastic zeal of our colleagues' but found the articles 'pontifically rhetorical, intense and unsatisfying'; he did not like Mason's poem.[30] The weekly *New Zealand Observer* was also generous to *Phoenix*'s 'rebellious' spirit, albeit in slightly mocking tones: 'it takes itself terribly seriously'. Firth's contributions provided an easy target for mockery. Mason's and Fairburn's verse was judged 'first-rate'.[31] All reviewers agreed that the design and illustrations – bold, angular wood- and lino-cuts – were superb.

Truth aside (and the Catholic review *The Month*, which dourly observed, under the heading 'Objectionable Papers': 'We have read the March number, and found it inexpressibly dull and empty of serious thought, the product of the saxophone mind'),[32] Mason's makeover of *Phoenix* caused more consternation inside the college than outside. Hector Monro in the student newspaper *Craccum* regretted that the evangelists of the new faith, 'so aggressively conscious of being the chosen people . . . should have been given a pulpit by the literary club, which has, after all, other work to do', and had unqualified praise only for Mason's review of *Plain Talk*, 'a really brilliant piece of writing' (which was so well received, in fact, that Lowry reprinted it as a 2d pamphlet).[33] Even before the issue had come out Monro and John Mulgan, apparently already suspicious of Mason's intentions, had called for a meeting of the Literary Club committee to discuss its policy in relation to *Phoenix*; and it was Mulgan who moved at an emergency meeting of the Students' Association executive in April that 'Groundswell' be deleted or the entire issue suppressed. Early in May the *Phoenix* committee met and passed a motion put by Lowry and Allen Curnow confirming its full confidence in the editor. But it also resolved, on a motion from Curnow and Monro, 'THAT the policy of this magazine be expressed in the balancing as nearly as possible of the quantity of poems, lino cuts and stories published with the quantity of miscellaneous articles of a political, sociological and critical nature and that efforts be made to secure the best available material of both kinds.' An earlier, more censorious motion (that 'In the opinion of this committee the prime purpose is the publication of original creative work and that articles of a political, sociological and critical nature should be definitely subordinated') had been defeated.[34] In fact, the proportion of original literary material to political and critical articles was slightly higher in Mason's issues than in those edited by Bertram – but that was not entirely the point.

'Yes, I am still father to the "Phoenix"', Mason wrote to Jack Stewart in June, ' – or, at any rate, am responsible for the juicy bits in it. There is a committee that cramps my style most horribly, or otherwise I should make things really move. As it is, I do all I can in the face of the Students' Association, the Literary Club, the Phoenix committee, the College Council, the Prof. Board, the University Senate, public opinion, King George, Rex Fairburn, and Jehovah.'[35]

HIS SECOND issue came out in June, and was very much on the same lines as the first, in both its content and its contributors. There was no sign that he was mellowing: 'Communist it is, and Communist it will remain', the *New Zealand Observer* remarked.[36] Along with the second instalment of Firth's dissertation on Soviet cinema, and a review by him of Eisenstein's *Que Viva Mexico*, there was a contribution from Jack Prince on Maxim Gorky, revolutionary and literary hero of the Russian people; an article by Jack Stewart on the famous Oxford Union debate of January 1933 (in which the motion had been passed 'that this House will in no circumstances fight for its King and Country') and why the English universities were turning red; a review of John Strachey's *The Coming Struggle for Power* by Norman Richmond; an exposé of the recently formed and right-wing New Zealand Legion; and an article by Blackwood Paul entitled 'Crankishness in religion', on the current upsurge of religious cults and fringes (which attracted the most favourable notice).

Mason's editorial notes began, as he could hardly resist, with a sarcastic dig at *Truth*: 'We have always admired that great instrument of emancipation and enlightenment. There is something at once so restrained, so radiant, so like Aurelius or St Francis, so (if we may say it) Christ-like about *N.Z. Truth*. Ever does that God-gifted organ-voice of New Zealand roll in honour of decency, respectability, chastity, God, king, country, and slave-camps.' But the matter was one for serious comment: 'More than ever is New Zealand coming under the sway of fear', he warned, and 'Those men to whom we should turn for stability, they are often panic-gripped worst of all. We do not ask our elders to see eye to eye with us, we only ask them to let us see.' Noting the banning also of *Oriflamme* at Canterbury, he observed: 'It may be argued that the objection is to frankness on sexual matters, leaving us free to talk politics as we will. That is rot, for the two aspects of life are bound up so intimately in a thousand ways. . . . Sex is the very basis of social life'.[37] His concern here was not only the prudish narrow-mindedness of the readers of *Truth*, but the larger question of the connection between sexual and social relations. It was a subject he had explored in his novel 'Dreams Come True' and in 'This Bird May Swing', and in a longer note on the banning of 'Groundswell' that he did not publish. Sex, 'Verboten. Taboo', was 'not the most urgent question in the world to-day, but it comes a good second to the politico-economic.' Out of the revolution, he hoped, 'will emerge some form of marriage more suited to human requirements than crude monogamy'.[38]

His commentary on general affairs this time was wider-ranging, and no less grim. 'The State is . . . slowly edging towards Fascism', he observed darkly. The old political groupings were breaking up, and in their place 'Leagues, societies, Legions and Associations thrive and more spring up every month' – fascists, by whatever name: 'You must remember that the first essential of a Fascist is unconsciousness and most of them do not so much as know that they are Fascists. That is revealed by scientific analysis ("A rat doesn't know it's a rat, but it is one all the same.")' It was some encouragement, however, that working-class militancy was also on the rise, evidenced by the respectable showing made by the Communist Party in the recent municipal elections, and the seamen's strike. He saw alarming evidence of growing anti-Semitism in New Zealand: 'The idea that there is a "New Zealand Spirit" which will prevent our ever imitating Germany is all my eye. Granted similar economic conditions we should act in much the same way. Women, Jews, artists and workers would do well to remember that.' The cruel fact of 'Poverty by the side of Plenty', not only here but in 'dear old Mother England', led him to muse on the colonial cringe:

Will our native-born writers *never* grow tired of flogging themselves into an intensely respectable ecstasy over a country they know only at second-hand? Will these sweet romantic souls go on until the end of time galvanising themselves into officially-inspired frenzies whenever they read that some English village is named Ousle-in-the-Wold? . . . And finally will they *never* learn that intelligent Englishmen only laugh at them for doing it?

This led him in turn to quote Marx on Edward Gibbon Wakefield and explain how colonisation was a capitalist adventure, which led in turn to a brief note about Samoa.[39] Denis Glover, reviewing this issue in the Canterbury student newspaper, captured his tone well: 'As controversialists and propagandists the *Phoenix* is far and away the best that New Zealand can boast of. . . . In his notes [Mason] ranges like a hungry lion up and down the field of New Zealand life and politics, and he makes his kill every time. His style is striking and his humour savage.'[40]

The literature, again, was different – indeed more so. There was poetry by Curnow, Milner, Beaglehole, C.R. Allen (an older, blind Dunedin writer of nostalgic, mannerist verse), and from Mason himself 'Amores VI', his love poem for Teddy – 'easily the best piece of literature in the magazine', Glover remarked, 'a love poem of great beauty'.[41] Jean Alison thought so too: 'Only one decent thing in it – a charming poem of Mason's', she wrote to Blackwood Paul. 'I've grown so suspicious of M. that I read the thing through three times thinking it must be Communist propaganda in a very subtle form. It isn't however – entirely simple and sentimental and very refreshing.'[42]

The Students' Association executive, however, had had enough, and now tried to have Mason removed. The association's constitution, they reminded the Literary Club, stated that officers of clubs and societies must be *bona fide* students. Mason was not. The *Phoenix* sub-committee agreed to pay Mason's Students' Association fee for him, but this decision was not ratified by the Literary Club committee when it met the following day. Sullivan (who was a member of the Literary Club) moved unsuccessfully that they dissociate themselves from *Phoenix*, which was no longer carrying out 'the policy or the wishes of the Club', and that it be handed over to an affiliated society. Instead the committee passed a motion, put by Mulgan and seconded by Lowry (an unexpected but presumably strategic alliance on the part of Lowry, who was anxious to save his magazine) which would have constrained Mason's editorial independence: 'that a recommendation be made to the *Phoenix* committee that no editorial be published, that all articles be signed, that literary matter be not less than half the contents, and that political articles be written to show differing points of view.'[43]

Mason had another idea: to take *Phoenix* away from the university

altogether, although precisely what this involved is not clear. It appears that
he put some such proposal to the Students' Association executive in June. A
draft legal document surviving among his papers, dated 8 July 1933 and
appointing Mason 'sole broker to a public company of £10,000 . . . to be
floated by us to take over the NEW WORLD PUBLISHING COMPANY of Auckland',
may have been related to this.[44] He had also been talking to Robin Richards
about the market for political journals in England.

FOR MASON, *Phoenix* was part of the larger political struggle. In July and
August, while he was preparing his next issue, he corresponded with two
students in Wellington, Gordon Watson and Alfred Katz, both members of
Victoria's Free Discussions Club which had produced the brief and banned
Student. They had written to Mason to congratulate him on *Phoenix*: 'a triumph
of maturity, vigour and directness', Katz complimented him, to which Mason
dourly replied: 'I suppose it is fair going for this bloody backwash of a country,
but it is far from satisfying me yet. It has millions of faults, but I fear most of
them will remain, as I am up against so many difficulties – not the least of
them my own abominable psychological difficulties as an incurable romantic.'[45]
Katz acknowledged the failure of *Student*: 'I think we did some good,
penetrated through the tough crust and hazy fascism to make some converts.
We failed because we were afflicted with the infantile sickness [romanticism],
and were poor Bolsheviks: we had less student support than we had
conceived.'[46]

Katz had been up to Auckland not long before and had met Mason and
Lowry and Firth. He had been fired up by coming in contact with like-
minded people: with others who were interested in the relationship between
art and politics, who 'have made a blending of the art and the science, who
have derived, that is, creative stimulus from social inspiration'. It was Gordon
Watson, however, who was to dedicate himself completely to the cause. After
graduating MA with honours in classics and English in 1934, he would choose
not to pursue the academic career that was his for the taking but instead go to
work full-time for the Communist Party, which he joined towards the end of
1933. He became a member of the national executive in 1934, and edited the
Party paper for most of the rest of the 1930s. Here was a rare example in New
Zealand, along with Mason himself, of the intellectual-turned-activist, the
poet-and-revolutionary, a representative figure of the 1930s left but one which
existed more in myth (or intention) than reality. By contrast, Katz, as he
confided to Mason, was struggling to find his own level of commitment:

struggling with 'my congenital mental laziness' and 'the business of romance vs. reality about which I'm intellectually but not emotionally convinced. . . . For all the talk I'm nothing but a poor romantic bourgeois intellectual trying to kid myself I'm a realist. What can a man do? Do you know?'[47] On one level he was articulating the fundamental dilemma which confronted the left-wing artist or writer or intellectual in the 1930s, and more and more urgently so as the decade wore on: how to reconcile the demands of personal and public responsibility, the creative and the political impulse. It was also a personal problem, which Mason recognised. He didn't know what a man could do, but he did understand.

To Watson, on the other hand, he replied with a long letter discussing strategies for building the radical movement, in the first instance in the university, in a programme of which he clearly saw *Phoenix* as a part:

> Not as a matter of personal pride, but as a practical suggestion, I may say that I think my technique in making the University carry that baby was very sound. To put it in a few words, it consists of beating them on their own ground – first of all, in establishing superiority over any of them in literary matters and so gaining the position: secondly, in keeping all the rules which they have established: thirdly, insisting that they in return keep their own rules.

The aim of magazines like *Phoenix* and *Student* and of the radical clubs should not be to build a mass left-wing student movement, since the mass of students 'will always be fascistic dolts'. *Truth* and its gullible readers, he correctly observed, had been 'fools to make so much fuss about reds in the Universities' (who were so few) corrupting the nation's future leaders. Rather, the 'great aim should be to use University facilities to help the workers'. He did not mean by this only capturing control of student magazines and printing presses (as, in this context, he seemed to regard his editorship of *Phoenix*), but building within the universities an intellectual vanguard of the left. Watson's programme was 'the unification of student radical activity' – a national conference of student Labour clubs was planned – and Mason, somewhat in the manner of the experienced elder, offered him advice. Build the movement solidly, slowly and secretly, he told him. Establish 'independent organisations to stiffen up the opposition of liberals, pacifists, and christian socialists to fascism. Hold them up straight so that we can snipe from behind them.' 'Aim at capturing the key positions by sheer superiority' and recruit only 'the very best type of student' – 'We have some excellent young men and girls in up here already. They are only learning, but they have brains and are true rebels and not mere belly-slaves.' And 'Remember always that the revolution is not likely to be made in this country next week nor even next year.' In all matters (referring now to the left at large) they must be realists. 'The whole militant proletarian movement in N.Z. seems to me to have suffered in the past from revolutionary romanticism and left-wing lyricism, giving way at times to right-wing apathy, as despair inevitably succeeds hope. . . . The whole thing was too unreal, too much in the nature of a dream in which oratory played the part of dream-fulfilment.' Now, however, things were changing. 'Doubtless the rise of Douglas-fascism and Legion-fascism has brought us to our senses. We must build more solidly, even if more slowly, making sure of every position, leaving no enemy territory in our rear.' He signed the letter 'Yours fraternally'.[48]

Some time during the year he joined either the Young Communist League or the Communist Party, as did Firth, Firth's wife, Patricia, and Lowry, prompted by Hitler's accession to power in Germany in January 1933. Lowry was to be expelled after about a year for 'frivolity', and Mason and Firth, it appears, were thrown out as well. Exactly what the extent of Mason's involvement with the Communist Party was at this time – whether and for how long he was a member of the Young Communist League, and whether, and for how long, he also became a fully fledged member of the Party – is not clear. Members of the Young Communist League were not card-carrying Party members, although in theory they would go on to become so. Joining the Party proper, according to the rules laid down by the 1933 national conference, was a serious affair. It required first a written application, giving a statement of one's connection with the working-class movement; the application had to be endorsed by two members of the branch (the 'area group' or 'factory cell') in question; there had to be a majority vote after the prospective member had been 'interrogated'; and payment of a one shilling entrance fee and weekly dues of 3d (or 2d if unemployed).[49] It was easier to be expelled than to join, and it was not unusual to be expelled more than once. To describe the Party as rigorous, dour, prone to factionalism and suspicious of students, poets and intellectuals is a cliché, but largely true. It was primarily interested in recruiting its members from the ranks of factory workers and, of necessity, the unemployed, and in building a militant vanguard in the trade union movement, not the universities. Tiny though it was, its organisational structure ('democratic centralism') was an elaborate business. Discipline was a serious matter.

The Young Communist League was slightly more relaxed. The eligible age for membership was from sixteen to thirty. Frank Sargeson, who was on relief work, growing tomatoes in his Takapuna garden and yet to start writing the short stories for which he would soon become known, was briefly a member in 1932–33, as he later recorded in his memoirs: it was at this time that he first met Mason. Older by a few years than Mason, he was expelled as soon as he turned thirty. He recalled writing and distributing propaganda leaflets, fearing discovery by plainclothes police, street marches, beach demonstrations, picnics and parties. His fellow members were 'odds and ends . . . from about the suburb and its fringes, two sisters who were in service with well-to-do housewives, a young grocer's assistant, an out-of-work journeyman jeweller, the jobless young son of a keen trade unionist carpenter'.[50] Mason, though, was involved with what appears to have been, formally or informally, the university branch. Stephen Champ, a young Englishman who was teaching at the Elam School of Art (and did woodcuts for the last *Phoenix*), would later recall being introduced by Hector Monro to Lowry, and in turn to Mason and Firth, and invited by them to join 'a Marxian Socialist Group of mainly ex-University students – in fact a group of the then young Communist party'.[51] Alfred Katz when he wrote to Mason in 1933 also referred to the Marxist study group Mason had organised at the university – he thought it was a Friends of the Soviet Union (FSU) group.

It is quite likely that Mason joined the FSU, a 'fraternal' organisation the Party had been instrumental in establishing in 1931–32 (and, like the Party, a local branch of an international movement). The membership of the FSU was both larger and wider than the Party's: around 1000 in 1933, by its own count, with 200 in Auckland, including left-leaning university lecturers such as Anschutz, and the newly appointed professor of English, Arthur Sewell. It had twenty-six branches nationwide, and distributed literature, held meetings and organised lecture tours to counter the 'slander campaign' against the Soviet Union being waged by the capitalist press. Gordon Watson was the national secretary and edited its monthly *Soviet News*. The Auckland headquarters were in an upstairs hall across the road from the Newton Post Office on Karangahape Road; public meetings were held on Sunday nights and a Russian-language class on Tuesdays. Mason had been invited to speak there on intellectuals in the Communist Party in November 1931. ('If there is one thing on this earth I know less about than another it is Soviet Literature', he remarked to Fairburn.[52])

Did Mason also join the Communist Party? His obituary in the *People's*

Voice, written by a onetime general secretary and personal friend, would say that he did, in 1933, as would Firth. On the other hand, Connie Soljak, then the sixteen-year-old secretary of the Auckland Young Communist League, would later explain: 'Whether Ron was a card holder I don't know but he was in with the University Branch but at that time most either were or floating around or else under instruction not to join.'[53] As difficult as it is to be certain now, so Mason, it seems, was ambivalent about his position then, for he stressed in his letter to Gordon Watson that he did not want to be publicly associated with Watson's plans for building the student left. 'Do not mention this letter, do not use my name, and see that this does not get into anyone else's hands. . . . Generally, try not to spread the rumour that I run Phoenix or that I am connected with the radical students' movement.'[54]

IT WAS NOT Mason's politics, though, that brought about the demise of *Phoenix*, however much they fuelled the suspicion and opposition of the student authorities and the Literary Club. During July and August he was busy soliciting and preparing copy for the next issue. Alfred Katz had promised reviews of John Dos Passos's novel *1919* and cartoonist David Low's *Russian Sketchbook*, and was working on an article on 'the bankruptcy of individualism' for a later issue. Watson was writing something too. 'I like stuff written in the most vigorous praise or blame', Mason told Katz, ' – black be black, white white, and above all red, red.'[55] Beaglehole regretted that he had 'nothing at the moment but non-controversial verse & a short history of N.Z. You wdn't like a series of portraits of Grey, Seddon, Reeves & Massey? I am trying to get the Art in N.Z. people to publish it & the N.Z. Legion to buy it. It is a little inoffensive essay in Marxian interpretation – but for safety's sake I don't say so. I hope indeed it has enough long words to be considered thoroughly bourgeois.'[56] From Sydney Jean Devanny, author of the banned New Zealand novel *The Butcher Shop* and a prominent member of the Communist Party of Australia, sent an account of her visit to the Soviet Union in 1931; Mason had approached her through Miriam Soljak – Connie's mother, a longtime activist in the women's branch of the Labour Party and now in the Communist Party. Jean Alison wrote a review of *Douglasism or Communism?* by Sid Scott (originally to have been titled 'Whither Douglas? Hold your horses major'), which Lowry had printed in August for the Party.

Mason himself reviewed *Snobbery with Violence*, de Montalk's account of his experience in prison, which had been published by Wishart in London and well received there. Mason's review too was generous, looking back affectionately to the time when de Montalk had delighted in provoking 'the abhorrence of those prudes, the New Zealand middle-classes', and pleased to find that the 'rather crude, aggressive egotism of de Montalk's earlier work has mellowed' (although he was 'still too inclined to take individuals as final causes, not seeking deeply "to find out the causes of things"').[57] There was also a review by Hector Monro of Nelle Scanlan's novel *Tides of Youth*, the second in her *Pencarrow* saga of family life in Wellington, along with a survey of drama in Auckland and a scathing write-up of a Brahms centenary concert by Rex Fairburn's brother Geoff – suggesting an intention on Mason's part to broaden the appeal of the magazine with a view to establishing it as independent of the university.

In the meantime Lowry had been busy printing a volume of poems by Allen Curnow, *Valley of Decision*, which appeared as a 'Phoenix miscellany' – a stylised phoenix adorning the title page – in September. The 'decision' of the title was Curnow's to abandon his theological studies. Later he was to thank Mason for encouraging him to have this, his first book, published.[58] Lowry had also printed the 1933 *Kiwi*, which contained a short story by Mason, 'The Meth Fiend', another from the collection 'Men and Things'. This was not a 'psychological study', however, but a piece of social realism, featuring Grafton at night, an old wino, and a subtle allusion, perhaps, to the deadbeat-outcast-Christ.

Three galley pages of *Phoenix*, Volume 2, Number 3 had been printed by the third week of September, when Lowry all of a sudden left town – with Elsie Farrelly, who was hitchhiking down to Wellington for the meeting of student Labour clubs that Gordon Watson had convened. 'Auckland has got too much for me and I'm coming South', Lowry wrote from Te Kuiti to Denis Glover in Christchurch, where he was headed, with the idea of activating their long-standing plan to set up a publishing business together. 'Overwork has taken my nerves so badly that I can't think straight to clear up the mess, and I'm cutting my losses.'[59] Mason had tried to dissuade him: the issue was all but ready for printing, and if they could just get this one out they might be in a strong enough position, 'the way public support was growing', to establish *Phoenix* on its own – as, just possibly, they could have. No circulation figures have survived, but in Curnow's memory 250 copies of the first two numbers had been printed, 750 of Mason's two. He had even managed to secure one advertisement: for Rowlatt and Moore, a small bookshop in Wellesley Street East run by a socialist, Eve Moore (a founding member of the New Zealand Fabian Society). But to no avail. Cutting and running was a very Lowry thing to do in the face of trouble, Elsie Farrelly later commented: 'Throughout the hitchhike he acted like a small boy released from after-school detention.'[60] When they got to Wellington she lent him his ferry fare.

According to Mason, the mess Lowry was fleeing included 'an abortive affair with one of the girls associated with "Phoenix"',[61] but the main cause of his problems was more mundane: his inability to keep either his own or the press's financial affairs in order. He had already been in debt to the Students' Association by some £40 at the end of 1932. When they requested, in the wake of the 'Groundswell' controversy, that he submit quarterly estimates he flatly refused. His final mistake, however, was printing the Sid Scott pamphlet, not because of its author or content, but because his contract stipulated that he must not use the *Phoenix* printery for outside work. The pamphlet had in fact been considered by the *Phoenix* sub-committee, but (according to the Students' Association's business manager, Percy Postlethwaite) authority to publish it was never given; and, while the colophon may have given Lowry's home address as the place of publication, he had no printing press there. When he was formally reprimanded by both the executive and the college registrar, Lowry sought to renegotiate his contract, a move which the executive, with considerable relief, interpreted as his resignation.

When the dust settled and an investigation had been made, Lowry was found to have left behind some £342 in debts. Blackwood Paul got up a collection to cover his personal share of it, which came to £72, contributing £41 himself. Mason paid 'all I could afford . . . and, as for Bob personally I have given him a bit of a hand privately and shall probably do a bit more as I can', he wrote to Paul in April the following year. 'I think that no really serious sin remains on our collective conscience.'[62] There were more serious repercussions for Lowry than the money, however: when he got back to Auckland in February 1934 he found that his scholarship had been revoked and he had been suspended *sine die* from the university.

12

No New Thing

1934

NINETEEN THIRTY-THREE had been a 'damnably busy year', as Mason remarked to Katz and Watson, and not only on account of *Phoenix*.[1] He had moved house early in the year, to 7 Herbert Road in Mt Eden: about six doors down from their old place, he told Teddy, which suggests that they were letting the big house in Ellerslie already. In May and June he presented a radio series with Norman Richmond in the WEA's Thursday 'Evening Talks' slot on 1YA, on 'The Development of Political Ideas'. Mason surveyed the history of political thought from the Athenians to the Victorians in six programmes (and received favourable reviews in the *Radio Record*), while Richmond dealt with Marx up to the present in the following five. The WEA had had a regular schedule on the state-owned YA stations since 1932, subject to the policy of the Broadcasting Board that nothing controversial be discussed on the air. Mason feared the worst when he was called in to the 1YA office one day, only to be told that he had infringed a ban on advertising by referring too specifically to a book on communism.

In September he approached Dave Faigan (still at Holl's) with a proposal that they collaborate on a pamphlet about anti-Semitism. The Auckland Jewish congregation, of which Faigan was a member, would cover the bare cost of publication by guaranteeing to purchase a portion of the 5000 pamphlets, which Lowry would print. 'Already in New Zealand this rottenest of superstitions has taken hold', Mason wrote to Faigan. 'I cannot impress on you too strongly that a continuance of crisis here may release elements just as ignorant and brutal as Hitler's basher-gangs.'[2] However, either he never wrote the pamphlet or Lowry never got around to printing it. At the end of the year he attended the WEA summer school at Paerata again and gave a full series of lectures, this time on 'French literature since the revolution'. He had also been involved in founding the Auckland Film Society in September; Firth was the secretary. Its office address was 1 Durham Street East, the same as Dan's.[3]

There was fun and friendship, too, not only politics and work. The

Richardses had moved from Tauranga to Takapuna in 1933, and Mason became a regular visitor and the children's favourite. He also taught Mark Richards briefly that year when relieving at Takapuna Grammar School. Mark would later regard him as a mentor when he began writing poetry himself. He remembered Mason from this time as a familiar and friendly presence, writing and putting on plays with the family; and his striking appearance, with his 'very black rather sparse-looking hair cut en brosse . . . exactly like a clothesbrush upside down'. And Jessie, 'a black-haired dragon, alternately demanding and dying', while '[s]omewhere in the background there was the sinister presence and threat of his elder brother, Dan, who seemed to have criminal leanings . . . a dark, fat, toadlike man with a specious bonhomie'.[4]

On weekends he accompanied Jean Alison and Elsie Farrelly and their friends to Anawhata, north of Piha on Auckland's wild west coast, where the students rented a hut for a shilling a night. Lowry, Hector Monro, Curnow and Dick Anschutz were among other friends who sometimes joined them. The hut was high on a headland, looking out across flax and low scrub to the steep, jutting coastline and rugged sea. They read and talked (Jean always carried her Housman), and swam at the small black-sand beach below. There were other excursions to Waiheke Island with a group that included Honey O'Connor and her future husband, the left-wing lawyer Frank Haigh, and Rita Darby and John Harris, who were soon to marry too; both were (or soon would be) members of the Communist Party. They stayed in a small cottage on the island. Mason had a habit of going off on his own in the mornings and not coming back, Honey Haigh later recalled: 'He literally forgot. He loved it – the wilder the better.' At night there were games of charades (at which Lowry excelled), and shadowgraphy, where the friends took turns to pose as historical characters, their silhouettes cast onto a backlit white curtain. One night, Honey remembered, after her Queen Mother had been revealed, it was Mason's turn. He took an inordinately long time: 'He was Christ hanging on the cross . . . done out of a couple of sheets and a towel. He looked miraculous.'[5]

AT THE END of 1933 Mason dusted off *No New Thing* and tried once again to find a publisher overseas, sending it to the Atlantic Monthly Press in Boston and to Leonard and Virginia Woolf's Hogarth Press in London. 'I think – perhaps over-optimistically – that the book is worth including in the Hogarth Living Poets Series', he wrote to the latter. The Hogarth Press had been the early publisher of Katherine Mansfield and T.S. Eliot; their list included essays

on politics, economics, psychoanalysis and aesthetics, and European writers
in translation. The first volume in the second Living Poets series, C. Day
Lewis's *Magnetic Mountain*, had just come out that year. 'I should prefer the
very cheapest format, say plainly printed paper fold-in covers', Mason wrote
to both publishers, and told them that he was 'prepared to back my faith with
a guarantee – small, but sufficient, I think, to cover you at any rate for bare
costs'.[6] Still, both turned him down. In the end he was to publish *No New
Thing* himself, after all – although not in quite so half-pie a fashion as *The
Beggar*. *No New Thing* was one of the first publications of the Unicorn (or
Spearhead) Press which he and Bob Lowry set up in May 1934.

Lowry arrived back in Auckland in February, having spent his months in
Christchurch helping Denis Glover with the Caxton Club Press that Glover
had set up in the basement of Canterbury College. He set about trying to
rehabilitate himself with the university, succeeding only in getting himself
readmitted to the Students' Association, however. In April the 'bloody Black-
handed swine of the College Conservative Clique' – the Professorial Board –
upheld his suspension until the end of the year, he fumed to Glover.[7]
Meanwhile, and hardly helping his case, he busied himself with political plans,
sending out a circular outlining a 'scheme for the formation of Labour Clubs
in the four University Colleges'. This was to involve a national secretariat
and a monthly journal edited by Mason, which would include literary as well
as political material – a new *Phoenix*? The clubs themselves 'while not affiliated
to any political party shall study the aims and ideas of the international working
class and support its objects' while appealing to 'liberal and radical sympathies
on a broad basis', and 'further study the questions of free speech and of
victimisation of University students or lecturers'.[8] But this project progressed
no further, much to the relief of some: Anschutz (Monro reported to Paul)
was worried 'not for the good name of the College but for the good name of
the Labour movement, which he thinks will be held up to derision in Bob's
hands'. Anschutz suggested that they introduce Lowry to Alun Richards,
who as a Christian socialist would be a safer political mentor for him than the
communist Firth.[9]

Lowry's fellow organiser in this scheme was not in fact Firth but Ronald
Holloway, another printer, who was to become the third partner in the
Unicorn Press. Holloway had worked with Lowry on the four issues of *Phoenix*
after coming back to Auckland in 1932 from Dunedin, where he had been
printing chocolate wrappers for Cadbury Fry Hudson, and finding himself
unemployed. When Lowry abandoned the fifth *Phoenix* and decamped to

Christchurch, Holloway had gone into partnership with Percy Postlethwaite, who had bought the Students' Association press, which they reincarnated as another mythical bird, the Griffin. With the Griffin Press Holloway printed D'Arcy Cresswell's essay *Modern Poetry and the Ideal*, a few issues of the student newspaper *Craccum*, and at least one number of the Elam art students' magazine *Palette* (April 1934), which included Mason's 'Nox Perpetua Dormienda'. According to one story, Holloway incurred Mason's lasting displeasure by leaving a line off one of his poems in *Palette*, but it was not this poem; Lowry did repeat a line of one poem, 'Their Sacrifice', in *Kiwi* in 1932.

Postlethwaite, however, refused to employ Lowry. Nor was Lowry's reputation the only thing frustrating the young printer–publishers' larger plans: 'as to the proposed publishing society,' Holloway wrote to Pat Lawlor in April, 'nothing more has happened here; the proprietors of the Griffin Press were not interested, and became utterly obstructive when they heard that Lowry hoped to have a share in the concern. Apparently Lowry's presence in any such venture would imply the presence of R.A.K. Mason also; and whatever Mason's reputation as a poet may be, as a company promoter and financier it seems dubious. Besides which, they are both communists.'[10] Instead, Mason bought a small Pearl treadle press and some 12-point Garamond type, installed it at 451 Great South Road, and invited Lowry to stay.

A brochure for the new publishing house Spearhead Publishers announced that its first publication would be Mason's *No New Thing*: 'The publishers consider that they could not have chosen any better book in New Zealand to indicate the standard which they intend to maintain.' Lowry, who 'is now managing the Unicorn Press', was to be the typographer, and Stephen Champ 'associated with the house as illustrator and decorator'.[11] Holloway joined the team a little later, after some persuading: unhappy, according to Lowry, with the £1 a week starting wage offered, and because 'Mason once said his printing was bloody stupid'.[12] Lowry had hopes of Glover going in with them too: they would be living communally on the premises, he told Glover, but didn't know where yet. For Mason it was surely a relief to be going into business doing something he cared about: publishing books, rather than selling insurance or sweepstake tickets (or whatever else he and Dan were up to). He had remarked to Glover in March, by way of apologising, as usual, for his lengthy delay in replying to a letter: 'As a matter of fact I have been working like a Trojan trying to keep business together: it seems now however that business has taken it into its own hands to relieve me of all responsibility by simply disappearing.' This was probably an allusion to the struggling fortunes of International Concessions Ltd. 'I am always torn between the twin desires of making a dishonest living and trying to dabble in intellectual matters. I usually try to combine the two with disastrous results to both.'[13]

'We open out with Mason's poems, 1924–29 in one of the juiciest little editions that ever burst upon the enraptured gaze', Lowry announced to Glover in May.[14] But *No New Thing* was to take considerably longer to put through the press than they anticipated. In the meantime Lowry printed for the university *Illustrations and Specimens of Criticism to accompany six lectures on aesthetics* by Anschutz, under the imprint of the Unicorn, and *The Material Basis of Culture*, an essay on economic history by H.D. Dickinson, a visiting lecturer from Leeds, which was announced as the first publication of the Spearhead Press. While work on *No New Thing* continued, the press moved briefly to Clifton Firth's studio, then into rented premises at 34 Kitchener Street, below Albert Park, next door to the Law Courts. There the Unicorn Press became a meeting-place for Auckland's literati for the few years of its brief life – as, being a Lowry venture, its life was destined to be. Among the regular visitors was Robin Hyde, who penned sharp, affectionately mocking columns about students and communists in the weekly *New Zealand Observer*, and also wrote poetry, published not by the Unicorn but in London. Another was the novelist Jane Mander, who had recently returned to New Zealand from London and New York and was appalled to find New Zealand culture as dull and shallow as when she had left it, and by the struggle and neglect of its young writers, to whom she became a generous supporter and friend.

'My Unicorn Press begins to bound away', reported Lowry with characteristic confidence at the end of August, unbowed, apparently, by his arrest and conviction on charges of obstruction and incitement to disorder at a demonstration the month before.[15] He had printed 2000 handbills for an illegal Friday night meeting at the corner of Pitt and Beresford streets on 20 July, called by the recently formed Free Speech Council to protest at the curtailment of the rights of free speech and assembly: since the Queen Street fracas of 1932 the Auckland City Council had routinely denied radical organisations permits to hold street meetings. It was not his printing, however, that got Lowry into trouble. Sid Scott, who was to chair the meeting – had he been allowed to – was the first of several men arrested, one after executing a famous leap onto the roof of the Beresford Street men's toilets, from where he was able to address the crowd for a few minutes before the police hauled him down. Whereupon Lowry climbed onto the bonnet of a nearby car to take up the megaphone (figuratively speaking) and was arrested as well. He was sentenced to two years' probation with a seven o'clock curfew, meaning that he was not to be away from home at night without the permission of his probation officer. It was a lenient sentence, on account of his youth; the others also received terms in gaol. 'I'm going to carry on with printing and read Marx', he reportedly told the court.[16]

The Unicorn's next publication was the text of an address on freedom of speech given by Arthur Sewell, the university's left-wing professor of English, at a public meeting at the Strand Theatre in September, called by the Auckland Rationalist Association and Sunday Freedom League. Mason was for a time the secretary of the Rationalist Association, which held its Sunday night meetings, at which a short address would be followed by musical items and supper, in its rooms in Swanson Street, or later in the new Fabian Society clubrooms at the bottom of Queen Street (a favourite radical haunt in the 1930s). Most likely he also attended the further meetings and demonstrations called by the Free Speech Council over the following year. The City Council did take notice – an authorised Free Speech meeting on the traditional soapbox site in Quay Street later in September was the first to be held there in over two years, and a march up Queen Street in November was also the first since April 1932 – but it refused to rescind the bylaw requiring a permit to be obtained each time.

WHILE THE Unicorn Press found its feet (Lowry's report of it bounding away was a little optimistic) – by this time sporting a bold, angular, horned unicorn's head, in a similar style to the second phoenix, as its logo, and advertising that it 'does good printing of all kinds & specialises in the production of modern pamphlets & magazines'[17] – Mason spent at least a term of 1934 teaching at Mt Albert Grammar School, where his old Latin teacher Ken Dellow had become headmaster. He had plans as well to open a bookshop, so he told Pat Lawlor, who was also the New Zealand agent for the Sydney *Bulletin* and other Australian publications, 'in confidence' at the end of August, but these came to nothing.[18] *No New Thing* was held up by a dispute with the binders.

In Christchurch, meanwhile, Glover brought out *New Poems*, the third and last publication (and first book) he produced at his Caxton Club Press in the university basement, and harbinger of the Caxton Press he was to establish on his own the following year. *New Poems* was a mini-anthology, edited by himself and Ian Milner, containing 'an arbitrary selection of verse – published and unpublished – by younger New Zealand writers':[19] twenty-three poems by ten poets, including Glover, Milner, Curnow, Fairburn and Mason, who was represented by 'Stoic Overthrow' and 'Youth at the Dance'. It was published in a tiny edition of forty-five. Mason provided the title. Whatever the editors had first had in mind 'sounds altogether too too damnably Mistermiddletonmurry', he frankly told Glover when replying to his request for material in March. 'You are doubtless by this time heartily sick of people poking borax at it but still I must suggest a change of some sort. The titles of those two Hogarth Press anthologies New Countries and something else that I cannot remember were excellent. I must advise something symbolical without being over subtle, along the lines as those.'[20] Not that he wasn't happy to be included: 'I may say that I have been at times approached by various people asking me to contribute to Art in NZ anthologies and such muck but I make it a rule to turn them down. Your case is quite different however and if you want anything at all I have written just go ahead.' He regretted only that he could not offer something new. 'I have tried, since receiving your letter, to finish and type out an absolute snorter, but business has just absolutely ballsed up any hope of doing anything which takes a bit of time and surplus energy.' He sent copies of half a dozen poems, including 'Youth at the Dance' on request, but with reservations: 'I wish I had written something with a bit more kick in it: stuff like that might well be the work of a man fool enough to read Spengler', he wrote of the poem that is widely read as his most directly political.[21]

The volume's austere black paper cover (relieved only by the title in a white window) expressed both a typographical aesthetic and its seriousness of purpose. *New Poems* was not quite *New Country* or *New Signatures* (the title Mason couldn't remember), two landmark anthologies published by the Hogarth Press in 1933 and 1932 respectively, which included the work of W.H. Auden, Stephen Spender and C. Day Lewis – the so-called 'pylon poets', as they had already been dubbed. These were the poets who led and defined the 'poetry of the thirties' in England by their rejection of the esoteric, aloof and self-indulgent writing of the 'modernists', epitomised by T.S. Eliot, and by declaring in their poetry their allegiance to the left, their sympathy with the working class and their faith in the redemptive role of poetry and of the poet. The contributors to *New Country*, its preface made clear, believed in the revolution. *New Poems* was not so politically committed. But it too registered a sense of the writer's engagement in the historical and cultural moment, and 'a sense of the poet's responsibility' – to himself and to the moment in equal measure. 'The poet is the focal point of awareness in his time, and since we are living in a revolutionary age some interpretation of its influence is only to be expected', the editors observed. 'Several of these writers respond more definitely to social stimuli than others', yet it was not for this reason that they had been chosen: 'What compels our attention is the liberating effect of such interest on their verse. We certainly note their sensitiveness to veering social forces, their willingness to face unpleasant issues, their implied faith in a more creative way of living; but above all we are struck by the renewed poetic vigour and pliancy which springs from these qualities of social affinity.' While the English pylon poets were raising their standard against the 'complexity and introspection, the doubt and cynicism'[22] of Eliot and his kind, however, New Zealand's new poets were rebelling against their own enemy, older and more easily targeted: 'It has been termed "new" because we think its general tone marks a departure from that unfortunate tradition in which any sentimental rhapsodising over love, flowers or sunsets seems to pass for poetry. A predilection for decorative lyricising and emotional embroidery, weakly reminiscent of pre-war Georgian verse, has produced in this country a lifeless growth which, though not necessarily insincere, is in no sense creative.'[23] This was already a familiar refrain, but the anthology itself signified something new.

With the establishment of the Caxton and Unicorn presses, the publishing scene was transformed from what it had been ten years before, when Mason had hawked *The Beggar* and *Penny Broadsheet* on Queen Street. Here were two new publishing houses, small and meagrely capitalised though they were, dedicated both to publishing the work of new writers, poets especially, and to the highest standards of production and design that their limited resources, unabashed talent and unlimited enthusiasm allowed: Lowry with exuberant flair, Glover with elegant restraint. 'If you want to publish a pamphlet, you have to first of all set up a paper-mill', Mason had once written in his notebook.[24]

At the same moment, too, *Tomorrow* magazine appeared, a weekly at first and later fortnightly journal of news and comment that would be the main – indeed, really the only – forum of the intellectual left in New Zealand for the remainder of the 1930s. Its first issue came out in July 1934. *Tomorrow* was perhaps what *Phoenix* would have become or what Mason wanted it to become, had he succeeded in keeping it going on its own. Avowedly 'independent' of party or financial interest, but unashamedly and increasingly left-wing, it was modelled on A.R. Orage's *New Age*, and inspired first by an urgent belief in the need to counter the deadening and dangerous influence on New Zealand politics and culture of the capitalist press, which *Tomorrow*'s founder, Kennaway Henderson, depicted in his sardonic and macabre cartoons as a katipo spider weaving its web around the globe. Glover printed the magazine and was a member of its small editorial team, which included Winston Rhodes and Frederick Sinclaire, respectively lecturer and professor of English at Canterbury University College. *Tomorrow* was principally but not only a political journal. There were book and occasional film reviews, while Winston Rhodes in his regular column on 'Life and letters' explicated the central themes of left-wing cultural theory of the 1930s: applying a philosophy of humanist Marxism to subjects ranging from Milton, Chesterton and the Victorian novel to workers' art clubs and Soviet film, tracing a revolutionary Great Tradition in Western literature to which the new, socialist culture was the heir, and looking for signs of life in New Zealand. Although the editors did not actively solicit literary contributions, *Tomorrow* also became, by default, an important outlet for new writing. Glover and Fairburn were its most prolific literary contributors, mainly of short satirical squibs, at which both excelled; although more important was its role in publishing, and thereby nurturing, the stories of Frank Sargeson. Mason, however, contributed comparatively little.

Rhodes welcomed *New Poems* in *Tomorrow* as 'a new departure in that standardised product the New Zealand anthology', and as signalling a new spirit of realism and bad temper in New Zealand literature, but not without criticism of what he considered an element of immaturity:

> I cannot help noticing that the voices of the writers are uncertain and strident. Luckily the editors do not provide an index of first lines. Such an index would have revealed what I mean – Get your machine guns manned, Let us laugh with the dying, Too late to live in whited sepulchres, We are two skeletons who sleep . . . . . Much could be written on the sinister vocabulary and the repellent in imagery. There is a tendency to talk too much about maggots and lice, bones and skeletons, wombs and worms. No doubt this is intentional, no doubt it is symbolic of a state of mind, but it shows, I think, that the writers, with all their implied faith in a more creative form of life and their poetic vigour and pliancy, have not yet achieved the serenity of discontent which knows that there are other things to write about, there are other songs to sing.[25]

FOR ALL THAT the establishment of the Unicorn and the Caxton presses marked the beginning of a new era in New Zealand literary publishing, *No New Thing* made hardly more of an impression on the reading public when it first appeared, at the end of 1934, than had *The Beggar*. It was Lowry's first book, and ambitiously planned. There was to be a limited, signed edition of 120 copies, 100 of which were intended for sale at half a guinea. 'It has been set by hand, and the type distributed', explained a slip inserted in one of the few copies that was produced according to Lowry's intentions.[26] Lowry rose to the challenge of setting Mason's difficult verse – with its very short and full-measure lines and hanging indent – by 'a vivid use of large bold lower-case roman numerals at the head of each numbered poem, and the same . . . in square brackets at the tail' to centre the verse on the page, as Glover was to write admiringly, the effect being as austere and disciplined as the poetry demanded. 'Bound in hand-woven linen and printed on a de luxe antique laid [paper], this is a book for the collector to prize for its appearance no less than its contents. . . . The verso of each leaf is left unprinted, normally a precious practice, but here adding to the effect of a luxurious edition for private circulation.'[27] Remembering Mason's comment to the Atlantic Monthly Press and the Hogarth Press about his preference for a cheap and simple format with plain paper covers, one wonders if this was what he, as opposed to Lowry, had in mind.

The cloth for the cover was woven by Stephen Champ's wife, Marion, from fishing twine, which made a coarse-weave fabric of natural colour. A 3/4-inch band of black interwoven with cream at the top and bottom edges echoed the bold black horizontal line beneath the title, which was set on a small rectangle of paper pasted onto the cloth. The fishing twine, however, altered in tension when woven to produce much less fabric than expected. The title page designed by Patricia Firth did not meet with Lowry's approval. Several copies, Holloway later recalled, were ruined at the bindery when the endpapers were mislaid and the first and last pages glued down instead. The binders could not be paid. The result was that the 100 copies intended for sale were never issued, and only a handful of the numbered special edition were bound. A handful more were finished in plain cardboard covers over the next few years, on demand. Frank Sargeson told Glover two or three years later: 'Lowry says it would be useless writing to Mason's binder. He says you & Curnow want copies, & if you send the money it will enable about half a dozen copies to be bound & released. I've seen the book myself. Fairburn has a copy & so has Cresswell.' It was, he thought, 'the best lot of poetry that's yet come out in N.Z.'[28] Others were to agree, and *No New Thing* was to be critically regarded as Mason's best volume. But because so few copies were produced there were no reviews.

The prose preface to which Fairburn had objected Mason had reduced to a brief afterword: 'Some of these poems were intended to appear in a vast medley of prose and poetry, a sort of Odyssey expressing the whole history of New Zealand. This I designed long ago and did much work on. I may possibly yet resume it, but youth having smouldered in senseless drudgery I can scarcely expect age to supply the necessary fire.' In the original version he had referred to this abandoned master work, still more cryptically, as 'a sort of vast Human Comedy, mingled prose and verse . . . The underlying mental unfolding might have been plain if I had done my magnum opus. Now suffice it to say that an increasing Calvinism of outlook has gone hand in hand with a technical movement towards the Parnassians – I am not unaware in what contempt these two terms are usually held.' After facetiously apologising for any offence to sensitive readers, he had listed his 'main influences: Beddoes, Catullus, Housman, Milton, Baudelaire, roughly in that order of time and (decreasing) intensity.'[29]

No New Thing displays a greater technical assurance than *The Beggar* and *Penny Broadsheet*, and a wider range of subject and tone, as is only to be expected of a larger collection (twenty-five poems) written over a period of five years. But the poetic voice is instantly recognisable: in the attention to strict form, the curious and deft mixture of the classical and colloquial, the dense constructions, sure rhythms, subtly shifting tone, elusive meanings; and in the preoccupation with those large and personal themes, love, time and mortality, 'the gigantic fantasies of religion, the certainties of generation, pain, and death'.[30] It was subtitled 'Poems 1924–29', although some were certainly written slightly later (over the last Lichfield summer of 1930, for example), and dedicated 'ad matrem' – to his mother.

Whatever Mason's grand scheme might have been – the 'mental unfolding' of his abandoned Odyssey – the volume was carefully arranged thematically, and it is easier to imagine that it might have been conceived as part of a vast human comedy than of an epic history of New Zealand. It opened with the 'Preface to the Book of Pessimism' that had appeared in Ian Donnelly's article in the *Sun* in 1928, introducing his 'bitter verses' as 'sponges steeped in vinegar/ useless to the happy-eyed/ but handy for the crucified', defining both a tone and a frame of reference. This he followed with the 'Stoic Marching Song', previously published in the *Sun*, and a still briefer statement of what Curnow has called Mason's 'shocked faith',[31] his outraged scepticism: six cynical lines entitled 'Evolution', first published in the *Star* in 1927.

'On the Swag' (so titled here for the first time) is paired with 'Judas Iscariot', a poem in a similar metre but with an entirely different feel. Its origin, Mason would later record, was a passing remark he made to Fairburn one day about the saving grace of humour, to which Fairburn replied that humour could have its dangers too. To the humble beggar that is Mason's Christ, his Judas is a fat, smug, jovial character, a hearty English–public–school type. The poem's easy humour is given its bitter edge by the implicit, off-stage tragedy, the betrayal:

> Judas Iscariot
>   sat in the upper
>   room with the others
>   at the last supper
>
> And sitting there smiled
>   up at his master
>   whom he knew the morrow
>   would roll in disaster.
>
> At Christ's look he guffawed –
>   for then as thereafter
>   Judas was greatly
>   given to laughter.
>
> Indeed they always said
>   that he was the veriest
>   prince of good fellows
>   and the whitest and merriest
>
> All the days of his life
>   he lived gay as a cricket
>   and would sing like the thrush
>   that sings in the thicket
>
> He would sing like the thrush
>   that sings on the thorn
>   oh he was the most sporting bird
>   that ever was born.

In his notebooks, where the same Judas recurs, the bitterness and sarcasm are sharper:

> So chubby little Judas took his pudgy white hands and little baby face off into the darkness. As he toddled along the road beside his comfortable wife his fat paunch wobbled in front of him. Within him glowed a pleasant feeling of duty well done even at the cost of sacrificing a friend. 'You know, I'm a pretty tolerant and broad-minded man. I sometimes think that perhaps there was something in what he said'.[32]

Arguably, Mason's sharp and knowing humour makes 'Judas Iscariot' a better poem than its uncomplicated, gentle counterpoint 'On the Swag'. The gentleness that was so often remarked in his own character was a rare quality in his poetry.

'Footnote to John ii 4', which follows – poignantly preceding 'Ecce Homunculus', which so affected Fairburn when he read it in 1930 – draws its impact from just that quality of gentleness and simplicity, and beautifully demonstrates Mason's skill with that most difficult of forms, the sonnet. 'I have not kept a copy,' he had written to Fairburn after he sent the typescript of *No New Thing* to him in 1932, 'but seem to remember calling one "Footnote to Luke ii.4". Would you mind peeping into the Bible next time you're in the dock and verifying that? It is supposed to be, of course, one of the occasions when Christ repudiates his family. Fortunately those are pretty common, and Mark iii.33. will do if you find the one I have given is wrong.'[33] The cue is Christ's cryptic response to Mary at the marriage at Cana.

> Don't throw your arms around me in that way:
>   I know that what you tell me is the truth –
>   yes I suppose I loved you in my youth
>   as boys do love their mothers, so they say,
>   but all that's gone from me this many a day:
>   I am a merciless cactus an uncouth
>   wild goat a jagged old spear the grim tooth
>   of a lone crag . . . Woman I cannot stay.
>
> Each of us must do his work of doom
>   and I shall do it even in despite
>   of her who brought me in pain from her womb,

> whose blood made me, who used to bring the light
> and sit on the bed up in my little room
> and tell me stories and tuck me up at night.

The shift in emotion and tone is perfectly controlled, from the defiant rhetorical gesture and piling up of harsh images to the intimate scene and colloquial phrase. The son's brutal rejection of his mother, growing to an exaggerated pitch of intensity – exaggerated deliberately, as Mason would later explain, to provoke her into realising his dilemma – gives way to the soft nostalgia into which the poem and he fall in the sestet, in spite of himself. 'I know of few sonnets', Allen Curnow would remark in his earliest critical comment on Mason, 'where the form is so completely assumed into the statement, "as if the body thought."'[34]

Fairburn, to a correspondent in 1934, described this poem as typical of Mason in its masculinity, its brutality: 'his work, I have noticed, doesnt usually appeal to women. . . . I find that "Footnote to John ii.4. very moving: an extremely masculine poem again: only menchildren who inhabit a world of Freudian nightmare know *that* agony.'[35] Yet Jocelyn was so moved by it, when she read it in Clench Common in 1932, that she wrote to him to ask for a signed copy: 'I hardly know how to explain my asking though – only if I had a son who could say that to me, I think I would be the proudest woman on earth.'[36]

'The Young Man Thinks of Sons', and renounces the cycle of procreation – the poem which the editor of the *Sun* declined to print for fear of offending his readers by the mention of lust – is ironically placed before a group of nine poems, making up more than a third of the book, which deal with the theme of sexual love. But there is no celebration here of sexual or romantic fulfilment. Unrequited longing, and love counterpoised with mortality, are the theme of four of them: his two Catullan studies, 'Lugete o Veneres' and 'Nox Perpetua Dormienda', and 'Thigh to thigh', all written over the long Lichfield summer of 1930, and 'Since flesh is soon'. The tone of the last is typically ambiguous:

> Since flesh is soon
> as the spread dung
> and the soul no more
> than a song that is sung

Why should I care
    that my name then be known
    when at best I'll be
    a name alone?

Toil and honour
    flee like driven sands:
    only my love
    is true and stands.

Is not all I was made for
    bright on her lips?
    does not my whole purpose
    glow from her hips?

Should not my whole right be
    to kiss her eyes?
    is not all good
    held in her thighs?

The would-be lover is sometimes defiant, as in 'If it be not God's law' ('henceforth I serve Satan truly'), wistful in his beautiful poem for Teddy, 'Be swift o sun', and defeated in 'She Who Steals', a poem which shows Mason's fine control of the contrasting full-measure and short lines:[37]

The spirit that burnt up so clearly has all gone out from me:
    she has stolen my life:
and I thought like a fool that it was I who won and not she
    as we lay here at strife.

Now far up on the grey naked mountainside in the great stone's shadow
    here I sprawl at length
while ant-like in distance and almost down to the meadow
    strides the thief of my strength.

Wounded puzzlement works to better literary effect for Mason than defiant assertion. Here, as in the collection as a whole, the dramatic moment which the poem enacts is more focused than in the poems of *The Beggar*. Mason's images too are now more direct and stronger. The last poem in this group, and most nearly a love poem, is a simple and powerful statement of the paradox of love both defeating and defeated by time:

> Our love was a grim citadel:
>   no tawdry plaything for the minute
>   of strong dark stone we built it well
>   and based in the ever-living granite:
>
> The urgent columns of the years
>   press on, like tall rain up the valley:
>   and Chaos bids ten thousand spears
>   run to erase our straw–built folly.[38]

After love and passion come age and retrospection. 'Wise at Last' and 'The Just Statesman Dies' are related poems which can be said to have a political theme, but are far from straightforward expressions of the poet's socialist convictions. Like the narrator of 'Wise at Last' (and the dying poet of Mason's notebook, perhaps), the just statesman reflects on a life of well-meaning, but misguided or futile good intentions; less stoically pessimistic, less cynical, but no less disillusioned. He finds satisfaction in the memory of sexual and spiritual fulfilment: not in the days when 'I starved in my garret/ to serve Man my fellow', or 'when in time/ I came to rule/ I was wise and just/ and good and a fool', nor in 'Two books of fine sonnets/ some prose of merit/ . . . my leisure's rare fruit/ and vexation of spirit'; but in the times when 'I walked on misty hills/ all night vague and cold',

> And in one hot summer
>   I lay with a girl
>   more fragrant than cinnamon
>   lustrous than pearl:
>
> And again comes back to me
>   one holy day
>   near the Feast of Crucifixion
>   on lone cliffs I lay.

They were hands that held me
    far up towards the skies
    and their soft disdain
    of the sacrifice.

All the day like a god
    with spirit transcended
    in warmth light and colour
    my senses were blended.

This was time not wasted
    this was time well spent
    this was fulfilment
    and I die content.

Death returns in the next four poems, which include 'In Perpetuum Vale' (which a note at the back of the book explained had 'appeared in mutilated form in *The Beggar*', and is here printed without the twelve lines Harold Monro objected to) and 'The Leave-taking', the bleak, unsentimental funeral poem he had submitted to the *Auckland Star* in 1927 (a year after the death of Maxwell Rudd, and a few months after Horace Holl's). At the end he placed those two visions of destruction, pessimism and fear published in *Phoenix*, 'Stoic Overthrow' and 'In Manus Tuas Domine'. Indeed, this was not poetry born out of a 'serenity of discontent'. Robin Hyde, reviewing Mason in *Art in New Zealand* a few years later, and comparing *No New Thing* with *The Beggar*, thought of Milton: there was no weakness in Mason's verse now, she observed, but neither was there 'the confidence of any great vision. He portrays what he sees, and that is almost darkness made visible.'[39]

13

Darkness

IN THE EARLY hours of one morning in 1934 Mason arrived at Marie Gaudin's house, wet through, covered in clay, shaking, distraught. He had walked 30 miles to Piha and back: had stood in the dark on the rocks above The Gap where at high tide the surf thunders through a narrow channel to crash and churn against the steep rock. At Piha beach in any tide the sea is treacherous, swirling into invisible rips around the base of Lion Rock. Marie and Jean Alison would later refer to this incident as Mason's 'suicidal drama'. He told Marie, after she had taken him home, calmed and fed him, that he was upset over a problem with the petty cash (either at Dan's office or the Unicorn Press). But neither she nor Jean believed that this alone could have taken him out to Piha that night.

These were, it was true, hard and straitened times. And business (whatever it was), as he had casually remarked to Denis Glover in March, was not going well. In the spring of this year Jane Mander wrote consolingly to the young writer Monte Holcroft, whose dream of living by his novels alone was soon to be disillusioned: 'All the struggling boys up here have had to get regular work. Fairburn is doing some routine job in Farmers, Coppard is out working in a woolshed, R.A.K. Mason is doing some stupid office work. D'Arcy Cresswell is in a hut out on the beach somewhere living on his radio talks . . .'. She wrote a few months later: 'Really these harrowing struggles . . . My heart is being wrenched here at the moment by the tragic mess R.A.K. Mason is in . . . a worse state than yours – much worse indeed, though you may not believe it possible.'[1]

Fairburn wrote of Mason to a friend in June this year: 'He has been through the most shockingly bad time during the last four years, and hasn't yet got on top of it – "absorbed" it if you like. Its not unusual, or unreasonable, when pain becomes unsupportable, to grow a hard shell over one's sensitivity'. His correspondent was Muriel Innes, who was writing an article on New Zealand poetry for the London journal *Bookman* and had found Mason uncommunicative. Fairburn assured her that this was not unusual. 'Regarding Mason: he has a curious and original mind, as full of trap-doors and secret passages as a Katzenjammer castle. . . . I agree that satire is not his métier; hypochondria creeps in – I hesitate to call it masochism, though I have heard him do so himself.'[2]

Fairburn well knew of Mason's susceptibility to 'vast depressions'.[3] As did Mason himself that his 'abominable psychological difficulties' amounted to more than the normal moodiness of youth, that the pessimism that so infuses his poetry was not a literary conceit. When Alfred Katz had confessed to him in 1933 the problems he suffered as a 'bourgeois intellectual' in reconciling romance and reality, Mason felt he recognised his own. The long letter he wrote to Katz in reply is extraordinarily candid, and fascinating in the way it shifts between psychological and political analysis, being at one moment a frank acknowledgement of his own emotional struggles and then a critique of the weakness of the New Zealand left to 'revolutionary romanticism':

It is always some consolation to know that there are others in the same mess, so let me tell you that I have the most terrific battles with every form of un-realism. In particular do I suffer from infantile fluctuations between heaven and hell, ecstasy and despair, living now in a land of enchantment now in bitterest gloom. It is all most impracticable, for when I am up in the clouds there is no need for any action ever again and when I get into the depths there is no hope in action – absurd alternations between omnipotence and impotence. It all goes back to the cradle – or perhaps the womb: at any rate, I can quite clearly trace it in memory to four or five years old, when I was ruefully learning that there were in this grim-becoming world horrors that no mother could rescue me from.

Never mind that now. Doubtless you know the symptoms and causes as well as I do – the symptoms probably better, as I am gradually growing up and to some slight extent forgetting about them. (God knows I was infinitely worse than you when I was your age – so far from recognising any sickness, I revelled in it.)

What you want to know is the cure. Curse it all, there isn't any – except perhaps death, though even there the germs of our malady will linger on to poison the healthy society that will grow up. The only consolation is that from our rottenness will emerge proletarian growth. For ourselves, we can only go a little way – not far enough to give us peace of mind ever, but at least enough to let us continue to exist.

The first thing to do is to face our trouble as a fact, a sickness to be cured (at any rate partially) by slow degrees. There it does help us to see our own state objectively if we can see it in others. That is why I repeat that there is no form of masochistic ecstasy that I have not known – and, for that matter, still do to a fair extent.

The great fault then is to attempt a miraculous cure a la Jesus, to tackle the whole thing at one swoop. That, of course, fails and you relapse into the other romantic extreme of apathy once again. As a matter of fact, while the whole vast ramshackle building cannot be reformed in one dash, the thing can be done if you take it bit by bit, never taking more than you can fix at the time, and not abating your energy if you find that you *have* gone wrong. As we can reasonably hope to live another half-century (failing accidents or fascism), there is no need to hurry things unduly.

There can be no doubt that Marxism, taken in moderate doses, is a marvellous corrective. Old G.B.S. says 'Karl Marx made a man of me'. The fact that he didn't is no fault of Marx's. It would be a great help here if we could get into touch with some realistic movement, but alas! I fear that the militant proletarians of N.Z. have so far been afflicted with an aggravated form of our complaint without even our excuse for it.[4]

WINSTON RHODES first met Mason when he went to Auckland for the first time in 1934. He had known nothing about New Zealand writing when he arrived from Melbourne two years earlier to take up a lectureship at Canterbury College. But he soon heard of Mason, who, '[a]lready in his late twenties . . . was becoming something of a legend for those who like myself had rediscovered his diminutive publication, *The Beggar*', and was keen to seek out 'this reputedly elusive but much talked of and admired poet and dissident . . . I found him in a rather cramped and dingy office where some obscure business was being conducted, the nature of which I never discovered.' Or perhaps their first meeting was at a literary evening he was taken to by Rex Fairburn at Dick Anschutz's home in Remuera; the next day Mason and Rhodes took a long walk together along Auckland's east coast bays. They talked about people and politics rather than poetry. He was immediately struck by Mason's 'warmth of friendship' and genuine and patient sincerity – a 'complete lack of any form of exhibitionism', which must have been refreshing after an evening being escorted around the town by Fairburn – and by 'an impressive but exceedingly complex personality':

His good humour and deep throaty chuckle could not conceal an intensity of feeling, the very rhythms of which can be felt in his poetry. In some indefinable way both his appearance and his manner suggested that beneath his quarrel with life and society was buried a persistent and disturbing quarrel with himself. Later and as I came to know him a little better, I was able to recognise a sombreness of mood and a preoccupied air that seemed at odds with an open-hearted disposition and a frankness of approach.[5]

'The human mind is like an iceberg', Mason had written in his notebook. And: 'Dark thoughts that fester in some sordid narrow slum of my soul.' And:

There are gaps in the continuity of my being; a stream which purls along chattering all the while and suddenly the music ceases for a moment. Or rather these lapses are like the treacherous vacua in the air into which the aviator falls – the unsubstantial suddenly giving place to nothingness.

The little shaggy savages, too, who wield bitter-poisoned darts are marching up from the fens and swamps of my soul. Meanwhile that old bearded gladiator of my Sanity is doing doubtful battle, and at times he goes down beneath them.

At times the Spectator (Reporter) swoons at the dreadful battle of the gladiator-passions in the arena below. The noise and terror of the conflict rolls up in clouds from below to overwhelm him.

All the old evils are swarming up from the back of my brain: the old phantoms that I thought I had left behind when I lost the pimples and passions of puberty. Strange sorrows and terrors and anguishes that have no name and do battle under so dense a cloud that they can be seen only dimly and rarely.

I am the tumult of the hurricane but I am the core of peace at its heart.[6]

One of his early, uncollected poems was this Dante-esque sonnet:

> Come out my soul from the dark wood of thought:
> for nothing profitable is found there,
> only a mephitic and miasmic air
> with venom noxious to poor mortals fraught:

and he who drinks that air will grow distraught
    and the wrongs of man become his lonely care,
    and his joy wanes, doubts grow, he learns to stare
in wondering wrath at the web where he is caught.

But come, come out where are clear glades enough
    for men to revel all the glad day long,
    where no remorse is for a thing done wrong,
where is no surly conscience with a gruff
    moroseness to deaden merriment and song,
where no face is cheerless and no voice rough.[7]

Mason never published the following poem, and it is not known when it was written:

Beware the mask, lest the mask become the man:
    I walking beyond Taupo once over that great plain
    by the mountain snows, and seeking ease of some pain
    did not bridge straight the needed moment's span
    but fell back on some clever trick and began
    to affect cynic features: with a spurt of rain
    the wind changed, but the face set not to change again
    became as a thorn that into the very soul ran

And this was long ago, but the face awry
    ill-fitted and fixed like a wounded man's from war,
    unyielding, reflected from every ill-omened eye
    as a barrier between the twain, making a lie
    of my outgoings, like a leper's bell before
    all my life has gone and now shall until I die.[8]

14

New life

1935–36

TROUBLE AT the office might not have taken Mason out to Piha that night, or not that alone, but it did make him leave town. In April 1935 he went to Sydney with Dan – apparently, so his friends believed, to escape the growing interest of the police in the brothers' business affairs. This may well have had something to do with the collapse of International Concessions Ltd, which had gone into liquidation at the end of 1934. Dan (now in a partnership named Smith & Mason) was appointed liquidator, and then replaced at a meeting of shareholders ten weeks later. The company was wound up in May 1935, although the settling of claims was to take another year and a half. The liquidator's accounts recorded that Dan was paid travelling expenses in April 1935 and Ron 'witness expenses' (along with wages) in July.[1]

Perhaps, too, the trip to Sydney was made with some new scheme in mind. It was paid for, Mason would later remark, by 'a group of company promoters'.[2] He was given a dinner-suit to wear, and Marie Gaudin cleaned the nicotine stains off his teeth.

He stayed in Sydney for at least a month and looked for work, doing the rounds of the broadcasting stations: he was asked to do a voice test and submit a script for the Australian Broadcasting Corporation, but this appears to have come to nothing. He did give a lecture, however, to the newly established Writers' League, of which Jean Devanny was president. He had been keen to meet Devanny since they had corresponded in 1933 and she told him about the Workers' Art Club she had founded, with the aim of drawing 'the artistic and would-be artistic crowd' into the radical movement and fostering a progressive, proletarian cultural movement. She had hoped he might be able to get something similar started in Auckland.[3] He saw Devanny herself only for five minutes, however, before she left on a 'propaganda tour' of Queensland for the Movement against War and Fascism. He also visited family friends and acquaintances, including his old history professor J.P. Grossman, who had fled to Sydney after being dismissed from Auckland University College in 1932 when it was discovered that he had been systematically defrauding the professor of philosophy for ten years.

Mason came back on his own. Dan stayed away for several more months
– he got married while he was there, to his longtime girlfriend, Nell – and
the two brothers were not to become involved in business together again. It
is tempting to see Dan and his dubious schemes as the inspiration for the
three-act satirical play entitled 'This Monkey Business' which Mason wrote
sometime during the 1930s. It concerned a trio of would-be tycoons, who in
the opening scene are hanging about in 'a street in a business area' lamenting
their lack of fortune. One is large, florid and unscrupulous; the second tall,
dark and gangly, and wears a permanent air of defeated optimism; the third 'a
skinny little weasel, with bristling hair, flashing eyes, protruding mouth' and
a slightly crazed manner (a thinly disguised self-portrait, perhaps). They
introduce themselves to a dodgy sharebroker named Eric, who seems rather
like Dan – young, smooth-talking and insolent – whose business is being
bankrolled by his rich uncle, a science professor who is doing research into
eugenics. Eric blackmails his uncle into setting the group up as a company
breeding monkmen – the ideal worker. But the professor's conscience gets
the better of his greed and gullibility; he develops a reverse process which
turns men into monkeys and administers it to his nephew, and the monkmen
are liberated.[4] In plot, 'This Monkey Business' is strongly reminiscent of
Karel Capek's 1920 expressionist play *RUR* (in which the term robot was
coined – Spencer Tracy made his debut playing one when it opened on
Broadway), and in parts of Eugene O'Neill's *The Hairy Ape*. It was never
performed.

The satirical voice is one Mason used increasingly in the following years,
in drama and journalism, though not, unlike many of his contemporaries, in
his poetry. He was also working around this time on a long, Swiftian prose
satire entitled 'They Should Be Slaves', a 33-page manuscript purporting to
be a speech given by a business entrepreneur to the Waipoua Chamber of
Commerce in 1933, outlining a ten-year scheme to solve unemployment and
save the economy by giving workers and farmers the same rights and protection
as private property: the upper classes would be compelled to buy the proletariat,
in proportion to their income. Slavery was no crueller than the present social
system, and planned production – and reproduction – was 'the keynote of
the 20th. century'. The piece was modelled, possibly, on Swift's *Modest Proposal*
for alleviating Ireland's poverty by fattening the children of the poor to feed
to the rich. It was never published, although he did once deliver it to a trade
union meeting.[5]

In December 1935 *Tomorrow* printed 'The Mountain of the Gods', a short, cynical fable by Mason about a bishop and a bank manager as the enemies of youth, hope and imagination.[6] Whether it was with hope or cynicism that Mason greeted the election of the country's first Labour government on 27 November that year is not recorded. In his notebook he had once begun drafting the regulations of the First Soviet Government of the District of Auckland, drawn up after the collapse of the Labour Capitalist Government of New Zealand in 1935.

WHEN MASON came back from Sydney, Lowry had told Glover in May, 'we [will] have a hundred, possibly five or six, to put into the Unicorn' and '[w]e're going to start publishing in earnest'.[7] It seems unlikely, however, that Mason came back with a few hundred pounds to invest in the press, as Lowry appears to have been expecting. They printed only one book during 1935, *Academic Freedom in New Zealand, 1932–34* by F.A. de la Mare, a compendium of documents relating to the several controversies that had excited the university colleges in those years, along with some jobbing work. They printed stationery for Mason Sterling and the various other enterprises Ron and Dan were involved with, and invitations for Irene Jenkin's wedding in August. (For a wedding present Mason gave her Hardy's *Jude the Obscure* and Ibsen's *Ghosts*, which he promptly borrowed back.) They had undertaken to publish D'Arcy Cresswell's poem – as he styled it – *Lyttelton Harbour*, a kind of autobiography in thirty-four sonnets, but this faced a long and difficult passage through the press, owing largely to Cresswell's circumstances being as penurious as the Unicorn's own. When the pages had finally been printed but remained unbound, Cresswell removed them to his bach at Castor Bay on the North Shore, where he was scraping a living on the generosity of his friends, meaning to get them bound and distribute them himself. Lowry and his partners, he had discovered – and complained to Glover – were 'in a very bad way, can't get ahead with the binding, nor pay any bills, and might even have the premises closed and stock seized for rent any day – including my poem'.[8] The book came out, from the Unicorn Press nevertheless, in 1936, for private sale only in an edition of 150 – 'a curious thing, too obscure for most New Zealanders, and absurdly priced at five shillings', Jane Mander tartly remarked. 'I am afraid it will be a flat failure.'[9]

Of more literary note, in 1936 the Unicorn also published Frank Sargeson's first collection of short stories, *Conversations with My Uncle*, and a short critical essay on Katherine Mansfield by Arthur Sewell. Although still hardly bounding away, it was, it seems, getting to its feet. But Mason was no longer involved. In the autumn of 1936 he left the press. Managing a business with Lowry and virtually no money (there was barely ever even petty cash) had become more than he could take. For the remainder of the year, it appears that his only income was from part-time teaching at Takapuna Grammar.

In April he took part in the inaugural New Zealand Authors' Week, a programme of lectures, exhibitions and radio talks held in the four main centres, which was intended to be the first of an annual event but was not to be repeated for another fifteen years. Its aim was to focus attention on 'the high cultural level at which New Zealand stands, and the lofty panorama of its work in literature', a sentiment which Mason probably regarded with the same disdain as most of his literary friends.[10] It was organised by the New Zealand branch of the international writers' organisation PEN, which had been established, on the initiative of Pat Lawlor, two years previously. Mason had joined but he did not remain a member for long. In March he had thanked Lawlor, the secretary, for fixing his subscription for him, assuring him that 'I shall settle as soon as I possibly can. At the moment I simply can't', and adding, 'That is in strictest confidence – I *must* maintain before the world an appearance of affluence.'[11]

Already PEN was regarded by the younger writers as the preserve of the old guard – Marris and Mulgan and friends – and Authors' Week with the same cynicism as an exercise in self-congratulation and puffery. 'Terrible people are running it here. Damn them', Sargeson complained to Glover. 'I shall keep on writing for the overseas markets.'[12] Winston Rhodes gave the event a short and disappointed report in *Tomorrow*, lamenting the tameness of the local literary scene and calling for 'honest, forthright criticism' and literature that dealt with life, his predominant theme.[13] But Fairburn, Hyde, Mander, Cresswell and Arthur Sewell, along with Mason, were among those who participated in the Auckland programme, which was held at the Art Gallery in Kitchener Street and reportedly attracted large and appreciative audiences. It all 'went off with éclat . . . lots of cars parked outside and so on'.[14] Mason's subject was 'The future of New Zealand literature', chosen, he told Lawlor, 'as a nice easy one – no one can challenge me on a matter of fact'.[15] The text of his talk has not survived, but Robin Hyde – who as a late inclusion on the programme had given a hastily prepared talk on 'The writer and his audience' in the previous session – made this report on both his and Fairburn's contributions in *Art in New Zealand*:

... we had A.R.D. Fairburn rising to speak on Auckland poets, and, after a little scattering of birdshot among the stuffed turtledoves of the long ago, giving the impression that he had sailed right around the coasts of New Zealand, eventually discovering those wild shores to be inhabited solely by R.A.K. Mason, making ink with the greatest difficulty from the gallbladders of financial cuttlefishes. As for Mr. Mason, he, billed to speak on the future of New Zealand literature, hoped for a mighty political uprising coincident with a great literary outpouring, but in the absence of either could only put up his umbrella in the pious hope of red rain, and so depart.[16]

The accompanying booklet, *Annals of New Zealand Literature: a bibliography of New Zealand writers past and present*, prefaced by a handful of brief thematic essays, was not such a success. Large numbers remained unsold, and it had been subject to a boycott even during its preparation. Mason had apologised to Lawlor that, as both Fairburn and Cresswell were 'against it', he had 'decided to chip in with them' while assuring him that it was nothing personal.[17] The result was that *No New Thing* was listed only in the addendum at the back. It is curious, even so, that Marris, editor of the annual *New Zealand Best Poems*, in his survey of 'Our younger generation of writers' (by which he really meant poets), mentioned Fairburn, de Montalk, Cresswell and Hyde among several others, but failed to notice Mason, and Curnow too.

IT WAS PERHAPS because of Mason's falling out with Lowry (professionally, at least) that it was Glover who published his next volume of poems, *End of Day*. This came out late in May 1936, in an edition of 150 – a large one for the infant Caxton Press – in pale green covers with the title in blood red. It contained five poems, and was dedicated 'ad mariam' (to Marie).

Like *No New Thing* it was not all that new. 'Youth at the Dance' had first been published in 1932, and was now a verse shorter. 'Prelude', published in *Tomorrow* in January 1936 (and again in February, corrected), like the untitled prelude to *No New Thing* defined the poet's purpose and his style, and like the 'Song of Allegiance' in *The Beggar* acknowledged his literary mentors:

> This short straight sword
>   I got in Rome
>   when Gaul's new lord
>   came tramping home:

It did that grim
  old rake to a T –
  if it did him,
  well, it does me.

Leave the thing of pearls
  with silken tassels
  to priests and girls
  and currish vassals:

Here's no fine cluster
  on the hilt, this drab
  blade lacks lustre –
  but it can stab.

His was the sword of 'Caesar and Tacitus, Lucretius and Catullus', Mason
declared, a language of 'brevity, precision and an almost colloquial quality' by
contrast with the 'politicians' Latin' of 'that windbag Cicero';[18] this was tough,
plain poetry, readers were warned. But the poems which follow were not
battle cries. Two of them had appeared in *Kiwi* in 1934: 'Payment', a lament
for past passion, heavy with sadness and loneliness; and a sombre sonnet on
death and solipsism, a 'Fugue' in both structure and theme:

All the selves that have been slain
  have so drenched this place with pain
  how can any soul endure
  where the whole ground is impure
  with its own dead?
       I'll escape
  these charnel-clutches and I'll shape
  fresh selves under other skies:
  and where there new ghosts arise
  I shall drag away once more
  from that dead-polluted shore.

And so till the last mutation
  puts an end to all migration
  and I lie in that blank land

where Time cannot stretch his hand
and the future cannot daunt me
and there is no past to haunt me.

'New Life' had been published in *Tomorrow* in April 1936 (as 'Notes for a
New Life'):

Before I found
     how it is ungainly
     to stand your ground
     and struggle vainly

Have my assurance
     that I have known
     sweatstreaked endurance
     and screech of the bone

I have stripped for the fight
     I have stripped for the main
     I have stripped for lovenight:
     I shall not strip again.

Where the captains of events
     charged hordes and were shattered
     stand Time's stone regiments
     brave-brain-bespattered

Negro-softly hard
     bonelicked clean of desire's
     least hint come knots charred
     from ancient fires.

Now entertain no slow
     dark cynic blood
     veins which, I pray, no flow
     of zeal may flood.

The title is ironic, of course. 'New Life' sits thematically alongside 'Wise at Last' and 'The Just Statesman Dies' as a reflection on a former life of struggle and passion. The poem is an admission, it seems, that it was not worth the fight (and that the odds were not even); it is about 'the freeing of the self from desire, from struggle, from "zeal"'.[19] In this company, 'Youth at the Dance' reads less easily as a straightforwardly revolutionary poem. Such gestures towards, or in despair of, a redemptive moment in life or history, Curnow would speculate, 'may come to the same thing'.[20]

End of Day attracted a handful of reviews, which welcomed back 'one of our most original poets' (*Auckland Star*) after an absence of 'some years' (Christchurch *Press*) and remarked on his 'unusual power of expression' and 'uncompromising effects'. One senses that they still did not know what to make of Mason. In *Tomorrow*, at greater length, Rhodes admired his economy and mastery of form – 'He wastes no time or words, and perhaps better than other writer of verse in New Zealand he knows how to mould his matter into suitable shape' – while noting the 'occasional mannerism' that irritated: '"Negro-softly hard" whatever may follow it is not a line likely to fulfil its mission, because more is lost in the collision of ideas than is gained in the shock'. The *Press* reviewer also seems to have stumbled here, remarking that 'his conciseness is in "New Life" carried to such a pitch that his lines become incomprehensible'. But it was right, Rhodes observed, that poetry should be hard, and it was to be welcomed that Mason was not yet another writer of 'pretty verse nor Guidebook doggerel', nor of easy propaganda.[21]

IN MORE THAN one sense, 1936 marked a change in Mason's life. One was creatively. *End of Day* was the last new publication of his poems for five years. It was not as though he had been prolific. But now he turned his attention away from poetry, or at least from poetry as he had been writing it.

In the spring of 1936 he was engaged as 'audience-organiser' for a WEA drama group production of Clifford Odets's *Waiting for Lefty*. From this came the establishment of the People's Theatre, in which, for the next few years, Mason was to be keenly involved. Theatre was not a new interest. He had been trying his hand at writing plays at least since the late 1920s, and had shared Fairburn's enthusiasm for, though not presence on, the amateur stage when they were both in their teens. He had been interested, particularly, in the idea of forming a political or workers' theatre ever since Jean Devanny had suggested it to him in 1933. Now the opportunity arose. Theatre was the medium in which, he hoped, he could creatively combine his literary and political interests: 'bring my artistic feelings into line with my intellectual knowledge', as he would put it to Denis Glover the following year.[22]

The WEA drama group had been making its mark on the Auckland theatrical scene for the previous few years with its annual productions: of Chekhov's *The Cherry Orchard* in 1932, Pirandello's *Six Characters in Search of an Author* in 1933, Toller's *Masses and Man* in 1934, and *The Hairy Ape* in 1935. These were radical fare for an audience accustomed to 'the drawing-room plays, the polite comedies, the substitutes for levitation dreams of Sir James Barrie, the Noel Cowardice, and the spawn of Ibsen', in Fairburn's words, that constituted the familiar repertoire of the Little Theatre and the Grafton Shakespeare and Dramatic Society.[23] The WEA productions were impressive equally for their style and standard of production as for the choice of play. The man responsible for both was Arnold Goodwin (producer of *Lefty* as well), a commercial artist and set designer who had trained in London, Paris and New York before arriving in New Zealand in 1913, and in 1935 had been appointed head of design at Elam School of Art. Mason would later remark that the two people from whom he learned the most about the theatre were the Irish playwright J.M. Synge and Arnold Goodwin.[24]

The WEA's 1936 production was something else again. *Waiting for Lefty* was the play of the moment and a classic of its time. Based on the New York taxi-drivers' strike of 1933, it had been premiered by New York's Group Theatre in January 1935, directed by Elia Kazan, who, along with Odets, was a member of the Group Theatre's Communist 'cell'. The central action of the play is a union meeting, which is interspersed with a series of episodes typifying the lives of the union members and the implications of the strike; placing some of the actors among the audience turns the theatre itself into the union hall. The play ends with a rallying cry to industrial militancy as the actors on stage turn to the audience calling 'Strike! Strike! Strike!' *Lefty* ran for ninety-three nights on Broadway and quickly became an essential work in the repertoire of left theatre groups around the world. With its mix of agit-prop and naturalistic theatre forms and its successful Broadway run, it typified the development of left-wing theatre in the 1930s as 'the most mature outcome of the collaboration of Workers Theatre and professional sympathizers and the most potent result of the fusion of Agit-Prop and social realism'.[25] As such it was an expression of a larger cultural development which paralleled the political rise of the Popular Front, the broad-based mobilisation of progressive opinion against fascism which gained such clarity and urgency after the outbreak in July 1936 of the Spanish Civil War.

Ideologically, the Popular Front was founded on the policy change instituted by the Communist International at its seventh world congress in 1935. There the old sectarian line, which had eschewed the industrial and political labour movements as reformist and reactionary, was abandoned for a tactical alliance of all progressive forces in the fight against the dark forces, fascism, and in defence of the promised land, the Soviet Union. Intellectually and emotionally, its catalyst was the potent combination of the Depression (the clear evidence of both the evil and the imminent collapse of capitalism), the seemingly inexorable rise of fascism and the apparent inevitability of another world war. In New Zealand the comrades were a little slow on the uptake, but follow the new line they eventually did, seeking affiliation with the Labour Party (in vain) and campaigning for Labour in the 1938 general election (in 1935 they had stood their own candidates). They changed the name of their weekly newspaper in 1939 from the *Workers' Weekly* to the *People's Voice*, although it was *Tomorrow* which became the most significant organ of Popular Front opinion, and fostered factional activity in a range of progressive organisations.[26] Here, as in Western countries throughout the world, Spanish medical aid committees and support for the International Brigades, the Left Book Club with its monthly orange-covered paperbacks and discussion groups, the fellow-traveller like Mason, with but not in the Party, the new theatre movement, the signing of manifestos and arguments about art and engagement – all were manifestations of the Popular Front and of the peculiarly heightened atmosphere of this time.

For Mason, of course, though not for many others, this commitment was neither new nor fleeting. And the People's Theatre was not just about turning art to the purpose of anti-fascism, but was the promise of a new, popular cultural movement. It was to last for only about as long as the Popular Front itself.

AS 'AUDIENCE-ORGANISER' for *Waiting for Lefty*, Mason canvassed the trade unions with a special half-price ticket offer of one shilling for block bookings of at least twenty-four seats. He spoke on the new theatre movement at a Rationalist Association meeting at the Strand Theatre, and most likely wrote the publicity material and programme notes for *Lefty*, which gave a potted history of the theatre and described the international success of the play. For centuries theatre had ignored, and in turn been ignored by, the masses; drama had been 'reduced to a sham and a lie: theatre-going became a mere intellectual snobbery, a fashionable fad, a social duty affected by a few'. The brave Little Theatre movement which emerged in the 1880s had proved to be 'a sort of theatrical Fabianism' and had failed to win the popular audience. Today, however, Mason wrote, 'All the best elements of the old drama are being melted down and forged anew in the fire of democratic enthusiasm', and a new movement was arising which 'promises to give us a dramatic revival surpassing those under Elizabeth in England or in Athens under Pericles'. Theatre was coming back to the people. 'There is an old legend concerning a giant, Antaeus, whose strength must be refreshed by contact with the earth. Such a giant is Art. Once an art becomes divorced from contact with the masses, it becomes flabby and sterile. It is one of the most hopeful signs of our age that more and more experts in every branch of the arts are emerging from the "ivory tower" of isolation and renewing their strength by contact with the life of the masses.' Thus 'The performance you are seeing to-night is more than a play', the programme for *Waiting for Lefty* announced, 'it is the promise of a new artistic and social future.'[27]

The play ran for a week from 17 October in the WEA hall in Symonds Street (the old Grammar School), which had a stage 'the size of a country hotel bedroom' and seating (on old school forms) for an audience of about 300. It was preceded by a dance adaptation of Hilaire Belloc's 'Miranda' and *Suilven and the Eagle* by Gordon Bottomley, a 'mystic and thoughtful poem-drama', presented by the dramatic practice class.[28] 'All Auckland is Waiting for Lefty' was the title of one of Mason's leaflets. In reality, most of Auckland was waiting for Jean Batten, who landed at the Mangere aerodrome in her Piper Gull monoplane on the afternoon of Friday, 16 October to complete the first direct flight from England to New Zealand, and embarked on a lecture tour at the Civic Theatre the next night. Still, houses for *Lefty* were full. At least eleven unions and the Young Communist League had taken advantage of the block-booking offer, 150 tickets were sold at the Otahuhu railway workshops, and booking office returns from Lewis Eady's came to just over £37. The *Star* and the *New Zealand Herald* gave it complimentary notices, managing to look past its 'propagandist' purpose to admire the novelty of its technique and dramatic presentation – but only just. 'The play might be suitably renamed "How Communists are Made"', the *Herald* reviewer observed, and noted that 'while one can readily understand its appeal among the depressed classes of some of the big cities of the United States, New Zealand definitely lacks the conditions to give it semblance of reality or to point its satire with sting'.[29]

In *Tomorrow* it was reviewed with unqualified enthusiasm by Frank Sargeson, who was himself writing drama at this time and had recently completed a play 'written round Communist agitation' entitled 'The Struggle'.[30] For Goodwin's production, he wrote, 'no praise is high enough', and both new and unexpected actors gave 'thrilling performances'. The play itself 'is a Strike play, as most readers know, it is a revolutionary encitement, but it is true art'.[31] This prompted a three-page response from Fairburn in the next issue, arguing that *Lefty* was not art but 'a solid hunk of Communist propaganda, dressed for the theatre', in which art had been 'subordinated to political expediency'. Still, he commended it for its freshness and vigour and admitted to having 'enjoyed it tremendously'.[32] He even joined the cast for the next production – the first by the new People's Theatre – in December.

On the strength of the success of *Lefty*, a meeting was held at the WEA hall the following Saturday – attended by about a hundred, the *Herald* reported – to discuss the formation of a People's Theatre League to encourage the production and writing of plays 'with a special working class interest'.[33] It was chaired by the secretary of the Timber Workers' Union, Fred Craig, and addressed by representatives of the union movement and the WEA. Arnold Goodwin outlined his vision of a theatre that would be 'owned and controlled by the people with artisans and technicians paid at Trade Union rates', putting on a play a month. Mason discussed the production of *Lefty* and presented the results of an audience survey, a multiple-choice questionnaire in which over 90 per cent of the respondents had rated the performance excellent, agreed that such plays would assist in workers' education, and expressed their interest in seeing more; only one thought it was 'horrid'. The lawyer Dick Singer (to whom Mason had sent his first, home-made book, 'In the Manner of Men', in 1923) thought that any such movement must also aspire to artistic excellence: 'to produce the best exponents of the English language'.[34]

Arthur Sewell moved that a People's Theatre be formed, and a twenty-member organising committee was appointed. Before it had a chance to meet, however, Mason convened an 'irregular' meeting to 'ensure proper Trade Union representation on the committee'.[35] He was elected to the chair at the next meeting of the organising committee, which approved of this initiative, then discussed the mechanics of representation and democratic procedure as set out in the fifteen-page draft constitution drawn up by Singer. A general meeting the following Sunday, 15 November, chaired by Mason again and attended by about sixty members, formally adopted the constitution and elected a duly representative executive committee, consisting of three members of the Transport Union, two railway workers and a representative of the WEA. Sewell was elected president, and Goodwin, Craig and Singer vice-presidents;

Mason was appointed organiser, and Bill Deuchar, an electrician, secretary. The constitution defined the organisation's purpose: 'For a mass development of the Theatre to its highest social level: for a theatre dedicated to the struggle against all forms of reaction, such as war, fascism, censorship, and other interferences with democratic rights.' Unions which guaranteed to purchase tickets at a reduced price for each performance for 12.5 per cent of their membership became affiliated members; their representatives, together with the executive committee, formed the 'grand council' or governing body of the theatre. Individual membership was set at a shilling a year. 'For a theatre owned and controlled by the people', the membership application card declared.[36]

For its first production the People's Theatre revived *Waiting for Lefty*, which was performed for three nights in December (preceded by a Western, *Two in Revolt*) at the Haywards Municipal Theatre in working-class Avondale. This time the response was not so encouraging. Audiences were 'small and not very appreciative': perhaps, it was speculated, because 'they were meeting something entirely new to them and not easily understood. Moreover the speed and violence of that remarkable play possibly stunned them after the insipid pictures to which they had been accustomed'; perhaps also because it was so close to Christmas.[37] But the People's Theatre was not deterred, and plans were soon afoot to take *Lefty* further afield.

AT THE END of December Mason attended the WEA summer school, which was held that year at Hunua Falls in the ranges south-east of Auckland. He went down with the advance party, who cleared tracks, dug latrines and erected tents, and became the camp's unofficial botanical field guide, taking guided bush walks – probably in the rain, for the summer of 1936–37 was unusually cold and wet. 'See our beautiful bush, under the personal guidance of SHORT-CUT MASON the WOODLAND WIZARD', announced the 'Hunua. Sporting. Ungrammatic Review' (the title was a spoof on the *Illustrated Sporting and Dramatic Review*).[38]

In the formal programme Mason gave three lectures in a series on 'Literature in an Age of Change'. In the first, as reported in the WEA *Bulletin*, he defined 'the three schools of criticism, the Textual, the Formal, the Social': it was the last in which he was chiefly interested. 'The question was how is it that Elizabethan England had the glory of Shakespeare, then passed to the dullness of Pope and Blackmore, again to burst out with Keats and Shelley? Literature, to live, must be related to a virile society.' This was demonstrated by the plain fact that 'today where the workers, the rising class, have control, art is flourishing', while in countries where they were suppressed 'it does not exist – in Italy and Germany there is not one writer left who has any real standing'. If his thesis seems simplistic, Mason was only presenting the prevailing critical analysis of the cultural left at this time. It was hard to ignore, in the late 1930s, the banning of books and the exile of writers from the fascist countries, and, conversely, the flourishing of culture and the status accorded to the artist and writer by both the people and the state in the Soviet Union – facts which were enviously documented in the left-wing press, in *Tomorrow* as well as the *Workers' Weekly*. This was a time of theoretical simplification and ideological absolutes. Capitalism and fascism spelt the death of Western culture, socialism was to be its saviour. Only under socialism, it really seemed, would the arts be free, popular and vital.

The next lecture in the series was 'Literature at the Crossroads', given by Willis Airey, the Marxist lecturer in history at Auckland University College, with whom Mason became good friends. Airey was a gentle, kind and unassuming man of strong left-wing convictions and intellectual depth, like Mason himself, who liked him enormously. Mason's second lecture dealt with 'The Road to the Right', and began with an exposition of 'the relation between form and content, positive and negative, subjective and objective, evolutionary and revolutionary ways of thought'. He then retailed the sorry story of T.S. Eliot, the *bête noire* of the literary left, who had once been a great poet of 'the dreariness and shabbiness of life – portraying its misery but with no solution', and in his despair and his quest for formal perfection had become all surface and negativity, and finally had 'reached the stage where there is nothing left to polish'. In his third lecture Mason discussed 'The Road to the Left: Proletarian Literature'. Petty-bourgeois artists, such as the futurists and the surrealists – 'unstable, explosive and anarchistic' – had identified with the working class but their sympathy was superficial. The progressive cultural movement of today, Mason argued, must be engaged, and must learn equally from the popular literature of the past (from such forms as Negro spirituals, Wobbly poetry, Scottish ballads), from the great thinkers of the past, and from the rise of the oppressed classes today. He concluded by reading Kenneth Patchen's 'Joe Hill listens to the praying' (from Patchen's just-published first book, *Before the Brave*) and Day Lewis's 'Johnny Head-in-Air'.

In another lecture he applied his Marxist analysis to New Zealand's literary history, perhaps repeating some of his Authors' Week talk. With a few exceptions, the sturdy creative spirit of the pioneers had long ago been lost, while the ruling classes had 'failed to produce the least flicker of intelligence'

Above: Frank and Jessie Mason with their second son, Ronald,
known to the family as John.
Hocken Library, E5308/29

Above right: Jessie, 1930s.
Hocken Library, E3193/84

Below: Queen Street, 1910s, with Mason's Hairdressing Saloon
(centre), next door to the Auckland Savings Bank.
Auckland Star Collection, Alexander Turnbull Library, G-2886-1/1

Above: Ronald (far right) standing next to his aunt, Foster Kells, with a Lichfield School party at Whakarewarewa, Labour weekend 1915. Mason lived in Lichfield with his aunt for four years.
Archives New Zealand, Auckland Regional Office, BANN 1861/1g

Left: Jessie and 'John', about 1917.
Hocken Library, E5308/33

Opposite above: Two photos of Mason as a Grammar School boy, 1917.
Hocken Library, E3193/82
Hocken Library, E5308/32

Opposite below: Auckland Grammar upper sixth, 1921, with headmaster J.W. Tibbs, centre; Mason, 'with manly hair', in the back row, left.
Hocken Library, E3193/80

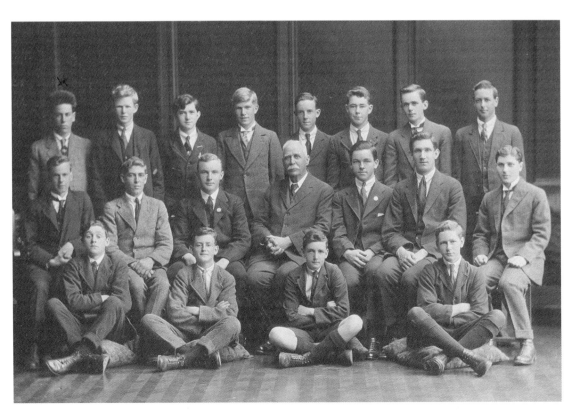

Opposite: Mason, about 1928, when he was a student at Auckland University College.
Hocken Library, E2231/12

Above left: Clifton Firth, friend and photographer, socialist and entrepreneur. Self-portrait.
Auckland City Libraries, 34-Z140

Above right: Geoffrey de Montalk, friend and fellow poet, 1924. He would later find fame as Count Potocki, pretender to the Polish throne.
Stephanie de Montalk

Right: Mason's closest friend, Rex Fairburn, and Jocelyn Mays, just married, at Clench Common, 1932.
Hocken Library, E2240/13

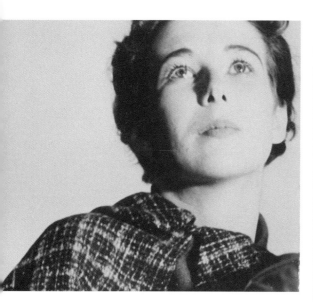

Above: Rita Chapman: 'a short-cut nose,
Venus, and child's eyes' ('Vengeance of
Venus'), 1941.
Hocken Library, E2053/25

Right: Edwynna (Teddy) Roussel, with whom
both Mason and Fairburn were in love.
Mason wrote 'Be swift o sun' about her.
A.R.D. Fairburn Literary Estate

Below: Marie Gaudin, Mason's 'steady date' for
ten years, at Piha, about 1930.
John Caselberg

Mason's older brother, W.T.F. Kells Mason (Dan), sometime lawyer and businessman. In 1931 he was found guilty of 'gross professional misconduct' and struck off.
Hocken Library, E503/148

R.A.K. Mason, November 1930.
Hocken Library, E5309/24

A WEA group at Anawhata, mid-1930s. From left: A.H. O'Keefe, W.B. Sutch, P. Williams, Horace Belshaw, Rex Fairburn (in plus-fours), Morva Sutch, Jack Basham, Mason (with cigarette), Ormond Wilson, Doris Basham, Dick Anschutz (obscured), Norman Richmond.
Hocken Library, E575/25

Opposite: Portrait of the young communist by Clifton Firth, late 1930s.

Right: Mason and Dorothea Beyda at Hunua Falls, January 1937, the summer they met.

Below: Summer school friends, Hunua, 1937. From left: Mary Dobbie, Jean Alison, Mason, Shirley Barton.

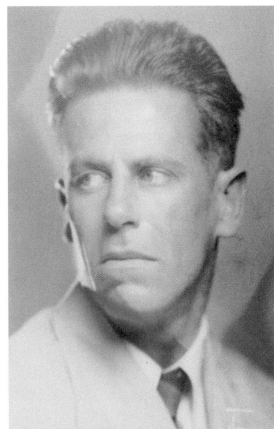

Opposite above: Mason (far right) in a WEA production of Jack Coppard's *Cartoon*, November 1939.
Auckland City Libraries, NZMS 867/6/5

Opposite below: Comrades at Castor Bay, November 1940. From left: Anne Purdy, Doolie Wilson, Elizabeth Richards, Vic Wilcox (the Communist Party's Auckland branch secretary), Gordon Watson ('general secretary'), Mason, Flora Gould and Sid Scott (just back from the Soviet Union).
Hocken Library, E2035/18

Above left: Mason and Dorothea, 1941.
Hocken Library, E579/6

Above right: Mason, editor of *In Print*, about the time he appeared in court in 1942 charged with breaching the wartime censorship regulations. Portrait by Bert Tornquist.
Hocken Library, E6893/12

Right: Jean Alison, Blackwood Paul and Mason (looking 'like a convict') at the Centennial Exhibition in Wellington, January 1940.
Hocken Library, E6893/1

WHOOPEE! EXHIBITION 1940 *FUN FOTO*

Mason's house at Crown Hill, designed by Vernon Brown, almost finished. Hocken Library, E576/29

Mason and Dorothea on holiday in the Bay of Islands, May 1949, the month his mother died.
Hocken Library, E575/24

At the Redvale 'Ranch', 1950.
Hocken Library, E576/30

Above: Mason in China, 1957: Rewi Alley, Dorothea, Mason, Irene Young, guide, Ramai Hayward.
Hocken Library, E578/11

Below: Mason and Ramai Hayward in fur coats, from Rudall Hayward's film *Inside Red China*, 1957.
Hocken Library, E578/9

Opposite: Clifton Firth's portrait of Mason for the *Collected Poems* (1962).
Hocken Library, E578/12

Right: Mason, John Griffin and Denis Glover at the launch of the *Collected Poems*, July 1962, from the *Dunedin Photo Review*.
Hocken Library, E2033/7

Below left: Mason at Charles Brasch's crib at Broad Bay, 1964. He lived here for several months during his time in Dunedin in 1962–65.
Hocken Library, E575/26

Below right: Auckland, 1971.
John Caselberg

Dunedin, 1963.
Hocken Library, E580/3

and had driven any creative talent there was to leave ('brains were amongst our largest exports'). Recent attempts to establish a middle-class culture (did he mean the *Kowhai Gold* or the *Phoenix* school?) were too late, for 'at the moment of its inception history is giving such culture death blows throughout the world', while of the 'intermediate classes' he cited Fairburn as characteristic in 'turning first to the left, then to the right in wavering hesitation'. Finally there was the working class, who needed assistance 'to take dominance in the intellectual field in such potentially valuable movements as Peoples Theatre'.

Mason was thin and nervous as a cat, Shirley Barton, who first met him there, later recalled; his hands shook and his trousers were frayed at the ends. But he was deeply impressive in his belief and passion. 'We sat on the floor on our straw palliasses, rain and cold outside and the fires of the mind within . . . To hear R.A.K. read "Johnny-Head-In-Air" was an experience not to be forgotten.'[39]

At Hunua Mason also met Dorothea Beyda, and fell in love. Dorothea was several years older than Mason – forty in 1936 – and separated, with a ten-year-old son. She had come to Hunua with her friend Mary Barkas, a psychologist who was living in retirement on the coast north of Thames after a career in practice in England, breeding schnauzers and studying Chinese philosophy; she gave a lecture in the 'Science and Social Needs' series at the school. Dorothea had arrived in New Zealand with her young son, Austin, and an unmarried sister in 1930, and lived at first on a farm near Cambridge with a friend, later in a converted garage on the Coromandel coast. She had been born Dorothea Mould in Southport, educated at convent schools in Skipton and Belgium, where she developed a talent for languages, and worked as a secretary and translator in London and Cologne. In 1923–24 she had sat with her friends on the floor of the Poetry Bookshop each week listening to the reading while Mason was putting together his first book and sending copies of *The Beggar* to Harold Monro. Her husband was a Syrian whom she had met in Madeira and who was by then in the United States. Dorothea was tall and handsome, with sun-bronzed skin, dark brown eyes and silver hair; sensual, affectionate and possessive – a lot like Jessie. She, too, was to call him John. They 'fell in love straight away'. Norman Richmond told her that Mason had been ill, 'and he looked it, thin, white and shaky, and with deep furrows in his face . . . ingrained with dirt'.[40] When the summer school was over she returned with him to Auckland and moved into 451 Great South Road. She found a job in the city as a copy-typist while Austin went to boarding school, and set about getting a divorce. Mason told Marie Gaudin, who was still his 'steady date', that he could not see her any more.

15

Waiting for Lefty

1937–38

IN THE NEW YEAR of 1937 Mason applied for a part-time job teaching English at Elam. He wrote hastily to the director, Archie Fisher, at the beginning of February, explaining that he was just going out of town, and 'If there is no application from me by the time you start considering them, for the love of Jesus and Mary would you mind giving my home a ring.'[1] Dorothea believed that he didn't get the job because of his politics, although it may have been more to the point that he didn't have a university degree. At least she had work. Jessie, now seventy-two, thought that Dorothea had money and would look after both her and Ron.

Mason did not have a job, but he threw himself energetically into the work of the People's Theatre. As organiser he set about signing up the trade unions, in 'accordance with its avowed policy of establishing in this country a theatre to be owned, controlled and operated by the workers'.[2] By the end of 1939 thirteen unions had affiliated, but only three did so in the first eighteen months. Mason's notes listed groups that should be approached for assistance 'in this order: workers, unemployed, farmers, churches, friendly societies, returned soldiers', and in due course the government; and identified potential sources of funding in addition to membership fees and ticket sales: business houses, 'public personages', 'art unions', etc.[3] He made contact with left theatre groups overseas, including the New Theatre Leagues in Melbourne and Sydney (formerly Jean Devanny's Workers' Art Club), and the Left Book Club Theatre Guild and the Unity Theatre in London, of which the People's Theatre became an affiliated member in July 1937. Establishing relations with the international movement provided not only comradely encouragement but also access to playscripts. Among Mason's papers are copies of *New Theatre* (London), *Theatre for the People* (published by the Left Book Club Theatre Guild) and *International Theatre* magazine. Long-term plans included acquiring a permanent theatre and establishing a library, and building a thriving workers' theatre movement nationwide. There was no reason, Mason told a meeting of theatre members, why over the next two or three years, 'barring the advent

226

of war or fascism' (a prescient qualification, as it turned out), they should not
extend their activities to become a national theatre. He also recorded in his
notes the resolution that 'every effort be made to concentrate on offering
first-class entertainment and that no person be allowed to turn a function into
a political meeting'.[4]

In his draft speech notes Mason addressed the intractable problem of
combining politics and art, which was also a central theme of his life. It was
best, he recommended, that they 'avoid abstract theorising as far as possible
for the present. Take the art V propaganda argument: if the question is
formulated & considered mechanistically then it is hopeless. The very moment
it is considered dialectically we see that art & propaganda are opposites, yes,
but they are interpenetrably opposites: well then we are well on the way to a
solution.' This reveals the influence of his reading of Marxist theory, but it
did not take him far towards a solution, theoretical or practical, of what was
to be a continuing cause of tension in the theatre (as in his life). But the first
principle, he believed, was that the People's Theatre must truly be a popular
one. '*Whether* a person is concerned primarily with propaganda & secondarily
with art *or* primarily with art & secondarily with propaganda there is only one
way of achieving his or her object – namely, ensuring the most democratic
possible form of organisation on a broad mass-basis. Anything else will finally
tend to artistic sterility & political reaction.'[5] Even this was more difficult
than it seemed, however.

In April they took *Lefty* to Waikato – into worker and farmer territory –
on a weekend tour, giving a matinée in Hamilton on Saturday and a
performance in Huntly on Sunday night. Mason took the part of one of the
union members in the audience. In Hamilton they met the same response, or
lack of it, as they had done in Avondale, from 'a small picture-going audience
which didn't quite understand what it was all about'. But Huntly was a coal-
mining town, and here, among 'probably the most militant workers in New
Zealand', they could hope for a more interested reaction. And they got one.
The Huntly miners and their wives 'rolled up and packed the Town Hall
. . . clapped, cheered, laughed and joined in the play when occasion
warranted'.[6] Only later was it learned that the play's coarse language ('foul
and blasphemous . . . to an extent to which New Zealand audiences have
not, as yet at any rate, become wholly accustomed', the *New Zealand Herald*
had observed[7]) had caused offence, the more so because the performance had
been on a Sunday night and many of the audience had come straight from
church. Indeed, the borough council had insisted that the play not start until

eight o'clock when church services were over. Bill Deuchar 'shrewdly suspect[ed] that the Communist propaganda in the play offended the orthodox Labour people and they hung their resentment on the most convenient peg'. But one of the locals assessed the situation more astutely: 'They don't like their own language thrown at them.'[8] The People's Theatre really was a workers' theatre as far as its membership went: more than three-quarters of those who have been identified (eighty-two in all) were workers or trade unionists, leaving aside the affiliated union membership. But engaging the interest of the working class was another matter. The militant miners of Huntly had proved as hard to please as the suburban proletariat of Avondale.

Others were not surprised. Frank Sargeson reported on the Waikato performances in *Tomorrow*, cheekily observing the irony of watching the Hamilton Left Book Club members arriving at the theatre in taxis to see a play about a taxi-drivers' strike. He had heard that the play 'didn't go down too well with the Huntly miners. They objected to THAT sort of language being used in front of their womenfolk, and a disgusted member of the cast told me that the people of this country are bone from the feet up. It is probably quite true. How otherwise would anyone have expected anything different from a performance of Waiting For Lefty in Huntly? After all, there can't be VERY many members of the Left Book Club in Huntly.'[9] Still, the tour had been a triumph of organisation, and it was some consolation to members, perhaps, that it had made a small profit, and to hear from the secretary of the Left Book Club Theatre Guild that *Lefty* had received a 'mixed' response in mining towns in England too.[10]

Their next production was Odets's anti-fascist play *Till the Day I Die*, a more ambitious undertaking requiring a cast of thirty-two (*Lefty* had fifteen). It was produced by Archie Fisher, with a cast drawn 'mostly from Trade Unions', and ran for seven nights at the WEA hall from 18 June, with an extra two performances in response to demand.[11] The Old Grammar School, they discovered, had the disadvantage not only of its size but that it was not licensed for public performances, which would have limited the audience to the hundred or so members of the theatre alone – a legal difficulty they overcame by selling combined membership cards and vouchers which could be redeemed for tickets on the night. Hiring a commercial theatre was for the moment beyond their means, and acquiring one of their own was to remain an ambition. Rehearsals thereafter were held either at the WEA hall or in a room provided rent-free by Dove-Myer Robinson, the former Auckland Communist Party secretary and a member of the People's Theatre committee, above his shop, Robinson's Motorcycles Ltd, in Grey's Avenue (opposite Town Hall corner), which they shared with the Auckland Motorcycle Club.

Till the Day I Die was a powerful indictment of the brutality and depravity of the Nazi regime, depicted in seven short, linked scenes. The first two nights were sold out before the season opened, thanks in part to strong trade union bookings. Public interest may well have been stimulated by the controversy that had recently surrounded the play in Australia, where police had attempted to shut down the Sydney New Theatre League's production during the first act following an official complaint from the German consul-general. Rumours ran that it would meet the same fate in Auckland but the acting Prime Minister, Peter Fraser, publicly stated that there would be no police interference with any theatrical production unless a play was 'obscene'. Fraser was invited to the opening night and went backstage afterwards to congratulate the cast.[12]

The reviewers too were impressed. A 'remarkable piece of dramatic writing (serious, tense and crammed with startling climaxes . . .)', said the *Herald*, a welcome relief from 'the inconsequential plots and drawing room settings of much modern drama' with 'exquisitely gowned young women or sleek-haired, sartorially perfect young men exchanging idle quips and sipping innumerable liqueurs'. However, some of the message had perhaps been lost in the intensity: 'As an instrument of propaganda its harrowing detail and stark cruelty leave with the open-minded an impression almost of incredibility.' 'Drama of terror' the *Star* headlined its review, calling the play 'a mingling of acid-etched drama and tragedy, reminiscent of the gloomy pessimism of the older Russian dramatists, carrying its message through a welter of harrowing emotional scenes': 'Sitting in a darkened hall, their attention claimed by the drama on a small flood-lit stage, the audience had the vivid feeling of being spectators, in a soft, dark void, gazing upon the demonistic toasting of souls in hell-fire, or of peeping from a forest gloom at some savage fire-lit rites accompanying the torture of human beings at the stake.' It was all too much for at least one member of the audience, who wrote to the *Herald* calling for the play to be banned on 'psychological grounds'.[13]

In keeping with the democratic principles of the left theatre movement, the cast remained anonymous. There were no stars in a People's Theatre, nor any of the 'petty jealousy' and 'petty personalities' that characterised the amateur theatre movement – in theory, anyway.[14] Mason played a minor part as a Jewish youth who has seven lines to say before being knocked down by a Nazi trooper, played by Pat Potter of the Auckland General Labourers' Union, who misjudged his stage punch on the first night and landed Mason a hefty blow on the jaw. Mason was excruciatingly bad on the stage, everyone agreed: he was far too self-conscious to be an actor. He did it because being involved was the best way to learn about writing for the theatre ('one must study and practice the art of the theatre as well as the special art of writing for it'), and because participating was all part of the democratic ethos of the People's Theatre movement.[15] But for the remainder of the season he managed to look convincingly frightened as the terrorised Jewish boy.

THE PEOPLE'S THEATRE brought Mason into contact with members of the trade union movement who were to be his close friends and colleagues for many years. One was Pat Potter, this incident notwithstanding; another was Roy Stanley, organiser for the Carpenters' Union and a member of the Communist Party. It was more than circumstance, though, that from this time Mason was associating largely with union and Party people. As Jean Alison saw it, he 'gave up' both poetry and 'the university people' in the mid-1930s to devote himself to the workers' struggle.[16] Or perhaps he was deliberately repudiating a life that he had once, cavalierly or inadvertently, given away. He also needed work.

He became part of the collective producing the new monthly journal of the Carpenters' Union, the *Borer*, which began publication in December 1936 with just a few cyclostyled pages. It was one effect of the introduction of compulsory unionism by the new Labour government in 1936, which saw union membership quadruple in three years. The *Borer* covered political and international as well as industrial and union news – it was one of only two union journals to report on the Spanish Civil War – and printed occasional book reviews and poems by Shelley, Upton Sinclair and Ian Milner: here one detects the hand of Mason, although all contributions were unsigned.

In the autumn of 1937 he became involved in attempts to establish a consumers' co-operative society. This movement, too, had burgeoned as a response to the Depression: there were six retail co-operatives in New Zealand in 1933 and nearly thirty or perhaps as many as sixty (according to different accounts) by 1937, but none so far in Auckland. The move to remedy this had the support of the unions – Tom Stanley, secretary of the Auckland General Labourers' Union (and soon-to-be Communist Party chairman), signed the flyer which called a meeting at the Trades Hall in February – and by June Mason was the organiser and *pro tem* secretary of the Metropolitan Co-operative Society. The key figure, however, appears to have been Denham von Sturmer, the author of a book promoting Danish dairy-farming methods as the cure for New Zealand's languishing butter prices, *New Zealand Down! Denmark Up! or, a modern market race*, and president of the recently formed New Zealand Co-operative Alliance. The Metropolitan Co-operative Society planned to open several stores concentrating on meat and clothing, but would operate first from Percy Landrell's Metropolitan Meat Mart in Karangahape Road.

Mason also bought a share, for £1, in the Progressive Book Society, which was incorporated in July 1937 to give a democratic structure and financial security to Auckland's radical bookshop, Progressive Books, which Jack and Doris Basham had opened in May 1936. Jack Basham was a watersider and communist and Quay Street regular, who had started his bookselling career distributing FSU leaflets on the Auckland waterfront before leasing premises at the top of Pitt Street – the Carpenters' Union fitted out the shop with shelves made from motor car cases. The Progressive Book Society was one of three such co-operative book societies (only tangentially related to the consumers' co-operative societies) which were established in Auckland, Christchurch and Wellington in the late 1930s (a fourth was founded in Dunedin in 1943), each taking over an existing left-wing bookshop that was run by or had links with the Communist Party. Their purpose, to make a wider range of socialist literature available at prices affordable by all, was identical with that of the Left Book Club, of which Mason was most likely a member as well: 'everyone' on the left in the 1930s was a member, at least to the extent of subscribing to the monthly 'choice', if not joining in the discussion groups, picnics and rallies. Mason's old *Phoenix* comrade, Blackwood Paul, by this time in Hamilton running his father's bookselling business, Paul's Book Arcade, had secured the New Zealand distribution rights for the Left Book Club publications when he met Victor Gollancz in London in 1936. They were to include (in 1938) *Poems of Freedom* edited by John Mulgan, an anthology of 'revolutionary' poems from the fourteenth century to the 1930s, in which Mason's 'Youth at the Dance' appeared between C. Day Lewis's 'Magnetic Mountain' and W.H. Auden's 'Brothers'.

The founding committee of the Auckland Progressive Book Society were virtually the same people who had been active in establishing the People's Theatre (although Mason himself was not involved): the triumvirate of radical academics at the university, Airey, Anschutz and Sewell, and Norman Richmond from the WEA; Tom Stanley, Fred Craig and J.G. Kennerley, the secretary of the Carpenters' Union; Jack Basham; a doctor, R.V. Shaw and the left-wing lawyer Frank Haigh – a Popular Front profile of the liberal left

and militant unions with a member or two of the Communist Party. It was
the Party's policy to maintain an active presence in these organisations, and in
the Left Book Club, the Friends of the Soviet Union and the Spanish Medical
Aid Committee, but they of course did not regard themselves as merely
communist fronts, and tensions arose. When Party leaflets were distributed at
the opening night of *Till the Day I Die*, the People's Theatre sent a formal
letter of complaint. The position of the Party in the union movement was
rather more complicated, as Mason was to discover.

A DIARY Mason kept in May–June 1937 records his busy life as an activist
and organiser:

> 4 [May] Tuesday
> Finalised arrangements with Mr Jenkins, general manager Otahuhu railway
> workshops, for Mr von Sturmer to speak. Had small poster sent out . . .
> Attended to Mr von Sturmer's mail & reported to him on long distance . . .
> Gave boys instructions for distribution of leaflets in Grey Lynn.
> Saw Messrs. Stanley, Burbridge & Campbell over T/U delegates, left leaflets:
> wrote Mr Moran of Painters Union.
>
> 5 Wednesday
> drafted names & tentative arrangements for Womens Guild & Educational
> Committee –
> made all preparations for Thursday meeting.
> made enquiries re suitable Hall for central meetings
> continued circularisation by small boys
> saw Miss Stone, went fully in to proposals for meeting of nucleus of Womens
> Guild.
> saw Mr & Mrs Pender & explained general scheme
> met Rationalist Association Executive & finalised plans for Sunday talk.
>
> 6 Thursday
> 7.30 organising c/tee
> conferred with Mr Titchens
> picked up green circulars from P.O. & set small boys to work in Newton area
> went to Otahuhu workshops with Ayres & von S. for mass-meeting –
> subsequently visited S.A.'s Otahuhu shop & went into whole position –
> preliminary inspection of possible sites.

visited Mr Petrie to go further into position of Croatian Benevolent Society: agreed to return with fuller facts.

made final arrangements for Organising committee meeting – attended meeting (see minutes) & spoke: enrolled members.

9 Sunday

afternoon with Mr von Sturmer at Peoples University & afterwards with Executive securing support

evening took chair at Strand for Mr von S – good meeting of 600 – secured enrolment, distributed leaflets

. . .

12 Wednesday

Coronation Day – saw Mr von Sturmer in morning & spent day with him & Mr Richmond – linking up Co-operative & WEA work

Women's Guild meeting in evening fell through

13 Thursday

drafted talk for education c/tee

saw Mr Corles re org. com.

called Mr Cuthbert – out.

spent afternoon attempting to secure enrolments Metro

called Mr Mason's: no meeting – saw Mr Williams – spent evening with Ball – arranged for my attendance at Thursday's meeting of NZWU men

14 Friday

. . .

fixed Wednesday meeting, drew up circular notice for organising c/tee & left with typist

saw Miss Stone & got position of Womens Guild meeting.

issued leaflets for boys

N.B. worst possible weather

16 Sunday

Attended Womens Guild at Dr Anschutz 2.30–5.30: good attendance

. . .

evening at Town Hall – farewell to nurses.

. . .

21 Friday
drew up list of streets in areas over Newton Ponsonby Grey Lynn, Arch Hill,
Eden Terrace & took for typing.
picked up circular from Auckland Service Print.

1 [June] Tuesday
prepared & posted further letters.
. . . got Borer from Mr Kennerley & arranged for page in Engineer with Mr
Burbridge
2.30–4 Women's Cheerio Club – spoke & got addresses
got list of additional addresses from Mr Richmond
prepared & attended organising committee meeting.

2 Wednesday
drafted article for Engineer & other letters.
attended to minutes & report organising committee.
saw Mr Stanley re Saturday
saw Mr Kennerley & explained misunderstanding.
. . .[17]

In mid-June he abruptly resigned from the Metropolitan Co-operative
Society. He cabled von Sturmer: 'Resigned. Position utterly impossible. Other
defections imminent stop. Doing all possible protect other venture. Its chances
excellent. Writing.' The 'other venture' was possibly the People's University
mentioned in his diary, of which nothing more was to be heard. He wrote
to von Sturmer a week later explaining the reasons for his precipitate
move:

the general hush-hush policy of secretiveness, the complete failure of the
Directors to clarify the position, the ignorance of co-operation displayed by
the Board, the contradictory & erratic behaviour of Landrells, the complete
domination of the Society by Landrells, the fact that every person genuinely
interested in co-operation became dissatisfied with methods when introduced
to the organisation & the fact that the Board was, from its composition,
utterly unfitted to represent the people of this city. The fight was hot & I had
to hope that someone would take my side. . . . I had a scheme of reconstruction
to offer, but the Directors kept us waiting till 9.15 & the chairman was hopeless:
as it was, the row lasted till 11. . . . It was impossible for me to either collaborate

with the little clique or to remove them or to further pretend that there was
solidity where actually there was only rottenness.[18]

An article appeared in the *Borer* the following month implying that the
Metropolitan Co-operative Society was not being established in the proper
co-operative manner (i.e., according to the rules laid down by the New
Zealand Co-operative Alliance) and calling for the Trades Council to intervene.
This may or may not have related to Mason's sudden decision to quit.

At the same time, straight after the successful season of *Till the Day I Die*,
he resigned from the People's Theatre committee: 'owing to pressure of private
affairs' is all that is recorded in the theatre's archive.[19]

It is inviting to speculate. And to see, perhaps, a pattern of behaviour –
one that Mason recognised himself, those 'abominable psychological
difficulties' he had confided to Alfred Katz, the 'absurd alternation between
omnipotence and impotence'. Winston Rhodes recognised it, in the way
that Mason would take things on and then sag in the middle, then accuse
himself, then as suddenly plunge into something else; in his continual struggle
to overcome the disillusionment that had beset him at an early age. 'I do want
to brighten life and make this world a better place for my being in it', he had
written to the imaginary German doctor. 'I do try and I sometimes do write
poems about pleasant things, but somehow they don't seem very good. The
optimistic things that I see and read and think and do all seem to slide away
from me when I sit down to write poetry'.[20]

Having resigned from all his unpaid offices, on 29 June Mason registered
as unemployed, which entitled him to a sustenance payment of £1 a week.
He was put on relief work stacking railway lines at the Public Works
Department's Penrose store.

'YOU ASK ME if I am still a marxist,' Mason wrote to Denis Glover in
November 1937.

> With the Manifesto continually happening in large quantities right under my
> nose! Possibly I may some day renounce, but then equally possibly I may
> clutch a crucifix to my dying bosom: & in neither case will it reflect any
> credit on me. As a matter of fact, one reason – only one – why I gave up
> writing was that I wanted to bring my artistic feelings into line with my
> intellectual knowledge. I fancy I have about got there & in the future hope to
> publish some reasonably decent proletarian stuff. It should be done. I have no

excuse for stuff of the old defeatist kind, but I do not want to sacrifice quality of form.[21]

All of the writers of this generation – the *Phoenix* generation, as they can be conveniently, if imprecisely, defined – felt the pressure of their time, the imperative of the 1930s to take a side. But Mason thought the hardest about the particular matrix of Marxism and art, or was the most demanding of himself, or perhaps was simply more of a believer. Glover himself was an ally of the left (and wrote his own bits of 'pylon poetry'), but was too idiosyncratic, or iconoclastic, to be a real fellow-traveller. And Sargeson, after his early flirtation with the Young Communist League, did not remain one of the fold. 'I can't make my mind up about machines & Karl Marx & Russia yet', he had written to Glover in 1936. 'Communist attempts to deal with anything beyond the mechanics of existence seem to me on a level with Y.M.C.A. summer camps' – a characteristically dry remark that has an element of truth.[22]

'That bit "faith in any better order of things" worries me', Sargeson responded to a letter from Glover in August 1937 (referring to what is not known, for Glover's letter has not survived).

> Would any other order of things alter Mason or any of us – much? Dostoevsky, I'm afraid, has had the last word on human nature for long years to come yet. We're all Dostoevskian up here – Mason, Cresswell, Robin Hyde, myself, even Fairburn. Mason of course is the last person in the world who should ever be a Marxist. Those two uncut umbilical cords of his – one leading to his mother & one to his poetry. If there is any fault in his poetry that's it. With Emily Bronte & Emily Dickinson you do feel that they did get out beyond themselves, but Mason never. 'Who touches this book touches a man.' Well, when I take up a book I don't quite want to touch a man. Both Mason & Cresswell are a little different from the rest of us in this way – that whereas life tortures all of us and it is delight & pain, Mason tortures himself, & Cresswell tortures other people, & that gives them a new delight & pain that most of us realise, happily, only in the imagination.[23]

Sargeson said nothing quite so direct in an article on Mason's poetry that he sent to J.H.E. Schroder at the Christchurch *Press* a few months later, entitled 'Food for Tender Stomachs' (after Philip Sidney), but his meaning was the same. Schroder kept the article for four months before returning it, objecting to its 'philosophising beginning' (he would prefer 'less exordium & more

Mason').[24] It was never published but a draft survives. '[P]oets are always being born who appear to be very little indebted to their times for the view they take of the most significant realities of human existence', Sargeson observed, whose theme was 'naked human experience', and who understood that '[s]ocial environments, no matter how perfectly organised, can never entirely relieve the individual from his feeling of loneliness' and his consciousness of the inevitability of decay and death. Mason was one of these, like Hesiod, Leopardi, Brontë and Housman. He referred to Mason's 'gloom' and 'bitterness' and admired his 'epigrammatic' style. The strength of Mason's poetry lay in 'his verbal facility, his feeling for exact epithet', and in his inventiveness of rhythm and form, Sargeson agreed with Harold Monro. He was not so sure he liked the way Mason thought.[25]

MASON HAD NOT, as he intimated to Glover, stopped writing poetry. Three poems which he later published were written over the summer of 1937–38. Each was a love poem, in a way.

'Flow at Full Moon' was for Dorothea. A slow, sensuous lyric, it is unique among Mason's poetry, not only his love poetry, in its calm, its theme of satisfaction and resolution. The flowing rhythm is reminiscent of a traditional form of Irish ballad and, within Mason's œuvre, of 'Nox Perpetua Dormienda', but this is a poem about fulfilment, not frustration:

> Your spirit flows out over all the land between
> > your spirit flows out as gentle and limpid as milk
> > flows on down ridge and through valley as soft and serene
> > as the light of the moon that sifts down through its light sieve of silk

> The long fingers of the flow press forward, the whole hand follows
> > easily the fingers creep they're your hair's strands that curl
> > along the land's brow, your hair dark-bright gleaming on heights
> > > and hollows
> > and the moon illumines the flow with mother of pearl

> Beloved your love is poured to enchant all the land
> > the great bull falls still the opossum turns from his chatter
> > and the thin nervous cats pause and the strong oak-trees stand
> > entranced and the gum's restless bark-strip is stilled from its clatter

Your spirit flows out from your deep and radiant nipples
    and the whole earth turns tributary all her exhalations
    wave up in white breath and are absorbed in the ripples
    that pulse like a bell along the blood from your body's pulsations

And as the flow settles down to the sea it nets me about
    with a noose of one soft arm stretched out from its course:
    oh loved one my dreams turn from sleep: I shall rise and go out
    and float my body into the flow and press back till I find its source.

There is no tension here – except perhaps in the use of 'noose' in the final stanza, which seems an uncomfortable word to evoke wilful surrender.

Dorothea later recalled the occasion of the poem's composition: 'It was while I was at the old house in Ellerslie. After a particular wonderful night in my little room with French windows open on the side garden and the moonlight streaming in, he couldn't settle and wandered out through the wide-open windows into the night and the moonlight. I couldn't keep awake. A few days later I saw the bones of the poem on his desk – with various gaps – a pencilled scribble.'[26] It was one, she said, that he especially loved.

'Twenty-sixth October' was written within a few days of 'Flow at Full Moon', Mason himself later recorded, and reflects his involvement with the People's Theatre at this time, with its 'very distinct Hamlet theme' and play on art and reality.[27] It is a dramatic poem, too, in a more familiar way, narrating a scene within a frame of reference that is at once immediate and immense, familiar and mythic. The poet is approaching the loved one's door

    . . . strode with a dry ironic gesture
        posing a high byronic posture
        towards your barred home, strutting the part
        of young man mocking broken heart

but at the last step turns away, unable to sustain the role. The genesis of this poem – the actual circumstance it describes – Mason did not divulge, only that there was one.

'Vengeance of Venus' was addressed to Rita Chapman, a young artist and keen member of the People's Theatre, whom he first met at rehearsals at the WEA in 1937. He would walk over to Glenfield to the farmlet where she lived with her mother and brother, she remembered, in the summer of

1937–38, and they would sit in the shade of the verandah and talk about politics and poetry. He would bring her poems and read them to her; 'and he spoke of love', but for her love outside marriage was unthinkable. (As Jean Alison would point out, the Shelleyan ideal of free love and the scruffy bohemian life of the poet and revolutionary that Mason led held little attraction for the young women of the 1930s, even for those, like her or Rita, who were less conventional in their political views: they were still expecting marriage and a home.) One hot summer day he came up the long path to the cottage and handed Rita a small page torn from a notebook on which was written a pencil draft of 'Vengeance of Venus', which he asked for back.[28] This is a more successful, less theatrical poem than 'Twenty-sixth October', a much better example of Mason's characteristic blending of 'tough colloquialism and rhetorical phrase':[29]

> But she was so small . . .
> > a short-cut nose, Venus, and child's eyes . . .
> > now does such a crime merit all
> > these disgraces and agonies?

> And you know it's not my habit
> > when a woman burns dark and slender
> > to run like a rabbit . . .
> > have mercy on a first offender

> And I had good cause,
> > a good presbyterian reason
> > for neglecting your laws
> > and just once commiting a treason.

> Now just savvy: a subtle
> > mind of modern complexities
> > may avoid a battle
> > through too much love of the prize:

> See, things aren't such straight sailing
> > these days as in Paphos of old
> > when your purple swans came trailing
> > a white chariot beneath skies of gold.

Yes . . . French blood and green-brown eyes,
        but then – for Christ's sake put down that whip,
        I confess all, abject apologies
        (I'm sorry too that I let Christ's name slip).

Owwww, no more red-hot bars:
        my last argument truly is spoken,
        have mercy on these scars
        for the criminal spirit is broken

The arrogant is humble
        and the fierce old wild-cat is tame:
        just drop that goad and I'll shamble
        once again through your damned hoops of shame.

The short-cut nose and child's eyes are Rita's, but the French blood and green–brown eyes suggest Marie (or perhaps Teddy). Mason's Venus is out of Horace and Lucretius.

THIS WAS not the last time Mason fell in love. Dorothea remained the woman in his life, but it was to be an unsteady relationship. She got her divorce at the end of 1937, but it was many years before they eventually married.

In 1938, after about a year, she moved out of the old house in Ellerslie, having grown sick of Jessie, of her jealousy and her histrionics. Dorothea's version of Mason's mother, although not uninfluenced by her own relationship with the son, is consistent with others': possessive, dominating and domineering. 'Ron had no chance against her.' Jessie was adept at what Dorothea saw as emotional blackmail. 'If she was thwarted, I remember her lying on the floor and having an attack of some sort, until she got her way, when she recovered' – a picture that accords with Mark Richards's of her 'alternately demanding and dying'. She would hand Ron half a crown for his bus fare and a cup of tea when he wanted to go to town. Shirley Barton remembered her ringing around all his friends when he had gone, pursuing him. Jean Alison recalled: 'When she said "my son",' in her deep, theatrical voice, 'it sent shivers up my spine.'[30] Dorothea moved in with a friend in Takapuna, and then took a flat in a house on the cliff top at Bayswater. (She would later buy a house in Tennyson Avenue, Takapuna.)

It seems that it was Dorothea – by her arrival in his life and her departure from Great South Road – who prompted Mason to make his own move from the family home, although the bond with his mother was too strong for it ever to be a complete break. After Dorothea left he bought some land on the North Shore, where Auckland's poets and bohemians tended to live – and a few trade unionists too: Pat Potter was one. He first bought a section half-way up Crown Hill behind Castor Bay, then later another section at the top of Crown Hill, with a wide view out to the Hauraki Gulf, Rangitoto in the foreground and Waiheke beyond. The architect Vernon Brown designed a house for him, in the modest, modern style that was Brown's contribution to the development of a vernacular domestic architecture in New Zealand: a low-pitched roof, creosoted weatherboard cladding and white-painted window frames. George Haydn, a Hungarian-Jewish refugee and thereafter close friend, built it (he also built Frank Sargeson's house in 1948), with help from Mason's Carpenters' Union friends. Mason himself was no handyman; his 'small, thin and nervous hands'[31] were better suited to nurturing native plants, which he was good at, than to handling builder's tools. In the nature of such things, and especially of these times, the house took some years to complete. In the meantime he stayed first for a time in the Castor Bay bach that D'Arcy Cresswell had rented for half a crown a week from the octogenarian and art patron Jane Stronach and her daughter between 1935 and 1938, and Robin Hyde stayed in briefly in 1937 – a two-roomed summer cottage at the bottom of the garden among 'a tangled forest of tea-tree and wattle and wild morning-glory' with 'a sly view of the sea'.[32] Later he lived on the Crown Hill section in an army hut, which, once the house was built – about 1947 – he continued to use as a study: it was basic but he loved it because it was all his own.

A cousin had moved into 451 Great South Road to look after Jessie after Dorothea left.

IN THE FIRST half of 1938 Mason wrote regularly for the *Workers' Weekly*, using the pseudonym 'P.W.D.' (for Public Works Department). He reported on the activities of the People's Theatre, and on the newly formed Auckland Left Book Club group, which held its first public meeting at the State Theatre on 10 April, chaired by Willis Airey, to raise awareness of the Japanese invasion of China and money for a relief fund. He wrote about Sir Stephen Allen, newly elected president of the right-wing Auckland Provincial Freedom Association, who had been New Zealand's administrator in Samoa and in charge when the Mau demonstrators were shot on Black Saturday, 1929. He also reviewed, favourably, Leon Feuchtwanger's *Moscow 1937*, a Left Book Club publication, in the course of which he dismissed Trotsky's later writings as politically 'stupid – such familiar formulae as stringing together quotations from Soviet papers and adding a commentary to the tune of "I alone am the true Communist"' and in a style 'as slovenly and boring as a book by Ramsay MacDonald'. Feuchtwanger's was one of the many outsiders' accounts of the Soviet Union which had become a minor industry in 1930s publishing. While the positive ones were not necessarily good books, Mason observed (although this one was), '[t]he attacks I find without exception dull, badly written and unreadable'.[33]

He wrote a satirical article about the capitalist press, 'Red Writer Denounces Communism – P.W.D. turns newspaper magnate', and another on the same subject in which he reminisced, with more cynicism than fondness, about his school years in Lichfield: in a 'remote Waikato village' twenty-five years ago where books had been scarce and newspapers treasured, pored over word by word in 'the little space in the long monotonous toil when cows were at last finished for the day, tea was over and the dishes cleared away'. The result was that the locals developed a split personality: 'the practical, good-humoured intelligence' of the rural working man co-existed with a 'narrow, venomous and bigoted' outlook inculcated by the press. 'The poor old aunt who brought me up was a bad case. She took not only the ordinary diet of the "Weekly News," but also the "Herald" (sent up in batches by another aunt after reading), the provincial daily and a little local bi-weekly', and read everything, 'advertisements and all, omitting only the sport news'. On the basis that an average *Herald* was twice the size of *Hamlet*, he calculated that Aunt Foster had read thirty million Wilson and Horton words a year for over fifty years. No wonder 'the poor old dear was a staunch Tory, and brought me up the same way', and that when he later visited as a young man and convinced socialist she welcomed her favourite nephew with conflicting emotions of love and disapproval.

He hoped he could get down for the harvest next summer, and see how things had changed.[34] But it was winter when he went back. Aunt Foster died less than three months later, on 12 July 1938. It seems likely that Mason took Jessie down to the funeral in the Putaruru Anglican Church.

He also wrote a debunking article about Edward Gibbon Wakefield and the New Zealand Company, prompted by New Zealand's approaching centennial in 1940 and publicity about plans for the official celebrations. This was an event which the left-wing intelligentsia regarded, for the moment, with aloof disapproval. '[W]e are afraid that the serious tasks that lie before us may to some extent be neglected in favour of merry-making. There can be no objection to pop-corn and toboggan slides, coloured fountains and brass band competitions. But they should not be allowed to hinder the business of pushing forward towards the establishment of a stable and just economy', *Tomorrow* pronounced sternly as plans for a centennial exhibition were announced.[35] Wakefield, Mason wrote, was not the noble and visionary coloniser of popular belief and conventional historical account, but 'a remarkably shrewd, go-getting, up-and-coming company promoter with all the qualities of his clan – hustle, crude ability, self-confidence, optimism, a boundless capacity for writing prospectuses, roping in notabilities to act as figureheads, lobbying, speechifying and intrigue', and the New Zealand Company, however enlightened it might have thought itself, 'grew more and more mercenary and sordid . . . they took the savings of the poor people in return for a promise of land, shipped them off to a far savage country, found that after all they could not give them the land, then attempted to swindle their unfortunate victims, even out of their legal rights.'[36] Mason was not the first to debunk colonial myths but such a view was not, especially at this time, widely accepted. The article was the beginning of a long-term project, never fully realised, to write the history of New Zealand 'from the scientific marxian viewpoint'.[37]

In 1938 he also enrolled, for the fourth time, in History I and passed, to complete his BA degree. That he did so at this time may have been a result of his deepening interest in New Zealand history, or of his friendship with Airey, or perhaps of being turned down for the job at Elam. Or perhaps it was the influence of Dorothea, who blamed Jessie and Dan for his having neither a trade nor a degree.

THE 'reasonably decent proletarian stuff' he had written of to Glover, however, was not these articles for the Party press. It was the theatre that occupied him creatively at this time, and increasingly so.

In April 1938 *Tomorrow* published a short political sketch, 'To Save Democracy', based on Harry Holland's 1919 pamphlet *Armageddon or Calvary* about New Zealand conscientious objectors in the First World War. The scene was a 'bare cell just behind the lines in France'. Two privates, 'a small, soft-voiced, quick-speaking Irishman' and 'a rangy, uncommunicative New Zealander', are standing guard over a prisoner, an objector, with whom the Irishman discusses the rights and wrongs of the war, the futility of fighting it

and of resisting it. The irony of the title is pointed up in the final exchange
when their brutal, disdainful captain, identifying the prisoner as a 'Labour
man', tells him exactly what they'll do to the socialists when the war is won:
'stand the whole rotten pack of them with their backs against the wall and
riddle them with bullets in their guts and finish them off at the point of the
bayonet'.[38]

This was mere agit-prop stuff: theatre for a political point. He put more
work into *Squire Speaks*, a six-page 'play for radio' that was published by the
Caxton Press and printed by the Unicorn later that year. Mason once said
that he first wrote *Squire Speaks* in 1928, and Dorothea remembered him
digging it out and reworking it, pruning ruthlessly, in 1937–38.[39] The play is
a dramatic monologue in free verse, set in a squire's hall in rural England at
the time of the 1926 general strike. The squire speaks as his faithful butler
advances on him with a rifle, mounting a one-man socialist revolution, until
the squire's son takes 'that old Afghan gun off the wall' and shoots the butler
dead:

> look the old fool had a bit of red flannel stuck on his barricade thing
> old Perkins gone socialist
>
> you'd as soon expect the grandfather-clock in the hall
> to put out its pendulum and knock you on the head
> like that fool bisney film we saw
> disney then disney
> it's a damn silly name in any case
> . . .
>
> phew what a nasty thing to happen in a man's own house
> just shows you just shows you
> I've noticed quite a bit of surliness about lately
> what I've always said
> working-classes all the same every one of them
> and the Government panders to them
> Manchester Guardian sort of stuff.

A group of armed villagers then arrive. Naïvely, the squire thinks they have
come to rescue him: they shoot him instead.[40] The artificiality of the setting
and consciously clichéd language give the play a fabular character. That *Squire*

Speaks contains no local reference, has nothing specifically to do with New Zealand (except insofar as the socialist revolution is international) despite Mason's developing interest in writing the real history of his country, has as much to do with his literary models as with its (uncertain) date of composition. There are similarities with the political dramas of Auden and the early propagandist poetry of C. Day Lewis in its viewpoint and tone, and Mason's squire is a familiar figure in folk and comic literary traditions. The form too has older antecedents.

Squire Speaks was Mason's first attempt, he later observed, 'to proceed from dramatic poetry to poetic drama', a natural progression. He later wrote explicitly on the subject of drama in poetry and poetry in drama, and about what he was attempting to do with his writing from this time. J.M. Synge, and the popular traditions of Irish and Scottish literature, was his reference point: 'with Synge, I felt strongly the need for poetry and drama to move more closely together, I mean not as a mechanical revival of so-called poetic drama but in some form fitting to our age, with drama benefiting by the bite and precision of poetry, while poetry should learn again the simple and open texture of drama'. Of his poetry, 'On the Swag', for example, was one poem which he felt had succeeded in combining 'the structural compression of poetry with the ease of prose'. It was Synge, he wrote elsewhere, who 'showed me the need to go to the people, share the common speech and common problems', and inspired him with the 'possibility of building towards a modern form of poetical plays (real plays, I mean, not closet-drama of the Tennysonian–T.S. Eliot type)'. And if 'our poets studied dramatic needs, then not only would that art perhaps benefit, but also it might act as a cross-fertilising agent on poetry: which – despite Verlaine and even possibly at the cost of a slight rash of "oh, Liberty"'s – could profit by a little rhetoric with its resulting comprehensibility.'[41] It was not so much that Mason abandoned poetry for drama, or for politics, but that he wanted to write a different kind of poetry – was seeking for his poetry a new purpose, a new form and a new audience.

Squire Speaks was to have been released by the middle of the year, but the Unicorn Press was in trouble again, or still. In July Lowry quit, signing over the plant to Holloway in payment of his debts, and went north, where he had found a job as relieving 'infant mistress' at Ngataki primary school, near Ninety Mile Beach, almost as far north as he could get. He left Holloway to complete the books in press: Mason's play and Roderick Finlayson's first collection of stories, *Brown Man's Burden*. As irrepressible as ever, Lowry wrote to Glover from Ngataki at the end of July that he had 'a couple of things to turn out for

Mason' when he returned to Auckland the following month, and that he was 'in the process of acquiring one or two largish and good type fonts, free of debt, hire-purchase, other people's ink incrustations, neurotic part-proprietors and all encumbrances whatever. And this shall form the framework or skeletal os of the old Unicorn, former Phoenix, in the act of becoming a new woodpecker'.[42] But he did not go back to Auckland until the following year, and was not to set up in publishing again until 1945. It was the end, finally, of the Unicorn Press, which Holloway and his wife, Kay, reincarnated as the Griffin Press and kept running for another thirty years. Those 'one or two things' Lowry was meant to have been doing for Mason appear to have been a couple of political leaflets, and the prose satire 'They Should be Slaves', which Mason had also sent to Glover the previous year: 'It seems again fairly topical, as Schemes & Crusades are again in the air (embryonic fascist opposition to overthrow Labour Government) . . . it would be a good deed & might attract the intellectual proletarians'.[43] One of the first things to appear under the revived imprint of the Griffin Press was a pamphlet compiled by Fairburn, Mason and others in advance of the 1938 general election, *Who Said Red Ruin?*, an analysis of the *New Zealand Herald*'s historical prejudice against the left.

Squire Speaks was out by August. Sargeson distributed it around the bookshops as Glover's Auckland agent. The reviewers were impressed but bemused: 'it represents, one supposes, the stream-of-consciousness style of writing', the *Auckland Star* observed. 'Much admiration is due to "Squire Speaks," a dramatic scene in some kind of free, blank verse', the Christchurch *Press* wrote, and confidently asserted that while the 'B.B.C. might admire [its] radio-acting properties . . . they would never produce it.' This was neither the Mason, nor the kind of play, they recognised. In *Tomorrow*, however, Winston Rhodes gave it less qualified praise, admiring, as he had before, Mason's conciseness and control: 'It isn't easy to write a play suitable for the radio because a new form and a new technique are required. It isn't easy to write a play in six pages which is completely satisfying as far as it goes from almost every point of view.' Mason had 'performed a most difficult task in a manner that could hardly be bettered. . . . Not a word could be cut out, not a word need be added. All action is reported through the mouth of the Squire, yet nothing is lost in dramatic intensity. The form is everything and hearing is believing.' Rhodes also feared, however, that it would not be heard on the radio, because 'the theme is not one that is likely to be chosen by radio producers'.[44] He was right.

16

Decent proletarian stuff

1938–40

MASON HAD resigned only from the executive and as organiser of the People's Theatre in June 1937. He had not severed his ties with it altogether. He had a part in its major, and only, production for 1938, and became more deeply involved again the following year, until the theatre's demise in 1940 – a casualty, as he had once predicted, of the war.

After the sell-out season of *Till the Day I Die* there had been several requests for further performances, including one from the loyal comrades of Huntly, but the logistics of touring a large play and defections from the cast made this impossible. A planned benefit performance for the Spanish Medical Aid Committee was also cancelled and a £10 donation made instead. Bill Deuchar was practically running the theatre by this time, and reorganised it. A new executive was elected. Archie Fisher became president, replacing Sewell, who was going on sabbatical leave to England (where they hoped he might be able to find them some good plays). The membership subscription was raised from 1s to 2s 6d. Sub-committees were established, along with an Agit-prop Group which was to put on short plays to 'prepare the minds of the people for the larger productions, and gradually help to arouse enthusiasm for the cause of Socialism'.[1] A concise *Waiting for Lefty*, adapted by Deuchar himself, was performed by the Agit-prop Group at meetings of the Carpenters', General Labourers' and Local Bodies Labourers' unions. The performance was so effective, reported the *Borer*, that some late-comers thought it was part of the meeting itself and one complained that it was the noisiest AGM he had ever attended.

Despite the evident advisability of concentrating on short, easily staged plays, the executive aimed high for their 1938 production: *Judgment Day* by American playwright Elmer Rice – 'perhaps the most ambitious project ever attempted by a New Zealand amateur group', a publicity circular announced, 'the casting especially presenting immense difficulties'.[2] They had first considered a Spanish Civil War play, Michael Blankfort's *The Brave and the Blind*, then *Roar China* by Russian playwright Sergei Tretyakov, but they couldn't find any local Chinese actors and the Chinese community was concerned that the play's anti-British theme might arouse hostility towards them. *Judgment Day* was a court-room drama, set in the Palace of Justice in 'a capital of South-eastern Europe': three people, members of the banned People's Party, are standing trial for the attempted assassination of the fascist dictator. It had been running for a year in London's West End, and had three performances by the People's Theatre in the Auckland Town Hall Concert Chamber in June. Bill Deuchar was the producer. (Fisher had resigned as both president and head of the production sub-committee in January, partly because of pressure of work at Elam, and partly because he was finding his involvement with the theatre 'exceedingly irksome': he was 'temperamentally ill-fitted', he explained to the secretary, to work under the 'extremely democratic form of control' insisted on by the People's Theatre.)[3]

Rita Chapman played the female lead, Lydia Kuman, one of the accused, to complimentary notices, although it was felt that she lacked credibility as the mother of a fourteen-year-old girl. Mason was Parvan, one of the witnesses for the prosecution. In the final scene, he raises his revolver to kill Lydia's husband, the revolutionary leader Alexander Kuman (played by Arnold Goodwin), whom everyone believed had committed suicide in prison but had in fact escaped and given evidence at the trial disguised as a priest, but is disarmed before he can fire. The play is subtitled 'A Melodrama in Three Acts'.

Putting it on, if Mason's testimony is anything to go by, had been a melodrama in itself. In May he wrote to the executive to 'protest against the disgraceful way in which the business of the organisation is being conducted. . . . I have so far served under three producers, been cast in four parts & memorised Murusi, Parvan & a large part of Dr Bathory.' He complained about rehearsals being turned into political meetings, and pointed out that when the theatre was founded the name Workers' Theatre had been unanimously rejected: 'If Mr Edwards or Mr Deuchar want a purely working-class theatre' they should go away and form their own (Jim Edwards, better known as the unemployed workers' leader whose batoning by the police sparked the Queen Street riot in April 1932, played General Rakovski, the Minister of Culture and Enlightenment). It was that intractable problem: how to mix politics and art happily. With it came a tension that was integral to the cultural movement of the Popular Front: between the idea of a workers' culture and a people's culture. As for the challenges of the production itself, it would be better to give major plays a try-out for a few nights in a small venue like the Trades Hall, Mason sensibly argued, before risking them in a large one like the Concert Chamber.[4]

The production was not a great success. Audiences were good (and a profit made) but the critics were unimpressed. The *Herald* found it unconvincing and sometimes farcical, though conceded that the problem was probably more with the play itself than the production: at the climax 'Many of the audience simply laughed.' The *Star* remarked that the People's Theatre should not be judged too harshly for 'a great deal of contemporary history smacks broadly of melodrama when viewed from the democratic security of a British community'.[5]

In *Tomorrow* Frank Sargeson was also disappointed. It was not one of Rice's best plays, he admitted, being 'melodramatic and sentimental', but his harshest criticism was for the People's Theatre itself for changing the ending and thus negating what he considered the play's one redeeming feature, the point at which the playwright's artistic integrity transcended his propagandist purpose. In the final moment one of the five judges, the only one whose commitment to justice and God has proved to be stronger than his obedience to the Party, rises from his chair and shoots the dictator from the bench, then immediately turns the gun on himself – realising, as Sargeson observed, that by that action he has become no better than the fascist gangster regime he despises. The People's Theatre cut out the suicide and brought the curtain down on the judge's final words as the dictator falls: 'Down with tyranny! Long live the people!' Sargeson commented sternly on the theatre's honesty, and wondered how this boded for the play-writing competition it had announced.[6]

Mason's own relationship with the People's Theatre was also tense. There was evidently some disagreement about the kind of production they should be attempting. He wrote to the new secretary, Rita Chapman, in July, telling her that he was 'still unable to see any reason why I should not make suggestions to the Executive' and offering to 'withdraw the first part of my proposal and simply to repeat the part concerned with the provision of a programme of New Zealand plays' (his own). In the absence of the other side of this correspondence, it is impossible to know just what was being discussed. His suggestion, Mason explained, had seemed to him 'to provide the simplest means of beginning to enlist local writers, with the ultimate aim of getting plays with an immediate and local appeal'.[7] What the People's Theatre had in mind was a Living Newspaper presentation, which Mason then agreed was 'a far better' idea. Living Newspaper had developed out of the Russian Proletkult theatre and become popular throughout the workers' theatre movement in

Europe in the 1920s, before reaching America in the mid-1930s. Unity Theatre
in London had produced its first Living Newspaper in March 1938. As the
name suggests, it was fast, flexible, political theatre, which used a range of
techniques borrowed partly from avant-garde cinema – highly stylised
movement, rapidly juxtaposed images, placards, voice-over, spotlighting and
projection – to dramatise topical issues: a classically 1930s mixture of agit-
prop and documentary realism. Sargeson appears to have been involved in
the plan to pioneer this particular brand of new theatre in New Zealand,
although with mixed feelings, as he remarked to Glover in August: 'At the
moment up here we're also balled up with the People's Theatre – they're
trying the latest American stunt – a Living Newspaper & we've all been
dragged in. I've a horrible fear at the moment it will turn out a cross between
a students' extravaganza & Masses and Man.'[8] In September *Tomorrow* published
'Two Sketches for a People's Theatre' by Sargeson which could well have
been part of a student capping extravaganza ('Crisis in Czecho-slovakia',
featuring Benza, Futler and Chamberfax, and 'Women in Politics', a
conversation between society girls Kay and Chloe).[9] In October the People's
Theatre prepared a sketch for performance at a Labour Party election rally in
the Town Hall but were prevented from putting it on by 'a legal ruling that
it was a piece "of entertainment"' and so could not be performed at a political
meeting.[10] In the end both the Living Newspaper and Mason's earlier proposal
were abandoned in favour of a production of the winning entry in the People's
Theatre play-writing competition, which was to be put on in March 1939.

THE COMPETITION had been announced at the beginning of March
1938, and closed at the end of June. There is no record of how many scripts
were received. Mason was possibly disbarred by virtue of being an active
member of the theatre, as the judging was to be done by the executive
committee. Sargeson was thinking of entering his 'working-class' play ('The
Struggle'), but perhaps he changed his mind after *Judgment Day*.[11] The prizes
were £5 and £3 (plus royalties if produced) for the winning full-length and
one-act entries – rather more modest than the £75 and £20 being offered in
the centennial literary competition, which opened in July 1938. The brief
was more specific, and more modest, too: 'While it is not anticipated that the
plays submitted will be of outstanding dramatic merit, it is expected that their
authors will endeavour to deal fearlessly and truthfully with problems of worldwide significance, in their special relation to the lives and happiness of our
own people', the announcement of the competition noted. The success of

Waiting for Lefty and *Till the Day I Die* had shown 'the possibilities which the future holds for a strong and virile drama in our country', one based on plays as vital as these 'but dealing with our own problems and outlook. . . . We need plays which will make the people think; which will help them to realise that however remote the trends and movements in the rest of the world may seem, nevertheless they have their reactions in New Zealand and must be understood if New Zealanders wish to cope intelligently with their own problems.'[12] In response to an inquiry the political implication of this was stated more carefully: 'We hope to find the point of view of working men and women expressed in dramatic form; we want, moreover, to promote the writing of plays with a definite bias against War, Fascism, and all forms of reaction.'[13]

Sargeson had taken too dim a view of the People's Theatre's intentions and integrity, perhaps. Of the three joint winners in the one-act category, 'Left Right' by R.E. Baeyertz, described by its author (a barrister and solicitor) as 'a stark brevity based upon the New Psychology', would have won outright had the author demonstrated more knowledge of the stage, said the judges' report – and notwithstanding his covering letter, in which he had discoursed on the dangers to the left movement of extremism and superstition and compared it to the Catholic church. 'Send Us, Lord, a Little War' by G.L. Hogben the judges thought was an excellent idea unconvincingly executed, but nearer to the Living Newspaper style the People's Theatre was interested in. 'Survival of the Fittest' by Robert Verrier, while another good idea, failed as propaganda because 'the doctrines advanced repel instead of attract through the writer making his propagandist a cold, inhuman doctrinaire when the need arises for human sympathy' (perhaps the People's Theatre had misunderstood his point).[14]

The winning three-act play, *Falls the Shadow*, was written by Ian Hamilton, an Englishman who had come to New Zealand in 1929 and taken up farming in Hawke's Bay. He was a socialist with means, and a pacifist who was to spend two years of the coming war in a detention camp as a conscientious objector. He became a friend of both Mason and Sargeson. He had already written a number of radio plays, and three one-act stage plays which explored Freudian and Jungian theories of the mind – which probably would not have gone down too well with the People's Theatre. *Falls the Shadow*, however, was a pacifist play. Set in the home of a retired major-general in the country south of London on the eve and in the aftermath of war, it dealt, in its first act, with the discord wrought within the family (gathered together for the first time in eight years) by the pacifist beliefs of the younger, artist-intellectual son, Michael. War comes in the second act, conveyed by a blacked-out stage, set-piece speeches by a number of symbolic figures (a Recruiting Officer, a Politician, a Strike Leader, etc) and off-stage sound effects of aeroplanes and bombs, a departure from the play's otherwise naturalistic mode which impressed the *Workers' Weekly* but which Sargeson, reviewing the play in *Tomorrow,* thought would have been more effective if it had employed the techniques and rapidity of the cinema. Britain defeats the invading fascist power (Italy), but not the forces of fascism at home. The third act shows the elder son, John, an airman, disillusioned by the experience of war and now a member of a subversive group within his fascist militia, thus turning 'away from the bloodshed and cruelty of national warfare to the plotting and bitterness of party strife' (as interpreted by the *New Zealand Herald*).[15] The last word is with Michael, who returns home from a concentration camp after soldiers refuse an order to execute him, an act he sees as symbolic of the ultimate victory of tolerance and non-resistance. The message is stated explicitly in the play's introductory monologue: that violence will breed violence and fascism whether exercised by the bosses or the workers.

Falls the Shadow was presented by the People's Theatre in the Concert Chamber in March 1939, directed by Bill Deuchar, and was published by the Griffin Press. The cast (listed in the programme this time) included several '[w]ell-known personalities in Auckland theatricals', with trade union and People's Theatre members in the minor roles (Mason did not appear).[16] 'A drawing room drama that is different' the advertisements described it and, as Sargeson observed, 'in view of the theme (pacifism), no one can seriously object to the conventional upper-middle class setting, because aerial warfare doesn't discriminate much between classes'.[17] The controversy that the play aroused within left-wing circles was to do not with its class credentials, however, but with its political line. There was already, perhaps, a defensive note in the circular that had gone out to trade unions, recommending it as 'easily the best play written to date by a New Zealander' and 'quite in accord with our policy of opposition to War, Fascism and other threats to Democracy.'[18] Being anti-war and pacifist were not the same thing, however. The *Workers' Weekly* was compelled to point out the play's 'serious weaknesses' ('[n]otwithstanding the excellence of the acting'): that 'it did not make plain the issues confronting democratic people today, nor point the way forward for them in the struggle against Fascism'. It was unlikely that the fascists would come to power in Britain once the fascist invading power had been defeated, as the play proposed; on the contrary, the democratic forces in Britain would be strengthened. 'The play concludes by suggesting the ultimate collapse of Fascism though a general weariness and hate of brutality and repression. Fascism will not fall – it must be overthrown.'[19] In short, *Falls the Shadow* did not meet the requirements of socialist realism (the official cultural policy of the Soviet Union since 1935) that art be realistic, optimistic and heroic. But finding the right line on the war was not that easy, as the Party itself was to discover.

In reply, the People's Theatre admitted that the play had limitations, but it had been the best submitted in the competition and met its policy of encouraging New Zealand plays. It was hardly relevant, of course, that although the play was written by a New Zealander (more or less) it could not be said to deal particularly with 'our own problems and outlook'.[20] In the last months of the 1930s everyone's attention was elsewhere.

Sargeson was also unconvinced on both political and aesthetic grounds, wondering whether Michael in his pacifism was not really just a victim of 'bourgeois illusionism' (he had been reading the English Marxist literary critic Christopher Caudwell). But it was a very good play, he thought, and deserved a better response. Audiences were disappointing, despite the railways union having bought 120 tickets, as was the ailing Prime Minister's declining his invitation to attend the opening night.

AT THE theatre's annual general meeting at the end of April 1939, Mason was re-elected onto the executive committee as one of three vice-presidents. Jean Alison was on the committee too, having returned to Auckland after three or four years away in England. So was Charles Bartlett, whom she was shortly to marry: both were members of the fellow-travelling faction within the theatre, she recalled, along with Mason. Four major productions had been planned for 1939, but Fisher had declined to produce *Bury the Dead* (an anti-war play by American writer Irwin Shaw) and a proposed revival of *Till the Day I Die* was abandoned. *Marching Song* by John Lawson, another large-cast production and an 'ardent and fiery strike play' which 'mingle[s] the colour problem, unemployment, the "law and order" racket, citizens' committees and blacklisting' and the 'woman problem' into its story of a labour dispute in a company town, was scheduled for October in the Prince Edward Theatre, but in the event this too would be cancelled.[21] The meeting discussed possible productions for the following year, including Odets's *Plant in the Sun* or *Golden Boy*, *Six Men of Dorset*, a play about the Tolpuddle martyrs, and *Professor Mamlock*, and decided to investigate hiring their own premises.

In the meantime, People's Theatre members presented a poem by Mason at a memorial service organised by the Spanish Medical Aid Committee for the five New Zealanders, among the thousands of others, who had died fighting with the International Brigade, and for the Spanish Civil War itself. That war ceased at the end of March 1939 when Franco's Nationalist forces entered Madrid, and with it the hope that had been steadily fading over the previous year, as the fighting had dragged on and the democratic powers persisted in their policy of non-intervention while Italy and Germany sent Franco money and arms. The memorial service, at the Regent Theatre on 14 May, opened with the Dead March played by the Watersiders' Band, followed by a poem (perhaps Hemingway's) in memory of the battle of Jarama (where 300 members of the Abraham Lincoln battalion were killed in February 1937), songs by Paul Robeson and a Basque children's choir, and ended with Mason's poem 'International Brigade: memorial service for the fallen'. It was presented 'en tableau': seated on the stage was 'a refugee peasant woman, child in arms' while the poem was read off-stage over a microphone, the first eleven stanzas in the voice of a Spanish woman, the next five by a member of the International Brigade, the final two in chorus. While the war had ended in defeat for the Republican forces, Mason's poem was not a lament but a celebration of the spirit of brotherhood and the ongoing struggle:

> . . .
> Yet a people's torment
> found friends of the people:
> to our aid they came
> from mine, wharf, desk, ship, farm, factory –
> from Peru & Canada,
> Australia, England, Sweden,
> France, Mexico, the States –
> from the furthest ends of the earth.
>
> These were not conscripts,
> these were not drugged by ignorance,
> these were not adventurers,
> these were no mercenaries:

But free, straight, with wise eyes,
young fellows whistling,
like our own sons whistling home from work –
like your son or my son.

. . .

Spain is not defeated:
Spain will fight on
the fight of humanity,
though in other forms:
these invaders will go out by the same road
as Hannibal went & the Romans,
as the Moors went & Napoleon –
& with them will go all traitors
who sold their own land
to oppression & darkness.
. . .[22]

It was meant to be spoken simply and emotionally. Mason was unhappy with the result. He hated expression marks in poetry, Shirley Barton recalled, and would be furious when a young woman at a WEA summer school recited Housman's 'In Summertime on Bredon' with wistful pathos. Rhythm was the thing. (It is curious, she reflected, that while Mason had such an appreciation of the singing rhythms of Burns, for example, he 'couldn't tell one musical note from another' and once on Queen Street on Christmas Eve, walking past a band playing 'O Come All Ye Faithful', asked her why they were playing 'God Save the King'.[23])

'International Brigade' was printed in the second issue of the new Party newspaper, the *People's Voice*, which was launched in July 1939 'for the welfare and freedom of the New Zealand people' and unity against fascism. It was edited by Gordon Watson, who had recently taken over the *Workers' Weekly* from Sid Scott. In 1938 the Party had also moved its headquarters from Wellington to Auckland, where a third of its members were, into the Auckland branch office in St Kevin's Arcade on Karangahape Road. Like its predecessor, the *People's Voice* contained mostly international news. It also had a literary page, with a short story by Henri Barbusse, an obituary for the German playwright Ernst Toller by Winston Rhodes, a book review and Mason's 'Youth at the Dance' in the first issue; along with film reviews, a sports column, and a woman's column edited by Elsie Freeman (Elsie Farrelly of *Phoenix* days, who had married the Party's former (by then expelled) general secretary, Fred Freeman).

Mason contributed a message of congratulations to the first number, along with others from Rhodes, Arthur Sewell and Horace Belshaw. He began:

> New Zealand speaks with two voices. . . . One is the true voice of our people. It is clear, bold and direct. It indulges in no high heroics, it is lacking in sentimentality, it turns and laughs at itself. Above all it is marked by vigorous independence. Rough it may be at times, but it is the roughness of quartz from which fine gold may be extracted. That is the voice of the masses. The other is an old half-witted sheep [quoting J.K. Stephen parodying Words-worth]. It is the voice of a front-page article in the 'Herald,' of a leader in the 'Dominion,' of a speech by – well, you know who. It is not the voice of the people at all. It speaks only for a few thousand money-addled reactionaries; and they are only New Zealanders by accident of birth, in all else they are merely local agents for the interest-extractors. Which voice will prevail? In the tough days ahead we must make the peoples' voice prevail.[24]

Mason's people's voice evokes a working-class character type that is already familiar – laconic, straightforward, and usually tall. It is like Joe the labourer in 'This Bird May Swing', 'tall [and] impassive in the proletarian way' with a 'twisted, whimsical face', and the 'rangy, uncommunicative' private in 'To Save Democracy'. It is like the Quay Street crowd he described in his unfinished novel 'Dreams Come True', 'working men with black silk or grey flannel shirts. Much the same appearance as a workman's crowd the world over – sombre, quiet, drab, grim', and the PWD worker in one of the sketches he wrote for the People's Theatre later that year, 'tall, & rangy: quiet, unemotional, direct . . . the embodiment of the New Zealand working-class'.[25] It is a rural as well as a working-class culture he evokes, which draws on his own experience in his childhood years and harvesting summers in Lichfield of the 'casual rural worker' like old George: 'in the backblocks you'll find evidences of a blunt, free, frank manner. It's disappearing even there', a character in one of the prose dialogues he wrote around 1930 observed. 'In the towns, of course, the ideal is to be a third-rate imitation of a timid insipid suburban Englishman.'[26]

In July and August Mason contributed a five-part series of articles entitled 'The Spirit of the Pioneers', '[b]ased on material not published before in N.Z.', as the *People's Voice*'s contribution to the centennial. He had done his research. The first article quoted extracts from letters written by new immigrants to their families back home, printed as an appendix to a New Zealand Company recruiting pamphlet published in Britain in 1842, to show that New Zealand's labourer–settlers had been intelligent, skilled workers escaping exploitation in 'the hell of the homeland' and determined to build a new society in the new world. The subsequent articles described the struggle for better conditions (noting the first documented strike in the colony), the development of agriculture and industry, and the spirit of friendship between the pioneers and the Maori. They had forged their new world with a high sense of social consciousness: 'At times these men and women show a rough piety. It is not, however, the remote and meaningless formalism of the upper classes, but a version marked with the qualities which made the earliest forms of Christianity a humane and democratic creed.' They had learned to fraternise with, understand and 'even admired' the Maori 'in a rough, good-natured fashion'; the war of the 1860s was not a settlers' war but a capitalists' war, brought by 'English lords and financiers, together with their local agents'. The final instalment quoted from the 1840s letters of John Shepherd, a typical New Zealand worker by virtue not of 'his breadth of outlook and personal integrity alone, but the fact that these are combined with a spirit of sturdy and spontaneous independence. For it cannot be too strongly stressed that the earliest stirrings of our popular spirit came, not from starved slaves driven to the edge of despair, but from men and women exuberant with a new hope. Resistance to oppression was not so much a duty as a joy.' These were words for the times.[27]

Over the next year or two Mason continued to work on a history of the New Zealand Company, entitled 'Cheaper Labourers', expanding the article he had written for the *Workers' Weekly* in 1938 into a draft of some 15,000 words. The Party planned to publish it as part of its centennial contribution 'in recalling and reviving the democratic traditions of our people and in making itself the heir of all the best traditions of New Zealand' (an expression of its adherence to the populist ideology of the Popular Front).[28] His foreword explained the need for a separate history of the New Zealand Company, of which there was none. The need was all the greater at that time because, in contrast to the earlier historians who had had few illusions about the nature of the enterprise and its entrepreneurs, recent writers 'have tended to swathe the whole scheme in a mist of pinkish romance'. What was needed was a scientific history, which would expose 'this pretty myth' of Wakefield as 'a martyr iniquitously victimised because of his early indiscretions and sacrificing his life in the cause of democracy'. His sources included the published writings of Wakefield and his contemporary critics, Dandeson Coates and Thomas Beecham; official publications of the New Zealand Company; volume two of Marx's *Capital*; and the histories published by the 'old colonists', Selwyn, Swainson, Rusden, Thomson and Saunders. Mason paid particular attention to the economic basis of the Wakefield scheme, the sufficient price for land and supply of cheap labour, and to the New Zealand Company's 'appalling and wilful ignorance concerning the Maoris' and the alienation of Maori land. By the time the company was wound up in 1858, he wrote:

> All the issues of the colony had been confused in a swarm of lies, an oligarchy had been clamped on to our democracy, the new colony was bent under a load of debt, honest men had been blackguarded, land-purchasers had been swindled[,] labourers swindled and starved, Russell had been sacked, homesteads and pahs had been burnt, farms had been pillaged, from Oheawai to the Wairau ran the graves of white men and Maoris, all the seeds had been sown for the horrible harvest of war which was to come in less than two years time . . . but the shareholders were paid in full.[29]

The work was never published, although Mason was to return to his researches into 'the origins of New Zealand' later in his life.

For the remainder of 1939, however, his regular contribution to the *People's Voice* — still as 'PWD' (he was probably still working at the Penrose Public Works store[30]) — were film reviews, in which he appraised the latest offerings from the Hollywood and British studios — Westerns, war movies and romantic dramas — in the sharp sardonic tone that was one of his own most recognisable voices. Zoltan Korda's *Four Feathers*, for example, was 'weak, dull and vicious — anaemia alternating with hysteria', and marked 'the final surrender of the "great" Mr. Korda to the most reactionary ideas of British imperialism'. The Egyptian desert had been shot like 'a succession of those greenery-yallery lithographs used for trade calendars', and the cinematography had nothing of the sweep and movement of Paul Rotha and John Grierson, pioneering British documentary film-makers. *In Name Only*, starring Cary Grant and Carole Lombard, was 'One of those films where you breathe a sigh of relief when you see a wealthy and handsome hero dive into a pub or a hamburger bar. You know that there, at least, there will appear someone at least resembling a human being — a barkeeper, drunk or waitress — but what a change from the wealthy nitwits!' 'Some day', he hoped, prefacing his comments on *Union*

Pacific, 'someone will make a film showing a band of devoted Indians besieged by a horde of land-hungry whites . . . the ring of murderous eyes gradually closing in . . . then in the distance the Indian reinforcements galloping madly up to the rescue . . . then, at last gasp, the relieving Indians tear up, scatter the besiegers, rescue the gallant besieged. I'd like to see that film. I'd like to live, too, to see the day when films show the truth about the intrigues of companies, about the exploitation of the pioneers, about the brutalities of capitalist agents.' Although he found it not as good as John Ford's *Stagecoach*, *Union Pacific* did at least 'produce a real impression of the power and ruthlessness of capitalism at its period of expansion'.[31] Mason's reviews were not invariably negative. He might have found more to like, though, if he had still been writing them a year later after Natan Scheinwald had opened his De Paris Theatrette in the Civic on Queen Street to show Continental and progressive films, the first commercial distributor in New Zealand to do so.

THE PEOPLE'S THEATRE was struggling with more serious problems than the competing attraction of the cinema as 1939 slid steadily, inevitably, into war. A sub-committee set up to investigate the finances reported an 'alarming drop in revenue'. *Falls the Shadow* had made a loss and, although forty people attended the annual general meeting, there were only twenty individual paying members at the end of April. 'Union apathy' was also a concern: more unions were affiliated but they bought fewer tickets. A publicity drive was launched, with letters soliciting support going out to unions, sympathetic newspapers and the Prime Minister, promoting the theatre as 'a working-class organisation' that was 'striving to give a dramatic expression to the voice of the inarticulate masses'.[32]

In October *Marching Song* was 'indefinitely postponed' at the last minute. It had been impossible to keep the cast together after war was declared in September. In the circumstances, the theatre decided to concentrate for the foreseeable future on short plays and small venues. 'It says a lot for the members that they unhesitatingly rejected any defeatist suggestions and decided not only to start again immediately, but even to try out new and progressive methods', Mason reported in the *People's Voice*. More frequent 'shows' would be held in suitable small halls, and would include 'a fair number of plays of immediate local interest'.[33]

Mason provided the local content. 'BMA', a sketch about the opposition of the New Zealand branch of the British Medical Association to the health provisions of the Labour government's social security legislation (free and

universal general practitioner, hospital, pharmaceutical and maternity services
– a subject of long and angry debate), had already been performed at several
Labour Party branch meetings, and in the 'pulpit session' at the Auckland
Unitarian Church in Ponsonby on 1 October. It opened the first of two
Sunday night programmes of one-act plays at the Fabian clubrooms on 12
November. The programme also included a satirical farce entitled *Good Blood
Bad Blood*, and *Rehearsal*, by Albert Maltz, an 'inside view of a labour theatre'
which was also presented at a WEA social.[34] 'BMA' features a country doctor,
dour and middle-aged, whose 'strong conscience gnaws at his strength' while
'a sense of hopelessness weighs him down'. He is called in the middle of a
winter night from a public works camp forty miles away to attend a gravely
sick child, and refuses. His wife remonstrates with him: she is younger, and
her 'certain amount of natural gaiety gives her the feminine quality of capacity
for cutting Gordian knots while he is still brooding over their complexity'.
When he falls asleep the doctor hears the unctuous voice of the president of
the BMA (alternately spotlit with the doctor's wife on an otherwise blacked-
out stage) urging him to stand firm for liberty and 'the ethics of our profession'
against 'unionists dabbling in politics', 'ignorant labourers drinking in low
pubs' and 'ill-advised demagogues in the name of a muddled humanitarianism'.
Of course, his conscience and his wife prevail.[35]

The 12th of November was a busy day in a busy month. That afternoon
'Skull on Silence', a dramatic monologue written by Mason for Armistice
Day, had been presented at a meeting in Quay Street, read by Bill Dickinson,
a member of the Communist Party. It describes the aftermath of the last war
in the voice of a worker who had enlisted and fought

> . . . for God, King and country –
> that is to say, for Wilson & Horton,
> and Colonial Sugar,
> Imperial Chemicals,
> Ernie Davis, New Zealand Insurance,
> Vesteys, Bill Goodfellow and Union
> Steamship

then came home to struggle on a rehab farm and finally died from his war
wounds, and ever since has listened, not to the silence of the grave but to the
crisis of capitalism:

I could even hear the scratch of the pen
as the bank foreclosed on the mortgage
and the soft dropping of a handful of earth
with the last farewell on my child's coffin.

And then I heard the wail of freedom in torture
and I heard the tramp of jack-booted tyranny
and the shuffle of men in queues
and the creaking of rickets in children's bones
and the slur of sandshoes in slavecamps
and then again I heard the thump of drums
and then again I heard the thud of armies
again the thud of armies.
Does it all start over again?[36]

The style is that of 'Service for the Fallen': simple and declamatory, using repetition and rhythm to carry its impact and ending on a note of uplift, a call for peace in keeping with the occasion and the Party's current line on the new war.

The previous weekend the People's Theatre had performed a sketch at a meeting to celebrate the anniversary of the Russian revolution, a regular date in the Party's social calendar. During the week Mason had also had a small part in the WEA's annual production, and its first major one of a local play: *Cartoon* by Jack Coppard, a satire on 'the shams of our present-day systems and sacred institutions' in which '[p]olitics, commerce, religion and art are all pilloried with the irony and humour of the newspaper cartoon'.[37] Mason had known Coppard since he was a boy, when their families regularly picnicked together. Well known as a writer of university revues, Coppard had also been making a small reputation in England with a handful of expressionist plays, which were as different as were agit-prop sketches and dramatic monologues from the conventionally realist fare that made up the bulk of New Zealand drama in this decade: from the domestic and rural dramas penned by members of the New Zealand branch of the British Drama League for its annual competitions (described by Ian Hamilton, reviewing the 1938 winners in *Tomorrow*, as nursery-level tripe) and the mainly historical dramas inspired by the centennial competition (Wakefield and Hobson were popular subjects), in which no first prize was awarded. Mason did not enter.

The People's Theatre's second Sunday night programme on 10 December included two pieces by Mason, together with an armistice play, *Eleventh Hour*, and *People's Court*, which 'purports to be a picture of court procedure in Moscow in 1933. . . . We've tried to whoop it up a bit'.[38] *Squire Speaks* opened the programme, perhaps spoken by Arnold Goodwin, who had given Mason's play its first public presentation at the WEA hall (from behind the dropped curtain) for the drama group's end-of-term show in September. The evening concluded with 'This Dark Will Lighten', a 'poem for mass recitation' which had appeared in the *People's Voice* in September. The form, a mass chant, was 'common in progressive theatres abroad', Mason explained. He had written the poem 'the day after War was declared, at a time when I thought it might become a genuine war against Fascism. I was wrong. Events soon showed that it was just another gangster's [*sic*] quarrel.'[39]

In fact, responding to the war ideologically for the left, and for the Party especially, was not as easy even as Mason suggests. The signing of the Nazi-Soviet non-aggression pact on 23 August had been a shock to no one so much as the communist movement. Bewilderment quickly gave way to realpolitik, and the pact was explained away on tactical grounds as an act of self-preservation by the Soviet Union. When war was declared the Party at first came out in support of it, then about a month later changed its mind and reverted to its earlier position, that it was an imperialist war – 'just another gangsters' quarrel'. In all this the local Party was following the Comintern line, but not without its own intense debates and a succession of policy statements in the *People's Voice*. It was a hard line to follow. The fight against fascism had finally come, and the Soviet Union was not part of it. For the left, the first eighteen months of the Second World War was a confusing and disheartening time.

'This Dark Will Lighten' was written in those few days when everything had seemed much clearer. The *People's Theatre Magazine* provided a synopsis:

A group of men and women who have worked together in the Labour movement are meeting perhaps for the last time. The doom of war is on them. They lament their fate and recall the life they are leaving, the lessons they have learnt in the struggle for bread, the lessons of the slump. Torn between the spirit of despair and the spirit of struggle, a firm resolve grips them – the resolve to forge out of this world of darkness a new world of eternal light.[40]

The verses are read by one, some or all of the speakers:

SOME:
The little shack on the cliffs
is poor and eaten with rain
bitten with storm of sou'-westers
and gnawed by the cold of the Tasman;
but at least there is light inside there
and a bit of fire and above all
the yarns and laughing of our comrades,
of those who are more than our kindred,
of those fellow-workers and dear companions –
good companions come by many roads,
strangers, yet intimate in unity of heart and head,
needing only to talk in half-words, in bits of jokes, mere sketch of hands . . .
hardly needing words to understand one another.

SOME:
But now leave the hut, break in twos and threes, face the storm, boys:
now the doubtful cliff-edge, fumbling path, swirl of sea-fog,
now in darkness the skirl of murmur and menace that swell and grow still,
shifting and groping, cling of cloud, clodding of clay,
now no comrade beside us.

ALL:
Remember then what we have all learnt
what we have learnt together:
fling the old tunes in the teeth
of the gnawing weather.

Dark and shifting is the way
and we must leave each other:
apart, alone we'll not forget
what we have learnt together.

ONE:
We learnt our lessons too hard to forget lightly:
on the cold chair at night after work in the old Marxian class . . .
dull room . . . clothes unchanged, sweat-stiff . . . dropping eyes . . .
throbbing head.

And the word of some comrade comes from overseas
the refugee, international brigadesman,
or from some old-timer from Waihi, red fed, or returned man.

VOICES:
But above all we learned in hard life
yes, year after year sweated, exploited, bullied, despised,
kept in ignorance, preached at, lied to.

Year after year dull in mill, wharf, truck, ship, factory –
on picket-line, hunger-march, strike, demo, clash with scabs,
skirmish with specials. . . .[41]

Some phrases and rhythms here are familiar from Mason's other, lyric poetry
(the little shack on the cliffs is recognisable too as the students' hut at Anawhata).
But there is a sentimentality and simplicity, a lack of tension, that make it
quite different. '[S]imple plays for special purposes', Mason later described
the political theatre he was writing at this time.[42] By definition this was
rhetorical literature, and it was meant not to be read but to be heard. The
production was by Archie Fisher. Shirley Barton many years later remembered
the impact it made on her: the players standing on the stage 'huddled together
barely visible in dim lighting, each wearing a sort of dark grey shift and with
bare feet that glimmered white in the darkness',[43] and the beautiful, sonorous
voice of Mason's friend Matt Te Hau,[44] who read the solo lines, including
the verses before the final chorus:

The blessings of a king cannot conjure out
the devils that darkness built up in our spirits:
no paper can wipe off
scars etched into the flesh with acid:
holy water cannot wash away
what is burnt into the living bone.

Let the toad crawl and the owl hoot,
the weasel yelp and the rat squeak:
we'll not squeal.

We take the gun of darkness and leave the world of light
to the politician, bishop, beer-baron, press-lord, war-profiteer;
you have taken all the rest, my dear lords –
take our hut too.

We leave the light to them
we leave our little light
and go apart agrope on the dark paths.

FULL CHORUS:
But we've still got a light within us
each one a light within us
that will yet light up a world of light,
fiery crosses, armada-beacons on hills of light
a chain of light to go ringing round the world
till the whole globe dances in space alive with light:
and many a rich man's blaze will go to feed that light
and every poor man in the wide world round
will crawl from his dark hole to feel that light
and kindle the torch of his eyes at that mighty light
and warm his hands at that never-dying light.

It is curious, perhaps, that the poem was performed at this time, when the Communist Party had just reaffirmed its policy of opposition to the war. But more than a call to arms it was a reminder that the war had to be the right one ('We shall fight for freedom/ – but we'll make sure it is freedom we're/ fighting for'). And the People's Theatre was not, of course, beholden to the Party.

THE PEOPLE'S THEATRE was in confident mood at the dark end of 1939. Volume 1, Number 1 of the *People's Theatre Magazine* came out at the beginning of December: sixteen typed, cyclostyled pages, with a cover printed by the Griffin Press. It was sold for 3d. It contained articles and news about the international left theatre (reprinted from overseas sources) as well as People's Theatre news, and saw promising signs of the beginnings of a thriving workers' theatre movement nationwide. The Dunedin Left Book Club had staged *The Insect Play*, *Professor Mamlock* and *Squire Speaks*, and *Till the Day I Die* had been performed in several Waikato towns by the newly established Hamilton

People's Theatre. Articles on the theatre art of Stanislavsky, the Federal Art Theatre in America, Chinese revolutionary drama, documentary film and 'The Theatre in New Zealand: history and perspective' were promised for the next issue, which, however, never came.

While plans were made for the following year's programme there were also socials and dances. *Better Bayonets*, a 'sketch concerning attempts at renewing the War of Intervention against the Soviet Union, with special reference to Finland', was performed at a Friends of the Soviet Union dance and a meeting in the Druids' Hall. *Perkins and the Butler*, an 'amusing short sketch' possibly written by Mason, was performed at a People's Theatre dance.[45]

The shadow of war notwithstanding, this was a good time. Shirley Barton had become a close friend of Mason and Dorothea. She had a small public typing agency (which she had persuaded her father to buy her) on the top floor of the Victoria Arcade at the corner of Queen and Shortland streets, the chief virtue of which, she found, was as a meeting-place for friends. On Friday afternoons Mason would meet Dorothea at Bycroft's biscuit factory further up Shortland Street, then they would collect Shirley and go for a drink or two. The evening often ended up at the Golden Dragon restaurant at the foot of Grey's Avenue, a regular haunt of intellectuals and the left. 'Ron would be in merry mood, laughing and quipping, happy, delighted to have found in Dorothea both beauty and kindness.'[46] Gordon Watson would often join them, and Vernon Brown, who was a member of the People's Theatre. Clifton Firth too, perhaps, though his friendship with Mason was becoming more distant. With his wife, Patricia, he had opened a photographic studio at 110 Queen Street in 1938, specialising in portraiture: glamorous, Hollywood-style shots using dramatic contrasts of light and shade. It made him a lot of money during the war, and a circle of 'bourgeois' friends with whom Mason did not feel comfortable, yet Firth would continue to profess his socialism.[47]

Noel Counihan and Judah Waten might be there as well. These two Australians, an artist and writer respectively, were both members of the Communist Party of Australia and had arrived in Auckland from Melbourne in May 1939, planning to find work and earn enough money to take them to Europe, but found themselves stranded by the war. Counihan got a contract with the *New Zealand Observer* to do a weekly series of caricatures of 'New Zealand notables', and also made drawings of his new literary friends, including Mason. It was Waten, however, with whom Mason had a closer affinity. He was a Russian Jew, born in Odessa, who had emigrated to Australia with his family as a child: a burly, curly-headed, dark-eyed man with a 'mordantly witty sense of humour, at its best in grim situations', an inexhaustible interest in people and a 'sharp eye for their pretences, quirks and failings'.[48] Mason – who was living at home with his mother at this time, Waten remembered – was 'full of fun, humorous and liked meeting friends and talking and drinking with them'. 'Remember', Counihan wrote to Mason a few years later, 'the "Southern Colonel", the "Reverend", the fish, chips etc and the voluble one silently horizontal, all to the tune of good NZ beer?' Yet Waten also discerned something melancholic about him.[49]

Frank Haigh would recall Friday afternoon drinks at his office in the late 1930s attended by Mason, Fairburn and some others: not quite a club but a regular assignation. Haigh was one of a group of people, along with Arthur Sewell, Archie Fisher and Dick Anschutz, 'academics or professional men with radical sympathies and money to spare for a cause', whom Mason tried to interest in backing a new journal of literature and current affairs in 1939.[50] He never quite gave up the dream of reviving *Phoenix*. He apparently had Lowry in mind to print it. But Anschutz had already given money to bail out Lowry once, and there were others who suspected that Mason would turn it into a communist paper. He was to be, as so often, bitterly disappointed.

There were weekend excursions on Pat Potter's yacht, too. Potter told a familiar story about Mason's habit of wandering off. One weekend when they had sailed over to Thames, Mason went for a walk across the mudflats at low tide, about ten o'clock at night. When he wasn't back by low tide the next morning they called the police. He had walked on through the night, slept by the side of the road, caught a ride in an early-morning milk truck to Coromandel and a boat back to Auckland, and sent a message back to his friends via the police to let them know where he was.[51]

MASON LECTURED on drama in New Zealand at the WEA summer school of 1939–40, at Paerata. Around the hall there were remnants of Christmas decorations, and as he spoke he walked around the stage twisting paper streamers into strange shapes, out of nervousness or passion. 'In the end this became more compelling, almost, than the lecture', one of his audience recalled.[52]

From there he went by car down to Wellington with Jean Alison and Blackwood Paul to attend the first public meeting of the newly formed Peace and Anti-conscription Council. Ian Milner, recently back from Oxford, was the secretary, and Counihan and Waten, in Wellington by this time, were both involved. The group had been denied use of the Town Hall by the mayor, and an estimated 1200–1500 people crowded into the Trades Hall instead on the evening of 18 January while a further 300 stood outside. The speakers were Milner and Counihan, Archie Barrington and Ormond Burton (whose younger brother Robert had been Mason's first Grammar School friend), founders of the Christian Pacifist Society, and Keva Bronson, an English socialist who had emigrated to New Zealand in 1939. Sixty pounds was collected for the cause, and a national conference planned for Easter.

Mason and his friends stayed in a boarding house at first, then with Doug Martin, a Presbyterian minister turned socialist and pacifist, in Miramar. Ron 'asked me to sleep with him', Jean later recalled – adding '[h]e often did' – and she said no, as she always did.[53] Yet he wrote to Dorothea from Wellington with love and longing. He was charmed by Wellington, its smallness and its closeness to the edge: 'I like the way you walk out your suburban back-gate & you're in the wilderness.' The weather was perfect. Martin's house was in Nevay Road, which runs along the top of the Miramar peninsula. 'A most gorgeous ridge we're on. One side looks down into a valley full of city, the other on to the harbour backed by wild hills.' 'It is like our honey-moon time & I only wish we were together again in it.' He considered looking for a job in Wellington, 'but I did not think for a second you would like the idea, so have done nothing'.[54]

From Nevay Road they watched the First Echelon sail on 6 January. Mason spoke at a Left Book Club picnic in the Hutt Valley, and the three visited the Centennial Exhibition in Rongotai, three of the nearly three million people who did so between November 1939 and May 1940. The exhibition was the centrepiece of the centennial celebrations, a huge government trade fair. The 55-acre site featured a series of purpose-built courts and pavilions showing off 100 years of material progress and the benevolent state, and the largest amusement park yet constructed in the southern hemisphere: a 10-acre 'Playland' which boasted such attractions as the cyclone roller-coaster, a dodgem track and scoot boats, a chamber of horrors which reconstructed local murders (and was censored by the police), a shark aquarium and the Daredevil International Lady Stunt Motorcyclists. The three posed for photographs standing behind cut-out apes and cartoon characters. 'The Exhibition photos are marvellous', Jean wrote to Blackwood later, 'especially the one of you & I doing Boomps-a-Daisy. You've got a sedate clerical or perhaps angelical look thats perfeckly sweet. Mason looks like a convict. I have a sneaking suspicion that RAK deliberately looked like that so that he wouldn't be recognised if our photos. were stuck up on the outside of the booth. Silly ass at times, our Mason. I expect he thought the police might get a copy.'[55]

They went home via Palmerston North and Wanganui, where Mason spoke at peace meetings. Travelling up the Whanganui River was 'grand', he told Dorothea, but the town itself Mason was less enchanted by: 'a tough & hungry town. . . . It is notorious being the deadliest town in NZ (of any size that is). It is a rather dead-end, intensely respectable & when they die they put their University degrees on their tombstones. Dinkum, they do, darling. I've seen it. Think of it. Here lies the dearly-beloved body of R.A.K. Mason BA safe in the arms of Jesus.'[56]

Back in Auckland, he was involved in the formation of an Auckland branch of the Peace and Anti-conscription Council, and was acting secretary for a time.[57] Jean, a few days after they returned, 'up & married' Charles Bartlett, without telling anyone; 'it must have been a shock for Ron', she later reflected.[58]

If Mason had really feared discovery by the police at the centennial fair, as Jean only half-jokingly suggested, his paranoia was not entirely misplaced. Under wartime emergency regulations promulgated in September 1939 and February 1940, opposition to the war effort and to conscription – which was to be introduced in July 1940 – was vigorously suppressed. From early 1940 communists and pacifists were regularly arrested as they got up to speak on street corners, and given fines or prison sentences of up to twelve months with hard labour. In May *Tomorrow*, which had been making itself increasingly unpopular with the Labour government over the previous two years in its self-appointed role as the government's socialist critic and conscience, was closed down, in effect, when its printer was warned that continued publication would be in breach of the regulations. The same month the *People's Voice* press was seized. For the next year a quarto-sized mimeographed version, in several local editions, was illegally circulated. The Party itself was not declared illegal, as it was in Australia, but it effectively went underground. The constitution was suspended, branches were dispersed into smaller groups, prominent members were sent out into the provinces, and a safe house was established in Auckland. When Roy Stanley was gaoled Mason took over the editorship of the *Union Record*, as the *Borer* had, sadly, been renamed.

Noel Counihan and Keva Bronson were deported. Counihan went into hiding for a month after deportation orders and warrants for their arrest were issued in May 1940, before going back to Auckland. There he was arrested talking to Judah Waten in Customs Street and put on board the *Wanganella* for Sydney. Bronson had been arrested in Wellington and was sent back to England with his heavily pregnant wife, Golda, in June. Mason wrote a story, 'Babe Unborn', which he intended to publish as a pamphlet, recounting these events and the personal tragedy that followed. Golda was expected to pay her own passage home, but after a public campaign was allowed to leave with her husband on the tramp steamer *Port of Wellington*, which had no doctor or medical facilities; the baby was still-born.

Public support for the Peace and Anti-conscription Council fell away as quickly as it had spread, only in part because of the government's determination to stamp it out. The 'phoney war' had become a real war when Hitler advanced into Norway and Denmark in April, and opposition to it was now a very unpopular cause.

THE PEOPLE'S THEATRE met its demise at the end of April as well, but not through any official act of suppression. At the beginning of the year the executive had been looking forward to the new season, beginning with a major production, possibly *Marching Song*, in April. Meanwhile two Sunday night programmes were being prepared for February, with George Bernard Shaw's *O'Flaherty VC* and Mason's 'To Save Democracy' in the first, and *In that Zone* and *Where's that Bomb?*, directed by Mason, for the second. When these were abandoned they decided on a revival of 'Skull on Silence', *Eleventh Hour* and 'This Dark Will Lighten', and to do a rewritten version of *Newsboy*, a popular American agit-prop play first presented in New York in 1933 by the Shock Troupe, a militant workers' theatre on the lower East Side, and updated after 1935 in line with the Popular Front. Finally, it was decided to abandon the Sunday night programme altogether. There were still hopes of reviving *Till the Day I Die* as well, also in a modified form. Goodwin declined the invitation to produce it, saying that he was too busy, but adding that he disapproved of 'the idea that by mutilation or inversion any play can be trimmed to suit the political demands of the moment. It is in just this that I see the limitations and weakness of a Theatre based solely on a political ideology. . . . My opinion is, as you know that People's Theatre must be first (and last) *Good* Theatre.'[59] But the larger goal of building a vital, popular, local theatre movement had not been lost entirely to the imperatives of the moment, it appears. The executive made contact with the local Penwoman's Club play-distributing circle, asking about scripts by New Zealand authors, and were sent a list of what were described as romantic comedies, farce and melodrama.

When a meeting called for 2 April failed to reach a quorum, it was proposed that the theatre 'go into recess as a producing theatrical organisation & turn its activity towards forming a drama school'. The report of a special committee documented the continuing 'downward trend' in the theatre's membership, finances, and participation other than by a devoted few. A few weeks later, a notice was sent out cancelling the annual general meeting scheduled for the end of the month. It had been decided to go into 'temporary recess', this explained, partly for financial reasons, and partly because it was felt 'that at the present time the drama was too slow & laborious a method of propaganda . . . People's Theatre was formed to fight War, Fascism & Censorship' and these things could be done better through the Peace and Anti-Conscription movement, 'your Union or other political organisation'.[60] Propaganda had prevailed over art.

17

In Print

1941–45

POLITICS WAS removing Mason from poetry just when the reputation of his poetry was suddenly growing.

In February 1941 the Caxton Press brought out an anthology simply entitled *Recent Poems*, containing nine by Curnow, twelve by Glover, four by Fairburn and five by Mason: 'Vengeance of Venus', 'Twenty-sixth October', 'Flow at Full Moon', and two other previously unpublished poems about love and death. One was a sad celebration of love ('Song Thinking of Her Dead': the poet thinking about his dead lover), the other a bloody image of betrayal (involving a guillotine, 'a lock/ of hair in the blood where it fell', pressed 'once to her lip/ and once to the breast he had betrayed').

In December Caxton published Mason's selected poems, titled *This Dark Will Lighten*. Glover had been hoping it would be more of a collected poems. 'Go right ahead & make your selection; but don't make it a small one', he had written to Mason in February. 'All your work goes through the fire before going through the press, and we might as well have a decent collection rather than a selection. I do hope you will have a good rake through the entrails of all your old stuff' – and he could not refrain from listing his own favourites.[1] Mason was hoping that Glover would publish 'Cheaper Labourers' as well but this was not to be, possibly only because of Glover's departure for the navy at the end of 1941 and the virtual suspension of Caxton publishing for the next three years: 'Cheaper Labourers' was listed as 'in preparation' in the front of *This Dark Will Lighten*, although only under considerable pressure, Mason later admitted.[2]

In making his selection Mason was, as Glover anticipated, rigorous. Just over half of his published work went into *This Dark Will Lighten*, and nothing recovered from manuscript: three poems from his very first collection, 'In the Manner of Men', half of *The Beggar* and three from *Penny Broadsheet* (all of which Mason regarded as his 'juvenilia'), only fifteen from *No New Thing*, four out of the five in *End of Day*, and only one of the *Recent Poems*, 'Flow at

Full Moon'. From *No New Thing* he omitted half of the love poems. He dedicated the selection 'Ad Dorotheam'.

His earliest poems he revised in the style he had adopted since 'On the Swag', removing punctuation and setting them out with the Horatian hanging indent. He made few other changes. One was that the 'friendless, utter verge of space' at the end of the 'Sonnet of Brotherhood' became the more familiar 'outer edge' of space. As Glover recognised, Mason's poems were thoroughly wrought, 'bonelicked clean' before they ever reached the printed page; he did not rewrite. There was one new poem, 'Prelude', his manifesto. This combined the bitter sardonic tone of his earlier preludes with a mood of revolutionary optimism, or rather moved from one to the other, proffering a vision of a new, post-revolutionary dawn:

> Here are the children
>> of the best part of a lifetime
>
> Not as they should have grown
>> but twisted stunted maimed
>> by poverty chastity
>> and obedience
>
> I have no child of the flesh
>
> Yet now I do not grudge that lack
>> of some fat priest's easy sacrifice
>> to these gross and avid gods
>
> Nor do I grudge the lines
>> that should have been but are not
>
> For the day is almost here –
>> look see scarlet in the sky of the east
>> the splash of blood that means dawn –
>> when the idols will be thrown down
>> and children will dance through our land
>
> Children of brain and of body
>> will link hands and laugh through our land

making green their feet with fresh grasses
and purple their mouths with the fruit
and golden their foreheads with the flowers
springing from trees rich with ashes
of old black idols of desolation.

This is clearly a political as well as a personal statement. Poetically, however, the Blakean socialist vision feels no more convincing than the brusque repudiation of his previous work. It seems typical that the poem, opening up a vision of a new dawn, should end with the stress on 'old black idols of desolation'.

Mason's collected poems, Caxton announced, 'will be one of the most notable books of poetry anywhere published in 1941'.[3] It was a large but not unreasonable claim. Certainly, the publication of *This Dark Will Lighten* made Mason's poems accessible to a much larger reading public than ever before, rather than just those who had happened across a rare copy of *The Beggar* or *No New Thing*, or had seen his few poems in *Phoenix*. He became the subject, too, of serious critical attention. Most of this came from Allen Curnow. In a five-page article in the second issue of Glover's occasional Caxton 'miscellany' *Book* (published in May 1941), Curnow considered Mason as a 'native poet', while repudiating the search for obvious indigenous traces. On the contrary, to understand Mason as a native poet, he argued, and by implication to anticipate the development of a real New Zealand literature, 'one must blot out the notion that New Zealand is a place which it is curiously vital for poets to write *about*; and substitute the attitude that New Zealand is a place in which poets may happen – by Divine forbearance – to live and work'. Mason's verse was conspicuous in being 'almost entirely lacking in explicit reference to the New Zealand scene and people', and in his 'awareness of the elemental immediacy of birth, life, pain, and death, with a corresponding appreciation of the problem of evil'. Still, Curnow was compelled to find the imprint of location, 'some glimpse into the unconscious mind of this island community': not in anything so obvious as an occasional mention of Penrose or the lone hand digging gum, but in 'the image of isolation, the raw edge', the sense of hostile territory. It was the assimilation of this nervous consciousness into at once larger and more personal themes that made Mason New Zealand's completest, 'most integral and mature poet', he believed. That his achievement was not better recognised was due partly to the exoticness of this universality, and of his Latin titles, and partly to the deceptive simplicity of his verse (for those who thought that, to be difficult, poetry must look difficult). He chose 'Be swift o sun' and 'Footnote to John ii 4' – quoted in full – to illustrate Mason's technical skill.[4]

Curnow reviewed *This Dark Will Lighten* twice. Briefly, in the Christchurch *Press*, he was more forthright about the regard in which he held Mason's verse – 'Here are sonnets which would rank high in any company. Here is a keen wit, salted by suffering. Here are a command of form and phrasing, a rhythmic control and balance, such as no other New Zealand poet has approached' – while reiterating (and developing) his argument that Mason's attention to the local scene and the contemporary world 'is often more significant by its obliquity'.[5] In the *New Zealand Listener* (anonymously, as 'Ibid') he expanded on his themes and admired Mason's rigour of selection, while admitting his disappointment that this was not the collected poems he had been expecting. Here was a poet 'mature and well-equipped and sure – sure of himself (or rather of the bitter certainty of his conflicts) and of his medium'. 'There is no doubt', Curnow declared, 'that this small book is an event, and even if it is a day or two late for Christmas presents, I am going to urge everyone with the least appreciation or care for verse to buy it.'[6]

Further afield, in the metropolis, Mason was also reviewed in John Lehmann's *Folios of New Writing*, in an article by William Plomer in the autumn 1941 issue on 'Some books from New Zealand'. The article was mainly about Frank Sargeson, for whom Plomer – author, publisher's reader, friend of the Woolfs as well as of Lehmann – had become an important contact on the London literary scene. Writing of *No New Thing*, which Sargeson had sent him and which he called a 'remarkable book', Plomer memorably and precisely described Mason's poetry as '[g]loomy, sexy and sardonic', but criticised what he saw as a typical colonial habit of rhetoric, of 'dramatiz[ing] himself into a romantic attitude', which, he thought, 'suggests an honest, if vain, effort to get to grips with New Zealand'.[7] It is interesting to see that Plomer, who was a South African not an Englishman, was more concerned with the 'New Zealandness' of Mason, or rather with reading in him an expression of the 'colonial condition', than was Curnow at this stage.

Mason's critics were not interested in his drama. E.H. McCormick, in his official centennial survey of New Zealand letters and art which came out towards the end of 1940, devoted only his final chapter to the last decade of the century under review. His critical approach was sociological (after F.R. Leavis, whose influence he had absorbed at Cambridge, where the survey started out as his doctoral thesis), and he especially noted the invigorating effect on the young New Zealand writers of the Depression, exemplified by the appearance of *Phoenix*. McCormick was a demanding critic, however, or perhaps a cautious one, finding only 'a residue – passages in A.R.D. Fairburn's *Dominion*, some of the shorter poems by Allen Curnow and R.A.K. Mason, with a handful of Denis Glover's good-humoured lampoons' among the work of this generation to have 'added considerably' to the thus-far small (indeed tiny) corpus of New Zealand verse that was of lasting literary value. McCormick was pleased that these enterprising young poets had 'abandoned their isolation to give New Zealand verse a social content lacking since the nineties, and with this a vigour and an intellectual distinction hitherto unknown', but displeased with them for being too swayed by literary and political fashion, and for 'an undiscriminating devotion to the younger English poets, whose influence is deplorably evident in Denis Glover's facile tributes to the proletariat and in R.A.K. Mason's *Squire Speaks*'.[8]

M.H. Holcroft, in his prize-winning entry in the centennial essay competition, *The Deepening Stream*, which was published by the Caxton Press in October 1940, also worried about the radicalising influence of the Depression. Remarking too on the 'noticeably radical trend in the serious writing now being done in New Zealand', he discoursed at length on the danger of 'undigested Marxism', dismissed 'didactic verse' (citing Fairburn's 1938 epic *Dominion* and the large amount of fashionable satirical verse, much of which was by Fairburn and Glover) and warned against adherence to a single political or social theory. He was confident, however, that this was only a transitional phase, albeit a necessary one, and that eventually this 'confusion of values and naivete of outlook' would be replaced by a distinctively New Zealand literary mind, which was what he was determined to discover.[9] *The Deepening Stream* was a philosophical speculation on the possibility and nature of a national culture, and an attempt to define New Zealand's 'national soul', the collective unconscious of its people, which derived, Holcroft believed, from the landscape and received its fullest expression in the work of its creative writers. Poets would lead the way, but the springs of New Zealand's cultural psyche lay in the very forms of the land and in the silence of the primeval forest.

Holcroft's essay was a curious, idiosyncratic, ruminative and meandering work compared with McCormick's brisk but eloquent survey, but its thesis was arguably more influential. Curnow's reference to the 'unconscious mind of this island community' and to a 'repressed yet living past' suggests that he had been reading *The Deepening Stream*.[10] It was not until the second of what was to be a trilogy of essays, *The Waiting Hills* (1943), that Holcroft turned to consider New Zealand literature in detail. Like McCormick, he found the Depression to have been 'a fortunate season' for New Zealand poets: it had unsettled them and given them 'time to think'. Of Mason specifically, he surmised that his 'proud agnosticism' – artistic and religious – had 'received at least part of its sinew from the impact of the slump years', although of course the attitude had been formed already. (Knowing that much of Mason's poetry had been written in the 1920s while fitting him into what quickly came to be identified as the 'thirties generation' would remain a critical challenge.) His 'consistent indifference to the New Zealand scene' Holcroft interpreted as an expression of the essential alienation of the artist, though perhaps intensified by this particular 'hostile place' in which he found himself: 'an unconscious reaction to the discovery of his solitariness as a poet in an unfriendly social climate'. Mason's preoccupation with 'the decay that lives in beauty', with death, showed not only the influence of the English literature he had read, but might also manifest, Holcroft suggested, 'the first natural response, in a New Zealand poet, to the shock of revelation which comes to every sensitive mind detaching itself from the quick rhythms of a secure existence'. Thus Holcroft found in Mason's pessimism an indication of an authentically New Zealand experience of that 'creative separateness' that was the necessary condition of artistic endeavour. He welcomed, however, the sign in Mason's recent poems – 'Flow at Full Moon' in particular – of a lightening of his mood. Holcroft was not the only critic to see a new beginning here in Mason's work.[11] For all this, he was keen to state that, while 'a powerful and original talent', Mason was not a role model for the New Zealand poet, except insofar as he exemplified the integrity of the artist. For he 'would have made his verse in any country and in any period'. He was not a useful precedent, in other words, when the role of poets was to 'acclimatize the muse, to open their minds and the minds of their readers to influences that can be found in this country and nowhere else'.[12]

WHILE MASON'S poetry was being worked into an emerging nationalist critical discourse, the poet himself had moved on. It was theatre that continued to engage his creative attention, as the artistic form that he believed was the only one valid for these times and consistent with his political ideals. But he found little outlet for this interest over the next few years – although he did take part in the WEA's annual productions in September 1940, playing the

estate manager Shamraev in Chekhov's *The Seagull*, 'quite strikingly badly',[13]
and May 1941 as Mickey, the boxer's masseur, in Odets's *Golden Boy*. His
acting had not improved: when told by the director to do something, not just
stand there, he chewed on a thumbnail.

The Party had more important work for Mason than writing plays and
running theatres. In 1941 he became the editor of a new weekly, *In Print*,
which was published from September 1941 until July 1943. It was not officially
a Party paper – the *People's Voice* was still banned – but in effect it was. Mason
was asked to be the editor because he was not a Party member.[14]

In Print was an expression of the Communist Party's new status after 22
June 1941, when Hitler's army marched into the Soviet Union. All of a sudden,
Party policy switched from lonely opposition to the war to all-out support
for it. 'This is the decisive moment of world history', a communiqué from
the national executive declared.[15] The choice was clear: *Help Russia or – Help
Hitler!* as the title of a sixteen-page pamphlet Mason wrote on behalf of the
newly formed Aid to Russia Committee put it. The pamphlet was both a
defence of the Soviet system and a call for co-operation with Russia to defeat
fascism and end the war. By the time it was printed Britain had declared the
Soviet Union an ally. It would be going too far to say that the Party became
respectable, but it was tolerated for the next three years to an extent it had
never been before, or ever would be again. Against the background of the
heroic Russian resistance to the German invasion during the five-month siege
of Stalingrad in the Russian autumn and winter of 1942–43, red flags flew
alongside the New Zealand ensign on Russia's national day, civic mayors
presided over public meetings to mark the 25th anniversary of the Red Army,
and even the Returned Services' Association formally expressed its 'profound
admiration for the magnificent resistance of our Russian ally to the onslaught
of the common enemy'.[16] The signing of a twenty-year Anglo-Russian alliance
in June 1942 was marked in Auckland by a mass rally in the Domain and a
parade led by the Watersiders' Band which culminated in the singing of 'The
Internationale', and a screening of the Russian film *Chapayev* at the Strand
Theatre in the evening to an audience of 1200. Mason described the rally:
'Thousands of voices repeating in steady unison a pledge of co-operation
with Russia in war and peace. . . . A thunderous yell of greeting to similar
gatherings throughout New Zealand. . . . A blaze of banners, flags and slogans,
carried by marching units of trade unions and national groups. . . . An unbroken
hush as the great gathering paid silent tribute to the dead, while flags dipped
slowly in impressive salute.'[17] Party membership trebled between June 1941

and the beginning of 1943, to reach 1800 – 1100 in Auckland.[18] It was the Party's strongest moment numerically, and its least revolutionary.

Auckland's trade union-based Aid to Russia Committee was superseded by a branch of the Society for Closer Relations with Russia, which was founded in Wellington in July 1941. This was a more broadly based movement than the old Friends of the Soviet Union, which had self-destructed through political infighting at the end of the 1930s. The Society for Closer Relations with Russia explicitly stated that it was 'not committed to Marxianism', but only to the promotion of 'closer cultural, diplomatic and economic relations between the New Zealand people and the people of the USSR'.[19] Its members included prominent intellectuals, members of Parliament and church leaders (Methodist, at least). By late 1944 there were thirty-five branches around the country. Mason sent apologies when he was invited to attend a meeting to discuss the formation of an Auckland branch in late August 1941 – he might not be able to go because he was 'not too well' – but stressed the importance of the new organisation's being representative. The draft list of sponsors did not include any artists or writers, he noted, suggesting Fairburn, Firth, Jane Mander, Archie Fisher and Vernon Brown, nor representatives of the workers, farmers or national minorities.[20] The front page of the first issue of *In Print* carried a report of a 3000-strong rally in the Auckland Town Hall on 4 September, called by the new society to 'endorse the pledges of Churchill and add their own greetings to the Soviet people' and chaired by Arthur Sewell.[21]

In Print was devoted primarily to encouraging the war effort – that is to say, propagating the Communist Party policy of a national and international united front against fascism. 'For the Peoples' Unity and Victory' was its slogan. 'Our interest is the overthrow of fascist aggression, a speedy end to the war, a sound and just peace', the first issue declared. The paper campaigned for the maximisation of the war effort, industrial efficiency and the war against waste, deep air-raid shelters, exposure of fifth-columnists, the opening of a second front in Europe, and Victory Loans. Its long-term manifesto was also the Party's: better wages, better housing and working conditions, equal pay for women, '[f]ull recognition of the rights of the Maori people' and freedom of speech.[22]

Its address was 451 Great South Road. Mason edited it there, while it was printed by the Times Printing Works, in Otahuhu at first and later in Chapman Street, Newton. He came over on the early-morning Bayswater ferry each day with a group that included Pia Richards, Arnold Goodwin, Ernest Blair, founder of the WEA Dramatic Club, and photographer Bert Tornquist. 'There was Ron coming on to the ferry every morning', Goodwin's daughter Barbara later recalled, 'sitting alongside the funnel with his bootlaces undone' and never noticing her doing them up for him each day. He grew a moustache at this time and wore a working-man's cap 'like Molotov – the top buttoned onto the peak'.[23] Jean (now Bartlett) worked for him as a reporter for 10s a week, spending one day out at Ellerslie and a day at the printery. Mason wrote all of the editorials and probably a good deal of the unsigned copy as well. The style was declamatory and exhortatory, studded with exclamation marks and capital letters. '[W]e have fought hard to give the working people a lead, a clear, practical and constructive lead. We have sought to show you how the Fascist beasts menace everything human and how this menace must be met by solid organisation of the working people from below. That is the basis for victory in this war and it will equally be a sure guarantee of winning the peace. Unity of the workers' forces, unity of all anti-Fascist forces to crush the mad beast', his first anniversary editorial ran.[24] When Jean asked him how a poet could write this jargon week after week, he replied that it was what the people expected and what he had to do.

One wonders how easily the Party's new-found enthusiasm for the war came to someone like Mason, whose gentle, generous nature suggests an instinctive pacifism. The justification for war and revolution was something he had struggled with in his notebooks years before. 'I think perhaps this is Armageddon after our fall from grace (what the Marxians call the downfall of the capitalistic regime). I begin to believe in those ancient prophesies and feel quite certain that this war will usher in the Golden Age. So a man should surely fight for that', he had written about the time he ceased correspondence with the German doctor.[25]

Sid Scott wrote a weekly war commentary for *In Print* and there was a page of 'News from the Anti-fascist Front' overseas. In the fifth issue Mason announced a new feature, 'a general article by an expert on subjects of national importance', such as drama, medicine, diet, law, New Zealand literature, printing and film-making. The first, on China, was by Winston Rhodes, who became a regular contributor, mostly on the war in the Pacific; the second, a profile by theatre owner Henry Hayward of Anna Pavlova. Willis Airey contributed on Soviet foreign policy; educationalist Walter Scott on advertising and capitalism. From October 1941 the paper printed the Soviet constitution in serialised instalments. There were book reviews, usually of works on topical or political subjects, a brief film column, theatre reviews (of

WEA productions) and the occasional poem, but not by Mason − William Blake, for example, and some by Gordon Watson.

Labour and industrial matters were treated when the larger subject was the war effort, but union matters were explicitly outside *In Print*'s brief. This was probably just as well. Harold Silverstone, the Wellington Party secretary and editor of the *Industrial Worker*, sent Mason some advice when he suspended his paper in favour of *In Print* in November 1941: be wary of industrial and trade union news, particularly of the 'tendency on the part of many people to attempt to use a workers' newspaper for sectarian purposes' (and 'be particularly careful of anything that comes from the Waikato coalfields'), avoid anything controversial, and above all work in as close as possible harmony with the Party.[26]

It was a hard job editing *In Print*, and a struggle just to keep it afloat. Not accepting trade advertising and not being an official Party concern, the paper was financed by subscriptions, fund-raising socials and dances, and donations to a succession of maintenance, fighting and Christmas funds. From time to time it was printed on stiff brown or shiny pink wrapping paper. When he was forced to cut back the number of pages to six because of the paper shortage, Mason reduced the type size so as not to compromise *In Print*'s mission. When his one-legged business manager, Ernie Coster, was called up in the middle of 1942 (followed soon after by the sub-editor, Nat Gould), an elderly Party member, Jack Summers, reluctantly took on the job.

Mason enrolled as a reservist in July 1941, and was himself called up but turned down for health reasons, according to Dorothea. When he presented himself, thin, pale and visibly shaking, the doctors told him to sit down for while and, as he was still shaking when they came back, sent him home.

He regularly met with the Party hierarchy, and 'more or less took his directions from them'.[27] They were friends as well as comrades. Sid Scott was one, as was Vic Wilcox, a former farm labourer who had become the Auckland branch secretary in 1940 and joined the national committee the following year, and who had married one of Pia Richards's daughters, Ann. Gordon Watson had enlisted at the end of 1941 (and was to be killed in action at Faenza two weeks before VE day). Occasionally Mason got into trouble. A mildly facetious piece about the Semple tank − the prototype 'home-made' tank built by the Public Works Department from a converted tractor, and named for the Minister of Public Works, Bob Semple: an irresistible target for Mason's satirical pen − brought a po-faced letter from Sid Scott and an apology and withdrawal from *In Print*. 'Admittedly the "Semple tank" is not the finest example of armament-production', Scott wrote. 'But it is desirable that New Zealand should establish an armaments-production industry, and, crudities or no crudities, we should regard these first beginnings as something to be encouraged – not made the subject of witticisms.'[28]

Toeing the Party line did not necessarily endear *In Print* to all of the rank and file, however, and the Party leadership had to remind its members to support the paper and that it was, indeed, representing the Party view. The steady fall in circulation (from a peak of 13,000) after March 1942 was interpreted as a reflection in part of the difficulty many members had in adjusting to the new policy on the war. Criticism 'is not infrequently heard', an Auckland branch bulletin noted, from those who felt that *In Print* did 'not sufficiently attack the Government and New Zealand capitalism'. Moreover, *In Print* had 'found itself unable to adequately combine the vigorous journalism of the earlier Party press, with the National Front policy', a report from the National Committee observed.[29] This was the Party's problem, not *In Print*'s, of course. It is always more fun to be militant in opposition. This may have been the most decisive moment of world history, but being on the side of the nation was not really where revolutionaries liked to be. Increasingly in the latter stages of the war, the Party's policy of no strikes in support of the war effort – the end result of its strategic rapprochement with the capitalist state – was a position with which many members did not feel comfortable.

THERE WERE more serious risks in the job than offending against political purity, or the Party's lack of a sense of humour. In February 1942 Mason appeared in court on six charges of breaching the Censorship and Publicity Emergency Regulations. He was a mass of nerves. Eileen Elphick, Dorothea's housemate at Tennyson Avenue (and who would later marry Ian Hamilton), saw him on the ferry that morning, dressed in a white suit, 'terribly thin . . . terribly shaking'.[30] Mason was defended by Frank Haigh. The two articles in question, in the 14 and 28 January issues, had described the working conditions provided for 1200 members of the Civilian Construction Unit who were sent to Fiji in November 1941 to build an aerodrome at Nadi. They had arrived to find that no accommodation, building materials or tools were provided, or mosquito nets, there was an inadequate supply of fresh water, and the food that had been shipped from New Zealand was already going bad when it arrived. When union delegates organised industrial action, twelve of them – among them Mason's friend from the Carpenters' Union, Roy Stanley – were deported back to Auckland, where they told their story to *In Print*. The court case, however, had nothing to do with the paper's sympathetic reporting of the workers' grievances and accusations of government suppression and victimisation, but with its having made public specific information about military preparations. The charges were swiftly dismissed, the magistrate observing that defence preparations in Fiji were already public knowledge and reprimanding the police for wasting his time with a 'far-fetched' and *prima facie* case.[31] Afterwards Mason was 'ordered away for a fortnight's rest'.[32]

Mason also played a walk-on part in the strange story of Sydney Gordon Ross, Captain Calder and the fifth column. Ross was a habitual petty criminal who was serving a sentence for breaking and entering at Waikeria Prison when he met up with Charles Remmers, a former policeman and convicted fraudster. Together they concocted an elaborate tale about a nationwide sabotage cell, recruited by German agents who had landed in New Zealand by submarine and were plotting to kidnap and assassinate the Cabinet in advance of a German invasion. When Ross was released from prison in March 1942 he took this story to Bob Semple. It convinced the police and Major Kenneth Foulkes, the British intelligence officer who had recently been appointed head of New Zealand's newly established Security Intelligence Bureau. Equipped with an official alias as Captain Calder of the merchant marine and a British naval hero, Ross went off to find evidence of the conspiracy. One of his first stops was *In Print*, where, as he later told the police, he interviewed Mason, who sent him to the headquarters of the saboteurs in Wellington. (Ross/Calder had not realised, perhaps, that by then the Communist Party was behind the war and in the business of exposing, not harbouring, fifth columnists.) Mason, when interviewed by Detective Jones at the *In Print* office on 15 July, denied ever having met Ross, sold him advertising space in the paper or printed any pamphlets for him; 'he had never asked any person to procure gelignite for him for any purpose'; though it was true that he 'sometimes had a drink at the Naval and Family Hotel . . . he usually drank sherry during working hours'. Perhaps because of Mason's visible nervousness, the detective thought that he was not being entirely truthful, and that he had at least met Ross.[33] The hoax was eventually revealed when a doctor failed to be convinced by the self-inflicted wounds which Ross claimed he had received at the hands of German spies, who had tortured him and forced him at gunpoint to dig his own grave. Neither Ross nor Remmers was charged with any offence in relation to this escapade, but Major Foulkes lost his job and was sent back home.[34]

More important, through *In Print* Mason met Hone Tuwhare, a young apprentice boilermaker and newly recruited member of the Party who distributed *In Print* and the *People's Voice* at the Otahuhu railway workshops, for long a stronghold of Party influence among Auckland's industrial working class. His father wrote the column in Maori which appeared (without translation) in *In Print* from September 1942. Tuwhare was also trying to write poetry, but it was not until a few years later that he discovered Mason was a poet too, and in time Mason became his literary mentor as well as a good friend. Mason never talked to him about poetry before that, only about political work and union matters. Like most people, Tuwhare assumed then that Mason was a card-carrying member of the Party, although he couldn't be sure; he was clearly a 'trusted man'.[35] It was their likeness in character – Tuwhare's humility, modesty and earthy sense of humour – as well as the politics and poetry that cemented an enduring bond between them.

In Print, with the Party and its union allies, took a real and not only an ideological interest in the issue of Maori rights and Maori welfare. In 1943 this was focused on Orakei, the two and a half acres occupied by the Orakei marae at Okahu Bay on Tamaki Drive, which was the last remaining piece of land in Auckland held by Ngati Whatua, who had gifted the site of the city to Governor Hobson a century before. The government claimed Orakei, and the Auckland City Council was keen to be rid of what was seen as an ugly and unsanitary blot on the suburban landscape. Unsanitary it certainly was: the decades-old and continuing legal dispute over the ownership of the land meant that Ngati Whatua had been prohibited from making any improvements to it, resulting in the slum-like conditions that Mason described in the first of several articles about Orakei in *In Print* (in January 1942). It was intended to demolish the village and resettle the people elsewhere – which is what in due course happened, but only after a fight.

This was not Mason's first involvement in the Orakei cause. Back in 1937, when the government had first told the City Council that the Orakei Maori must go – because a new garden suburb was planned for the hilltop above the bay, and its residents could hardly be expected to look down on a shabby marae – an Association of the Friends of Orakei was formed. Mason joined its eighteen-member committee, along with Fairburn, and Robin Hyde was the secretary. After several months of vigorous lobbying, the group disbanded when the immediate threat of eviction appeared to have passed.[36] Or so they thought.

In 1943 Te Puea Herangi came up to Auckland from Ngaruawahia to lend her mana and the backing of the Maori King movement to the campaign.

She enlisted the support of the trade union movement through Pat Potter, who was by this time secretary of the Auckland General Labourers' Union and soon to be appointed the Auckland Trades Council's 'Maori liaison officer'. On 5 April Te Puea visited Orakei with Potter and a delegation of union leaders to lend a practical hand in cleaning up the grounds, and announced plans for renovating the meeting house, constructing a new dining hall, and erecting a palisade around the marae. Tom Karaka, one of Mason's friends in the Labourers' Union, believed that the palisade had been Mason's idea but with his typical modesty he did not take the credit. Mason would later credit it to Potter, describing it as an 'Irish trick'.[37] On the afternoon of Saturday, 29 May, 200 unionists – carpenters, labourers and Mason – gathered at the marae to build a 300-foot long modern version of a traditional Maori palisade: a two-foot concrete base surmounted by eight-foot peeled and sharpened manuka stakes interspersed with heart of totara posts eight feet apart. 'You'll be building not only a ponga palisade', Potter, who organised the 'day of action', told them, 'but also the basis for a better world order.'[38] (Less than ten years later, Ngati Whatua were evicted and resettled in state rental housing up on the hill at Bastion Point, and the marae was destroyed.)

When she heard a few months after this that Mason was 'very sick', Te Puea invited him down to Ngaruawahia to rest: 'dear Ron just make up your mind and come', she wrote to him, 'sit down and [write] a short note and say you are coming'.[39] He was off work for three months before Christmas, but whether he spent any of this time in the King Country is not known.

THE *People's Voice* resumed publication in July 1943. Its resurrection was celebrated with a fund-raising dance at the Masonic Hall to which readers were invited to come 'and meet these Comrades, SID SCOTT, RON MASON, JACK SUMMERS, and the rest who have so ably built the working-class press'.[40] Mason's last editorial for *In Print* expressed the theme with which he had titled his selected poems, light in darkness: 'When we began, night was darkening over the world, big with storm: night gathered and the storm rolled its full strength. To-day there is still night and thunder, but at least we discern, surely though afar, the certain tokens of a sunny dawn.'[41]

He stayed on as co-editor of the *People's Voice* alongside Sid Scott, who was rapidly losing his sight from glaucoma, for which he had sought treatment in London and Moscow in 1939. *In Print* became a smaller-format monthly 'magazine of Marxism', the Party's 'theoretical organ'. Its first issue, in December 1943, had articles by Scott, Harold Silverstone and Lenin ('Socialism and War', dating from 1915, introduced by Mason). Mason contributed two articles to the new *In Print*, one on Pacific affairs (the Australia-New Zealand agreement on Native Peoples of the Pacific), and a long discourse on 'The churches and the United Front' in response to an article in the previous issue by Elsie Locke (formerly Freeman). He contested her claim that unity among religions and between believers and non-believers to resist oppression had been unknown before the Russian revolution. Describing a long history of progressive religious movements, from the Levellers to the rise of Christian socialism in the nineteenth century, he stressed the importance for theoreticians of the left of distinguishing between religion as a faith and religion as an ethic. Dialectical materialism was irreconcilable with the 'supernatural element in religion', but Christianity and communism shared a common ground in their belief in the brotherhood of man.[42]

Mason's name no longer appeared as publisher of *In Print* and the *People's Voice* after April 1944. He was 'railroaded out' by Sid Scott, according to Pat Potter.[43] What was behind this is not clear – possibly nothing more than that the Party wished to reassert authority over its press and that Mason was not in fact one of the fold. He had a go at working as a gardener for a while, tree-pruning and landscaping, before Potter gave him a job with the Labourers' Union.

18

New theatre

1945–48

IT WAS A relief, probably, to be out of the Party press. 'For the last couple of years I have been working harder by ten times than ever before in my life', Mason wrote in 1944 to Norman Richmond, who was by then teaching history at the University of Queensland. He had dropped all of his WEA connections, 'except for a bit of interest in the drama side'.[1] By this he was referring not only to his occasional, undistinguished contribution as an actor. In the first half of the 1940s his hopes for the growth of a popular, progressive theatre movement were briefly revived.

In 1941 he had reviewed in *In Print* a performance of six dance-dramas by members of the WEA theatre class taught by Margaret Barr. Barr, who had arrived in Auckland two years before, had studied with Martha Graham in New York in the 1920s and taught at Dartington Hall in Devon for four years, before setting up her own Workers' Dance-Drama Theatre Group in the mid-1930s in London, where she also joined Unity Theatre. She left England for New Zealand with her husband, a conscientious objector, on the eve of the war, and after a six-month stint in a munitions factory took up a post as drama tutor with the WEA in 1940. For the next five years she was a vivid figure on the Auckland WEA and theatre scene, with her striking, Katharine Hepburn looks and unconventional attire (mackintosh, hair-snood and sandals), Stanislavskian teaching methods and autocratic style. She lived on a yacht moored at the Akarana Yacht Club which she and her husband had bought after selling the MG they had shipped out with them from England.

These pieces 'are more than plays or ballets', *In Print* wrote of her first WEA production in October 1941. 'They have not only beauty and artistry, but also social significance.' 'Factory' was the title of one. The following year's programme included dance-dramas about deep shelters and the Spanish Civil War. 'The whole work is at a high level of intelligence, yet at the same time it re-creates the primitive elements of drama, when men and women moved in dances which were at once simple and full of faith, vigour and fire', observed *In Print* of the 1941 production.[2] The blending of forms as well as the social and political commitment in Barr's work interested Mason, and he wrote a script for her third show in 1943. The programme also included a work she had written at Mason's request for that year's May Day rally in Myers Park, at which the speakers had included Pat Potter, Auckland Communist Party secretary Alec Drennan and Te Puea, who concluded her words with the last three verses of Thomas Bracken's 'Not Understood'.

China, Mason's dance-drama poem, presented, in the words of the *People's Voice*, 'an epic story of China's unity and resistance against the Japanese, foreshadowing her final emergence victorious as a great and democratic nation. The story is told through the symbolic actions of two groups of villagers, who unite under the terroristic attacks of the Japanese.' It was written 'by the well-known poet, R.A.K. Mason' (not by the editor of the *People's Voice*, Ron Mason).[3] The style was that of Mason's mass chants:

> Hear how, as the rice is cast to rot in dung and slime,
> so did we rot in despair that was made ever deeper
> until at last like the rice we rose up
> and out from the slime we lifted up the spears of our green leaves
> and we hammered up our way
> through the muck dunged with our own corpses
> and from ground made fat with our own blood
> came silver of an enduring harvest.
>
> This is how it once was:
>
> Flood and plague and famine
> came and went like the generations:
> dynasts rose and fell:
> war-lords and their armies
> like willow leaves sprung green,
> turned yellow, choked the drains.
>
> But ever the families and the land
> and the rice they planted in the land.
> . . .

and his *In Print* editorials:

Said the agitators
by day in the rice-field,
at evening in the village,
in word and song and dances,
in plays, posters and pictures:
'Rise up, rise up like the waters of the flood,
arise, unite, free in your own discipline,
unite our endless numbers:
in unity is power,
force to face the struggle,
strength to win victory:
unity for victory!'[4]

Sections of the poem, read by Barr herself, alternated with a series of dances – the Dance of the Planting of the Rice, Dance of Unity, Dance of the Killing of the Tiger – performed to music by Dorothea Franchi. Mason also had the poem printed as an eight-page pamphlet for sale at the performances (it made 'a quick profit', to his surprise).[5] He had no deep knowledge of China, he stated in his foreword, but hoped that through his words would 'shine forth a little of that glorious spirit of resistance to barbarism which is being shown to-day by so great a part of the human race and is manifest so particularly in the heroic Chinese people', and that 'its publication may possibly be some incentive towards a progressive drama in this country. . . . It has been my invariable experience' – referring to his political sketches and verse dramas for the People's Theatre – 'that such plays are welcomed by the working people. To me it seems certain that the majority of our people would take as ardent an interest in dramatic artistry as do our Maori fellow-citizens: provided only that the work was done honestly and without condescension by authors and players, and that it was progressive both in outlook and presentation.'[6]

The existence among his papers of several playscripts dating from the 1940s from Unity Theatre's 'New Theatre' script service testifies to Mason's continuing ambition of reviving the People's Theatre, or something like it. And there were encouraging signs of the national progressive theatre movement which the *People's Theatre Magazine* had looked forward to in the establishment in 1942 of Wellington's agit-prop, Party-connected Unity Theatre and the still-active Hamilton People's Theatre. Both of these groups were to turn into something else in the post-war era, however, and moved away, in different degrees, from their political origins and agit-prop style. In Auckland, the

New Theatre Group was founded in 1945 under the lead of Margaret Barr, along with Owen Jensen, the WEA music tutor. Its prospectus described it as 'a representative community theatre . . . interested in furthering the aims of progressive drama in all its aspects'. Weekly classes were offered in improvisation, body technique, eurhythmics and lyrical movement at the Trades Hall, and in musical appreciation at 'Madame Valeska's studio'. Fees were 30s a term or 3s a class; membership for 'active participants in any sphere of dramatic work . . . e.g. actors, authors etc' was 10s 6d a year.[7] Mason joined. Shirley Barton remembered the rehearsals where he 'simply suffered like others of us who were conscripted by the forceful Margaret and made to mime picking a daffodil or, in Ron's case, taking a shower. As he struggled with the motions again and again a friendly voice was heard to remark, "That's the best wash Ron has had in years".'[8]

The New Theatre Group gave its inaugural public performance on 3 October 1945 at St Andrews Hall in Symonds Street, opening a four-night season. The programme consisted of a curtain-raiser by Mason entitled 'The Buccaneering Banker', satirising opposition to the nationalisation of the Bank of New Zealand (which had been discussed in Labour circles since the beginning of the war); a series of short dance-drama pieces from Barr's early repertoire (including her first, *Hebridean*, set to folksongs arranged by Edmund Rubbra); a technique display; a reprise of *China*; and a one-act play by Mason entitled 'Refugee'. The setting of 'Refugee' was a conference of the Returned Services' Association at which a delegation of refugees from Europe seeks permission to speak; its theme, in the words of their spokesman, was that 'all we refugees are good New Zealanders, just as all good New Zealanders are refugees'. He is grudgingly given leave by the belligerent chairman to put their case, and the six short scenes which follow represent the experience of various groups of people who came to New Zealand to escape from oppression: the Maori, '[f]leeing from war, enslavement, death'; the Irish rebel, wondering if 'even in New Zealand there might still be English'; the escaped convict from Sydney; the New Zealand Company labourer; dispossessed Highland crofters; and most recently the refugees from Nazi Europe – several of whom Mason by then numbered among his friends.[9] The show was positively reviewed in the *People's Voice* as 'a revelation of the value of good drama as a weapon for progressive purposes' and 'vigorous, colourful and original', and in the new *Year Book of the Arts in New Zealand* by Ernest Blair, who admired the group's energy and enthusiasm: 'It was home-spun stuff, much of it, but with a genuine quality of texture very pleasant to see. Where stage experience was occasionally lacking in the plays, it was replaced by an enthusiastic belief in the subject matter which triumphed over all the rules, actually creating a new technique.'[10]

'The form and quality of the New Theatre Group is closely bound up with the personality of Miss Barr', Blair continued, and he hoped that 'she will remain in New Zealand long enough to see the Group solidly established'. She did not, however. The programme had announced the group's first Living Newspaper, 'based on the housing problem', for early the following year. But Barr had already parted company with the WEA – acrimoniously, according to her biographer; Mason would later refer to the '[g]rim story behind kiss of death to Margaret Barr's work and nascent drama in Auckland'.[11] Little is known of how she spent her remaining time in Auckland before she left for Sydney in 1949, aside from obtaining a qualification in seamanship and helping her husband build the new yacht on which they sailed. But there were no more performances by the New Theatre Group.

THE New Theatre Group's variety programme of October 1945 was the last full production of any of Mason's plays, for some twenty years at least. 'Economic necessity', he explained some time later, 'never allowed me to make a full-scale attempt' at writing for the stage, and only to write these 'simple plays for special purposes'.[12] He would leave among his papers numerous other scripts, written but not performed, or started and not finished. 'The Man from Verstchaginski' is annotated in his hand 'v. early' and was probably written in the 1920s, when, by his own account, he first tried his hand at drama and Fairburn was playing juvenile lead for the Grafton Shakespeare and Dramatic Society. It is a comic sketch. The scene is the local Communist Party office in a small agricultural centre somewhere in the Soviet Union, staffed by a young Party official. Into the office comes an old peasant, 'an enormous, bearded, ancient, brute' looking as if he has 'just walked out of page 1972 of a Tolstoy novel'. He has walked through the snow from a village several days away that the revolution has not yet reached. 'Yes, yes I know', the young official interrupts him impatiently. 'Those things interest us no longer: we do not read the Tolstoy and the Gogol and the Dostoievsky books any longer. We are more cosmopolitan now: *I* have read many English books – books which deal with interesting wholesome subjects – Edgar Wallace . . .'

Most of the scripts or fragments of scripts are short sketches, some with a classical theme: a sketch featuring Spartacus the slave, for example; another about Gaius Marius. More typical are small comedies of social comment. In

'Rearguard Action' a young Maori mother inveigles a naval widow's pension out of a social security clerk, although her husband has in fact deserted and she is already receiving one. In 'Almost a Tragedy' it is the clerk, a phlegmatic railway attendant – another of Mason's working-class types: 'a big unemotional man with a Western sheriff moustache' – who gets the better of the smart businessman anxious to get to Wellington for an important meeting. While the mischievously loquacious station attendant is still issuing a ticket the train speeds through; he sells the businessman a ticket for the bus instead, and later news arrives that the train has crashed. 'Toilers Triumphant' (subtitled 'a pure, pure play'), a broad satire on capitalism, depression and war, clearly belongs to Mason's People's Theatre days. It features Tom and Dick, two tough-looking labourers leaning on their shovels, and young Harry, who is a keen attender of WEA plays, the corrupting influence of which they jovially tease him about. The good, simple life of ditch-digging is for them. 'We are lost once we start all this politics, and art and education and socialism and stuff.' Their mock-literary banter is interrupted by the arrival of the boss with news that Drains and Ditches Ltd has been forced out of business by Russian dumping, but they are not to fear: with a subsidy from the state they are going into business digging trenches instead, 'about six foot long and six foot deep'. The play ends, after *Waiting for Lefty*, with audience and cast joining in a chorus of 'War . . . War . . . War'.

'Escape At All Costs', which is not a comedy, appears to have been written in the very early 1930s, and was perhaps one in the book of plays Mason told Fairburn in 1932 he was 'keeping to work on'. Like the novel he was working on then too, it is about life choices, and it has something in common also with some of the short stories he was writing at that time – little dreams of escape. It is 1931 and two old friends are meeting up for the first time in ten years: Dick, a George Westbrook-like character who has been to sea and knocked around in the south Pacific making his living as a trader, planter and beachcomber; and John, who went into the church, then married. They reminisce about the days when they were 'wild-headed young bachelors. All beer and tobacco and philosophy and the mad whirling talk of young men.' Dick reflects that it was John 'who seemed to have the adventurous stirrings in your blood, while actually it's I who have become the outlaw'. All that remains of John's rebellious spirit is the 'far-off sardonic impenetrable way at times' that his wife Rose does not understand. It becomes clear that Rose married the wrong man ten years ago, and the play ends with her embracing Dick as John decides to leave.[13]

MASON TURNED forty in January 1945. In February he joined Dorothea at Mary Barkas's place on the Coromandel coast – 400 'wild and woolly' acres between Tapu and Waiomu (which they often visited)[14] – for a much-needed break. 'I have sweated over the last three years & over the last six months I have suffered from it', he wrote to Noel Counihan the previous October. 'I have been below par all winter & am just aching for summer.'[15] Long periods of ill health were becoming a pattern. He walked back to work: left at midnight with a pack on his back and '[w]alked till about 2 a.m., then turned in under a pohutukawa tree, swigged the O.P. rum and had a good sleep. Woke as the colours were just beginning to show ever so faintly & had a swim. Got to Coromandel at 12.40', in time to catch the Sunday boat back to Auckland. 'Went over to the bach, slept 11 hours & woke without the slightest trace of weariness or soreness. . . . Of course I lobbed right into P.V. Press day . . . AND domestic duties in a big way.'[16]

In addition to his union job he was back at the *People's Voice* temporarily, helping out Sid Scott, who was by then almost totally blind. Their printer, John Helleur, was fined for tax evasion in March and faced another charge of conducting a black market in tyres, and Mason was anticipating trouble over a pamphlet they had printed without a permit, about the civil war in Greece.[17] When he was not at work, for the union or the Party, or looking after Jessie, who was sick, and straightening up the house at Great South Road (Jessie, said Mason's friend Peter Purdue, secretary of the Carpenters' Union, was 'the untidiest woman I'd ever come across in my life'[18]), he was developing his garden at Crown Hill and fixing up the army hut, and finally getting to work on the new house. It had been held up first by the wartime unavailability of timber, and this time its progress would be frustrated by the 'property and building . . . rackets'. A 38-line satirical poem in rhyming couplets entitled 'He Got His Timber At Last', published anonymously in the union journal in January 1947, was by him.[19] The garden posed no such frustrations. 'Tomatoes & beans are flourishing & corn should not be long', he reported in March 1945 to Dorothea, who was then staying with friends in Ngongotaha. 'Trees sprouting in all directions. And you should see my hibiscus!'[20]

Mason worked for the Auckland General Labourers' Union for ten years as assistant secretary and editor of its monthly journal, *Challenge* – the job Pat Potter had found for him when he was 'railroaded out' of the *People's Voice*. *Challenge* began publication in August 1944 with just four pages at first, but within a year growing to twelve to sixteen pages, with a letterhead designed by Denis Knight Turner (who also drew regular cartoons) and an editorial board. Mason was the general editor, Potter industrial editor and business manager. *Challenge* reported international and political news as well as union affairs (awards, conditions and strikes), and reviewed books supplied by Progressive Books. Mason wrote, or wrote up, most of the content himself, including a satirical column entitled 'Crazy Clarence', a commentary on current affairs by a ludicrously right-wing capitalist, depicted by Knight Turner as a mad professor in a mortarboard, who wrote to the editor each month 'from the little cell where I am so unjustly confined . . .'. There was a smattering of items of cultural interest, including a generous review of the New Theatre Group's debut performance in 1945:

> We are more than a little interested in this initial showing, as our own R.A.K. Mason, better known as Ron, editor of 'Challenge,' and a familiar figure with his little notebook and pencil on all jobs, is the author of the plays, 'Buccaneering Banker,' 'Refugee,' and 'China.' Ron has been busy hiding his light under a bushel, and while telling you all about the other people in the theatre, entirely fails to mention his part in it, and also the fact that he is one of N.Z.'s finest (if not the finest) poets and writers of to-day.[21]

As assistant secretary of the union, and Potter's right-hand man, Mason attended meetings, took minutes and wrote reports. During 1945 he prepared a report on the brick industry, which began with a 'brief historical sketch' starting from the Old Testament and the building of the Tower of Babel in order to show 'not only the vast value and durability of brick, its adaptability and universal use, but also to correct a certain sort of suggestion that the industry was born into the world about the year 1929 in the vicinity of Auckland'. This was perhaps not quite what union officials were accustomed to reading. His conclusions, however, no doubt were: that 'The basic cause of the industry's decline . . . lies not in technical difficulties, supply problems, war circumstances, nor (Oh blessed word!) manpower difficulties – but in the financial set-up of the capital concerned.'[22]

The Labourers' Union offices were in the Union Bank Buildings on Karangahape Road, just across and along the road from the Party headquarters. In the Rising Sun over the road Mason would meet friends and colleagues, like Vic and Ann Wilcox, for a drink. Dorothea also worked in the union office for a time. The trouble with Mason, Potter found, was to get him to stick with the job. He was inclined to launch himself into some new project or enthusiasm, leaving the last one unfinished. And he was a poor office worker, but good with people: he was so humble that he made others feel important.[23]

He had an ease and affinity with Maori and Pacific Islanders which was of particular value to the union, as it was to the Party. In the second half of the 1940s the Auckland General Labourers' Union became closely involved in the political and economic affairs of the Cook Islands, which had been a New Zealand territory since 1901. This came about through a visit to the union offices in June 1945 by a delegation led by Albert Henry – a future Cook Islands premier, but at this time a bus driver and the informal leader of the Auckland Cook Island community. They came with evidence of the sordid working conditions at the French phosphate mine on Makatea. This was 'the worst labour scandal in New Zealand history', Mason was later to write, in which several hundred Cook Island Maori were virtually 'blackbirded' with the connivance of the island administration to save the mining company.[24] It was Te Puea who suggested that they approach Potter, because of his and the union's support for the Maori struggle over Orakei. *Challenge* published the Makatea story and, on the initiative of the Labourers' Union, the Auckland Trades Council called for the government to conduct an inquiry, which it reluctantly did. An Auckland branch of the recently formed Cook Islands Progressive Association (CIPA) was established, with Albert Henry as its secretary, and adopted a conspicuously more militant and political programme than the parent organisation in Rarotonga.

As labour unrest in the Cook Islands escalated in 1946 under the CIPA's lead, the government moved to support the establishment of a Cook Islands trade union affiliated with the New Zealand Federation of Labour, with the aim of neutralising the influence of the communist-dominated Auckland Trades Council, to which the CIPA, in the view of a Labour government growing increasingly hawkish and anti-communist in the early days of the Cold War, was undesirably close. In June 1946 Potter and Mason drove Albert Henry down to Wellington to address the annual conference of the Federation of Labour and meet with the Prime Minister, Peter Fraser. On their way home, at Mason's request they detoured through Lichfield, to Potter's annoyance. 'We went miles out of our way. Ron wanted to sit outside a house for hours, meditating. He didn't go inside.'[25]

All through these months Mason was taking notes, working on a 'history and general survey' of the Cook Islands which was published by the union in January 1947: a 100-page illustrated volume, its cover designed by Denis Knight Turner, entitled *Frontier Forsaken: an outline history of the Cook Islands.*[26]

He didn't put his name to it because, he explained elsewhere, although he was confident of the authenticity of the information he had been given (mostly by Albert Henry), he had not been to the islands to see for himself.[27] He had, however, done his own research. He quoted extensively from accounts by early visitors to the islands, such as Edward Tregear, and from other secondary sources to describe the beauty and bounty of this south seas archipelago before New Zealand annexed it. But New Zealand's administration had quickly degenerated into 'sheer, naked, unadulterated despotism', and through official neglect this once-prosperous tropical garden had been reduced to a state of economic degradation. In content the book ranged from the prehistory of the islands and the relationship between the New Zealand and Cook Islands Maori to a detailed account of the negotiations between the CIPA, the unions and the government. Its style mixed lyrical description with political rhetoric and historical figures and facts: 'in the scope of this Group we find every variety of island, from fertile and populous Rarotonga to lonely Suwarrow, where only the sea-birds scream on the reef enclosing the great harbour where lie pearls and fabled treasure – Suwarrow, so strangely named after that grim old Russian General Suvarov, whose forces defeated the armies of Napoleon in Italy', Mason wrote about a place where he had never been, though surely it reminded him of Samoa, as the CIPA and its nationalist aspirations did of the Mau.[28]

Frontier Forsaken was a polemic, but not without historiographical value. It was, as Mason's preface pointed out, the first printed general history of the Cook Islands. When a young Fulbright scholar was commissioned by the Department of Island Territories to prepare a report on the islands for the government in 1950, he made use of Frontier Forsaken, but criticised Mason for, in effect, romanticising the democratic nature of Cook Island society by failing or choosing not to examine how traditional political and social structures had been altered under protectorate rule.[29] Unsurprisingly, Mason's book did not please the government of the day. Peter Fraser sent a letter, which Mason printed in Challenge, to the several businesses who had taken out advertising in it, describing it as a 'virulent, biased and inaccurate attack' on the government promoted by 'persons who were openly and avowedly members of the Communist Party, or fellow-travellers with it'.[30]

A government-sponsored Cook Islands trade union was duly registered in July 1947, and industrial action on the Cook Island wharves ended in disarray in 1948. Albert Henry then distanced himself from the militant Auckland unions – 'has taken things off at a tangent with a co-operative trading venture', as Mason put it, accepting a government loan on the condition that he sever all ties with the communist unions.[31] But his dalliance with Potter and the Party, and the brief militant life of the CIPA, had laid the basis for Henry's future political career. For the Cook Islands, the agitation over economic conditions in the 1940s spurred the New Zealand government towards formulating a policy for the islands based on economic development and increased political autonomy.

MASON WAS writing no poetry in these years, save for a few satirical lines in the union or Party press. Politics had finally displaced art – or was it simply that life had? That was Mason's view, or so he insisted in a talk he gave after Rex Fairburn's death in 1957, on the subject of myth-making:

> Recently a doctor asked me why I had for long given up writing poetry. I answered 'I find it so hard to make a living that at the end of it I have no energy left. For instance, to-day I have been cutting back someone's 12 ft tecoma hedge to 5 ft & I'm tired out'.
>
> He said 'Isn't it a fact that you became a marxist & found that marxism can't be reconciled with poetry?'
>
> I said 'No. I certainly found that a problem, but at one time I had it down for the count – if it hadn't been for the tecoma hedges'.
>
> He scowled & said 'Why-don't-you-tell-the-truth?' & moved away with a look that was darkly significant.[32]

His poetry continued to have a life of its own, however. The year 1945 saw the publication by the Caxton Press – revitalised now that Glover was back from the war – of Allen Curnow's seminal anthology, *A Book of New Zealand Verse 1923–45*. The modest title belied the book's seriousness of purpose and the extent of its influence, which Curnow himself anticipated: 'Now & then, when zeal gets the better of me, I convince myself that this book, with its ambitious Introduction, is a most remarkable & valuable document in our "spiritual" – or call it "imaginative" – history of N.Z.', he wrote privately on the eve of its publication.[33] It was a small, rigorous selection – 'selective to the point of austerity', in the words of one reviewer[34] – from sixteen poets over twenty years, compared with the fifty-seven poets and twelve years represented in Quentin Pope's *Kowhai Gold*, which it explicitly set itself against. Curnow was leaving behind all that 'trivial, fanciful, simply bad verse' that filled the pages of *Kowhai Gold* and had dominated New Zealand verse from the 1890s, literature that was 'disembodied from any living and tangible surrounding': 'My intention has been to cut our losses'. The beginning of New Zealand poetry was to be found here, instead, in literature that dealt 'direct with life'. Now were poets 'making a home for the imagination', now they understood the poet's task as one of 'trying to keep faith with the tradition in the language while his imagination must seek forms as immediate in experience as the island soil under his feet'. The common themes of the new poetry were 'there, plainly' to see: the themes of land and time and people, and so much 'sea-coast stuff' – from Mason's early sea-bondage sonnets to 'Be swift o sun', for example – as to suggest 'some common problem of the imagination', something which derived from New Zealanders' unique experience of being 'interlopers on an indifferent or hostile scene'.[35] These phrases quickly entered the critical lexicon.

Curnow's moment of beginning, 1923, was the year that Mason put together his first collection, 'In the Manner of Men' (which he believed to have been a tiny, lost, printed edition). Mason and D'Arcy Cresswell, in that order of importance, were his two founding fathers of New Zealand verse. They were two poets who could hardly be less alike, except in their sense of vocation: they took poetry seriously. Their appearance 'marked the end of the undisputed reign of whimsy in New Zealand verse'. (Of course, it was not enough just to be serious: de Montalk, who had taken his vocation as a New Zealand poet the most seriously of all in the 1920s, was written out of the canon here.) Mason was represented in the anthology by eighteen poems, ranging from his schoolboy translation of Horace to 'Flow at Full Moon'. His maturity was always startling. Unlike Fairburn, Curnow observed, he had no need to transform himself, to make himself into the poet he desired to be. There was no clumsy apprenticeship, no false steps. His poetry is 'nearer than any here to that least questionable kind of all, which is like an occurrence in nature'. While he 'professes Communism', Curnow noted, 'that has barely touched his verse in any direct or dogmatic way', but he was also right not simply to dissociate Mason's political from his poetic impulse: 'both political faith and tragic lyric must come of some deeper conflict in him, never reconciled, a sense of the unexpiated evil between man and man'.[36]

More complicated is Curnow's contention that in Mason 'we have none so uncompromising in the point of departure, in acceptance of the New Zealander's natural, if remote vantage of vision, where echoes blur all speech'. Curnow here extended the argument he had made in his 1941 *Book* article, about Mason's unconscious but essential New Zealandness; he found in the final lines of 'Sonnet of Brotherhood' – 'here in this far-pitched perilous hostile place/ this solitary hard-assaulted spot/ fixed at the friendless outer edge of space' – a perfect expression of the disjunction between imagination and place, 'the tension between the New Zealander and the land his body inhabits but his spirit has not won'.[37]

There is little on record of Mason's response to his critics at this time, although he was to develop a deepening dislike for the practice of academic criticism – which is nothing unusual. Winston Rhodes, however, saw in it more than the normal reaction of a poet to his critics: an antagonism stemming from frustration that the meaning of and the tensions between his life and work, the strength of his social compulsions, were not understood. Mason did object specifically, however, to the appropriation of 'Sonnet of Brotherhood' to a nationalist critical argument. He had intended those lines to refer not specifically to New Zealand, Mason insisted (though Curnow never said that he had), but to the condition of the whole of humanity, which was always his theme. He also maintained a grievance over the critics' refusal to pay serious attention to his dramatic writing, and to read it on its own terms: that they insisted on judging it by the same standards as his poetry and then found it lacking.

He can only have been angered by J.C. Reid's *Creative Writing in New Zealand: a brief critical history*, which appeared in 1946. Reid was a Catholic layman as well as a lecturer (later professor) in English at Auckland University College, and his critical judgment was founded strongly on his religious beliefs: the main want of New Zealand literature, he believed, was 'spiritual stiffening'. He was glibly disparaging of the influence of left-wing ideas on the young intelligentsia of the 1930s and, after identifying Mason as the most notable of this generation, observed brusquely and disapprovingly his 'retreat into Marxism', which had 'resulted in the production of inferior material'.[38]

A more welcome appreciation of his poetry came this year from the young composer Douglas Lilburn. When Lilburn met Mason for the first time in Auckland early in 1946 he talked about setting some of his poems to music. 'You were so good-natured over a glass of beer when we met recently', he wrote subsequently in telling Mason which poems he had chosen and asking permission for them to be produced for radio. He had selected 'O Fons Bandusiae' and 'Song Thinking of Her Dead'. Lilburn later wrote to him: 'Perhaps the most a composer can hope for is to do no violence to your words! All I have tried to do is to capture some of the emotional colouring that emanates so clearly from these poems, & to follow as best I can the superb rhythms that you set flowing. They're moving, they're not didactic, & they have that easy regular rhythmic flow & the singing quality that you give to words when you handle them.'[39] The poems were broadcast on 3YA Christchurch on 29 November, in a short programme simply entitled 'Music for voice and piano', along with two piano works by Lilburn and his setting of the Willow Song from *Othello*. The *New Zealand Listener* reviewer was most impressed: the pieces 'showed that a poem can, contrary to normal usage, become a song without being distorted, sentimentalised, or rendered inaudible, and can even gain in charm and significance. This "O fons Bandusiae" perfectly caught the humour and sensuous joy of Mason's translation; and I doubt if any who heard the second will re-read the line "where her small powerful face lies strong and dead" with quite the same feelings.'[40]

Mason was anthologised a second time in 1945 in very different company. In September 1944 Noel Counihan had written from Melbourne soliciting a contribution to an anthology that he and Judah Waten were compiling, to be the first publication from their newly established Dolphin press. The book was intended to 'constitute as formidable a statement as possible of a progressive, "realist" position in contemporary literature and art', a challenge to the prevailing modernist avant-garde centred on the Sydney-based *Angry Penguins* magazine. It was to be 'widely distributed in the Labor movement'. Responding to Counihan, Mason agreed with him that *Angry Penguins* was 'pretentious cack'. He sent extracts from 'International Brigade' and *China*, for which Counihan thanked him enthusiastically: 'bloody fine poems which we are all frankly delighted with and which we are confident will burst like three hand grenades among the writing brigade here . . . Your work is *vastly* different from the poetry familiar here and will sit quite a few people up on their beam ends.'[41] Sargeson was the only other New Zealand writer represented in this anthology, with an extract from his novel-in-progress, *When the Wind Blows*. Titled *Southern Stories, Poems and Paintings*, it came out at the end of 1945. Mason was asked to promote it in Auckland and to send material for further editions, but there was to be none.

In the cosier New Zealand literary world of the 1940s, there was (as yet) no such ideological battle as the one being waged between the modernists and realists in Australian art and letters. And no place for Mason's politically informed experiments with literary form. In autumn 1945 he had broached with Denis Glover the possibility of Caxton publishing a collection of his verse dramas and prose satires, but Glover had to disappoint him. He was already far too busy with his autumn list and other titles planned for later in what was to be Caxton's most productive year yet, and dealing with the collapse of the Progressive Publishing Society (PPS), which was about to go into liquidation owing Caxton 'vast moneys'.[42] The Curnow anthology was one of the projects – along with the third part of Holcroft's essay trilogy, *The Encircling Seas*, and the short story anthology *Speaking for Ourselves* which Sargeson was editing – that Glover had to rescue from the ruins of the PPS. The society had been formed in 1941 as a joint venture between the country's three co-operative book societies with the aim of publishing both left-wing and New Zealand literature, and had effectively filled the gap left by Caxton's diminished output while Glover was overseas. In just over three years it published some sixty-five titles before self-destructing through a combination of overconfidence, inexperience and ineptitude, £2500 in debt. One would have expected Mason to support at least the aims of the Progressive Publishing Society, founded as it was on both socialist and literary ideals (though not without tension between them), and probably he did, but he was ungracious to Glover about its demise. 'You may jeer at the pricking of that preposterous balloon the PPS', Glover replied to him, but he was not amused.

'But do not despair', Glover reassured Mason. 'If I see any chance' of doing the book Mason had asked about 'I shall let you know – and there is always the future.' The PPS had also suggested to Glover a reprint of Mason's selected poems 'a while ago', but even this he felt he could not manage at that time. 'The Anthology will flaunt you very adequately before your rapturous public, & this must serve for a while.'[43] Two years later Glover was thinking about what was to become his Caxton Poets series: 'a few volumes of New Zealand verse in an easy standard format, done cheap but neat', he described the idea to Fairburn, 'about 32 pages, close-ish set in a small 10-point . . . Fact is neither you nor Mason – no, nor Curnow – has a selected poems available just now'.[44] Mason, however, would not be included in this series. At the same time, in February 1947, Glover wrote to tell Mason 'that I am brooding over a new collection of your poems, such as we discussed briefly in Bertram's house' when he had been in Auckland late the previous year. This was evidently to be a more comprehensive collection than the rigorously selected poems he had got out of Mason in 1941, or the cheap but neat volume he had in mind for the Caxton Poets. 'The book must be suitably casebound, and the edition large enough to ensure that it does not go out of print within five years.'[45] But it was not to get into print for another fifteen.

IT IS DIFFICULT to place Mason on the literary scene in these years, however integral a figure he was in the literary history that was being written. There were enough writers in Auckland by this time, most of them on the North Shore, to create a tangible sense of literary community, as there had not been when Mason and Fairburn hiked their lonely way across the Auckland isthmus with Housman in their pockets twenty years before. It included not only Mason's near-contemporaries, like Fairburn and Sargeson, but also a younger generation of writers, like Maurice Duggan, John Reece Cole and Kendrick Smithyman, who looked on Sargeson as their mentor. There were also the educated exiles from Europe who attracted and were attracted to the writers in turn in their mutual need for sophisticated conversation and coffee. One such was Greville Texidor, who had come from London with her German husband in 1940 and who sharply caricatured this bohemian sub-culture in the fiction she wrote while she was here: 'those masochistic coffee parties with all the intelligentsia squirming with culture, hearing what's wrong with them in a foreign accent'; the Saturday night gatherings attended by 'Professor Salmonson with half a dozen bottles of beer, John Priest who had written some very good poetry once and was reckoned a brilliant conversationalist, the refugee doctor Lewenthal with his case of classical records, the painter Peake with his beard . . .'.[46] Mason, however, remains a shadowy and elusive figure.

'R.A.K. Mason writes nothing save for the "People's Voice" & flits mysteriously from one pathetic shack to another', Jane Mander wrote to Monte Holcroft in 1945, continuing her report on the desolate existence of the New Zealand intellectual.[47] Kevin Ireland as a schoolboy in the 1940s knew of Mason as legendary and mysterious. He had a friend whose father was helping Mason build his house at Crown Hill, and '[i]n the hope of seeing him we used to bike past the house often', but they never did. Of the man he did come to meet in time, in the pub or the Golden Dragon or on the ferry, he remembered 'bristly hair, stern face, shy eyes'.[48]

Mason was not close to Sargeson in these years; it was only later, in the last decade of his life, that they became close friends. He still saw something of Fairburn, but theirs was not the friendship it had once been. His aversion to letter-writing placed him at a further remove from the other pole of the New Zealand literary world of this period, Christchurch, where Glover, Caxton and Curnow were. (Glover, Sargeson and Fairburn, by contrast, were prolific correspondents.) The letter Mason sent to Glover in April 1945 wondering if Caxton would publish his verse dramas had been written three years before.

('Thank you for finally dispatching my 1942 letter, it was a touching thought, & shows the unwavering fidelity of a great mind', Glover replied. He would later remember receiving five letters from Mason at once one day, letters that had been written previously but not posted, after not having had one for eight years.[49]) When Charles Brasch asked Mason for a contribution for the first issue of *Landfall*, the literary quarterly that he and Glover and Bertram had been musing on for three years and was launched in March 1947, Mason sent apologies. 'PROFOUNDLY REGRET UNABLE SEND CONTRIBUTION BEST LUCK', he cabled. But he did write a supportive piece about the new journal for *Challenge*, few of whose readers are likely to have gone out and subscribed.[50] Among the recorded accounts of the genesis of *Landfall* – the centre and arbiter of the New Zealand literary scene for so many years – Maurice Duggan has the meeting at which the title was chosen taking place 'on the verandah of Ron Mason's house', which was 'small, and made of pine stained with a mixture of creosote and stockholm tar: the facings – frames, architraves, mullions, bargeboard were painted white', around it 'black wattle, solanum, hakea, a eureka lemon, a poor man's orange'. Brasch, Jim and Jean Bertram, Douglas Lilburn, Mason and Dorothea were there, and possibly others.[51] But Mason's creosote cottage at Crown Hill does not have the same place in the literary history, and mythology, as Sargeson's fibrolite bach in Esmonde Road.

Mason and Dorothea were to be seen at Greville Texidor and Werner Droescher's house just a few streets away at Forrest Hill, where the North Shore writers and their friends regularly gathered on Saturdays over Mediterranean-style food and Lemora, the citrus wine brewed by Russians at Matakana which is remembered with mingled horror and affection in almost every literary memoir of this period. The young John Reece Cole, whom Mason had introduced to Sargeson, lived in the caravan at the bottom of the section. Werner Droescher worked at the Forrest Hill market garden of Len and Gladys Salter, former proprietors of the Takapuna general store, who were long-standing friends of Mason's and Dorothea's. They were guests at the small wedding party of Maurice and Barbara Duggan, whom they first knew through Eileen Hamilton (Dorothea lent them her wedding ring). And Mason did attend some of the famous parties hosted by Bob and Irene Lowry at their Epsom home on the slopes of One Tree Hill, where he was likely to be found sitting in a corner, observing. '[N]ot given to bookish chatter or to chatter of any kind', Eric McCormick recalled of these usually raucous occasions, he 'was a conspicuous figure, somewhat aloof from the frivolous throng, smiling benignly, saying little'.[52] He appears not to have been present, however, at the party thrown in honour of Glover's visit to Auckland in September 1946, when Texidor brandished a kitchen knife across the table at Glover after he made a slighting remark about the left-wing intellectuals who had gone to Spain (she had been there, he hadn't).

Mason's closest literary friendship in these years was with the German-Jewish poet Karl Wolfskehl, who had arrived in New Zealand in 1938, aged sixty-nine and nearly blind, with his much younger partner, Margot Ruben. They moved from their small Mt Eden flat to Takapuna in 1943. '[T]hat noble old Jewish refugee poet', Mason later described him, 'a giant with a great mass of curly hair and a leonine head', and as large in intellect, imagination and emotion as he was in physical stature.[53] Wolfskehl epitomised what the European exiles represented for the New Zealand intelligentsia: exoticness, and direct contact with a culture that was also theirs, but not theirs. He possessed a vast and deep knowledge of German and Romantic literary cultures, had been a leading figure among the German Symbolists (the 'Cosmic Circle') in the 1890s and in the bohemian-literary set in Munich through the next two decades, had translated poetry from older forms of German, ancient and medieval Latin, French, Italian, English, Flemish, Swedish and Hebrew and reworked translations from Arabic and Persian. The writers were infatuated. 'I feel like a man who has heard of Shakespeare, but by some extraordinary mischance has never been able to get a copy of his work', Sargeson wrote to a friend in 1942.[54]

It was Mason, among the New Zealand writers who befriended him, whom Wolfskehl liked the most, valued the most 'as truly and deeply as a man as as a poet'. And it was only Mason, felt Margot Ruben, who 'fully appreciated Wolfskehl's significance and fate'.[55] They would sit together for hours, chuckling over glasses of red wine, discussing literature and language, classical philology and European history, or Mason would be fulminating about the perfidy of the English and the suffering of the Irish and Scots. Wolfskehl and Ruben spent their last summer together before Wolfskehl's death in June 1948 at Dorothea's house in Tennyson Avenue. There he wrote his last work (*Das Satyrspiel*, the Satyr-play) and received the proofs of his last volume of poems (*An die Deutschen*, To the Germans). They celebrated New Year's Eve with Mason and Phoebe Meikle, and a bottle of Tauranga riesling provided by Pia Richards which Wolfskehl opened with great ceremony and solemnity at midnight.

19

John ii 4

1948–49

MASON'S Crown Hill house was hardly finished when Jessie moved into
the only bedroom, uninvited. The Ministry of Works had been negotiating
to buy the old place at 451 Great South Road to enlarge the grounds of
neighbouring Penrose High School. When the government settles, 'which
won't be long', Jessie wrote to Mason in January 1948 from Cambridge,
where she was staying for several weeks with her sister, 'we will be free of all
mortgages & should carry on easily'.¹ She had been going down to Cambridge
for Christmas and New Year for the previous few years. The letters she wrote
to him from there were the same as she had been writing twenty years before,
to Lichfield or Samoa: 'Am glad I was able to free you from me for a time
. . . Do not work heavy dear Jack – things will be right'. 'Am so longing to
hear from you. Wanted to say a lot to you before I left – but could not –
Hope things may never be so hard for us again. You may get a surprise for
things I may do when I come home'. '[T]ry & not work *too* hard – we will be
alright very soon dear & we can make things as we like – Thanks for *all*
you've done & I *know* & *appreciate* everything'. '*Do* try & not slave too hard,
we'll do well for you very soon dear. Perhaps you do not ever dream of how
I appreciate all you have done for me, – but Jack, I *do* – & will do much for
you I hope soon'.² She was in her eighties by this time, and frequently ill.
Mason tried to get her into several nursing homes but none would keep her.
When she was well she was a familiar sight in Crown Hill, walking barefoot
down to the shops at Milford.

Early in May 1948 Mason resigned from the Labourers' Union, apparently
because it was in financial difficulty: 'As I understand that the Union is finding
it difficult to maintain its present staff', he began his letter of resignation.³
The testimonial Potter wrote for him a few months later noted his 'rare
capacity for analysis and expression, combined with a deep sense of
responsibility'.⁴ He appears not to have gone back to the union until the
beginning of 1949, when Crazy Clarence reappeared in *Challenge*. He had
bought some land at Redvale, ten miles up the East Coast Road north of

Crown Hill, 140 acres of rough bush which he and Dorothea nicknamed the Redvale Ranch, and spent much of the winter of 1948 breaking it in and building a small bach, travelling up on the bus from Crown Hill. He kept a diary, of clearing, burning, planting and roughing out tracks, and carefully recorded his bus fares.

In September he went down to Dunedin, on his first-ever visit to the South Island, to give two public lectures at the University of Otago. The student Literary Society had proposed that the university host a lecture or series of lectures on 'New Zealand letters', and submitted a list of possible speakers. Omitting the several writers who had spoken in the city the year before under the auspices of the WEA (Curnow, Glover, Rhodes, Holcroft and Fairburn), they nominated Sargeson, Mason, McCormick, the poet J.R. Hervey, J.C. Beaglehole or W.J. Scott. The Professorial Board placed Mason first.[5]

He stayed with old friends, Rita and John Harris, who were about to leave for Nigeria, where John, who was the Otago University librarian, had been appointed librarian at the new University College of Ibadan; and with the Dunedin city librarian, Archie Dunningham. Interviewed by the *Otago Daily Times* on the day he arrived, Mason congratulated the university for sponsoring 'the expression of free, unfettered opinion' at a time when this was never more urgent, and for its initiative in bringing the academic specialist into contact with the people, adding cryptically that the invitation was 'a welcome change from treatment which I have received elsewhere'.[6]

Willis Airey's daughter Deirdre, who was studying medicine at Otago, attended his two lectures and would remember both his nervousness and his polemic. He gave the first, under the title 'The mechanisation of culture', on the evening of 20 September. He began by quoting Thomas Carlyle in the nineteenth century: 'Things are in the saddle and they are riding us to the devil.' Now things were 'at the throttle . . . sweeping us down at twentieth-century tempo, with atomic intensity, at supersonic speed', and mankind was left 'lost in the forest, bewildered, benighted and beset by storm'. He spoke stridently about the Second World War, 'that incredible outburst of barbarism' when 'the madmen of the self-styled anti-Comintern bloc, the Axis powers, made their insane assault on all towards which the dreams and aspirations of men have strained up from out [of] the original slime', and about the threat of another posed by 'the utter spiritual vacuity of the present leaders of the United States and their sycophants in other countries', before getting on to his real subject, the arts. Mason was not one of those who feared modernity and believed that mechanisation inevitably led to the degradation of the arts.

The cinema, for example, could be as legitimate an art form as that of 'Homer or Goya, Bach or the dramatists', although little of what was seen in New Zealand theatres was. The problem was when the mechanised and 'non-participant arts' (like the cinema) began to 'overlay and smother' the participant arts (the theatre), instead of each flourishing and stimulating the other. The argument that all the people wanted were Hollywood films was 'a dangerous falsehood, a damnable devil's doctrine' propagated by capitalists and abetted by 'cultural snobs and highbrows'. New Zealand was particularly vulnerable because culturally it had 'only recently found the urge to swim, is just poking its nose out of the old backwater into the mainstream of the world, at the very moment when such a rip-roaring tide of rubbish comes sweeping down the river'. But he had no time for 'complacent excuses accepted for our cultural backwardness' – a reference, as he made clear, to the current preoccupation with the theme of cultural nationalism. 'Our cultural weakness stems from one basic fact – a false humility, a fawning, cringing & sycophantic subservience of spirit' which 'is certainly not a fault of our common people'. He concluded the lecture by thanking the university again for recognising its historical role as a place of wisdom and disputation, for only in this way

> have we a chance to fight against the increasing menace of mechanisation, under monopoly conditions, militarism, degradation of the human mind and spirit, a chance to get away from insane specialisation and to develop that old 'bush sense', what might be called the mastery of the art and science of integration, the study of total circumstance. Something of all this I have endeavoured to outline sketchily on a broad canvas, aiming to bring not more learning but some touch of that inspiration of Apollo, without which all the learning in the world remains but dead wood. These are considerations for your reflection and action, here in our brief hour, as we stand poised on this perilous knife-edge of time, upon this tiny speck of a globe swinging in the wasty vastness of space.[7]

What Mason meant by 'the study of total circumstance' is made clearer in an address he gave to the Auckland University College Literary Society in March that year. He prefaced this talk, which was devoted mainly to discussing the American socialist literary magazine *New Masses*, by emphasising the need for the writer to be socially engaged, as Milton, Shakespeare, Shelley, Voltaire and Tolstoy had been. There was a disturbing, pervasive and powerful tendency in contemporary culture towards specialisation and the evasion of reality 'which makes modern literature a mystery', like a doctor's prescription, which may conceal a good remedy or mere Epsom salts. The writer must rather be like 'a doctor of social science'. 'In fulfilling his obligation to society, a writer must ensure that his work is significant and important – he must guard against shallowness and superficiality. In addition he must be a good writer so that his work is clothed in telling language. The problem in New Zealand', he added, 'is that so much effort is needed to publish that many are crushed in the struggle.' His student audience appears not to have been impressed by Mason's political argument, however, or at least the chairman of the society, who reported on the meeting in the student newspaper, was not: 'Mr. Mason's sympathetic handling of his subject was much appreciated, as was his humour, the only discordancy being the political assumption that he made. At the beginning of the meeting Mr. Mason stated his intention of keeping his communistic views out of the discussion but, not unnaturally, he was unable to do so for long.'[8]

His second Dunedin lecture, on the evening of 23 September, was on 'The problem of a national theatre'. This was a subject being widely debated at the time in the context of the recent establishment of the National Orchestra, which had given its inaugural concert in March 1947 as the latest in a succession of state-funded cultural institutions founded by the Labour government in the 1940s, which included the National Film Unit, Library Service, Cultural Fund and Literary Fund. The debate was further fuelled by the highly successful visit to New Zealand in 1948 of the Old Vic Theatre Company with Laurence Olivier and Vivien Leigh (their Dunedin season opened at the end of September). Mason had already joined this debate when he contributed to a small symposium in the March 1948 number of *Landfall* – the symposium was his own suggestion, and was his first and only contribution to the magazine; Brasch had waited in vain for the short story he had been promised for the second issue. There, he had condemned the appropriation of the name 'New Zealand Theatre' by the Auckland cinema magnate and entrepreneur Robert Kerridge for his latest venture, a commercial touring company whose members had been recruited mostly in Britain and whose productions to date, light comedies and mild thrillers, had not even reached the standard, Mason harshly observed, of 'a decent local amateur effort'. This was commercial opportunism, and one more example of the monopolistic tendency of 'Big Business' – Kerridge had recently sold half of his cinema chain to the J. Arthur Rank Corporation, creating the Kerridge Odeon empire. It was not the promise of the growth of 'serious drama' which would challenge the dominance of the cinema. For that one must look instead to '[s]tate theatre, municipal theatre, national theatre run by its members, people's theatre'.[9]

In his Dunedin lecture Mason argued for a state-funded national theatre, which would show 'the best modern plays, the classics and the works of local playwrights' and 'restore to us what we have too long been denied'. He referred to children's, Greek, Roman, medieval, modern English, Chinese and Polynesian theatre, and defined the value of theatre as a popular and social art: 'practise or enjoyable participation in art is like a good walk over windy hills'. The dynamic and collective nature of the theatre was 'like mixing concrete from sand, shingle, cement, and water, or like building a compost heap, in which you might use dead cats and cabbage stalks to create a useful product' (both the *Otago Daily Times* and the Dunedin *Evening Star* admired his 'brilliant' use of metaphor).[10] As he had put it less colourfully in *Landfall*: 'The drama, more than any other art, calls for popular stimulation, for co-operation between artists, technicians, audience and the whole community, perpetually re-creating a centre of energy, which is at once a recipient and source of social stimulus.'[11]

'When I saw you here you hoped to start writing again', Brasch wrote to him several months later. '[I]f you have any poems or stories at any time, will you remember *Lf*?' Mason had been stimulated by the trip south – as some of those who had invited him hoped that he would be[12] – and perhaps also by an approach from an American literary journal earlier that year inquiring after new poems. But Brasch would still wait in vain.[13]

Mason was away for two to three months. From Dunedin he went on to Christchurch, where he stayed with Denis Glover at Clifton, high on the hills above Sumner, eight miles from the city – in 'a beautiful little earth cottage at the foot of the garden'. He spent much of his stay there 'just loafing round the garden or playing with the small boy' (the Glovers' three-year-old son), he reported to Jessie, as well as rewriting his lecture on the national theatre for the Christchurch *Press*.[14] He made a weekend excursion to Timaru, and sailed around Lyttelton harbour with Glover to visit Glover's good friend Anton Vogt for an afternoon of poetry and home-brew. Mason had been unwell before he left Auckland, and the trip was a tonic. 'It seems strange to me now to think that a few weeks ago I was on the point of cancelling my trip to the South Island', he wrote to Archie Dunningham. 'To have done so would have been to have missed the happiest moments of my life'. 'I have only got as far as here on my odyssey', he wrote from Christchurch to a family friend in Dunedin. 'I am enjoying myself too much to want to shift on

. . . Ugh, I don't want to get back to Auckland.'¹⁵ His mother he reassured
that he hoped to be starting for home the following week, and that 'I have
been feeling ever so much better the last week or so, with the change and rest
just beginning to take effect.' In reply she promised to send him down £10
'if you say where to – Son I want you to get *quite* better & let all else go for
present', and reported on the garden at Crown Hill: 'Phenomenal growth
. . . I just love it here now. Pines at back about 7 or 8 feet – Tree tomatoes,
guavas & feijoas look promising – Never have to buy any more wood – Tons
here. Now if you can just get well.'¹⁶

Glover would later recall finding Mason in the garden one day at Clifton,
standing at the very cliff edge 'looking over the beautiful stretch of Pegasus
Bay', trembling: he handed him a bottle of rum and without a moment's
hesitation Mason took it and downed the lot and stopped shaking.¹⁷ This is
the recollection of a recognised alcoholic. Bill Pearson, then a student at
Canterbury University College, met Mason for the first time at Glover's in
1948, but it was his own and Glover's drinking that he remembered, not
Mason's. He had met Glover in a bar near the Caxton Press and they had
stopped at another in Sumner on the way home. Unable to keep pace with
his host, Pearson fell asleep over dinner and was awakened a few hours later
by Mason, who escorted him down the hill to catch the last tram.¹⁸

While he was in Christchurch Mason applied for a job as Adult Education
tutor for North Canterbury, enclosing testimonials from Dave Faigan, Pat
Potter and Winston Rhodes. He stated his particular interest in dramatic
work, and that 'I have always maintained a wide reading in literary and artistic
matters, the social sciences and current affairs and have become increasingly
interested in soil problems.' Rhodes's testimonial especially recommended
his ability to 'discuss problems of the day with exceptional clarity and
knowledge', his ease with people and unassuming manner. The following
month he applied for a junior lectureship in the English Department at Victoria
University College in Wellington. He was offered neither.¹⁹

This trip south was like the time he visited Wellington in January 1940:
when he got away, he didn't want to go back.

RETURNING TO Auckland, he went back to work for the union, and
back out to Redvale when he could. In February and March he spent several
days there, burning off paspalum and making a fire-break. Towards the end
of April he went out for nine days with Dorothea. 'Adzed & soured cocksfoot
on sidings near bach – marked out & cleared contour clearings . . . – put

palisade round nursery bed & dug over re-dug bed to transplant c/gooseberries – consolidated odd compost heaps – Did path to road & metalled round bach – cut line for road fence 3 ch. – tidied bach, put up long shelf, attended tools, fixed door &c . . . NB Power-lines just coming through.'[20] At the beginning of May they went up to the Bay of Islands to stay with Ian and Eileen Hamilton: Mason 'badly needed a holiday'.[21] The Hamiltons had bought 200 acres at Separation Point on the Kerikeri inlet, where they planned to establish a communal farm and Ian was applying his new-found enthusiasm for organic gardening. It was a beautiful and isolated place, accessible only by launch from Kerikeri or along the beach on foot at low tide.

On 13 May his diary recorded simply, 'Mother died.'[22] They had managed to get Jessie into a nursing home in Bayswater before they left, but had been in the Bay of Islands only about a week when a telegram arrived with news that her health was rapidly deteriorating. Mason set out immediately, walking seven miles over the hills in the semi-dark to Kerikeri, where he went to the home of friends of the Hamiltons. Finding that they had already gone to bed, he spent the night in their dog kennel, then caught the first train to Auckland in the morning. He got there too late.

He was desolate at his mother's death, and at the fact that he hadn't been there when she died. Dan, however, was there. At the funeral 'they had to prop him up', Honey Haigh recalled. Afterwards she helped him to sort out Jessie's things but 'he wouldn't let anything go . . . the tie was almost physical'. 'I was afraid that with the shock Ron would crack up again', Dorothea would recall.[23]

Mason found refuge at Redvale, with the land. From June he rented a cottage opposite the ranch and Dorothea went up to stay with him there. '[H]e spent the days slashing & burning gorse and tea-tree, aki aki etc, while I boiled the billy on an open fire on the ground, & got a meal at night on the cottage range. It was almost fun, if he had not been so miserable.'[24] In late July he wrote to Charles Brasch, who had asked him for another article for *Landfall*: 'just now I am very unsettled, both in my mind and in my affairs. Since my return from the South, it has been little else but illness, trouble and sorrow, ending in my mother's death.'[25]

He and Dorothea stayed at Redvale for about six months, before Mason went back and tidied up Crown Hill for sale, with Dan's help. Then he bought a two-bedroomed bach at Torbay over the sea, 'a dreary little cottage' with a large garden and a lovely view. They built on a kitchen and sundeck. Mason developed the garden while Dorothea painted and distempered inside: 'I hoped we should settle down at last.'[26]

20

The swamp

1950–53

THE NEXT few years were anything but settled. This was a time of hard, dark political and personal struggle. Behind it lay the Cold War.

Being on the left at this time was very different from in the heady days of the Popular Front and Stalingrad, as anti-communist sentiment deepened within the government, the press and the population at large, and in the labour movement. The Communist Party lost control of the Auckland Trades Council in the executive elections of April 1948, having held the positions of president, vice-president and secretary for three years, and Alec Drennan was defeated again for the presidency in 1949. Party membership had fallen by more than half since 1943. The deregistration of the Auckland Carpenters' Union in March 1949 was a clear warning of the fate of the militant unions, of which the Auckland General Labourers' Union was one, in this chilly climate, at the hands of a Labour government intent on defeating the red menace. '[S]ocialist outsides trying to hide capitalist insides, like a nice-looking apple full of grubs', wrote Mason in 'Daddy, Paddy and Marty. A Farce In One Act', which was published in the *People's Voice* in April 1950. This simple sketch expressed the bitter disillusionment of the left at the reactionary and treacherous turn of the Labour government in its last years in office.[1] 'Instead of pursuing a policy based on Labour's Militant past, they have hitched New Zealand's economy and foreign policy to the Roman Candle of American Imperialism', Potter wrote in *Challenge*.[2]

In August 1949 compulsory military training was introduced, after a referendum in which half a million people voted for it and 150,000 against. *Challenge* had backed the opposition campaign, which was led by newly established Peace and Anti-Conscription Councils strongly supported by the Trades Councils. A Peace and Anti-Conscription Federation was formed at a conference in Wellington in March 1949, and its national office soon after moved to Auckland. Around this time Mason was one of a group of sponsors, along with Frank Haigh, Sargeson, Fairburn and Lowry, who raised subscriptions to assist the publication of Ian Hamilton's *Till Human Voices*

Wake Us, a fierce and angry account of his incarceration as a military defaulter during the Second World War.

Peacetime conscription, and the government's enthusiasm for the Cold War, was only one cause of the disenchantment that contributed to Labour's defeat at the general election in November 1949 by the more hawkish, right-wing National Party led by Sid Holland. There was widely felt frustration in the years immediately after the war that the spoils of victory were being withheld. Industrial unrest grew, particularly on the wharves, as the government imposed a regime of economic stabilisation with the support of the moderate leadership of the Federation of Labour (FOL), whose powerful vice-president, Fintan Patrick Walsh, once a founding member of the Communist Party, was now deeply hated by the militant left. The Black Prince, they called him, riding 'his trusty steed, old Stabiliser' and carrying his 'good sword, Arbitrator', as Mason depicted him in *Challenge*.[3]

The deregistration of the Carpenters' Union precipitated the split between the left and right wings of the labour movement that had long been threatened. During the carpenters' dispute the leadership of the Waterside Workers' Union had accused the national executive of the FOL of 'strike-breaking' in a 'gross betrayal of the affiliated members' and of being 'agents of the employing class' in not supporting the Auckland carpenters.[4] When, at the FOL's annual conference in Wellington in late April 1950, they were requested to withdraw and apologise for these remarks or be expelled from the federation – a threat not being made for the first time – the watersiders walked out, after a further day of mud-slinging and procedural manoeuvring. They were followed by about sixty other delegates, including those of the Auckland General Labourers' Union, and cheered by Communist Party leaders as they left the hall, according to one report. The next day the breakaway delegates, who represented about a third of the FOL membership, met at the Trades Hall and set up a separate New Zealand Trade Union Congress (TUC).

In the May issue of *Challenge* Potter explained to his members why their delegates had joined the walkout: in part out of loyalty to the wharfies and freezing workers, and in protest at the bureaucratic behaviour of the FOL executive in orchestrating the effective expulsion of the watersiders, its interference in affiliated unions' internal affairs, its too cosy relationship with the Labour government and its support for stabilisation. 'The formation of the Trade Union Congress takes us one more step forward on the road to our socialist objective', he declared, exhorting the members to endorse the executive's stand, which they did unanimously.[5] In retrospect, he was to paint the picture a little differently.

Potter became the president and Mason secretary of the first district council
of the TUC to be established. Meanwhile, in *Challenge* Crazy Clarence formed
his own CIO: Clarence's Independent Organisation of Red-Spotters and Red-
Baiters.[6] At a meeting of the TUC's national committee held in Wellington
in June, at Potter's instigation, Mason was elected assistant national secretary
and authorised to publish a journal. The first issue of *Congress News*, edited by
Mason, a monthly four-page news sheet, came out in May. (He was far too
busy, Mason told Charles Brasch in June, to review Allen Curnow's verse
play *The Axe* for *Landfall*.) The TUC's first political activity was to call national
demonstrations to coincide with the opening of Parliament on 28 June to
protest at the rapidly rising cost of living, the consequence of the new
government's lifting of stabilisation controls. The novelist Maurice Shadbolt,
then a member of the university Socialist Club, recalled first encountering
Mason there. Descending from the speaker's platform in Myers Park after
addressing the crowd on behalf of student socialists, on a palely sunny winter
day, Shadbolt met 'a battered and kindly-faced man, scruffily dressed, with a
stub of cigarette in his mouth. He wanted to know how to spell my name; he
was writing a report for a trade union journal. He informed me that his name
was Ron Mason.' Shadbolt didn't know who he was until an impressed fellow
student came up and told him: '"R.A.K. Mason," he informed me with awe.
"New Zealand's greatest poet." "Him?".'[7]

At the inaugural national conference of the TUC, held at the Wellington
Trades Hall on 9–11 August, Mason was the secretary, and 'amazed delegates
with the detail contained in the minutes'.[8] Potter was elected national president,
but despite his sterling performance Mason was defeated for the position of
secretary-treasurer by Archie Grant of the Canterbury Rubber-workers'
Union, by 156 votes to 80. The conference was attended by thirty-four
delegates representing nearly 23,000 workers – half of them watersiders and
carpenters, the only national organisations to join. Many of the unions whose
delegates had participated in the original walkout had returned to the fold on
the vote of their members. The most militant of the militants, the watersiders,
maintained a low-key presence in the TUC. While it was the Auckland
General Labourers who 'forced the pace' (as Mason was later to write) in
getting the movement under way organisationally, opinions differ, however,
as to whether they were its real or nominal leaders. To Crazy Clarence, Sid
Holland and F.P. Walsh, it was all a communist plot. In fact, the Waterside
Workers' Union was not a 'communist union': Alec Drennan, its Auckland

president, was the only prominent communist among its leadership; the national president and secretary, Jock Barnes and Toby Hill, were not members of the Party, but militants of a different – industrial syndicalist – kind. But this was academic to those who were inclined to see reds everywhere.

The TUC adopted a constitution which stated its principles of practical militancy, socialisation of the means of production, distribution and exchange, and freedom of individual unions to manage their own affairs. Its eight-point manifesto included higher wages, equal pay for equal work, a shorter working week, protection of civil liberties, and support for the peace and anti-conscription campaign and for a ceasefire in Korea.

THE SUDDEN escalation of the Cold War with the outbreak of the war in Korea in May 1950 revitalised the local peace movement, with which Mason was again involved. It also prompted him to poetry. 'Sonnet to MacArthur's Eyes' was published in the *People's Voice* in September 1950, and translated into several languages in the bulletin and monthly review of the World Federation of Trade Unions, a communist-aligned body from which the Federation of Labour had disaffiliated at its 1949 annual conference, further fuelling the disaffection of the left. The poem was inspired by a newspaper report of United States General Douglas MacArthur's reaction on seeing the dead bodies of four young Korean soldiers: 'That's a good sight for my old eyes.'

> I have known old eyes that had seen many more
>   Aspects of warfare than this man has seen –
>   Eyes that had looked on Gallipoli or the keen
> Edge of battle with the Boers or, in even older war,
>
> Had known Balaclava and the Mutiny's evil score:
>   Such eyes, as I've known them old, have always been
>   Eager to see spring flowers and the youth who mean
> Mankind's Spring after war's winter. Never before
>
> Have I known of anyone whose old eyes rejoice
>   To see young men lying dead in their own land,
> Never have I known one who, of his own choice,
>   Follows up the machines of death to take his stand
> Over the slain and in a quavering voice
>   Declaim his joy at youth dead beneath his hand

– not quite a strict Petrarchan sonnet, as Mason later pointed out, and deliberately so. He wrote it 'in a state of cold fury' after reading MacArthur's words, which furnished the poem's epigraph, in the *New Zealand Herald*: 'fury at General McArthur and all other old people who might be pleased to think they had caused the death of young ones'.[9] It was the last poem he wrote that would be included in his *Collected Poems*.

As 'R.A.K. Mason, Poet' he was one of the sponsors of a Youth Peace Conference held at the Yugoslav Hall in Hobson Street in August, along with Pat Potter ('Trade unionist') and Denis Knight Turner ('Artist'). At the end of October he took part in a Trade Union Peace Conference at the Auckland Trades Hall organised by the New Zealand Peace Council (as the Peace and Anti-Conscription Federation had renamed itself), and attended by fifty-five delegates, thirty observers and some forty visitors. Drennan was head of the organising committee. Mason introduced the session on 'The Press and Public Opinion', which discussed and passed resolutions demanding that the daily press 'cease preparing for war by propaganda, provocation and appeals to narrow prejudice', and urging 'those engaged in the dissemination of propaganda, printing trade workers, journalists, radio workers' to 'work for peace in the interests of the people'. He was elected onto a permanent Trade Union Committee for Peace representing the General Labourers' Union.[10] An old peace movement friend, Doug Martin, was the secretary. Mason's name continued to be associated with peace movement activities in Auckland through the 1950s. A reading of his Armistice Day poem 'Skull on Silence' was part of the advertised programme for a Women's Peace Festival held in December at the Lewis Eady Hall.[11]

IN DECEMBER Mason was back in Wellington, with Potter and other officials of the union, putting the TUC's case for a general wage order before the Arbitration Court. They were challenging the FOL at its own game, not merely by appearing before the court (the militant unions were opposed to the compulsory arbitration system), but by asking for more than the federation did. The general wage order of 15 per cent issued on 31 January was lower than both the FOL and TUC had asked for, but the TUC claimed credit for forcing the Arbitration Court to make a higher award than it had intended to. 'Comic Opera Court', Mason titled his personal report of the hearing. He was dismayed at how blatantly 'class bias' had been shown, not only in the court's judgment, which was to be expected, but in its proceedings, and disparaged the weak-kneed position of the FOL. The TUC's case had been 'infinitely superior' to the FOL's and 'in fact, far and away the most searching and profound that has ever been presented to an industrial Court in this country'.[12]

In February he was back at the Wellington Trades Hall again, taking the minutes at the TUC's national wages conference. But the conference had been upstaged by what was rapidly developing into the most prolonged, bitter and divisive industrial confrontation in the country's history.

Dispute over how the January general wage order would be passed on to the watersiders (who were not covered by the Arbitration Court decision) had led to the union imposing a nationwide overtime ban, which led to the ship-owners locking them out. A state of emergency was declared on 21 February under the Public Safety Conservation Act, which had been hastily passed after the riots of April 1932, and sweeping Waterfront Strike Emergency Regulations were issued the following day. These empowered the Minister of Labour to suspend awards, freeze union funds and use the armed forces to replace striking labour; prohibited pickets, demonstrations, meetings and posters; and made it an offence to give support to the watersiders in any way. They were to be enacted if the watersiders did not return to work by 26 February. The watersiders voted not to. Two days later their union was deregistered and its funds seized.

The TUC wages conference opened on 27 February, the day the emergency regulations came into effect and troops went onto the wharves. That evening a TUC delegation went to see the Prime Minister and Minister of Labour to ask the government to revoke the regulations.[13] They were accompanied by delegates from the Waterside Workers' Union, but the FOL and the Labour Party had refused to join them. The TUC declared its support for the watersiders, while the FOL, at a special conference a week later, resolved to call on them to abandon their action. The TUC leaders, who were back (or still) in Wellington, stood outside the hall handing out leaflets.

The union overtime ban was only the ostensible cause of a confrontation that had long been expected, and even looked forward to by the ship-owners and by a government determined to smash the militant watersiders' union, strike a blow in the international struggle against communism, and mark a decisive end to fifteen years of Labour rule. It was not only, or even, an industrial dispute but an ideological one. 'Which Way New Zealand?' asked the May editorial in *Challenge*, which sounds like Mason rather than Potter: 'Two roads lie ahead – the Tory Government's and the Labour Movement's.

The Tory road is broad and attractive, well surfaced and edged with flowers. The Labour way is narrow and muddy, only a bullock-track winding through the scrub. Why not accept and amble amiably along that pleasant Tory road? Why not? Because all our experience shows that a Tory road is "the broad road that leadeth to destruction," "the primrose path of dalliance that leads to the eternal bonfire."'[14] The FOL was largely successful in isolating the watersiders, although some 14,000 other workers also went out, but not the Auckland general labourers or the carpenters. Few of the unions which did so were to last the distance. In addition to editing *Congress News*, Mason's contribution to the propaganda war that was waged through the course of the dispute, in spite of the emergency regulations, included publishing an expanded second edition of the most popular of the many leaflets issued by the underground press, titled *If It's Treachery Get Tuohy* (the name by which Fintan Patrick Walsh had been known when he joined the Wobblies in America in his youth), which quickly became a collector's item, selling for £1 and then £5 on the street.[15]

The lockout lasted for five months. With their own offices shut down, the Auckland watersiders used rooms offered by the Auckland General Labourers' Union. Mason had the job of interviewing the watersiders' wives, listening to their harrowing stories of being ostracised by friends and neighbours and trying to keep their families fed on what meagre strike pay the union could provide. It was an offence even to give food to the watersiders' families, although this was one clause of the regulations that the police were inclined not to enforce. Dorothea recalled: 'A tougher type could have coped better, but poor Ron got so upset for them. And it went on for day after day after day.' It was a long trek in from Torbay, with only an occasional bus running to Bayswater, then the ferry and a tram up to Karangahape Road. With meetings going on through the evenings Mason spent cold, dark hours on the winter nights waiting for trams, ferries and buses, often having to walk the last stretch from Brown's Bay to Torbay, arriving home white and exhausted. 'And then he would drink too much' and not sleep.[16]

During the second week of May Mason attended a five-day New Zealand Peace Congress organised by the Peace Council: there was still the war to be fought on the larger front. Held in the Auckland Town Hall and Manchester Unity Hall, it was attended by some 270 delegates, observers and visitors, including three invited overseas speakers – peace activists from Australia and Britain (the organisers had been hoping to get D.N. Pritt, Paul Robeson and Madame Sun Yat Sen). Mason was not one of the listed speakers, but one friend remembers him at one of the sessions getting up to recite from Milton's *Areopagitica*.[17]

The same week, a New Zealand Writers' Conference was taking place in Christchurch, organised by the university English Department's Professor John Garrett and Winston Rhodes. It was the first such national gathering of the literati since 1936. Here another war was being fought as the literary generations squared off against each other. Much discontent was aired about the administration of the State Literary Fund by its elderly advisory committee, and the precocious James K. Baxter stole the show with his address on 'Recent Trends in New Zealand Literature'. The poet must be 'a cell of good living in a corrupt society', Baxter declared, and by both his writing and his example attempt to change it – an argument for moral engagement against Romantic isolation with which Mason would have agreed.[18] Almost everyone who was anyone in New Zealand letters was there. Fairburn was the other notable absence, having refused to attend because the organisers would not pay his fare. Mason had other things to do.

Several thousand people attended a rally in the Domain organised by the TUC on Sunday, 13 May, the day after the Peace Congress closed, where Walter Nash, the new leader of the Labour Party, famously declared that Labour was neither for nor against the watersiders, to the disgust of the assembled crowd. A week later Jock Barnes addressed a meeting in the Town Hall called by a combined trade union committee, again chaired by Potter: £240 was collected for the watersiders' families. On 3 June a reported 17,000 attended another rally in the Domain, two days after 'Black Friday', when a march up Queen Street led by the Waterside Women's Auxiliary had been stopped by police batons. Eric McCormick later described seeing Mason on one of these occasions: 'in the Domain at a rally of striking (locked out?) wharf labourers . . . grim-faced, in a row of union officials. He might have been a commissar, I reflected, but was as usual on the losing side'.[19]

The watersiders went back to work in mid-July, defeated, as there had never really been any doubt, except in their own minds, they would be. From May it had been clear that the dispute was nothing more nor less than a war of attrition, which the watersiders could only lose, pitted against the combined forces of the employers and the state in a Cold War climate of loathing and fear. Even the Party was having doubts by then about the wisdom of continuing the struggle. The day after the watersiders' executive recommended a return to work, the government called a snap election on the strength of its hardline handling of the crisis. 'Let's put Sid out and Walter in', Potter exhorted a rally in the Trades Hall on 22 July (also addressed by Barnes), to the embarrassment of the Labour Party, who were not keen at that moment to be associated with the bad old days of union militancy.[20] At the poll on 1 September, the National government increased its parliamentary majority by four seats.

The end of the waterfront dispute also spelled the end of the Trade Union Congress. The final issue of *Congress News* came out in September. Although there was no formal dissolution, the TUC had ceased to function by the end of the year.

THE FALLOUT from 1951 was lasting and cruel. Striking watersiders were blacklisted and the union leaders gaoled. Within the left there was recrimination.

At the Auckland area conference of the General Labourers' Union in December 1951, the executive presented a ten-page report on the 'National Industrial Situation', written largely by Mason, which considered the dispute and the events leading up to it in the light of its outcome, and cast the General Labourers' Union in the role of loyal but unwilling comrades. 'During the battle, we had to refrain from statement and suffer for the mistakes of others', but now it was time for '[s]harp criticism'. Had it been wise to walk out of the Federation of Labour, rather than continue to build the progressive forces within 'the machine'? In hindsight, it seemed not. The walkout 'was wished on to us without consultation, but we had no option except to go with our long-standing associates' – which was not quite how things had appeared at the time. The watersiders had then abandoned their faithful allies and it 'fell to this Union to force the pace' and get the Trade Union Congress up and running. From February, when the watersiders' executive had been too busy to meet with them and give support to the wages conference, the TUC had been 'cold-shouldered, ignored and forgotten'. It had been wrong, Mason's report contended, to continue the struggle once it had become clear that victory could only be Pyrrhic.[21] The leadership of the Waterside Workers' Union, he observed to the publications editor of the World Federation of Trade Unions (WFTU) in London at the same time, 'between ourselves, was neither as capable nor as straightforward as it should have been, whether in the commencement, conduct or outcome of the struggle'. He was anxious here to stress that the losses the left-wing unions had suffered as a consequence of the dispute far outweighed its success as a demonstration of staunchness and organised militancy, which is what the WFTU was happier to hear.[22]

The report was unanimously accepted by the area conference, but it led to a series of fractious encounters between the Auckland watersiders and labourers over the next six months. At the monthly meeting of the Labourers' Union in February 1952, during a heated debate on the question of reaffiliating with the Federation of Labour, Drennan was expelled for calling Potter a liar and banned from further meetings until he had apologised in writing. Two further meetings were convened in June between the Labourers' Union executive and the deregistered watersiders, who were smarting from the criticism levelled at them in Mason's report. Mason took the minutes, and made a written statement of his own role as 'the Recording Angel of this outfit' – as 'Beelzebub to Mr. Potter's Satan': 'I am not a big noise in the Trade Union Movement – little more than a murmur – but I do feel that when abuse is being showered round so liberally as it was by the delegation I am entitled to at least a little of it.' Acknowledging that he had been largely responsible for 'what has now apparently been re-christened "that scurrilous document"', he went on to suggest 'a simple and reasonable path by which the Watersiders can extricate themselves from the swamp into which they have charged with all the light-hearted irresponsibility of stallions in spring-time'. His light-hearted tone belied the intensity of feeling that 1951 and its aftermath had aroused.[23]

The question of reaffiliation with the Federation of Labour then caused a rift between the General Labourers' Union and the Communist Party which was to develop into a vitriolic exchange of accusation and abuse, personal and political, as Party disputes had a tendency to do. In the May 1952 issue of *Challenge* Potter stated that he personally disagreed with the Party's policy of rejoining the FOL in the interests of labour unity, a position which was subsequently endorsed by the union. The FOL had become only more reactionary and dictatorial since the end of the dispute: 'Better be out on the naked hills with Rob Roy McGregor than sit in palaces with the subservient creatures of those who seek to enslave us', as Mason (perhaps) wrote in a later issue of *Challenge*. By November Potter was accusing the Party of conducting 'a campaign of disruption and character assassination' within the union aimed at discrediting its leadership as right-wing. In February, he claimed, it had been joined by 'two or three disgruntled and embittered individuals', prominent (but unnamed) members of the Party, who had embarked on 'a concerted campaign of abuse directed at the Union officers', Potter in particular, which 'reached a crescendo when one disrupter indulged first of all in a whispering campaign, then in open outbursts assailing my personal integrity in the lowest terms of the gutter, acting the real "lumpen proletarian"'.[24]

While this antagonism vented itself in the pages of *Challenge* and the *People's Voice* over the following months, the Labourers' Union called for the Trade Union Congress to be resuscitated. In May a conference of 'independent and progressive' unions was held, and decided instead to form a looser alliance of 'Non-F.O.L. Unions'.[25] But Mason was probably not there.

The falling-out between the Party and his union was deeply upsetting to Mason: '[t]his cruel conflict', he said of this time.[26] He found himself ostracised by those who had been his friends, colleagues and allies in the struggle for years. And, in the widening division within the Party, Mason was also, it seemed, on the wrong side. Sid Scott, to whom Mason was closest among the Party leadership – he had known him for some twenty-five years – was asked to resign as general secretary at the 1951 Party conference, and was replaced by Vic Wilcox. There was an element of farce in what Scott later saw as a conspiracy to remove him. He had been rebuked for ringing a Party member on the Peace Council office telephone in May 1951, thus conducting internal Party business 'in a manner which would easily supply our class enemy with all that is necessary to completely publicly link such organisations as the Peace Council with our Party'. For this he was reprimanded for 'extremely incorrect behaviour' in relation to security and for his 'liberal Social Democratic attitude'.[27] During the waterfront dispute, Scott claimed, he had been excluded by the secretariat who took over the running of the Party, operating in a clandestine manner, holding meetings in the crater of Mt Eden or in a parked car on reclaimed land. In Scott's account he had been the first to have doubts about the watersiders' strategy in leaving the FOL and in prolonging the lockout.[28] But differences of opinion over the waterfront dispute were only one element in a larger personal and political contest, of a kind to which the Communist Party was peculiarly prone.

> COME, SOUL, and tramp the jagged
>   flint-knives on the peak
>   of peril where the ragged
>   mists of death swirl & reek.[29]

The stresses of this time precipitated on Mason's part 'a bad and long breakdown', although its causes were deeper – he had not been the same,

Dorothea said, since his mother died.[30] In the autumn of 1953 he took sick leave from the union. He 'has been off the scene for the last three months with a serious illness', *Challenge* readers were informed in August, but was now on the mend. In reality this breakdown was to last about a year: 'a terrible year'.[31]

Abruptly, and without consulting Dorothea, he sold the Torbay cottage. A friend of hers who had just returned from Australia had been looking at properties for sale in the area and left the keys for the real estate agent to collect from Mason. He had been fretting for some time about the foundations of the house, whose previous owner had begun digging out an air-raid shelter under it, and after talking about this with the agent, over a few drinks, was persuaded to sell: it went in three days. Furious, Dorothea left him. She went to stay for a while with Mary Barkas, then took a job as a receptionist for a doctor friend in Christchurch. It was a relief, she said, to find herself among 'a very pleasant, cheerful and NORMAL lot of people'.[32] She had no intention of going back.

Mason stayed with Dan at Whenuapai for a few months, before moving into a bach at Mairangi Bay, in Matipo Road. It was one of the first places to have been built in what was still a largely undeveloped new subdivision, the properties separated by manuka- and gorse-lined tracks. The bach was at the bottom of a gully, built on swampy ground, and he set about developing a swamp garden – while doing battle with the 'little shaggy savages . . . marching up from the fens and swamps of my soul'.[33]

When Shirley Barton arrived back in Auckland towards the end of 1953, after several years in China working with Rewi Alley as liaison officer for the aid agency CORSO, she was shocked at how she found Mason: '[he] was in a highly nervous state, blaming himself for every move he'd made and repeating it over and over again', and physically as well as mentally unwell. A doctor had told him he should avoid exertion because he had a weak heart: hard advice for a man for whom huge walks and strenuous gardening were two of his great pleasures. 'He became an old man, still in his forties, walking with a stick, listening to his heart, fearful of any rash move.'[34] After about six months Dorothea came back to look after him, when she heard how ill he was: 'looking like a ghost, thin white & shaky again' and 'crawling about with a stick'. They lived at Mairangi Bay on his social security benefit (£2 7s 6d a week, probably topped up by sick pay from the union), while he tried to build his swamp garden. He had slashed the gorse, dug 'ditches and channels all over the place' and planted masses of ferns. It was 'an interesting experiment', but he was too sick to work at it properly, and their goat ate the new fern shoots. He drank and could not sleep.[35]

At Mairangi Bay he wrote 'In Time of Testing', for Dorothea:

> All that was hope turns at one stroke to horror
>   One sudden flame
> Fuses all joy to grief, wisdom to error
>   And pride to shame
>
> And now has struck the terror and the hour
>   Of utmost need
> And in that flash there falls back every flower
>   Of hopeful seed.
>
> The day drags out in cold sorrow and rain
>   Till longed-for night
> Worse than denying promise brings more pain
>   More evil plight.
>
> Now who stands steadfast not for the mere moment
>   But through the long
> Linked hours unheeding prospect or repayment
>   Stands and is strong.
>
> There was but one who loved and I thought careless
>   And so I fell:
> And now it is her love which follows fearless
>   Along my Hell.[36]

In October he wrote to Rex Fairburn, to ask him how to go about applying for a grant from the State Literary Fund. He had written to Fairburn a few months earlier, sending condolences on the death of Fairburn's father and apologising for not having been to see him 'in your bereavement, but I was at the time fighting an affliction which has since put me out of action for the time'. Remembering the depth of hostility Arthur Fairburn had felt towards his son's red-talking, poetry-scribbling friend all those years ago, when he had banned him from the Fairburn home, Mason remarked: 'In a way, I regret that I did not try to open up negotiations with the Old Man when I had the chance on the ferry some months ago. In another way – and I know you will understand what I mean – I am glad that I did not. He did not relax his attitude, & I admire him for it.' He also regretted that he had seen so little of Fairburn for so long: recently it 'just seems to be everlasting rush & strain & all so unnecessary'.[37]

It is a measure of Mason's isolation from the literary scene that it was Fairburn to whom he turned for advice about applying for a literary grant, as Fairburn was very publicly opposed to state support for writers. 'I heartily agree with you in principle', Mason told him, but 'circumstances are such that I feel my best course would be to try to get one. *Believe me*, I have not made the decision lightly.' He was thinking of applying for £500 'to do a History of the N.Z. Company. I did a lot of work on it at one time & I think I could pick up the threads fairly easily.' But he had no idea how to go about it, who the secretary was and what lobbying might be required, '& cannot as yet get myself back into circulation in order to find out'.[38] There is no evidence that Mason applied for a grant at this time; but he did go and see Fairburn.

Winston Rhodes, worried by what he had heard about the state of Mason's health, wrote towards the end of the year suggesting that he come down south for a holiday, but he heard nothing back. In November Mason and Dorothea went up to Okura, near Redvale, to a friend's farm. They stayed there for about three months. Mason 'just sort of vegetated'. He worried incessantly about his heart. But what was really worrying him was that he couldn't write, and that he wasn't doing anything.[39]

21

Tecoma hedges

1954–57

EARLY IN 1954 Mason and Dorothea sold the swamp section and the 'ranch', and with two mortgages bought a large old villa in Esplanade Road, Mt Eden. It was 'another gloomy house', Dorothea found, but big enough for them to take in boarders so that she could stay at home and care for Mason rather than going out to work. They furnished it from auction sales and let two of the rooms. A third became an expansive (24 by 27 foot) study for Mason. There was a large back garden which Mason made his own. He built himself a 'bush-house', a shelter made with the branches of a poplar tree, overlaid with netting across which pumpkin vines trailed: 'a primitive boy-scout sort of thing . . . He would hide in there.'[1]

Still he was 'ill, depressed and discouraged'. He had been cast out by the Party. 'His life as a poet had been sacrificed for his even stronger compulsion to fight social injustice. Now he had no comrades in the fight.'[2]

Bill Pearson came to know Mason well at this time, having returned from London in 1954 (with the manuscript of his novel, *Coal Flat*) and moved from Christchurch to take up a lectureship at the University of Auckland. Pearson was also editing the Peace Council's monthly magazine, and mixed with a group of Party members and sympathisers (although, despite pressure to, he never joined himself). Like Shirley Barton, he saw Mason at this time as 'an embattled loner', disapproved of by the people in the Party that Pearson was close to, for reasons that were never made clear; his 'loyalty to the cause of freedom and the dignity of the common man was no less for the defeats and the slights he had suffered from his allies'.[3] The Party at this time was earnestly extolling the virtues of self-criticism and distancing itself from the sectarianism associated with older members like Sid Scott. Mason was also tainted, perhaps, by his connection with the Peace Council, with which the Party had a fraught relationship (as it invariably did with 'friendly' organisations). Pearson became a regular visitor at Esplanade Road on Sunday nights, usually taking a half-bottle of whisky which they would drink after dinner. Mason would proudly show him his garden.

In May 1954 Shirley invited Mason to become chairman of the New
Zealand–China Friendship Association, of which she had recently been elected
secretary. 'He and I sat on hard benches in a dingy milk bar in Karangahape
Road . . . He was still far from well', but he agreed with enthusiasm, and was
to apply himself to the role with dedication – but only after seeking an assurance
from the Party that there would be no interference, intrigue or factionalism
on their part.[4] Shirley approached him as much because she felt that Mason
needed a new interest, a focus for his political and social concerns, as because
the association particularly needed Mason. Some months earlier she had written
to Rewi Alley in Peking of her hope that Mason could visit China: 'My old
friend R.A.K. Mason is in a bad way and needed a shot of new inspiration
from the new world even more than I thought when I suggested he come as
a delegate', she told Alley. 'I hope we can rescue him. Makes the heart ache
to see the casualties and such a waste to the movement.'[5] Shirley saw Mason's
crisis not only as personal but as symptomatic of a wider malaise. For her,
coming home from China after six years had been a disillusioning experience.
She had been shocked by the pervasiveness and vehemence of Cold War
feeling, and at the culture of individualism, cynicism and hedonism that seemed
to her to have taken the place of the idealism, activism and altruism of the
1930s. 'So many erstwhile progressives have become anti-Soviet, anti-
communist, anti-"political" . . . "disillusioned", self-seeking, turn off any
serious talk with flippant wisecracks', she wrote to Alley. 'Sensitive souls are
bewildered by the collapse of beautiful ideals; they get dulled and scared and
semi-paralysed. "The winter of decadence has set in and good men feel the
chill." Too many sit huddled in their overcoats, isolated and rapidly losing
any faith they had in mankind.' It was in this context that she saw Mason's
suffering, and wanted him to discover what she had in China. 'What is it
about China and the Chinese people', she asked Alley, 'that seems to draw on
the deepest springs of love and loyalty. Something that rests one's heart.'[6]

　　She was also pleased to be able to oust the incumbent chairman of the
fledgling New Zealand–China Friendship Association. It had been founded
two years before by Mabel Lee (Sing), an English-born postmistress who had
married a Chinese (to her family's horror), was now in her late sixties and
widowed; 'a devoted little elderly woman' who had been a well-known figure
in Auckland left-wing circles for many years (she was to join the Communist
Party at the age of eighty-one).[7] Lee had asked Shirley to take over the
position of secretary when her eyesight began to fail. The association's object
was to promote friendship and cultural and trade relations between the two

countries, and to encourage the New Zealand government to officially recognise the new People's Republic of China. Once she had become secretary in March, Shirley set about straightening the association out (as she reported to Alley), which meant removing 'difficult' members from the committee, including the chairman, Leo Sim, a former communist turned Trotskyist ('I think it's called a Fourth Internationalist'), to get it 'out of the narrow sectarian category into which it has already fallen, and to develop it into a genuine broad friendship association'. There were 165 members by June 1954.[8] Along with Mason, Dorothea joined the committee. In time, China was to become for Mason the hope and tonic that both Dorothea and Shirley hoped it would.

BUT OVER the next few years Party squabbles and union troubles cast a dark shadow, precipitating another breakdown in the early months of 1955.

Mason had begun to feel uneasy towards the end of 1954 about the financial administration of the union, although it was to be another year before these worries finally impelled him to resign. It was another two years after that before the details and extent of the misdealing he had been the first to suspect were revealed. In February 1958 Pat Potter was convicted in the Auckland Supreme Court on nineteen charges of theft from the union, of sums totalling £1780, and sentenced to three years' gaol. The charges (there had initially been fifty-seven) related to the period August 1954 to April 1957, and the funds Potter was alleged to have misappropriated included sick pay allocated to Mason. In his defence Potter admitted that he had borrowed but denied that he had stolen from the union. In a long and bitter statement to union members written some months before the case went to court, he maintained that every official in the union had known that the money paid to Mason, along with one or two others, 'to supplement their meagre Social Security payments', was 'camouflaged' in the accounts and charged to him personally, just as it was normal practice for unions to indulge in loose book-keeping practices to protect their (illegal) strike funds.[9] Potter believed that he was being made a scapegoat for the union's financial crisis – it was broke by Christmas 1956 – for which others were equally culpable, and that the real reason he was being victimised was his outspoken disagreement with the Communist Party over the Soviet Union's invasion of Hungary in 1956 and his support of Sid Scott, who was expelled (after he had resigned) in 1957 for publicly dissenting from the Party line on Hungary (as were quite a few others, while many more left).

This was not the first time, nor would it be the last, that a union official was found stealing union funds; nor the only time the Party was in some way involved. Notoriously, there was the case of Wally Ashton, the communist secretary of the Auckland Trades Council who went missing in April 1948 and was presumed drowned when his empty car was found at Piha, and was subsequently found to have embezzled £2000 of Trades Council funds – a scandal the moderate unions were quick to capitalise on in their campaign against the militant left. For Mason, however, Potter's disgrace was a shocking betrayal by one who had been his close friend and colleague for fifteen years. It was a similar sense of personal betrayal as he had felt twenty years before when Dan had been found guilty on a similar charge of dealing dishonestly with his clients' money. It was as well that Mason had left the union by the time the police were called in, as Potter and the union executive engaged in an acrimonious exchange of accusation and counter-accusation, and the case went to court closely reported in the press. Back in 1954 or 1955 Mason had confided his concerns to Vic Wilcox, and was advised to keep well out of the business.

IN JANUARY 1955 – the month he turned fifty – Mason attended a Forest and Bird Society camp at Lake Waikaremoana with other members of the China friendship committee. He was happy there, away from pressure and worry: swimming, 'telling yarns about Princess Te Puea, flirting with the girls, playing cards', and surrounded by the peculiar, remote and sombre beauty of the lake, nestled deep in the rugged Urewera ranges, where 'evening now is a girl who lets fall/ Her grey and scarlet shawl/ Over the filigree of a footstool made/ Of amber and of jade'.[10] The bush was always a first place of refuge and recuperation. The lines are from a poem written there which evoked the region's Maori history as well as its natural beauty.

Two months later he was on sick leave from the union, and booked himself a week's stay at the Huia Guest Lodge at Ruatahuna, in the heart of the Ureweras. He was packing to go down there when he learned that Dan had collapsed and died suddenly from a heart attack while helping to put out a fire at a neighbour's house. He would write later to a friend about the death of 'the last of my close family': 'I had for a long time been working up to telling him that all my life I felt I had been wrong in not understanding him better and now there was no chance to tell him so.' He went down to the Ureweras as planned after the funeral, a day late. 'Wasn't much of a holiday . . . but it was still the right thing.'[11]

Mason's illness in the first half of 1955 meant that he was unable to join Tom Karaka, president of the Labourers' Union, and its Auckland organiser,

Harold Kay, on a three-week visit to China in April–May, at the invitation of the Chinese building trades union. A year later he was invited to be part of a ten-member cultural delegation, along with former Labour MP Ormond Wilson and Jim Bertram, but again he couldn't go. The Chinese government at this time was busily inviting foreign parties on carefully conducted, expenses-paid tours to see the new communist China, as part of its policy of 'people's diplomacy'. The latter invitation had come from the Chinese People's Association for Cultural Relations with Foreign Countries, addressed to Mason, as president of the New Zealand-China Friendship Association, and Ormond Wilson, who had initiated it. Mason went down to Wellington in March to discuss the details of the trip and who would make up the delegation – along with the setting-up of a Wellington branch of the China association – with Bertram, Wilson and others. He also attended the first meeting of the Victoria University College Literary Society, where he read 'Stoic Overthrow', which must have seemed to him an evocative poem for these times.[12] But he told them that he wouldn't be going to China himself because, Bertram subsequently remarked, 'improbably he was just embarking on a course of landscape gardening'.[13]

He had resigned from the union by this time and was setting himself up in the gardening business as Eden Garden Services, 'Specialists in New Zealand Native Plants'. He did this for the next five years, working intermittently and informally in partnership with a fellow member of the China committee, Ben Wood. He started his nursery with cuttings taken from the Waitakere ranges and turned the back garden of Esplanade Road into 'a small forest of native trees and shrubs'.[14] For a time he persuaded his friend Wolf Strauss to go in with him in a commercial seaweed compost scheme. In Strauss's truck they made trip after trip over the gravel road out to Muriwai Beach on the west coast to collect the seaweed, which Mason turned into excellent compost, but Strauss tired of the enterprise before he did.

There was nothing improbable, in fact, about Mason taking up gardening, which he had always loved and had a talent for. It made him only a modest and insecure living, but it was a better place for him to be than the tough and sometimes treacherous world of union and Party politics: it is hard not to feel that that was a world for which a person of Mason's gentleness and sensitivity – and in the end, too, his honesty and strong instincts of loyalty and responsibility – was ill suited. Once he was out of the union, his health, physical and mental, improved. Dan's death at the age of fifty-five caused him to worry again about the condition of his own heart, but when he eventually consulted another doctor he was told that exercise was, on the contrary, just what he needed.

At this time both of the rented rooms at Esplanade Road were let to friends and the atmosphere in the household was relaxed and almost familial. A niece of Dorothea lived there through 1955 and 1956 while attending university, and when she married in January 1957 Mason and Dorothea went down to New Plymouth for the wedding. Mason stayed on for a week at a Forest and Bird Society camp on Mt Taranaki, spending his time walking in the bush making notes on the alpine flora. Margot Ruben stayed with them before she returned to Europe finally in April 1956, and she and Mason became close: they shared the same sharp wit and brittle sense of humour, as well as their connection with Wolfskehl. '[W]hen I heard that you had become a full-time gardener – well, that seemed, as we say in German, "Wink del Götter": a favourable sign from heaven', she wrote to him from Paris in April. She also suggested that he grow mushrooms commercially in his basement, as she had been making inquiries at the Laboratoire de Cryptogamie about the conditions needed for growing champignons, with the thought of introducing them into New Zealand.[15] As Winston Rhodes observed, for all the pressures and conflicts that Mason suffered, despite the periods of depression, 'the martyrdom of the man and the tragedy of unfulfilled aims and hopes' that Rhodes came more and more to see, to his friends Mason was not gloomy company but 'dynamic, indignant, compassionate' and fun.[16] The writer Sarah Campion, who had been Mason's neighbour at Mairangi Bay, when thinking of Mason at this time remembered his 'potent charm' and the rough, unkempt, 'Canadian lumberman' appearance that belied the softness of his nature.[17]

HE HAD been buoyed too by a letter from Denis Glover, who was thinking again about the volume of collected poems he had suggested to Mason ten years before. Glover was by then living in Wellington, having been fired from the Caxton Press by his business partner, Dinny Donovan, for his drunkenness and erratic work habits, and then from his friend Albion Wright's Pegasus Press. He was working as an advertising copywriter and had joined Harry Tombs's tiny Wingfield Press as typographer and production manager. He wrote to Mason at the beginning of April 1956: 'There's so much interest in your verse, bubbling up now as ever but more like a good yeasty brew, that you positively have a public duty to see that something is done about it.'[18]

That interest was being stimulated in part by a flurry of anthologising, in what was an especially fertile and disputatious time in New Zealand poetry. A second, enlarged edition of Allen Curnow's *Book of New Zealand Verse* had come out in 1951, and Curnow was already working on the Penguin anthology that would be published in Britain in 1960. In the winter of 1956 the *Oxford Anthology of New Zealand Verse*, edited by two young Auckland academics, Robert Chapman and Jonathan Bennett, appeared. This was a rival anthology not only in being an Oxford production as opposed to a Penguin or Caxton one, but also in overtly challenging Curnow's perceived bias against the younger poets and his privileging of his own, 1930s, generation, as well as rejecting the 'South Island myth' – the determining theme of land and time and alienation as New Zealand's poetic muse – which he was held to have authored. It was another salvo in the generational war that had been raging – usually less politely than in the introductions to poetry anthologies – since the late 1940s. Mason's representation in the Oxford anthology was smaller than in Curnow's, twelve poems to Curnow's selection of sixteen (which Curnow revised little across his three editions), but, for all this anthology's revisionism, Chapman's introduction did not challenge Curnow's evaluation of the 1920s as New Zealand's moment of literary awakening, nor, thereby, Mason's seminal position.

Mason replied to Glover's letter in July, to Glover's astonishment: 'I can't think what cataclysm has struck Auckland that I should be favoured within 3 months of a reply from you. Unprecedented, my dear sir, unprecedented!'[19] There was the small snag of the rights that the Caxton Press held over *This Dark Will Lighten*, which meant 'not only a moral but a more or less legal obligation to consult them'. Glover suspected that Donovan would block them, out of jealousy, or else want to do the book himself, and told Mason not to let on that they had anything more in mind than a reprint. Mason's own remark to Glover about the new Caxton was surprisingly vitriolic, perhaps out of loyalty to his old friend: 'I haven't heard of their publishing anything. I doubt if they are even sound business people. Donovan personally is just a once-seen memory that looked more suited to publishing for Fintan Patrick Walsh than for myself.'[20] Glover's strategy of concealment evidently worked, for the situation was resolved easily enough (helped by the intercession of Curnow, who was having his own problems with Caxton over his Penguin anthology), with Mason specifically excluding in his contract with Glover any right of reprint by Caxton. 'So fire right ahead, if you wish', he told him in July, 'you've got me quite keen'. Mason's only stipulation was that he wanted to do a separate volume of his plays, but he hastened to assure Glover that he was not asking him to publish this as well, he would like his typographical advice only.[21] Glover was keen that Mason get on with the preparation of a proper collected poems at last: 'For God's sake, bestir yourself: it's no good just poking sticks at an existing collect., deleting here & adding there. Let's go into the whole thing.' He was planning a 'definitive edition', casebound, with a print run of 1000, anticipating a good demand from the universities.[22]

The same day that he had replied to Glover Mason also wrote to Charles Doyle, a young poet and critic who had recently arrived from England and was later to join the English Department at Auckland University. He was interested in writing a critical study of Mason's work, a proposal to which Mason was (for the moment) happy to agree. Glover was interested in publishing whatever Doyle produced as well. But this book was to take longer to get to press than the collected poems. In October Glover was pressing Mason to 'take the big step in the frontward direction'. By February he had Curnow lined up as editor and hoped to be publishing before the end of the year. 'I have set my (few remaining) teeth on this job', he told Mason. But Mason appeared to have lapsed back into his normal habit of procrastination, finally provoking Glover into verse:

> You dig up the Esplanade
> Your shovel holding tight
> And you drink down lemonade
> But never a word you write.[23]

MASON HAD been too busy, he might have said, with his gardening business – 'my Given Vocation of mucking up the landscape'[24] – and with the affairs of the New Zealand–China Friendship Association.

His duties as chairman included welcoming and escorting visiting delegations. In June 1956 two Chinese trade unionists were jointly hosted by the association and the Auckland General Labourers' Union; their itinerary included a mayoral reception and dinner with the management of the Auckland Harbour Bridge project. In October the Classical Theatre of China came, to the excitement of not only the local Sino-philes. The eighty-strong troupe performed to capacity audiences in Christchurch, Wellington and Auckland during a three-week tour, presenting excerpts from classical Peking opera and folk dances. Mason welcomed them at a reception given by the Auckland

Chinese community as 'ambassadors of peace' and 'the senior theatre of China, that is to say, the senior theatre of the world. In all seriousness, I say that in the Chinese people, in their lovable qualities and their great ancient arts – in these factors lies our main hope for the salvation of the human race'. Beforehand, the *New Zealand Herald*, in an editorial pondering the political and moral rightness of developing closer trade and cultural relations with Communist China, noted with more cautious approval that 'The Chinese visitors apparently intend to present classical offerings and not the depressing propaganda of the Communist stage. Provided they confine their activities to legitimate artistic endeavour, they are entitled to the respect due to all true artists.'[25] The tour was a spectacular success: audiences were delighted and beguiled by the beauty and strangeness of what they saw. 'What coarse barbarities our own theatre seemed to offer by comparison!' wrote the young playwright Bruce Mason, who went to three consecutive performances in Wellington. By the end of the first he 'felt slightly drunk, stunned by the weird noise and fierce colour, awhirl with its vivacity, charmed by its delicacy, wonderfully stimulated and exhilarated'.[26]

Mason accompanied the troupe every day they were in Auckland and on a sight-seeing tour to Hamilton, Rotorua, Wairakei, the Tongariro Chateau and the Waitomo caves. The itinerary ended in Auckland, with the final performance followed by 'a wow of a party on stage': 'All poets painters musicians trade unionists and Maoris and the Chinese community – quite a change from the usual Chamber of Commerce Remuera set-up', Sargeson reported to Glover.[27] Mason's (and Sargeson's) friend Bob Sillis, of the Carpenters' Union and Communist Party, would remember driving Mason to the theatre that night, with Mason's trousers strategically held up by a safety pin, and the bunch of chrysanthemums he carried wrapped in newspaper to present to the troupe in farewell. Later Mason wrote to the theatre's deputy director, Ma Shao Po: 'I often think of the days we spent together and count them as among the happiest in my life.'[28]

THE SHADOW which fell over this time was the death of Rex Fairburn in March 1957, from the cancer with which he had been diagnosed the previous October. Mason visited him at his home in Devonport nine days before he died.

They appear to have seen each other little, if at all, in the previous four years, but they had corresponded. In November 1956 Fairburn had replied to a letter from Mason, which has not survived but was evidently written in response to an article Fairburn had contributed to *Landfall*, entitled 'The Culture Industry'. In his article Fairburn complained that the current boom in cultural activity, and in particular criticism ('this huge critical pullulation'), really expressed only a shallow and pretentious aestheticism, before returning to his ongoing argument against the organisation of this 'dabbling' in the arts by the state. His letter to Mason, however, discussed historicism with reference to Arnold Hauser's *A Social History of Art*, which had just been published; Mason was apparently concerned by the historicism of Hauser's Marxist analysis. Fairburn touched only briefly on the contentious issue of state patronage: 'You seem to think I have lost my kick, and have become some sort of reactionary', he remarked. Only a casual postscript referred to his illness: 'Since last writing I've been in hospital – my left kidney had to be lifted out, on account of cancer. Convalescence satisfactory.'[29]

A few weeks after Fairburn's death, Mason spoke to the Auckland University Literary Society about their friendship. This was on his own initiative – he phoned Bill Pearson – after he had been offended at being asked to contribute five minutes to a radio tribute.[30] He gave a long and somewhat rambling talk – 'a few facts, reflections and illustrative anecdotes', he introduced it – recalling their Grammar School days and youthful escapades – the onion-growing scheme, Fairburn's abortive working summer at Lichfield, the long walks and earnest talk – and reading at length from Fairburn's letters, which he had carefully kept. Mason presented himself as a 'skinny, lonely, ill-fitting little wretch' when he first met Rex at the age of fifteen, then as the rather too serious friend and righteous revolutionary who admonished Fairburn for not getting a job and castigated him for sabotaging his Socialist Club, and by this time 'an impoverished and infirm old working man, isolated, at war with the world'. He said little about poetry, other than to warn against the temptations of literary canonisation (with reference to both himself and Fairburn) and reading the poem Fairburn had written for him, 'Lines for a Revolutionary', when speaking of their political and personal parting. But their friendship, he insisted, the fundamental bond, had remained: 'For all our differences, we were heretics & rebels. He didn't recant & I hope I don't.' It was a fond, sad, witty reminiscence, and concluded: 'I never knew any man better, I never liked any man more, I never mourned nor shall I mourn any more greatly.'[31]

He went to Fairburn's funeral. But he didn't go to the wake, telling Bill Pearson as he strode off to catch the ferry that there was a China association meeting he had to go to.

22

China

1957–61

IN APRIL 1957 Mason was invited for the third time to visit China, and this time he was able to accept. So when W.H. Oliver wrote to him that month asking if he could have the text of Mason's talk on Fairburn for a forthcoming commemorative issue of *Landfall*, Mason told him he was too busy.

The invitation, from the Chinese People's Association for Cultural Relations with Foreign Countries, was for Mason and four others to come for a month-long tour. To make up his party he asked film-makers Rudall and Ramai Hayward, who were to make a documentary film of the trip; Irene Young, the secretary of the Christchurch branch of the New Zealand-China Friendship Association; and Dorothea. They were all friends. Ramai and Irene had shared Dorothea's Bayswater flat in the late 1930s, and Rudall and Ramai, who had married in 1943, lived just across the road from Mason and Dorothea in Mt Eden. All were members of the New Zealand-China Friendship Association, Mason told their Chinese hosts, and 'Mrs. Hayward and Miss Young have special status also, as being part-Maori and part-Chinese respectively, with particular knowledge of those sections of the community.'[1] Dorothea would act as secretary to the group.

Mason went not as a poet, but as a gardener. He took with him nearly a hundred native seedlings and a collection of botanical books, and was to spend much of his time in China visiting gardens and nurseries and admiring the government's programme of reafforestation, while the Haywards and Dorothea were off filming elsewhere.

For the three months before their departure he devoted himself to research and preparation for the trip, while 'going flat out to complete my landscaping projects, a strenuous job in winter' which put him in bed for a week with flu. He also found time to involve himself in the protests against H-bomb testing in the Pacific, despite having made 'a rule to keep all spare time and energy for China business'.[2] He refused to fly, so he and Dorothea travelled by sea. On 9 August they sailed on the *Wanganella* for Sydney, where they spent some days talking with the New South Wales branch of the Australian China Society and Mason obtained a commission from the Australian Broadcasting Corporation to send them radio tapes, while his plants were held in quarantine. On 19 August they embarked on MS *Changsha* for Hong Kong, going via Brisbane and Cairns, where Mason spent a day on 'an agricultural-horticultural tour of the hinterland', and the Philippines, which appalled him: Cebu was 'just a chaotic junk-heap of unrelieved misery', while in Manila one could admire the beauty of the modern architecture and gardens but 'the horrible huts are only around the corner, and there is an overall stench of enslavement and corruption'. The voyage itself, however, afforded him 'some real relaxation for the first time in many years', marred only, perhaps, by his concern for the welfare of his two cases of seedlings as they passed through the tropics.[3]

They were met in Hong Kong on 10 September by the Haywards and Irene Young, who had taken the fast route. Hong Kong too horrified Mason: 'Luxury and poverty hand in hand everywhere particularly at night . . . beggars in dozens . . . Darkened shop windows showed workers asleep *under* their sewing machines', he wrote to Shirley. It was two days before they were 'liberated' from 'that Hell-hole' and crossed the border by train into mainland China.[4]

In China Mason was immediately impressed by the trees – 'hundreds of miles of eucalypts' they saw from the train on the way to Canton – and by the vastness of the land. The group's itinerary took them from Canton north to Wuhan, at the confluence of the Yangtze and Hanshui rivers, north again to Peking, then down to the eastern port city of Shanghai. In Canton, while the Haywards and Dorothea filmed the Pearl River boat people living on their junks on the river, Mason delivered his plants to the Botanical Institute. Half of them, including kauri, miro, nikau, tanekaha and beech seedlings, would not survive. He also visited Mabel Lee, who was in hospital in Canton for a cataract operation. In Wuhan they saw the newly built, 1100-metre Wuhan Bridge, the first bridge to span the Yangtze River, and attended the rehearsals for the bridge-opening ceremony. There they renewed old acquaintances, as some of the members of the Chinese Classical Theatre who had been to New Zealand the year before were performing with the Wuhan Opera Theatre. The Haywards and Dorothea filmed at the new iron and steel works while Mason and Irene visited the Hupei Forestry nurseries, where he was given gingko, *Metasequoia* and *Cunninghamia* (Chinese fir) seedlings to take back to New Zealand. On the 700-mile journey north to Peking he observed, day after day, 'the people peacefully cultivating, irrigating, harvesting and everywhere tending their land'. On a visit to a farm co-operative near Peking he commented, 'I am a gardener and work like a pe[a]sant', and extended 'greetings from the pe[a]sants of N.Z. to the pe[a]sants of China'. Asked if he had seen the 'backward things' as well as the good things, he replied that he had once lived, fifty years ago, 'in a little village that was as remote and isolated and primitive as your Chinese villages'.[5]

The group spent two and a half weeks in Peking, doing the usual sights: the Forbidden City (the Imperial Palace), the Summer Palace, the Temple of Heaven, the Imperial Hunting Lodge, the Ming Tombs and the Great Wall. They went to the opera, acrobatics, a Chinese film and an English ballet; visited lacquer- and ivory-workers' co-operatives, the Institute of National Minorities and the Institute of Forest Science. From the secretary of the Academica Sinica of Agriculture Mason received a gift of twenty varieties of litchi tree (before leaving Auckland he had obtained permission from the Department of Scientific and Industrial Research (DSIR) to bring back ninety-five plants, including forty camellias and forty litchi seedlings for an experimental planting in Northland). They were welcomed to the 'very humble home' of Ma Shao Po of the Classical Theatre, and saw Rewi Alley, as almost all New Zealand visitors to Peking did. Alley would later recall the day he spent with Mason out in the western hills of the city: 'one glorious Autumn day. We roamed through the old temples there, and at times the beauty of the scene caught on so well that his face lit with enthusiasm for it all.'[6] With Alley they attended China's National Day celebrations in Tiananmen Square on 1 October, and watched half a million people parade past in 'only 3 1/2 hours . . . laughing, singing, dancing, cheering in gay, bright and colourful procession'.[7] In the evening, after the fireworks and folk-dancing displays, they were introduced to Mao Tse-Tung, whom Ramai presented with a Maori feather cloak.

Mason was utterly captivated by China. Its appeal for him was political and cultural, and something else as well. Mason's China, James Bertram would observe, was revolutionary China: not just the new People's Republic and the Great Leap Forward and production statistics but

a long stretch of modern history, from the 'Great Revolution' of the 1920's . . . up to the Japanese war and the triumph of the Red Armies. This, for RAK, was the episode of our times which most exactly corresponded to his romantic revolutionary vision – all the tough poems about red dawns and machine gun fire – plus a background of folklore & classical culture wh. he had tried hard to appreciate for its own sake. . . . China as seen through early Russian films, through Malraux's eyes, & Brecht's, & I suppose Ron's & Trotsky's too.[8]

The importance of theatre, mime, dance and oratory in Chinese arts corresponded with his own fascination with these forms, and he seemed to find an affinity between Chinese and Celtic modes of cultural expression. Making a speech at a farewell dinner in Canton he 'recalled that, on an occasion when too much demanded saying for prose to express, my Celtic forebears would invoke the right to use the poetic principle. The murmur of agreement showed that this was a well understood custom in China also.'[9] What Mason responded to in China at a deeper, or simpler, personal level may be sensed in the tribute that Ma Shao Po had paid to him when the Chinese Classical Theatre left New Zealand in November 1956: when he spoke of the poet who 'leads a hard and simple life' and of his 'firmness, courage, simplicity, humour and cherished love for friendship'.[10] Glimpsed in the background of Rudall Hayward's film *Inside Red China*, Mason appears, Bertram observes, 'as a kind of Byronic Daemon, arrived at his proper place. . . . He is *at home* in China in an almost uncanny way.'[11]

Having extended their stay in Peking, the party abandoned their original plan to visit Nanjing and Suzhou and travelled directly on to Shanghai, where they spent just a few days – making the usual visits: to a kindergarten, a housing development, and a state nursery to which Mason offered to send hebe, lancewood, totara and miro specimens – before returning to Canton on 14 October. Mason and Dorothea then crossed over to Hong Kong to catch their boat, the SS *Nieuw Holland*, home. While their sailing was delayed they spent a few days visiting friends of Shirley Barton and were interviewed by the local papers. An item in the *Hong Kong Tiger Standard* quoted Mason's observation of the 'absolute freedom of religion' that existed in Communist China, and of the 'trees everywhere . . . from Canton to Shanghai to Peking'. It also printed a Chinese translation of the poem he had composed and read at a farewell dinner given for the group in Canton. The poem was 'based on an old Irish saying, "One Hundred Thousand Blessings Be Upon Your Home",' he said:

> May a hundred thousand blessings fall upon your house, O China,
> May they fall like the small drops that spatter the dust,
> When, after long drought, the land lies warm and waiting,

May they alight on your roof-tops like the quiet doves of peace,
Gliding down through the air as softly as the autumn poplar-leaves.
And may these blessings be all around you in all your paths,
You and your children forever.[12]

'The wonder and the glory of it all have been beyond belief,' he wrote to
Shirley, in the midst of final packing. 'God, I seem to have a combination of
all the travellers' nightmares in my baggage – unsorted notes, plants,
cinematograph film, a case of art objects' – in addition to the thirty-two items
of luggage the party were already carrying, Rewi Alley had given him a case
of art works and another of books to take back for the Canterbury Museum.[13]
They left Hong Kong finally on 22 October. The *Nieuw Holland* took them
via Singapore, where they had time for a visit to the Botanical Gardens and a
drink at the Raffles Hotel 'just to see it', then Java and Bali. On the journey
Mason organised and summarised the notes he had made. He recorded
'thousands of miles farms kept like gardens . . . whole great cities being
remodelled'. 'Bewildering complexity, tumultuous appearance of life,
incredible wealth of individual expression – children in shoals, all so different'.
As for the 'assumption that Western capitalism produces diversity, socialism
makes for uniformity. Forget it for China.'[14] No constraints had been placed
on their movements, he observed. 'We went anywhere we wanted to, at any
time, and met whom we liked. We met leaders of the country . . . , millionaires,
peasants, professors, industrial workers, artists, foreign residents, visitors like
ourselves, foresters, shopkeepers and all.'[15] There were others who approached
China in a more sceptical frame of mind – most of the members of the cultural
delegation that had gone in 1956, for example. But Mason went to China as
a believer and everything he saw confirmed his expectations and his political
faith. In a speech he made at a banquet in Peking he described his first
impressions of the country, and expressed a theme that echoes in some of his
earliest poems:

On the one hand, all was strange and foreign.
    In another way, nothing was foreign. I have never felt with such force the
words of the old Roman playwright – Homo sum et humani nihili alienum
a me puto. I am a human being and nothing in humanity seems foreign to
me.
    On the one hand, I felt humility before the priceless treasures of the Chinese
people.

On the other hand, I had some feeling of participation in this supreme culmination of the culture of mankind.

To that culture, no people has contributed so much as yours. Yet all have made some contribution.

From time immemorial, the tides of human thought have flowed the world. Not only along the great routes, from here across to Sweden, over to the American continent, down to India and its neighbours, through the myriad islands of the Pacific. But also minor streams in infinite variety, according to the complexity of the constituent element, the raindrop, the human being.[16]

They arrived back in Auckland on the *Wanganella* on 26 November, after spending several days in Sydney. A fortnight later Mason wrote to Winston Rhodes: 'In my own small way, I feel that China has wakened me up, like herself, after a long sleep.'[17]

THE GROUP were welcomed home by their fellow Auckland China enthusiasts at a reception organised by Shirley Barton. Mason wasted no time in dispatching the Alley books and art works to the Canterbury Museum and presenting litchi, gingko, *Metasequoia* and *Cunninghamia* seedlings to the DSIR.

The Haywards made three films with the footage they had taken: two short colour films, one about the children of China and the other about its art and architecture (*New China* and *The Wonders of China*), and a half-hour black and white documentary, *Inside Red China*, in which Mason appears trying on a sheepskin coat in a crowded narrow street in Peking, taking tea in the garden with David Kwok, the director of the Wing-on Cotton Mills ('one of the slowly disappearing class of Chinese capitalists'), and joining the people of Wuhan carting baskets of stones on carrying poles for the construction of the approaches to the new bridge, smiling and joking.[18] The films were released commercially in late 1958, screening with Rank feature films in cinemas around the country, and were subsequently acquired by the Department of Education for its National Film Library for schools.

Mason never went back to China, although he hoped to. For the next few years, however, in several ways, China remained a focus of his life. One day not long after he had returned, when walking up Grey's Avenue he met a young Chinese who appeared troubled and disoriented, and invited him home. His name was Jimmy Lum, and he told Mason that he had just been thrown out of his home by his brothers. He was to live with Mason and Dorothea for the next three years, helping Mason with his gardening work while Mason taught him English, helped him to gain New Zealand citizenship and eventually to buy his own house. In February 1958 the inaugural national conference of the by then renamed New Zealand China Society was held in Wellington. Mason spoke about his trip and was elected the national president, and Shirley Barton secretary; Dorothea became secretary of the Auckland branch, and Tom Karaka its president. Their monthly meetings were usually held at Esplanade Road. In February and March 1960 Rewi Alley visited New Zealand for the first time in twenty-three years. He stayed for the two weeks he was in Auckland with Willis and Isobel Airey, because Mason and Dorothea had no spare room, but Esplanade Road was filled with people and planning. A mayoral reception was organised, along with a packed public meeting in the Town Hall, and a China Society picnic on the beach at Piha, at Mason's suggestion – he had always loved picnics.

At some point, possibly before he went to China or else when they met in Peking, Mason conceived the idea of writing a biography of Alley. He certainly discussed it with him there: Shirley wrote to Mason on the eve of his return that she was sorry 'the R.A. biography didn't come off'.[19] After he was back, she and Mason planned instead to work together on a combined edition of Alley's two journals-cum-travelogues, *Yo Banfa* and *The People Have Strength*, which Shirley had edited when she worked with Alley in Shanghai as his secretary and translator in 1951–52. This arrangement was abandoned, however, when the London publisher Robert Hale approached Alley in 1960 about a biography, and he referred them to Mason, who 'had the idea once'.[20] The Alley biography was to remain a work-in-progress for several years. Mason spent January of 1961, with Shirley's assistance, preparing a synopsis for Hale, which he delivered to them in February. Alley was a willing although not wholly enthusiastic subject, telling Shirley that he hoped Mason 'will not really have time to get down to' it, but warned them that the project would not be regarded with favour in Peking, in a political culture that had little regard for the individual story: 'No interest in personal heroes, especially when most of the Chinese people are heroes anyway.' Nor did he see much value in Mason coming back to China to do more research: 'He would be busy with sight seeing if he did, and as much in a tizzy as most [China Society] delegates get to be after they hurtle around.'[21]

It was local opposition from Alley's sponsors in Peking, however, rather than his lukewarm encouragement that appears to have scuttled the project, temporarily at least, by the middle of 1961. Quite what happened is unclear. Shirley wrote to Alley in May that 'you know Ron (Mason) could have handled it properly', and that the best thing now would be for Mason to submit to Hale 'something of his own instead', to capitalise on their interest, and for Alley to make some explanation 'to save Ron's reputation. (Could be simply that you "felt unable to endorse such a personal story even though convinced if anyone could handle it in good taste, RAK could.").'[22] Mason, however, decided to continue with the work anyway, with Hale's encouragement and Alley's good will.

TO A SIGNIFICANT extent it was China that brought Mason back to writing. After the long, hard years of working for the union, his life was becoming, in a number of ways, a literary one again. This was what he hoped. Two early unpublished poems, which were to be included in his forthcoming collected poems, appeared in the Auckland University literary magazine *Nucleus* (co-edited by Allen Curnow's son Wystan) in April 1958. The collected poems, it was noted, was 'in preparation for the Mermaid Press', Glover's latest enterprise in Wellington.[23] In August Mason took part in a WEA weekend writers' school, along with Bill Pearson and poet Kendrick Smithyman. The class continued to meet for several months afterwards, with Mason persevering the longest among the tutors. The following February he chaired a Robert Burns evening at the Manchester Unity Hall organised by Unity Artists (a left-wing group that had formed a few years earlier to develop working-class literature and drama) to mark the Scottish poet's bicentenary,[24] and he was then involved in the establishment of an Auckland Burns Association, becoming one of its vice-patrons. For their first Burns Anniversary Dinner in January 1960 he wrote and read this poem:

> Stone and steel is Scotland, but they are the dam and sire
>> of fire
> so the bright issue of her people's injustice and wrong
>> is song
> and they, of all peoples, hold foremost in hero's regard
>> the bard
> and highest that loving honour for him who stands tall
>> above all.[25]

Mason began to take the Celtic literary tradition extremely seriously at this time. He had always made much of his Scottish and Irish (and emphatically not English) inheritance as the source of both his politics and his poetry. But as he returned to writing this became a more insistent, even obsessive, theme. During 1959 he contributed to a radio programme entitled 'The Making of a Poem', in which poets introduced and read one of their own works. Mason chose 'On the Swag'. He invoked the image of a gathering storm to describe the process of poetical composition, before outlining the genesis of this particular poem – although it was more of a poet's manifesto: the 'three general concepts I then felt strongly, and have since found no reason to reject'.

> First, I felt with John Millington Synge, that poetry could, and should, be as it was so long in Scotland and Ireland, a thing of the people, but at the same time profound. So this poem has a simple surface appearance, but with deeper layers of significance beneath. . . . Language and rhythm are deliberately made easy and casual, to allow for conformity with human thought: now plunging, but not uncontrollably; now soaring, but not out of sight of earth. Secondly and once again with Synge, I felt strongly the need for poetry and drama to move closely together.

Third, 'and most important', was the poem's meaning: 'Ever since childhood, and thanks primarily to ancient family traditions brought by pioneer forefathers, I have been impressed most powerfully by the unity of the human race, as opposed to its diversity.' In an age and a culture in which historians and scientists seemed interested only in the points of discontinuity and difference, it was left to 'philosophers, poets, and exponents of true religion' to 'recall how, since time immemorial, the whole human race has seethed over the vast arc of the continents, and their islands, all humanity intermingling, and either directly or indirectly, interconnected'.[26]

The critics' failure to consider his work in the context of these principles angered Mason. In 1959 Oxford University Press published E.H. McCormick's *New Zealand Literature: a survey*, a considerably enlarged revision of his 1940 *Letters and Art* (and the only full-length general study for another three decades). The two pages he devoted to Mason in this volume emphasised his 'cold austerity' and bleakness of vision – McCormick wrote, for example, of the 'dark obsessional world of *No New Thing*', where with 'a grim, self-probing, self-mortifying tenacity of purpose he proceeds to evoke a private hell of unfulfilled or rejected love, of strangulating parental affection, of dissolution, decay, and betrayal' – to an extent which suggests that he found it not only uneasy but also unpleasant reading. But what aggravated Mason was the swift dismissal of his 'political' writing once again. 'Most of his later verse',

McCormick concluded, 'has been dedicated to the revolutionary cause which has proved no more amenable to him than to the majority of poets. *Squire Speaks* (1938) reads like a sketchy caricature of Auden and Isherwood, while the humane sentiments of *China* (1943) fail to compensate for the banality of its verse. Mason was the supreme poetic casualty in the political strife of the thirties.'[27] Mason's response to this was equally blunt: 'Among worst criticism ever written are seven lines foot of pp 116-117.' McCormick, he felt, 'doesn't understand my conception of poetry', although it was one 'common to most of mankind'.[28]

Curnow, in the introduction to his Penguin anthology which came out the following year, offered a more circumspect and sensitive interpretation of Mason's lapse into silence after the 1930s, so early and so young: 'Mason exhausted his subject (or it exhausted him) within ten years, and has written almost nothing since'. In this essay Curnow restated and refined his by then much-contested thesis about the essential relationship between poetry and place — the 'vital discovery of self in country and country in self' — and worked Mason more securely into this 'nationalist' theme. Might not the mother rejected in 'Footnote to John ii 4' be the Mother Country? for example. To Curnow, Mason's 'condition of shocked faith' was one that a New Zealander could particularly recognise as his own. It was evidently a subject he had discussed with Mason. Acknowledging the poet's objection to the popular reading (which he had been the first to offer) of 'Sonnet of Brotherhood' as an allegory of the New Zealander's physical and spiritual isolation, Curnow went on: 'He is willing to suppose, nevertheless, that here and elsewhere in his earlier lyrics, both the choice of theme and the intensity of feeling point to an under-level of allegory implicating the poet as a New Zealander.'[29] But this was not a critical project in which Mason was interested.

On a Friday night in August 1960 Mason attended the first of a series of fortnightly readings of New Zealand literature, at which the work of ten writers was featured, including Mansfield, Fairburn, Sargeson, Robin Hyde and himself. 'Stocky, jovial R.A.K. Mason, a landscape gardener, thoroughly enjoyed his evening', the *New Zealand Woman's Weekly* reported. '"I have written little in the last 20 to 25 years," he said. He thinks that since poetry is based on the spoken word it should be read', and cited his favourite poet as W.B. Yeats.[30]

In June 1961 he applied to the State Literary Fund for £320 to work on a book of short stories 'largely on Maori themes', about which he had 'just now been approached by an English publisher' (possibly Hale).[31] It was not that he had changed his mind about the efficacy or ethics of government support for writers, since he had expressed his reservations about it to Fairburn when he had thought of applying back in 1953. This view he had made clear when he responded to a *Landfall* questionnaire on state patronage in December 1959. To the question, what else could be done to assist writers (in addition to the £2000 then dispensed annually by the Literary Fund)? he replied:

> Sorry I cannot be more enthusiastic about all this, but what little I know of the writer's craft I learnt in the early twenties. (For those who like over-simplified economic explanations, my first publications coincide neatly with the slump of 1923–4.) One lesson learnt in that tough school is that the fundamental ambition of the New Zealand state is to ensure conformity and uniformity by fair means or foul. That lesson has been well reinforced by subsequent experience. Nothing in my experience conduces me to the belief that a wide extension of patronage by such a state can provide the necessary conditions for stimulating a literature.

In answer to the question, what is the most you have earned in one year from writing? he replied, 'Perhaps a fiver.' He remarked to Brasch when he returned the questionnaire: 'I just cannot get enthusiastic about all this tendency to seek easy ways for a hard craft.'[32]

Mason's application was a question of need. He contracted pneumonia in the winter of 1961, after doing a job planting an exposed golf course. This not only meant that he was unable to work for many weeks, but made him 'troubled' about his future as a landscape gardener. He was, after all, in his late fifties by then and frequently in poor health. To write he had to have means. He also applied, in late August, for the recently established Robert Burns Fellowship at the University of Otago, after much encouragement from Bill Pearson. This was a more lucrative prospect than £320 from the Literary Fund. The first literary fellowship to be established at a New Zealand university, the Burns had been endowed in 1958 by a group of anonymous benefactors – rumoured (correctly) to be primarily Charles Brasch – 'to encourage and promote imaginative New Zealand literature and to associate writers thereof with the University'.[33] It was named to mark the Burns bicentenary and Dunedin's particular connection with the bard through his nephew, Otago's first Presbyterian minister. It provided a room in the English Department for a year and a stipend of at least £1200 (the starting salary of a full-time lecturer). Preference would be given, the criteria stated, to candidates under forty years of age, which led Mason to believe that he was not eligible to apply, until Pearson assured him otherwise: it meant only that where there were two candidates of equal merit the younger one would be preferred. Pearson had written to the head of the English Department, Alan Horsman, about Mason's application, telling him that he believed there was new poetry on the way.

In September Mason learned that he had been awarded a Literary Fund grant, to assist him in his writing 'without restriction to prose'.[34] He began making plans to go to Coromandel the following month, find some accommodation and spend at least until Christmas there, to recuperate from his pneumonia and write. He would come over on the boat about 20 October, he wrote to Deirdre Airey (who now had a medical practice in Coromandel), 'complete with clothes, typewriter, a box of Chinese food, paper, rough drafts +c'. If he didn't get the fellowship, perhaps he would stay until the next winter: 'I might do a bit of fossicking, if I can't sell a book, & end up as a venerable, silver-haired dirty old hermit, the pride of Coromandel'.[35] He cancelled these plans when he heard at the beginning of October that he had also been awarded the Burns.

23

A separate country

1962

WHEN HE heard that he had been awarded the Burns Fellowship, Mason wrote to the registrar at the University of Otago, 'My first feeling was of reprieve from death.'[1] He was referring to his bout of pneumonia and his fears about his future. But it was more than that. To Judah Waten, from whom he heard a few months later for the first time in almost twenty years, he was more frank: 'It came at a time when things had been too grim too long for me. I could see no show of ever starting a literary life again and honestly, Judah, not much show of keeping on with life itself.'[2] The fellowship rescued him not only from financial insecurity and 'months of sickness',[3] but from the 'dark wood' of another depression. When he was seeing his doctor about his pneumonia he had received, for the first time, it seems, professional advice about his 'psychological difficulties'. He evidently had a new doctor, Victor McGeorge, who had a special interest in mental health and 'rather surprised me', Mason confided to Deirdre Airey, 'with a very delicate bit of psychological probing, which clarified some bits of my malady in a way I had surmised myself. Of course, he did not know that I have a bit of formal knowledge of psychology & he was restoring a bit of my shattered faith therein, as he did in medical science.'[4]

There had been thirty-two applicants for the Burns that year, the fourth it had been awarded. The selection committee noted that the appointment was 'the best . . . made to the Fellowship since it was instituted' and that 'they consider Mr. Mason to be the foremost living poet' in New Zealand.[5] He was offered a salary of £1275 and travelling expenses of £10 5s 9d. Accommodation was not provided but assistance was offered in finding some, and Mason outlined to the registrar his needs: 'I am a most old-fashioned country-born New Zealander in regard to living habits. I propose to have one good meal out daily and do most of my own housework (perhaps arranging with a student to give things an occasional once-over) . . . A small flat or perhaps one of those old pensioners' cottages close in seems to summarise my ambitions.'[6] He was to go down alone; Dorothea would remain in Auckland.

He received many messages of congratulation when the award was publicly announced. One was from Marie Gaudin, whom, like Judah Waten, he had not seen for some twenty years. By chance they met in the street a few days later, and 'as two people well into middle age, we resumed old friendship with ease', Mason would later recall, 'each with the knowledge that more than friendship had been involved.'[7] Shirley Barton sent him some lines from Herbert:

> And now in age I bud again,
> After so many deaths I live and write;
> I once more smell the dew and rain,
> And relish versing . . .

In the literary community, by his friends, and by Mason himself, the award of the Burns was seen as his chance of a comeback, after his silence for so long. 'His literary river will flow again', ran the headline of a front-page article in the Dunedin *Evening Star* the day after he arrived in the city. He 'does not fit the picture of the grey-flannel-suit type young writer usually awarded university literary scholarships', the reporter observed: 'Tanned and fit, seeming much younger than 57, Mr Mason has none of the accepted air of a poet about him.' And he 'makes no bones about his lay-off from writing'. Asked why he had written so little for the past twenty to thirty years he replied simply, 'I was broke'. To another journalist he explained that he had had 'neither encouragement nor real opportunity' during that time. When asked about his plans after his Burns year, he hoped 'the award will mark his return to full-time writing and that he can put his spade away. "If it doesn't I'll never get back".'[8] But he was less relaxed about it than he let on. To Deirdre Airey he confessed, 'Frankly, I am a bit diffident about starting again after all these years.'[9]

He made, or was to make, a raft of literary plans for Dunedin, although in his letter of application he referred specifically to only the book of short stories for which he had also applied to the Literary Fund. He had 'at various times undertaken several books which I have had to abandon for purely economic reasons', he stated. 'My first job, if appointed, would be to work on these', starting with the short stories.[10] Did he mean 'Men and Things', and the 'fables and tales' he had sent to Fairburn in England in 1931? Perhaps he was also intending to return to his history of the New Zealand Company. He told the press that his main project would be the biography of Rewi

Alley, and that he 'may, if the spirit moves him, write some more poetry'. Writing to Hale in September 1961, he had also mentioned a 'satirical fantasy in novel form, but capable of dramatisation'.[11] His 'main interest, apart from those suggested,' he told the Burns selection committee, 'is the re-establishment of native plants.' In another, longer application which he drafted but did not send, he expounded the basis and purpose of his writing in the same terms as he had in his 1959 radio broadcast:

> My intention some thirty years ago was to use our common speech as basis for a literary idiom adaptable to poetry, narrative, plays or oratory, with appropriate modification in each case, but without unnatural distortion. This is largely, of course, local adaptation of old Celtic practice, in which divisions such as that between prose and poetry are not regarded as rigid. . . . Given a reasonable amount of leisure, I am confident that I can satisfactorily apply it to the projected book of stories and possibly other work.[12]

Although there was no obligation to do so, nor even any expectation, Mason took the fellowship's nominal connection with Robert Burns seriously. 'He went completely Scottish in Dunedin', Dorothea later observed. 'It is a particular personal pleasure to know that I am coming with the blessing of our Burns Association to a city with the old traditions of Scotland and in the name of her greatest writer', he wrote in his letter of acceptance. 'My only hope is that I can, in my own way, prove not unworthy of those traditions and the confidence reposed in me', sentiments he also expressed to the president of the Auckland Burns Association: 'My hope is that I shall be able to wear the mantle not unworthily.'[13]

BEFORE HE left Auckland he began collecting and sorting his papers with the intention of depositing some 'literary-historical material' in either the Otago University Library or the Hocken Library. J.E. Traue at the General Assembly Library in Wellington had sent him an 'accurate and uncannily full' preliminary draft of a bibliography of his writing, and he was aware that a student ('a lad called Broughton') was working on a thesis on Cresswell, Fairburn and himself.[14] For all that he appeared to be enjoying this attention, however, he remained ambivalent about critical scrutiny. Charles Doyle had finally sent him a draft of a 20,000-word critical study for comment. He had been up to Auckland to see Mason (with the help of a grant of £20 from the Literary Fund) in January 1957, at which point he had expected to have the essay largely completed by the end of that month. Mason replied to him in 1962 by registered mail. He objected angrily to Doyle's use of 'some old, undated, unpublished matter' that he had lent him as the basis for 'judgment and speculation', with no consideration of its origin or context, when 'I clearly understood that your main purpose was not final evaluation but provision of material for possible future scholarship'. He ended his letter by refusing Doyle permission to quote not only from unpublished but from copyright material as well (which, as Doyle pointed out, he could not do).[15] Eighteen months later, in a less acrimonious exchange, he recalled to Doyle that he had been 'not wildly enthusiastic about biographies generally' at the outset, 'as it tends towards silly chit-chat, but personally I was sick of people who couldn't even get main lines clear, through inability to comprehend even the elements of Celtic family tradition'. He went on to complain about McCormick's 'insist[ence] on setting the verse of my plays against my lyric poetry'. He had objected to the draft because it had 'become gummed up with all sorts of nonsense like a brash American college graduate'.[16] By this time he had worked out an understanding with Doyle, who was to substantially rewrite his essay more than once before it was finally published in 1970. But he remained suspicious of biographical projects: 'these slick jobs based on kindergarten play-way with a smear of pseudo-scientific anthropology and an odd trip to the DNB.'[17]

With money given to him by his aunt Winifred (Frank Mason's sister, whom he visited in Whangarei at Christmas) and Clifton Firth's assistance, he bought himself a new tweed suit for the south. He took the overnight train to Wellington on 14 January 1962 and spent a day in the capital, seeing Glover, who was finally working on his collected poems, and John Reece Cole, now assistant librarian at the Alexander Turnbull Library. Cole upbraided Mason for taking his papers down to Dunedin rather than giving them to the Turnbull, which liked to be recognised as the country's national research library, to which Mason replied that, as Dunedin was the only city that had ever done anything for him, they could have first pick. To the Turnbull librarian, Clyde Taylor, when he raised this issue with Mason again a year later, he facetiously suggested that Taylor consider moving the Turnbull to Dunedin: 'The civilisation–savagery contrast would then be pretty complete.'[18] It was not that he had anything against Wellington (which he hardly knew). The warmth that Mason came to feel for Dunedin, as the only New Zealand city that 'has done anything to earn my gratitude at a time when I want it, in my lifetime', was matched, and to a considerable extent inspired, by the strength of the resentment he felt especially towards Auckland and 'the supercilious Aucklanders', for reasons that were never clear. He once claimed, obscurely, that there had been a campaign against his getting the Burns: 'there was some reasonable-sized consternation in some Northern quarters, and one crowd even tried to nerve themselves for a public attack, but simply weren't game to go the University of Otago'.[19]

He spent four or five days in Christchurch on the way south, meeting Rewi Alley's brother Pip and gathering information for the biography. Alley was sending batches of material to Christchurch for Mason to look at, and had told his brother to be as helpful to Mason as he could: 'He is a moody chap, a sensitive one too, who responds to a bit of warmth and friendliness.' Alley also wanted to make sure he got the story right: 'Remember', he told Pip, 'that the Chinese revolution produced its people, and any of us who have helped it are products of it'. '[H]elp him a bit to see that the hero is an ordinary human, and that any hereoes [sic] there are, are the Chinese.' It was advice Mason would understand.[20] From Christchurch, he took the bus to Dunedin on 21 January.

HE HAD arranged to stay for a few days with Charles Brasch in Heriot Row on the City Rise, before moving into rented rooms in a two-storey brick house at 8 Heriot Row. 'Good trip, good reception – good digs: handy to University & quite comfortable', he reported to Dorothea. He had '[o]ne huge room, detached kitchen, share convs. with other men, but they seem pretty quiet.'[21] It was a short, steep walk down to town and the university, where the English Department occupied an old wooden house in Leith Street, beside the stream which the city's fathers had grandiosely named after Edinburgh's Water of Leith. In a few days he had 'roughly established' himself in the Burns Fellow's room at the top of the stairs.

One of his first social engagements was an invitation to the home of the president of the Dunedin Burns Club, of which he was made an honorary member. He attended their annual Burns celebrations, which included a concert in the Town Hall and a wreath-laying ceremony, and was photographed by the *Otago Daily Times* standing in front of the Burns statue in the Octagon on 25 January – the 203rd anniversary of the poet's birth – holding the tartan-covered volume of Burns he had been given at the age of eight. He had first read Burns when he was six, he said, when a relative had given him a guinea to learn 'Tam O'Shanter' by heart. Like Burns – and the sixteenth-century poet David Lindsay, to whom he also paid tribute: Lindsay who 'wrote for colliers, carters, cooks and not for cunning' – 'Mr Mason has always tried to be a poet who is one of his own people', the paper reported.[22]

He was charmed by Dunedin, by its Scottishness and its smallness, its friendliness and its seriousness. 'So lovely in this quiet old grey backwater of a city, with its emphasis on the scholarly life', he wrote to Dorothea. The 'polite obduracy' of the people reminded him of the Chinese: 'the solid citizenry, I mean, not the students and Bohemians (of whom there are a surprising number)'.[23] He loved the proximity of the Town Belt, dense and dark along the hillside above the city, through which he walked almost daily. Even the weather was not too bad. The locals had told him that they were having an unusually good summer, and this was true: 1962 was the warmest year New Zealand had experienced for a century, and the winter was to be the mildest for fifty years. His neighbour at Heriot Row would remember him blithely sunbathing naked on the back lawn on sunny days, in full view of the Mater Misericordiae Hospital nearby. Still, by late April he had felt colder than he had ever been since Lichfield.

He made contact soon after he arrived with a cousin (once removed), Lorna Brown, whose husband had just been appointed lecturer in design at the university, and he was to see much of them and their young family during his time in Dunedin. In the autumn they made trips to Tuapeka, in the goldfields country south-west of Dunedin, where they owned a 100-year-old cottage, and Mason found that the landscape reminded him of China 'towards the Great Wall'.[24]

He was, however, singularly unfitted for bachelor life in a foreign town, however hospitable it might be. 'I am baching and keep house marvellously', he told Clifton Firth in February.[25] In reality he was to find domestic responsibility a growing struggle. For one thing, he could not cook. 'Have discovered how great culinary discoveries are made', he had written to Dorothea a few days earlier, ' – by lone men, preferably on diets, using up fag ends. Some time you MUST try odd bits of mushroom sort of poached in skim-milk-powder milk. Add bits of chopped up cheese, if available. Do try it. I just have. It stinks.'[26] It was a wonder she did not come down and rescue him straight away. He was under strict dietary instructions from his doctor because of his heart and a propensity to put on weight rapidly as he grew older. 'Still dutifully eating the lollies and chewing the lettuce', he reported to McGeorge in February. 'Haven't lost any weight, but haven't gained any'.[27] But he found it was a '[d]amn hard place to slim in: no sooner do I start to get the proper gaunt and haggard look than some kind woman determines I must be starving myself and she must do something towards fattening me up.'[28]

  He found his first few months in Dunedin strenuous. The city's Festival
Week ran for the last week of January, and he took part in a lunchtime poetry
reading at the Globe Theatre and attended the exhibitions, including one of
Czech art. He and Brasch began making plans for an evening of New Zealand
poetry set to music, although this apparently did not eventuate. There was a
party hosted by Patric and Rosalie Carey at the Globe Theatre for newly-
weds Barry Crump and Fleur Adcock early in February: 'A very happy affair,
but I just sat quietly and drank beer and talked to everyone in succession
without trying to make passes even at the prettiest. Just as well, as it gradually
came out some of them are to be my students.'[29] He was invited to a morning
tea at the Royal Overseas League, addressed the Burns Club's monthly meeting
(with whisky and haggis) in the RSA Hall, and spoke on Scottish literature at
a businessmen's luncheon. At the end of March he went down to Invercargill
for the inaugural meeting of the Invercargill Burns Club, which was held in
a 'beautiful central Scottish societies hall that just made my mouth water.
Enormous supper afterwards.' He was hosted by the president and spent 'nearly
two full days just being whisked round Southland', which was 'terrifically
fertile and just stiff with sheep', and wrote lyrically to the Auckland Burns
Association about the Caledonian hospitality of the south.[30] 'Never so much
at home as along at the Burns Club,' he wrote to the writer O.E. Middleton
a few days later, 'with their quietly humorous, shrewd understanding and
way of summing things up.'[31]

  Back in Dunedin Mason spoke at the first meeting for the year of the
university Literary Society (held 'in Mr. O'Leary's living room'). His topic,
as reported in the student newspaper Critic, was the current 'self-conscious
search for a theme that would unify New Zealand literature', and the popular
thesis that to its writers New Zealand was remote, isolated, alien and alienating,
a 'backwater of the English-speaking world': 'This self absorption in self-
analysis was futile, and the very thing that stifled creativity.'[32] For a poetry
reading at the university on 10 April, which he had helped to organise with
Charles Brasch and also introduced, the two poems he read (very badly,
according to Brasch) were 'Sonnet of Brotherhood', persistently misappropriated as a key text of that thesis but nevertheless one of his favourites, and
another favourite, 'Flow at Full Moon'.[33]

  In the middle of April he moved from the Heriot Row boarding house
into a self-contained flat at 33 Drivers Road, Maori Hill – the 'poshest part'
of the city, he told Dorothea, although the place itself hardly was. It was a

'gigantic rambling wooden structure', reputed to be the largest single-storey house in Dunedin, set well back from the road.[34] He had the north-west corner of one wing. The flat was unfurnished, and his cousin Lorna and Suzanne Edson (wife of his old Grammar School classmate Norman Edson, who was then professor of biochemistry at the Otago Medical School) helped him get it established. He was like a child, they found, in his helplessness in such matters.

In May he addressed the New Zealand Library Association on New Zealand poetry anthologies. When Shirley Barton and Jim Bertram invited him to come to Wellington that month for a China Society conference and to give a lecture to the English honours class at Victoria (and address the Literary Society, Bertram also suggested), he declined, saying he was too busy; but he began making plans to organise an exhibition in Dunedin of Chinese photography and films. He had resigned as president of the China Society when he was awarded the Burns, but was now talking about setting up a branch in Dunedin.

WITH ALL this activity he had not found much time for writing. At the end of February he was still sorting and editing his papers for deposit in the Hocken Library (as he would be a year later), although he had written a one-act play: a short sketch based on a story Dorothea had told him about an old gold-digger who refuses to leave a camping ground in Thames, claiming squatters' rights on the strength of his prospector's licence. He had also been preparing for publication an edited version of his 1957 radio talk about Fairburn. Keith Maslen of the English Department, who ran the university Press Room – a former wash-house out the back of the department housing an ancient Albion press – was in the habit of asking the Burns Fellow for a short text to print. He also liked to ask them to help with the printing and setting, but Mason's hands shook so much that he could barely place the papers on the points, let alone set any type.[35] The three-page pamphlet, simply titled *Rex Fairburn* and issued in a numbered edition of 100, was a brief, heartfelt contribution to the Fairburn legend of the New Zealand Renaissance man – poet, sportsman and democrat: 'No man better epitomised our people, our virtues and our weaknesses – competent, interested in everyone and everything, always seeking, never acquisitive, easy-going to a fault, often ready to sacrifice the argument for the wisecrack, liking his own country and respecting the rights of other peoples to their way.'[36] Mason sent a copy to Firth, among other friends, who was unimpressed: 'What a romantic you are. I'm buggered if I'd do a thing like that for the old reprobate. Have you forgotten his sabotage of

Phoenix and his essay on the Marx Bros?' In reply Mason distinguished between the 'made-married-and-marred-in-England article' and 'the other one, the native Fairburn'. Among the papers he had been sorting through was some *Phoenix* material, he told Firth, and 'I was very pleased to find out how right, on the whole, we were'.[37]

In the second half of April Mason was checking the galley proofs of his collected poems, which he returned to Glover and Albion Wright at the Pegasus Press on 11 May, with the postscript, 'I particularly liked the shadows that crapt on the sand and the boy who came to his girl-friend vowing great oats. Seems a pity to change them.' There was one substantial change he did want to make, however: to remove 'Lugete o Veneres', 'a difficult decision, but [the poem] has no value, is out of line with other stuff and always in the past has had too much prurient attention paid to it'. 'I don't think much of it', he wrote to Curnow defending the decision: 'it is mildly amusing in an ironical sort of way, if taken in conjunction with the original Catullus, but no one wishes to do anything so straightforward as that anymore – much prefer to read deeply autobiographical meanings into things where they don't exist.'[38] Glover and Curnow were having none of this. Glover suspected the hand of Horsman: 'What's gone wrong with you?' he challenged Mason.

> Are you so soft in the head that you think poetry has to be piddled down to the level of the intelligent young brats Elderly Withered-Widdled Professors think will be Good for Them? You have no obligation to *anyone* for this bloody fellowship. You have not even got to do anything. If some punk Professor wants to get in the way, tell him to get rooted. . . . As a Burns Fellow you are an honoured guest of their mouldered walls. The Water of Lethe. Jump in, cock, if you're silly enough not to know that you have no obligation but to yourself. Remember this, you silly old bastard – Carpenters' Union, Friends of all the World, Inc., Failed Socialist, Incompetent Communist, Good Gardener, Wonderful Friend, Silly Bloody Sucker – remember the street of 1000 Doughnuts and remember those who have been behind you all these years.[39]

Urgent telegrams were dispatched – the book was due to come out in six weeks, and a party was already being planned – before Mason replied, backing down:

> All right all right. Me and Pontius Pilate and McLeod of Assynt and Ramsay Mac. in that order of time and seniority in iniquity. All I did was say I didn't

like one poem, just one: as a matter of fact, there's a whole lot I don't like but I just said one and you are unkind enough to equate me with the CARPENTERS' union.[40]

He denied that anyone in the university had influenced him, although his colleagues in the English Department had helped him with the proofs.

As usual, he had been rigorous in his selection. Although he made no attempt to suppress any other previously published poems, he included only a handful of unpublished ones dating from 1924–30, including 'Ad Mariam', his poem for Marie Gaudin. Apart from the 'Sonnet to MacArthur's Eyes' there was nothing later than 'Flow at Full Moon'.

Mason had written some new poems, however. Three were published in the university Students' Association's annual literary review in July, collectively titled 'Tria Carmina' and dedicated 'ad Miram'. They were love poems: three poems about lost, remembered or elusive love. One, a long rhetorical poem to which he later gave the title 'ad Miram', was addressed to a young woman he had tutored in the 1930s. The dedication, he would later explain, 'is a complicated pun, such as is dear to my heart: ad Miram can either mean for Mira (Maori name) or for the marvellous woman (Latin) or both – as it does'.[41] 'Honey' may have been inspired by a more recent attraction:

I read somewhere once or was it Fairburn that told
　Me of the man who, falling to death, yet a moment clung
To an outcrop where grew a flower, and to it, as his hold
　Weakened, stretched out his mouth for one drop of honey on his tongue.

Now into the Pascalian abyss that reveals no end
　It is I have fallen, and clutch clay for a short hopeless holding,
And you are that flower on the fall to Hades, but you bend
　Beyond reach at the breach of my mouth, and the handhold is yielding.

Mason fell in love in Dunedin, more than once. The first time was with an English and German student, Kay Flavell, whom he met at the Careys' party in February, and who invited him to dinner a few weeks later. She shared a flat in Elder Street with three other students. It was not far from Heriot Row and Drivers Road, and Mason would often call around there in the evenings, usually when they were preparing dinner, and talk or just sit for an hour or two, or several. To them he was an old man, 'a rugged, rough-hewn sort of person', sitting by their fire talking about poetry, their studies, or himself in his sadder moments, spilling cigarette ash onto his old brown jersey, his hands shaking. When he arrived 'he often looked deadbeat: "On the Swag" was exactly like he was to us', but when he spoke about China, for example, he would become animated by 'an almost schoolboy enthusiasm'.[42] Eventually Kay recognised and rejected his more than friendly and scholarly intentions. From the outside it looked like a lonely old man making improper advances to attractive female students (Kay was not the only one). To Kay, with more sympathy, it seemed that she represented 'some sort of fantasy', which had something to do with a nostalgia for his own university days. He gave her a copy of *Phoenix*, as well as an anthology of French verse, and wrote her poems. He needed, too, the affirmation he received from students like Kay, to whom Mason was the famous poet, a legendary figure, at a time when he was struggling with the burden of reputation. It also had something to do with his regret, which would become a growing preoccupation, about not having had children. Being surrounded by students in this university town made him intensely aware of his age.

 Kay remembered him later in a poem of her own:

> You taught me to drink neat whisky,
> Gave me a silver hipflask,
> Called me 'kid'.
> Gentle, defenceless, fierce,
> Like the ageing Goethe
> In the grip of a young man's passion.
> Weeping in the Chinese restaurant
> You dreamed of a child
> But you were the lonely child,
> Always coughing.[43]

BY JUNE, loneliness and the onset of winter were beginning to dispel the initial charm of Dunedin. The chest pains he had suffered since his pneumonia were getting worse, as were his piles, a long-standing affliction which Dorothea had tried to persuade him to have treated. 'Sorry if I sound a bit blue,' he apologised. 'Don't worry, just phase. All well really, but sometimes feel long way from home and you.' A fortnight later he wrote: 'Fit of blues has passed. Must expect some & have been remarkably free.' They had just had their first snow, he told her, 'much more friendly than I had expected'.[44]

To cheer him there was the launch of his *Collected Poems*. This was the highlight of his Burns year, and part of its undoing. It was held at the University Bookshop on the evening of Saturday, 7 July, and organised by John Griffin, the bookshop manager. Alan Horsman spoke on behalf of the English Department, over Glover's loud fulminations about the stupidity of academics and critics. Glover, drunk as usual, read *Squire Speaks*. Albion Wright had a speech prepared and afterwards complained bitterly that no one had asked him to deliver it (although 'everyone knew he had disappeared with a blonde and a bottle', Mason told Dorothea).[45] Mason had invited his student friends from Elder Street, and they would later remember Glover's performance, and how thrilled Mason was by the whole occasion: how 'he really glowed that night'.[46] The party continued afterwards at Griffin's home in Mornington, where Glover and Wright were staying. It was later that night, at Elder Street, according to one of her friends, that Kay rebuffed Mason's advances. The next morning when he went around to the Mornington house to accompany Glover and Wright to the airport, Glover saw him coming up the steps: 'There he is, there he is with his bloody tormented face and his Jesus Christ look', he called out to Griffin.[47]

The *Collected Poems* was dedicated to Dorothea. It had an abstract, 'rather sultry'[48] black and red cover design (to Glover's dislike), and a more subtle and sensitive seven-page introduction by Allen Curnow which affirmed Mason's position as 'his country's first wholly original, unmistakably gifted poet'. Curnow mainly recounted the little-known publishing history of Mason's handful of slim volumes and seventy-odd poems, but in his concise assessment of their quality he caught something that the usual critical emphasis on the dark pessimism and grim stoicism overlooked when he observed (quoting Yeats): 'paradoxically there is almost everywhere joy in the sheer vitality and momentum of the verse – Gaiety transfiguring all that dread'.[49] The reviews which came out over the following weeks were consistently good, weighing the evidence of the complete, though small, œuvre against the legend, and finding that the reputation was still deserved. The full range of Mason's poems confirmed his status as 'the good grey eminence of modern New Zealand poetry', 'the first of the few'; although, observed Louis Johnson, it also humanised him by showing that he could sometimes write badly, in some of the early work which shared 'the common faults of fashion in a feeble tradition' (the blight of Georgian lyricism) before the '[d]irectness and toughness' took over. The 'freshness and contemporaneity of the language in his later work' still surprised, Johnson found. 'The control seems complete;

the effects masterful.' He ventured to hope that there might yet be more.[50]

Winston Rhodes's piece in the *New Zealand Monthly Review*, appropriately titled 'R.A.K. Mason: an appreciation', seems less a review of the poems than a tribute to the man he knew:

> One senses too, but refrains from exploring, those personal compulsions where, for reasons one must be content to leave obscure, the person behind the craftsman has been entrapped in a series of paradoxes which impart to his lines an urgency, a passion, and an intensity beyond the reach of those who have never plumbed the depths of despair or risen to the heights where it is possible to glimpse man's unattainable hopes. . . . His poetry is to be felt in the blood, a poetry that is a challenge to those subterranean feelings about life and death and the stresses and strains of human existence. He is a fatalist who knows the need to struggle, a zealot convinced that time destroys all, a pagan with a Marxist outlook, a Marxist drawn to Christian symbols, a lover who knows that love conquers time. This is no trivial form of inconsistency, but a profound awareness of the central paradoxes of life.[51]

Hone Tuwhare, whom Mason was at this time encouraging to have his own poems published, sent a more direct personal response: 'Yep – You're a fuckin' god, but not too far away for me to feel that you're the muscle and blood of my own choice season.'[52]

The book sold out early in 1963, taking Albion Wright by surprise: he had melted down the type and had to have it reset for a second printing. It shared with Curnow's *A Small Room with Large Windows* the Jessie Mackay Award given by PEN for the best book of poetry published in 1962, earning Mason a cheque for £50.

The publication of his *Collected Poems*, closely following Curnow's 1960 Penguin anthology, put Mason before a wider audience than the local literary community, still looking for or arguing about the need for an indigenous literary tradition. The reviewer of the Penguin anthology in the British weekly the *New Statesman* identified Mason's 'deceptively simple lyrics – pessimistic, sceptical and deeply ironical' as 'the most arresting pieces in the collection', and wondered why the poet was not better known in Britain. The *Times Literary Supplement*, which reviewed the *Collected Poems* in January 1963, rated Mason as 'a major minor in English poetry': the influence of Housman was evident, but

Mr. Mason was not harmed and he emerged a better poet than Housman, if only because there is as much self-mockery as self-pity in him, and his wryness of emotion is stretched taut over a surging compassion for the despised and rejected among men. . . . 'this far-pitched perilous hostile place' is himself, his country, and the whole tragic scene of beleaguered man. He can suffer, he can mock, and he can be realistically satirical. But the past continues to lacerate him while the future daunts him, and that is perhaps why, for all his adaptability with verse forms, he has written so little, and almost nothing since 1941.[53]

This was a more suggestive speculation on the mystery of why Mason had stopped writing poetry than most local commentators made.

ON THE Monday after his book launch Mason gave the first of three lectures to the first-year students in the English Department. It was hoped, although not insisted on, that the Burns Fellow would make a contribution to the department's teaching. In his letter of application Mason had noted that his special field was Latin literature: 'I feel that I could still make a contribution to this subject, with emphasis on Lucretius as the focal point of literary history.'[54] But of course it was on New Zealand poetry that he was asked to speak. He was scheduled to give three more lectures to the senior students in the second term. He was extremely nervous, terrified of lecturing to the large stage I class, and of the English Department itself, with its threatening aura of academic austerity, or so he perceived it. He spent hours beforehand at Elder Street drinking cup after cup of coffee, and asked Kay and her friends to come with him.

In the first lecture he discussed the Curnow anthology, whose poets, he said, were 'a mixed bunch, ranging from the cloistered to some whom I can only describe as heroic'. He told some anecdotes about Fairburn, and described Glover the sailor–poet in his naval days during the war, 'standing on the bridge of a small ship and straining his eyes to peer through Arctic gloom for possibilities of interception by air or sea from Nazi-occupied Norway', and Rewi Alley 'galloping headlong over the far uplands of Tibet, while passing a bottle of their head-lifting spirit with the booted, cloaked and bedaggered horsemen of those parts' (a highly romanticised image of Alley in China, which Mason had paraphrased from Edgar Snow). His point seemed to be that the poet must be one of the people. His notes for the lecture included: 'Poetry has proper place in community, proper relationship to prose', 'Reciprocal responsib. between writer & community' and 'Should be friendship and helpfulness between all writers, provd. men of good will'.[55]

For the next two lectures he asked the students to submit written questions to which he prepared answers, with his characteristic sharp humour. He began one of the sessions with the observation that there was nothing in the Curnow anthology 'that wasn't written over 20 years ago & that makes it easier for me to comment: I can feel that it is somebody else, whom I just happen to have known fairly well'. To the question, 'Is there always a superior meaning to be elicited from your poems'? he replied, 'Only in the good ones', before discussing the background, intention and 'inner symbolism' of 'On the Swag', 'Judas Iscariot', 'Sonnet of Brotherhood', 'Twenty-sixth October' and 'Flow at Full Moon'. He spoke about the influence of Latin on his style, and about the importance of rhythm, of which he had made 'a bit of a special study . . . largely in one of the greatest schools, listening to songs in Gaelic. . . . so far as you can isolate the various factors of poetry and its related arts of prose, singing and music, rhythm is the fundamental factor.' His scripted answers to more general questions about New Zealand poetry and poets were perhaps disappointingly vague: such as that poets must 'act as leaders of thought and leaders are with their people but in advance: they should aim at an interpretation of the positive and negative factors, in such a way as to allow of a positive outcome' – an argument, if the students were listening carefully, for the role of the poet as social agent. The 'important point' in defining a New Zealand literature was 'how successfully you interpret the fundamental characteristics of your people, with implicit comment, at least aspects of the NZ spirit. In the process, as I have tried to make clear, you reach down into the rivers underlying the whole of humanity.'[56]

Nervous though he may have been, he evidently established some rapport with the students, for he was offered a part-time tutoring position in the second term. He did not take it up.

On 14 July he wrote to Victor McGeorge about his piles and chest pains, and depression, and asked him if he could recommend a doctor in Dunedin. 'I would not ask if I could stick it, but there [are] times when it is just too much.' In the letter (which he may not in fact have sent) he heavily scored out this sentence: 'The hardest part is to get the old happy come-hither & be afraid to respond, in case of pain too great for performance.'[57] Four days later he wrote to Dorothea, suggesting they meet in Picton or Nelson during the university vacation for a holiday. He had been working too hard and was 'fed up with my own housekeeping', and should have come up to Auckland for a break and to see McGeorge as he had planned. He was lonely, sad and regretful.

I know there is no use moaning about the past, but at least we can learn from it and one thing clear is that we have not had enough time together . . . We can find a place where no one will know us and I can see no reason why you should not call yourself Mrs M., as I have suggested before. It would surprise your English soul to know what a proper New Zealand custom that is and no one thinks a thing of it, provided the relationship is right. And I will try hard to stop my silly snarls and be sweet.[58]

A few days later he replied to a letter he had received in April from his old friend Norman Richmond, who had been a patient on and off at Sunnyside psychiatric hospital in Christchurch for the last few years, and whom Mason had visited in January on his way south. It was a disturbed, manic letter:

Can't be bothered to tell you how I got in here again, but it won't be for long. Moreover I am about to embark on some massive research – partly into the intellectual & emotional development of my family during 5 generations – say 1840–1980 – & partly into what Blake called multiple vision, you remember?

> May God us keep
> From Single Vision & Newton's sleep.

Isn't this up your street a bit? I'd like to know. I've invented a term POLYCHROMATIC thinking or vision.

In his reply Mason made no mention of Blake or polychromatic vision (he wrote only of how 'bracing and stimulating' he had found Dunedin), but he must have recognised the condition.[59]

The following day he replied to Dorothea, who was planning to come down in August and meet him at Abel Tasman National Park. He told her that he had made an appointment at the hospital, but not to 'hope for too much: you know I am far from recovered yet, but at least we shall be together again and I do so need you. . . . pain is a bitter thing and you must just try to pardon me for wrongs done to you'. He enclosed a poem, entitled 'Reunion', the writing of which 'at least has done me a lot of good'. It was like a coda to 'Flow at Full Moon':

> The snow is soft,
>> from the winter sky wheeling and turning
>> or the ashes that waft
>> over hills from unseen summer burning:

> So softly and calm
>> your spirit gleams the length of the land
>> and there glints a balm
>> to heal all ills from your hand:
>
> Your breasts are more strong
>> than any false idol to allure me
>> and of that too long
>> I have lacked their sight to assure me.

'There must be more affirmation in my poetry again and you must be the cause of it', he wrote to her. 'My mind has been dark without reason, but love between us can illuminate it once again.'[60]

Among his unpublished papers are also these two stanzas, dated 10 July 1962:

> The moon resumes the field
>> that small insane men have assailed
>> & resurrects the heavenly shield
>> where Hell's horde has not prevailed:
>
> And the moon is your bosom
>> that must triumph over the infernal
>> & your breast is the blossom
>> of the lotus & it is eternal.[61]

On 26 July he went into Dunedin Hospital to have his piles treated, and was admitted for depression. He was placed under the care of the professor of psychological medicine, Wallace Ironside, and given the anti-depressant drug Amitriptyline. His medical file would subsequently record that he was suffering from a 'bout of depression which was so severe that he contemplated suicide'.[62] What Mason had long ago described as his 'absurd alternations between omnipotence and impotence', 'infantile fluctuations between heaven and hell, ecstasy and despair', was now diagnosed as manic depression.[63] He explained later to McGeorge: 'Sorry to have to report that, since my last letter I have had a bit of a bad spell. . . . The continuous strain of trying to look after a flat and do literary work, without a proper break, seemed just more than I could manage.'[64] As much as anything it was the pressure of expectation, that he would start writing again, and his distress at his lack of achievement that had become too much.

From hospital he wrote to Dorothea, desperate that she come down: 'The days without you seem ever so long in passing & ever so short in sum' . . . 'We could make it all official with a visit to the Registrar, if you like. In any case, darling, know that you are my one true & beloved wife; I am sorry I am not a better provider, but it hasn't always been easy.'[65] After two weeks she flew to Dunedin. She was shocked to find him 'looking like a grey ghost again', shaking as he had during his breakdown ten years before.[66] He was discharged into her care, and on 27 August they were married at the Dunedin Registry Office.

He had been in hospital – for the first time in his life – for just over two weeks, but recovery took much longer. 'I am only just crawling round, quite a bit shaken', he wrote to Hone Tuwhare in late September, describing his breakdown as 'a queer kind of crack-up . . . I thought at first I had had a stroke'.[67] He was still taking Amitriptyline and going back three times a week for sessions with Wallace Ironside. Ironside was later to describe Mason as 'an extraordinarily fine man', whose 'complex yet modest and simple personality' had made a deep impression on him.[68] Every weekend his cousin Lorna would take him and Dorothea out to the beach or the bush with her family. In October he wrote to Shirley Barton: 'I am only just picking up where I left off when afflicted with the Mysterious Malady about a couple of months ago.' It had something to do with an inability to assimilate vitamin B, he told her, and quipped, 'Probably couldn't stand the sight of my cooking: don't blame it.' To McGeorge later that month he described it as 'an unexpected attack of "the blues" in a way that I had never had before. . . . I cling to the hope that I will come out of it with fresh creative ability'.[69]

24

Strait is the Gate

1963–65

AS HE SLOWLY regained his equilibrium in the last months of 1962 Mason got down to work, at last, on his Alley biography – or at least he said he was getting down to work on it. Dorothea had been dismayed to discover when she came down that 'he had done practically nothing on it, except muddle up all Rewi's letters to his mother'.[1] How much work he had in fact already done on it, and how much more he would do, is unclear. Eventually, in 1965, he handed the project on to Willis Airey. He had by then a rough 'second working draft' of 55 quarto pages (covering about half the synopsis he had delivered to Hale).[2]

In December he published *China Dances*, a small booklet (printed by John McIndoe) containing his 1943 verse drama *China*, his speech of welcome for the Classical Theatre in 1956, and his poem 'A Hundred Thousand Blessings'. Its preface restated a familiar theme: the publication was intended 'to vindicate the right of poetical method in fields too often lightly abandoned to prose', as a challenge to

> those who insist on judging all forms of expression in verse by principles applicable to poetry intended for printing only and who fail to consider that any such expression may be intended for any other purpose. . . . For my own part, I cannot agree with this, nor, indeed, tolerate those Jeremiahs of poetry who, often with protestations of regret, prophesy a continual narrowing in theme and purpose until ultimately nothing shall be left save a wisp to blow away with the wind. These theorists are no more endearing when they present their opinions under a spurious sociological face of inevitability. On the contrary, I still consider that poetry should break the charmed circle to seek its ancient allies of music, drama and oratory, in such form and with such a theme as may benefit the case.[3]

Alternatively, to the editor of the *People's Voice* he explained that his main purpose in publishing it was 'affirmation of faith in Movement'.[4] He distributed it privately, like the Fairburn booklet, and it was barely noticed, although Winston Rhodes sent him a supportive response ('Of course the lovers of tortuous little ego-verses won't like it, but I don't believe the future is for them') and encouraged him to go on writing in this line.[5] It was what he intended to do.

At the end of August, shortly after he came out of hospital, he had applied for an extension of his Burns Fellowship for a second year (which was allowed for in the regulations), listing his achievements to date: in addition to the lectures, interviews and poetry readings, sorting his papers and superintending the publication of the *Collected Poems*, *China Dances* and the Fairburn talk, he had written several one-act plays, '[f]urthered studies regarding Scottish and New Zealand literature', and commenced work on his Alley biography. This was as far as he got towards making a formal report on his Burns year. His plans for the next were to complete the biography and write some more plays.[6] The application was unsuccessful but by December he had decided to stay on in Dunedin anyway, for a time at least and possibly for good, despite lingering reservations about the climate, and the isolation ('There is always plenty doing here, but one has a peculiar sensation of being in the capital of a separate country', he remarked to Jim Bertram), and Dorothea's mixed feelings.[7] He had been invited to edit and present the monthly *Poetry* programme for radio in 1963, and this would give him at least some regular income after the fellowship ceased – or pocket money, at least: it paid ten guineas after tax per programme. Bertram had been the editor in 1962 and it was perhaps he who suggested that Mason do it next.

Mason and Dorothea spent the summer, and a good part of the following year, living at Broad Bay, ten miles out along the peninsula road, where Charles Brasch had given them the use of his crib. It was a small, one-roomed cottage perched on the cliff edge, facing north-east with a perfectly framed view past Port Chalmers to the harbour heads. In front a steep path led down to the rocky shoreline; behind was a small garden which Mason cultivated, digging in stranded whale-feed and, on one occasion, a dead shark. It was probably here that he wrote the following sad sonnet, entitled 'Encomie' and dated 19 February 1963:

> I cannot see beyond this one clear end:
>   I have glimpsed an inn that holds a moment's light
>   over the swirl of the wild mountain night:
>   and suddenly the hopeless paths all trend

to one straight meaning and your lit doors send
                    direction through the void, give the blind plight
                    of the lost purpose once again the sight
                    of some bright goal towards which all things may tend.

    I do not know if I have even pence
                    towards recompense of cost to you nor heed
                    whether you know the way the paths run thence:
                    I know not if you know where or when they will lead
                    or can foretell it with some wise woman's sense
                    of future from past: I do but know my need.[8]

HE SPENT much of February still tidying up his literary 'remains' for the Hocken.[9] (He had declined an invitation from Margaret Dalziel of the English Department to attend the annual student congress at Curious Cove in the Marlborough Sounds.) At the end of the month he went up to Christchurch, on his own, to take part in a 'festival of poetry' being organised by the Theatre Arts Guild, along with James K. Baxter, Father John Weir from St Bede's College (a future Baxter and Mason scholar), Ruth France and another local poet, Wendy de la Bere. It was held in the Civic Theatre on Friday, 1 March, with a matinee for schoolchildren (1000 of them) and another session in the evening. A 'glorious, hilarious shambles', Mason subsequently described the event to Denis Glover.[10] Only Mason and Baxter made as much impression on the reviewers as the art direction did. Weir was seated centre-stage in a high-backed red armchair, Baxter on a high stool to one side in front of 'a picture painted in heavy lines that were somewhere between a spiral and a scrawl', while '[i]n deep shadow before a curtain on the steps leading to the elevated armchair R.A.K. Mason sat on the stage left', with France and de la Bere at the far left 'under a large flower arrangement'. Weir spoke for forty minutes. Mason, on last, 'crammed into about 10 minutes' some of his early poems and finished with a powerful rendition of 'Sonnet to MacArthur's Eyes'.[11] Winston Rhodes was there and remembered it well: 'Indignation, passion as well as compassion could be heard in every accent of his voice and, in the midst of the tumultuous applause, I had time to reflect that although this was a sonnet, the way in which it had been declaimed gave me an inkling of the kind of agitational but simple rhetoric about which he had been talking years before.'[12] Mason, in a short review of the festival for the New Zealand Monthly Review, neglected to say anything about what anyone had read or said but did remark on the organisers' 'tendency to confuse a reading with a stage show, so that readers got a bit lost amongst the scenery'.[13]

Afterwards he had coffee with a young woman he had met during the preparations for the reading, Jennifer Barrer, a schoolteacher and actor in her early twenties. They felt an instant empathy. 'I think we each saw the good in each other and responded to it', he wrote to her later. 'I think it was the good in you that helped you to see that I was in pain of mind and body and made you offer me at once the chance of a sit down and a cup of coffee and a pleasant chat.'[14] What she saw, in her own words, was his loneliness and 'a slightly broken quality'. After coffee they sat on the banks of the Avon, and 'rather like a ritual' he formally told her that she was his adopted daughter, 'the child he wished he'd had'. She had recently had an abortion (unwillingly) and Mason told her about the abortion Dorothea had had in 1944, feeling that she was too old, or perhaps just not wanting to have another child.[15] She invited him to stay at her parents' house on the Cashmere Hills, and he spent a week there, advising them on planting their several acres of land, listening to Jenny rehearse her roles, and reading her all of his *Collected Poems*. 'I think we understand each other in friendship that is rarely given in this life', he wrote to her a few days after he got back to Dunedin, in the first of some twenty letters he wrote to her over the next year. 'There seems to me to be something between us that is more than either of us apart and for me at least brings a feeling of truth and innocence; strength and kindness.'[16] It was, she would later describe it, 'a genuine true love affair': the love that is friendship.[17] He was devastated when she told him in August that she was moving to Auckland. He had thought about going back to Christchurch to work for several months – he had spied a suitable quiet bach at Governor's Bay, he had told Winston Rhodes in early April – but never did.

There were poems for Jenny. And among the group of lyric poems Mason wrote in Dunedin, the older man and young woman – age, love, death and longing – was a recurring theme. In 'Bags Dog Boat', for example:

> The bags are locked, the labels clear,
> My mind has marshalled all the gear
> And reason reigns and has no fear.
>
> Girl, you are young and I am old.
> Only my heart will not be told
> But cries apart and unconsoled.

It is a shambling dog that's fled
From the feast and lifts its head
To scan the clouds and wail the dead.

My mind is sound, my reason clear.
The boat rocks at the Lethean pier.
My dog and I go aboard, my dear.

And 'Against John Knox':

All the farewells are said,
    and well – save the one I most wished to say,
    but I was betrayed
    by pain that lurked traitor in the way,
    by pain and a tongue
    black and ill–gallows-hung.

The one among all
    most innocent – unless it be sin
    to exist and be small
    and young and lovely and put out a thin
    paw to confide
    in a friend by her side –

I saw in completeness
    in the whole glory and splendid
    strength of her sweetness:
    all I had of sweetness responded,
    but the words came distorted
    like the babe aborted.

Wrong is done, no avail
    saves, for wrong results by definition:
    aye, but 's that the whole tale?
    is there not yet some act of contrition
    to ease the dark burden,
    with glimpsed hope of pardon?[18]

'HAVE BEEN getting steamed up about my "Poetry" broadcasts,' he told Jenny in the third week of March, 'but things now seem reasonably clear. First won't be as good as I wanted, but what the Hell'.[19] The half-hour programme was broadcast at 8 pm on the YA stations every third Wednesday of the month. It was 'designed to appeal to all listeners who have a taste for poetry in its various manifestations, both in New Zealand and overseas', the talks officer in Wellington, Peter Bland, instructed him in January. The content was left largely to the editor's discretion, with the proviso that each programme contain a good proportion of poems. '[W]e look to the editor to impress on the programme something of his own personality'.[20] Bertram's theme in 1962 had been to pair New Zealand poets with 'good but minor' English ones: in his first programme he had featured Mason and the Tudor poet Thomas Wyatt.[21] Mason's theme was to be 'the conflict between the popular and the cloistered'. As he explained to the Dunedin producer, George Blackburn: 'at the risk of over-simplification, I may define policy as that of preferring poetry based on the spoken word to that of the bookish school. More specifically, such policy is in accord with the Scottish tradition as it first found clear form in Dunbar and lives to-day in MacDiarmid. . . . an essential aspect of such a concept is the close connection between poetry, singing, music (and, indeed, other arts).'[22]

In his first programme, which was broadcast on 17 April, Mason announced that his 'general aim' was to 'do something towards drawing closer our poets and our people', before discussing the history of Scottish literature, illustrated with readings of 'The Twa Corbies', Burns's 'It was A' for our Rightful King' and a Gaelic lullaby. Scottish poetry, he observed, was popular both 'in the sense of conforming basically to the lives, arts, aspirations and speech of the people' and in 'being appreciated, even loved, by the people'. Its essential features were its 'simplicity, picturesque imagery symbolising deeper thought beneath, humour, often of a grim variety, dramatisation, easy interplay between the everyday and exalted, the close connection with music and singing'.[23] He might have been talking about his own verse. It is not hard to see the appeal to Mason of the classic Scots, or 'Lallans', literature which flourished briefly in the fifteenth and sixteenth centuries, and reached its peak in the work of William Dunbar, Robert Henryson and Gavin Douglas, Renaissance writers who were educated in Greek and Latin prose and verse but at the same time 'in love with the blunt, carnal and comic quality of popular Scots'.[24] This was not a new interest, although perhaps the intensity of Mason's interest in it was new. He had been reading these writers all his life. 'I like old Dunbar, by

God I do', he had written in his notebook once. 'I like him like I like potato-chips.'[25]

In his second programme he took the American poets Robert Frost (who had died in January 1963) and T.S. Eliot to exemplify in the twentieth century the conflicting tendencies of popular and cloistered, or 'fugitive' (quoting Milton), poetry. Frost wrote 'as he was, a weather-beaten much-experienced farmer, vigorous yet profound, and with a certain dry humour', while Eliot epitomised that kind of poetry that 'tends to become humourless, bookish and unnecessarily obscure'. In June he surveyed 'influences from our poetic heritage', beginning with classical Greek and Latin, then the translations, 'from Bishop Douglas's great version of the Aeneid in the early sixteenth century to Day Lewis's translations of the Eclogues', with 'a very pleasant by-way, medieval Latin poetry', and read 'The Ballad of Sir Patrick Spens'.[26] There were reviews as well, although Bertram had advised him to avoid these as far as possible, good reviewers being as hard to find as good readers. For Allen Curnow's latest book Mason asked Alan Horsman, wanting, as he observed to Bertram, 'someone a bit au-dessus du combat, as Curnow seems to be such a contentious centre in the confounded obscure feuds that seem to rage to-day'.[27]

His relationship with the broadcasting staff from the outset was not easy. Comparing notes with Bertram, he complained of the Dunedin personnel's 'exaggerated fear of Head Office' and 'positive panic on the copyright question'.[28] To Jenny, in June, he described his 'guerilla warfare with a few radio elements . . . They are a bit dazed by my letters at the moment, but still don't actually do anything except teach me the elements of New Zealand poetry.'[29] They were finding him as difficult as he was finding them.

'I am simply soaked in raw Scots poetry tonight', he wrote to Jenny at the beginning of April, after recording his first programme. 'Unsettling stuff, if you have a taste for it.' He went on: 'Funny way Scots writers sometimes manage get inside minds of opposite sex, with all complexities . . . The most shattering, devastating deflation of the male ego ever written was by old Dunbar . . . "Two Married Women and the Widow." Wicked piece of work and all done dead-pan. Fortunately for us men, it is in such broad Scots that it is a specialist's job to decipher.'[30] He was in the midst of writing his own Scottish tale of love and tragedy and devastating deflation of the male ego. He had begun work on a 'short play', which he hoped to finish over Easter. By mid-May he had 'twenty intense pages of typescript', by June 'nearly a thousand lines, all in blank verse and all but five lines in broad Scots'. He was working on it out at Broad Bay, going back into town to prepare his *Poetry* programmes. 'You are not in it,' he told Jenny, 'but your spirit is all through it.'[31]

Strait is the Gate, subtitled 'a Scottish morality', was the major literary product of Mason's time in Dunedin. It was not the poetry people had been expecting.[32] A 'poetic historical drama', it was set in Dunedin and on the Otago goldfields in 1861 and, by the time he had added a prologue and an epilogue, at the gates of heaven 'and half-way down to Hell'.[33] In brief, its story centres on Jean McDonald, 'a half-starved and fiery girl' of seventeen, and the love she declares for a young, fanatical Minister – 'actually a street-preacher . . . about 24, but aged by suffering' (modelled partly on Norman McLeod, the charismatic leader of the Nova Scotian settlement at Waipu in the 1850s). After the Minister spurns Jean, calling her a whore, she agrees to marry the 'flashy young man' her mother favours, but he turns out to be the fool she thought he was, who spends all his money on drink and women, and when she becomes pregnant tells her that they were not properly married at all and that she is, therefore, nothing but a whore. She once again comes to the Minister, who refuses her again, whereupon she throws herself from a cliff to her death. The irony, as Mason points out in his production notes, is that, as Jean knows, it is the Minister's youth and ignorance – his 'first-night fear' – rather than his rigid, bigoted morality that makes him incapable of responding to or even recognising her love, until it is too late. He denies her a Christian burial, then spends three tortured days sitting by her grave. In the epilogue St Peter turns the Minister away from the gates of heaven, whereupon the Minister laughs and tells Peter the joke is on him and he will go and join Jean in hell. Peter then tells the Minister that the joke is really on him because Jean is already in heaven; it is only on her instruction that he finally lets the Minister in.

Needless to say, such a summary does not convey the texture of the play, in which the tragedy is interwoven with rich comic dialogue, particularly between the Minister and the clan, or 'the Five', who recruit him to be the spiritual leader of their goldfields community. They, and other minor characters, represent a type Mason had drawn before, in their 'capacity for dead-pan humour, often of a grim variety, for self-dramatisation, yarn-spinning, leg-pulling and the like', 'a strongly marked New Zealand characteristic to this day', which he sees as a product of the country's Celtic and working-class traditions – they are the ditch-diggers in 'Toilers Triumphant', for example. In Mason's introduction to the play, the Minister is described as 'one variation of a type recurrent in Scottish history. He is Burns, Byron, Stevenson, any

one of those whose contradictions remain conflicts, generating their own hell
as they go along'. In his lengthy production notes, Mason depicts him as 'a
reformed drunkard, a virgin, strong in his appetites . . . predominantly saturnine
in character, grotesque in appearance, but has to encompass every role from
incarnation of evil to voice of God – they include Saint Francis, John Knox,
Baudelaire and business-man'. St Peter, 'bearded, stooping and sardonic',
represents 'All the cranky, contradictory, philosophical, tender, cantankerous
old Scots that ever reached the century'. Before the gates of heaven the Minister
greets him:

> Min: It's gratifying my first taste o' heaven is
>   To find ye've studied the language.
> Peter: Mebbe it's my ain.
> Min: Are ye no' that Peter, who, when in Rome the cock – . . .
> Peter: Many hae tried that cock trick tae blackmail their way.
>   I am weary o' crowing cocks – I could thraw their necks.
>   Peter, Saint, Rock o' Holy Church an' now
>   The Guardian o' Heaven's Gate.
> Min: Then are
>   Ye no' that Peter that once lived by Galilee?
> Peter: Aye, but I might hae come there frae Aberdeen
>   For the Scots, ye ken, are a much-travelled race.

In the play's final, or at least fullest, version there were thirty-two characters.
It was written in 'fairly orthodox blank verse' – the general effect to be 'of
speech sometimes coinciding with, sometimes conflicting with rhythmical
emphasis' – and was to be spoken in 'standard Scots, with a only mild flavour
. . . suitable for English or Scottish audiences'. The aim was 'to preserve the
twang, bite, and above all, the rhythms of Scottish speech'. Its general style
'may be described as a regional type of romantic realism, with symbolistic
overtones', his introductory notes explained. To Jenny he had described both
the language and the play as 'very closely woven, almost in a Maori manner,
with exalted and homely all knitted together to produce results that are tragic
and comic at the same time'.[34]

Undaunted, the university Dramatic Society scheduled a reading for August
and began rehearsals in July. A full production – 'together with other plays by
R.A.K.M.', he hoped[35] – was planned for March the next year.

BY THIS TIME he had decided to stay on in Dunedin. 'Yes, Dunedin for keeps, I think', he wrote to Jean Bartlett at the beginning of June. 'If you have to live in New Zealand – and I made up my mind on that – then one might as well live in a city that retains a high measure of civilisation, even in the University.' He had 'struck a fairly happy vein' with his writing, at last. But the deciding factor was that the university librarian, Jock McEldowney, had created 'a mild part-time position' for him in the library, 'sufficient for needs and not too strenuous'.[36] (In fact, said Dorothea, he didn't like the job and hardly ever went.) Dorothea reluctantly agreed, and they put their Mt Eden house on the market and started looking for something in Dunedin. By early September they had bought a place in Stonelaw Terrace, on the north-eastern ridge of Maori Hill. The house needed alterations and while the work was being done they spent the summer of 1963–64 at Broad Bay, having given up the Drivers Road flat. By now Mason had become a familiar figure at the bay, walking on his own over the peninsula and drinking at the Portobello Hotel, and having to be assisted by the publican on occasions when he went off walking after a session at the hotel. The poet Ruth Dallas, who often looked after the crib for Brasch, remembered Mason there as 'a large, thoughtful, brooding man, quiet, but none the less warm'.[37]

He had been corresponding with Jean Bartlett about the foreword he had written for Hone Tuwhare's first book, *No Ordinary Sun*, which was being published by Blackwood and Janet Paul, for whom Jean was now working as an editor. For the past several years Mason had been reading and commenting on the poems Tuwhare sent him from Mangakino, and had insisted that it was '*quite time* you started to publish' when the Pauls approached Tuwhare, who had demurred. It was Mason who had first told Tuwhare that he should stop trying to write sonnets and express himself freely 'without hedging'; to forget about 'iambuses and dactyls' because 'the most important things a poet needs to know about composition come from the inside'.[38] He discovered writing, Tuwhare later commented, partly to fill the vacuum left in his life when he left the Communist Party after the invasion of Hungary in 1956, while his lifelong love of words, and particularly the language of the Old Testament, had derived from being brought up in five religions, and communism.[39] *No Ordinary Sun* was to be a spectacular début, a literary event of a kind *The Beggar*, in its quieter way, had been too (although no one knew it then). The first print-run of 700 copies would sell out in ten days.[40] Bob Lowry was designing and typesetting it, and it gave him, he told Tuwhare, 'a real thrill . . . such as I have not experienced since setting Mason's *No New*

Thing 30 years ago'.[41] Mason's influence in the poetry was plain, in turns of phrase and word inversions, the look of the poems (the hanging indent and pared-down punctuation), their rhetorical style and muscularity.

In his foreword Mason acclaimed Tuwhare as a worker-poet: 'In these days when so much poetry is clouded with caution, sickness, weak cynicism, it is good to find a man seeing things with the clear vision of one who knows life by work, by hard work with his hands', reassuring that 'the stuff of poetry can still be found in such store, can be given form by the pen of a Maori boilermaker on an outback construction job'. He acclaimed Tuwhare also as a Maori poet, the first one to qualify 'as a poet in English and in the idiom of his own generation, but still drawing his main strength from his own people. Time and again, as one reads a poem, it becomes apparent how, in treating some aspect of present-day life, the inspiration is buoyed and thrust up by the power of tradition, the force of a people organised for life.'[42] What Jean Bartlett and Blackwood Paul objected to was Mason invoking, with reference to his Irish grandfather, the soldier George Kells, the country's 'Celtic debt' that was owed by the pioneers to the Maori who helped and befriended them. 'I never thought to see the day when you'd go all soft and mushy over your bog Irish grandaddie and his Celtic debts (which you are going to pay the Scotch way – through a free foreword)', Jean responded. Not all the pioneers were Celtic, she reminded him. But he would not change it.[43]

Dennis McEldowney recorded in his diary Mason coming around to see him one Sunday morning in July 1963 with a book of poetry (Charles Doyle's) that he wanted him to review for his radio programme: 'I've told him I am not really competent to review poetry, but he disregards this. He had long underpants on but no socks, shakes a little, has suffered from the cold lately but otherwise is delighted with Dunedin, talked mainly of the survival of Scottish clan feuds in New Zealand.'[44] The following week the *Otago Daily Times* ran an article on Mason, who has 'decided to settle in Dunedin and resume the writing of poetry', it reported. *Strait is the Gate* would mark his 'return to serious poetic writing'. It was 'vastly different' from what he had done before, Mason commented, but 'I think the work I am doing now is as good as that of the twenties, because it has a more developed quality of objectivity than before. I have got outside anything of the nature of my own personal experience.'[45] Alongside was printed a poem, 'Song for Dunedin', which, he was careful to stress, was written expressly as a song in the 'old Celtic tradition, with internal rhymes and a muted lilting rhythm', and meant to be set to music:[46]

Soft by a hill that lay all still,
    As I was walking sorely,
I came by a town and I laid me down,
    And she was waking early.

'O, quiet town, in your grey-gold gown,
    In your grey and golden mantle,
The way lies drear and I in fear,
    And your eyes are grey and gentle.

'By night and alone by hill and by stone,
    O, it is ill to wander:
I would lie warm a while between the storm
    And the long night lying yonder:

'My feet they are bruised and my heart ill-used
    And I would rest for a moment.'
'For a year you may rest your head on my breast,
    And a song at the most for payment:

'Lie by me here for all a year
    And I'll cradle you full sweetly:
But if you will stay for a year and a day,
    Then I'll have your heart completely.'

Much of the *Otago Daily Times* article quoted one he had written for the newsletter *University Week*, in which he contended that Dunedin was on the verge of launching a period of 'intensified development' in New Zealand literature comparable to that of the 1930s. While the *Phoenix* group had not constituted a 'literary movement in the sense of close unity along clearly formulated lines', he observed, there had been at that time a feeling of 'friendly co-operation' and 'sense of some common purpose'. Since then, there had been 'isolated achievement in plenty', combined with 'a sort of wistful harking back to the thirties' and 'at times almost a glorification of depression as a factor in causing literary quickening'. But now he thought he saw the 'sharply-marked stirring among younger people' that heralded a new movement, citing the Otago students' annual literary *Review* and recent dramatic revue (with which he had assisted): 'For crisp, clear, hard-hitting creative work there has probably been nothing to touch this in our history'. Mason was not the only one to be impressed by this production – Brasch too, for example, thought it was 'by far the best thing of the sort I've ever seen in this country'[47] – and the establishment of the Burns had undoubtedly contributed to the literary vitality of the city. Still, one has the sense that Mason was generalising his own feeling of a new start into the signs of a renaissance of New Zealand literature as a whole.[48]

He had said these same things in his July radio broadcast, and also in Balclutha, where he had been invited to talk to an adult education class on 18 July and spoke generally about the history of New Zealand verse, having made it clear to the organiser that he did not like to be a critic of fellow poets' work. Writing the following day to Louis Johnson about the trials of editing the *Poetry* programme, he had lamented the partisanship that reigned in New Zealand letters: 'one of my aims is to show that there is an over-riding brotherhood of poetry, regardless of differences, and that this applies to all except those who have put themselves outside the pale'.[49]

James K. Baxter, it seems, was one who was outside the pale. Mason had been hurt by Baxter's trenchantly critical review of Curnow's Penguin anthology in 1961, for Curnow's sake as well as his own. In condemning Curnow's 'intense preoccupation with landscape poetry, time, and the cult of isolation', and the consequent selectivity of the literary–historical landscape he had defined, Baxter had also criticised what he would refer to a few years later as 'the literary canonisation of R.A.K. Mason', with the observation that 'Mason, though he wrote well, has been overrated: his range is very narrow indeed.'[50] Mason was not the only one who felt that Baxter had squandered, or simply failed, his early promise – Curnow was one, Bertram another – and he was contemptuous of Baxter's recent conversion to Catholicism, of course. But there seems to have been a personal element too in Mason's dislike of the younger poet, who was 'apparently going further into crankiness than ever', he remarked to Bertram. Mason was not wholly aloof from the 'clan feuds' that raged in the New Zealand literary world, and he was deeply sensitive to criticism. 'Speaking of Baxter's peculiar habits,' he wrote to Bertram in May 1963, 'I saw a copy of an avant-garde sort of journal called Argo recently' (meaning *Argot*, a little magazine published by students at Victoria University): 'To my utter astonishment, there was a poem of my own modified by Master Baxter & the whole without acknowledgement of any sort.' The poem, 'The Seventh Wound', was a reworking of Mason's 'The Seventh Wound Protests', first published in his *Collected Poems*. It was not a parody, as 'To the Last Hero (RAKM)' was a parody of 'Sonnet of Brotherhood' in Baxter's mischievous 1957 collection *The Iron Breadboard*, but '[w]hat reduced me to mingled annoyance & amusement was that his improvement consisted of giving it some sort of feeble Left-wing slant: I feel that if I want any Left-wing touches introduced, I am quite capable of doing it myself!' Baxter, he would later remark, 'would be lucky to scrape home in the first half dozen' of New Zealand poets.[51]

He also complained about Baxter to Charles Doyle, with whom he was corresponding again about Doyle's critical study. Doyle was now rewriting his monograph for the fourth time, and assured Mason that he had 'curtailed' his biographical observations 'so that they are not markedly different from those in the *Collected Poems*'.[52] In February 1964 he advised Mason that he had been offered a contract by Twayne of New York to write a critical biography for their World Authors series, to which Mason (three months later) happily agreed – while continuing to deny Doyle access to the material he was depositing in the Hocken, which was 'tabu to everyone until I have finished working on it myself, and I can assure you it would not help you'.[53] Doyle warned Mason, though, that he must expect to be written about more and more and that 'there will be a lot more of the Savage and Stead kind of assessment'.[54]

C.K. Stead had published a review of the *Collected Poems* in the July 1963 issue of the quarterly *Comment*, entitled 'R.A.K. Mason's poetry – some random observations'. It was, in fact, a serious and important critical essay, which read closely a handful of the poems while surveying Mason's complete œuvre, and did no damage to his reputation. If Mason was upset by this review, it was perhaps simply by the level of scrutiny and by the essentially speculative nature of such a reading, although Stead was as interested in the way the poems worked as in what they meant, or rather in the extent to which these were the same. That was his point: how the poems 'reconstruct in poetic form . . . primary acts of self-consciousness'. Mason may not have appreciated Stead's contention that he was a poet by nature rather than by nurture, 'a poet without a craft, a poetic medium rather than a maker of poems, a man who has been the victim of poetic occasions and a poet who is victim of the failure of those occasions'. This was, in fact, a recurrent critical theme already: what Stead called the poems' 'natural, urgent lyricism' – combined with sheer surprise that poems that were so good had been written by one who was so young – and the effect this gave of their having been written by compulsion rather than design. From this point, Stead interpreted Mason's 'silence since about 1940' as 'the failure of a gift for which the will could provide no substitute', and saw the later political poems – such as 'Youth at the Dance' and 'Sonnet to MacArthur's Eyes' – as attempts 'to substitute good intentions for poetic occasions' which 'lamentably fail'.[55] This certainly would not have pleased Mason.

Roger Savage, however, simply did not think his poems were very good. Reviewing them in the September 1963 issue of *Landfall*, he found Mason's 'protesting masochism' sincere but immature, and his technique not up to the task of turning his 'biographical reality' into meaningful verse. His work revealed 'a poet who has something pressing to say but is beaten to the post by the dialect in which he has chosen to say it', and 'a man indulging himself, revelling almost, in attitudes and environments which hurt . . . beating his head a shade melodramatically against the walls of the smug, degraded colonial church and society he has been born into'. Then, after *No New Thing*, 'the pessimistic *diable du corps* in him died and he dried up'.[56] This review drew letters of protest from Charles Doyle and from Ian Milner in Prague. 'You owed it to Mr Mason (and, incidentally, to us) to commission a review from a critic long familiar with the poet's work and background', Doyle wrote (Savage was a young English lecturer with a Cambridge degree, recently appointed to Victoria). 'A *Collected Poems* seems an occasion for summing up rather than cutting the poet down.'[57] Frank Sargeson too was angry, writing privately to Bill Pearson, whose novel *Coal Flat* had just been harshly reviewed in *Landfall* as well: 'do these younger people know nothing about the desert such as Mason broke into. And does it not occur to them that the fact of that desert must be taken into account?'[58]

THE SAVAGE review was one of a series of unhappy events in the last months of 1963, on top of an unusually bad winter which saw Mason succumb to the flu in August and a severe cold in September. A reading of *Strait is the Gate* was held at the university's Allen Hall on 18 August during the university arts festival, in which Mason also took part in a series of 'literary gatherings' at the Zodiac Coffee Shop on George Street (to which 'All beatniks, pseudo-intellectuals, itinerant troubadours and C.N.D. supporters' were welcomed[59]). Brasch had been worried – 'Reports about Ron Mason's play gloomy,' he wrote to Bertram a few days before – but Mason was pleased with the reading, and particularly gratified that 'every Scot present seemed to accept the play as a serious study in Scottish affairs'.[60] The 'thing had become a sort of a test-case for my own literary revival', as he told Pip Alley.[61] He set to work revising it, eventually expanding it from three acts and a running time of just under an hour to five acts and two and a quarter hours. But a month later the Dramatic Society decided not to stage it as a major production the next year.

In November his radio programme was abruptly dropped. On the 14th the producer wrote to advise him that it 'has been decided to make November's edition the last one for this year', adding, 'in view of your need for a good rest, you will probably be very glad to be free from this burden' and wishing him 'a speedy return to good health'. The programme was broadcast at 10.30 pm instead of the usual time of 8.[62] His relationship with the 4YA staff had grown increasingly fraught. In June he had sent the producer a four-page letter complaining, among other things, about the way his scripts were being edited:

> One point that especially concerns me is the tendency towards excision of passages of one particular type. These are brief remarks of a mildly jocular nature or containing personal reminiscence or giving a 'news' interest – such passages at the end of a more serious or general one are designed to provide relaxation of tension, ease of transition and confidence among listeners when one is dealing with material where cultivation of a familiar attitude is desirable.

The continuity for the last programme had also been 'a shambles'. In reply the producer reminded Mason that they needed one month's notice to clear copyright for New Zealand poems and two months for overseas material, and asked for clearer information, in plenty of time, about who was reading what.[63] In December he received a polite letter from the supervisor of talks in Wellington, thanking him for having

> done a great deal to make the programme accessible to a wider audience and I am sure many New Zealanders interested in their own country's literary history have been eager to hear the voice and views of one of New Zealand's most important and significant poets. Your endeavour to explain and illustrate the popular movement in poetry, taking the Scottish tradition as your principal examplar, was singularly original and worthwhile.

But it was probably not what they wanted.[64]

On 15 November Mark Firth, the son of Clifton and his second wife, Melva, to whom Mason had been close, died suddenly from a brain haemorrhage. Mason had sent him for his twenty-first birthday four months earlier a copy of Engels's *Origin of the Family, Private Property and the State*. Three weeks later came the suicide of Bob Lowry, after years of struggle with alcoholism and depression.[65]

'RON MASON is going queer', Keith Maslen told Dennis McEldowney in February.[66] Signs of the manic phase in the manic-depressive cycle were apparent in the early months of 1964. One was his deepening obsession with (in John Griffin's words) 'wanting to pass on his genes'.[67] There had been another, real affair in Dunedin, after Dorothea had come down, which ended over Mason's pressure that the woman have his child. Among the poems he wrote in Dunedin was this one:

> Up the hill with the sea-gulls skirling
> > braide our heads & the sea-mists swirling,
> > a flash of blue sky in the lifts between
> > or a glint of the sea's grey or the land's green:
> > and there were only on all the earth
> > my love & I and the child of our birth.
>
> We came to a rock where the path cleft,
> > one way ran right & one ran left,
> > one to the left & one to the right
> > one to the dawn and one to the night.
>
> For a moment we stood together,
> > then she & I turned our ways for ever:
> > each glanced back once where we had been
> > and the little boy never was seen.

Mason also developed a strange obsession, according to Griffin, with the idea of hiring a white horse, which he would ride between Broad Bay and Dunedin, and would give him inspiration. He came to Griffin one day asking if he could have room behind the bookshop for stabling. The Australian writer Henry Lawson, he told Griffin, when he had lived for a time on the east coast of the South Island, had been frequently seen around Kaikoura on a white horse.

Literary and other plans and projects accumulated. He sent to the University of Auckland for his academic record with the idea of enrolling at Otago. In March he went up to Christchurch for two and a half weeks, and discussed with Albion Wright an anthology of New Zealand poetry he had begun working on. Entitled 'We Speak Our Own Words', it was to be 'the first national anthology to be published in New Zealand', the notes he had drafted declared. Full consideration would be given for the first time to literature in languages other than English, namely '[t]he Scots Tongue', along with Welsh, Irish and Gaelic, and Maori, both classical and 'post-European'. The work of women poets would be properly recognised (especially Jessie Mackay), as would 'the role of poetry in making the modern Trade Union and Labour Movement' and the many 'actual worker-poets': 'the generally inculcated idea that New Zealand poetry is primarily a University affair should be subtly made to appear ludicrous'. In concept this was some years ahead of its time. Mason got as far as a typescript of poems selected from the Alexander and Currie and Curnow anthologies, and a list of some forty younger poets for consideration.[68]

In Christchurch he also talked to Pip Alley about the Alley biography. He was now planning to edit a collection of Rewi's poems, while the biography appears to have transmuted into, or been joined by, a play: among his papers is a page headed 'Rewi Alley: A Maker of Modern History. A play in five acts by R.A.K. Mason'. Shirley Barton, meanwhile, was still reassuring Alley that Mason was working on the biography, although they both realised that completing it was more important for Mason than it was for Alley himself. Alley, in fact, had long given up any real expectation that Mason would do it, and had been urging his brother not to put pressure on him: 'Peggy Garland says that he is a disintegrated personality and will never write again', he had written to Pip in 1962. 'I did not agree with her, for Ron has in him the spark of greatness that take[s] flame again if the tinder is right', but perhaps now he had 'disintegrated too far'.[69]

Strait is the Gate, meanwhile, Mason told Jenny Barrer, he had 'set . . . aside a bit to mature'.[70]

He bought some land, with a deposit of £5, in Puketai Street, off Highcliff Road, on the Otago Peninsula: eight mostly gorse-covered acres with a derelict house. The land sloped steeply to the east and was exposed to the coldest winds, but he intended to develop it as a market garden. He had plans to start a publishing company, called 'Otakou Publishers – Printers, Publishers, Booksellers', and an Otago School of Scottish Studies, and was devising a new radio programme. 'He tried to found some sort of Trust which I never could understand,' Dorothea recalled, 'went in and out by taxi to Dunedin, day and night' and 'became altogether irresponsible'. At night he built huge fires in the garden at Broad Bay, only metres from the crib.[71]

In May 1964 he and Dorothea finally moved into their house in Stonelaw Terrace. The next day Mason admitted himself to Dunedin Hospital. The 'little shaggy savages', the 'small insane men', were back.

He was in hospital for at least two months this time, under the care once again of Wallace Ironside. Writing to Melva Firth on 13 July, 'the first [day] that I have managed to write for some months', he described the symptoms he by now knew so well: 'It began as a period of uncontrollable elation, cut short by a plunge into depression so bad that I have not wanted to see anyone but Dorothea. . . . They have all sorts of new drugs & methods of treatment, but so far I have not responded very well. Time assumes a strange quality under these circumstances – infinitely long in passing, unnaturally short in retrospect.'[72] To Jenny he wrote the following day of a 'massive depression' that had been 'building up and held me back from any sensible activity'.[73]

After he was discharged they stayed on in Dunedin for some months more, with Mason seeing Ironside weekly, and then fortnightly. Charles Brasch saw him in late September looking 'decidedly better', but 'pretty dejected' still.[74] Brasch had also spoken to Ironside, and Ironside, 'a gentle sympathetic man who seemed pained for him', told Brasch that Mason's heart condition would only get worse and that his manic-depressive states would continue. He thought that Mason would have benefited from electric shock treatment, but Mason had been too afraid to agree to it. Ironside 'does not think he will write any more – or write anything good; but I wonder how he can be so sure', Brasch wrote in his journal. 'How will Ron endure to live, knowing his one talent gone? It frightens me.'[75]

When they were finally able to sell the Stonelaw Terrace house, Mason and Dorothea went back to Auckland. They were not able to dispose of the Puketai Street property for several years.

25

Bags dog boat

1965–71

THEY RETURNED to Auckland towards the end of May 1965, and moved back into Dorothea's old house in Tennyson Avenue, Takapuna, which her son Austin had bought in 1950 (after they moved to Torbay) and now rented back to them. For the next few months Mason did little except play patience for hour after hour. Bill Pearson found him 'rather subdued and stouter than he had been'.[1]

He had seen a naturopath friend of Dorothea's and was 'a lot better for it – and a lot thinner', she reported to Brasch in September.[2] Brasch received 'such a cheerful letter' from him in November, he told Sargeson: 'a great change this; marvellously encouraging'.[3] But Mason continued to struggle with his health, both physical and mental, in his remaining years. The letter of referral he brought from Dunedin recorded that he had suffered from coronary disease and angina for the last twelve years, had arrhythmia, and had been under treatment for depression. His new GP, Charles Howden, found him to be 'a pleasant but generally depressed personality', who was overweight and persisted in smoking heavily against advice. Haemorrhoids also continued to trouble him, until he had a second operation in 1967.[4]

Mason did not see Glover when he was in Auckland for a few days at the end of the year: 'just could not manage it', he apologised, while Glover apologised that he did not know Mason's address. But it is also possible that Mason was avoiding Glover, who had been pursuing him about the 'wodge of letters from Rex' he believed Mason had in his possession.[5] Glover was planning to a publish an edition of Fairburn's letters and had been collecting them for the previous few years. The ones Mason had indeed kept – over thirty of them – were among the material he was depositing in the Hocken Library, but Glover suspected that there was something else behind his reluctance to give them up. 'It wld be unfair to withhold them on private or "sacred" grounds', he told Mason when he had first approached him in February 1964; and he need not worry about them being published immediately, Glover assured him: 'The general editing may well take years while we await more timely deaths.' But what his objections, if any, were, Mason did not say. When Glover finally sent Harold Innes around to Tennyson Avenue in July 1966 to collect him along with the letters for 'instant copying', Mason sent Innes away.[6]

The North Shore by this time was a different place from the one Mason knew. Since the Auckland Harbour Bridge had opened in 1959 the population of the Shore and the East Coast Bays, once a ragged stretch of baches and ti-tree, had burgeoned. He felt more isolated there without a car, Mason complained to Pearson, than he had in the days when everyone relied on the bus and ferries: 'I never cease to curse the people who built that Bridge without a footway.' And he missed 'the pleasant up-country walks that I can no longer indulge in', although this was a consequence of his poor health rather than the proliferation of the despised motor car.[7] One consolation was being just around the corner from Frank Sargeson, who had even more reason to be aggrieved about the bridge that had turned quiet Esmonde Road into a commuter thoroughfare, along which 'cars stream by like a chain-belt of sausages with ersatz stuffing'.[8] They became good friends at this time. They talked about literature, with Sargeson frequently seeking Mason's advice on matters of classical scholarship – asking him to identify or translate passages of Latin – and gaining a deep respect for Mason's erudition in a field in which his own was, he regretted, woefully lacking.

STRAIT is the Gate also found a champion in Sargeson. He had heard that Mason's play had been dismissed in Dunedin and Christchurch as 'no good theatrically, and old hat poetry into the bargain', but he disagreed, and sent it at the beginning of March 1966 to the Auckland University Drama Society. Two months later he was trying to get back the two copies of the script he had given them, which had been 'booted round the common rooms and ridiculed' by students who had no idea what to do with blank verse – an experience which only reinforced Sargeson's already well-developed antipathy towards the academy.[9] Instead he decided to do it himself, as a production of the New Independent Theatre which he had set up in 1962 with Christopher Cathcart and the artist Colin McCahon. It would be their first production in three years.

A production of Sargeson's own historical drama dealing with sex, religion and guilt – A Time for Sowing, based on the life of the disgraced Anglican missionary Thomas Kendall – had been the catalyst for the establishment of the New Independent Theatre, with which Sargeson hoped to support the development of 'theatre with life in it which will be closely connected with the particulars of New Zealand experience' (a statement of aim strikingly similar to that of the People's Theatre).[10] He had met Cathcart, a 'little nuggety Scot' who had been involved in amateur theatre in Scotland before coming out to New Zealand, where he had trained as a meat inspector,[11] at the first reading of his play. The first production of the New Independent Theatre, in June 1962, was Sargeson's *The Cradle and the Egg*, but it was not a critical success. Subsequent productions were even less so, and the company went into recess when Cathcart returned to Britain at the end of 1963, with an Arts Council bursary to study directing. By this time he was back, and *Strait is the Gate* presented an opportunity to revive the New Independent Theatre.

Even getting the play started, Sargeson found, was 'like one of the labours of Herakles'.[12] They were preparing to put it on in November and issued a press release in July, hoping to raise some of the cost of the production through subscription. The themes of the play, the press release stated, were as universal as those of Mason's poetry: the 'long uncertain voyage or journey from lands distant from one's own' which had 'been told ever since story-telling began', 'the tormented love of a girl for a man . . . and the equally tormented love of that man for the God he desperately endeavours to serve'. The production 'may depend for its success as much upon good Scottish voices as an ability to act', Sargeson added.[13] At Mason's suggestion they got in touch with the Auckland Burns Association, with which he had re-established contact, although it was to go into recess itself in 1967. Auditions were held and rehearsals began in July. Jennifer Barrer was cast as Jean. 'Thank heaven Mason's play will be done', Brasch wrote to Sargeson. 'He wrote quite cheerfully not long ago, before he knew; this should give him fresh hope.'[14] But it was not done. The difficulties of assembling a large cast of amateur actors who could deliver blank verse in convincing Scottish accents proved too great. And perhaps this was not the only reason. Dorothea, for one, was worried about the effect a negative critical reception would have on Mason's state of mind.

He was prescribed the new anti-depressant drug Allegron in May and again in August that year. When his doctor next saw him in November he was exasperated to find that Mason had stopped taking it because he felt it made him more depressed, and that he was still smoking twenty-five cigarettes a day. 'Difficult to make any progress with this man', he recorded.[15]

Having abandoned a stage production of *Strait is the Gate* for the moment, Sargeson then tried the New Zealand Broadcasting Corporation (with whom he was negotiating for the broadcast of his own two plays), with more success.

'Mason, I may say,' he told W.G. Austin, the chief producer, after describing the merits of the play, 'is in very poor shape, ill and very depressed, and almost any kind of break would be an excellent tonic for him. Whatever happens, we are hoping to produce the play ourselves eventually.' Sargeson was hardly surprised that it was turned down, for the same reason that everyone else had dismissed it, he disdainfully suspected: 'the play isn't the fashionable sort of thing being looked for, therefore'. 'Our reason for approaching you', he went on, 'was that we felt the play needed a rest from being shoved around talked about and mainly spat upon. We thought it could work out splendidly for sound radio, and this would help to break down opposition and enable us to start [from] scratch instead of wearing out our energies knocking back the prejudices.'[16] Austin protested that the script presented 'a great number of difficulties' for radio, including its very large number of characters, the Scottish accents and a lack of dramatic focus, and suggested that in view of Mason's fragile state of health they would be better to wait for a stage performance first, 'when the worries from that point of view could be ironed out', than for him to 'have to digress into radio problems' now. After being persuaded to read the play himself more closely, however, Austin changed his mind, coming to appreciate, with Sargeson, Mason's 'strong, tangy writing' and the play's 'granite quality' (which he compared to Arthur Miller's *The Crucible*).[17] In November the Broadcasting Corporation purchased the script from Sargeson (representing the New Independent Theatre) as agent for Mason. Over the first half of 1967 Mason revised it in consultation with an NZBC scriptwriter, reducing the number of characters from thirty-two to sixteen to focus the action more closely on the Minister and Jean, and its running time to about an hour. But he refused to remove the prologue and epilogue, which were essential for their liveliness and to 'the "Scottish" flavour of the play', as Sargeson endeavoured to explain: 'St Peter is no Anglican, a Scottish Presbyterian. Points too fine, perhaps.'[18]

The play was recorded in October and November at the Broadcasting Corporation's Christchurch studio, because there were 'more acceptable Scots radio performers' down there.[19] It was broadcast on the YC stations on the evening of 6 January 1968. Mason and Dorothea were holidaying in Coromandel at the time and heard it only indistinctly on a transistor radio. But Mason was extremely pleased with the result: 'a grand job', he told Austin, especially the most difficult part of the Minister whose 'whole interplay of toughness & gentleness came out splendidly'.[20]

MASON RECEIVED $98 less tax for the broadcast rights to *Strait is the Gate*, and reimbursed Sargeson most of the £70 the New Independent Theatre had spent on their aborted production. He could hardly afford to do so. His financial circumstances were difficult. He was living on the social security age benefit, which Wallace Ironside had arranged for him to start receiving a few months before he became eligible in January 1965, along with Dorothea's, supplemented for a time from 1968 by a part-time job teaching Latin at St Anne's, a private girls' school in Takapuna, and his very small earnings from his writing. In addition to royalties on the *Collected Poems* there were occasional paltry payments for rights to broadcast or anthologise poems. Penguin, for example, had paid (to Curnow's embarrassment) only five guineas for the sixteen poems included in the 1960 anthology; he had received ten guineas for the broadcasting rights to the six poems Bertram had used on his *Poetry* programme in March 1962. More generously, the Australian Broadcasting Corporation paid fourteen guineas for the six poems Anton Vogt used the same year in one of a series of profiles of New Zealand writers entitled 'The Poet's Tongue', in which he presented the author of *The Beggar* as 'a gloomy, morose, bitter young man – an "angry young" man, a generation before it became fashionable'.[21] A commission to write a song for the Girl Guides' Association (based on a medieval Nordic poem), forwarded to Mason by Albion Wright in 1964, presumably paid something, although there is no record of how much. He answered regular requests by this time for poems to be included in overseas anthologies – 'On the Swag' was the most popular – usually for the fee of a guinea a poem.[22]

They sometimes appeared in unlikely places: his early 'Sonnets of the Ocean's Base' in the newsletter of the Auckland University Underwater Club, for example – as 'remarkable examples of truly submarine literature', the secretary wrote to Mason.[23] In 1962 Alfred Katz, his fellow romantic revolutionary and troubled young man from *Phoenix* days, wrote to him from California, where he was now an associate professor of social welfare in medicine at UCLA, to ask if he could use 'Sonnet of Brotherhood' as 'a kind of thematic frontispiece' for a book he was editing on public health.[24]

Still suffering from angina, still smoking, 'and has the same chronic slightly depressed personality', his doctor recorded at the end of March 1968. Mason's refusal to follow dietary instructions was also giving cause for concern: his weight had risen from twelve stone nine pounds in August 1967 to over fourteen stone in June 1968. '[M]anic phase entered recently', Howden recorded in November.

At the beginning of 1969 Mason threw himself, with classically manic energy, into the organisation of a six-week literature course for the North Shore branch of the WEA. It had been 'jacked up', Sargeson told Brasch, to provide Mason with 'a little monetary help'.[25] Mason had the six lectures planned, with Sargeson and Tuwhare lined up as speakers and plans to invite Curnow and C.K. Stead as well, by the end of January. The course would be run 'along ordinary democratic WEA lines, with opportunity for question and discussion along the lines of a Trade Union meeting', he told Peter Purdue of the Carpenters' Union. The subject, 'Some Aspects of New Zealand Literature',

> may seem a bit remote from working-class matters, but I hope that my name will be a guarantee at least to some (including yourself) that the subject will, with assistance, be tackled in good radical, proletarian, marxian fashion. The assistance I mean is partly the support of the members, who must be taken into account, and it would certainly help me no end to have half a dozen chippies, experienced in struggle, ready at hand to help me on such subjects as literature & the depression.

Representative university, Maori and trade union speakers would participate, an advertisement for the course in the local paper announced. The general tone would be 'vigorous, clear-cut and democratic, in line with the nature of the people'.[26]

At the beginning of February he 'seem[ed] to be well', Howden noted, although his weight had gone up to fourteen and a half stone. In early March he appeared 'slightly restless'.

The course, which was held at the Takapuna Public Library, began on 20 March. Seventy people came to the first evening, when Mason gave an introductory talk about New Zealand literature and the importance of the 1930s. The second session featured the poetry of Fairburn, with a panel discussion between Mason, Sargeson, Clifton Firth and John Graham (a playwright and close friend of Sargeson's), chaired by Alistair Paterson (a poet and naval officer at the Devonport Naval Base). For the third Sargeson spoke on the short story. The fourth, on 10 April, may have been the one Tuwhare was supposed to speak at but he stopped at the pub on the way there and never showed up. The next meeting was devoted to theatre, and the final one on 24 April to publishing, with Janet Paul. By this time Mason was planning a second term to run from July to September, with a theatre workshop and a literature class – thirty people had expressed an interest in each – and had produced two issues of the *North Shore Seminar*, 'A Journal Devoted to the Arts and Sciences'. The first, 'Souvenir Edition' on six cyclostyled pages, issued on 27 March, included an article by Mason on the literary tradition of the North Shore, beginning with D'Arcy Cresswell, Robin Hyde and the Castor Bay bach in the 1930s, and a profile of Bill Pearson as the first of a regular column on 'Who's who in New Zealand literature'. Volume 1, Number 2 (17 April) featured Tuwhare and had a review of Denis Glover's latest book *Sharp Edge Up*, as well as course news. On 23 April Seminar Publications Ltd was registered as a limited liability company, with Mason as the director and a capital of $2000. He had leased a room in a Takapuna office and opened a bank account, unbeknown to Dorothea, asked the sculptor Anthony Stones to design a cover and ordered a print-run of several hundred copies for the next issue, which he never completed – 'without any backing or capital . . . no advertisements, no accountants and writing the whole thing himself'.[27] Then the bills came in.

In May he was 'back to the depressive phase', Howden recorded. On 5 June he was admitted as a voluntary patient to Oakley psychiatric hospital. He made 'a good recovery in less than a month', treated with anti-depressants and tranquillisers.[28] But once he was back home he 'just vegetated'.[29] Howden found him 'deeply depressed' again in July. 'Had a Hell of a winter, ending in hospital', Mason wrote to a friend at the end of the year. 'Everything I tried to do just blew up in my face & I gave up until I could get my strength back.'[30]

IN FEBRUARY Dorothea told Howden that he was going 'manic again'. He was writing another play – possibly 'Montrose was a Graham', for which fragments of a script in shaky handwriting survive among his papers, another Scottish play set in Dunedin but 'neat and trim', not 'rambling and shambling' like *Strait is the Gate*.[31] He had also resumed work on his history of the New Zealand Company. Later, however, Dorothea would find no trace among his papers of all the work he had apparently done on this project other than the notes he had taken in the 1930s.

For a study he had the use once more of his much-loved army hut from Crown Hill. When Mason sold the Crown Hill house after Jessie died, Willis Airey had bought the hut and moved it to his own new section at Brown's Bay, and had it re-roofed, repainted and reglazed. Then, after Airey's death, since his widow had moved away, it was dismantled once again and re-erected

in the back garden at Tennyson Avenue. From further back in the past he also
recovered at the beginning of 1970 a small stash of *Beggars*: eleven copies that
had 'turned up among the effects of a deceased relative'.³² These were the
ones that, according to family legend, had been rescued from incineration in
the washhouse copper. He wrote to Christchurch bookseller John Summers
and John Griffin in February offering five of them for sale, at $20 each on
receipt and the rest on the usual trade terms:

> Remember, these are genuinely unissued, a continuation of the first edition
> of 1924, signed and dated . . . author's signature, the word Takapuna and the
> actual date of signature, after nearly half a century . . . what a literary find
> . . . the man that gets the reputation of founding modern New Zealand
> poetry, literature even . . . mentioned in all the official works . . . international
> reputation . . . the Beggar, mind you . . . itself a legend [. . .] You have only
> to whisper it round a small circle of literati (or would-be-ones), scholars,
> genuine collectors, speculators posing as genuine collectors, wealthy dilettanti
> and the rest, in order to inflame their passions – possessiveness, intellectual
> snobbishness, cupidity &c. &c. Think how that, done with all dignity and
> discretion, could inflame the lusts of minds already fairly well inflamed by
> alcohol . . .

He was hoping to 'capitalise on five and wait for a rise on the others'.³³
Summers offered to take one for $6, while Griffin regretted that 'the BEGGAR
is probably totally out of my class'. Mason sold one to another bookseller a
few months later for $50, having taken Griffin's advice on its likely market
price and that he would be better off selling them 'one at a time with patience
and cunning'.³⁴

He told Griffin that he hoped 'to start publishing some material inside six
months'. Albion Wright was considering doing *Strait is the Gate* – which
Mason then retitled 'More Joy in Heaven': 'This seems to me to reflect better
the basic theme of compassion'³⁵ – possibly in conjunction with a Scottish
publisher. Through the agency of Jean Ann Andersen, an editor for Blackwood
and Janet Paul, it had been sent to the newly established South Side Press in
Edinburgh. It had also been sent to Sydney Goodsir Smith, the New Zealand-
born poet, critic and leading figure in the twentieth-century revival of literature
in Scots, whose eventual response, however, was not as enthusiastic as they
had hoped: he thought the play dramatically and poetically convincing but
was critical of the Scots. Wright told Mason that he would need Literary

Fund assistance. Mason replied that he should have a script ready for him by Christmas.

Meanwhile, Sargeson had been making his own efforts to get the play into print, if not onto the stage (for the abandoned 1966 production had after all proved to be the last gasp of the New Independent Theatre). He had approached John Weir in August 1968 about the possibility of the Christchurch literary magazine *Frontiers*, of which Weir was the poetry editor, devoting an issue to it. The antipathy of the theatrical community to the play, Sargeson remarked to Weir, was typical of the 'illiteracy' of theatre people and, he suspected, 'all tied up with the current provincial notion that value is to be found in our time and our experience and nowhere else. . . . I am of course much concerned with Mason's personal troubles,' he added, 'but let that be irrelevant to what I suggest.'[36] The magazine declined the offer.

Mason was himself in correspondence with Weir about a 'Poetry for Schools' series of short monographs that Weir had begun planning in 1967, and Caxton and Pegasus were intending to publish. The volume on Mason was to be the first in the series and Weir had made a selection of twenty-five poems. Mason asked him to replace 'Body of John', which 'I do not like', with 'O Fons Bandusiae', which had 'a rhythm and gaiety . . . which should help to lighten the book', and to find room for 'Ad Miram' and 'Song for Dunedin', which had 'something of the narrative ballad quality that appeals to young people, quite naturally. I would gladly sacrifice some of the earlier stuff for them'. He declared that the 'whole thing must end with Song for Dunedin, otherwise it will end on a sour note'.[37] Mason missed Dunedin, and his simple poetic tribute to the city was a poem he was especially fond of, although he had to write to the *Otago Daily Times* for a copy of it when he could not find it among his papers. In August 1970 he wrote to John McIndoe (on Douglas Lilburn's advice) about publishing the score that had been written for the poem by a Takapuna neighbour and music teacher, Susan Rhind. He suggested an edition of 250 or 300: 'My stuff always tends to sell well – poetry, that is – and Dunedin is very loyal.'[38]

Mason was gratified by a growing interest from composers in his poems and their awareness of an affinity between poetry and music that had for long been of such importance to him. Later that year Peter Platt, the professor of music at Otago, approached him for permission to write an orchestral song cycle based on *No New Thing*. They had discussed the general question of verse and music when Mason was in Dunedin. 'Pleased to find that at last I am beginning to understand what the Hell I want to say in regard to music and poetry', he had written to Platt in 1963. 'Your remark on instrumental difficulty of expressing both aspects of Heine and Housman just hit the point.'[39]

In the middle of 1970 Mason applied for the recently established Katherine Mansfield Memorial Fellowship, based in Menton, and in October for the Literary Fund's annual Scholarship in Letters, listing as his projects: poetry, revision and production of *Strait is the Gate*, an edition of the journal of Thomas Shepherd (a member of the first New Zealand Company expedition of 1826) and a history of the New Zealand Company, and work on his papers for the Hocken Library 'with the further aim of writing an autobiography'.[40] The same month he ordered copies of A.H. McLintock's *History of Otago: the origins and growth of a New Zealand Company settlement* (1949) and Michael Turnbull's *The New Zealand Bubble: the Wakefield theory in practice* (1959). When he consulted the professor of history at Auckland University, Keith Sinclair, about his New Zealand Company project, Sinclair was surprised at how out of date with the literature Mason was. He also approached Sydney Musgrove in the English Department about the possibility of a research grant, but was told that these were available only to staff.

None of these proposals came to fruition.

WHEN Bill Pearson returned to Auckland at the end of 1970, after three years at the Australian National University in Canberra, he found Mason 'grossly fat, short of breath, smoking heavily, his trousers fastened only by the top button'.[41] After a much longer interval away, Ian Milner met Mason again in the new year for the first time since 1932, having come back from Prague to spend a year as a visiting professor at the University of Otago. 'He'd put on weight, the face was fuller but with a wax-like pallor. His tempo of being seemed slowed down – not from age alone. But the root elements of mind and spirit, while mellowed, were little changed.' When Milner asked him about China he talked animatedly.[42] His weight had gone up to over sixteen stone by this time. Never a good sleeper, he was getting up throughout the night to make himself cup after cup of milky coffee, going through three quarts of milk a day. Sargeson later told of walking on Takapuna beach one day around this time with Mason and a friend who chastised Mason for neglecting his health. You should remember, she told him, that our bodies are the temples of God – to which Mason, after several minutes' silence and pausing to catch his breath, replied, 'I think the bats have got into my temple.'[43]

The winter of 1970 had been hard. 'Unsuspected bronchitis and a coughing fit led me to go out and crack my skull on the kitchen floor. . . . The doctor has put an absolute ban on smoking. It's Hell' – harder evidently than he had found having to give up drinking. He wrote to another friend in May 1971, after apologising for not having replied to a Christmas letter, that they had had 'a bad spell of sickness last year and things got disrupted. Now I know what time does. It lurks behind a big artichoke and suddenly jumps out and hits me on the head when I am not expecting it.'[44] Yet these years after Oakley were, in Dorothea's memory, 'a calm, peaceful time. I think Ron was happy in a quiet way, or as happy as with his temperament he could be.'[45]

Sargeson was a regular visitor, usually one evening a week. And he took it upon himself to try to get something done about Mason's financial situation, in the form of a special pension. He raised the matter first with the Minister of Internal Affairs at the end of 1970, when writing to complain about recent decisions by the Literary Fund advisory committee, and was told that there were special benefits for which Mason could apply. 'I imagine Mr R.A.K. Mason would know about his chances of supplementary social security assistance', Sargeson replied tartly. 'I was intending to stress the constrictions suffered by a very distinguished New Zealander in his time of poor health and old age', who was 'suffering a heart complaint, lacks even the simple amenity of a telephone, and continues to write without a good many of the working materials which add up to a basic minimum for any serious writer' (and, he did not say to the minister, was 'a little uncertain in his wits').[46] Mason had given up his part-time teaching job by this time, and his only regular income apart from his age benefit was royalties. His bank balance in November 1970 was $15.18. Albion Wright was happy to send him an advance of $20 on his royalties when he asked for one (from 'Saint Albion the Blessed') in March 1970, November and again in March 1971. Sargeson also wrote to George Gair, MP for North Shore (and parliamentary under-secretary) and Labour MP Eddie Isbey, noting the 'dazzling honour' (an Order of Merit) recently conferred on the historian J.C. Beaglehole by the Queen. By comparison, a 'salvaging gesture by the New Zealand Government' to rescue Mason from his poverty seemed not too much to ask, as he 'is distinguished for his poetry no less worthily than is Dr J.C. Beaglehole for his scholarship'.[47]

Meanwhile, in Wellington James Bertram and Ian Gordon, professor of English at Victoria University and chairman of the Literary Fund advisory committee, were doing their bit. Formal proposals were before the government early in 1971 for special annuities for both Mason and Janet Frame, whose case Charles Brasch had been advancing for several years. In April Gordon was advised that the Frame case would shortly go before Cabinet but that

Mason's could not be dealt with until they had received financial details from him. Mason sent these to Bertram in May, belatedly and apologising 'I am a poor man at figures and slow'.[48]

Sargeson was, perhaps, the more acutely aware of Mason's precarious financial position because of the contrast with his own. He had never been well off, nor needed to be; but he had received a special literary pension for nearly twenty years, arranged for him (and only him) by the literary-minded under-secretary for Internal Affairs, Joe Heenan, in the 1940s. Similarly, he must have thought about the contrast in their writing lives. For Sargeson since the mid-1960s had been enjoying a late literary florescence after many fallow years, while Mason's last years were clouded by disappointment and sadness, by a sense of failure. Mason deeply regretted not having been able to – or not having taken his opportunity to? – pursue a career in classical scholarship. Teaching elementary Latin to the students at Holl's or the girls at St Anne's was hardly satisfying. And for all the plans, and the sudden bursts of creative energy, and however much he wanted to, he was not writing.

At the beginning of 1971 he obtained entry forms for the New Zealand Theatre Federation Rothman Play of the Year award and the Ngaio Marsh Television Playwriting Competition. He wrote in April to Cecil Hall, brother of Kathleen Hall, the New Zealand Anglican missionary to China who had died in April 1970 and whom he had known through the China Society. He was planning to write a short biography of her, he told Cecil, and would like to talk to him about her early years. He would be coming down to Hamilton in about ten days' time, and would book into a boarding house or motel.[49] Later that month a composer, Bruno Nicholls, wrote to him from Piha, suggesting that he adapt 'More Joy in Heaven' (*Strait is the Gate*) to an opera. Mason replied that he would be pleased to collaborate with him, but just then he was busy preparing the script for a straight drama production; it appears that Mercury Theatre were considering it.[50] In May, after consulting Bill Pearson, he inquired about a research fellowship at the School of Pacific Studies at the Australian National University. Among his papers remain a manuscript draft in his shaky handwriting of the announcement of the formation of a publishing company by Mason and Janet Paul, specialising in books and pamphlets concerning New Zealand, Australia and the Pacific Islands, and a mocked-up title page for 'Pacific: a quarterly devoted to Pacific Affairs (ed. R.A.K. Mason)'. These may date from these last few years, or perhaps from an earlier period of manic activity, from 1964 in Dunedin.

In March Albion Wright wrote to tell him that the Pegasus Press was

planning a third edition of the *Collected Poems*, to come out that year (the
second having sold out in September 1970). Mason would receive an advance
copy at the beginning of July. Another welcome boost to his income as well
as morale came in April when he was asked to contribute to *New Zealand's
Heritage*, a popular encyclopedia being published in weekly instalments by
Hamlyns. He nominated his special interest as the period before 1870 and in
particular the New Zealand Company – 'In fact, I am undertaking a history
of the Company, on a five year basis', he told the editor-in-chief, Ray Knox
– and was commissioned to write a 3000-word profile of Edward Gibbon
Wakefield (at the rate of $25 per 1000 words).[51] He submitted the article,
entitled 'The Grand Plans of Edward Gibbon Wakefield', in June. But he
would not see it in print. A few weeks later he wrote to Knox about his plans
to expand his research into 'a history of New Zealand culture, showing the
influence not only of English but also of Scottish (both Gaelic and Lallands),
Maori and minor streams, such as Irish, Welsh, French, Yugoslav, Jewish and
even Chinese. It is a big subject and has never been properly done.'[52] He
applied for the Katherine Mansfield fellowship again. And was waiting
hopefully to hear about the annuity.

On 13 July an official in the Internal Affairs Department telephoned Bertram
with the news that the Cabinet had approved the payment of a special annuity
for Mason.[53] But it had come too late. Mason died at 5 o'clock that morning.
He had been returning to bed when he collapsed from a heart attack – 'and I
knew', said Dorothea, 'he looked different at once'.[54]

MASON'S funeral service was held two days later at the Maclaurin Chapel
at Auckland University – chosen by Dorothea, remembering Willis Airey's
funeral held there three years before. Two hundred and fifty people came.
Allen Curnow spoke and poems were read by C.K. Stead. Many of Mason's
trade union, Party and China Society friends, Pearson recalled, were
uncomfortable in the academic setting and felt excluded from the service,
while Frank Sargeson expostulated privately about the university's gall in
paying tribute to Mason then when they had treated him so shabbily over his
play.[55] Even in death, it seemed, poetry and politics would not easily mix.

26

Exegi monumentum

THE QUESTION of a permanent public memorial to Mason was being talked about before the end of 1971. A campaign was under way, with Allen Curnow publicly lambasting the Auckland City Council for its reluctance to properly recognise the 'first among New Zealand poets'. His own idea was for 'a simple stone pedestal with a bronze plaque in Albert Park'.[1] Four years later a totara tree was planted outside the new city library. This had been Colin McCahon's suggestion. Mason had often enough expressed a cynicism about the setting-up of monuments 'in crumbling stone, or perdurable bronze', although he had also always had an acute awareness of posterity, of the fate of that 'old neglected Masonic book in some quiet slumbering library': a kind of self-consciousness to contradict his humbleness. When he was introduced at the inaugural meeting of the Victoria University Literary Society in 1957, and the speaker (probably Jim Bertram) remarked that if New Zealand was a civilised country there would be statues of Ron Mason in the parks, he stood and flicked an imaginary spot from his sports jacket while replying with a grin, 'When you talk of statues, it makes me think of seagulls.'[2] But one imagines that he would have been pleased by the planting of a tree.

There were several poetic tributes, too. Bertram's four lines, headed with an epigraph from Juvenal ('Probitas laudatur et alget': honesty is praised and left to starve) expressed the feeling among Mason's literary peers at the time of his death that he had been shamefully neglected by the establishment in his last years:

> Deprived of heaven but sure enough of hell
> You kept your nerve and kept your loyalties,
> Your verse rang out like strokes on a bronze bell –
> They praised the tone, and let the poet freeze.[3]

It is Hone Tuwhare's more personal elegy, though, that represents Mason's enduring literary influence, and the cross-currents of his life:

> Time has pulled up a chair, dashed
> a stinging litre from a jug of wine.
> My memory is a sluggard.
>
> I reject your death, but can't dismiss it.
> For it was never an occasion for woman
> sobs and keenings: your stoic-heart
>
> would not permit it. And that calcium-covered
> pump had become a sudden road-block bringing
> heavy traffic to a tearing halt.
>
> Your granite-words remain.
> Austere fare, but nonetheless adequate for the
> honest sustenance they give.
>
> And for myself, a challenge.
> A preoccupation now more intensely felt, to tilt
> a broken *taiaha* inexpertly
>
> to my old lady, *Hine-nui-te-Po*, bless the old
> bitch: shrewd guardian of that infrequent *duende*
> that you and Lorca knew about, playing hard-to-get.
>
> Easy for you now, man. You've joined your literary
> ancestors, whilst I have problems still in finding
> mine, lost somewhere
>
> in the confusing swirl, now thick now thin,
> Victoriana-Missionary fog hiding legalized land-rape
> and gentlemen thugs. Never mind, you've taught me
>
> confidence and ease in dredging for my own bedraggled
> myths, and you bet: weighing the China experience
> yours and mine. They balance.

Your suit has not the right cut for me except around
the gut. I'll keep the jacket though: dry-cleaned
it'll absorb new armpit sweat.

Ad Dorotheum: She and I together found the poem
you'd left for her behind the photograph.

> *Lest you be a dead man's*
> > *slave*
> *Place a branch upon the*
> > *grave*
> *Nor allow your term of*
> > *grief*
> *To pass the fall of its*
> > *last leaf*

'Bloody Ron, making up to me,' she said, quickly:
too quickly.

But Time impatient, creaks a chair. And from the
jug I pour sour wine to wash away the only land
I own, and that between the toes.

A red libation to your good memory, friend. There's
work yet, for the living.[4]

Notes

Abbreviations:

RM: R.A.K. Mason
HL: Hocken Library, University of
      Otago, Dunedin
ATL: Alexander Turnbull Library, National
      Library of New Zealand, Wellington

1   The Beggar

1   Geoffrey de Montalk, 'God's Own
    Country' (Earl's Court London 4 a.m.
    14:3:30), MS-Papers-1128-49, ATL.
2   Marie Gaudin, interviewed by John
    Caselberg, MS-1265/II/1/9, HL; John
    Child to Caselberg, 1970, MS-990/16/
    13, HL; Dave Faigan, interviewed by
    Caselberg, MS-1265/II/1/12.
3   RM to Denis Glover, 5 Nov. 1937, MS-
    990/16/13.
4   Denis Glover, *Hot Water Sailor*, A.H. &
    A.W. Reed, Wellington, 1962, p.103.
5   Allen Curnow, 'The Unhistoric Story',
    Selected Poems, Penguin, Auckland, 1982,
    p.31.
6   C.K. Stead, 'R.A.K. Mason's Poetry –
    some random observations', *Comment*,
    July 1963, p.38.
7   RM to Glover, 5 Nov. 1937.
8   'R.A.K. Mason on Rex Fairburn', 1957,
    manuscript version, MS-592/F-2, HL.
9   Charles Brasch to Roger Savage, 17 May
    1963, MS-996/2/348, HL.
10 RM, 'Sonnet of Brotherhood';
    'notebooks', MS-990/10.

2   Penrose and Lichfield *1905–16*

1   I am reliant on John Caselberg's research
    for the genealogical information in this
    chapter.
2   J.C. Mogford, 'Forbes, Margaret',
    Dictionary of New Zealand Biography,
    Vol.1, Allen & Unwin/Department of
    Internal Affairs, Wellington, 1990,
    pp.133-4; Mogford, *The Onehunga
    Heritage*, Onehunga Borough Council,
    Auckland, 1989, pp.15, 122; G.G.M.
    Mitchell, 'Early settlers in the Manukau',
    Journal of the Auckland Historical Society,
    No.2 (Apr. 1963), pp.19-23 (reprinted in
    *Journal of the Auckland–Waikato Historical
    Societies*, No.19 (Sept. 1971), p.16).
3   W.J. Houston, 'Kells Families in N.Z.',
    typescript, 1974 (copy held by John
    Caselberg).
4   RM, foreword to Hone Tuwhare, *No
    Ordinary Son*, Janet and Blackwood Paul,
    Auckland, 1964.
5   'Lawlessness in country districts',
    Auckland Weekly News, 13 Dec. 1884,
    p.26.
6   *Panmure District School Centennial 1873–
    1973*, Panmure District School,
    Auckland, 1973.
7   Interviews with John Caselberg, MS-
    1265/II/1/4, 9, HL.
8   *New Zealand Herald*, 4 Oct. 1904, p.4.
9   *Auckland Evening Star*, 28 Aug. 1879,
    p.[2].
10 Ibid.
11 *Auckland Weekly News*, 20 May 1882, p.7.
12 Ian Bodle to Dorothea Mason, MS-
    1265/II/3/18.
13 *The Historic Highway*, Auckland, 1967, p.1.

14 Quoted in E.J. Searle, *City of Volcanoes: a geology of Auckland*, 2nd edition, Longman Paul, Auckland, 1981, p.123.
15 Interviews with John Caselberg.
16 '"New Zealand's first wholly original, unmistakably gifted poet." Sam Hunt interviews R.A.K. Mason', *Affairs*, No.2 (June 1969), p.25.
17 RM to Alfred Katz, 7 Aug. 1933, MS-592/B, HL.
18 RM to Geoffrey de Montalk, 5 Jan. 1930, MS-990/16/13, HL; M.C. Cox, *Lichfield*, Waikato Times, Hamilton, 1948, p.13.
19 RM to Jean Ann Scott Miller, 12 Feb. 1970, MS-990/16/13; RM to de Montalk, 5 Jan. 1930.
20 Cox, p.5.
21 C.I. Baldwin, 'Kells, Isabella Foster Rogers', *Dictionary of New Zealand Biography*, Vol.3, AUP/Department of Internal Affairs, Wellington, 1996, p.255; Miss Kells, retirement speech, quoted in *Lichfield School Centennial, 1884–1984*, p.5.
22 'R.A.K. Mason on Rex Fairburn', 1957, transcript, Auckland University Library, p.6.
23 Cox, p.27.
24 MS-990/1.
25 Coroner's report, J46 COR 1913/467, Archives New Zealand.
26 Ian Bodle, interviewed by John Caselberg, MS-1265/II/1/4.
27 Notes to 'Dreams Come True', p.1, MS-592/C pt 1.
28 RM, 'notebooks', MS-990/10. (In the margin he noted 'upas' for the tree of pain.)
29 Baldwin.
30 RM to Jessie and Dan, 28 Oct. 1925, MS-990/15/11.
31 *Panmure District School Centennial, 1873–1973*, p.25.
32 RM, 'notebooks'.

3 The boy with manly hair 1917-22

1 Robert Burton to John Caselberg, 23 Apr. 1978, MS-1265/II/3/45, HL; Alexander Turner, interviewed by Caselberg, MS-1265/II/1/9.
2 Burton to Caselberg.
3 K.A. Trembath, *Ad Augusta: a centennial history of Auckland Grammar School, 1869–1969*, Auckland Grammar School Old Boys' Association, Auckland, 1969, p.96.
4 'R.A.K. Mason on Rex Fairburn', 1957, transcript, Auckland University Library, p.2.
5 Burton to Caselberg; Norman Leonard to Caselberg, 4 Dec. 1978, MS-1265/II/2/4.
6 Ian Bodle to Caselberg, 24 July 1978, MS-1265/II/3/26.
7 RM, 'notebooks', MS-990/10, HL.
8 E.M. Blaiklock, in 'R.A.K. Mason 1905–71: some tributes', *Landfall*, Vol.25, No.3 (Sept. 1971), p.229.
9 Manuscript fragment, MS-990/10.
10 Blaiklock, *Landfall*, Sept. 1971, pp.229, 232-3; *Between the Valley and the Sea: a West Auckland boyhood*, Dunmore Press, Palmerston North, 1979, p.67; *New Zealand Herald*, 29 Nov. 1977, section 1, p.6.
11 Leonard to Caselberg.
12 Ian Bodle to Dorothea Mason, MS-1265/II/3/18.
13 Burton, interviewed by Caselberg, MS-1265/II/1/4. (According to Mason's wife, Dorothea, his Uncle Roy was deputed to tell him the circumstances of his father's death.)
14 Irene Jenkin, interviewed by Caselberg, MS-1265/II/1/10.
15 'R.A.K. Mason on Rex Fairburn', manuscript version, MS-592/F-2, HL.
16 Ibid.
17 The account of Mason and Fairburn discovering their family connection in a churchyard comes from Rex's brother Geoffrey, as retold by Thayer Fairburn to John Caselberg, 18 Sept. 1981, MS-1265/II/2/2.
18 Auckland Grammar School *Chronicle*, third term, 1920, p.24.
19 Thayer Fairburn to Caselberg, 25 Oct. 1981, MS-1265/II/2/2; Burton to Caselberg.
20 She did not sell the Penrose property until 1923.

21 *Chronicle*, third term, 1921, p.23.

22 Ibid., second term, 1921, p.41.

23 Ibid., first term, 1922, p.35.

24 Ibid., second term, 1922, p.42.

25 Allen Curnow, *A Book of New Zealand Verse, 1923-1945*, Caxton Press, Christchurch, 1945, p.32.

26 RM, *The Beggar*, Auckland, 1924, p.24.

27 *Chronicle*, third term, 1922, p.35.

28 J.W. Tibbs, 23 Nov. 1922, MS-990/1.

4   In the Manner of Men *1923–25*

1 MS-990/8, HL.

2 Registrar, University of New Zealand, to J.W.Tibbs, 26 July 1923, MS-990/15/1.

3 [Seddon Memorial Technical College to RM, 19 Sept. 1923], MS-990/15/1.

4 Notes to 'In the Manner of Men', MS-592/E-5, HL.

5 Ibid.

6 RM, 'notebooks', MS-990/10.

7 C.K. Stead, 'R.A.K. Mason's poetry – some random observations', *Comment*, Vol.4, No.4 (July 1963), p.38.

8 MS-990/6. The poem is dated Nov. 1923.

9 RM, 'notebooks'.

10 R.A. Singer to V.R.N. Bird (RM), 11 Dec. 1923, MS-990/15/1.

11 RM, 'notebooks'.

12 Ibid.

13 V.R.N. Bird to Henry Hemus, 24 Feb. 1924; Hemus to RM, 18 Feb. 1924, MS-592/E-6.

14 A.R.D. Fairburn to RM, 12 Feb. 1924, MS-592/F-1.

15 RM to Fairburn, Nov. [1921?], Fairburn Literary Estate.

16 RM to Fairburn, 22 Aug. 1923.

17 'R.A.K. Mason on Rex Fairburn', 1957, transcript, Auckland University Library, pp.15-16.

18 RM, 'notebooks'.

19 RM, 'notebooks'. Mason is paraphrasing (in Pooterish fashion) an epigram which first appeared in *Sands of Time* (Walter Sichel, 1923): 'The rain, it raineth on the just/ And also on the unjust fella:/ But chiefly on the just, because/ The unjust steals the just's umbrella.'

20 *Auckland Star*, 12 July 1924, p.18.

21 Ibid.

22 Harold Monro to RM, 27 Dec. 1924, MS-990/16/18.

23 Stead, p.35.

24 Mason would later comment that Mary and Flora in this poem 'are a martyr and a saint out of my imagination. I firmly believed in them until challenged by Curnow to produce evidence.' RM to J.E. Weir, 9 Oct. 1970, MS-990/16/16.

25 E.M. Blaiklock, *Landfall*, Vol.25, No.3 (Sept. 1971), p.232; *New Zealand Herald*, 29 Nov. 1977, section 1, p.6.

26 RM, 'notebooks'.

27 Ibid.

28 Ibid.

29 Ibid.

30 Allen Curnow, introduction to R.A.K. Mason, *Collected Poems*, Pegasus Press, Christchurch, 1962, p.9.

31 Allen Curnow, *The Penguin Book of New Zealand Verse*, Penguin, London, 1960, p.38.

32 RM, 'notebooks'; RM to Geoffrey de Montalk, 5 Jan. 1930, MS-990/16/13.

33 *Auckland Star*, 12 July 1924, p.18.

34 N.A. Winter to RM, 15 July 1924, MS-990/15/1.

35 Penelope Fitzgerald, introduction to J.H. Woolmer, *The Poetry Bookshop, 1912–1935: a bibliography*, Woolmer/Brotherson, Winchester, 1988, p.xxix.

36 Ibid., p.ix; R. Tomalin, preface to H. Monro, *Collected Poems* (ed. A. Monro), Duckworth, London, 1970.

37 Monro to RM, 27 Dec. 1924.

38 *The Chapbook: a miscellany*, No.39 (1924), p.5.

39 RM to Denis Glover, 6 Mar. 1934, MS-Papers-0418-24, ATL.

40 Ibid.

41 This was the printer's error, not Monro's. On his proof copy of *The Beggar* Mason had marked that the two verses should be on a new page.

42 Monro to RM, 27 Dec. 1924.

43 Denis Glover to RM, 3 Feb. 1962, MS-990/16/14.

44 RM, 'notebooks'.

45 'R.A.K. Mason on Rex Fairburn', p.2.
46 RM, 'notebooks'.
47 Ibid.
48 Jean Bartlett to John Caselberg, 25 Feb. 1978, MS-1265/II/3/21, HL.
49 RM, 'notebooks'.
50 Robert Burton, interviewed by John Caselberg, MS-1265/II/1/4.
51 *Auckland Star*, 5 Jan. 1929, magazine section, p.1.
52 RM, 'notebooks'.
53 RM to de Montalk, 5 Jan. 1930.
54 *Auckland Star*, 5 Jan. 1929.
55 RM to S. Slater, 28 Aug. 1963, quoted in Caselberg, 'R.A.K. Mason, 1905-1971: a record of his life and writings', 1986, p.73, MS-1265/II/6.
56 RM, 'notebooks'.
57 Ian Bodle, interviewed by John Caselberg, MS-1265/II/1/4.
58 RM, 'notebooks'.
59 '"New Zealand's first wholly original, unmistakably gifted poet." Sam Hunt interviews R.A.K. Mason', *Affairs*, No.2 (June 1969), p.25.
60 *Times Literary Supplement*, 4 Jan. 1963, p.10.
61 MS-990/6.
62 RM, 'notebooks'.
63 *Auckland Star*, 17 Oct. 1924, p.18.
64 Monro to RM, 1 Oct. 1925, MS-592/E-5.

5 Poets and princes *1926–27*

1 A.R.D. Fairburn to RM, 9 Jan. 1932, MS-592/F-1, HL.
2 *Times* obituary quoted in *Kiwi*, 1933, p.78; E.M. Blaiklock, *Between the Morning and the Afternoon*, Dunmore Press, Palmerston North, 1980, p.53.
3 E. Locke, *Student at the Gates*, Whitcoulls, Christchurch, 1981, p.43.
4 Fairburn to Geoffrey de Montalk, 21 July 1926, MS-Papers-2461-1, ATL.
5 'R.A.K. Mason on Rex Fairburn', 1957, transcript, Auckland University Library, p.4.
6 Fairburn to de Montalk, 21 July 1926.
7 De Montalk to Fairburn, 2 Aug., 14 Oct. 1926, Micro-MS-131, ATL.
8 De Montalk to Fairburn, 2 Aug. 1926.
9 Fairburn to de Montalk, 7 Sept. 1926; RM, review of *Snobbery with violence: a poet in gaol*, 1933, MS-592/B.
10 De Montalk to Fairburn, 2 Aug. 1926; Fairburn to de Montalk, 6 Aug. 1926.
11 De Montalk to RM, 28 Oct. 1926, MS-592/E-5. Mason had asked Fairburn at the beginning of October for de Montalk's address, but this does not necessarily mean that he wrote to him. In *Recollections of My Fellow Poets*, published when he was in his late seventies (in 1983), de Montalk stated that 'I cannot clearly remember exactly when I first met Mason. But it was probably at one of Shaw's talks on literature at the Y.M.C.A. Quite likely in 1923.' But his memory appears to have been faulty by that time. The correspondence confirms that he did meet Fairburn at a Shaw talk at the WEA. His recollection of lunching with Rudd and Mason in 1923–24 confuses the picture, because Rudd was dead by the time de Montalk came back to Auckland from Christchurch.
12 De Montalk to RM, 16 Feb. 1927, MS-592/E-5.
13 De Montalk to Fairburn, St Bartholomew's Day 1926, Micro-MS-131.
14 Fairburn to de Montalk, 24 Jan. 1927, MS-Papers-2461-2.
15 Fairburn to de Montalk, 21 July, 7 Sept. 1926, MS-Papers-2461-1.
16 De Montalk to RM, 11 Aug. 1926; de Montalk, 'About poetry – and Maxwell Rudd', 1927, MS-Papers-1128-419, ATL.
17 Fairburn to de Montalk, 26 Oct. 1926, MS-Papers-2461-2.
18 Quoted in D. Trussell, *Fairburn*, Auckland University Press/Oxford University Press, Auckland, 1984, p.52.
19 Fairburn to de Montalk, 19 Aug. 1926, MS-Papers-2461-1.
20 RM to Lola, MS-592/E-5.
21 Lola to RM, 19 Oct. 1926, MS-592/E-5.
22 RM, 'notebooks', MS-990/10, HL.

23 RM to Fairburn, 2 Oct. 1926, nd,
    Fairburn Literary Estate.
24 RM to Fairburn, nd.
25 Fairburn to RM, 26 Sept. 1926, MS-
    592/F-1.
26 RM to Horace Holl, 29 Dec. 1926, MS-
    990/5/1.
27 Fairburn to de Montalk, 13 Dec. 1926,
    MS-Papers-2461-2.
28 Fairburn to RM, nd, 27 Jan. 1927, MS-
    592/F-1.
29 Fairburn to RM, 3 Feb. 1927, MS-592/
    F-1.
30 RM to de Montalk, 5 Jan. 1930, MS-
    990/16/13.
31 Lola to RM, 9 Feb. 1927, MS-592/E-5.
32 Fairburn to RM, 26 Sept. 1926.
33 Fairburn to RM, 29 Jan. 1932, MS-592:
    F-1.
34 RM to Fairburn, [Dec. 1931].
35 Fairburn to de Montalk, 21 July 1927,
    MS-Papers-2461-3.
36 Blaiklock, *Between the Valley and the Sea*,
    Dunmore Press, Palmerston North, 1979,
    p.67.
37 RM, notes for poetry lectures, 1962,
    MS-1134/2, HL.
38 Fairburn to de Montalk, 5 May 1927,
    MS-Papers-2461-3.
39 Fairburn to de Montalk, 13 June 1927,
    MS-Papers-2461-3.
40 De Montalk to Fairburn, 28 Oct. 1926;
    RM, 'notebooks'.
41 De Montalk to Fairburn, 21 June,
    Whitsunday 1927, Micro-MS-131.
    Mason's 'motor-car lines' are from 'After
    Death' and 'The Beggar' respectively.
42 'R.A.K. Mason on Rex Fairburn', p.18;
    New Zealand Herald, 9 Sept. 1926, p.8; 11
    Sept. 1926, p.12.
43 Fairburn to de Montalk, 21 July 1927,
    MS-Papers-2461-3.
44 Clifton Firth to RM, 18 July 1962, MS-
    990/15/6.
45 Stephen Champ to John Caselberg, 22
    Feb. 1982, MS-1265/II/2/1, HL; Irene
    Jenkin, interviewed by Caselberg, MS-
    1265/II/1/10.
46 'R.A.K. Mason on Rex Fairburn', p.16.
47 Firth, interviewed by John Caselberg,

MS-1265/II/1/3.
48 Notes to 'Dreams Come True', p.2, MS-
    592/C pt 1.
49 Of the 47 members of the Communist
    Party between 1921 and 1927 whose ages
    are known, more than 60 per cent were
    under 30 when they joined (K. Taylor,
    'Workers' Vanguard or People's Voice?
    The Communist Party of New Zealand
    from origins to 1946', PhD thesis, VUW,
    1994). Mason's first, informal, contact
    with the Party may have been in
    November 1926, when he and Geoff
    Fairburn attended a 'Communist Social
    and Dance' (RM to Fairburn, nd).
50 'Dreams Come True', episode H, pp.10-
    11.
51 Robin Hyde, 'Comrades of the Hammer
    and Sickle: Auckland communists on
    their native heath', *New Zealand Observer*,
    27 Aug. 1931, reprinted in G. Boddy & J.
    Matthews (eds), *Disputed Ground*,
    Victoria University Press, Wellington,
    1991, p. 254.
52 'Dreams Come True', Episode H, p.9.
53 *New Zealand Herald*, 3, 6 Nov. 1928,
    p.13, 7 Nov. 1928, p.15.
54 Jessie Mason to ?, 25 May 1927, MS-
    592/E-6.
55 Fairburn to de Montalk, 13 June, 30 May
    1927, MS-Papers-2461-3.
56 De Montalk to Fairburn, Armistice Day
    and St Bartholomew's Day 1926.
57 De Montalk to Fairburn, Easter Sunday
    1927.
58 De Montalk to Fairburn, Whitsunday
    1927, 5 Apr., 3 Aug., 28 Mar., 24 May,
    19 Aug. 1927. (Evidently Mason did, for
    there were six more copies in stock by
    the end of May, which the shop had sold
    by August.)
59 Fairburn to de Montalk, 13 June 1927; de
    Montalk to Fairburn, 24 May 1927,
    Easter Sunday 1927.
60 De Montalk, *Wild Oats*, Christchurch,
    1927, 'Envoy'.
61 Fairburn to de Montalk, 30 May 1927.
62 De Montalk to Mason, 16 Feb. 1927.
63 Fairburn to de Montalk, 14 June 1927.
    The review has not survived.

64 Fairburn to de Montalk, 16 July 1927;
   RM to de Montalk, 5 Jan. 1930;
   Auckland *Sun*, 7 Sept. 1927; S. de
   Montalk, *Unquiet World: the life of Count
   Geoffrey Potocki de Montalk*, Victoria
   University Press, Wellington, 2001.
65 Fairburn to de Montalk, 21 July 1927.
66 RM to de Montalk, 5 Jan. 1930.
67 Robin Hyde, *Journalese*, National
   Printing Company, Auckland, 1934,
   p.191.
68 RM, 'notebooks'.
69 'Sonnet', *Auckland Star*, 8 Oct. 1927,
   p.21. Mason included 'The Leave-taking'
   (printed on 17 Sept. 1927) and
   'Evolution' (3 Dec. 1927) in *No New
   Thing* (1934); another untitled sonnet
   printed in the *Star* on 25 February 1928
   was republished in the *Collected Poems* in
   1962. The *Star* had published one poem
   by Mason previously, in February 1925:
   'Poverty – a threnody' (21 Feb. 1925,
   p.18).
70 *New Zealand Worker*, 21 Sept. 1927, p.11;
   12 Oct. 1927, p.16. Beneath the first
   contribution the paper printed a notice
   'To Correspondents. R.A.K. Mason. – A
   letter to the University wrongly
   addressed to us. Please send address for
   return.'
71 Fairburn to de Montalk, 2 Aug. 1927.
72 De Montalk to Fairburn, Trinity Sunday
   1927.
73 'R.A.K. Mason on Rex Fairburn', p.16.
74 De Montalk to RM, 21 Dec. 1927.
75 Fairburn to de Montalk, 21 July 1927.

6   Why we can't write for nuts *1928–29*

1 RM to A.R.D. Fairburn, 24 Dec. 1927,
   Fairburn Literary Estate.
2 'R.A.K. Mason on Rex Fairburn', 1957,
   transcript, Auckland University Library,
   p.6; RM to Fairburn, 24 Dec. 1927.
3 Fairburn, 'The truth about harvesting –
   by one who has suffered', Auckland *Sun*,
   21 Jan. 1928, p.24; 'R.A.K. Mason on
   Rex Fairburn', p.5.
4 Notes to 'Dreams Come True', p.2, MS-
   592/C pt 1, HL.
5 Jessie Mason to RM, 18 Jan. 1928, MS-
   592/E-6.
6 Fairburn, 'The truth about harvesting';
   Fairburn to RM, nd, MS-592/F-1.
7 Fairburn to RM, 18 Jan. 1928, MS-592/
   F-1; RM to Geoffrey de Montalk, 5 Jan.
   1930, MS-990/16/13, HL.
8 De Montalk to RM, 5 Mar. 1928, MS-
   592/E-5; de Montalk to Fairburn, 25
   Apr., 29 May 1928, Micro-MS-131,
   ATL.
9 'Quant à moi', the postcard continued,
   'it looks as if he is convinced of my
   poetic gifts and intends to help me. He is
   very pleasant and beautiful.' De Montalk
   to RM, 11 Feb. 1928, MS-990/15/1.
10 De Montalk to RM, 5 Mar. 1928.
11 Harold Monro to Humbert Wolfe, 22
   Sept. 1926; Monro to Hamish Maclaren
   (*Spectator*), 16 Mar. 1928, Harold Monro/
   Poetry Bookshop Papers, Add 57741,
   British Library.
12 RM to de Montalk, 5 Jan. 1930.
13 De Montalk to RM, 5 Mar. 1928.
14 Jean Alison, in 'R.A.K. Mason, 1905–
   1971: some tributes', *Landfall*, Vol.25,
   No.3 (Sept. 1971), p.226.
15 He was referring to Katherine Mansfield,
   as other notes make clear.
16 S. Anderson, 'Freak English', Auckland
   Sun, 15 June 1928, p.14; RM, 'Free verse
   – the historic position', *Sun*, 22 June
   1928, p.14; *Sun*, 29 June 1928, p.14. De
   Montalk speculated on the identity of the
   Horahora correspondent: 'Do tell me,
   immediately', he wrote to Fairburn, 'was
   it Miss Anderson who rent to R.A.K.? If
   so, it was no less a nymph (pit-a-pat, pit-
   a-pat, my heart!) than Ada.' De Montalk
   to Fairburn, 12 Aug. 1928.
17 Auckland *Sun*, 7, 14, 21 Dec. 1928, p.14.
18 RM to Donnelly, 14 Dec. 1928, MS-
   Papers-7650-1, ATL.
19 Among the small changes Mason later
   made to this poem, the son of Joseph
   became the son of Mary.
20 Auckland *Sun*, 4 Jan. 1929, p.12; 18 Jan.,
   8 Feb. 1929, p.14.
21 De Montalk to Fairburn, 10 Feb. 1929,
   MS-Papers-1128-10, ATL.

22 De Montalk to Fairburn, 21 Dec. 1929.

23 De Montalk to the editor, *Sun*, [Mar. 1930], MS-Papers-1128-10; *Sun*, 23 May 1930.

24 D.H. Monro, *Fortunate Catastrophes: an anecdotal autobiography*, Quokka Press, Melbourne, 1991, p.64.

25 Fairburn, 'A New Zealand Poet', *New Zealand Artists' Annual*, Aug. 1929, p.69.

26 RM to Pat Lawlor, 20 May 1929, MS-Papers-4046, ATL; Lawlor to RM, 29 Apr., 20 May 1929, MS-592/E-5.

27 De Montalk, 'God's Own Country' (dated 'Earl's Court London 4 a.m. 14:4:30'), MS-Papers-1128-49.

28 Douglas Glass to RM, 17 Apr. 1929, MS-592/E-5.

29 *Auckland Star*, 5 Jan. 1929, magazine section, p.1, 19 Jan., p.7, 3 Aug., p.1. The poem was here titled 'Saith the Preacher', later published as 'Away is flown each petty rag'.

30 The sexual theme of this poem is more explicit in the revised version which Mason later published, replacing the final couplet, 'Still, in the long run they'll win, and not I,/ They'll have the last laugh when Eternity's gone by', with 'There's balm for flesh, flesh that's alive and raving/ to smell and touch these girls, with a fiendish craving'. No doubt this version would have been rejected by the *Sun* as well.

31 Percy Crisp to RM, 21 June [1929], MS-592/E-5.

32 Lawlor to RM, 4 June 1930, MS-990/15/2.

33 RM, 'Why We Can't Write for Nuts', MS-1134/1, HL.

34 RM to Lawlor, 6 June 1930, MS-77-067-4/1, ATL.

35 Crisp to RM, 22 Sept. 1930, MS-592/E-5.

36 Harold Monro to RM, 26 Apr. 1929, MS-990/16/18; Glass to RM, 17 Apr. 1929.

37 Monro to RM, 5 Nov. 1929.

38 H.E. Monro (ed.), *Twentieth Century Poetry*, Chatto and Windus, London, 1929, pp.7-11.

39 RM to de Montalk, 5 Jan. 1930.

40 RM to Fairburn, 13 Jan. 1930.

41 Auckland *Sun*, 7 Feb. 1930, p.14; *Auckland Star*, 1 Mar. 1930, magazine section, p.2.

42 Fairburn to RM, 13, 6 Feb. 1930, MS-592/F-1.

43 A.C. Paterson, testimonial, 28 Oct. 1930, MS-990/1; annual report of the Department of Classics, 1929, quoted by L.A. Wilson (academic registrar, University of Auckland) to John Caselberg, 16 Nov. 1983.

44 RM to de Montalk, 5 Jan. 1930.

7 The Book of Pessimism *1930*

1 Jessie Mason to RM, 23 Dec. 1929, MS-592/E-6, HL.

2 RM to A.R.D. Fairburn, 13 Jan. 1930, Fairburn Literary Estate.

3 N.M. Richmond to RM, 16 Dec. 1929, 24 Feb. 1930, MS-592/E-5.

4 RM to Geoffrey de Montalk, 5 Jan. 1930, MS-990/16/13, HL.

5 RM, 'notebooks', MS-990/10.

6 RM to de Montalk, 5 Jan. 1930.

7 Ibid.; de Montalk to Fairburn, 21 Jan. 1930, MS-Papers-1128-10, ATL.

8 RM to de Montalk, 5 Jan. 1930.

9 RM to Jessie Mason, 8 Jan. 1930, MS-990/15/10.

10 RM to de Montalk, 5 Jan. 1930.

11 Notes for poetry lectures, 1962, MS-1134/2, HL.

12 Fairburn to RM, 3 Sept. 1932, MS-592/F-1.

13 Draft introduction to *No New Thing*, MS-1134/2, HL.

14 Fairburn to RM, 18 Mar. 1930.

15 Ibid.

16 RM to de Montalk, 5 Jan. 1930.

17 Firth, quoted by Fairburn to RM, 13 Feb. 1930; and by RM to Jessie Mason, 20 Feb. 1930. Markey was a devotee of the Abrams reflexoscope, a quack cure for cancer (using vibration), and had initially come to New Zealand in 1925 to promote it, having also persuaded Universal Studios to finance a film.

When he left New Zealand in 1930, taking with him props to finish *Hei Tiki* in America, Ngati Tuwharetoa accused him of stealing their taonga and tried (unsuccessfully) to recover them through the courts.

18 Fairburn to RM, 18 Feb. 1930; de Montalk to Fairburn, 3 Jan. 1930, MS-Papers-1128-10.

19 RM to de Montalk, 5 Jan. 1930.

20 Marie Gaudin, interviewed by John Caselberg, MS-1265/II/1/9, HL.

21 'Myself, I still refrain from worshipping at the ecstatic shrine of Venus Aphrodite', he also wrote in his long letter to de Montalk, after inquiring after the state of de Montalk's own love life and reminding him of Balzac – 'every emission of semen costs me a novel' (RM to de Montalk, 5 Jan. 1930).

22 Jean Bartlett, interviewed by the author, 13 Dec. 1999.

23 RM to Marie Gaudin, 29 Jan. 1930, MS-1265/II/3/44, HL.

24 RM to Fairburn, 24 Mar. 1930.

25 RM to Marie Gaudin, 7 Mar. 1930.

26 RM to Marie Gaudin, 7 Mar., 29 Jan., 26 Feb. 1930.

27 RM to Jessie Mason, 15 Mar. 1930, MS-990/15/10; to Marie Gaudin, 26 Feb. 1930.

28 RM to Marie Gaudin, 7 Mar., 26 Feb. 1930.

29 MS-990/6. A typescript of this poem, along with 'Nox Perpetua Dormienda', is pasted into a scrapbook of Fairburn's dated 1925–30 (MSS & Archives A-11, 11.4, Auckland University Library).

30 RM to de Montalk, 5 Jan. 1930.

31 Edwynna Roussel (Teddy) to RM, 8 Mar., 5 May, 21 Mar. 1930, MS-592/F-4.

32 Fairburn to RM, 3 Feb. 1930, MS-592/F-1.

33 Fairburn to RM, 29 Dec. 1929.

34 Fairburn to RM, 3 Feb. 1930.

35 Teddy to RM, 14, 1 Mar. 1930.

36 Jessie Mason to RM, 26 Mar. 1930, MS-592/E-6.

37 Teddy to RM, 21 Mar. 1930.

38 Teddy to RM, nd; Fairburn to RM, 18 Feb. 1930.

39 Teddy to RM, 1 Mar., [Apr.] 1930.

40 Teddy to RM, 14 Mar.; RM to Teddy, 26 Apr. 1930.

41 Fairburn to RM, 18 Mar. 1930.

42 RM to Fairburn, 24 Mar. 1930.

43 Fairburn to RM, nd.

44 Teddy to RM, 21 Mar., 25 Apr., 14 Mar. 1930.

45 Fairburn to Teddy, nd, MS-592/F-1; RM, 'notebooks', MS-990/10.

46 Fairburn to Firth, 9 Feb. 1930, MS-80-390, ATL; Fairburn to RM, 18 Mar. 1930.

47 RM to Teddy, 26 Apr. 1930.

48 Ibid.

49 Court of Appeal civil register, 1921–34, ABIO 7242/415; case file, ABIO 6085/1910, Archives New Zealand.

50 RM to Fairburn, 12 Dec. 1930.

51 Teddy to RM, 5 May 1930.

52 Notes to 'Dreams Come True', pp.3-4, MS-592/C pt 1.

53 RM to Marie Gaudin, 29 Jan. 1930.

54 Notes to 'Dreams Come True', p.4.

55 'Dreams Come True', Episode B, pp.1-2, 6-10.

56 Notes to 'Dreams Come True', p.5.

57 'Dreams Come True', Episode C, pp.3-4.

58 RM to Marie Gaudin, 29 Jan. 1930.

59 Notes to 'Dreams Come True', p.6.

60 'Dreams Come True', Episode F, pp.1-3, G2, p.2.

61 Notes to 'Dreams Come True', p.6.

62 'Dreams Come True', Episode F, p.3.

63 Notes to 'Dreams Come True', p.9.

64 'R.A.K. Mason on Rex Fairburn', 1957, transcript, Auckland University Library, pp.15-16.

65 Fairburn to RM, 13 Oct., 3 Dec. 1930.

66 Ibid.

67 RM to Fairburn, 12, 24–25 Dec. 1930. Mason's academic record shows that he passed in history and sociology, failed philosophy, and did not sit either psychology or Greek HAL.

68 A.C. Paterson, testimonial, 28 Oct. 1930, MS-990/1.

69 RM to Fairburn, 24–25 Dec. 1930.

70 Teddy to RM, 3 Nov. 1930.

8   **The islands** *1931*

1   RM, preface to 'An Old Trader in the South Seas', MS-Papers-0061-82, ATL; RM to George Westbrook, nd, MS-Papers-0061-27.
2   RM to the registrar, Auckland University College, 26 Dec. 1929, MS-990/1, HL; RM to Fairburn, 24–25 Dec. 1930, Fairburn Literary Estate. Mason may also have been working for Nelson in some other capacity, as well as tutoring his daughter. In a job application in 1948 he listed his secretarial and organising experience as including 'a year's work for the late Hon. O.F. Nelson . . . resulting in the grant of three months' furlough in the Islands'. RM, application for Adult Education position, Canterbury, 18 Nov. 1948, MS-990/1.
3   RM, preface to 'An Old Trader'.
4   Majorie Perham, *Pacific Prelude: a journey to Samoa and Australasia, 1929*, Peter Owen, London, 1988, p.122.
5   RM to Fairburn, 24–25 Dec. 1930.
6   RM to Geoffrey de Montalk, 5 Jan. 1930, MS-990/16/13.
7   RM to Jessie Mason, 1 Jan. 1931, MS-592/E-4, HL.
8   RM to Jessie Mason, 1, 6–7, 8 Jan. 1931.
9   Preface to 'An Old Trader'; RM to Jessie Mason, 1 Mar. 1931.
10 Preface to 'An Old Trader'.
11 RM to Eric, 30 May 1931, MS-990/15/2.
12 RM to Jessie Mason, 16 Feb, 25 Feb., 20 Jan. 1931.
13 Draft introduction to *Strait is the Gate*, MS-990/4.
14 RM to Jessie Mason, 25 Feb. 1931.
15 RM to Jessie Mason, 26 Jan. 1931; to F.M. Keesing, 5 May 1931, MS-990/15/2.
16 RM to Jessie Mason, 26 Jan., 8 Jan., 20 Jan. 1931.
17 Jessie Mason to RM, 5 Jan., 2 Mar., 1 Apr. 1931, MS-592/E-6.
18 Jessie Mason to RM, 17 Feb 1931. On the back of this letter she also wrote this verse:

'Ate Dirt' did you say?
Come, Come, my Son, stay –
And put on your cap for a while –
For tho' the dirt massed –
When R.A.K. passed
He whisked it away with a smile.

19 Jessie Mason to RM, 21, 5 Jan. 1931.
20 RM to Jessie Mason, 16 Feb. 1931; Jessie to RM, 11 Mar. 1931.
21 RM to the registrar, Auckland University College, 26 Dec. 1929.
22 RM to Jessie Mason, 26 Jan. 1931; Jessie Mason to RM, 30 Jan., 17 Feb. 1931.
23 RM to Jessie Mason, 16, 25 Feb. 1931.
24 RM to Eric, 30 May 1931.
25 RM to Jessie Mason, 16 Feb. 1931.
26 RM to Westbrook, 17 Apr. 1931; to Eric, 30 May 1931.
27 RM to Westbrook, nd.
28 Mason had been prescribed glasses in 1923: 'I have to wear goggles', he reported to Fairburn (RM to Fairburn, 18 Aug. 1923).
29 RM to Westbrook, 1 [Apr.], nd, 12 June 1931.
30 RM to Fairburn, 18 June 1932.
31 RM to Westbrook, 1 [Apr.], 17 Apr. 1931.
32 Mason had been planning to send it to Putnams but whether he did or not is not known.
33 Julian Dana to Westbrook, 27 Feb., 22 May, 4 June 1933; agreement dated 13 June 1933, MS-Papers-0061-28.
34 Westbrook to Dana, 14 June 1933, MS-Papers-0061-29.
35 Westbrook to RM, 15 June, 8 Dec. 1933, MS-Papers-0061-27.
36 Dana to Westbrook, 20 July 1933.

9   **On the swag** *1931*

1   RM to George Westbrook, nd, MS-Papers-0061-27, ATL.
2   Ibid.
3   RM, 'notebooks', MS-990/10, HL.
4   RM to Westbrook, 1 [Mar.] 1931.
5   RM to F.M. Keesing, 5 May 1931; to Cecil Gardiner, 12 July 1931, MS-990/15/2.

6 RM to Keesing, 5 May 1931; to Westbrook, nd.
7 Jessie Mason to RM, 22 Feb.–15 Mar. 1931, MS-592/E-6, HL.
8 E.M. Blaiklock to RM, nd, MS-592/E-5.
9 RM to A.R.D. Fairburn, 23 Apr. 1931, MS-990/15/2.
10 RM to Edwynna Roussel (Teddy), 9 May 1931, MS-990/15/2.
11 The cheapest boat fare to London in 1932 was £39, according to Charles Brasch in his memoir *Indirections*, Oxford University Press, Wellington, 1980, p.189.
12 Both Irene Jenkin and Marie Gaudin believed, in fact, that Paterson offered to assist Mason financially to go to England but Jessie wouldn't let him go.
13 RM to Fairburn, 23 Apr. 1931.
14 Ibid.
15 *Kiwi*, 1931, p.34.
16 Marie Gaudin, interviewed by John Caselberg, MS-1265/II/1/3, HL.
17 Pia Richards to RM, 12 Mar. [1931], MS-592/F-5.
18 Ibid.
19 RM to Teddy, 9 May 1931.
20 Teddy to RM, 11 June 1931, MS-592/F-4.
21 Teddy to RM, 11 June, 2, 30 July, 22 Sept. 1931.
22 Teddy to RM, 16 Sept. 1932. By this time she was some months pregnant. When Mason wrote to her apparently for the last time in April 1933 it appears that she was intending to return, possibly just for a visit, but if he did see her again there is no evidence of this among his papers and none of his later friends ever met her.
23 Fairburn to RM, 15 Aug. 1931, MS-592/F-1.
24 Fairburn to RM, 11 Nov. 1930.
25 Fairburn to RM, 3 Dec. 1930; to Clifton Firth, 8 Jan. 1931, MS-Papers-1128-013, ATL; to RM, 20 Jan., 22 Mar. 1931.
26 Teddy to RM, 13 Jan. 1931.
27 Pope had approached Donnelly for Mason's poems, not realising, as he subsequently apologised to Mason, 'that you are still resident in New Zealand' (Donnelly to RM, nd; Pope to RM, 5 Feb. 1930, MS-990/17/27). The release of the anthology was held up, Fairburn told Mason (in October), because de Montalk was miffed that his permission had not been sought.
28 Fairburn to RM, 16 Oct. 1930, MS-990/16/14.
29 Fairburn to RM, 3 Dec. 1930.
30 Fairburn to RM, 3 Dec. 1930, 20 Jan. 1931.
31 RM to Fairburn, 23 Apr., 25 May 1931.
32 RM to Westbrook, 12 June 1931.
33 RM to Fairburn, 5 Sept. 1931, Fairburn Literary Estate.
34 Fairburn to RM, 23 July 1931.
35 Fairburn to RM, 3 Sept. 1932.
36 *Phoenix*, Vol.1, No.2 (July 1932), pp.5-16.
37 RM to Fairburn, 6 May 1932.
38 Fairburn to RM, 31 Aug. 1931.
39 RM, 'notebooks'.
40 RM to Fairburn, 7 Nov. 1931.
41 Jocelyn Fairburn to RM, 8 Jan. 1932, MS-592/F-1.
42 RM to Fairburn, 4 Oct. 1931; Lucretius, *On the Nature of the Universe* (trans. R. Melville), Clarendon Press, London, 1997, p.36.
43 Fairburn to RM, 20 Jan. 1931.
44 RM to Fairburn, 25, 14 May 1931.
45 RM to Fairburn, 23 Apr. 1931; to Westbrook, 9 Aug. 1931.
46 RM to Cecil Gardiner, 12 July 1931; to Westbrook, 12 June 1931. This was evidently money Dan had not been paid by Associated Investment Underwriters (NZ) Ltd of Hamilton.
47 RM to Fairburn, 14 May 1931.
48 RM to Fairburn, 5 Sept. 1931.
49 *New Zealand Worker*, 12 Aug. 1931, p.4.
50 RM to Fairburn, 5 Sept. 1931; report by Hector Monro and Blackwood Paul in *Phoenix*, Vol.1, No.2 (July 1932), p.40.
51 RM to Fairburn, 7 Nov. 1931.
52 RM to Fairburn, 5 Sept. 1931.
53 RM to Westbrook, 12 June 1931; *Auckland Star*, 21 May 1931, p.8, *Farming*

First, 10 June 1931, *New Zealand Samoa Guardian*, 9 July 1931.

54 Ian Donnelly to RM, 14 July [1931], MS-592/E-5.
55 RM to Keesing, 5 May 1931.
56 RM to Westbrook, 12 June 1931.
57 RM to Fairburn, 23 Apr. 1931; notes on *Phoenix* (1962), MS-592/B.
58 RM to Fairburn, [Dec. 1931].
59 Pia Richards to RM, 16 Nov. [1931].
60 RM to Fairburn, [Dec. 1931], 7 Nov. 1931, 1 Nov. 1930.
61 *Auckland Star*, 29 Aug. 1931, magazine section, p.5.
62 Ibid.; RM, Notes to 'Dreams Come True', MS-592/C pt 1. He re-used part of the Communist Reporter's soap-box speech from his novel, Mason recalled here.
63 *New Zealand Observer*, 8 Oct. 1931, p.11.
64 Ibid., 29 Oct. 1931, p.8. The film screened nightly from 24 to 28 October (along with two travelogues, *Beautiful Waiheke* and *A Trip through New Zealand*, and a short comedy, *What a Night*). There were also reviews in the *Herald* and the *Star*, both on 26 Oct. See also J. McCartney, 'Robert Fearn Steele', MA thesis, University of Auckland, 1997.
65 *New Zealand Observer*, 8 Oct. 1931, p.11.
66 RM to Fairburn, 5 Sept. 1931; to Westbrook, 9 Aug. 1931. 'I have not yet made up my mind about standing', he told Westbrook. 'I think I have not told you that I might – keep that under your hat.'
67 RM to Westbrook, 9 Aug. 1931.
68 RM to Fairburn, 17 July 1932.
69 RM to Westbrook, 4 Oct. 1931.
70 K. Taylor, 'Workers' Vanguard or People's Voice? The Communist Party of New Zealand from origins to 1946', PhD thesis, Victoria University of Wellington, 1994.
71 RM, 'notebooks'.
72 '"New Zealand's first wholly original, unmistakably gifted poet." Sam Hunt interviews R.A.K. Mason', *Affairs*, No.2 (June 1969), p.24.
73 Fairburn to Firth, 23 Dec. 1931, MS-80-390, ATL.
74 Fairburn to RM, 28 Dec. 1931.
75 'This Bird May Swing', MS-990/3.
76 Jessie Mason to RM, 4 Jan. 1932, MS-592/E-6.
77 RM to Pia Richards, 19 May 1931, MS-990/15/2.
78 Pia Richards to RM, [May? 1931].

10 A crack-brained socialist *1932*

1 RM to A.R.D. Fairburn, 20 May 1932, Fairburn Literary Estate.
2 Among Mason's papers is a page in manuscript headed 'New Fruit from Old Stocks', possibly an early title for *No New Thing*, with the clearly facetious epigraph: 'This is the book which I have written well:/ If you don't like it you can go to Hell.' (MS-990/6, HL.)
3 RM to Robert Graves, 17 Mar. 1932, MS-990/16/18.
4 Fairburn to RM, 4 Dec. 1931, MS-592/F-1, HL.
5 Fairburn to RM, 21 Mar. 1932.
6 RM to Fairburn, 6 May 1932. He did care that the publishers did not touch the poems, however. 'One other thing', he told Fairburn: 'in "The Young Man Thinks of Sons" I have "I'll take care that the lust of my loins never bring to fruition." Don't let the cows change it to "brings". It is, of course, a Subjunctive ("ne . . . unquam pari*a*t, not parit). Pedantry if you like but . . . '.
7 Fairburn to RM, 16 June 1932; draft introduction to *No New Thing*, MS-990/6.
8 Fairburn to RM, 31 July, 24 June 1932.
9 Harold Raymond to Fairburn, 24 Aug. 1932, MS-990/6.
10 RM to Terry Bond, 25 Nov. 1932, MS-990/16/18. Mason referred in this letter to meeting Bond 'just before the Rangitikei sailed' – possibly when Bond was returning to England: he had come back to New Zealand for a holiday in October 1932 on the same sailing of the *Rangitikei* as Fairburn.
11 RM to Graves, 17 Mar. 1932. It had, he might have added, been 'hopelessly

mismanaged' by himself. When *No New Thing* was eventually published in 1934, Harold Innes wrote to him: 'Since ordering a copy of "The Beggar" I have heard persistent rumours that that unfortunate gentleman has long since come to an untimely end. If you would care to send me a copy of "No New Thing" instead of "The Beggar" I would very much like to have it and then we could call it quits.' Innes to RM, 19 Sept. 1934, MS-990/16/19.

12 Fairburn to RM, 16 June 1932.
13 RM to Fairburn, 6 May 1932.
14 Fairburn to RM, 21 Mar. 1932.
15 Charles Lahr, quoted by Fairburn to RM, 21 Mar. 1932.
16 Fairburn to RM, 29 Feb. 1932.
17 RM to Fairburn, 20 Apr. 1932; *Auckland Star*, 8 Apr. 1932, p.6.
18 Fairburn to RM, 16 June 1932, 22 Dec. 1931.
19 Fairburn to RM, 16 June 1932.
20 Fairburn to RM, 29 Jan., 2 Mar., 16 June 1932.
21 Fairburn to RM, 31 July 1932.
22 'R.A.K. Mason on Rex Fairburn', 1957, transcript, Auckland University Library, p.15.
23 RM to Fairburn, 20 Apr. 1932.
24 Fairburn to RM, 16 June 1932.
25 RM to Fairburn, 20 Apr., 6 May 1932.
26 Fairburn to RM, 31 July 1932.
27 Fairburn to RM, 29 Jan., 16 June, 2 Mar., 15 July 1932.
28 In his autobiography Kay described his backers as 'an investment corporation, with extensive Australian interests, who were willing to finance a small holding company for development purposes' (*The Restless Sky: the autobiography of an airman*, Harrap, London, 1934, p.134).
29 Company files CO–A1/707, no.4633, A1/667, no.4308, Archives New Zealand, Auckland Regional Office. Its prospectus described the company's activity as the purchase and acquisition of sporting concessions, from New Zealand and overseas (the actual employment of the concessions was left to subsidiary companies from which International Concessions Ltd would extract royalties and fees). Firth, many years later (interviewed by John Caselberg), would remember that Mason always supported his brother and defended him at every opportunity; but he did not recall the nature of his own involvement in Dan's business other than being persuaded to buy shares. (Nor did he mention his own enterprises: Market Research Ltd was one, which he established in 1932 in partnership with Jack Stewart.) Stephen Champ, another left-wing friend, recalled that Mason disliked his job because it represented the antithesis of what he believed in.

30 RM to Fairburn, 6, 20 May 1932.
31 Pia Richards to RM, [1932], MS-592/F-5.
32 Bob Lowry to Denis Glover, 1 Dec. 1931, MS-Papers-0418-4, ATL.
33 Lowry to Glover, 29 Sept. 1931. Lawrence and Middleton Murry's *Adelphi* became the *New Adelphi* in 1927.
34 Lowry to Glover, 1 Dec., 3 May, 1931, 25 Feb. 1932, MS-Papers-0418-5.
35 *Phoenix*, Vol.1, No.1 (Mar. 1932), 'The cause of it all', p.[1].
36 *New Zealand Herald*, 23 Apr. 1932, supplement, p.8.
37 RM to Fairburn, 6 May 1932.
38 James Bertram to RM, 1 Jan. 1932, MS-592/E-5.
39 Lowry to Glover, 29 Sept. 1931. Curnow had had six poems in *Kiwi* the previous year.
40 J.C. Beaglehole to RM, 14 Mar. 1932, MS-592/E-5.
41 'Modernism and literature', draft lecture for WEA, 11 May 1932, MS-990/8.
42 RM to Atlantic Monthly Press, 25 Nov. 1933, MS-990/16/18.
43 RM, 'notebooks', MS-990/10.
44 *Phoenix*, Vol.1, No.2 (July 1932), pp.55-6. A review by John Mulgan of the second *Phoenix* in the student newspaper *Craccum*, which praised 'His End was Peace' as 'the mainstay of the number', suggests that some, however, found

Mason's psychological interest just puzzling: 'This [Mason's story] has received considerable praise artistically, while being criticised from the side of technical details. The average man has not the necessary knowledge of psychology to adjudicate on the question of Maddox's stroke and whether or not such a state of mind is possible in a man. I have heard people with knowledge of farming criticise the details of the twenty-five acre farm, and while such criticisms may seem trifling they have a certain importance which no author can afford to overlook. The story remains, however, a striking piece of prose.' *Craccum*, 22 Sept. 1932, p.5.

45 Lowry to Glover, 24 July 1932.
46 Allen Curnow, introduction to R.A.K. Mason, *Collected Poems*, Pegasus Press, Christchurch, 1962, p.13.
47 Jean Bartlett (Alison) to John Caselberg, 29 July–7 Aug. 1980, MS-1265/II/3/21, HL. Allen Curnow recalled hearing the second account from Rona Munro. Curnow, annotations to Caselberg manuscript, 'The Mirror and the Sword', MS-1265/II/5/1.
48 'R.A.K. Mason on Rex Fairburn', pp.13-14.
49 Ibid.
50 RM to Edwynna Roussel, 30 Apr. 1933, MS-990/15/2.
51 'R.A.K. Mason on Rex Fairburn', p.14. Fairburn would later title the poem when it was published 'Lines for a Rebel'.
52 MS-990/6. When this poem was written is not known.

11 **Romantics and revolutionaries *1933***

1 *Landfall*, Vol.25, No.3 (Sept. 1971), pp.225-6.
2 Jean Bartlett (Alison), interviewed by John Caselberg, MS-1265/II/1/12, HL; Elsie Locke (Farrelly), interviewed by John Caselberg, MS-1265/II/1/9.
3 Ian Milner, *Intersecting Lines*, Victoria University Press, Wellington, 1993, pp.99-100.

4 Quoted by John Caselberg, 'R.A.K. Mason, 1905–1971: a record of his life and writings', 1986, p.192, MS-1265/II/6.
5 Pia Richards to RM, nd, 9/10 Oct. 1932, MS-592/F-5.
6 Jean Alison to Blackwood Paul, 2 Jan. 1933, MS-Papers-5523-12, ATL; Bob Lowry to Denis Glover, 5 Feb. 1933, MS-Papers-0418-4, ATL.
7 Jean Alison, *Landfall*, Sept. 1971, p.226; Ron Holloway, 'Remembering Bob Lowry', *Landfall*, Vol.18 No.1 (Mar. 1964), p.56.
8 James Bertram, 'A note on the war generation', *Landfall*, Vol.19, No.2 (June 1965), p.139.
9 Elsie Locke, *Student at the Gates*, Whitcoulls, Christchurch, 1981, p.158.
10 Pia Richards to RM, 2 Sept. 1932.
11 Allen Curnow, interview with MacD. Jackson, *Islands*, Winter 1973, pp.144-5.
12 Quoted in K. Sinclair, *A History of the University of Auckland, 1883-1983*, Auckland University Press/Oxford University Press, Auckland, 1983, p.154.
13 Jean Alison to Blackwood Paul, 2 Jan. 1933.
14 *Phoenix*, Vol.2, No.1 (Mar. 1933), pp.7, 5.
15 Ibid., pp.7-9.
16 Ibid., p.6.
17 Ibid., pp.14, 20, 22.
18 *Auckland Star*, 13 May 1933, magazine section, p.2.
19 *Phoenix*, Vol.2, No.1 (Mar. 1933), pp.33-4.
20 Auckland University College Professorial Board minutes, 15 May 1933.
21 Quoted in 'Censors and "The Phoenix"', *New Zealand Observer*, 4 May 1933.
22 Draft 'Notes' for *Phoenix*, Vol.2, No.2, p.5, MS-592/B.
23 Eric Cook, 'Groundswell', pp.34-5, MS-592/B.
24 Draft 'Notes' for *Phoenix*, Vol.2, No.2, p.2.
25 RM, notes on *Phoenix* (1962), MS-592/B; 'Groundswell', p.35.
26 RM, notes on *Phoenix* (1962).
27 *New Zealand Truth*, 31 May 1933, quoted in P. Hughes, '"Sneers, jeers . . . and red

rantings": Bob Lowry's early printing at Auckland University College', *Turnbull Library Record*, Vol.12, No.1 (May 1989), p.18.

28 RM to Jack Stewart, 10 June 1933, MS-990/15/2, HL.

29 *Auckland Star*, 13 May 1933, magazine section, p.2.

30 *Art in New Zealand*, June 1933, p.233.

31 *New Zealand Observer*, 4 May 1933, p.7.

32 *The Month*, July 1933.

33 *Craccum*, 11 May 1933.

34 Minutes of *Phoenix* sub-committee meeting, 6 May 1933, MS-Papers-5233-12.

35 RM to Jack Stewart, 10 June 1933.

36 *New Zealand Observer*, 6 July 1933, p.7.

37 *Phoenix*, Vol.2, No.2, pp.1–4.

38 Draft 'Notes' for *Phoenix*, Vol.2, No.2.

39 *Phoenix*, Vol.2, No.2 (June 1933), pp.4–6.

40 *Canta*, 19 June 1933.

41 Ibid.

42 Jean Alison to Blackwood Paul, 30 May 1933.

43 Minutes of Literary Club meeting, 5 July 1933, quoted in Hughes, p.22.

44 MS-990/1. The signatories were R. Hall Thomson, A. Atkinson and L. Gallagher.

45 Alfred Katz to RM, 10 July 1933; RM to Katz, 7 Aug. 1933, MS-592/B.

46 Katz to RM, 10 July 1933.

47 Ibid.

48 RM to Gordon Watson, [Aug. 1933], MS-592/B.

49 Roth Papers, MS-94-106-01/2, ATL.

50 Frank Sargeson, *Sargeson*, Penguin, Auckland, 1981, p.174.

51 Stephen Champ to John Caselberg, 22 Feb. 1982, MS-1265/II/2/1.

52 RM to A.R.D. Fairburn, 7 Nov. 1931, Fairburn Literary Estate.

53 Connie Purdue to John Caselberg, 11 Jan. 1982, MS-1265/II/2/5. The writer Maurice Shadbolt's account of trying to join the Party as a student in 1950 is consistent with this account. He went to see the Auckland branch secretary, Alec McLeod:

'You've thought about this?'
'I have,' I claimed.
'And you're sure about it?' he asked. 'Do you have to?'
'I'm not sure what you mean.'
'You might be more use if you weren't a dues-paying member.'
'I see,' I said, though I didn't.
'You could be,' he explained, 'a Party member in all but name. You could attend branch meetings and take part in policy discussions. But you wouldn't be known as one. If challenged you could deny membership. You could find that helpful at university and elsewhere. We might too. Having someone who isn't known as a communist can be an advantage.'
'If you say so,' I said with some frustration.
I was never to learn whether I was or I wasn't.
(Shadbolt, *One of Ben's*, David Ling, Auckland, 1994, pp.156-7.)

54 RM to Watson, [Aug. 1933].

55 RM to Katz, 7 Aug. 1933.

56 J.C. Beaglehole to RM, 26 July 1933, MS-592/B.

57 MS-592/B.

58 It was in fact Mason's suggestion that he do a volume of Curnow's poems on the *Phoenix* press. Curnow to RM, 3 [Jan? 1933], MS-592/E-5.

59 Lowry to Glover, 22 Sept. 1933.

60 Locke, *Student at the Gates*, p.180.

61 RM, notes on *Phoenix* (1962).

62 RM to Blackwood Paul, 23 Apr. 1934, MS-Papers-5523-10.

12 No New Thing 1934

1 RM to Alfred Katz, 7 Aug. 1933, MS-592/B, HL.

2 RM to Dave Faigan, 10 Sept. 1933, MS-990/15/2, HL.

3 Mason's name was listed as one of the founding members when the society was registered as an incorporated society in September 1933. (Thanks to Simon Sigley for this information.)

4   Mark Richards, 'My recollections of R.A.K. Mason', MS-1265/II/3/18, HL.

5   Honey Haigh, interviewed by John Caselberg, MS-1265/II/1/4.

6   RM to Hogarth Press, 1 Dec. 1933; to Atlantic Monthly Press, 25 Nov. 1933, MS-990/16/18.

7   Bob Lowry to Denis Glover, 20 May 1934, MS-Papers-0418-5, ATL.

8   Lowry to Glover, 'The scheme for the formation of Labour Clubs in the four University Colleges', 19 Feb. 1934.

9   Hector Monro to Blackwood Paul, [1934], MS-Papers-5523-10, ATL.

10 Ronald Holloway to Pat Lawlor, 21 [Apr.] 1934, MS-Papers-77-067-4/3, ATL. (Holloway dated this letter '24 vi'; Lawlor annotated it 'April'.)

11 Prospectus, Spearhead Publishers [1934], MS-990/6.

12 Lowry to Glover, 30 Aug. 1934, MS-Papers-0418-6. Holloway's version of the negotiations differs: Mason was intending to pay him £2 a week and Lowry £1, but they agreed to accept 30s each. (Holloway, interviewed by John Caselberg, MS-1265/II/1/11.)

13 RM to Glover, 20 May 1934, MS-Papers-0418-24.

14 Lowry to Glover, 20 May 1934.

15 Lowry to Glover, 30 Aug. 1934.

16 R. Hyde, 'Flaming youth and free speech', New Zealand Observer, 16 Aug. 1934, p.5; New Zealand Herald, 21 July 1934, p.10, 1 Aug. 1934, p.4; H. Roth, 'In the fight for free speech', New Zealand Monthly Review, May 1969, pp.7-9.

17 W.A. Sewell, Freedom of Speech, Auckland, 1934, back cover.

18 RM to Pat Lawlor, 22, 29 Aug. 1934, MS-Papers-77-067-4/1.

19 D. Glover and I. Milner (eds), New Poems, Christchurch, 1934, foreword.

20 RM to Glover, 6 Mar. 1934.

21 Ibid.

22 M. Roberts (ed.), New Country, Hogarth Press, London, 1933, p.18.

23 New Poems, foreword.

24 RM, 'notebooks', MS-990/10.

25 H.W. Rhodes, 'The art of quarrelling', Tomorrow, 5 Sept. 1934, pp.16-17.

26 No New Thing, copy held by the Alexander Turnbull Library. This (signed) copy was given by Frank Sargeson to William Plomer in 1937 and returned to Sargeson after Plomer's death.

27 Glover, 'Bob Lowry's books', Book, No.8 (Aug. 1946), p.[37].

28 Frank Sargeson to Glover, 27 June [1938], MS-Papers-0418-18. Of the very few linen-bound and numbered copies known to have been produced, one went to Marie Gaudin, another to Jean Alison.

29 No New Thing, Notes; draft introduction, MS-990/6.

30 Allen Curnow, 'The poetry of R.A.K. Mason', Book, No.2 (May 1941).

31 Curnow, introduction to The Penguin Book of New Zealand Verse, Penguin, London, 1960, p.44.

32 RM, 'notebooks'.

33 RM to Fairburn, 6 May 1932, Fairburn Literary Estate.

34 Curnow, 'The Poetry of R.A.K. Mason'.

35 Rex Fairburn to Muriel Innes, 14 June 1934, MS-Papers-1128-12, ATL.

36 Jocelyn Fairburn to RM, 21 July 1932, MS-592/F-1.

37 This poem uses the same metre as 'The Young Man Thinks of Sons' and 'Lugete o Veneres'. Writing of the latter poem to Fairburn, Mason had likened the effect to that of a water-wheel: 'This idea of mine in metre: the long line is supposed to drag along until the beat is almost gone out of it and she is petering out – then the little run of two beats gives you a sense of definite rhythm again.' RM to Fairburn, 24 Mar. 1930.

38 Marie Gaudin, when he showed her this poem, recognised that 'straw-built' came from Paradise Lost.

39 R. Hyde, 'Poetry in Auckland', Art in New Zealand, Vol.9, No.1 (Sept. 1936), p.31.

13 Darkness

1   Jane Mander to M.H. Holcroft, 11 Oct. 1934; nd [1934], MS-Papers-1186-16, ATL.
2   Rex Fairburn to Muriel Innes, 14 June 1934, MS-Papers-1128-12, ATL.
3   Fairburn to RM, 22 Dec. 1931, MS-592/F-1, HL.
4   RM to Alfred Katz, 7 Aug. 1933, MS-592/B.
5   Winston Rhodes, 'R.A.K. Mason. Some memories', 12 Aug. 1976; and interviewed by John Caselberg, MS-1265/II/3/18, II/1/8, HL; D. Trussell, *Fairburn*, Auckland University Press/Oxford University Press, Auckland, 1984, p.151.
6   RM, 'notebooks', MS-990/10, HL.
7   'Come out my soul' was included in Mason's *Collected Poems* in 1962 as a previously unpublished poem but it had appeared in the *Auckland Star*, titled simply 'Sonnet', on 25 February 1928.
8   MS-990/6.

14 New life *1935–36*

1   CO-A1/667, no.4308, Archives New Zealand, Auckland Regional Office. Jessie as well as Dan, Ron, and Clifton Firth had a few hundred shares in the company.
2   'Writers in New Zealand: A Questionnaire', *Landfall*, Vol.14, No.1 (Mar. 1960), p.59. In a 1948 job application Mason stated that he had done secretarial and organising work in both New Zealand and Australia.
3   Jean Devanny to RM, 2 July 1933, MS-592/B, HL.
4   'This Monkey Business', MS-990/3, HL.
5   'They Should Be Slaves', MS-990/7.
6   *Tomorrow*, 18 Dec. 1935, pp.14-15.
7   Bob Lowry to Denis Glover, 15 May 1935, MS-Papers-0418-5, ATL.
8   D'Arcy Cresswell to Glover, 19 Jan. 1936, in H. Shaw (ed.), *The Letters of D'Arcy Cresswell*, University of Canterbury, Christchurch, 1971, p.102.

9   Jane Mander to M.H. Holcroft, 14 Dec. [1935], MS-Papers-1186-16, ATL.
10 *New Zealand Authors' Week Bulletin*, No.1, Oct. 1935.
11 RM to Pat Lawlor, 18 Mar. 1936, MS-Papers-77-067-4/1, ATL. Mason's name appears on a PEN membership list of July 1937 but he is not there in May 1940 (*P.E.N. Gazette*, No.1, Aug. 1937; No.4, May 1940). He participated in an unsuccessful campaign to get Lawlor rather than Johannes Andersen elected as the New Zealand representative to the international conference in Argentina in 1936; this appears to have been his only active involvement.
12 Frank Sargeson to Glover, 28 Apr. 1936, MS-Papers-0418-18.
13 *Tomorrow*, 13 May 1936, p.21.
14 A.R.D. Fairburn to Glover, 6 May 1936, in L. Edmond (ed.), *The Letters of A.R.D. Fairburn*, Oxford University Press, Auckland, 1981, p.100.
15 RM to Lawlor, 12 Mar. 1936.
16 *Art in New Zealand*, Vol.9, No.1 (Sept. 1936), pp.31-2.
17 RM to Lawlor, 25 Mar. 1936. Johannes Andersen, not Lawlor, was the editor of the publication.
18 Notes for poetry lectures, 1962, MS-1134/2, HL.
19 Allen Curnow, introduction to R.A.K. Mason, *Collected Poems*, Pegasus Press, Christchurch, 1962, p.13. 'Prelude' but not 'New Life' was included in the second *Verse Alive* (1937), an anthology of poetry from *Tomorrow* edited by Denis Glover and Winston Rhodes.
20 Ibid.
21 *Auckland Star*, 27 June 1936, magazine section, p.2; Christchurch *Press*, 18 July 1936, p.17; *Tomorrow*, 8 July 1936, p.21.
22 RM to Glover, 5 Nov. 1937, MS-990/16/14.
23 Fairburn, 'Waiting for Lefty: meditations on the new drama', *Tomorrow*, 25 Nov. 1936, p.52.
24 Notes on drama, MS-990/1.
25 S. Cosgrove, 'From Shock Troup to Group Theatre', in R. Samuel et al.

(eds), *Theatres of the Left, 1880-1935*, Routledge & Kegan Paul, London, 1985, p.264.

26 Mason, perhaps, had anticipated this change with the advice he had given to Gordon Watson in 1933 about building the radical movement in the university (at least he seemed to suspect that it was not quite in line with current policy): 'You may regard it all as hopelessly right-wing and reactionary: it attempts at any rate to be realistic and to be a basis for a line of action which can run absolutely straight to the very end', he had remarked (RM to Watson, [Aug. 1933], MS-592/B).

27 Leaflet, 'All Auckland is Waiting for Lefty!'; *Waiting for Lefty* programme, Oct. 1936, MS-990/5.

28 *New Zealand Herald*, 19 Oct. 1936, p.12; Sargeson, 'Auckland braves censors who were waiting for Lefty', *Tomorrow*, 11 Nov. 1936, p.21.

29 *New Zealand Herald*, 19 Oct. 1936; *Auckland Star*, 19 Oct. 1936, p.9.

30 Sargeson to Glover, 3 Nov. 1935, 3 Jan. 1936.

31 *Tomorrow*, 11 Nov. 1936.

32 Fairburn, 'Waiting for Lefty: meditations on the new drama', p.50.

33 Circular letter, Oct. 1936, MS-990/5; *New Zealand Herald*, 2 Nov. 1936, p.14.

34 Minutes of public meeting in the WEA hall, 31 Oct. 1936, NZMS 821/1, Auckland City Libraries; MS-990/5.

35 Circular letter, MS-990/5.

36 Minutes of general meeting, 15 Nov. 1936; Rules of People's Theatre Incorporated, NZMS 821/1; membership application, MS-990/5.

37 Bill Deuchar to Victor Arnold, Sydney New Theatre League, 27 July 1937, NZMS 821/1; letter dated 18 Dec. 1936, MS-990/5.

38 *Auckland WEA Bulletin*, Vol.2, No.1 (Feb. 1937), p.21.

39 Shirley Barton, 'R.A.K. Mason – some memories and notes', MS-1265/II/3/27, HL.

40 Dorothea Mason to John Caselberg, MS-1265/II/2/25.

15 Waiting for Lefty 1937–38

1 RM to A.J.C. Fisher, 5 Feb. 1937, MS-990/15/2, HL.

2 People's Theatre to the secretary, Transport Board Employees' Union, 18 May 1937, NZMS 821/1, Auckland City Libraries.

3 Manuscript notes, MS-990/5.

4 Ibid.

5 Ibid.

6 Bill Deuchar to Victor Arnold, Sydney New Theatre League, 27 July 1937, NZMS 821/1.

7 *New Zealand Herald*, 19 Oct. 1936, p.12.

8 Deuchar to Arnold, 27 July 1937; H.W. Crook to the People's Theatre, 25 Apr. 1937, NZMS 821/2.

9 *Tomorrow*, 18 Aug. 1937, p.657.

10 Secretary, LBC Theatre Guild to People's Theatre, 27 Apr. 1938, NZMS 821/2.

11 Deuchar to Arnold, 27 July 1937.

12 *New Zealand Observer*, 17 June 1937, p.7.

13 *New Zealand Herald*, reprinted in *Workers' Weekly*, 25 June 1937, p.4; *Auckland Star*, 14 June 1937, p.3; *New Zealand Herald*, 21 June 1937, p.12.

14 RM, speech notes, MS-990/5.

15 RM, draft preface to three plays, [1960s], MS-990/1.

16 Jean Bartlett (Alison), interview with the author, 13 Dec. 1999.

17 MS-990/2.

18 RM to Denham von Sturmer, 24 June 1937, 84-055, HL.

19 Minutes of general meeting, 23 June 1937, MS 821/1; Deuchar to Arnold, 27 July 1937.

20 RM, 'notebooks', MS-990/10.

21 RM to Denis Glover, 5 Nov. 1937, MS-990/16/14.

22 Frank Sargeson to Glover, 26 Jan. 1936, MS-Papers-0418-18, ATL.

23 Sargeson to Glover, 9 Aug. [1937].

24 Sargeson to Glover, 1 June, 2 July 1938;

J.H.E. Schroder to Sargeson, 30 May 1938, MS-Papers-0418-18.

25 Sargeson, 'Food for Tender Stomachs. The poetry of R.A.K. Mason', MS-Papers-0432-379, ATL.

26 Dorothea Mason to John Caselberg, 3 Jan. 1981, MS-1265/II/3/25, HL.

27 RM, notes for poetry lectures, 1962, MS-1134/2, HL.

28 Rita Johnstone (Chapman) to John Caselberg, 31 Oct. 1980, MS-1265/II/2/3.

29 Allen Curnow, introduction to R.A.K. Mason, *Collected Poems*, Pegasus, Christchurch, 1962, p.14.

30 Dorothea Mason to Jean Bartlett, 26 Sept. 1976, MS-1265/II/2/25; Shirley Barton, Jean Bartlett, interviewed by John Caselberg, MS-1265/II/1/12, 4.

31 Dorothea Mason, MS-1265/II/2/25.

32 W. D'Arcy Cresswell, *Present Without Leave*, Cassell, London, 1939, p.223.

33 *Workers' Weekly*, 13 May 1938, p.4.

34 'The papers got Auntie', *Workers' Weekly*, 29 Apr. 1938, p.4.

35 *Tomorrow*, 17 Aug. 1938, p.642.

36 'Our origins', *Workers' Weekly*, 18 Feb. 1938.

37 Notes for an article on New Zealand history, MS-990/6.

38 *Tomorrow*, 27 Apr. 1938, pp.408, 411.

39 Draft preface to three plays.

40 *Squire Speaks*, Caxton Press, Christchurch, 1938, pp.4-5.

41 Draft preface to three plays; 'The Making of a Poem', 1959, Radio New Zealand Sound Archives; draft application for the Burns Fellowship, 24 Aug. 1961, MS-990/1; *China*, Auckland, 1943, foreword.

42 Bob Lowry to Glover, 31 July 1938, MS-Papers-0418-6, ATL.

43 RM to Glover, 5 Nov. 1937, MS-990/16/14.

44 *Auckland Star*, 15 Apr. 1939, Week-end Pictorial, p.10; Christchurch *Press*, 30 July 1938, p.18; *Tomorrow*, 22 June 1938, pp.538-9.

16 Decent proletarian stuff *1938-40*

1 Report on the progress of the People's Theatre, Jan. 1938, NZMS 821/1, Auckland City Libraries.

2 Circular, 1 Dec. 1937, NZMS 821/3.

3 A.J.C. Fisher to Bill Deuchar, 12 Jan. 1938, NZMS 821/3.

4 RM to the executive committee, People's Theatre, 6 May 1938, MS-990/15/2, HL.

5 Only the *New Zealand Woman's Weekly* was enthusiastic, describing it as 'one of the most exciting dramas for many years . . . gripping from start to finish' – its controversial theme 'will make it the most talked-of production of the year'. *New Zealand Herald*, 27 June 1938, p.12; *Auckland Star*, 27 June 1938, p.11; *New Zealand Woman's Weekly*, 23 June 1938.

6 *Tomorrow*, 6 July 1938, pp.566-7.

7 RM to the executive committee, 11 July, 8 Aug. 1938, NZMS 821, 821/2.

8 Frank Sargeson to Denis Glover, 30 Aug. 1938, MS-Papers-0418-18, ATL.

9 *Tomorrow*, 14, 28 Sept. 1938.

10 *People's Theatre Magazine*, p.15.

11 This was probably not the same play that Sargeson told Glover he was putting in for the centennial literary competitions, along with several short stories and two novels.

12 Press release, NZMS 821/1; *Workers' Weekly*, 8 Apr., *Tomorrow*, 13 Apr. 1938, pp.354-5.

13 Secretary to T. Angus, 8 July 1938, NZMS 821/1.

14 Report on competition entries, NZMS 821/1. ('As the R.C. looks for the imprimatur of the bishop', Baeyertz had written, 'so Leftists find satisfaction in the blessing by the Left Book Club.' R.E. Baeyertz, 28 June 1938, NZMS 821.)

15 *New Zealand Herald*, 20 Mar. 1939, p.12.

16 *Workers' Weekly*, 10 Mar. 1939, p.4.

17 *New Zealand Herald*, 18 Mar. 1939, p.28; *Tomorrow*, 12 Apr. 1939, p.377.

18 Undated circular letter, NZMS 821/2.

19 *Workers' Weekly*, 31 Mar. 1939, p.4.

20 *Workers Weekly*, 8 Apr., *Tomorrow*, 13

Apr. 1938, pp.354-5. Hamilton left for England soon after the production of *Falls the Shadow*, hoping to get it staged in London, but he was stranded in Norway when war broke out and never got there.

21 Programme copy, NZMS 821/1; *Tomorrow*, 13 Sept., p.733, 11 Oct. 1939, p.800.

22 'International Brigade: memorial service for the fallen', MS-Papers-94-106-01/3, ATL.

23 Indeed, one friend believed that he was tone deaf. Shirley Barton, 'R.A.K. Mason – some memories and notes', 1983, MS-1265/II/3/27, HL; Eileen Hamilton, interviewed by John Caselberg, MS-1265/II/1/11.

24 *People's Voice*, 7 July 1939, p.4.

25 'This Bird May Swing', pp.1, 8, MS-990/3; *Tomorrow*, 27 Apr. 1938, p.408; 'Dreams Come True', episode H, p.10, MS-592/C pt 1, HL; 'BMA', p.1, MS-990/3.

26 'God in Hell', p.13, MS-990/3.

27 *People's Voice*, 21 & 28 July, 11, 18 & 25 Aug. 1939, p.7.

28 1939 conference report of the Central Committee of the CPNZ, MS-Papers-94-109-01/3, ATL.

29 'Cheaper Labourers: a brief history of the New Zealand Company' (by PWD), pp.[3], 29, 37, MS-1265/II/3/3.

30 He worked there for two years, Mason later recorded, being eventually 'in charge of central steel stocks'.

31 *People's Voice*, 20 Oct., 10 Nov., 1 Dec. 1939, p.8.

32 Secretary to *People's Voice*, 19 Aug. 1939, to M.J. Savage, 28 Aug. 1939, NZMS 821/2.

33 *People's Voice*, 10 Nov. 1939, p.8.

34 *People's Theatre Magazine*, p.5.

35 'BMA', pp.1, 10-12. 'Most regrettable' was Mason's own verdict on this play many years later. 'A man in a Public Works camp was phoning a doctor for his sick wife: the doctor would not come and a chorus (probably moreporks) intoned B-Murder Artists.' RM to J.E.

Traue, 25 July 1962, MS-1134/1, HL.

36 *People's Voice*, 24 Nov. 1939, p.7.

37 *People's Voice*, 3 Nov. 1939, p.8.

38 *People's Theatre Magazine*, p.8.

39 *People's Voice*, 15 Sept. 1939, p.7; *People's Theatre Magazine*, p.8.

40 *People's Theatre Magazine*, p.8.

41 MS-1134/1.

42 Draft preface to three plays, [1960s], MS-990/1.

43 Shirley Barton, 'R.A.K. Mason – some memories and notes'.

44 In 1939 one of the first intake of Maori students at Auckland Training College, Te Hau was later awarded an OBE for his work in Maori education.

45 *People's Theatre Magazine*, p.10.

46 Shirley Barton, 'R.A.K. Mason – some memories and notes'.

47 Patricia Firth was to write to Mason in 1942 about how deeply hurt Clifton had been by Mason's withdrawal of friendship. Patricia Williams (Firth) to RM, 8 July 1942, MS-990/15/3.

48 Ian Milner, *Intersecting Lines*, Victoria University Press, Wellington, 1993, p.163.

49 Judah Waten to John Caselberg, 25 May 1982, MS-1265/II/2/6; Noel Counihan to RM, 21 Oct. 1944, MS-990/15/3.

50 Jean Bartlett (Alison) to John Caselberg, 11 Aug. 1981, MS-1265/II/3/21.

51 Pat Potter, interviewed by John Caselberg, MS-1265/II/1/11.

52 Owen Jensen to John Caselberg, 20 July 1983, MS-1265/II/2/3.

53 Jean Bartlett to John Caselberg, 29 July–7 Aug. 1980, MS-1265/II/3/21.

54 RM to Dorothea, 18, nd, 25 Jan. 1940, 83-032/1, HL.

55 Jean Bartlett to Blackwood Paul, 30 Jan. [1940], MS-Papers-5523-12, ATL.

56 RM to Dorothea, Wed. [Jan. 1940].

57 The secretary was Pat Potter, and both the Auckland General Labourers' and Carpenters' unions were affiliated. As acting secretary Mason signed a notice calling a meeting at the Carpenters' Union rooms on 15 February (MS-990/2); the *People's Voice* (15 Mar. 1940)

recorded the formation of the branch at a meeting at the Trades Hall.

58 Jean Bartlett to Blackwood Paul, 30 Jan. [1940]; to John Caselberg, 29 July–7 Aug. 1980.

59 Arnold Goodwin to the secretary, 24 Jan. 1940, MS 821/3.

60 MS 821/1.

17 In Print 1941–45

1 'The Spark's Farewell, The Miracle of Life, The Body of John, After Death & perhaps others from "The Beggar" (but not perhaps Latter-Day Geography Lesson). Amores VI certainly, & In Manus Tuas. And I have a weakness for that little Song of Allegiance.' Denis Glover to RM, 20 Jan. 1941, MS-990/16/14, HL.

2 J.E. Traue to H.O. Roth, 3 May 1962, MS-Papers-6164-64, ATL.

3 *Recent Poems*, Caxton Press, Christchurch, 1941, inside back cover.

4 Allen Curnow, 'The Poetry of R.A.K. Mason', *Book*, No.2 (May 1941).

5 Christchurch *Press*, 10 Dec. 1941, p.10.

6 *New Zealand Listener*, 26 Dec. 1941, p.16.

7 William Plomer, 'Some books from New Zealand', *Folios of New Writing*, autumn 1941, reprinted in Penguin *New Writing*, 17 (Apr.-June 1943), pp.151-2.

8 E.H. McCormick, *Letters and Art in New Zealand*, Department of Internal Affairs, Wellington, 1940, pp.188, 182, 189.

9 M.H. Holcroft, *The Deepening Stream*, Caxton Press, Christchurch, 1940, pp.64, 70, 71, 76.

10 Curnow, 'The Poetry of R.A.K. Mason'.

11 The Christchurch *Press* reviewer of *Recent Poems*, for example, felt that Mason's poems may 'mark the close of a period': this was Mason still wrestling with the enemies in his own mind but 'the struggle seems not to have found as full issue as in some earlier pieces'. Quoted in *Book*, No.2, (May 1941).

12 M.H. Holcroft, *The Waiting Hills*, Progressive Publishing Society, Wellington, 1943, pp.70, 72, 81, 88.

13 Mark Richards, 'My recollections of R.A.K. Mason', MS-1265/II/3/18, HL.

14 Mason may already have had his own plans for launching (another) new magazine. Winston Rhodes wrote to him in June 1941: 'We're going ahead now with Tomorrow's money hoping to get 90% permission to use it in the direction we think best. Personally I favour the Industrial Worker now that your plan has fallen through'; though it is possible this referred to the proposal Mason had been trying to float earlier, in 1939. Rhodes was writing to him first about an 'exposure of the Meat Trusts' Mason had written, or was writing, to be included in a pamphlet series that the Christchurch Co-operative Book Society was launching; no such pamphlet was published, however. (Rhodes to RM, 23 June [1941], MS-990/16/15.)

15 National secretariat, CPNZ, statement to Party sections, 23 May 1941, MS-Papers-94-106-02/1, ATL.

16 *New Zealand Herald*, 1 Nov. 1941, quoted in N. Taylor, *The Home Front*, Department of Internal Affairs, Wellington, 1986, p.601.

17 *In Print*, 24 June 1942, p.1.

18 *Forward to Victory in 1943*, report of the national committee, CPNZ, Jan. 1943, and notes by Bert Roth, MS-Papers-94-106-02/1.

19 *New Zealand Soviet Bulletin*, Vol.1, No.1 (Jan.-Feb. 1946), p.4; New Zealand Society for Closer Relations with the USSR, constitution, MS-Papers-3826, ATL.

20 RM to Bob, 28 Aug. 1941, MS-990/15/3.

21 *In Print*, 10 Sept. 1941, p.1.

22 *Forward to Victory in 1943*; *In Print*, 10 Sept. 1941, p.5, 8 Oct. 1941, p.2.

23 Barbara Thompson, interviewed by John Caselberg, MS-1265/II/1/11; Charles Bartlett, interviewed by Caselberg, MS-1265/II/1/4.

24 *In Print*, 16 Sept. 1942, p.[4].

25 RM, 'notebooks', MS-990/10.

26 Harold Silverstone to RM, 11 Nov. 1941, MS-990/17/32.

27 Jean Bartlett, interviewed by John Caselberg, MS-1265/II/1/4.

28 *In Print*, 5 Nov., 12 Nov. 1941, p.4.

29 Auckland CP branch bulletin, 10 Aug. 1942; *Forward to Victory in 1943*, MS-Papers-94-106-02/1.

30 Eileen Hamilton, interviewed by John Caselberg, MS-1265/II/1/11.

31 *In Print*, 14, 28 Jan., 4 Mar. 1942; *Auckland Star, New Zealand Herald*, 25 Feb. 1942; Taylor, p.923; *People's Voice*, 14 July 1971.

32 *In Print*, 25 Mar. 1942, p.4.

33 New Zealand Police, report of Detective R.D.L. Jones, No.3272, 21 July 1942. (I am grateful to Hugh Price for bringing this document to my attention.)

34 Navy Department file N2, 08/1/25, Archives New Zealand. See also S. Young, 'Ross, Sydney Gordon', in *Dictionary of New Zealand Biography*, Vol.5, Auckland University Press/ Department of Internal Affairs, Wellington, 2000, and D. Filer, 'The Great Spy Lie', *New Zealand Listener*, 25 Sept. 1982.

35 Hone Tuwhare, quoted in J. Hunt, *Hone Tuwhare: a biography*, Godwit, Auckland, 1998, p.42.

36 The first meeting was held on 7 August 1937 and the penultimate one on 10 November. See D. Challis & G. Rawlinson, *The Book of Iris: a life of Robin Hyde*, Auckland University Press, Auckland, 2002, p.438; Robin Hyde, 'Who says the Orakei Maori must go?', *New Zealand Observer*, 8 July 1937; 'No more dancing at Orakei', ibid., 19 Aug. 1937.

37 RM, obituary for Te Puea, *Challenge*, 1 Nov. 1952.

38 *In Print*, 9 June 1943, 12 May 1943, p.1.

39 Te Puea Herangi to RM, 14 Aug. 1943, MS-990/15/3.

40 *In Print*, 7 July 1943, p.3.

41 Ibid, p.4.

42 *In Print: a magazine of Marxism*, Dec. 1944, pp.23-8.

43 Pat Potter, interviewed by John Caselberg, MS-1265/II/1/10.

18 New theatre *1945–48*

1 RM to Norman Richmond, [1944], MS-990/15/3, HL.

2 *In Print*, 22 Oct. 1941, p.5, 5 Nov. 1941, p.8.

3 *People's Voice*, 1 Dec. 1943, p.7.

4 *China: script by R.A.K. Mason for a dance-drama by Margaret Barr*, Times Printing Works, Auckland, 1943, pp.3, 6.

5 RM to Richmond, [1944].

6 *China*, foreword.

7 New Theatre Group prospectus, MS A-194/1/6, Auckland University Library.

8 Shirley Barton, 'R.A.K. Mason – some memories and notes', 1983, MS-1265/II/3/27, HL.

9 RM, 'Refugee', MS-Papers-2370, ATL.

10 *People's Voice*, 17 Oct. 1945, p.8; *Year Book of the Arts in New Zealand*, 1945, pp.120-1.

11 New Theatre Group programme, ephemera collection, ATL; RM to Winston Rhodes, 17 Aug. 1962, MS-990/16/15; C. von Sturmer, *Margaret Barr: epic individual*, L. von Sturmer, Sydney, 1983. Barr spent the rest of her life in Australia, where she established the Sydney Dance-Drama Group in 1952; she died in 1991.

12 Draft preface to three plays [1960s], MS-990/1.

13 MS-990/3.

14 Dorothea Mason to John Caselberg, 13 Mar. 1978, MS-1265/II/2/25.

15 RM to Noel Counihan, 12 Oct. 1944, MS-990/15/3.

16 RM to Dorothea, 23 Feb. 1945, 83-023/1, HL.

17 *The Truth about Greece*, published by Sid Scott for the In Print Publishing Co.

18 Peter Purdue, interviewed by John Caselberg, MS-1265/II/1/12.

19 RM to Alan Mulgan, 12 Feb. 1948; *Challenge*, Feb. 1947, p.5.

20 RM to Dorothea, 15 Mar. 1945.

21 *Challenge*, [Oct.] 1945.

22 'Draft Report on the condition of the Brick Industry done for the Union', MS-990/13.

23 Pat Potter, interviewed by John Caselberg, MS-1265/II/1/11. Winston Rhodes would also comment on Mason's reputation on the left for being unreliable – saying he would do something and then simply not turning up.

24 *Frontier Forsaken: an outline history of the Cook Islands*, Challenge Publications, Auckland, 1947, p.81. The account that follows of the Cook Islands Progressive Association and Albert Henry's activities in the late 1940s is taken from H.O. Roth, 'Albert Henry as Labour Organizer: a struggle for power in the Cook Islands', *Journal of Pacific History*, Vol.12 (1977), pp.176–87.

25 Pat Potter, interviewed by John Caselberg. Mason would later refer to the 'great personal trouble' he was suffering during this time. 'Some notes on source material for "Frontier Forsaken"', MS-1134/2, HL.

26 *Frontier Forsaken*, p.5.

27 'Some notes on source material for "Frontier Forsaken"'. Mason subsequently did make his name known, he recorded here, when he 'found that the Union Secretary was beginning to behave in a most peculiar manner & even to suggest that he himself was the writer'.

28 *Frontier Forsaken*, pp.65, 5.

29 R.P. Gilson, 'Notes on Rarotongan Administration (for New Zealand Government, 1950 – unpublished)', in R.P. Gilson, drafts and research materials, folder 25a, Records Room, Division of Pacific and Asian History, Australian National University (copy made available by Doug Munro).

30 *Challenge*, July 1948.

31 RM to the secretary, World Federation of Trade Unions, 26 Nov. 1951, MS-990/17/32.

32 'R.A.K. Mason on Rex Fairburn', 1957, manuscript version, MS-592/F-2, HL.

33 Allen Curnow to Joe Heenan, 7 May 1945, MS-Papers-1132-42, ATL.

34 *Southland Times*, 14 July 1945, p.8.

35 Allen Curnow, introduction to *A Book of New Zealand Verse, 1923–45*, Caxton Press, Christchurch, 1945, pp.15-18, 21, 33, 45, 52.

36 Ibid., pp.26-7, 31.

37 Ibid., p.31, 28.

38 J.C. Reid, *Creative Writing in New Zealand: a brief critical history*, Whitcombe & Tombs, Auckland, 1946, pp.28, 34.

39 Douglas Lilburn to RM, 16 Apr., 17 Nov. 1946, MS-990/16/15.

40 *New Zealand Listener*, 13 Dec. 1946, p.10.

41 Counihan to RM, 13 Sept., 1, 21 Oct. 1944, MS-990/15/3.

42 Denis Glover to RM, 26 Apr. 1945, MS-990/16/14.

43 Ibid.

44 Glover to A.R.D. Fairburn, 17 Feb. 1947, MS-Papers-1128-84, ATL.

45 Glover to RM, 12 Feb. 1947.

46 Greville Texidor, 'Goodbye Forever', in *In Fifteen Minutes You Can Say A Lot*, Victoria University Press, Wellington, 1987, pp.204, 209.

47 Jane Mander to M.H. Holcroft, 13 May 1945, MS-Papers-1186-16, ATL.

48 *Landfall*, Vol.25, No.3 (Sept. 1971), p.241.

49 'Have been sorting over old papers & find they largely consist of letters from you to me & replies (unposted) from me to you', Mason was to write to Glover in 1961. Glover to RM, 26 Apr. 1945; Glover to John Caselberg, nd, MS-1265/II/3/24; RM to Glover, 18 Sept. 1961, MS-Papers-0418-24, ATL.

50 RM to Charles Brasch, 24 Jan. 1947, MS-996-2/244, HL; *Challenge*, Mar.1947, p.4.

51 Quoted in Ian Richards, *To Bed at Noon: the life and art of Maurice Duggan*, Auckland University Press, Auckland, 1997, p.96.

52 *Landfall*, Sept. 1971, p.235.

53 'R.A.K. Mason on Rex Fairburn', 1957, transcript, Auckland University Library, p.2.

54 Frank Sargeson to E.P. Dawson, 15 Apr. 1942, quoted in M. King, *Frank Sargeson: a life*, Penguin, Auckland, 1995, p.224.

55 Margot Ruben, 'Karl Wolfskehl. Exul immeritus: Erinnerungen an Neuseeland', in *Karl Wolfskehl*

Kolloquium, Castrum Peregrini,
Amsterdam, 1983, pp.52-3.

19 John ii 4 *1948–49*

1   Jessie Mason to RM, 6 Jan. 1948, MS-990/15/10, HL.
2   Jessie Mason to RM, 22 Dec. 1946, 30 Dec. 1947, nd.
3   RM to the secretary, AGLU, 21 Apr. 1948, MS-990/17/32. (He gave two weeks' notice.)
4   Pat Potter, 14 Sept. 1948, MS-990/17/32.
5   University of Otago Professorial Board minutes, 10 Mar., 12 May 1948, HL.
6   *Otago Daily Times*, 20 Sept. 1948, p.4. The previous year Mason had written an article for the *New Zealand Labour Review* – formerly Sid Scott's *In Print* – warning of witch-hunts against radicals in the universities, recalling the early 1930s, after comments made in Parliament about his friend Willis Airey and the WEA. 'Reaction discovers Adult Education', *New Zealand Labour Review*, Sept. 1947.
7   'The Mechanisation of Culture', MS-990/13, MS-1134/1, HL; *Otago Daily Times*, 21 Sept. 1948, p.8; Dunedin *Evening Star*, 21 Sept. 1948, p.3.
8   *Craccum*, 26 Apr. 1948, p.16.
9   'Mr Kerridge tries culture', *Landfall*, Vol.2, No.1 (Mar. 1948), pp.34-8.
10 *Otago Daily Times*, 21, 24 Sept. 1948, p.8; *Evening Star*, 21 Sept. 1948, p.3, 24 Sept. 1948, p.4.
11 'Mr Kerridge tries culture', p.35.
12 It was Deirdre Airey's impression that in fact the invitation had been engineered by John Harris to 'give Mason a boost'.
13 Charles Brasch to RM, 1 June 1949, MS-996-2/244, HL; *Virginia Quarterly Review* to RM, 13 Jan. 1948, MS-990/17/27. (The editor had seen an article on New Zealand poets by an American writer, she told Mason. The poetry quarterly *Voices* published 'Poetry in New Zealand' by H.W. Wells in its Commonwealth issue in 1948.)

14 RM to Jessie Mason, 9 Nov. 1948, MS-990/15/10; Christchurch *Press*, 29 Nov. 1948.
15 RM to Archie Dunningham, 9 Nov. 1948; RM to Joy Childs, 9 Nov. 1948, MS-990/15/3.
16 RM to Jessie Mason, 9 Nov. 1948; Jessie Mason to RM, 18 Nov. 1948, MS-990/15/10.
17 Denis Glover, interviewed by John Caselberg, MS-1265/II/1/1, HL.
18 Bill Pearson, 'Memories of Ron Mason', 1979, MS-1265/II/3/1.
19 Application dated 18 Nov. 1948; Winston Rhodes, testimonial, 15 Nov. 1948, MS-990/1; application dated 16 Dec. 1948, MS-990/15/3.
20 'Redvale Ranch 1948' diary, MS-990/1.
21 Dorothea Mason, memoir, MS-1265/II/3/25.
22 In fact, Jessie died on 14 May. In her will, which she made in November 1944, she left bequests of £50 to a niece and nephew, £400 to Ron, and the remainder of her estate (valued at less than £1200 in total) to Ron and Dan in equal shares. The £400 for her younger son was the 'reward', perhaps, that she had so long promised him. (Probate file, BBAE 1570, 611/1950, Archives New Zealand, Auckland Regional Office.)
23 Honey Haigh, interviewed by John Caselberg, MS-1265/II/1/4; Dorothea Mason, memoir.
24 Dorothea Mason, memoir.
25 RM to Brasch, 23 July 1949, MS-996-2/244.
26 Dorothea Mason, memoir.

20 The swamp *1950–53*

1   *People's Voice*, 26 Apr. 1950, p.3.
2   *Challenge*, Dec. 1948–Jan. 1949, p.2.
3   Ibid., Apr. 1951, p.1.
4   Quoted in H.O. Roth, *Trade Unions in New Zealand*, Reed, Wellington, 1973, p.71.
5   *Challenge*, May 1950, p.2.
6   Ibid, June 1950, p.2.
7   M. Shadbolt, *One of Ben's*, David Ling,

Auckland, 1994, p.155.

8 *Challenge*, Sept. 1950, p.7.

9 *People's Voice*, 27 Sept. 1950, p.3; notes for poetry lectures, 1962, MS-1134/2, HL.

10 The Trade Unions and Peace, 28 Oct. 1950, programme and minutes, MS-Papers-82-213-11, ATL.

11 *Challenge*, Nov. 1950, p.7, Mar. 1951, p.2. A review of the festival did not specifically mention Mason's poem, however. Mason was also one of the seventeen sponsors, along with Roy Stanley, Vic Wilcox and Clifton Firth, of a Youth Weekend for Peace in November 1952, which featured a comic opera, a Grand Peace Picnic, bowls, darts, chess, table tennis and other sports to bring people together 'in sport and culture' as the Helsinki Olympics had 'brought thousands from all nations in a friendly and peaceful spirit'.

12 RM, 'Comic Opera Court', 20 Dec. 1950, MS-Papers-0658-1, ATL.

13 Minutes of Wages Conference of the NZTUC, 27–28 Feb. 1951, MS-Papers-0658-1; *Evening Post, Dominion*, 28 Feb. 1951.

14 *Challenge*, May 1951, p.1.

15 Dick Scott, address to the Trade Union History Project's 1951 anniversary conference, Wellington, 2001. Tuohy was Walsh's birth name; he adopted the Fintan and Walsh before he returned to New Zealand from the United States in 1920.

16 Dorothea Mason, memoir, MS-1265/II/3/25, HL.

17 MS-Papers-82-213-11; Elizabeth Schliessel, interviewed by John Caselberg, MS-1265/II/1/7.

18 James K. Baxter, 'Recent trends in New Zealand poetry', in F. McKay (ed.), *James K. Baxter as Critic*, Heinemann, Auckland, 1978, p.11.

19 *Landfall*, Vol.25, No.3 (Sept. 1971), p.235.

20 *Challenge*, Aug. 1951, pp.4–5; *New Zealand Herald, Auckland Star*, 23 July 1951.

21 'Report to Area Conference on National Industrial Situation'(1951), MS-1265/II/3/47.

22 RM to World Federation of Trade Unions, 26 Nov. 1951, 22 Jan., 11 Mar. 1952, MS-990/17/32.

23 RM, reply to allegations made by watersiders' delegation, 19 June 1952, MS-1265/II/3/47.

24 *Challenge*, May 1953, p.1; Potter, 'Fight fair – or disruption', *Challenge*, Nov. 1952, p.8.

25 *Challenge*, June 1953, p.1.

26 Shirley Barton, 'R.A.K. Mason – some memories and notes', 1983, MS-1265/II/3/27.

27 Sid Scott to Harold Silverstone, 5 July 1951; district executive (Auckland) to the national secretary, 1 June 1951, MS-94-106-02/2, ATL.

28 S.W. Scott, *Rebel in a Wrong Cause*, Collins, Auckland, 1980; *NZ Truth*, 30 Aug., 9 Sept. 1960.

29 RM, 'notebooks', MS-990/10.

30 Dorothea Mason, memoir; note to Shirley Barton, MS-1265/II/3/27.

31 *Challenge*, Aug. 1953, p.7; Dorothea Mason, memoir.

32 Dorothea Mason to John Caselberg, 3 Jan. 1981, MS-1265/II/3/25.

33 RM, 'notebooks'.

34 Subsequent medical notes record that Mason suffered from this time from ischaemic heart disease and angina. Shirley Barton, 'R.A.K. Mason – some memories and notes'; Charles Howden to John Caselberg, 20 Oct. 1980, MS-1265/II/2/3; death certificate, 1971/3081, Registrar General's Office.

35 Dorothea Mason, memoir.

36 MS-990/6.

37 RM to A.R.D. Fairburn, 21 July 1953, MS-Papers-1128-50, ATL.

38 RM to Fairburn, 13 Oct. 1953.

39 Winston Rhodes to Sid Scott, 11 Jan. 1954, MS-Papers-94-106-5/7; Dorothea Mason, memoir.

21 Tecoma hedges *1954–57*

1 Dorothea Mason, memoir, MS-1265/II/3/25, HL; Ramai Hayward, interviewed by John Caselberg, MS-1265/II/1/12.
2 Shirley Barton, 'R.A.K. Mason – some memories and notes', 1983, MS-1265/II/3/27.
3 Bill Pearson, 'Memories of Ron Mason', 1979, MS-1265/II/3/1.
4 Barton, 'R.A.K. Mason – some memories and notes'; Pearson, 'Memories of Ron Mason'.
5 Barton to Rewi Alley, 28 Oct. 1953, MS-Papers-87-083-1/01A, ATL.
6 Barton to Alley, 20 Feb., 23 Apr., 5 Oct. 1954.
7 Barton to Alley, 20 Oct. 1953; obituary (unsourced clipping), MS-1265/II/3/27.
8 Barton to Alley, 6 Mar., 27 Mar. 1954, 20 Oct. 1953, 23 June 1954.
9 Pat Potter, 'To Members Auckland Labourers' Union: union administration', MS-Papers-94-106-40/07, ATL. This file contains extensive documentation of the Potter case, including the auditors' reports and correspondence.
10 Elizabeth Schiessel, interviewed by John Caselberg, MS-1265/II/1/10; 'Evening Waikaremoana', MS-990/6, HL.
11 RM to Jennifer Barrer, 9 Aug. 1963, in the possession of Jennifer Barrer, Christchurch.
12 *Salient*, 22 Mar. 1956; Anton Vogt, 'The Poet's Tongue: R.A.K. Mason', MS-Papers-2435, ATL. Vogt, Charles Brasch, Denis Glover and James K. Baxter were among those present at the meeting.
13 J. Bertram, *Return to China*, Heinemann, London, 1957, p.17.
14 *New Zealand Listener*, 29 Dec. 1967, p.5.
15 Margot Ruben to RM, 29 Apr. [1956], MS-990/15/4.
16 Winston Rhodes, 'R.A.K. Mason. Some memories', 12 Aug. 1976, MS-1265/II/3/18.
17 Sarah Alpers, 'Some memories of R.A.K. Mason', MS-1265/II/3/18. When Campion and her husband, Antony Alpers, moved to Stanley Bay a few years

later where they built a new house, Mason landscaped their garden.
18 Denis Glover to RM, 2 Apr. 1956, MS-990/16/14.
19 Glover to RM, 22 July 1956.
20 RM to Glover, 14 July 1956, MS-Papers-0418-24, ATL.
21 Ibid.
22 Glover to RM, 22 July, 2 Apr. 1956.
23 Glover to RM, 27 Oct. 1956; 3 Feb. 1957.
24 RM to Glover, 18 Sept. 1961.
25 RM, 7 Nov. 1956, reprinted in *China Dances*, John McIndoe, Dunedin, 1962, p.12; *New Zealand Herald*, 8 Oct. 1956.
26 *Landfall*, Vol.11, No.1 (March 1957), p.72. Mason was asked to write about the tour by the Auckland left-wing journal *Here and Now*, but never got around to it.
27 Frank Sargeson to Glover, 9 Nov. 1956, MS-Papers-0418-18.
28 RM to Ma Shao Po, 23 Aug. 1957, MS-1432, HL
29 *Landfall*, Vol.10, No.3 (Sept. 1956), pp.199, 200; A.R.D. Fairburn to RM, 15 Nov. 1956, quoted in L. Edmond (ed.), *The Letters of A.R.D. Fairburn*, Oxford University Press, Auckland, 1981, p.259.
30 He did contribute to the radio tribute as well, which was broadcast on 17 April, alongside James K. Baxter.
31 'R.A.K. Mason on Rex Fairburn', 1957, manuscript version, MS-592/F-2, HL.

22 China *1957–61*

1 RM to Mr Chen, June 1957, MS-1432, HL.
2 RM to Rewi Alley, 12 June 1957, MS-1432; notes for a speech against nuclear bomb tests on Christmas Island, MS-990/13, HL.
3 Dorothea Mason, memoir, MS-1265/II/2/25, HL; RM to Shirley Barton, 10 Sept. 1957, quoted in John Caselberg, 'R.A.K. Mason, 1905-1971: a record of his life and writings', 1986, p.328, MS-1265/II/6; to Alley, 23 Aug. 1957, MS-1432.
4 RM to Barton, 10 Sept. 1957, quoted in Caselberg, 1986, p.331.

5   RM, reports: 'Farming in China (1) The Co-operative Movement'; farm co-operative near Peking, 20 Sept. 1957; Wuhan, 16 Sept. 1957, MS-1432.

6   Ramai Hayward, interviewed by John Caselberg, MS-1265/II/1/12; Alley to Dorothea Mason, 25 Nov. 1975, MS-1265/II/3/18.

7   RM, script for Australian Broadcasting Corporation, MS-1432.

8   James Bertram to Charles Doyle, 1 Oct. 1965, MS-1265/II/3/23.

9   RM, preface to *China Dances*, McIndoe, Dunedin, 1962, p.3.

10 Ma Shao Po, 7 Nov. 1956, reprinted in *The Traveller*, Feb. 1957, MS-990/1.

11 Bertram to Doyle, 1 Oct. 1965.

12 *Hong Kong Tiger Standard*, 18 Oct. 1957, p.1; 'A Hundred Thousand Blessings', reprinted in *China Dances*, p.13.

13 RM to Barton, 21 Oct. 1957, MS-1432.

14 Dorothea Mason, memoir; RM, notes on China, MS-1432.

15 RM, 'China wants Peace', *Peace*, Feb. 1958, p.5.

16 MS-1432.

17 RM to Winston Rhodes, 9 Dec. 1957, quoted in Caselberg, 1986, p.343.

18 *Inside New China*, dir. Rudall Hayward, script by Ramai Hayward, Hayward Film Productions, 1957, New Zealand Film Archive. The films had, in fact, been a source of tension during the trip. Mason had been annoyed to find when he reached Hong Kong that the Haywards had brought a large amount of colour film as well as black and white film with them, as he complained to Shirley Barton. 'I also had to assert as clearly but quietly as possible that we were more than a film unit, that we were here on a N.Z. China Society invitation as guests of the Cultural Association and that I was the leader of the delegation, expected to act as such.' RM to Barton, 21 Oct. 1957.

19 Barton to RM, 10 Nov. 1957, MS-1432.

20 Alley to Barton, 28 Aug. 1960, MS-Papers-6533-43, ATL; Alley to Pip Alley, 23 Aug. 1965, MS-Papers-74-047-3/01, ATL.

21 Alley to Barton, 2 Oct., 29 Dec. 1960, MS-Papers-6533-43.

22 Barton to Alley, 15 May 1961, MS-Papers-6533-27. Hale had already sent Mason a contract for the book (offering him an advance on royalties of £150) by the time Alley informed them that he had had second thoughts because of the personal nature of the project – as Shirley had suggested he should. It is clear, however, from correspondence between Mason and Alley and between Alley and Barton, that the decision had not been his.

23 The poems were 'She Kept Cows' and 'Lullaby and Neck-verse'. *Nucleus*, Vol.1, No.2 [1958], pp.2, 8, 9.

24 The Unity Artists writers group published *Fernfire* magazine (1957–66), which published work by Hone Tuwhare and Noel Hilliard among others. It is perhaps curious that Mason did not otherwise have anything to do with this group; but the founder and *Fernfire*'s editor, Murray Gittos, does not recall him being involved and there is no record of it among his surviving papers.

25 MS-990/6.

26 'The Making of a Poem', 1959, Radio New Zealand Sound Archives.

27 E.H. McCormick, *New Zealand Literature: a survey*, Oxford University Press, London, 1959, pp.114-17.

28 Notes for poetry lectures, 1962, MS-1134/2, HL.

29 Allen Curnow, *The Penguin Book of New Zealand Verse*, Penguin, London, 1960, pp. 46, 21, 43, 44.

30 *New Zealand Woman's Weekly*, 22 Aug. 1960, p.59. (Mark Richards was one of the three readers.)

31 RM to the secretary, State Literary Fund advisory committee, 6 June 1961, MS-990/16/21.

32 *Landfall*, Vol.14, No.1 (Mar. 1960), pp.58-60; RM to Charles Brasch, 27 Dec. 1959, MS-996-2/224, HL.

33 University of Otago Registry, Burns Fellowship file, 00-156/52, HL.

34 Secretary, State Literary Fund advisory

committee to RM, 14 Sept. 1961, MS-990/16/21.

35 RM to Deirdre Airey, 27 Sept. 1961, MS-990/15/5.

23 A separate country 1962

1 RM to the registrar, University of Otago, 17 Oct. 1961, MS-990/16/21, HL.
2 RM to Judah Waten, 22 Feb. 1962, MS-990/16/16.
3 RM to Jean and Hone Tuwhare, 16 Oct. 1961, MS-990/16/22.
4 RM to Deirdre Airey, 27 Sept. 1961, MS-990/15/5.
5 Registrar to Brasch, Thompson & Millar, 19 Oct. 1961, University of Otago Registry, Burns Fellowship file, 00-156/52, HL.
6 RM to the registrar, 17 Oct. 1961.
7 Notes to 'Dream Come True', p.6, MS-592/C pt 1, HL.
8 Dunedin Evening Star, 22 Jan. 1962, p.1; Otago Daily Times, 26 Jan. 1962, p.1; Christchurch Press, 17 Jan. 1962, p.13.
9 RM to Deirdre Airey, 27 Sept. 1961.
10 RM to the registrar, University of Otago, 26 Aug. 1961.
11 Press, 17 Jan. 1962; Otago Daily Times, 26 Jan. 1962, Dunedin Evening Star, 22 Jan. 1962; RM to G. Chesterfield, at Robert Hale, 25 Sept. 1961, MS-1432, HL.
12 Draft application, 24 Aug. 1961, MS-990/1.
13 Dorothea Mason to John Caselberg, MS-1265/II/3/25, HL; RM to the registrar, 17 Oct. 1961; RM to Auckland Burns Association, 16 Oct. 1961, MS-990/16/22.
14 RM to Alan Horsman, 7 Jan. 1962, MS-990/16/21. The 'lad' was W.S. Broughton, whose PhD thesis, 'W. D'Arcy Cresswell, A.R.D. Fairburn, R.A.K. Mason: an examination of certain aspects of their lives and works', was submitted to the University of Auckland in 1968.
15 RM to Charles Doyle, 10 Jan. 1962, quoted in John Caselberg, 'R.A.K. Mason, 1905-1971: a record of his life

and writings', 1986, p.355, MS-1265/II/6, and in Doyle to RM, 19 June 1963, MS-990/16/14.
16 RM to Doyle, 26 June 1963, MS-990/16/14.
17 RM to W.S. Broughton, 16 Feb. 1970, MS-990/17/29.
18 RM to C.R.H. Taylor, 18 Dec. 1962, MS-990/16/19.
19 Ibid.; RM to Deirdre Airey, 16 Apr. 1962, MS-990/15/6; to Elizabeth Nurse (Richards), 3 June 1963, MS-990/15/7.
20 Rewi Alley to Pip Alley, 30 Oct., 22 Dec., 11 Oct. 1961, MS-Papers-74-047-4/06, ATL.
21 RM to Dorothea Beyda, 24 Jan. 1962, 83-032, HL.
22 Otago Daily Times, 26 Jan. 1962.
23 RM to Dorothea, 5 Mar., 8 Feb. 1962.
24 RM to Dorothea, 26 Apr. 1962.
25 RM to Clifton Firth, 19 Feb. 1962, MS-990/15/6.
26 RM to Dorothea, 15 Feb. 1962.
27 RM to Victor McGeorge, 16 Feb. 1962, MS-990/15/6.
28 RM to Dorothea, 26 Apr. 1962.
29 RM to Dorothea, 15 Feb. 1962.
30 RM to Katie Weir, 16 Apr. 1962, MS-990/17/34.
31 RM to O.E. Middleton, 6 Apr. 1962, MS-990/16/15.
32 Critic, 5 Apr. 1962; RM to O.E. Middleton, 6 Apr. 1962.
33 Charles Brasch to James Bertram, 11 Apr. 1962, MS-Papers-93-133-09, ATL. Mason also read Curnow's 'House and Land' and 'The Unhistoric Story'.
34 RM to Dorothea, 26 Apr. 1962.
35 Keith Maslen to the author, 17 Feb. 2003.
36 Rex Fairburn, Press Room, University of Otago, Dunedin, 1962, p.[3].
37 Clifton Firth to RM, 24 July 1962, MS-990/16/22; RM to Firth, 15 Aug., 19 Feb. 1962, MS-990/15/6.
38 RM to Denis Glover, 11 May 1962, MS-990/16/14; to Allen Curnow, 23 May 1962, MS-592/D.
39 Glover to RM, 20 May 1962, MS-990/16/14.

40 RM to Glover, 28 May 1962.

41 RM to J.E. Weir, 9 Oct. 1970, MS-990/
16/16. (The young woman was Mira
Szaszy.)

42 Coralie Marshall, interviewed by John
Caselberg, MS-1265/II/1/9.

43 Kay Flavell, interviewed by John
Caselberg, MS-1265/II/1/9; to the
author, 22 May 2003.

44 RM to Dorothea, 19 June, 2 July 1962.

45 RM to Dorothea, 14 July 1962.

46 Coralie Marshall, interviewed by John
Caselberg.

47 John Griffin, interviewed by John
Caselberg, quoted in Caselberg, 1986,
p.364.

48 Bertram, notes for 1962 *Poetry* broadcasts,
1962, MS-990/8.

49 Allen Curnow, introduction to R.A.K.
Mason, *Collected Poems*, Pegasus Press,
Christchurch, 1962, pp.9, 11.

50 *New Zealand Herald*, 21 July 1962, section
3, p.2; *New Zealand Listener*, 7 Sept. 1962,
p.35; *Auckland Star*, 20 July 1962, p.4;
Hawkes Bay Herald Tribune, 28 July 1962,
p.4.

51 *New Zealand Monthly Review*, Sept. 1962,
pp.20-1.

52 Hone Tuwhare to RM, 24 Aug. 1962,
MS-990/16/17.

53 *New Statesman*, 13 Jan. 1961, p.62; *Times
Literary Supplement*, 4 Jan. 1963, p.10.
The *TLS* review (of Curnow's *A Small
Room with Large Windows* and *Australian
Poetry 1961* as well as Mason's *Collected
Poems*) was by Colin Horne, professor of
English at the University of Adelaide.

54 RM to the registrar, 26 Aug. 1961.

55 Notes for poetry lectures, 1962, MS-
1134/2, HL.

56 Ibid.

57 RM to McGeorge, 14 July 1962.

58 RM to Dorothea, 18 July 1962.

59 N.M. Richmond to RM, 11 Apr. 1962;
RM to Richmond, 23 July 1962, MS-
990/15/6. (Richmond had been forced
to retire from teaching in 1950 because
of mental illness and had been
institutionalised intermittently in
Australia before he returned to New

Zealand in 1959.)

60 RM to Dorothea, 24 July 1962.

61 MS-990/6.

62 V.J. McLean, acting superintendent,
Carrington (formerly Oakley) Hospital,
to Dorothea Mason, 12 Apr. 1983, MS-
1265/II/2/1.

63 RM to Alfred Katz, 7 Aug. 1933, MS-
592/B.

64 RM to McGeorge, 23 Aug. 1962.

65 RM to Dorothea, 6 Aug., 1 [Aug.] 1962.

66 Dorothea Mason, memoir, MS-1265/II/
3/25.

67 RM to Tuwhare, 23 Sept. 1962.

68 Wallace Ironside to John Caselberg, 21
July 1978, MS-1265/II/2/3.

69 RM to Shirley Barton, 11 Oct. 1962;
RM to McGeorge, 27 Oct. 1962.

24 Strait is the Gate *1963-65*

1 Dorothea Mason, memoir, MS-1265/II/
3/25, HL.

2 Mason's notes, synopsis and draft are in
the Alley papers in the Turnbull Library
(MS-Papers-74-047-6/15); there are also
notes and a draft of the synopsis among
his own papers in the Hocken Library
(MS-1432). His biography, as far as it
went, portrayed Alley as a product less of
the Chinese revolution than of his New
Zealand upbringing: 'He had reached his
goal [Shanghai, in 1927], the gigantic,
ancient and tumultuous world of China,
entering now upon the period of its
greatest conflicts and resolutions. To a
rare degree among men of European
descent, he was formed by nationality,
family training and mental compulsion to
penetrate into the inner meaning of this
world, to feel with it and understand it in
study but even more by participation.' It
began with a chapter about Rewi
Maniapoto and the battle of Orakau.

3 *China Dances*, John McIndoe, Dunedin,
1962, pp.3-4.

4 RM to Alec McLeod, 7 Mar. 1963, MS-
990/16/25, HL.

5 Winston Rhodes to RM, 15 Dec. 1962,
MS-990/16/15. Jim Bertram also sent

him positive comments, for which Mason thanked him: 'You are one of the few people who took it that I was serious in regard to the possibilities of prose learning from poetry.' RM to Bertram, 2 May 1963, MS-Papers-5075, ATL.

6   RM to the registrar, University of Otago, 31 Aug. 1962, MS-990/16/21.

7   RM to Bertram, 2 May 1963.

8   MS-990/6.

9   RM to J.E. Traue, 28 Feb. 1962, MS-990/16/19.

10   RM to Denis Glover, 2 Apr. 1963, MS-990/16/14.

11   Christchurch *Press*, 2 Mar. 1963, p.13; *Star*, 2 Mar. 1963.

12   Winston Rhodes, 'R.A.K. Mason. Some memories', 12 Aug. 1976, MS-1265/II/3/18.

13   *New Zealand Monthly Review*, Apr. 1963, p.19.

14   RM to Jennifer Barrer, 9 Aug. 1963, in the possession of Jennifer Barrer, Christchurch.

15   Jennifer Barrer to John Caselberg, 5 Sept. 1978, 7 July 1982, MS-1265/II/2/1.

16   RM to Jennifer Barrer, 12 Mar. 1963.

17   Jennifer Barrer, interviewed by John Caselberg, MS-1265/II/1/9.

18   MS-990/6. Jennifer Barrer would later publish two poems of her own about Mason: 'Letter to Ron', in *Follow the Sun* (Hazard Press, Christchurch, 1992) and 'Ronald Allison Kells Mason', in *Looking Up* (Caxton Press, Christchurch, 1997).

19   RM to Jennifer Barrer, 21 Mar. 1963.

20   Peter Bland to RM, 15 Jan. 1963, MS-990/16/24.

21   Bertram, notes for 1962 *Poetry* broadcasts, MS-990/8.

22   RM to Winston Rhodes, 15 Mar. 1963; to George Blackburn, 16 Mar. 1963, MS-990/17/24.

23   Notes for 1963 *Poetry* broadcasts, MS-990/8.

24   N. Ascherson, *Stone Voices*, Granta, London, 2002, p.137.

25   RM, 'notebooks', MS-990/10.

26   MS-990/8.

27   RM to Bertram, 2 May 1963.

28   RM to Bertram, 9 May 1963.

29   RM to Jennifer Barrer, 21 June. 1963.

30   RM to Jennifer Barrer, 3-4 Apr. 1963.

31   RM to Jennifer Barrer, nd [Apr.], 12 May, 3 June 1963.

32   In Mason's papers there is also a typed set of a dozen poems written in Dunedin, but there is no evidence that he tried to get them published.

33   RM to Jennifer Barrer, 3 June 1963.

34   Ibid.; *Strait is the Gate*, script, draft introduction and notes preliminary to reading, MS-990/4; RM to Jennifer Barrer, 12 May 1963.

35   RM to Jennifer Barrer, 3 June 1963.

36   RM to Jean Bartlett, 4 June 1963, MS-990/16/24; to Elizabeth Nurse (Richards), 3 June 1963, MS-990/15/7.

37   R. Dallas, *Curved Horizon*, University of Otago Press, Dunedin, 1991, p.138.

38   RM to Hone Tuwhare, 19 Feb. 1962, Tuwhare to RM, 23 Jan. 1962, MS-990/16/17; Tuwhare, quoted in J. Hunt, *Hone Tuwhare: a biography*, Godwit, Auckland, 1998, pp.43, 77, and in 'Boilermaker by trade. Poet by inclination', unsourced newspaper clipping, 84-055, HL.

39   Tuwhare, interviewed in *New Argot*, May 1975, p.2. His mother had been a Mormon; his father had been a member, in turn, of the Anglican, Methodist, Jehovah's Witness and Ratana churches.

40   Hunt, p.71.

41   Bob Lowry to Tuwhare, 4 Oct. 1963, MS-990/16/17.

42   RM, foreword to Tuwhare, *No Ordinary Sun*, Blackwood and Janet Paul, Auckland, 1965.

43   Jean Bartlett to RM, 18 July 1963, MS-990/16/17; RM to Jean Bartlett, 4 June 1963, MS-990/16/24.

44   D. McEldowney, *Full of the Warm South*, John McIndoe, Dunedin, 1983, p.36.

45   *Otago Daily Times*, 27 July 1963, p.4.

46   Ibid.; RM to Douglas Lilburn, 23 June 1970, MS-990/16/15.

47   Charles Brasch to Bertram, 26 June 1963, MS-Papers-93-133-09, ATL.

48   *Otago Daily Times*, 27 July 1963; notes

for 1963 *Poetry* broadcasts.

49 RM to Louis Johnson, 19 July 1963, MS-990/16/24.

50 James K. Baxter, 'Aspects of Poetry in New Zealand', 1967, in F. McKay (ed.), *James K. Baxter as Critic*, Heinemann, Auckland, 1978, p.75; Baxter, 'The Kiwi and Mr. Curnow', *Education*, Vol.10, No.1 (Feb. 1961), pp.27-8.

51 RM to Bertram, 2 May 1963; to Albion Wright, 7 Sept. 1970, MS-990/16/23.

52 Charles Doyle to RM, 19 June 1963, MS-990/16/14.

53 RM to Doyle, 21 May 1964, ibid.

54 Doyle to RM, 2 Feb. 1964.

55 C.K. Stead, 'R.A.K. Mason's poetry – some random observations', *Comment*, July 1963, pp.34-8.

56 *Landfall*, Vol.17, No.3 (Sept. 1963), pp.286-90.

57 Ibid., Dec. 1963, p.421; Jan. 1964, pp.189-90. Bertram had recommended Savage to Brasch, and Brasch was pleased to have someone 'look at [Mason's] work with a fresh eye', he told Savage when he commissioned the review. 'What you say is, I think, the sort of thing that needs saying', he replied when Savage sent him the first draft, after two angry reminders; but he became less pleased when Savage failed to revise it as he wanted. At least one sentence he had found 'gratuitously unkind'. MS-996-002/348, HL.

58 Frank Sargeson to Bill Pearson, 6 Oct. 1963, MS-Papers-4261-191, ATL.

59 *Critic*, 8 Aug. 1963, p.6.

60 Brasch to Bertram, 14 Aug. 1963; RM to H. Thornton, 28 Aug. 1963, MS-990/16/25.

61 RM to Pip Alley, 22 Aug. 1963, MS-1432, HL.

62 George Blackburn to RM, 14 Nov. 1963, MS-990/17/24.

63 RM to Blackburn, 9 June 1963; Blackburn to RM, 14 June 1963.

64 B.G. Broadhead to RM, 11 Dec. 1963, MS-990/16/24. There is other evidence that Mason's programmes were not well received. Brasch described his July broadcast as 'querulous' (Brasch to Bertram, 19 July 1963). Ormond Wilson reported to Peggy Garland in January 1964 that 'Ron Mason has settled with Dorothea in Dunedin and gives pompous and very bad radio broadcasts' (P. & D. Beatson (eds), *Dear Peggy: letters to Margaret Garland from her New Zealand friends*, Sociology Department, Massey University, Palmerston North, 1997, p.82).

65 One of the projects Lowry left unfinished was Tuwhare's *No Ordinary Sun*, which did not come out until September 1964.

66 McEldowney, p.58.

67 John Griffin, quoted in John Caselberg, 'R.A.K. Mason, 1905–1071: a record of his life and writings', 1980, p.404, MS-1265/11/6; interview with the author, Apr. 2003.

68 Notes for proposed anthology, MS-990/9.

69 Rewi Alley to Pip Alley, 31 May 1962, 7 Oct. 1963, MS-Papers-74-047-4/07, -4/08, ATL. Pip was less understanding in his comments to Rewi about Mason's failure to produce the book, writing to him in March the following year: 'I am afraid Ron got too heavily weighed down with beer drinking or perhaps just getting old to be of any use' (MS-Papers-74-047-3/02). Mason finally wrote to Hale in April 1965 to tell them that he had had to give the project up on medical advice; he had told Alley that he did not think he could go on with it in December 1964, and suggested that his friend Willis Airey take it over. Airey began work on his biography in the middle of 1965: *A Learner in China: a life of Rewi Alley*, it was published in 1970, two years after Airey's death.

70 RM to Jennifer Barrer, 27 Mar. 1964.

71 Dorothea Mason, memoir.

72 RM to Melva Firth, 13 July 1964, MS-1265/II/3/8.

73 RM to Jennifer Barrer, 14 July 1964.

74 Brasch to Bertram, 22 Sept. 1964.

75 Brasch, Journal, Aug. 1964, MS-996-9/33, HL.

25 Bags dog boat 1965–71

1 Bill Pearson, 'Memories of Ron Mason', 1979, MS-1265/II/3/1, HL.

2 Dorothea Mason to Charles Brasch, 15 Sept. 1965, RM to Brasch, 3 Nov. 1965, MS-996-2/244, HL.

3 Brasch to Frank Sargeson, 15 Dec. 1965, MS-Papers-0432-149, ATL.

4 Charles Howden, medical notes, 1965–70; Howden to John Caselberg, 20 Oct. 1980, MS-1265/II/2/3.

5 RM to Denis Glover, 18 Dec. 1965, Glover to RM, 7 Feb. 1964, MS-990/16/14, HL.

6 Glover to RM, 7 Feb. 1964, 21 July, 9 Oct. 1966.

7 RM to Pearson, 6 June 1966, MS-1265/II/3/11.

8 Frank Sargeson to Kevin Ireland, 30 May 1959, quoted in M. King, Sargeson, Viking, Auckland, 1995, p.349.

9 Sargeson to J.E. Weir, 2 Aug. 1968; Sargeson to Bob [Chapman?], 15 July 1971, MS-Papers-0432-141, 197.

10 Sargeson to Harold Innes, 23 Nov. 1962, MS-Papers-0432-492.

11 Sargeson to Winston Rhodes, 1 June 1964, MS-Papers-0432-140.

12 Sargeson to C.K. Stead, 26 June 1966, MS-Papers-0432-141.

13 Auckland Star, 21 July 1966, p.6.

14 Brasch to Sargeson, 25 June [1966], MS-Papers-0432-149.

15 Howden, medical notes.

16 Sargeson to W.G. Austin, 13 & 24 Sept. 1966, MS-Papers-0432-194.

17 Austin to Sargeson, 20 Sept., 24 Nov. 1966.

18 Sargeson to Austin, 29 Nov. 1966.

19 Austin to Sargeson, 25 Sept. 1967.

20 RM to Austin, 24 June 1968, MS-990/16/25. The Minister was played by Donald Farr, Jean McDonald by Pamela Merwood. Austin directed another radio production of Strait is the Gate in 1974, with Russ Burton as St Peter, Brett Shand as the Minister and Cilla McQueen as Jean. A full stage production was done at the Globe Theatre in October 1979, directed by Jennifer Blumsky (Jennifer Barrer), with Russ Burton playing the Minister and Shirley Griffiths as Jean. For Jennifer Barrer, the Globe Theatre production was the fulfilment of a dream both she and Mason had had that they would one day collaborate. In June that year the Globe had staged a programme of Mason's short plays, including China and Squire Speaks.

21 Anton Vogt, 'The Poet's Tongue. R.A.K. Mason', 1962, MS-Papers-2455 and 5201-29, ATL; MS-990/17/27.

22 He refused permission for 'On the Swag' to be included in a South African anthology for schools, however.

23 G.J. Tee to RM, 30 June 1970, MS-990/17/28.

24 Alfred Katz to RM, 20 Sept. 1960, MS-990/17/27; A. Katz & J.S. Felton, Health and Community: readings in the philosophy and science of public health, Free Press, New York, 1965.

25 Sargeson to Brasch, 9 Mar. 1969, MS-996-3/101.

26 RM to Peter Purdue, 29 Jan. 1969, MS-990/17/35; publicity notes and clippings, MS-990/8.

27 Dorothea Mason, memoir, MS-1265/II/3/25.

28 Howden, medical notes; V.J. McLean, acting superintendent, Carrington Hospital to Dorothea Mason, 12 Apr. 1983, MS-1265/II/2/1.

29 Dorothea Mason, memoir.

30 RM to Jean Ann Scott Miller, 17 Dec. 1969, MS-990/16/13.

31 RM to Jean Ann Scott Miller, 12 Feb. 1970.

32 RM to John Summers, 17 Feb. 1970, MS-990/16/19.

33 RM to Summers and to John Griffin, 17 Feb. 1970.

34 Summers to RM, 24 Feb. 1970, Griffin to RM, 27 Feb. 1970, MS-990/16/19; Griffin to RM, 14 May 1970, Misc-MS-0010a, HL. In July 1971 a short profile of Mason in the New Zealand Herald (in its 'Makers of Auckland' series) stated that

he had 'sold his only remaining copy to a university professor for $10'. *New Zealand Herald*, 1 July 1971, section 1, p.16.

35 RM to John Weir, 9 Oct. 1970, MS-990/16/16.

36 Sargeson to Weir, 2 Aug. 1968.

37 RM to Weir, 8 June, 2 Mar. 1970.

38 RM to John McIndoe, 31 Aug. 1970, MS-990/15/9.

39 RM to Peter Platt, 3 Sept. 1963, MS-990/15/7. Platt's song cycle *No New Thing*, for mezzo-soprano and orchestra, was recorded for radio broadcast by the Dunedin Civic Orchestra with Honor McKellar. Other musical settings of Mason's poems, held in the music collection at the Alexander Turnbull Library, include a score for 'Song of Allegiance' for baritone and viola by Lilburn, 'Tribute' for the Orpheus Choir by Bruce Mason, and 'Be swift o sun' for guitar by Willow Macky.

40 Application for Scholarship in Letters, 12 Dec. 1970, MS-990/17/26.

41 Pearson, 'Memories of Ron Mason'.

42 Ian Milner, 'Ron Mason: a memoir', 2 Aug. 1982, MS-1265/II/3/18.

43 *Landfall*, Vol.25, No.3 (Sept. 1971), p.240.

44 RM to Willow Macky, 9 Oct. 1970; to Lenore Harty, 12 May 1971, MS-990/15/9.

45 Dorothea Mason, memoir.

46 Sargeson to David Seath, Minister of Internal Affairs, 28 Dec. 1970, 27 Jan. 1971; to J.W. Winchester, 9 May 1971,

MS-Papers-4261-195, 196.

47 Sargeson to George Gair, 12 Feb. 1971, MS-Papers-4261-196.

48 RM to James Bertram, 10 May 1971, MS-990/16/13.

49 RM to Cecil Hall, 16 Apr. 1971, MS-Papers-6407-6, ATL.

50 Bruno Nicholls to RM, 29 Apr. 1971, and reply, MS-990/17/25; Sargeson to Winchester, 9 May 1971.

51 RM to Ray Knox, 29 Apr. 1971, MS-990/17/26.

52 RM to Knox, 5 July 1971.

53 Bertram, interviewed by John Caselberg, MS-1265/II/1/1. Several years later Bertram wrote to Dorothea: 'You know how strongly I felt about the pension Internal Affairs finally approved for Ron, just before he died'. Bertram to Dorothea Mason, 14 Apr. 1977, 83-032/4, HL.

54 Dorothea Mason, memoir.

55 Pearson, 'Memories of Ron Mason'.

26 Exegi monumentum

1 *New Zealand Herald*, 11 Jan. 1972.

2 Anton Vogt, 'The Poet's Tongue. R.A.K. Mason', 1962, MS-Papers-2455 and 5201-29, ATL.

3 James Bertram, *Occasional Verses*, Wai-te-ata Press, Wellington, 1971, p.31.

4 Hone Tuwhare, 'Ron Mason', *Something Nothing*, Caveman Press, Dunedin, 1974. (The draft Tuwhare sent to Dorothea is in MS-990/18, HL.)

Sources

Note on manuscript sources:

The bulk of R.A.K Mason's papers, along with the papers of his wife, Dorothea, are held in the Hocken Library, University of Otago, Dunedin. Also in the Hocken Library are John Caselberg's research notes and the drafts of his biography of Mason. Mason's letters to A.R.D. Fairburn, 1921–32, are in the possession of the Fairburn family in Auckland. His letters to Jennifer Barrer are in the possession of Jennifer Barrer, Christchurch. Sadly, I did not find his letters to Harold Monro (the few that there were) in the Harold Monro/Poetry Bookshop papers in the British Library.

The extensive holdings of the Alexander Turnbull Library, Wellington, of the papers of New Zealand literary figures were also an important source for this biography, in particular the papers of A.R.D. Fairburn, Geoffrey de Montalk, Denis Glover, Frank Sargeson, James Bertram, Pat Lawlor and Janet Paul. The Bert Roth papers contain material relating to Mason's involvement with the Auckland General Labourers' Union and Trade Union Congress, and are also an invaluable source on the history of the Communist Party of New Zealand, and left-wing movements generally. The Turnbull Library also holds the Samoa correspondence between Mason and George Westbrook and Mason's Westbrook manuscript, and his research notes for and draft of his biography of Rewi Alley, as well as correspondence in the Alley and Shirley Barton papers bearing on Mason's China experience. The records of the Auckland People's Theatre are held by Auckland City Libraries. Detailed references to these and other manuscript sources can be found in the endnotes.

Published works by R.A.K. Mason:

The Beggar, Whitcombe & Tombs, Auckland, 1924
China, Auckland, 1943
China Dances, John McIndoe, Dunedin, 1962
Collected Poems, Caxton Press, Christchurch, 1962
End of Day, Caxton Press, Christchurch, 1936
Frontier Forsaken: an outline history of the Cook Islands, Challenge Publications, Auckland, 1947
Help Russia or – Help Hitler!, Aid to Russia Committee, Auckland, 1941
No New Thing, Spearhead Publishers, Auckland, 1934
Penny Broadsheet, Auckland, 1924
R.A.K. Mason at Twenty-five, Nag's Head Press, Christchurch, 1986
Rex Fairburn, Press Room, University of Otago, Dunedin, 1962

Squire Speaks, Caxton Press, Christchurch, 1938
This Dark Will Lighten, Caxton Press, Christchurch, 1941

Journals edited or contributed to by R.A.K. Mason:

Auckland Grammar School *Chronicle*, 1916–22
Challenge, 1944–56
Congress News, 1950–53
In Print, 1941–43
In Print: a magazine of Marxism, 1943–45
Kiwi, 1931–33
Landfall, 1948
Nucleus, 1958
Otago University *Review*, 1962
Palette, 1934
People's Theatre Magazine, 1939
People's Voice, 1939–45
Phoenix, 1932–33
Tomorrow, 1935–38
Union Record, 1940
Workers' Weekly, 1938–39

Anthologies, critical essays and other works about R.A.K. Mason:

Broughton, W.S. 'W. D'Arcy Cresswell, A.R.D. Fairburn, R.A.K. Mason: an examination of certain aspects of their lives and works', PhD thesis, University of Auckland, 1968
The Chapbook: a miscellany, No.39, 1924
Chapman, R.M. & J. Bennett (eds), *An Anthology of New Zealand Verse*, Oxford University Press, London, 1956.
Curnow, Allen (ed.), *A Book of New Zealand Verse*, Caxton Press, Christchurch, 1945
Curnow, Allen, 'Conversation with Allen Curnow', *Islands*, Vol.2, No.2 (Winter 1973), pp.142–62
Curnow, Allen (ed.), *The Penguin Book of New Zealand Verse*, Penguin, London, 1960
Curnow, Allen, 'The poetry of R.A.K. Mason', *Book*, No.2 (May 1941)
Daalder, Joost, 'R.A.K. Mason and the passing of time', *Landfall*, Vol.35, No.2 (June 1981), pp.226–44
Doyle, Charles, *R.A.K. Mason*, Twayne, New York, 1970
Hamilton, Stephen, 'Red hot gospels of highbrows: R.A.K. Mason and the demise of Phoenix', *Kotare*, Vol.1, No.1 (October 1998), pp.5–11
Harley, Ruth, 'R.A.K. Mason: Poetry and politics', *Landfall*, Vol.8, No.2 (June 1980), pp.142–64
Holcroft, M.H., *The Deepening Stream*, Caxton Press, Christchurch, 1940
Holcroft, M.H., *The Waiting Hills*, Progressive Publishing Society, Wellington, 1943
Jackson, MacD.P. & E. Caffin, 'Poetry', in T. Sturm (ed.), *The Oxford History of New*

Zealand Literature in English, 2nd edition, Oxford University Press, Auckland, 1998

McCormick, E.H., *Letters and Art in New Zealand*, Department of Internal Affairs, Wellington, 1940

McCormick, E.H., *New Zealand Literature: a survey*, Oxford University Press, London, 1959

Middleton, O.E., 'R.A.K. Mason at the Gobe', *Landfall*, Vol.8, No.2 (June 1980), pp.138–42

Milner, Ian & Denis Glover (eds), *New Poems*, The Caxton Club Press, Christchurch, 1934

Monro, Harold (ed.), *Twentieth Century Poetry*, Chatto and Windus, London, 1929

Murray, Stuart, *Never a Soul at Home: New Zealand literary nationalism and the 1930s*, Victoria University Press, Wellington, 1998

'"New Zealand's first wholly original, unmistakably gifted poet." Sam Hunt interviews R.A.K. Mason', *Affairs*, No.2 (June 1969), pp.23-25

Plomer, W., 'Some books from New Zealand', *Folios of New Writing*, autumn 1941, reprinted in Penguin *New Writing*, 17 (Apr.–June 1943)

Reid, J.C., *Creative Writing in New Zealand: a brief critical history*, Whitcombe & Tombs, Auckland, 1946

'R.A.K. Mason 1905–1971. Some tributes', *Landfall*, Vol.25, No.3 (Sept. 1971), pp.222-42

Robinson, Roger and Nelson Wattie (eds), *The Oxford Companion to New Zealand Literature*, Oxford University Press, Melbourne, 1998

Simpson, Peter, 'New Thing/*No New Thing*: R.A.K. Mason and Robert Lowry', unpublished paper

Stead, C.K., 'R.A.K. Mason's poetry: some random observations', *Comment*, 16, Vol.4, No.4 (July 1963), pp.34–39

Weir, J.E., *R.A.K. Mason*, Oxford University Press, Wellington, 1977

Wells, H.W., 'Poetry in New Zealand', *Voices*, Commonwealth issue, No.33, 1948

Other secondary sources:

Barker, F., *Lichfield School Centennial, 1884–1984*, Lichfield, 1984

Barnes, Jock, *Never a White Flag: the memoirs of Jock Barnes, waterfront leader*, Victoria University Press, Wellington, 1998

Barrowman, Rachel, *A Popular Vision: the arts and the left in New Zealand, 1930-1950*, Victoria University Press, Wellington, 1991

Bassett, Michael, *Confrontation '51; the 1951 waterfront dispute*, Reed, Wellington, 1972

Beatson, Peter & Diane (eds), *Dear Peggy: letters to Margaret Garland from her New Zealand friends*, Sociology Department, Massey University, Palmerston North, 1997

Bertram, James, *Return to China*, Heinemann, London, 1957

Birchfield, Maureen, *She Dared to Speak: Connie Birchfield's story*, University of Otago Press, Dunedin, 1998

Blaiklock, E.M., *Between the Foothills and the Ridge: a tale of two climbers*, Dunmore Press, Palmerston North, 1981

Blaiklock, E.M., *Between the Morning and the Afternoon: the story of a pupil teacher*, Dunmore Press, Palmerston North, 1980

Blaiklock, E.M., *Between the Valley and the Sea: a West Auckland boyhood*, Dunmore Press, Palmerston North, 1979

Borrows, J.L., *Albertland*, Reed, [Wellington], 1969

Boyd, Mary, 'The Record in Western Samoa to 1945', in A. Ross, *New Zealand's Record in the Pacific in the Twentieth Century*, Longman Paul, Auckland, 1969

Brady, Anne-Marie, *Friend of China: the myth of Rewi Alley*, RoutledgeCurzon, London, 2003

Brasch, Charles, *Indirections: a memoir, 1909–1947*, Oxford University Press, Wellington, 1980

Brett, H. & H. Hook, *The Albertlanders: brave pioneers of the sixties*, Capper Press, Christchurch, 1969

Challis, Derek & Gloria Rawlinson, *The Book of Iris: a life of Robin Hyde*, Auckland University Press, Auckland, 2002

Colgan, Wynne, *The Governor's Gift: the Auckland Public Library, 1880–1980*, Richards Publishing/Auckland City Council, Auckland, 1980

Cox, M.C, *Lichfield*, Waikato Times, Hamilton, 1948

Cresswell, W. D'Arcy, *Present Without Leave*, Cassell, London, 1939

Cresswell, W. D'Arcy (ed. H. Shaw), *The Letters of D'Arcy Cresswell*, University of Canterbury, Christchurch, 1971

Dallas, Ruth, *Curved Horizon*, University of Otago Press, Dunedin, 1991

De Montalk, G. Potocki, *Recollections of My Fellow Poets*, Prometheus Press, Auckland, 1983

De Montalk, Stephanie, *Unquiet World: the life of Count Geoffrey Potocki de Montalk*, Victoria University Press, Wellington, 2001

Dennis, Jonathan & Jan Beiringa (eds), *Film in Aotearoa New Zealand*, Victoria University Press, Wellington, 1992

Dictionary of New Zealand Biography, Vols 1–5, Department of Internal Affairs, etc., Wellington and Auckland, 1990–2000

Edmond, Lauris (ed.), *The Letters of A.R.D. Fairburn*, Oxford University Press, Auckland, 1981

Fairburn, A.R.D., *Selected Poems*, introduction by MacD.P. Jackson, Victoria University Press, Wellington, 1995

Ferrier, Carole, *Jean Devanny: romantic revolutionary*, Melbourne University Press, Melbourne, 1999

Field, Michael J., *Mau: Samoa's struggle against New Zealand oppression*, Reed, Auckland, 1984

Glover, Denis, 'Bob Lowry's books', *Book*, No.8 (August 1946)

Glover, Denis, *Hot Water Sailor*, A.H. & A.W. Reed, Wellington, 1962

Grant, J., *Harold Monro and the Poetry Bookshop*, Routledge and Kegan Paul, London, 1967

Hamilton, Stephen, 'The risen bird: *Phoenix* magazine, 1932–1933', *Turnbull Library Record*, Vol.30 (1997), pp.37–64

Hancock, K., *Sir Albert Henry: his life and times*, Methuen, Auckland, 1979

The Historic Highway, Auckland, 1967

Hughes, Peter, '"Sneers, jeers . . . and red rantings": Bob Lowry's early printing at

Auckland University College', *Turnbull Library Record*, Vol.12, No.1 (May 1989), pp.5–32

Hunt, Janet, *Hone Tuwhare: a life*, Godwit, Auckland, 1998

Hyde, Robin (ed. G. Boddy & J. Matthews), *Disputed Ground: Robin Hyde, journalist*, Victoria University Press, Wellington, 1991

Hyde, Robin, *Journalese*, National Printing Company, Auckland, 1934

Jamison, Kay R., *Touched with Fire: manic-depressive illness and the artistic temperament*, Free Press, New York, 1993

Jensen, Kai, *Whole Men: the masculine tradition in New Zealand literature*, Auckland University Press, Auckland, 1996

Kay, C.E., *The Restless Sky: the autobiography of an airman*, Harrap, London, 1964

King, Michael, *Sargeson: a life*, Penguin, Auckland, 1995

King, Michael, *Wrestling with the Angel: a life of Janet Frame*, Viking, Auckland, 2000

Locke, Elsie, *Student at the Gates*, Whitcoulls, Christchurch, 1981

McCartney, J., 'Robert Fearn Steele', MA thesis, University of Auckland, 1977

McEldowney, Dennis, *Full of the Warm South*, McIndoe, Dunedin, 1983

McGregor, Rae, *The Story of a New Zealand Writer: Jane Mander*, Otago University Press, Dunedin, 1998

McKay, Frank (ed.), *James K. Baxter as Critic*, Heinemann, Auckland, 1978

Meikle, Phoebe, *Accidental Life*, Auckland University Press, Auckland, 1994

Milner, Ian (ed. Vincent O'Sullivan), *Intersecting Lines: the memoirs of Ian Milner*, Victoria University Press, Wellington, 1993

Mitchell, G.G.M., 'Early settlers in the Manukau', 1963, *Journal of the Auckland Historical Society*, No.2 (Apr. 1963), reprinted in *Journal of the Auckland-Waikato Historical Societies*, No.19 (Sept. 1971), pp.16–20

Mogford, Janice, *The Onehunga Heritage*, Onehunga Borough Council, Auckland, 1989

Monro, D.H., *Fortunate Catastrophes: an anecdotal autobiography*, Quokka Press, Melbourne, 1991

Monro, Harold (ed. A. Monro), *Collected Poems*, Duckworth, London, 1970

Munro, Doug, 'The Westbrook Papers', *Turnbull Library Record*, Vol.5, No.2 (Oct. 1972), pp.18–35

Ogilvie, Gordon, *Denis Glover: his life*, Godwit, Auckland, 1999

Parker, D., B. Andersen & W. Brewer (comps), *'51: 50th Anniversary Waterfront Lockout and supporting strikes*, Auckland '51 Waterfront Reunion Committee, Auckland, 2001

Panmure District School, 1873–1963: 90th jubilee souvenir booklet, Panmure District School, Panmure, 1963

Panmure District School Centennial, 1873–1973, Panmure District School, Panmure, 1973

Perham, Marjorie, *Pacific Prelude: a journey to Samoa and Australasia, 1929*, Peter Owen, London, 1988

Rhodes, H. Winston, *New Zealand and the Soviet Union: an historical account of the NZ-USSR Society*, New Zealand-USSR Society, Auckland, 1979

Richards, Ian, *To Bed at Noon: the life and art of Maurice Duggan*, Auckland University Press, Auckland, 1997

Roth, H.O., *100 Years Fighting Back: the story of the Auckland Carpenters' Union, 1873–1973*, The Old Mole for the Auckland branch, N.Z. Carpenters' Union, Auckland, [1973]

Roth, H.O., 'Albert Henry as labour organiser: a struggle for power in the Cook Islands', *Journal of Pacific History*, Vol.12 (1977), pp.176–87

Roth, H.O., *A Century of Struggle: the Auckland Trades Council, 1876–1976*, Auckland, 1977

Roth, H.O., *Trade Unions in New Zealand*, Reed, Wellington, 1973

Rowe, N.A., *Samoa Under the Sailing Gods*, Putnam, London, 1930

Ruben, Margot, 'Karl Wolfskehl. Exul immeritus: Erinnerungen an Neuseeland', in *Karl Wolfskehl Kolloquium*, Castrum Peregrini, Amsterdam, 1983

Samuel, Raphael, et al. (eds), *Theatres of the Left, 1880–1935*, Routledge & Kegan Paul, London, 1985

Sargeson, Frank, *Sargeson*, Penguin, Auckland, 1981

Scott, Dick, *151 Days: official history of the great waterfront lockout and supporting strikes, February 15–July 15, 1951*, Labour Reprint Society, Christchurch, 1977

Scott, S.W., *Rebel in a Wrong Cause*, Collins, Auckland, [1980]

Searle, E.J., *City of Volcanoes: a geology of Auckland*, 2nd edition, Longman Paul, Auckland, 1981

Shadbolt, Maurice, *From the Edge of the Sky: a memoir*, David Ling, Auckland, 1999

Shadbolt, Maurice, *One of Ben's*, David Ling, Auckland, 1994

Sinclair, Keith, *A History of the University of Auckland, 1883–1983*, Auckland University Press/Oxford University Press, Auckland, 1983

Smith, Bernard, *Noel Counihan: artist and revolutionary*, Oxford University Press, Melbourne, 1993

Smithyman, Kendrick, *A Way of Saying*, Collins, Auckland, 1965

Taylor, Kerry. 'Workers' Vanguard or People's Voice? The Communist Party of New Zealand from origins to 1946', PhD thesis, Victoria University of Wellington, 1994

Taylor, Nancy M., *The Home Front*, Department of Internal Affairs, Wellington, 1986

Texidor, Greville (ed. K. Smithyman), *In Fifteen Minutes You Can Say A Lot*, Victoria University Press, Wellington, 1987

Thompson, R.C., 'Britain, Germany and New Zealand in Polynesia', in Kerry Howe, et al. (eds), *Tides of History: the Pacific Islands in the twentieth century*, University of Hawaii Press, Honolulu, 1994

Trembath, K.A. (with Wynne Colgan), *Ad Augusta: a centennial history of Auckland Grammar School, 1869–1969*, 2nd edition, Auckland Grammar School Old Boys' Association, Auckland, 1969

Trussell, Denys, *Fairburn*, Auckland University Press/Oxford University Press, Auckland, 1984

Tuwhare, Hone, *No Ordinary Sun*, Blackwood and Janet Paul, Auckland, 1964

Urlich, J., *Journey Towards World Peace: a history of the New Zealand Peace Council*, Lake Ohia Publications, Wellington, 1998

von Sturmer, C., *Margaret Barr: epic individual*, L. von Sturmer, Sydney, 1993

Westbrook, G.E.L., *Gods Who Die: the story of Samoa's greatest adventurer, as told to Julian Dana*, Macmillan, New York, 1935

Woolmer, J. Howard, *The Poetry Bookshop, 1912–1935: a bibliography*, Woolmer/Brotherson, Winchester, 1988

Index

WORKS

anthologies including, see: *Book of New Zealand Verse*; *Kowhai Gold*; *Modern Muse*; *New Poems*; *Oxford Anthology of New Zealand Verse*; *Penguin Book of New Zealand Verse*; *Recent Poems*; *Southern Stories, Poems and Paintings*; *Twentieth Century Poetry*

compilation: *China Dances*, 366-7

non-fiction: 'An Old Trader in the South Seas' (Westbrook memoir), 127, 131-3, 147; 'Cheaper Labourers' (history of New Zealand Company), 243, 257-8; *Frontier Forsaken: an outline history of the Cook Islands*, 295-6

poems: 'Ad Mariam', 109, 357; 'ad Miram', 357, 393; 'Ad Regem', 168; 'After Death', 52, 56, 89-90, 92; 'Against John Knox', 370; 'Amores VI', *see* 'Be swift o sun'; 'The Agnostic', 48-9; 'Away is flown each pretty rag', 93; 'Bags Dog Boat', 369-70; 'The Beggar', 42-3, 48, 52, 56; 'Be swift o sun' ('Amores VI'), 140-1, 172, 181, 203, 275, 298; 'Beware the mask', 210; 'Body of John', 57-8, 64, 69, 87, 393; 'Come Out My Soul', 83-4, 209-10, 357; 'A Doubt', 62-3, 89; 'Ecce Homunculus', 103-4, 202; 'Eheu Fugaces', 39-40; 'Encomie', 367-8; 'Evolution', 199; 'Flattering Unction', 93; 'Flow at Full Moon', 237-8, 272-3, 276, 298, 354, 357, 362, 363; 'Footnote to John ii 4', 201-2, 275, 345; 'The Four Limbs of the Heretic', 40; 'A Fragment', 62; 'Fugue', 216-17; 'Gaudio Quod Nescio', 64; 'He Got His Timber at Last' (satirical), 293; 'Honey', 357; 'A Hundred Thousand Blessings' (China), 339-40, 366; 'I cried out in the wilderness', 48; 'If it be not God's law', 203; 'In Manus Tuas Domine', 175-6, 205; 'In Perpetuum Vale', 48, 52, 56, 89, 205; 'In Time of Testing', 324; 'I Send My Mind Aquest', 40-1; 'Judas Iscariot', 199-201, 362; 'The Just Statesman Dies', 204-5, 218; 'Latter-day Geography Lesson', 57, 90; 'The Leave-taking',

83, 205; 'The Lesser Stars', 51-2, 56, 89-90; 'Lugete o Veneres', 106-7, 202; 'Lullaby', 42, 52; 'Lullaby and Neck-verse', 64; 'Man and Beast', 83; 'Miracle of Life', 51, 56, 97; 'The moon resumes the field', 364; 'Nails and a Cross', 103; 'New Life', 217-18; 'Nox Perpetua Dormienda', 107, 192, 202, 237; 'O Fons Bandusiae', 36-7, 48, 298, 299, 300, 393; 'Oils and Ointments', 63; 'Old Memories of Earth', 49-50, 56; 'On a Dead Cripple', 144; 'On the Swag', 101-3, 143, 147, 166, 199-200, 201, 273, 362, 389; 'Our love was a grim citadel', 204; 'Payment', 216; 'Preface to the Book of Pessimism', 90, 199; 'Prelude' (*End of Day*), 215-16; 'Prelude' (*This Dark Will Lighten*), 273-4; 'Progress', 57; 'Reunion', 363-4; 'The Seventh Wound Protests', 378-9; 'She Who Steals', 203; 'Since flesh is soon', 202-3; 'Song for Dunedin', 376-7, 393; 'A Song of Allegiance', 60-1, 215; 'Song Thinking of Her Dead', 272, 299; 'Sonnet of Brotherhood', 51, 92, 273, 299, 345, 354, 362, 389; 'Sonnet of my Everlasting Hand', 62; 'Sonnets of the Ocean's Base', 41-2, 48, 389; 'Sonnet to MacArthur's Eyes', 315-16, 357, 368, 380; 'The Spark's Farewell to its Clay', 56, 96; 'Stoic Marching Song', 82-3, 199; 'Stoic Overthrow', 164, 175, 195, 205, 330; 'Stone and steel is Scotland', 343; 'Their Sacrifice', 152-3, 166, 192; 'Thigh to thigh', 106, 107, 202; 'Tribute', 90; 'Twenty-sixth October', 238, 239, 362; 'Up the hill with the sea-gulls skirling', 382; 'Vengeance of Venus', 238-40; 'Wayfarers', 50-1, 62; 'Wise at Last', 137-8, 204, 218; 'The Young Man Thinks of Sons', 93, 202; 'Youth at the Dance', 166-7, 175, 195, 215, 218, 231, 255, 380

poetry collections: *The Beggar* – contents of, 48-53, 57-8, 199, 203, 272; destruction of, 13-14, 53, 92;

Unity Theatre, London, 226, 250, 289
Unity Theatre, Wellington, 289
University Bookshop, Dunedin, 359
University Coaching College (Holl's), 13-14,
    46, 67, 72-3, 79, 88, 98, 109, 135, 189,
    396
University of Otago: Dramatic Society, 374,
    377-8, 381, 382; English Department,
    346-7, 352, 355, 357, 359, 361-2, 368;
    Library, 350, 375; Literary Society, 354;
    Press Room, 355; role of, 307; staff of,
    306, 393; *University Week*, 377-8; *see also*
    Burns Fellowship

Verrier, Robert, 251
Victoria University (College): 67, 355, 380;
    Literary Society, 330, 355, 398
Virgil, 39, 40, 46, 51, 66, 100
Vogt, Anton, 309, 389
von Sturmer, Denham, 230-1, 232-4 *passim*

Waiheke Island, 190, 241
Waikato, 19, 159, 227; *see also* Lichfield
Waiting for Lefty: described, 219; influence on
    RM, 292; People's Theatre productions
    of, 223, 227-8, 247, 250-1; WEA
    production of, 218, 219, 220-2; *see also*
    People's Theatre
Wakefield, Edward Gibbon, 181, 242, 243,
    257-8, 261, 397
Walker, Prof. Maxwell, 66-7
Walsh, Fintan Patrick, 313, 314, 318, 332
Wanganui, 19, 269
Ward, Sir Joseph, 79
Waten, Judah, 266-7, 300, 348, 349
Waterfront dispute, 1951, 317-18, 319-21
Waterside Women's Auxiliary, 319
Waterside Workers' Union, 313, 314-15,
    317, 318, 320-1
Watson, Gordon, 182, 183, 185, 186, 187,
    189, 255, 281
Weir, John, 368, 393

Wellington: RM's visits to, 267-8, 295, 310,
    314, 316, 317, 351; mentioned, 17, 188,
    270, 355
Westbrook, George, 126-7, 130-3, 134, 135,
    147, 150, 292
Whitcombe & Tombs, 48, 80
Wilcox, Ann (née Richards), 281, 294
Wilcox, Vic, 281, 294, 322
Wild Oats, 80-2, 142
Wilkinson, Iris, *see* Hyde, Robin
Williams, Nicholas (Dick), 33
Wilson, Ormond, 330
Wolfe, Humbert, 87, 156
Wolfskehl, Karl, 304, 331
Wonders of China, The (Hayward film), 341
Wood, Ben, 330
Workers' Art Club, Sydney, 211, 226
Workers' Educational Association (WEA):
    drama productions by, 218-19, 220-2,
    261, 262, 277-8, 280, 287; radio
    broadcasts of, 189; RM seeks
    employment with, 99, 122, 123, 129;
    RM's lectures and classes for, 151, 164,
    189, 223-5, 267, 343; RM's 1969 NZ
    literature course for, 390-1; summer
    schools, 151, 189, 223-5, 267;
    mentioned, 233, 238, 259, 290, 292, 306
Workers' Weekly, 220, 224, 241, 252-3, 255,
    257
World Federation of Trade Unions, 315,
    320-1
Wright, Albion, 331, 356, 359, 360, 383, 389,
    392-3, 395, 396-7
Writers' League (Australian), 211
Wyatt, Thomas, 371

Year Book of the Arts in New Zealand, 290-1
Yeats, W.B., 69, 70, 157, 345
Young Communist League, 184, 185, 186,
    221, 236
Young, Irene, 336, 337-9 *passim*
Youth Peace Conference, 316